LAND OF TALES

LAND OF TALES

Stories of Ireland for Children

——— Chosen by ———
Joan Ryan and Gordon Snell

GLENDALE PRESS

First published in Ireland by
THE GLENDALE PRESS
1 Summerhill Parade
Sandycove
Co. Dublin, Ireland

© 1982 G. Snell, J. Ryan and The Glendale Press
Published in hardcover 1982
Second impression 1983
First paperback edition 1989

ISBN 0 907606 74 1

Cover and Book Design by Q
Typeset by Print Prep (Ireland) Ltd
Printed in Great Britain at
The Camelot Press Ltd, Southampton

Contents

Acknowledgements

The editors and publishers gratefully acknowledge the following sources for their kind permission to reproduce stories: *The Twelve Silly Sisters*, copyright 1924 by Macmillan Publishing Co., Inc., renewed 1952 by Padraic Colum; *The Wishing Chair* from *The Four Leaved Shamrock* by Sinéad de Valera, published by C.J. Fallon Ltd. Dublin 1979; Mr. D.H. Sealy for *The Piper and The Puca* translated by Douglas Hyde from *Leabhar Sgeulaigheachta* in the W.B. Yeats Collection *Fairy and Folk Tales of the Irish Peasantry* published by Walter Scott, London 1888; *The White Road of Druagh* by Patricia Lynch was reproduced from *The Black Goat of Slievemore and Other Irish Fairy Tales*, published by J. M. Dent & Son, Ltd., London 1950; *The Birth of Bran* by James Stephens, the Society of Authors on behalf of the copyright owner Mrs Iris Wise and in the USA, copyright 1920 by Macmillan and Co. Inc. renewed 1948 by James Stephens.

Grateful acknowledgement is given to the following sources for illustrative material: *Empire Style Designs and Ornament* by J. Beunat, Dover Publications, New York; *Instant Archive Art,* The Graphic Communications Centre Ltd. Kent; *A Portrait of the Irish in America* by W. D. Griffin, Academy Press, Dublin; *Ireland* by Mr. and Mrs. G. Hall; *Illustrated London News; 1800 Woodcuts by Thomas Bewick and his School,* edited by B. Cirker, Dover Publications, New York; Bord Fáilte; The Trustees of the British Museum; *Catchpenny Prints,* Dover Publications, New York, and *Pictures from Punch.*

In the event of any copyright holders having been overlooked the publishers will be only too pleased to come to an arrangement at the first available opportunity.

Introduction

Once upon a time, before radio and records and television, listening to stories was a favourite form of entertainment. Storytellers who knew the old tales and legends by heart were valued guests at any gathering or round any fireside.

Ireland is a land with a long and rich tradition of such tales, and some of them were passed on through many generations, without ever being written down. There were tales of heroes and battles long ago; of haunted places and deeds of daring; of witches and ghosts, giants and mermaids, and the mischievous horse-like pookas; and of the fairy people who used their magic powers to help or to harm human beings.

During the last century, and even earlier, people started collecting and publishing the old stories. Some of these collections were cheap books, sold at fairs or by travelling pedlars. Others were the work of scholars and folk-lore collectors, such as Douglas Hyde, Ireland's first president.

Today, many of these stories can be found only by delving in old libraries — and that is just what has been done, to gather the tales in this book and bring them to a wider, modern audience. Some better-known stories have also been included as well as some by more recent authors.

All the tales are good for telling aloud in the way the old storytellers did, as well as for reading to yourself. Either way, they show why Ireland deserves to be called a "Land of Tales".

Joan Ryan and Gordon Snell

FOR LEONARD AND MAEVE
WITH MUCH LOVE

Sour and Civil

by FRANCES BROWNE

Once upon a time there stood upon the seacoast a certain village of low cottages, where no one lived but fishermen. All round it was a broad beach of snow-white sand, where nothing was to be seen but gulls and cormorants, and long tangled seaweeds cast up by the tide that came and went night and day, summer and winter. There was no harbour nor port on all that shore. Ships passed by at a distance, with their white sails set, and on the landside there lay wide grassy downs, where peasants lived and shepherds fed their flocks. The fishermen thought themselves as well off as any people in that country. Their families never wanted for plenty of herrings and mackerel; and what they had to spare the landsmen bought from them at certain village markets in the hills, giving them in exchange butter, cheese, and corn.

The best two fishermen in that village were the sons of two old widows, who had no other children, and happened to be near neighbours. Their family names were short, for they called the one Sour, and the other Civil. There was no relationship between them that ever I heard of; but they had only one boat, and always fished together, though their names expressed the difference of their humours — for Civil never used a hard word where a soft one would do, and when Sour was not snarling at somebody, he was sure to be grumbling at everything.

Nevertheless they agreed wonderfully, and were lucky fishers. Both were strong, active, and of good courage. On winter's night or summer's morning they would steer out to sea far beyond the boats of their neighbours, and never came home without some fish to cook and some to spare. Their mothers were proud of them, each in her own fashion — for the saying held good, 'Like mother, like son.' The Widow Civil thought the whole world didn't hold a better than her son; and her boy was the only creature at whom the Widow Sour didn't scold and frown. The village was divided in opinion concerning the young fishermen. Some thought Civil the best; some said, without Sour he would catch nothing. So things went on, till one day about the fall of winter, when mists were gathering darkly on sea and sky, and the air was chill and frosty, all the boatmen of the village went out to fish, and so did Sour and Civil.

That day they did not have their usual luck. Cast their net where they would, not a single fish came in. Their neighbours caught boatsful, and went home, Sour said, laughing at them. But when the sea was growing crimson with the sunset their nets were empty, and they were tired. Civil himself did not like to go home without fish — it would damage the high repute they had gained in the village. Besides, the sea was calm and the evening fair, and, as a last attempt, they steered still further out, and cast their nets beside a rock which rose rough and grey above the water, and was called the Merman's Seat — from an old report that the fishermen's fathers had seen the mermen, or sea-people, sitting there on moonlight nights. Nobody believed that rumour now, but the villagers did not like to fish there. The water was said to be deep beyond measure, and sudden squalls were apt to trouble it; but Sour and Civil were right glad to see by the moving of their lines that there was something in their net, and gladder still when they found it so heavy that all their strength was required to draw it up. Scarcely

11

had they landed it on the Merman's Seat, when their joy was changed to disappointment, for besides a few starved mackerel, the net contained nothing but a monstrous ugly fish as long as Civil (who was taller than Sour), with a huge snout, a long beard, and a skin covered with prickles.

'Such a horrid ugly creature!' said Sour, as they shook it out of the net on the rough rock, and gathered up the mackerel. 'We needn't fish here any more. How they will mock us in the village for staying out so late, and bringing home so little!'

'Let us try again,' said Civil, as he set his creel of mackerel in the boat.

'Not another cast will I make tonight;' and anything more Sour would have said, was cut short by the great fish, for, looking round at them, it spoke out —

'I suppose you don't think me worth taking home in your dirty boat; but I can tell you that if you were down in my country, neither of you would be thought fit to keep me company.'

Sour and Civil were terribly astonished to hear the fish speak. The first could not think of a cross word to say, but Civil made answer in his accustomed manner.

'Indeed, my lord, we beg your pardon, but our boat is too light to carry such a fish as you.'

'You do well to call me lord,' said the fish, 'for so I am, though it was hard to expect you could have known my quality in this dress. However, help me off the rock, for I must go home; and for your civility I will give you my daughter in marriage, if you will come and see me this day twelvemonth.'

12

Civil helped the great fish off the rock as respectfully as his fear would allow him. Sour was so terrified at the whole transaction, that he said not a word till they got safe home; but from that day forward, when he wanted to put Civil down, it was his custom to tell him and his mother that he would get no wife but the ugly fish's daughter.

Old Widow Sour heard this story from her son, and told it over the whole village. Some people wondered, but the most part laughed at it as a good joke; and Civil and his mother were never known to be angry but on that occasion. Widow Civil advised her son never to fish with Sour again; and as the boat happened to be his, Civil got an old skiff which one of the fishermen was going to break up for firewood, and cobbled it up for himself.

In that skiff he went to sea alone all the winter, and all the summer; but, though Civil was brave and skilful, he could catch little, because his boat was bad — and everybody but his mother began to think him of no value. Sour having the good boat got a new comrade, and had the praise of being the best fisherman.

Poor Civil's heart was getting low as the summer wore away. The fish had grown scarce on that coast, and the fishermen had to steer further out to sea. One evening when he had toiled all day and caught nothing, Civil thought he would go further too, and try his fortune beside the Merman's Rock. The sea was calm, and the evening fair. Civil did not remember that it was the very day on which his troubles began by the great fish talking to him twelve months before. As he neared the rock the sun was setting, and

much astonished was the fisherman to see standing upon it three fair ladies, with sea-green gowns and strings of great pearls wound round their long fair hair: two of them were waving their hands to him. They were the tallest and stateliest ladies he had ever seen; but Civil could perceive as he came nearer that there was no colour in their cheeks, that their hair had a strange bluish shade, like that of deep sea-water, and there was a fiery light in their eyes that frightened him. The third, who was less of stature, did not notice him at all, but kept her eyes fixed on the setting sun. Though her look was mournful, Civil could see that there was a faint rosy bloom on her cheek — that her hair was a golden yellow, and her eyes were mild and clear like those of his mother.

'Welcome! welcome! noble fisherman!' cried the two ladies. 'Our father has sent us for you to visit him,' and with one bound they leaped into his boat, bringing with them the smaller lady, who said —

'Oh! bright sun and brave sky that I see so seldom!' But Civil heard no more, for his boat went down miles deep in the sea, and he thought himself drowning; but one lady had caught him by the right arm, and the other by the left, and pulled him into the mouth of a rocky cave, where there was no water. On they went, still down and down, as if on a steep hill-side. The cave was very long, but it grew wider as they came to the bottom. Then Civil saw a faint light, and walked out with his fair company into the country of the sea-people. In that land there grew neither grass nor flowers, bushes nor trees, but the ground was covered with bright-coloured shells and pebbles. There were hills of marble, and rocks of spar; and over all a cold blue sky, with no sun, but a light clear and silvery as that of the harvest moon. The fisherman could see no smoking chimneys, but there were grottoes in the sparry rocks, and halls in the marble hills, where lived the sea-people — with whom, as old stories say, fishermen and mariners used to meet on lonely capes and headlands in the simple times of the world.

Forth they came in all directions to see the stranger. Mermen with long white beards, and mermaids such as walk with the fishermen, all clad in sea-green, and decorated with strings of pearls; but every one with the same colourless face, and the same wild light in their eyes. The mermaids led Civil up one of the marble hills to a great cavern with halls and chambers like a palace. Their floors were of alabaster, their walls of porphyry, and their ceilings inlaid with coral. Thousands of crystal lamps lit the palace. There were seats and tables hewn out of shining spar, and a great company sat feasting; but what most amazed Civil was the quantity of cups, flagons, and goblets, made of gold and silver, of such different shapes and patterns that they seemed to have been gathered from all the countries in the world. In the chief hall a merman sat on a stately chair, with more jewels than all the rest about him. Before him the mermaids brought Civil, saying —

'Father, here is our guest.'

'Welcome, noble fisherman!' cried the merman, in a voice which Civil remembered with terror, for it was that of the

great ugly fish; 'welcome to our halls! Sit down and feast with us, and then choose which of my daughters you will have for a bride.'

Civil had never felt himself so thoroughly frightened in all his life. How was he to get home to his mother? and what would the old widow think when the dark night came without bringing him home? There was no use in talking — Civil had wisdom enough to see that: he, therefore, tried to take things quietly; and, having thanked the merman for his invitation, took the seat assigned him on his right hand. Civil was hungry with the long day at sea, but there was no want of fare on that table: meats and wines, such as he had never tasted, were set before him in the richest of golden dishes; but, hungry as he was, the fisherman perceived that everything there had the taste and smell of the sea.

If the fisherman had been the lord of lands and castles, he could not have been treated with more respect. The two mermaids sat by him — one filled his plate, another filled his goblet; but the third only looked at him in a stealthy, warning way when nobody perceived her. Civil soon finished his share of the feast, and then the merman showed him all the splendours of his cavern. The halls were full of company, some feasting, some dancing, and some playing all manner of games, and in every hall was the same abundance of gold and silver vessels; but Civil was most astonished when the merman brought him to a marble chamber full of heaps of precious stones. There were diamonds there whose value the fisherman knew not — pearls larger than ever a diver had gathered — emeralds, sapphires, and rubies, that would have made the jewellers of the world wonder; the merman then said —

'This is my eldest daughter's dowry.'

'Good luck attend her!' said Civil. 'It is the dowry of a queen.' But the merman led him on to another chamber: it was filled with heaps of gold coin, which seemed gathered from all times and nations. The images and inscriptions of all the kings that ever reigned were there; and the merman said —

'This is my second daughter's dowry.'

'Good luck attend her!' said Civil. 'It is a dowry for a princess.'

'So you may say,' replied the merman. 'But make up your mind

which of the maidens you will marry, for the third has no portion at all, because she is not my daughter; but only, as you may see, a poor silly girl taken into my family for charity.'

'Truly, my lord,' said Civil, whose mind was already made up, 'both your daughters are too rich and far too noble for me; therefore I choose the third. Her poverty will best become my estate of a poor fisherman.

'If you choose her,' said the merman, 'you must wait long for a wedding. I cannot allow an inferior girl to be married before my own daughters.' And he said a great deal more to persuade him; but Civil would not change his mind, and they returned to the hall.

There was no more attention for the fisherman, but everybody watched him well. Turn where he would, master or guest had their eyes upon him, though he made them the best speeches he could remember, and praised all their splendours. One thing, however, was strange — there was no end to the fun and the feasting; nobody seemed tired, and nobody thought of sleep. When Civil's very eyes

closed with weariness, and he slept on one of the marble benches
— no matter how many hours — there were the company feasting
and dancing away; there were the thousand lamps within, and the
cold moonlight without. Civil wished himself back with his mother,
his net, and his cobbled skiff. Fishing would have been easier than
those everlasting feasts; but there was nothing else among the sea-
people — no night of rest, no working day.

Civil knew not how time went on, till, waking up from a long
sleep, he saw, for the first time, that the feast was over, and the
company gone. The lamps still burned, and the tables, with all
their riches, stood in the empty halls; but there was no face to be
seen, no sound to be heard, only a low voice singing beside the
outer door; and there, sitting all alone, he found the mild-eyed
maiden.

'Fair lady,' said Civil, 'tell me what does this quietness mean
and where are all the merry company?'

'You are a man of the land,' said the lady, 'and know not
the sea-people. They never sleep but once a year, and that is at
Christmas time. Then they go into the deep caverns, where there is
always darkness, and sleep till the new year comes.'

'It is a strange fashion,' said Civil; 'but all folks have their way.
Fair lady, as you and I are to be good friends, tell me, whence come
all the wines and meats, and gold and silver vessels, seeing there are
neither corn-fields nor flocks here, workmen nor artificers?'

'The sea-people are heirs of the sea,' replied the maiden; 'to
them come all the stores and riches that are lost in it. I know not
the ways by which they come; but the lord of these halls keeps the
keys of seven gates, where they go out and in; but one of the gates,
which has not been opened for thrice seven years, leads to a path
under the sea, by which, I once heard the merman say, in his cups,
one might reach the land. Good fisherman, if by chance you gain
his favour, and ever open that gate, let me bear you company; for

18

I was born where the sun shines and the grass grows, though my country and my parents are unknown to me. All I remember is sailing in a great ship, when a storm arose, and it was wrecked, and not one soul escaped drowning but me. I was then a little child, and a brave sailor had bound me to a floating plank before he was washed away. Here the sea-people came round me like great fishes, and I went down with them to this rich and weary country. Sometimes, as a great favour, they take me up with them to see the sun; but that is seldom, for they never like to part with one who has seen their country; and, fisherman, if you ever leave them, remember to take nothing with you that belongs to them, for if it were but a shell or a pebble, that will give them power over you and yours.'

'Thanks for your news, fair lady,' said Civil. 'A lord's daughter, doubtless, you must have been, while I am but a poor fisherman; yet, as we have fallen into the same misfortune, let us be friends, and it may be we shall find means to get back to the sunshine together.'

'You are a man of good manners,' said the lady, 'therefore I accept your friendship; but my fear is that we shall never see the sunshine again.'

'Fair speeches brought me here,' said Civil, 'and fair speeches may help me back; but be sure I will not go without you.'

This promise cheered the lady's heart, and she and Civil spent that Christmas time seeing the wonders of the sea country. They wandered through caves like that of the great merman. The unfinished feast was spread in every hall; the tables were covered with most costly vessels; and heaps of jewels lay on the floors of unlocked chambers. But for the lady's warning, Civil would very much have liked to put away some of them for his mother.

The poor woman was sad of heart by this time, believing her son to be drowned. On the first night when he did not come home, she had gone down to the sea and watched till morning. Then the fishermen steered out again, and Sour having found his skiff floating about, brought it home, saying, the foolish young man was doubtless lost; but what better could be expected when he had no discreet person to take care of him.

This grieved Widow Civil sore. She never expected to see her son again; but, feeling lonely in her cottage at the evening hour when he used to come home, the good woman accustomed herself to go down at sunset and sit beside the sea. That winter happened to be mild on the coast, and one evening when the Christmas time was near, and the rest of the village preparing to make merry, Widow Civil sat, as usual, on the sands. The tide was ebbing and the sun going down, when from the eastward came a lady clad in black, mounted on a black horse, and followed by a squire in the same sad clothing: as the lady came near, she said —

'Woe is me for my daughter, and all that have lost by the sea!'

'You say well, noble lady,' said Widow Civil. 'Woe is me also for my son, for I have none beside him.'

When the lady heard that, she alighted from her horse, and sat down by the fisherman's mother, saying —

'Listen to my story. I was the widow of a great lord in the heart of the east country. He left me a fair castle, and an only daughter, who was the joy of my heart. Her name was Faith Feignless; but, while she was yet a child, a great fortuneteller told me that my daughter would marry a fisherman. I thought this would be a great disgrace to my noble family, and, therefore, sent my daughter with her nurse in a good ship, bound for a certain city where my relations live, intending to follow myself as soon as I could get my lands and castles sold. But the ship was wrecked, and my daughter drowned; and I have wandered over the world with my good Squire Trusty, mourning on every shore with those who have lost friends by the sea. Some with whom I have mourned grew to forget their sorrow, and would lament with me no more; others, being sour and selfish, mocked me, saying my grief was nothing to them: but you have good manners, and I will remain with you, however humble be your dwelling. My squire carries gold enough to pay all our charges.' So the mourning lady and her good Squire Trusty went home with Widow Civil, and she was no longer lonely in her sorrow, for when the widow said —

'Oh! if my son were alive, I should never let him go to sea in a cobbled skiff!' the lady answered —

'Oh! if my daughter were but living, I should never think it a disgrace though she married a fisherman!'

The Christmas passed as it always does — shepherds made merry in the hills, and fishermen on the shore; but when the merrymakings and ringing of bells were over in all the land, the sea-people woke up to their continual feasts and dances. Like one that had forgotten all that was passed, the merman again showed Civil the chamber of gold and the chamber of jewels, advising him to choose between his two daughters; but the fisherman still answered that the ladies were too noble, and far too rich for him. Yet as he looked at the glittering heap, Civil could not help recollecting the poverty of where he came from, and the thought slipped out —

'How happy my old neighbours would be to find themselves here!'

'Say you so?' said the merman, who always wanted visitors.

'Yes,' said Civil, 'I have neighbours up yonder whom it would be hard to send home again if they got sight of half this wealth;' and the honest fisherman thought of Widow Sour and her son.

*   *   *

The merman was greatly delighted with these speeches — he thought there was a probability of getting many land-people down, and by and by said to Civil —

'Suppose you took up a few jewels, and went up to tell your poor neighbours how welcome we might make them?'

The prospect of getting back to his country rejoiced Civil's heart, but he had promised not to go without the lady, and therefore, answered prudently what was indeed true —

'Many thanks, my lord, for choosing such a humble man as I am to bear your message; but my people never believe anything without two witnesses at the least; yet if the poor maid whom I have chosen could be permitted to accompany me, I think they would believe us both.'

The merman said nothing in reply, but his people, who had heard Civil's speech, talked it over among themselves till they grew sure that the whole of the country would come down, if they only had news of the riches, and petitioned their lord to send up Civil and the poor maid by way of letting them know.

As it seemed for the public good, the great merman consented; but, being determined to have them back, he gathered out of his treasure chamber some of the largest pearls and diamonds that lay convenient, and said —

'Take these as a present from me, to let your people see what I can do for my visitors.'

'Civil and the lady took the presents, saying —

'Oh, my lord, you are too generous. We want nothing but the pleasure of telling of your marvellous riches up yonder.'

'Tell everybody to come down, and they will get the like,' said the merman; 'and follow my eldest daughter, for she carries the key of the land gate.'

Civil and the lady followed the mermaid through a winding gallery, which led from the chief banquet hall far into the marble hill. All was dark, and they had neither lamp nor torch, but at the end of the gallery they came to a great stone gate, which creaked like thunder on its hinges. Beyond that there was a narrow cave, sloping up and up like a steep hill-side. Civil and the lady thought they would never reach the top; but at last they saw a gleam of daylight, then a strip of blue sky, and the mermaid bade them stoop and creep through what seemed a crevice in the ground, and both stood up on the broad sea-beach as the day was breaking and the tide ebbing fast away.

'Good times to you among your people,' said the mermaid. 'Tell any of them that would like to come down to visit us, that they must come here midway between the high and low watermark, when the tide is going out at morning or evening. Call thrice on the sea-people, and we will show them the way.'

Before they could make answer she had sunk down from their sight, and there was no track or passage there, but all was covered by the loose sand and sea-shells.

'Now,' said the lady to Civil, 'we have seen the heavens once more, and we will not go back. Cast in the merman's present quickly before the sun rises;' and taking the bag of pearls and diamonds, she flung it as far as she could into the sea.

Civil never was so unwilling to part with anything as that bag, but he thought it better to follow a good example, and tossed his into the sea also. They thought they heard a long moan come up from the waters; but Civil saw his mother's chimney beginning to smoke, and with the fair lady in her sea-green gown he hastened to the good widow's cottage.

The whole village were woke up that morning with cries of 'Welcome back, my son!' 'Welcome back, my daughter!' for the mournful lady knew it was her lost daughter, Faith Feignless, whom the fisherman had brought back, and all the neighbours assembled to hear their story. When it was told, everybody praised Civil for the prudence he had shown in his difficulties, except Sour and his mother: they did nothing but rail upon him for losing such great chances of making himself and the whole country rich. At last, when they heard over and over again of the merman's treasures, neither mother nor son would consent to stay any longer, and as nobody persuaded them, and they would not take Civil's direction, Sour got out his boat and steered away with his mother toward the Merman's Rock. From that voyage they never came back to the village. Some say they went down and lived among the sea-

people; others say — I know not how they learned it — that Sour and his mother grumbled and growled so much that even the sea-people grew weary of them, and turned them and their boat out on the open sea. What part of the world they chose to land on nobody is certain: by all accounts they have been seen everywhere, and I should not be surprised if they were in this good company. As for Civil, he married Faith Feignless, and became a great lord.

(from *Granny's Wonderful Chair*)

The Ghosts
and the Game
of Football

by PATRICK KENNEDY

There was once a poor widow woman's son that was going to look for service, and one winter's evening he came to a strong farmer's house, and this house was very near an old castle. 'God save all here,' says he, when he got inside the door.

'God save you kindly,' says the farmer. 'Come to the fire.'

'Could you give me a night's lodging?' says the boy.

'That we will, and welcome, if you will only sleep in a comfortable room in the old castle above there; and you must have a fire and candlelight, and whatever you like to drink; and if you're alive in the morning I'll give you ten guineas.'

'Sure I'll be 'live enough if you send no one to kill me.'

'I'll send no one to kill you, you may depend. The place is haunted ever since my father died, and three or four people that slept in the same room were found dead next morning. If you can banish the spirits I'll give you a good farm and my daughter, so that you like one another well enough to be married.'

'Never say't twice. I've a

27

middling safe conscience, and don't fear any evil spirit that ever smelled of brimstone.'

Well and good, the boy got his supper, and then they went up with him to the old castle, and showed him into a large kitchen, with a roaring fire in the grate, and a table, with a bottle and glass, and tumbler on it, and the kettle ready on the hob. They bade him good-night and God speed, and went off as if they didn't think their heels were half swift enough.

'Well,' says he to himself, 'if there's any danger, this prayer-book will be more useful than either the glass or tumbler.' So he kneeled down, read a good many prayers, then sat by the fire, waiting to see what would happen.

In about a quarter of an hour, he heard something bumping along the floor overhead till it came to a hole in the ceiling. There it stopped, and cried out, 'I'll fall, I'll fall.'

'Fall away,' says Jack, and down came a pair of legs on the kitchen floor. They walked to one end of the room, and there they stood, and Jack's hair had like to stand upright on his head along with them. Then another crackling and whacking came to the hole, and the same words passed between the thing above and Jack, and down came a man's body, and went and stood upon the legs. Then comes the head and shoulders, till the whole man, with buckles in his shoes and knee-breeches, and a big flapped waistcoat and a three-cocked hat, was standing in one corner of the room. Not to take up your time for nothing, two more men, more old-fashioned dressed than the first, were soon standing in two other corners. Jack was a little cowed at first, but found his courage growing stronger every moment, and what would you have of it, the three old gentlemen began to kick a football as fast as they could, the man in the three-cocked hat playing again' the other two.

'Fair play is bonny play,' says Jack, as bold as he could; but the terror was on him, and the words came out as if he was frightened in his sleep; 'so I'll help *you*, sir.'

Well and good, he joined the sport, and kicked away till his shirt was ringing wet, savin' your presence, and the ball flying from one end of the room to the other like thunder, and still not a word was exchanged. At last the day began to break, and poor Jack was dead beat, and he thought, by the way the three ghosts began to look at himself and themselves, that they wished him to speak.

So, says he, 'Gentlemen, as the sport is nearly over, and I done my best to please you, would you tell a body what is the reason of your coming here night after night, and how could I give you rest, if it is rest you want?'

'Them is the wisest words,' says the ghost with the three-cocked hat, 'you ever said in your life. Some of those that came before you found courage enough to take a part in our game, but no one had energy enough to speak to us. I am the father of the good man of next house, that man in the left corner is *my* father, and the

man on my right is my grandfather. From father to son we were too fond of money. We lent it at ten times the honest interest it was worth; we never paid a debt we could get over, and almost starved our tenants and labourers.'

'Here,' says he, lugging a large drawer out of the wall; 'here is the gold and notes that we put together, and we were not honestly entitled to the one-half of it; and here,' says he, opening another drawer, 'are bills and memorandums that'll show who were wronged, and who are entitled to get a great deal paid back to them. Tell my son to saddle two of his best horses for himself and yourself, and keep riding day and night, till every man and woman we ever wronged be rightified. When that is done, come here again some night; and if you don't hear or see anything, we'll be at rest, and you may marry my grand-daughter as soon as you please.'

Just as he said these words, Jack could see the wall through his body, and when he winked to clear his sight, the kitchen was as empty as a noggin turned upside down. At the very moment the farmer and his daughter lifted the latch, and both fell on their knees when they saw Jack alive. He soon told them everything that happened, and for three days and nights did the farmer and himself ride about, till there wasn't a single wronged person left without being paid to the last farthing.

The next night Jack spent in the kitchen he fell asleep before he was after sitting a quarter of an hour at the fire, and in his sleep he thought he saw three white birds flying up to heaven from the steeple of the next church.

Jack got the daughter for his wife, and they lived comfortably in the old castle; and if ever he was tempted to hoard up gold, or keep for a minute a guinea or a shilling from the man that earned it through the nose, he bethought him of the ghosts and the game of football.

(from *Legendary Fictions of the Irish Celts*)

31

The Piper and the Púca

by DOUGLAS HYDE

In the old times, there was a half fool living in Dunmore, in the county Galway, and although he was excessively fond of music, he was unable to learn more than one tune, and that was the 'Black Rogue'. He used to get a good deal of money from the gentlemen, for they used to get sport out of him. One night the piper was coming home from a house where there had been a dance, and he was half drunk. When he came to a little bridge that was up by his mother's house, he squeezed the pipes on, and began playing the 'Black Rogue'. The Púca came behind him, and flung him up on his own back. There were long horns on the Púca, and

the piper got a good grip of them, and then he said —

'Destruction on you, you nasty beast, let me home. I have a ten-penny piece in my pocket for my mother, and she wants snuff.'

'Never mind your mother,' said the Púca, 'but keep your hold. If you fall, you will break your neck and your pipes.' Then the Púca said to him, 'Play up for me the "Shan Van Vocht" *(An t-Sean-Bhean Bhocht).'*

'I don't know it,' said the piper.

'Never mind whether you do or you don't,' said the Púca. 'Play up, and I'll make you know.'

The piper put wind in his bag, and he played such music as made himself wonder.

'Upon my word, you're a fine music-master,' says the piper then; 'but tell me where you're bringing me.'

'There's a great feast in the house of the Banshee, on the top of Croagh Patrick tonight,' says the Púca, 'and I'm bringing you there to play music, and, take my word, you'll get the price of your trouble.'

'By my word, you'll save me a journey, then,' says the piper, 'for Father William put a journey to Croagh Patrick on me, because I stole a white gander from him last Martinmas.'

The Púca rushed him across hills and bogs and rough places, till he brought him to the top of Croagh

Patrick. Then the Púca struck three blows with his foot, and a great door opened, and they passed in together, into a fine room.

The piper saw a golden table in the middle of the room, and hundreds of old women sitting round about it. The old women rose up, and said, 'A hundred thousand welcomes to you, you Púca of November. Who is this you have with you?'

'The best piper in Ireland,' says the Púca.

One of the old women struck a blow on the ground, and a door opened in the side of the wall, and what should the piper see coming out but the white gander which he had stolen from Father William.

'By my conscience, then,' says the piper, 'myself and my mother ate every taste of that gander, only one wing, and I gave that to Moyra-Rua, and it's she told the priest I stole his gander.'

The gander cleaned the table, and carried it away, and the Púca said, 'Play up music for these ladies.'

The piper played up, and the old women began dancing, and they were dancing till they were tired. Then the Púca said to pay the piper, and every old woman drew out a gold piece, and gave it to him.

'By the tooth of Patrick,' said he, 'I'm as rich as the son of a lord.'

'Come with me,' says the Púca, 'and I'll bring you home.'

They went out then, and just as he was going to ride on the Púca, the gander came up to him, and gave him a new set of pipes. The Púca was not long until he brought him to Dunmore, and he threw the piper off at the little bridge, and then he told him to go home, and says to him, 'You have two things now that you never had before — you have sense and music.'

The piper went home, and he knocked at his mother's door, saying, 'Let me in, I'm as rich as a lord, and I'm the best piper in Ireland.'

'You're drunk,' said the mother.

'No, indeed,' says the piper, 'I haven't drunk a drop.'

The mother let him in, and he gave her the gold pieces, and, 'Wait now,' says he, 'till you hear the music I'll play.'

He buckled on the pipes, but instead of music, there came a sound as if all the geese and ganders in Ireland were screeching together. He wakened the neighbours, and they were all mocking him, until he put on the old pipes, and then he played melodious music for them; and after that he told them all he had gone through that night.

The next morning, when his mother went to look at the gold pieces, there was nothing there but the leaves of a plant.

The piper went to the priest, and told him his story, but the priest would not believe a word from him, until he put the pipes on him, and then the screeching of the ganders and geese began.

'Leave my sight, you thief,' says the priest.

But nothing would do the piper till he would put the old pipes on him to show the priest that his story was true.

He buckled on the old pipes, and he played melodious music, and from that day till the day of his death, there was never a piper in the county Galway was as good as he was.

(from *Leabhar Sgeulaigheachta*, and included in W.B. Yeats's collection, *Fairy and Folk Tales of the Irish Peasantry*)

The Wishing Chair

A story of the Olden Time

by SINÉAD DE VALERA

'We are a happy family,' said Shane MacFadden, as he and his wife and daughter Róisín were having their supper one fine summer evening.

'Yes, indeed, Shane,' said his wife, 'but you have to work hard to keep us in such comfort.'

'You know, Nóra, I am well helped by you and Róisín.'

'And, Father,' said Róisín, 'you also have managed to give me a good education and the opportunity to learn to play the harp.'

Róisín gave much pleasure to her parents by playing for them in the long winter evenings.

They were indeed a happy family with no thought of the trouble that was to come to them.

Sickness broke out in the neighbourhood. The inmates of the little house did not escape. Both father and mother died. Róisín recovered. A sad and lonely girl she was.

Her aunt, who lived some distance away, said she would leave her own house and come with her two daughters to live with her.

'I will be a mother to you, Róisín,' she said, 'and Mella and Gobnait will be just the same as sisters.'

It was a sad day for Róisín that the three women came to the house. All three were lazy and idle. They left all the work to Róisín.

37

The two girls were always arguing and quarrelling.

'I am tired of this life,' Mella said one day. 'I wish some handsome, rich man would come and marry me.'

'You with your yellow face and long, lanky figure the wife of a rich, handsome man!' said Gobnait.

'Well, Gobnait, I would rather have my nice, slight figure than be a fat, heavy creature like you. It is well you have such huge feet for if they were small they would never support your big, bulky body. If you did not eat so much you might have a nice, slight figure like mine.'

Róisín tried to make peace between them.

'You would both be much happier if you did not quarrel so much,' she said.

'Oh, you need not talk, Róisín,' said Mella. 'Everyone loves you.'

'Yes,' added Gobnait, 'and with your beauty you prevent anyone from looking at either of us.'

'You were lucky, too, in having had such devoted parents and in getting a good education.'

'Our parents took very little care with our upbringing,' said Mella. 'Even now my mother does not bother about us. She is either dozing at the fire or talking to the neighbours.'

There was neither peace nor comfort in the house and Róisín was very unhappy.

One night the sisters were looking out the window while their mother was sitting at the fire. Róisín was trying to tidy the kitchen.

'There is the new moon,' said Gobnait. 'I see it clear in the sky and not through a tree. Perhaps it will bring me good luck.'

'I don't care about the moon,' was Mella's remark. 'It never brought good luck to me.'

'Oh, look!' exclaimed Gobnait as a woman passed by the

window, 'there is Ana Críona (wise Ana). I will call her in. She has always plenty of news.'

The woman, as her name implied, was believed to be very wise. She had wonderful stories of the olden time. For miles round she was welcomed in the different houses, but she never stayed longer than a couple of days in each.

'Céad míle faílte (a hundred thousand welcomes), Ana,' said Róisín as she placed a chair near the fire.

'Though the day was warm the evening is chilly,' said Ana, 'and for an old woman like me the heat is pleasant.'

'Well, Ana, what news have you tonight?' asked Gobnait.

'Good news,' Ana replied, 'there is a new owner in Dunbawn Castle.'

'That is the castle,' said the mother, 'where the rich widow lived. She pined away after the death of her beautiful daughter Maeve.'

'Yes,' said Ana. 'The new owner is the widow's nephew. He is the last of the family and will inherit all the wealth.'

'What is his name?' asked Gobnait.

'Brian is his name. He is a fine, handsome young man.'

'And who will live with him in the Castle?' asked Mella.

'Oh! there are many attendants, but the principal one is Nuala, his old nurse. She has been with him since he was born. Both his parents have been dead for some years. I must be going now, for I have some distance to walk to the next house.'

'Oh, Ana, don't go till you tell me my fortune,' said Mella.

'And mine,' said Gobnait and Róisín, speaking together.

'Now, girls, I cannot tell you your fortune, but I can tell you

how to get good luck for yourselves. I am doing this for your sake, Róisín.'

The three girls gathered round her, anxiously waiting to hear what she would say.

'Your face is your fortune, *a stór*,' she said to Róisín, 'but it is your kind heart that will bring you the good luck.'

Ana smiled as she said:

'Now listen, girls.'

'You all know the high bank at the back of the strand near the Black Rock.'

'Yes,' came in a chorus.

'If you climb the bank you will come to a field. Walk through the field to the stone fence at the end.'

'Is it a long field?' asked lazy Gobnait.

'Yes, and when you have crossed the fence you will come to another field, a larger one.'

'Must we walk through that too?' asked Mella.

'Yes. And when you have crossed the fence at the far end you must walk through another field, much larger than either of the others.'

'Oh! I could never do that,' said Gobnait.

'Well, if you could not, it is useless for me to tell you any more.'

'Oh, go on, Ana,' said Mella. 'Don't mind lazy Gobnait.'

'Yes, go on,' said Gobnait, 'perhaps I could try the long walk.'

Ana continued:

'At the end of the third field there is a little wood. The trees form a kind of circle. In the centre of the circle there is a stone chair. This is the Wishing Chair. Anyone who sits in it can wish three times. In this way they can get three things which they desire.'

'I'll start off in the morning,' said Gobnait.

'No,' said Ana. 'You must go in the order of age. Mella first, then Gobnait and then Róisín. I must leave you now. I wish you all good luck. Good night.'

'I'll get up at cock crow in the morning,' said Mella.

'You will,' laughed Gobnait, 'if the cock begins to crow at midday. That is your usual time for rising.'

'You are not such an early riser yourself,' was the angry retort from Mella. Turning to Róisín, she said: 'You call me when you yourself are getting up.'

Next morning Mella left the house at an early hour. She walked briskly to the sea shore. When she reached the high banks she thought she would hardly be able to climb to the top of them. She made a great effort but by the time she had crossed the third field she was exhausted and parched with thirst.

With lagging steps, she came to the little wood. As she sat down in the chair she forgot everything but her desire for a drink. She cried aloud, 'Oh, how I wish I had a drink of clear, cold water.' Immediately the leaves on the trees overhead seemed to sing the words, 'Your wish will be granted.'

There at her feet she saw a well of sparkling water and a vessel at the brink.

She took a long drink and then remembered that one of her wishes was gone.

'My second wish is that I will have roses in my cheeks like the lovely colour that Róisín has in hers.'

Again the leaves seemed to sing —

'Your wish will be granted.'

All at once nice pink roses appeared in her cheeks, but there were thorns in each which pricked her.

'Oh,' she cried, 'my third wish is that these thorny roses will go away. Bad as my yellow face was it did not hurt like this.'

The voices in the leaves answered —

'Your wish will be granted.'

The water in the well turned yellow and in it she saw her face reflected.

'You don't look very happy,' said Gobnait as her sister reached home, weary and footsore.

'Never mind how I look,' snapped Mella.

'Well,' said Gobnait, 'I will try my luck tomorrow and I hope I will come home happier than you are after your adventure.'

Next morning, Gobnait rose early. She ate a good substantial breakfast, for she had always a great appetite.

Her experience was much the same as her sister's till she reached the wishing chair.

The fresh air made her very hungry.

'I'm starving,' she cried out.

'I wish I had a good dinner.'

The voices in the leaves called out —

'Your wish will be granted.'

There beside her, on a crystal tray, she saw a delicious meal. She ate heartily. Then she remembered that one of her wishes was gone.

'My second wish is that I will have a nice slight figure instead of being so fat and bulky.'

The voices in the leaves said —

'Your wish will be granted.'

Thereupon she felt her body shrinking and shrinking till her clothes hung so loosely round her that she looked like a long pole. Her feet seemed now to be enormous under her thin, lean body.

'Oh,' she said, 'I wish I had my own figure back again.'

Again came the song in the leaves —

'Your wish will be granted.'

All at once her own appearance returned.

She went home and ate a fine supper. Then she went to bed and tried to sleep off her disappointment.

On the third morning, Róisín got up very early. She left every-thing in order for the three lazy women who were still sleeping.

After a hasty meal she set out for The Wishing Chair.

The beauty of the morning made her glad. The sea was calm and sparkling under the golden rays of the sun. As she went through the fields she stopped for a moment to gather some of the wild scabious that grew on the borders of the fields. All was calm and peaceful in the brightness of the lovely summer day.

Still it was a weary girl that reached The Wishing Chair. She sank down on the chair, worn out for want of food and rest.

Unconsciously she called out —

'I wish I could rest and slumber a while.'

The voices in the leaves sang —

'Your wish will be granted.'

Suddenly she was asleep and dreaming. In her dream she saw a tall, handsome man. He smiled at her and seemed about to speak. While still half-dreaming, she exclaimed —

'Oh! how I wish that such a man as that would be my husband.'

The voices in the leaves sang —

'Your wish will be granted.'

'My third wish is that I will soon have a home far away from my aunt and cousins.'

The voices in the leaves answered —

'Your wish will be granted.'

She began her return journey. After having walked about a mile she heard a cry from a small tree by the wayside. As she stopped she saw a bird hanging from one of the branches. A thread of hair had evidently got entangled in its foot. She climbed up the bank where the tree grew and set the captive free.

The bird flew to a neighbouring tree. It chirrupped gaily, as if to thank the friend who had given it its liberty.

As Róisín was descending from the bank she came upon a large stone and hurt her foot badly. When she tried to walk she found she could not move without severe pain.

Her home was far distant and very few people came along the way. To add to her troubles her dress had got badly torn.

Poor Róisín was in despair. She sat down by the wayside and cried. After a while she heard the sound of approaching footsteps. Round a bend in the road a woman came into sight. To her relief and delight she saw her friend Ana Críona coming towards her.

'What is the matter with my *cailín dílís?*' asked Anna.

While Róisín was telling her friend all that had happened, a sound of wheels was heard. Round the curve came a splendid carriage drawn by two fine horses.

Ana rushed forward and stood in front of the carriage. It stopped. The door was opened by the footman. A young man alighted. Róisín looked at his face and uttered a cry. She would have fallen if Ana had not caught her as she became unconscious.

The stranger was the man she had seen in her dream.

Ana recognised him as Brian, the new owner of Dunbawn Castle.

'Oh! Sir,' said Ana, 'have pity on this poor girl. She has hurt her foot and is not able to walk.'

'Where is her home?' Brian asked.

'A good distance from here, if indeed, it can be called a home

for there will be small comfort
when she goes there.'

Róisín had now partly re-
covered consciousness.

'Will you come with her if
I take her to my home?' asked
Brian.

'Gladly will I go. I would do anything for the girl I love so well.'

Turning to Róisín she said —

'Come now, my girl, good fortune has sent a carriage to bring
you to a nicer place than the home you have left.'

Still in a half-swoon, Róisín was helped into the carriage. Ana
sat beside her and talked cheerfully, telling her all would be well.

The carriage stopped outside a splendid castle. When the door
was opened an elderly woman with a kindly face came forward to
meet Brian.

'I have brought visitors, Nuala,' he said.

Róisín, half dazed with wondering, was led to the door.

'Well, my son,' said Nuala, 'if kindness and beauty are recom-
mendations, the visitors have certainly a big share of both.'

She led them to a fine room and placed Róisín on a comfortable
couch.

Brian came into the room and soon Nuala had heard the whole
history of the meeting.

'I must go to some friends I promised to see this evening,' said
Brian. 'I will not be back for some days. Will you, Nuala, take care
of our guests till I return?'

'That I will do and welcome,' said Nuala. 'Indeed it will be nice
to have someone young in the house.'

Soon Róisín was in a comfortable room with a dainty meal
placed before her. Ana shared the meal and cheered the patient
with the interesting things she had to tell.

'Now, Róisín,' said Nuala, 'rest for a while. Ana and I will have a little chat.'

When the two women were talking together, Nuala said —

'I have taken Róisín to my heart. Her beautiful fair hair and blue eyes remind me of my dear boy's cousin Maeve. I will be lonely when she leaves.'

A far-away look came into Ana's eyes as she said, 'Yes, when she leaves.'

Gradually the sprained foot improved until Róisín was able to walk without trouble.

'Now, Ana,' she said, 'since I am able to walk again I should return home. I fear I have outstayed my welcome by remaining so long.'

'Oh, *alanna*,' said Nuala, 'don't think of going until my dear boy comes back. He would never forgive me if I let you go without seeing him again. What do you say, Ana?'

Ana paused and looked very wise. Then she said, 'My advice is that Róisín stays.'

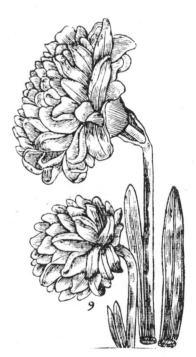

There was now the question of dress to be considered as Róisín's own had been so badly torn.

'Will the pair of you come with me to Maeve's room?' asked Nuala.

'There are many dresses there which the poor girl never wore.'

Ana was lost in admiration of Róisín when she saw her arrayed in a magnificent dress.

'I always knew you were beautiful,' she said, 'but you now look like some wonderful creature from fairyland.'

'Perhaps,' said Nuala, 'you would like to see the different rooms in the house.'

'Oh, yes,' was the answer from both.

'Here,' said Nuala, 'is the room where poor Maeve used to play the harp.'

'Oh, may I play, please?' asked Róisín.

'Of course, *a stór*, and welcome. Come, Ana, and I will show you the other rooms.'

Róisín forgot everything in her delight in the music. She played on and on and did not notice that the door of the room had been opened until she heard a voice say, 'Maeve.' She turned round and saw Brian standing in the room.

'I fear I have startled you,' he said. 'For a moment I thought my cousin Maeve was back again. Please continue to play.'

Róisín was unable to play. She felt as if she were again in The Wishing Chair dreaming of the handsome young man who now stood by her side.

Ana and Nuala came into the room. 'Now,' said Ana, 'I can start on my travels again. The roving life suits me best.'

'I wish you would stay, Ana,' said Brian, 'but I understand your longing to return to your old way of life, but I want to ask you to leave Róisín with us.'

'Oh, yes, Ana,' said Nuala, 'please leave Róisín with us.'

'Won't you stay, Róisín?' asked Brian, 'and stay always, for from the moment I first saw you I knew you were the girl I would like to make my wife.'

'And perhaps later on,' said Ana, with a knowing smile, 'she will tell you of the first moment she saw you.'

Nuala took Róisín in her arms, saying — 'Oh, we will now have a happy home. My dear boy won't be lonely any more.'

'But my aunt and cousins!' said Róisín.

'Your aunt and cousins!' exclaimed Ana. 'If ever they attempt to come near you I'll get all the bad fairies in the country to plague them day and night. *Slán agaibh* (good bye) now. My next visit will be for the happy wedding.'

With these words she hurried off.

The wedding was one of the grandest ever seen in the countryside and Brian and Róisín lived happy ever after.

(from *The Four Leaved Shamrock*)

Diarmuid Ulta and the King

by JEREMIAH CURTIN

There was a king in South Erin once, and he had an only daughter of great beauty. The daughter said that she would marry no man but the man who would sail to her father's castle in a three-masted ship, and the castle was twenty miles from deep water. The father said that even if the daughter was willing, he'd never give her to any man but the man who would come in a ship.

Diarmuid Ulta was the grandson of a great man from Spain who had settled in Erin, and he lived near Kilcar. Diarmuid heard of the daughter of the king of South Erin, and fixed in his mind to provide such a ship and go to the castle of the king.

Diarmuid left home one day, and was walking toward Killybegs, thinking how to find such a ship, or the man who would make it. When he had gone as far as Buttermilk Cliff, he saw a red champion coming against him in a ship that was sailing along over the country like any ship on the sea.

'What journey are you on?' asked the red champion of Diarmuid; 'and where are you going?'

'I am going,' answered Diarmuid, 'to the castle of a king in South Erin to know will he give me his daughter in marriage, and to know if the daughter herself is willing to marry me. The daughter will have no husband unless a man who brings a ship to her father's

castle, and the king will give her to no other.'

'Come with me,' said the red man. 'Take me as comrade, and what will you give me?'

'I will give you what is right,' said Diarmuid.

'What will you give me?'

'I will give you the worth of your trouble.'

Diarmuid went in the ship, and they sailed on till they came to Conlun, a mile above Killybegs. There they saw twelve men cutting sods, and a thirteenth eating every sod that they cut.

'You must be a strange man to eat what sods twelve others can cut for you,' said Diarmuid; 'what is your name?'

'Sod-eater.'

'We are going,' said the red man, 'to the castle of a king in South Erin. Will you come with us?'

'What wages will you give me?'

'Five gold-pieces,' said the red man.

'I will go with you.'

The three sailed on till they came to the river Kinvara, one mile below Killybegs, and saw a man with one foot on each bank, with his back toward the sea and his face to the current. The man did not let one drop of water in the river pass him, but drank every drop of it.

'Oh,' said the red man, 'what a thirst there is on you to drink a whole river! How are you so thirsty?'

'When I was a boy, my mother used to send me to school, and I did not wish to go there. She flogged and beat me every day, and

I cried and lamented so much that a black spot rose on my heart from the beating; that is why there is such thirst on me now.'

'What is your name, and will you go with us?'

'My name is Gulping-a-River. I will go with you if you give me wages.'

'I will give you five gold-pieces,' said the red man.

'I will go with you,' said Gulping-a-River.

They sailed on then to Howling River, within a mile of Dun Kinealy. There they saw a man blowing up stream with one nostril, and the other stopped with a plug.

'Why blow with one nostril?' asked the red man.

'If I were to blow with the two,' replied the stranger, 'I would send you with your ship and all that are in it up into the sky and so far away that you would never come back again.'

'Who are you, and will you take service with me?'

'My name is Greedy-of-Blowing, and I will go with you for wages.'

'You will have five gold-pieces.'

'I am your man,' said Greedy-of-Blowing.

They sailed away after that to Bunlaky, a place one mile beyond Dun Kinealy; and there they found a man crushing stones with the end of his back, by sitting down on them suddenly.

'What are you doing there?' asked the red man.

'My name is Ironback,' answered the stranger. 'I am breaking stones with the end of my back to make a mill, a bridge, and a road.'

'Will you come with us?' asked the red man.

'I will for just wages,' said Ironback.

'You will get five gold-pieces.'

'I will go in your company,' said Ironback.

They went on sailing, and were a half a mile below Mount Charles when they saw a man running up against them faster than any wind, and one leg tied to his shoulder.

'Where are you going, and what is your hurry? Why are you travelling on one leg?' asked the red man.

'I am running to find a master,' said the other. 'If I were to go on my two legs, no man could see me or set eyes on me.'

'What can you do? I may take you in service.'

'I am a very good messenger. My name is Foot-on-Shoulder.'

'I will give you five gold pieces.'

'I will go with you,' said the other.

The ship moved on now, and never stopped till within one mile of Donegal they saw, at a place called Kilemard, a man lying in a grass field with his cheek to the earth.

'What are you doing there?' asked the red man.

'Holding my ear to the ground, and hearing the grass grow.'

'You must have good ears. What is your name; and will you take service with me?'

'My name is Hearing Ear. I will go with you for good wages.'

'You will have five gold-pieces.'

'I am your man,' said Hearing Ear.

They went next to Laihy, where they found a man named Son-of-Knowledge, and he sitting at the roadside chewing his thumb.

'What are you doing there?' asked the red man.

'I am learning whatever I wish to know by chewing my thumb.'

'Take service with me, and come on the ship.'

He went on the same terms as the others, and they never stopped nor halted till they came to the castle of the king. They were outside the walls three days and three nights before any man spoke a word to them. At last the king sent a messenger to ask who were they and what brought them.

'I have come in a ship for your daughter, and my name is Diarmuid Ulta,' was the answer the king got.

The king was frightened at the answer, though he knew himself well enough that it was for the daughter Diarmuid had come in the ship, and was greatly in dread that she would be taken from him. He went then to an old henwife that lived near the castle to know could he save the daughter, and how could he save her.

'If you'll be said by me,' said the henwife, 'you'll bid them all come to a feast in the castle. Before they come, let your men put sharp poisoned spikes under the cushions of the seats set apart for the company. They will sit on the spikes, swell up to the size of a horse, and die before the day is out, every man of them.'

Hearing Ear was listening, heard all the talk between the king and the henwife, and told it.

'Now,' said Son-of-Knowledge to Diarmuid, 'the king will invite us all to a feast to-morrow, and you will go there and take us. It is better to send Ironback to try our seats, and sit on them, for under the cushion of each one will be poisoned spikes to kill us.'

That day the king sent a message to Diarmuid. 'Will you come,' said he, 'with your men, to a feast in my castle to-morrow? I am glad to have such guests, and you are welcome.'

'Very thankful am I,' said Diarmuid. 'We will come to the feast.'

Before the company came, Ironback went into the hall of feasting, looked at everything, sat down on each place, and made splinters of the seats.

'Those seats are of no use,' said Ironback; 'they are no better than so many cabbage stalks.'

The king had iron seats brought in, strong ones. There was no harm to Diarmuid and his company from that feast.

Away went the king to the henwife, and told how the seats had been broken. 'What am I to do now?' asked he.

'Say that to get your daughter they must eat what food is in your castle at one meal.'

Next day Diarmuid went to the castle, and asked, 'Am I to have your daughter now?'

'You are not,' said the king, 'unless your company will eat what food is in my castle at one meal.'

'Very well,' said Diarmuid, 'have the meal ready.'

The king gave command to bring out the hundred and fifty tons of provisions in the castle all prepared and ready for eating.

Diarmuid came with his men, and Sod-eater began; and it was as much as all the king's servants could do to bring food as fast as he ate it, and he never stopped till there was not a pound of the hundred and fifty tons left.

'Is this all you have to give me?' asked Sod-eater. 'I could eat three times as much.'

'Oh, we have no more,' said the servants.

'Where is our dinner?' asked Diarmuid.

The king had nothing for the others, and he had nothing for himself. All had to go away hungry, and there was great dissatisfaction in the castle, and complaining.

The king had nothing to do now but to go to the henwife a third time for advice in his trouble.

'You have,' said she, 'three hundred and fifty pipes of wine. If his company cannot drink every drop of the wine, don't give him your daughter.'

Next day Diarmuid went to the castle. 'Am I to have your daughter now?' asked he of the king.

'I will not give my daughter,' said the king, 'unless you and your company will drink the three hundred and fifty pipes of wine that are in my castle.'

'Bring out the wine,' said Diarmuid; 'we'll come to-morrow, and do the best we can to drink it.'

Diarmuid and his men went next day to where the wine was. Gulping-a-River was the man for drinking, and they let him at it. After he got a taste, he was that anxious that he broke in the head of one pipe after another, and drank till there wasn't a drop left in the three hundred and fifty pipes. All the wine did was to put thirst on Gulping-a-River; and he was that mad with thirst that he drank up the spring well at the castle, and all the springs in the neighbourhood, and a loch three miles distant, so that in the evening there wasn't a drop of water for man or beast in the whole place.

What did the king do but go to the henwife the fourth time.

'Oh,' said she, 'there is no use in trying to get rid of him this way; you can make no hand of Diarmuid by eating or drinking. Do you send him now to the Eastern World to get the bottle of

cure from the three sons of Seán Mac Glinn, and to have it at the castle before noon to-morrow.'

'Am I to get your daughter now?' asked Diarmuid of the king.

'You'll not get my daughter,' said the king, 'unless you have for me here to-morrow the bottle of cure which the three sons of Seán Mac Glinn have in the Eastern World.'

Diarmuid went to his ship with the king's answer.

'Let me go,' said Foot-on-Shoulder. 'I will bring you the bottle in season.'

'You may go,' said Diarmuid.

Away went Foot-on-Shoulder, and was at the sea in a minute. He made a ship of his cap, a mast of his stick, a sail of his shirt, and away with him sailing over the sea, never stopping nor halting till he reached the Eastern World.

In five hours, he came to a castle where the walls of defence were sixty-six feet high and fifty-five feet thick. Seán Mac Glinn's three sons were playing football on the top of the wall.

'Send down the bottle of cure to me,' said Foot-on-Shoulder, 'or I'll have your lives.'

'We will not give you the bottle of cure; and if you come up, it will be as hard to find your brains five minutes after as to find the clay of a cabin broken down a hundred years ago.'

Foot-on-Shoulder made one spring, and rose six feet above the wall. They were so frightened at the sight of what he did, and were so in dread of him that they cried, 'You'll get what you want, only spare us — leave us our lives. You are the best man that we have ever seen coming from any part; you have done what no man could ever do before this. You'll get the bottle of cure; but will you send it back again?'

'I will not promise that,' said Foot-on-Shoulder; 'I may send it, and I may not.'

They gave him the bottle. He went his way to his ship, and sailed home to Erin. Next morning the henwife dressed herself up as a piper, and, taking a rod of enchantment with her, went away, piping on a hill which Foot-on-Shoulder had to cross in coming to the castle. She thought he would stop to listen to the music she was making, and then she would strike him with the rod, and make a stone of him. She was piping away for herself on the hill like any poor piper making his living. Hearing Ear heard the music, and told Diarmuid. Son-of-Knowledge chewed his thumb at Diarmuid's command, and found out that the piper was the king's henwife, and discovered her plans.

'Oh,' said Son-of-Knowledge to Diarmuid, 'unless you take her out of that, she will make trouble for us.'

'Greedy-of-Blowing, can you make away with that old woman on the hill?' asked Diarmuid.

'I can indeed,' said Greedy-of-Blowing.

With that, he ran to the foot of the hill; and with one blast from both nostrils, he sent the old hag up into the sky, and away she went sailing so that neither tale nor word of her ever came back.

Foot-on-Shoulder was at the ship outside the castle walls half an hour before noon, and gave the bottle of cure to Diarmuid.

Diarmuid went that minute to the castle, and stood before the king.

'Here is the bottle of cure which I got from the three sons of Seán Mac Glinn in the Eastern World. Am I to get your daughter now?'

'I'll send you my answer to the ship,' said the king.

Where should the king go now in his trouble but to find the henwife. She was not at home. He sent men to look for the old woman; no tidings of her that day. They waited till the next day; not a sight of her. The following morning the king sent servants and messengers to look for the henwife. They searched the whole neighbourhood but could not find her. He sent all his warriors and forces. They looked up and down, searched the whole kingdom, searched for nine days and nights, but found no trace of the henwife.

The king consented at last to give his daughter to Diarmuid, and he had to consent, and no thanks to him, for he couldn't help himself. The daughter was glad and willing; she loved Diarmuid from the first, but the father would not part with her.

The wedding lasted a day and a year, and when that time was over, Diarmuid went home on the ship to Kilcar, and there he paid all his men their wages, and they went each to his own place.

The red man stayed some time in the neighbourhood, and what should he do one day but seize Diarmuid's wife, put her in the ship, and sail away with her. When going, she put him under injunction not to marry her for a day and a year.

Now Diarmuid, who was hunting when the red man stole his wife, was in great grief and misery, for he knew not where the red man lived nor where he should travel to find him. At last he sent a message of inquiry to the King of Spain; and the king's answer was, 'Only two persons in the whole world know where that man lives, Great Limper, King of Light, and Black Thorn of Darkness. I have written to these two, and told them to go to you.'

The two men came in their own ship through the air to Kilcar, to Diarmuid, and talked and took counsel.

'I do not know where the red man can be,' said Black Thorn, 'unless in Kilchroti; let us go to that place.'

They sailed away in their ship, and it went straight to the place they wanted. They had more power than the red man, and could send their ship anywhere.

In five days and nights they were at Kilchroti. They went straight to the house, and no one in the world could see the red man's house there but these two. Black Thorn struck the door, and it flew open. The red man, who was inside, took their hands, welcomed them heartily, and said, 'I hope it is not to do me harm that you are here.'

'It is not to harm you or any one that we are here,' replied they. 'We are here only to get what is right and just, but without that, we will not go from this.'

'What is the right and just that you are here for?' asked the red man.

'Diarmuid's wife,' replied Black Thorn, 'and it was wrong in you to take her; you must give her up.'

'I will fight rather than give her,' said the red man.

'Fighting will not serve you,' said Black Thorn, 'it is better for you to give her to us.'

'You will not get her without seven tons of gold,' said the red man. 'If you bring me the gold, I will give her to you. If you come without it, you'll get fight from me.'

'We will give you the gold,' said Great Limper, 'within seven days.'

'Agreed,' said the red man.

'Come to the ship,' said Great Limper to Black Thorn.

They went on board, and sailed away.

'I was once on a ship which was wrecked on the coast of Spain with forty-five tons of gold. I know where that gold is; we will get it,' said Great Limper.

The two sailed to where the gold was, took seven tons of it, and on the sixth day they had it in Kilchroti, in front of the red man's house. They weighed out the gold to him. They went then to find Diarmuid's wife. She was behind nine doors; each door was nine planks in thickness, and bolted with nine bars of iron. The red man opened the doors; all went in, and looked at the chamber. The woman went out first, next the red man; and, seizing the door, he thought to close it on Great Limper and Black Thorn, but Black Thorn was too quick for him, and before the red man could close the door he shot him, first with a gold and then with a silver bullet.

The red man fell dead on the threshold.

'I knew he was preparing some treachery,' said Black Thorn. 'When we weighed the gold to him, he let such a loud laugh of delight out of him.'

They took the woman and the gold to Diarmuid; they stayed nine days and nights with him in Kilcar, eating, drinking, and making merry. They drank to the King of Spain, to all Erin, to themselves, and to their well-wishers. You see, I had great work to keep up with them these nine days and nights. I hope they will do well hereafter.

(from *Hero Tales of Ireland* by Jeremiah Curtin, who was told the story by James Byrne of Glen Columkil, Co. Donegal)

The Fairy Dance

by LADY WILDE

One evening late in November, which is the month when spirits have most power over all things, as the prettiest girl in all the island was going to the well for water, her foot slipped and she fell. It was an unlucky omen, and when she got up and looked round it seemed to her as if she were in a strange place, and all around her was changed as if by enchantment. But at some distance she saw a great crowd gathered round a blazing fire, and she was drawn slowly on towards them, till at last she stood in the very midst of the people; but they kept silence, looking fixedly at her; and she was afraid, and tried to turn and leave them, but she could not. Then a beautiful youth, like a prince, with a red sash, and a golden band on his long yellow hair, came up and asked her to dance.

'It is a foolish thing of you, sir, to ask me to dance,' she said, 'when there is no music.'

Then he lifted his hand and made a sign to the people, and instantly the sweetest music sounded near her and around her, and the young man took her hand, and they danced and danced till the moon and the stars went down, but she seemed like one floating on the air, and she forgot everything in the world except the dancing, and the sweet low music, and her beautiful partner.

At last the dancing ceased, and her partner thanked her, and he invited her to supper with the company. Then she saw an opening in the ground, and a flight of steps, and the young man, who seemed to be the king amongst them all, led her down, followed by the whole company. At the end of the stairs they came upon a large hall, all bright and beautiful with gold and silver lights; and the table was covered with everything good to eat, and wine was poured out in golden cups for them to drink. When she sat down they all pressed her to eat the food and to drink the wine; and as she was weary after the dancing, she took the golden cup the prince handed to her, and raised it to her lips to drink. Just then, a man passed close to her, and whispered —

'Eat no food, and drink no wine, or you will never reach home.'

So she laid down the cup, and refused to drink. On this they were angry, and a great noise arose, and a fierce, dark man stood up, and said —

'Whoever comes to us must drink with us.'

And he seized her arm, and held the wine to her lips, so that she almost died of fright. But at that moment a red-haired man came up, and he took her by the hand and led her out.

'You are safe for this time,' he said. 'Take this herb, and hold it in your hand till you reach home, and no one can harm you.' And he gave her a branch of a plant called *athair-luss* (ground ivy).

This she took, and fled away along the sward in the dark night; but all the time she heard footsteps behind her in pursuit. At last she reached home and barred the door, and went to bed, when a great clamour arose outside, and voices were heard crying to her —

'The power we had over you is gone through the magic of the herb; but wait — when you dance again to the music on the hill, you will stay with us for evermore, and none shall hinder.'

However, she kept the magic branch safely, and the fairies never troubled her more; but it was long and long before the sound of the fairy music left her ears which she had danced to that November night on the hillside with her fairy lover.

(from *Ancient Legends, Mystic Charms and Superstitions of Ireland*)

Master and Man

by T. CROFTON CROKER

Billy Mac Daniel was once as likely a young man as ever shook his brogue at a festival, emptied a quart, or handled a shillelagh; fearing for nothing but the want of drink; caring for nothing but who should pay for it; and thinking of nothing but how to make fun over it; drunk, or sober, a word and a blow was ever the way with Billy Mac Daniel; and a mighty easy way it is of either getting into or of ending a dispute. More is the pity that, through the means of his thinking, and fearing, and caring for nothing, this same Billy Mac Daniel fell into bad company; for surely the good people are the worst of all company any one could come across.

It so happened that Billy was going home one clear frosty

night not long after Christmas; the moon was round and bright; but although it was as fine a night as heart could wish for, he felt pinched with cold. 'By my word,' chattered Billy, 'a drop of good liquor would be no bad thing to keep a man's soul from freezing in him; and I wish I had a full measure of the best.'

'Never wish it twice, Billy,' said a little man in a three-cornered hat, bound all about with gold lace, and with great silver buckles in his shoes, so big that it was a wonder how he could carry them, and he held out a glass as big as himself, filled with as good liquor as ever eye looked on or lip tasted.

'Success, my little fellow,' said Billy Mac Daniel, nothing daunted, though well he knew the little man to belong to the *good people*; 'here's your health, any way, and thank you kindly; no matter who pays for the drink;' and he took the glass and drained it to the very bottom without ever taking a second breath to it.

'Success,' said the little man; 'and you're heartily welcome, Billy; but don't think to cheat me as you have done others — out with your purse and pay me like a gentleman.'

'Is it I pay you?' said Billy; 'could I not just take you up and put you in my pocket as easily as a blackberry?'

'Billy Mac Daniel,' said the little man, getting very angry, 'you shall be my servant for seven years and a day, and that is the way I will be paid; so make ready to follow me.'

When Billy heard this he began to be very sorry for having used such bold words towards the little man; and he felt himself, yet could not tell how, obliged to follow the little man the live-long night about the country, up and down, and over hedge and ditch, and through bog and brake, without any rest.

When morning began to dawn the little man turned round to him and said, 'You may now go home, Billy, but on your peril don't fail to meet me in the Fort-field to-night; or if you do it may be the worse for you in the long run. If I find you a good servant, you will find me an indulgent master.'

Home went Billy Mac Daniel; and though he was tired and weary enough, never a wink of sleep could he get for thinking of the little man; but he was afraid not to do his bidding, so up he got in the evening, and away he went to the Fort-field. He was not long there before the little man came towards him and said, 'Billy, I want to go a long journey to-night; so saddle one of my horses, and you may saddle another for yourself, as you are to go along with me, and may be tired after your walk last night.'

Billy thought this very considerate of his master, and thanked him accordingly: 'But,' said he, 'if I may be so bold, sir, I would ask which is the way to your stable, for never a thing do I see but the fort here, and the old thorn tree in the corner of the field, and the stream running at the bottom of the hill, with the bit of bog over against us.'

'Ask no questions, Billy,' said the little man, 'but go over to that bit of bog, and bring me two of the strongest rushes you can find.'

Billy did accordingly, wondering what the little man would be at; and he picked two of the stoutest rushes he could find, with a

little bunch of brown blossom stuck at the side of each, and brought them back to his master.

'Get up, Billy,' said the little man, taking one of the rushes from him and striding across it.

'Where shall I get up, please your honour?' said Billy.

'Why, upon horseback, like me, to be sure,' said the little man.

'Is it after making a fool of me you'd be,' said Billy, 'bidding me get a horseback upon that bit of a rush? May be you want to persuade me that the rush I pulled but a while ago out of the bog over there is a horse?'

'Up! up! and no words,' said the little man, looking very angry; 'the best horse you ever rode was but a fool to it.' So Billy, thinking all this was in joke, and fearing to vex his master, straddled across the rush. 'Borram! Borram! Borram!' cried the little man three times, and Billy did the same after him; presently the rushes swelled up into fine horses, and away they went full speed; but Billy, who had put the rush between his legs, without much minding how he did it, found himself sitting on horseback the wrong way, which was rather awkward, with his face to the horse's tail; and so quickly had his steed started off with him that he had no power to turn round, and there was therefore nothing for it but to hold on by the tail.

At last they came to their journey's end, and stopped at the gate of a fine house. 'Now, Billy,' said the little man, 'do as you see me do, and follow me close; but as you did not know your horse's head from his tail, mind that your own head does not spin round until you can't tell whether you are standing on it or on your heels: for remember that old liquor, though able to make a cat speak, can make a man dumb.'

The little man then said some queer kind of words, out of which Billy could make no meaning; but he contrived to say them after him for all that; and in they both went through the key-hole of the door, and through one key-hole after another, until they got into the wine-cellar, which was well stored with all kinds of wine.

The little man fell to drinking as hard as he could, and Billy, no way disliking the example, did the same. 'The best of masters are you, surely,' said Billy to him; 'no matter who is the next; and well pleased will I be with your service if you continue to give me plenty to drink.'

'I have made no bargain with you,' said the little man, 'and will make none; but up and follow me.' Away they went, through key-hole after key-hole; and each mounting upon the rush which he left at the hall door, scampered off, kicking the clouds before them like snow-balls, as soon as the words, 'Borram, Borram, Borram,' had passed their lips.

When they came back to the Fort-field the little man dismissed Billy, bidding him to be there the next night at the same hour. Thus did they go on, night after night, shaping their course one night here, and another night there; sometimes north, and sometimes east, and sometimes south, until there was not a gentleman's wine-cellar in all Ireland they had not visited, and could tell the

flavour of every wine in it as well, ay, better than the butler himself.

One night when Billy Mac Daniel met the little man as usual in the Fortfield, and was going to the bog to fetch the horses for their journey, his master said to him, 'Billy, I shall want another horse to-night, for may be we may bring back more company than we take.' So Billy, who now knew better than to question any order given to him by his master, brought a third rush, much wondering who it might be that would travel back in their company, and whether he was about to have a fellow-servant. 'If I have,' thought Billy, 'he shall go and fetch the horses from the bog every night; for I don't see why I am not, every inch of me, as good a gentleman as my master.'

Well, away they went, Billy leading the third horse, and never stopped until they came to a snug farmer's house, in the county Limerick, close under the old castle of Carrigogunniel, that was built, they say, by the great Brian Boru. Within the house there was great carousing going forward, and the little man stopped outside for some time to listen; then turning round all of a sudden, said, 'Billy, I will be a thousand years old to-morrow!'

'God bless us, sir,' said Billy; 'will you?'

'Don't say these words again, Billy,' said the little old man, 'or

you will be my ruin for ever. Now Billy, as I will be a thousand years in the world to-morrow, I think it is full time for me to get married.'

'I think so too, without any kind of doubt at all,' said Billy, 'if ever you mean to marry.'

'And to that purpose,' said the little man, 'have I come all the way to Carrigogunniel; for in this house, this very night, is young Darby Riley going to be married to Bridget Rooney; and as she is a tall and comely girl, and has come of decent people, I think of marrying her myself, and taking her off with me.'

'And what will Darby Riley say to that?' said Billy.

'Silence!' said the little man, putting on a mighty severe look; 'I did not bring you here with me to ask questions;' and without holding further argument, he began saying the queer words which had the power of passing him through the key-hole as free as air, and which Billy thought himself mighty clever to be able to say after him.

In they both went; and for the better viewing the company, the little man perched himself up as nimbly as a cocksparrow upon one of the big beams which went across the house over all their heads, and Billy did the same upon another facing him; but not being much accustomed to roosting in such a place, his legs hung down as untidy as may be, and it was quite clear he had not copied the way in which the little man had bundled himself up together. If the little man had been a tailor all his life he could not have sat more contentedly upon his haunches.

There they were, both master and man, looking down upon the fun that was going forward; and under them were the priest and piper, and the father of Darby Riley, with Darby's two brothers and his uncle's son; and there were both the father and the mother of Bridget Rooney, and proud enough too the old couple were that night of their daughter, as good right they had; and her four sisters, with brand new ribbons in their caps, and her three brothers all looking as clean and as clever as any three boys in Munster, and there were uncles and aunts, and gossips and cousins enough besides to make a full house of it; and plenty was there to eat and drink on the table for every one of them, if they had been double the number.

Now it happened, just as Mrs. Rooney had helped his reverence to the first cut of the pig's head which was placed before her, beautifully bolstered up with white savoys, that the bride gave a sneeze, which made every one at table start, but not a soul said 'God bless us.' All thinking that the priest would have done so, as he ought if he had done his duty, no one wished to take the word out of his mouth, which, unfortunately, was preoccupied with pig's head and greens. And after a moment's pause the fun and merriment of the bridal feast went on without the pious benediction.

Of this circumstance both Billy and his master were no inattentive spectators from their exalted stations. 'Ha!' exclaimed the little man, throwing one leg from under him with a joyous flourish, and his eye twinkled with a strange light, whilst his eyebrows became elevated into the curvature of Gothic arches; 'Ha!' said he, leering down at the bride, and then up at Billy, 'I have half of her now, surely. Let her sneeze but twice more, and she is mine, in spite of priest, mass-book, and Darby Riley.'

Again the fair Bridget sneezed; but it was so gently, and she blushed so much, that few except the little man took, or seemed to take, any notice; and no one thought of saying 'God bless us.'

Billy all this time regarded the poor girl with a most rueful expression of countenance; for he could not help thinking what a terrible thing it was for a nice young girl of nineteen, with large blue eyes, transparent skin, and dimpled cheeks, suffused with health and joy, to be obliged to marry an ugly little bit of a man, who was a thousand years old, barring a day.

At this critical moment the bride gave a third sneeze, and Billy roared out with all his might, 'God save us!' Whether this exclamation resulted from his soliloquy, or from the mere force of habit, he never could tell exactly himself; but no sooner was it uttered than the little man, his face glowing with rage and disappointment, sprung from the beam on which he had perched himself, and shrieking out in the shrill voice of a cracked bagpipe, 'I discharge you from my service, Billy Mac Daniel — take *that* for your wages,' gave poor Billy a most furious kick in the back, which sent his unfortunate servant sprawling upon his face and hands right in the middle of the supper-table.

If Billy was astonished, how much more so was every one of the company into which he was thrown with so little ceremony. But when they heard his story, Father Cooney laid down his knife and fork, and married the young couple out of hand with all speed; and Billy Mac Daniel danced the Rinka at their wedding, and plenty did he drink at it too, which was what he thought more of than dancing.

(from *Fairy Legends and Traditions of the South of Ireland*)

The Thief

by PADRAIC PEARSE

One day when the boys of Gortmore were let out from school, after the Glencaha boys and the Derrybanniv boys had gone east, the Turlagh boys and the Inver boys stayed to have a while's chat before separating at the Rossnageeragh road. The master's house is exactly at the head of the road, its back to the hill and its face to Loch Ellery.

'I heard that the master's bees were swarming,' says Michileen Bartly Enda.

'In with you to the garden till we look at them,' says Daragh Barbara of the Bridge.

'I'm afraid,' says Michileen.

'What are you afraid of?' says Daragh.

'By my word, the master and the mistress will be out presently.'

'Who'll stay to give us word when the master will be coming?' says Daragh.

'I will,' says little Anthony Manning.

'That'll do,' says Daragh. 'Let a whistle when you see him leaving the school.'

In over the fence with him. In over the fence with the other boys after him.

'Have a care that none of you will get a sting,' says Anthony.

'Little fear,' says Daragh. And off forever with them.

Anthony sat on the fence, and his back to the road. He could see the master over his right shoulder if he'd leave the school-house. What a nice garden the master had, thought Anthony. He had rose-trees and gooseberry-trees and apple-trees. He had little white stones round the path. He had big white stones in a pretty rockery, and moss and maiden-hair Fern and common fern growing between them. He had . . .

Anthony saw a wonder greater than any wonder the master had in the garden. He saw a little, beautiful wee house under the shade of one of the rose-trees; it was made of wood; two storeys in it; white colour on the lower storey and red colour on the upper storey; a little green door on it; three windows of glass on it, one downstairs and two upstairs; house furniture in it, between tables and chairs and beds and delf, and the rest; and, says Anthony to himself, look at the lady of the house sitting in the door!

Anthony never saw a doll's house before, and it was a wonder to him, its neatness and order, for a toy. He knew that it belonged to the master's little girl, little Nance. A pity that his own little sister hadn't one like it — Eibhlin, the creature, that was stretched on her bed for a long three months, and she weak and sick! A pity she hadn't the doll itself! Anthony put the covetousness of his heart in that doll for Eibhlin. He looked over his right shoulder — neither master nor mistress was to be seen. He looked over his left shoulder — the other boys were out of sight. He didn't think the second thought. He gave his best leap from the fence; he seized the doll; he stuck it under his jacket; he clambered out over the ditch again, and away with him home.

'I have a present for you,' says he to Eibhlin, when he reached the house. 'Look!' and with that he showed her the doll.

There came a blush on the wasted cheeks of the little sick girl, and a light into her eyes.

'*Ora*, Anthony, love, where did you get it?' says she.

'The master's little Nance, that sent it to you for a present,' says Anthony.

Their mother came in.

'Oh, mameen, treasure,' says Eibhlin, 'look at the present that the master's little Nance sent me!'

'In earnest?' says the mother.

'Surely,' says Eibhlin. 'Anthony, it was, that brought it to me.

Anthony looked down at his feet, and began counting the toes that were on them.

'My own pet,' says the mother, 'isn't it she that was good to you! *Muise*, Nance! I'll go bail that that present will put great improvement on my little girl.'

And there came tears in the mother's eyes out of gratitude to little Nance because she remembered the sick child. Though he wasn't able to look his mother between the eyes, or at Eibhlin, with the dint of fear, Anthony was glad that he committed the theft.

He was afraid to say his prayers that night, and he lay down on his bed without as much as an 'Our Father.' He couldn't say the Act of Contrition, for it wasn't truthfully he'd be able to say to

God that he was sorry for that sin. It's often he started in the night, imagining that little Nance was coming seeking the doll from Eibhlin, that the master was taxing him with the robbery before the school, that there was a miraculous swarm of bees rising against him, and Daragh Barbara of the Bridge and the other boys exciting them with shouts and with the music of drums. But the next morning he said to himself: 'I don't care. The doll will make Eibhlin better.'

When he went to school the boys asked him why he went off unawares the evening before that, and he after promising them he'd keep watch.

'My mother sent for me,' says Anthony. 'She'd a task for me.'

When little Nance came into the school, Anthony looked at her under his brows. He fancied that she was after being crying; he thought that he saw the track of the tears on her cheeks. The first time the master called him by his name he jumped, because he thought that he was going to tax him with the fault or to cross-question him about the doll. He never put in as miserable a day as that day at school. But when he went home and saw the great improvement on Eibhlin, and she sitting up in the bed for the first time for a month, and the doll clasped in her arms, says he to himself: 'I don't care. The doll is making Eibhlin better.'

In his bed in the night-time he had bad dreams again. He thought that the master was after telling the police that he stole the doll, and that they were on his track; he imagined one time that there was a policeman hiding under the bed and that there was another hunkering behind the window-curtain. He screamed out in his sleep.

'What's on you?' says his father to him.

'The peeler that's going to take me,' says Anthony.

'You're only rambling, boy,' says his father to him. 'There's no peeler. Go to sleep.'

There was the misery of the world on the poor fellow from that

out. He used think they would be pointing fingers at him, and he going the road. He used think they would be shaking their heads and saying to each other, 'There's a thief,' or, 'Did you hear what Anthony Pharaig Manning did? Her doll he stole from the master's little Nance. Now what do you say?' But he didn't suffer rightly till he went to Mass on Sunday and till Father Ronan started preaching a sermon on the Seventh Commandment: 'Thou shalt not steal; and if you commit a theft it will not be forgiven you until you make restitution.' Anthony was full sure that it was a mortal sin. He knew that he ought to go to confession and tell the sin to the priest. But he couldn't go to confession, for he knew that the priest would say to him that he must give the doll back. And he wouldn't give the doll back. He hardened his heart and he said that he'd never give the doll back, for that the doll was making Eibhlin better every day.

One evening he was sitting by the bed-foot in serious talk with Eibhlin when his mother ran in in a hurry, and says she —

'Here's the mistress and little Nance coming up the bohereen!'

Anthony wished the earth would open and swallow him. His face was red up to his two ears. He was in a sweat. He wasn't able to say a word or to think a thought. But these words were running through his head: 'They'll take the doll from Eibhlin.' It was all the same to him what they'd say or what they'd do to himself. The only answer he'd have would be, 'The doll's making Eibhlin better.'

The mistress and little Nance came into the room. Anthony got up. He couldn't look them in the face. He began at his old clatter, counting the toes of his feet. Five on each foot; four toes and a big toe; or three toes, a big toe, and a little toe; that's five; twice five are ten; ten in all. He couldn't add to their number or take from them. His mother was talking, the mistress was talking, but Anthony paid no heed to them. He was waiting till something would be said about the doll. There was nothing for him to do till that but count his toes. One, two, three . . .

What was that? Eibhlin was referring to the doll. Anthony listened now.

'Wasn't it good of you to send me the doll?' she was saying to Nance. 'From the day Anthony brought it in to me a change began coming on me.'

'It did that,' says her mother. 'We'll be forever grateful to you for that same doll you sent to her. May God increase your store, and may He requite you for it a thousand times.'

Neither Nance nor the mistress spoke. Anthony looked at Nance shyly. His two eyes were stuck in the doll, for the doll was lying cosy in the bed beside Eibhlin. It had its mouth half open, and the wonder of the world on it at the sayings of Eibhlin and her mother.

'It's with trouble I believed Anthony when he brought it into me,' says Eibhlin, 'and when he told me you sent it to me as a present.'

Nance looked over at Anthony. Anthony lifted his head slowly, and their eyes met. It will never be known what Nance read in Anthony's eyes. What Anthony read in Nance's eyes was mercy, love and sweetness. Nance spoke to Eibhlin.

'Do you like it?' says she.

'Over anything,' says Eibhlin. 'I'd rather it than anything I have in the world.'

'I have the little house it lives in,' says Nance. 'I must send it to you. Anthony will bring it to you to-morrow.'

'*Ora!*' says Eibhlin, and she clapping her two little thin palms together.

'You'll miss it, love,' says Eibhlin's mother to Nance.

'No,' said Nance. 'It will put more improvement on Eibhlin. I have lots of things.'

'Let her do it, Cait,' said the mistress to the mother.

'Ye are too good,' says the poor woman.

Anthony thought that it's dreaming he was. Or he thought that it's not a person of this world little Nance was at all, but an angel come down out of heaven. He wanted to go on his knees to her.

When the mistress and little Nance went off, Anthony ran out the back door and tore across the garden, so that he'd be before them at the bohereen-foot, and they going out on the road.

'Nance,' says he, 'I s-stole it, — the d-doll.'

'Never mind, Anthony,' says Nance, 'you did good to Eibhlin.'

Anthony stood like a stake in the road, and he couldn't speak another word.

Isn't it he was proud bringing the doll's house home to Eibhlin after school the next day! And isn't it they had the fun that evening settling the house and polishing the furniture and putting the doll to sleep on its little bed!

The following Saturday Anthony went to confession, and told his sin to the priest. The penance the priest put on him was to clean the doll's house once in the week for Eibhlin, till she would be strong enough to clean it herself. Eibhlin was strong enough for it by the end of a month. By the end of another month she was at school again.

There wasn't a Saturday evening from that out that they wouldn't hear a little, light tapping at the master's door. On the mistress going out Anthony would be standing at the door.

'Here's a little present for Nance,' he'd say, stretching toward her half-a-dozen duck's eggs, or a bunch of heather, or, at the least, the full of his fist of *duileasg*, and then he'd brush off with him without giving the mistress time to say 'thank you.'

(from *The Mother and other Tales*)

The Three Clever Sisters

by JEREMIAH CURTIN

I n the county Cork, a mile and a half from Fermoy, there lived three brothers. The three lived in one house for some years and never thought of marrying. On a certain day they went to a fair in the town of Fermoy. There was a platform on the fair ground for dancing and a fiddler on the platform to give music to the dancers. Three sisters from the neighbourhood, handsome girls, lively and full of jokes, made over to the three brothers and asked would they dance. The youngest and middle brother wouldn't think of dancing, but the eldest said, 'We mustn't refuse; it wouldn't be good manners.'

The three brothers danced with the girls, and after the dance took them for refreshments.

After a while the second brother spoke up and said, 'Here are three sisters, good wives for three brothers; why shouldn't we marry?

Let the eldest brother of us take the eldest sister; I will take the second; the youngest brother can have the youngest sister.'

It was settled then and there that the three couples were satisfied if the girls' parents were. Next day the brothers went to the girls' parents and got their consent. In a week's time they were married.

Each of the three brothers had a good farm, and each went now to live on his own place. They lived well and happily for about ten years, when one market-day the eldest sister came to the second and asked her to go to Fermoy with her.

In those days women used to carry baskets made of willow twigs, in which they took eggs and butter to market. The second sister said she hadn't thought of going, but she would go, and they would ask the youngest sister for her company.

All three started off, each with a basket of eggs. After they had their eggs sold in the market they lingered about for some time looking at people, as is usual with farmers' wives. In the evening, when thinking of home, they dropped into a public-house to have a drop to drink before going. The public-house was full of people, chatting, talking, and drinking. The three sisters did not like to be seen at the bar, so they went to a room up stairs, and the eldest called for three pints of porter, which was brought without delay.

It is common for a farmer or his wife who has a ten-shilling piece or a pound, and does not wish to break it, to say, 'I will pay the next time I come to town;' so the eldest sister said now. The second sister called for three pints, and then the third followed her example.

'Tis said that women are very noisy when they've taken a glass or two, but whether that is true or not, these three were noisy, and their talk was so loud that Lord Fermoy, who was above in a room finishing some business with the keeper of the public-house, could not hear a thing for their chat, so he sent the landlord to tell the

women to leave the room. The landlord went, and finding that they had not paid their reckoning yet, told them it was time they were paying their reckoning and moving towards home.

One of the sisters looked up and said, 'The man above (God) will pay all. He is good for the reckoning.'

The man of the house, thinking that it was Lord Fermoy she was speaking of, was satisfied, and went up stairs.

'Have they gone?' asked Lord Fermoy.

'They have not, and they say that you will pay the reckoning.'

'Why should I pay when I don't know them? We'll go down and see who they are and what they mean.'

The two went down, and Lord Fermoy saw that they were tenants of his; he knew them quite well, for they lived near his own castle. He liked the sisters, they were so sharp-witted.

'I'll pay the reckoning, and do you bring each of these women a glass of punch,' said he to the man of the house.

The punch was brought without delay.

'Here is a half sovereign for each of you,' said Lord Fermoy. 'Now go home, and meet me in this place a week from to-day. Whichever one of you during that time makes the biggest fool of her husband will get ten pounds in gold and ten years rent free.'

'We'll do our best,' said the sisters.

Each woman of them was anxious, of course, to do the best she could. They parted at the door of the public-house, each going her own way, and each thinking of what could be done to win the ten pounds and ten years' rent.

It had happened that the eldest sister's husband became very sickly a couple of years after his marriage and fell into a decline. On the way home the wife made up her mind what to do. She bought pipes, tobacco, candles, and other articles needed at a wake. She was in no hurry home, so 'twas late enough when she came to the house. When she looked in at the window she saw her husband sitting by the fire with his hand on his chin and the children asleep around him. A pot of potatoes, boiled and strained, was waiting for her.

She opened the door. The husband looked at her and asked, 'Why are you so late?'

'Why are you off the table, and where are the sheets that were over you?' asked she as if in a fright; 'or the shirt that I put on you? I left you laid out on the table.'

'Sure I am not dead at all. I know very well when you started to go to the market, I wasn't dead then, and I didn't die since you left the house.'

Then she began to abuse him, and said that all his friends were coming to the wake, and he had no right to be off the table tormenting and abusing herself and the children, and went on in such a way that at last he believed himself dead and asked her in God's name to give him a smoke and he would go up again on the table and never come down till he was carried from it.

She gave him the pipe, but didn't let him smoke long. Then she made him ready, put him on the table, and spread a sheet over him. Now two poles were stretched overhead above the body and sheets hung over and down on the sides, as is customary. She put beads between his two thumbs and a Prayer-book in his hands. 'You are not to open your eyes,' said she, 'no matter what comes or happens.' She unlocked the door then and raised a terrible wailing over the corpse. A woman living opposite heard the wailing, and said to her husband:

'Oh, it is Jack that is dead, and it is a shame for you not to go to him.'

'I was with him this evening,' said the husband, 'and what could kill him since?'

The wife hurried over to Jack's house, found the corpse in it, and began to cry. Soon there was a crowd gathered, and all crying.

The second sister going past to her own home by a short cut, heard the keening and lamenting. 'This is my sister's trick to get the ten pounds and ten years' rent,' thought she, and began to wail also. When inside she pinched the dead man, and pulled at him to know would he stir; but it was no use, he never stirred.

The second sister went home then, and she was very late. Her husband was a strong, able-bodied man, and when she wasn't there to milk the cows he walked up and down the path watching for her, and he very angry. At last he milked the cows himself, drove them out, and then sat down in the house. When the wife came he jumped up and asked, 'What kept you out till this hour? 'Twas fitter for you to be at home long ago than to be strolling about, and the Lord knows where you were.'

'How could I be here, when I stopped at the wake where you ought to be?'

'What wake?'

'Your brother's wake. Jack is dead, poor man.'

'What the devil was to kill Jack? Sure I saw him this evening, and he's not dead.'

He wouldn't believe, and to convince him she said, 'Come to the field and you'll see the lights, and maybe you'll hear the keening.'

She took him over the ditch into the field, and seeing the lights he said, 'Sure my poor brother is dead!' and began to cry.

'Didn't I tell you, you stump of a fool, that your brother was dead, and why don't you go to his wake and go in mourning? A respectable person goes in mourning for a relative and gets credit for it ever after.'

'What is mourning?' asked the husband.

''Tis well I know,' said she, 'what mourning is, for didn't my mother teach me, and I will show you.'

She brought him to the house and told him to throw off all his clothes and put on a pair of tight-fitting black knee breeches. He did so; she took a wet brush then, and reaching it up in the chimney, got plenty of soot and blacked him all over from head to foot, and he naked except the black breeches. When she had him well blackened she put a black stick in his hand. 'Now,' said she, 'go to the wake, and what you are doing will be a credit to the family for seven generations.'

He started off wailing and crying. Whenever a wake house is full, benches and seats are put outside, men and women sit on these benches till some of those inside go home, then those outside go in. It is common also for boys to go to wakes and get pipes and tobacco, for every one gets a pipe, from a child of three to old men and women. Some of the boys at Jack's wake, after getting their pipes and tobacco, ran off to the field to smoke, where their parents couldn't see them. Seeing the black man coming, the boys dropped their pipes and ran back to the wakehouse, screaming to the people who were sitting outside that the devil was coming to carry the corpse with him. One of the men who stood near was sharper-sighted than others, and looking in the direction pointed out, said:

'Sure the devil is coming! And people thought that Jack was a fine, decent man, but now it turns out that he was different. I'll not be waiting here!' He took himself off as fast as his legs could carry him, and others after him.

Soon the report went into the wake house, and the corpse heard that the devil was coming to take him, but for all that he hadn't courage to stir. A man put his head out of the house, and, seeing the black man, screamed, 'I declare to God that the devil is coming!' With that he ran off, and his wife hurried after him.

That moment everybody crowded so much to get out of the house that they fell one over another, screeching and screaming. The woman of the house ran away with the others. The dead man was left alone. He opened one eye right away, and seeing the last woman hurrying off he said:

'I declare to the Lord I'll not stay here and wait for the devil to take me!' With that he sprang from the table, and wrapped the sheet round his body, and away with him then as fast as ever his legs could carry him.

His brother, the black man, saw him springing through the door, and, thinking it was Death that had lifted his brother and was running away with him to deprive the corpse of wake and Christian burial, he ran after him to save him. When the corpse screamed the black man screamed, and so they ran, and the people in terror fell into holes and ditches, trying to escape from Death and the devil.

The third sister was later than the other two in coming home from Fermoy. She knew her husband was a great sleeper, and she could do anything with him when he was drowsy. She looked into the house through a window that opened on hinges. She saw him sitting by the fire asleep; the children were sleeping near him. A pot of potatoes was standing by the fire. She knew that she could get in at the window if she took off some of her clothes. She did so and crawled in. The husband had long hair. She cut the hair close off to his head, threw it in the fire and burned it; then she went out through the window, and, taking a large stone, pounded on the door and roused her husband at last. He opened the door, began to scold her for being out so late, and blamed her greatly.

"Tis a shame for you,' said he. 'The children are sleeping on the floor, and the potatoes boiled for the last five hours.'

'Bad luck to you, you fool!' said the woman. 'Who are you to be ordering me? Isn't it enough for my own husband to be doing that?'

'Are you out of your mind or drunk that you don't know me?' said the man. 'Sure, I am your husband.'

'Indeed you are not,' said she.

'And why not?'

'Because you are not; you don't look like him. My husband has fine long, curly hair. Not so with you; you look like a shorn wether.'

He put his hands to his head, and, finding no hair on it, cried out, 'I declare to the Lord that I am your husband, but I must have lost my hair while shearing the sheep this evening. I'm your husband.'

'Be off out of this!' screamed the woman. 'When my husband comes he'll not leave you long in the house, if you are here before him.'

In those days the people used bog pine for torches and lighting fires. The man having a bundle of bog pine cut in pieces, took some fire and went towards the field, where he'd been shearing sheep. He went out to know  could he find his hair and convince the wife. When he reached the right place he set fire to a couple of pine sticks, and they made a fine blaze. He went on his knees and was searching for the hair. He searched the four corners of the field, crawling hither and over, but if he did not a lock of hair could he find. He went next to the middle of the field, dropped on his knees, and began to crawl around to know could he find his hair. While doing this he heard a terrible noise of men, and they running towards him, puffing and panting. Who were they but the dead man and the devil? The dead man was losing his breath and was making for the first light before him. He was in such terror that he didn't see how near he was to the light, and tumbled over the man who was searching for his hair.

'Oh, God help me!' cried the corpse. 'I'm surely done for now!'

Hearing his brother's voice, the black man, who was there, recognised him. The man looking for the hair rose up, and seeing his brothers, knew them; then each told the other everything, and they saw right away that the whole affair was planned by their wives.

The husbands went home well fooled, shame-faced, and angry. On the following day the women went to get the prize. When the

whole story was told it was a great
question who was to have the
money. Lord Fermoy could not
settle it himself, and called a
council of the gentry to decide,
but they could not decide who
was the cleverest woman. What
the council agreed on was this:

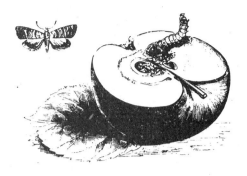

To make up a purse of sixty pounds, and give twenty pounds and
twenty years' rent to each of the three, if they all solved the problem that would be put to them. If two solved it they would get
thirty pounds apiece and thirty years' rent; if only one, she would
get the whole purse of sixty pounds and rent free for sixty years.

'This is the riddle,' said the council to the sisters: 'There are four
rooms in a row here; this is the first one. We will put a pile of apples
in the fourth room; there will be a man of us in the third, second,
and first room. You are to go to the fourth room, take as many
apples as you like, and when you come to the third room you are
to give the man in it half of what apples you'll bring, and half an
apple without cutting it. When you come to the second room you
are to do the same with what apples you will have left. In the first
room you will do the same as in the third and second. Now we will
go to put the apples in the fourth room, and we'll give each of you
one hour to work out the problem.'

'It's the devil to give half an apple without cutting it,' said the
elder sister.

When the men had gone the youngest sister said, 'I can do it
and I can get the sixty pounds, but as we are three sisters I'll be
liberal and divide with you. I'll go first, and let each come an hour
after the other. Each will take fifteen apples, and when she comes
to the man in the third room she will ask him how much is one-
half of fifteen; he will say seven and a half. She will give him eight

apples then and say: 'This is half of what I have and half an apple uncut for you.' With the seven apples she will go to the second room and ask the man there what is one-half of seven; he will say three and a half. She will give him four apples and say, 'Here are three apples and a half and the half of an uncut apple for you.' With three apples left she will go to the man in the first room and ask what is the half of three. He will answer, 'One and a half.' 'Here are two apples for you,' she will say then; 'one apple and a half and the half of an uncut apple.'

The eldest and second sister did as the youngest told them. Each received twenty pounds and twenty years' rent.

(from *Tales of the Fairies and of the Ghost World*)

The Selfish Giant

by OSCAR WILDE

Every afternoon, as they were coming from school, the children used to go and play in the Giant's garden.

It was a large lovely garden, with soft green grass. Here and there over the grass stood beautiful flowers like stars, and there were twelve peach-trees that in the spring-time broke out into delicate blossoms of pink and pearl, and in the autumn bore rich fruit. The birds sat on the trees and sang so sweetly that the children used to stop their games in order to listen to them. 'How happy we are here!' they cried to each other.

One day the Giant came back. He had been to visit his friend the Cornish ogre, and had stayed with him for seven years. After the seven years were over he had said all that he had to say, for his conversation was limited, and he determined to return to his own castle. When he arrived he saw the children playing in the garden.

'What are you doing here?' he cried in a very gruff voice, and the children ran away.

'My own garden is my own garden,' said the Giant; 'any one can understand that, and I will allow nobody to play in it but myself.' So he built a high wall all round it, and put up a notice-board.

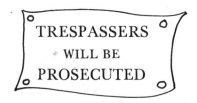

TRESPASSERS
WILL BE
PROSECUTED

He was a very selfish Giant.

The poor children had now nowhere to play. They tried to play on the road, but the road was very dusty and full of hard stones, and they did not like it. They used to wander round the high walls when their lessons were over, and talk about the beautiful garden inside. 'How happy we were there!' they said to each other.

Then the Spring came, and all over the country there were little blossoms and little birds. Only in the garden of the Selfish Giant it was still winter. The birds did not care to sing in it as there were no children, and the trees forgot to blossom. Once a beautiful flower put its head out from the grass, but when it saw the notice-board it was so sorry for the children that it slipped back into the ground again, and went off to sleep. The only people who were pleased were the Snow and the Frost. 'Spring has forgotten this garden,' they cried, 'so we will live here all the year round.' The Snow covered up the grass with her great white cloak, and the Frost painted all the trees silver. Then they invited the North Wind to stay with them, and he came. He was wrapped in furs, and he roared all day about the garden, and blew the chimney-pots down. 'This is a delightful spot,' he said, 'we must ask the Hail on a visit.' So the Hail came. Every day for three hours he rattled on the roof of the castle till he broke most of the slates, and then he ran round and round the garden as fast as he could go. He was dressed in grey, and his breath was like ice.

'I cannot understand why the Spring is so late in coming,' said the Selfish Giant, as he sat at the window and looked out at his cold, white garden; 'I hope there will be a change in the weather.'

But the Spring never came, nor the Summer. The Autumn gave golden fruit to every garden, but to the Giant's garden she gave none. 'He is too selfish,' she said. So it was always Winter there, and the North Wind and the Hail, and the Frost, and the Snow danced about through the trees.

One morning the Giant was lying awake in bed when he heard some lovely music. It sounded so sweet to his ears that he thought it must be the King's musicians passing by. It was really only a little linnet singing outside his window, but it was so long since he had heard a bird sing in his garden that it seemed to him to be the most beautiful music in the world. Then the Hail stopped dancing over his head, and the North Wind ceased roaring, and a delicious perfume came to him through the open casement. 'I believe the Spring has come at last,' said the Giant; and he jumped out of bed and looked out.

What did he see?

He saw a most wonderful sight. Through a little hole in the wall the children had crept in, and they were sitting in the branches of the trees. In every tree that he could see there was a little child. And the trees were so glad to have the children back again that they had covered themselves with blossoms, and were waving their arms gently above the children's heads. The birds were flying about and twittering with delight, and the flowers were looking up through the green grass and laughing. It was a lovely scene, only

in one corner it was still winter. It was the farthest corner of the garden, and in it was standing a little boy. He was so small that he could not reach up to the branches of the tree, and he was wandering all round it, crying bitterly. The poor tree was still covered with frost and snow, and the North Wind was blowing and roaring above it. 'Climb up! little boy,' said the Tree, and it bent its branches down as low as it could; but the boy was too tiny.

And the Giant's heart melted as he looked out. 'How selfish I have been!' he said; 'now I know why the Spring would not come here. I will put that poor little boy on the top of the tree, and then I will knock down the wall, and my garden shall be the children's playground for ever and ever.' He was really very sorry for what he had done.

So he crept downstairs and opened the front door quite softly, and went out into the garden. But when the children saw him they were so frightened that they all ran away, and the garden became winter again. Only the little boy did not run, for his eyes were so full of tears that he did not see the Giant coming. And the Giant stole up behind him and took him gently in his hand, and put him up into the tree. And the tree broke at once into blossom, and the birds came and sang on it, and the little boy stretched out his two arms and flung them round the Giant's neck, and kissed him. And the other children when they saw that the Giant was not wicked any longer, came running back, and with them came the Spring. 'It is your garden now, little children,' said the Giant, and he took a great axe and knocked down the wall. And when the people were going to market at twelve o'clock they found the Giant playing with the children in the most beautiful garden they had ever seen.

All day long they played, and in the evening they came to the Giant to bid him good-bye.

'But where is your little companion?' he said: 'the boy I put

into the tree.' The Giant loved him the best because he had kissed him.

'We don't know,' answered the children: 'he has gone away.'

'You must tell him to be sure and come to-morrow,' said the Giant. But the children said that they did not know where he lived, and had never seen him before; and the Giant felt very sad.

Every afternoon, when school was over, the children came and played with the Giant. But the little boy whom the Giant loved was never seen again. The Giant was very kind to all the children, yet he longed for his first little friend, and often spoke of him. 'How I would like to see him!' he used to say.

Years went over, and the Giant grew very old and feeble. He could not play about any more, so he sat in a huge arm-chair, and watched the children at their games, and admired his garden. 'I have many beautiful flowers,' he said; 'but the children are the most beautiful flowers of all.'

One winter morning he looked out of his window as he was dressing. He did not hate the Winter now, for he knew that it was merely the Spring asleep, and that the flowers were resting.

Suddenly he rubbed his eyes in wonder and looked and looked. It certainly was a marvellous sight. In the farthest corner of the garden was a tree quite covered with lovely white bloossoms. Its branches were golden, and silver fruit hung down from them, and underneath it stood the little boy he had loved.

Downstairs ran the Giant in great joy, and out into the garden. He hastened across the grass, and came near to the child. And when he came quite close his face grew red with anger, and he said, 'Who hath dared to wound thee?' For on the palms of the child's hands were the prints of two nails, and the prints of two nails were on the little feet.

'Who hath dared to wound thee?' cried the Giant; 'tell me, that I may take my big sword and slay him.'

101

'Nay!' answered the child: 'but these are the wounds of Love.'

'Who art thou?' said the Giant, and a strange awe fell on him, and he knelt before the little child.

And the child smiled on the Giant, and said to him, 'You let me play once in your garden, to-day you shall come with me to my garden, which is Paradise.'

And when the children ran in that afternoon, they found the Giant lying dead under the tree, all covered with white blossoms.

(from *The Happy Prince, and Other Tales*)

The
White Road
of Druagh

by PATRICIA LYNCH

Liam O'Malley lived in the small cabin below the humped bridge, where the Donomark river ends and Druagh fishing harbour widens out to the bay.

The cabin was so small it had only one window and a narrow door squeezed in beside it. But Liam was very proud of living in such a house, for his name was over the window in gold letters.

The first day of Christmas week Liam was crossing the bridge. The sky was grey, the wind blew harsh and cold down from the mountains. A sudden gleam of light shot out, like an arrow, between two dark clouds and caught the name. But now Liam saw not only his name but along with it a word he was sure hadn't been there before — TAILOR. There it was:

LIAM O'MALLEY, TAILOR

'That's queer!' muttered Liam. 'Who put that up over our house?'

And home he rushed to ask his mother.

'Sure, twas always there,' she told him. 'Twas yer own father painted it himself, God help him! Only he hadn't enough paint to give TAILOR the second coat. He was always meaning to buy more. But one Fair Day he hadn't the money and another Fair

103

Day he hadn't the time — that was the way of it. But when we've had rain to wash the letters clean an the wind comes from the north an has a bite in it — then TAILOR shines out grand, just as on the day the poor man painted it.'

'Tell me about me father,' coaxed Liam. 'You promised you would when I was old enough to understand.'

'I will, son. I will!' agreed his mother.

'He was the best tailor in the whole countryside from Cork to Bantry an beyant. He was always being sent for to make a weddin suit, or a grand coat for a lad going over to Cork, or mebbe up to Dublin. Indeed we'd have been made up only he was always fixin a coat for this wan, or a cloak for that wan that hadn't a penny piece to pay him.'

'I'm off to New York when I'm a man!' boasted Liam.

'Sure, there's so many Druagh people there ye won't know ye've left home,' laughed his mother. 'But listen, now!

'I was down at the stream washin a head of cabbage. Yer father was sittin on the table in the winda finishin a waistcoat for young Mr. Darley that was goin away to college — a red waistcoat, I remember well.'

'And what was I doing?' Liam wanted to know.

'God bless ye, child! Ye were swingin on the gate an singin to yerself as happy as Larry.'

The poor woman sighed.

'Keep on! Don't stop!' cried Liam impatiently.

'Himself had two buttonholes to stitch an he was determined to have them done before dinner, so that he'd have the money for the Fair. Twas Fair Day, ye see, just before Christmas.'

'Was there snow on the ground and ice in the bucket?' asked Liam.

'There was not, child. But twas bitter cold an me fingers were like icicles wid the harshness of the wather. An when I came back wid the cabbage for the dinner there wasn't a sign of yer father an, from that day to this, not a soul has set eyes on him.'

'And he took the waistcoat with him?'

'He did indeed!' cried Mrs. O'Malley. 'An a hooded cloak he'd been makin for some poor woman, an his needle an scissors an thimble an the spool of thread.'

'And what was I doing then?' demanded Liam.

'Ye were still swingin on the gate, an singin a quare little song.'

'Didn't I know where me da had gone?'

'Ye did not, Liam, though I axed ye, an the neighbours, an the polis, an the priest axed ye till they were tired. Ye knew nothin, wisha, God help ye! Twas a long time ago — seven whole years, a long time!'

'What was the song I was singing?' Liam wanted to know.

'Sure, I forget, child, if I ever knew. Sit down now, while I take up the praties an we'll ate our dinner. When yer father was here we'd have praties an bacon an cabbage into the bargain, an apple cake for our tay.'

The potatoes were so big and floury and Liam was so hungry he didn't miss the bacon and cabbage, though he did wish they could have apple cake for tea.

When they had eaten even the smallest of the potatoes his mother wrapped herself in her black-hooded cloak.

'I'm off to Jimmy Gallagher's wid the sewin I have finished,' she said. 'Mebbe I'll bring ye back a Peggy's Leg. Mind now — do yer lessons before ye go out to play an who knows what luck we may have before Christmas!'

Liam learned the rivers of Ireland, repeated his seven-times table, and began to read the story of Finn MacCool and the Fighting Tinker.

He read to the bottom of the page, then stood staring over the half-door at the gate set in the wall which went round the garden.

'I'm going to find me father!' said Liam. And putting the story of Finn MacCool back on the shelf he went out of the cabin and down to the gate.

Which way should he go? Up the river or towards the bay?

While he tried to make up his mind, Liam swung backwards and forwards.

Up the river or round by the harbour?

Two boys were skimming flat stones across the water under the bridge, and Liam had almost decided to join them when an old man who travelled the roads came along the boreen which went by the cabin. He was whistling as he marched along, a bulging sack over his shoulders and a battered caubeen pulled down to his ears. His coat was tattered and his toes poked through his boots, but his face was brown and his blue eyes twinkled cheerfully.

'Am I right for Druagh, avic?' he asked.

'Over the bridge,' replied Liam, swinging away.

'An might I ax, were ye on yer way in, or out?' chuckled the stranger.

'Out!' replied Liam. 'I'm wanting to find me father, only I don't know where to look.'

And he told the travelling man all he had heard from his mother. The man shook his head.

'Seven years is a shockin long time, me poor gossoon. A track grows faint in seven years. If he went far enough, a man might forget the way back. I'm thinkin the only ones who could help ye is them that doesn't know a day from a year, or a year from a day.'

He gave a hoist to his sack and was off and away before Liam could ask him where to find the people who didn't know a year from a day.

The boy climbed back on the gate, but swung very gently, so that he wouldn't make a noise, for he was thinking hard.

He didn't see any one along the bank, or hear footsteps on the boreen, but there was a little woman peering at him from under the hood of her pleated cloak.

'Are ye ridin far?' she asked.

'I don't know,' replied Liam. 'I want to find me father and I don't know how to start.'

'Is it Liam O'Malley, the tailor?' asked the little woman. 'He finished this grand new cloak for me only yesterday, an I'm on me way to pay him, for he's the one should be paid.'

She was turning away. Liam jumped down and caught her cloak.

'Let me come with you!' he cried. 'You're the one can help me. You don't know seven years from a day!'

But he was clutching cold, white mist, which was sweeping up from the river and he couldn't see a yard before him.

'She didn't go past me. I know she didn't. Where did she go?'

He could hear a voice singing through the mist:

'For a day is as long as a year,
An a year no more than a day,
When ye tread the road of the white stones
That leads across the bay.'

'I know that song,' thought Liam. 'I've heard it before.'

And he sang it under his breath.

He walked slowly, his hands held out before him and there he was at the edge of the river, with the setting sun shining across the water.

Down on the river, following a white path which rose above the water, was the little woman in the hooded cloak.

Liam's mother had once told him of the town across the bay, which had been overwhelmed in ancient times by a great tide one stormy night. A road of white stone had led to it, and now fishermen going out with their nets at Christmas or Easter time could see it glimmering through the water as their boats passed over.

Liam looked back. The mist had vanished and the golden letters were gleaming as if they had been painted only that morning.

Then he leaped down on the white road.

The tide was coming in and the waves were tossing against the bank, but the white road was dry as a town pavement.

Liam could see the little woman far out in the middle of the bay and she was standing on the last stone.

'Where she goes I'm going!' he declared.

And down she stepped into the water!

Liam could swim a few strokes, but he had never been far from the bank.

He went slower and slower.

'Mebbe I'd as well turn back!' he muttered. 'Wish I'd never looked at the white road.'

But he kept on as far as the last stone.

There were wide steps going under the water and the little

woman trotting down as comfortably as if she were on the main street. Before he knew what he was doing Liam was jumping two steps at a time to keep up with her.

At the bottom

of the steps was a street with houses on each side. Liam tried to look in at the windows, but the water was like a green mist and he could see nothing. The street opened into a square and a wrecked fishing-boat lay there, with fish swimming over its deck and about the mast.

The little woman kept to the pavement and went round the square. Liam gave a jump, meaning to land on the boat. Instead he went right across and landed on the other side.

In front of him was a shop with a wide window. There was a table piled with stuff — sea green, river green, blue and silver. There sat a man sewing the buttonholes of a red waistcoat and over the window in big golden letters was written:

LIAM O'MALLEY, TAILOR

'Father!' cried Liam, rushing to the door.
But the little woman was before him.

'By your leave, young sir!' she said and pushed past.

'There's manners!' thought Liam. But he didn't say a word out loud.

The tailor looked up from his work at the woman and the boy.

'I've come to pay ye for the hooded cloak ye finished yesterday,' said the little woman. 'Tis the best I ever wore.'

'And I've come to bring you home,' said Liam. 'Me mother doesn't think it's Christmas without you!'

'Don't listen to him!' cried the little woman. 'But count the money!'

She tipped a handful of gold out on the table.

'Who are you?' the tailor asked Liam.

'I'm Liam! Your son!' the boy told him. 'You left home seven years ago. Come back with me now. Me mother misses you terrible!'

The tailor nodded.

'What are ye talkin about?' he said. 'Twas only a couple of hours ago. I was stitchin the waistcoat when this little woman came along askin for her cloak an I went down to the strand wid her!'

'Twas seven years ago!' declared Liam. 'Wasn't I a little boy when you came away and amn't I a big boy now?'

'Seven years!' exclaimed the tailor, and he stepped away from the table.

'Take the gold!' pleaded the little woman. 'Didn't I promise I'd pay ye well!'

'Keep your gold!' said the tailor sternly. 'I made the cloak out of kindness for I never thought ye could pay a penny piece. Then ye play this trick on me. If I take your gold I'll never see me own home again!'

'Twas no trick!' cried the little woman angrily. 'I promised I'd show ye where the white road of Druagh led an I've kept me word!'

'Seven years!' groaned the tailor, making for the door.

Liam gathered up the gold and stuffed it in his pocket, then ran after his father.

But now the square was crowded with men, women, and children, who tried to push the tailor back into the shop.

'Who'll make our clothes?' they cried.

'Keep close to me!' whispered the tailor to his son.

He leaped over the fishing-boat with Liam beside him and ran down the street to the steps. Hands clutched their coats and caught at their arms but there was no strength in them.

Liam went first. He had jumped down the steps. Now he had to force himself up through the water. At last they were on the white road. But night had come and moonlight silvered the river. Behind them voices were crying out: 'The best tailor we ever had!' 'Who'll make our clothes?' 'Come back and you shall have all the gold in the sea!'

But neither the tailor nor Liam looked back.

There was a candle gleaming in the window of the cabin and the half-door stood open. Mrs. O'Malley was at the gate watching out for Liam.

'Did ye see a young lad as ye came along?' she asked as the tailor came up to her, for Liam was lagging behind, so tired he could scarcely lift one foot before the other and shivering with cold,

though his clothes were as dry as if he had never been within a mile of the water.

Then his mother gave a scream.

'Tis yerself's come back after seven long years! Where have ye been? What happened ye? An God be good to us,

111

ye still have the red weskit! Welcome home! Me poor fella!'

'Sure, I didn't know I'd been away!' declared the tailor. 'Why would I leave me good home?'

And they went up the path to the cabin.

That was a Christmas worth talking about! When the neighbours heard the tailor was back home they came down to the cabin to welcome him and hear his story. And there wasn't one came empty-handed.

Liam had never had such eating and drinking in his life and his father bought him the knife with four blades and a corkscrew that he'd been longing for.

When all the good things were eaten and the press was once more empty Liam took out the money he had brought up with him from the lost town. But the gold pieces had turned into sea-shells, though they were the loveliest he had ever seen.

Then the tailor set to work and the customers came from miles around, for there wasn't one but wanted a suit or a cloak made by the man who had been tailor to the town under the water.

(from *The Seventh Pig*)

Tom Daly and the Nut-eating Ghost

by JEREMIAH CURTIN

Tom Daly lived between Kenmare and Sneem, but nearer to Kenmare, and had an only son, who was called Tom, after the father. When the son was eighteen years old Tom Daly died, leaving a widow and this son. The wife was paralysed two years before Tom's death, and could rise out of the bed only as she was taken out, but as the fire was near the bed she could push a piece of turf into it if the turf was left at hand.

Tom Daly while alive was in the employ of a gentleman living at Drummond Castle. Young Tom got the father's place, and he looked on his godfather as he would on his own father, for the father and godfather had been great friends always, and Tom's mother was as fond of the godfather as she was of her own husband. Four years after old Tom died the godfather followed him. He was very fond of chestnuts, and when he came to die he asked his friends to put a big wooden dish of them in his coffin, so he might come at the nuts in the next world.

They carried out the man's wishes. The godfather was buried, and the bed-ridden widow mourned for him as much as for her own husband. The young man continued to work for the gentleman at Drummond Castle, and in the winter it was often late in the

113

evening before he could come home. There was a short cut from the gentleman's place through a grove and past the graveyard. Young Tom was going home one winter night, the moon was shining very brightly. While passing the graveyard he saw a man on a big tomb that was in it, and he cracking nuts. Young Daly saw that it was on his godfather's tomb the man was, and when he remembered the nuts that were buried with him he believed in one minute that it was the godfather who was before him. He was greatly in dread then, and ran off as fast as ever his legs could carry him. When he reached home he was out of breath and panting.

'What is on you,' asked the mother, 'and to be choking for breath?'

'Sure I saw my godfather sitting on the tomb and he eating the nuts that were buried with him.'

'Bad luck to you,' said the mother; 'don't be belying the dead, for it is as great a sin to tell one lie on the dead as ten on the living.'

'God knows,' said Tom, 'that I'd not belie my godfather, and 'tis he that is in it; and hadn't I enough time to know him before he died?'

'Do you say in truth, Tom, that 'tis your godfather?'

'As sure as you are my mother there before me 'tis my godfather

that's in the graveyard cracking nuts.'

'Bring me to him, for the mercy of God, till I ask him about your own father in the other world.'

'I'll not do that,' said Tom. 'What a queer thing it would be to bring you to the dead.'

'Isn't it better to go, Tom dear, and speak to him? Ask about your father, and know is he suffering in the other world. If he is we can relieve him with masses for his soul.'

Tom agreed at last, and, as the mother was a cripple, all he could do was to put a sheet around her and take her on his back. He went then towards the graveyard.

There was a great thief living not far from Kenmare, and he came that night towards the estate of the gentleman where Tom was working. The gentleman had a couple of hundred fat sheep that were grazing. The thief made up his mind to have one of the sheep, and he sent an apprentice boy that he had to catch one, and said that he'd keep watch on the top of the tomb. As he had some nuts in his pockets, the thief began to crack them. The boy went for the sheep, but before he came back the thief saw Tom Daly, with his mother on his back. Thinking that it was his appren-

tice with the sheep, he called out, 'Is she fat?'

Tom Daly, thinking it was the ghost asking about the mother, dropped her and said, 'Begor, then, she is, and heavy!' Away with him, then, as fast as ever his two legs could carry him, leaving the mother behind. She, forgetting her husband and thinking the ghost would kill and eat her, jumped up, ran home like a deer, and was there as soon as her son.

'God spare you, mother, how could you come!' cried Tom, 'and be here as soon as myself?'

'Sure I moved like a blast of March wind,' said the old woman; ''tis the luckiest ride I had in my life, for out of the fright the good Lord gave me my legs again.'

(from *Tales of the Fairies and of the Ghost World*)

The Twelve Silly Sisters

by PADRAIC COLUM

On Hallowe'en the Pooka goes galloping through the countryside, and he gives the Pooka's jaunt to this or that person that he meets going home late. Sometimes what the Pooka does is good, but more often it is bad. It would be a bad thing if he carried off the little girl who has gone down the road to fetch the fiddler in to play for us. But it was not a bad thing that the Pooka did when he carried off the twelve silly sisters of the Lord of Ballinakill.

The Lord of Omey had to marry the first of the twelve silly sisters, although there was his own third cousin for him to marry, and she was fair and wise and considerate. On Hallowe'en he went to his cousin's mother's house and found Nabla there, and she was molding candles, which was the right and proper thing for a young woman to be doing with the dark nights of winter coming on.

'My jewel you are,' said the Lord of Omey to her. 'Tomorrow we will go to the Abbey, and I will wed you there and give you the keys of my castle, upstairs and downstairs, the attic and the cellar.'

She gave him her word that she would go with him, because, as I have told you, Nabla was wise and considerate, and besides she loved O'Tool, the Lord of Omey, every bit as much as he loved her.

Now the Lord of Omey and Nabla, the lady he was to marry,

117

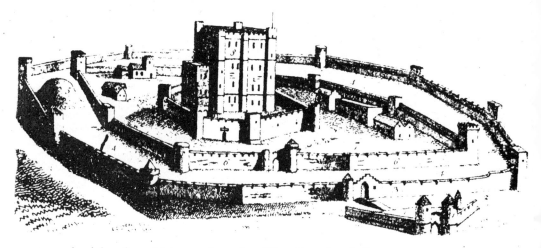

were inside the Abbey church. The Lord of Omey was standing before the altar with the ring between his fingers, when a tall, fiery-headed fighting man appeared at the church door. With the fright he got at seeing him there, O'Tool dropped the ring upon the flag-stones.

'My master sent me to tell you, O'Tool,' said the red-headed fighting man, 'that you're not to get married.'

'Not to get married!' said the Lord of Omey.

'At least, not to get married to the woman that's before you,' said the red-headed fellow. 'But my master isn't one to keep you from having a spouse; he is sending you one of his own daughters. The priest needn't go.'

Now, although the O'Tools were Lords of Omey, they had lords over them, and the lords that were over them were the O'Flaherties and the O'Flaherties were all terrible fighting men. Their battle shout was enough to make every one else leave the battlefield. The sight of their fiery-red heads coming across the country was enough to make the people put a bar on the gate of the town and a bolt on every house inside of it. And the O'Tools were the mildest clan in the whole of Connacht. Not a man of them would say 'boo' to a goose belonging to one of the O'Flaherties, let alone to one of their fighting men.

'My master is sending you one of his own daughters,' said the red-headed fighting man. 'The priest needn't go.'

And the priest did not go. The messenger did not go, either. Indeed, the only one who went out of the Abbey church was the fair and considerate Nabla. She went to the castle of Omey, and got there before any of the rest of them.

Did I tell you that she had got the keys of the castle before she came up to the altar? She had then. She opened the attic and went in, and her mother went along with her, and there the two of them stayed in O'Tool's castle.

The Abbey church was filled with red-heads, for all the O'Flaherties came in. And with them came the first of O'Flaherty's daughters, the one that was to be bride to the O'Tool.

There was nothing for the Lord of Omey to do but to pick up the ring he had let fall upon the flagstones, take the lady's finger out of her mouth, and put the ring on her finger. And so they were married, the Lord of Omey and Gibbie, the daughter of O'Flaherty.

And when they went back to O'Tool's castle the bride did everything that a silly person would do. That day she gave wine to the tax-gatherers and water to the poets. She left honey beside a boy and expected him not to eat it. She left milk beside a child and expected it not to drink it. She left food beside a generous man and expected him not to give it away to the hungry ones who came to the door. I could spend the whole of Hallowe'en night (and it is not the shortest night of the year) telling you of all the silly things that Gibbie did when she came into the castle of Omey.

She gave orders that O'Tool's horses were to have their shoes taken off before they came into the castle yard. This was to prevent their tramping and stamping while her kinsfolk ate around O'Tool's tables. And when the Lord of Omey heard that order given, he cried tears down. His gallant horses to be lamed by com-

ing without shoes over the sharp cobbles of the castle yard! But he could do nothing about it, for the order was given to one of the red-heads who had come out of her father's country. O'Tool cried for his horses that night as he sat at his wedding supper.

But Nabla, his wise and considerate cousin, was above in the attic. The order that was given was told her, and she came down the backstairs of the castle in the blackness of the night. She went out into the castle yard, and she took the straw from under the cows in the byres, and she strewed the stones of the castle yard with the straw. And no one knew what she did but Pincher, the watchdog that had one tooth. The horses came in, and they went silently upon the straw, and their hoofs were not hurt by the sharp cobblestones, and so they came safe.

Gibbie was silly, and her sisters were silly too. The eleven of them came to spend a while with her. So that they might not be lonely in O'Tool's castle, Gibbie had a bed made that would hold all the eleven of them. But she forgot to have a blanket made that would go across that bed. What she gave them covered this one and that one, but never all of them. They pulled the cover from one to the other of them, and they were cold sleeping and cold waking up every night they were in O'Tool's castle.

The eleven sisters got tired of having so little sleep and so much perishing in the bed that was made for them, and they made up their minds to go back to their father's castle in Ballinakill. Gibbie, their sister, knew what was due to ladies of their rank and degree, and she would not let them go unattended. And first she called to Nabla, thinking that she was the goose girl, to go with them. But then she decided that she herself was the best company that her sisters could have, and she made up her mind to go halfway with them. So they started off, the twelve of them. But the sisters could not let Gibbie go back without company, and so they went halfway back to the castle with her. And then she went halfway back with them. And they were going and coming, and coming and going, until the black night came down upon the ground.

And it was the night of Hallowe'en, the night that the Pooka goes abroad. He came upon the sisters as they were going backward and forward on the roads between Omey and Ballinakill. He was a horse so black that you could see yourself in his skin. He came galloping up, with fire in his eyes and froth on his jaws. He took the twelve sisters on his back, and away with him, through bushes and briars, over hills and through hollows, until he brought them to a certain place that I know about.

It is called the Townland of Mischance. Where the place is is written down, but then, they say, *An rud é scribheann an Púca leigheann sé féin é.* 'What the Pooka writes, only he himself can read.' In the Townland of Mischance the twelve sisters stayed, and every one in it was like themselves. They gave wine to the tax-gatherers and water to the poets. They left food near a generous man and expected him not to give it to the hungry ones who came to the door. And I think I was in that place myself a day or two ago.

But the place I was in then, and the place I am in now isn't alike. Here we're wise enough not to go abroad on Hallowe'en night unless we have business to bring us abroad. We're not the sort that would ever be given the Pooka's jaunt.

Well, there Gibbie and her eleven sisters stayed, and the O'Flaherties, for all their chasing up and down the country were never able to find them. The sisters were in their right place there, and they were well enough off.

And the Lord of Omey met his cousin, the fair and considerate

Nabla, some time after his wife and her sisters went away from him. He was walking near the Abbey church and she was walking near the same place. They went in together. There he married her with a ring that he found in a hoofprint near — in the Pooka's hoofprint. Ever afterwards he had a wise and considerate spouse.

(from *The Peep Show Man*)

Fairy Justice

by LADY WILDE

One day a young lad was out in the fields at work when he saw a little fellow, not the height of his hand, mending shoes under a dock leaf. And he went over, never taking his eyes off him for fear he would vanish away; and when he got quite close he made a grab at the creature, and lifted him up and put him in his pocket.

Then he ran away home as fast as he could, and when he had the Leprehaun safe in the house he tied him by an iron chain to the hob.

'Now tell me,' he said, 'where am I to find a pot of gold? Let me know the place or I'll punish you.'

'I know of no pot of gold,' said the Leprehaun; 'but let me go that I may finish mending the shoes.'

'Then I'll make you tell me,' said the lad.

And with that he made down a great fire, and put the little fellow on it and scorchéd him.

'Oh, take me off, take me off!' cried the Leprehaun, 'and I'll tell you. Just there, under the dock leaf where you found me there is a pot of gold. Go; dig and find.'

So the lad was delighted, and ran to the door; but it so happened that his mother was just then coming in with the pail of fresh milk, and in his haste he knocked the pail out of her hand, and all the milk was spilled on the floor.

Then when the mother saw the Leprehaun she grew very angry and beat him. 'Go away, you little wretch!' she cried. 'You have overlooked the milk, and brought ill-luck.' And she kicked him out of the house.

But the lad ran off to find the dock leaf, though he came back very sorrowful in the evening, for he had dug and dug nearly down to the middle of the earth; but no pot of gold was to be seen.

That same night the husband was coming home from his work, and as he passed the old fort he heard voices and laughter, and one said —

'They are looking for a pot of gold; but they little know that a crock of gold is lying down in the bottom of the old quarry, hid under the stones close by the garden wall. But whoever gets it must go of a dark night at twelve o'clock, and beware of bringing his wife with him.'

So the man hurried home and told his wife he would go that very night, for it was black dark, and she must stay at home and watch for him, and not stir from the house till he came back. Then he went out into the dark night alone.

'Now,' thought the wife, when he was gone, 'if I could only get to the quarry before him I would have the pot of gold all to myself; while if he gets it I shall have nothing.'

And with that she went out and ran like the wind until she reached the quarry, and then she began to creep down very quietly in the black dark. But a great stone was in her path, and she stumbled over it, and fell down and down till she reached the bottom, and there she lay groaning, for her leg was broken by the fall.

Just then her husband came to the edge of the quarry and began to descend. But when he heard the groans he was frightened.

'Cross of Christ about us!' he exclaimed; 'what is that down below? Is it evil, or is it good?'

'Oh, come down, come down and help me!' cried the woman. 'It's your wife is here, and my leg is broken, and I'll die if you don't help me.'

'And is this my pot of gold?' exclaimed the poor man. 'Only my wife with a broken leg lying at the bottom of the quarry.'

And he was at his wits' end to know what to do, for the night was so dark he could not see a hand before him. So he roused up a neighbour, and between them they dragged up the poor woman and carried her home, and laid her on her bed half dead from fright, and it was many a day before she was able to get about as usual; indeed she limped all her life long, so that the people said the curse of the Leprehaun was on her.

But as to the pot of gold, from that day to this not one of the family, father, or son, or any belonging to them, ever set eyes on it. However, the little Leprehaun still sits under the dock leaf of the hedge, and laughs at them as he mends the shoes with his little hammer — tick tack, tick tack — but they are afraid to touch him, for now they know he can take his revenge.

(from *Ancient Legends, Mystic Charms and Superstitions of Ireland*)

Simon and Margaret

by WILLIAM LARMINIE

Long ago there was a king's son called Simon, and he came in a ship from the east to Eire. In the place where he came to harbour he met with a woman whose name was Margaret, and she fell in love with him. She asked him if he would take her with him in the ship. He said he would not take her, that he had no business with her, 'for I am married already,' said he. But the day he was going to sea she followed him to the ship, and such a beautiful woman was she that he said to himself that he would not put her out of the ship; 'but before I go farther I must get beef.' He turned back and got the beef. He took the woman and the beef in the ship, and he ordered the sailors to make everything ready that they might be sailing on the sea. They were not long from land when they saw a great bulk making towards them, and it seemed to them it was more like a serpent than anything else whatever. And it was not long till the serpent cried out, 'Throw me the Irish person you have on board.'

'We have no Irish person in the ship,' said the king's son, 'for it is foreign people we are; but we have meat we took from Eire, and, if you wish, we will give you that.'

'Give it to me,' said the serpent, 'and everything else you took from Eire.'

He threw out a quarter of the beef, and the serpent went away that day, and on the morrow morning she came again, and they threw out another quarter, and one every day till the meat was gone. And the next day the serpent came again and she cried out to the king's son, 'Throw the Irish flesh out to me.'

'I have no more flesh,' said the prince.

'If you have not flesh, you have an Irish person,' said the serpent, 'and don't be telling your lies to me any longer. I knew from the beginning that you had an Irish person in the ship, and unless you throw her out to me, and quickly, I will eat yourself and your men.'

Margaret came up, and no sooner did the serpent see her than she opened her mouth, and put on an appearance as if she were going to swallow the ship.

'I will not be guilty of the death of you all,' said Margaret; 'get me a boat, and if I go far safe it is better; and if I do not go, I had rather I perished than the whole of us.'

'What shall we do to save you?' said Simon.

'You can do nothing better than put me in the boat,' said she, 'and lower me on the sea, and leave me to the will of God.'

As soon as she got on the sea, no sooner did the serpent see her than she desired to swallow her, but before she reached as far as her, a billow of the sea rose between them, and left herself and the boat on dry land. She saw not a house in sight she could go to.

'Now,' said she, 'I am as unfortunate as ever I was. There is no place at all for me to get that I know of, and this is no place for me to be.' She arose and she began to walk, and after a long while she saw a house a good way from her. 'I am not as unfortunate as I thought,' said she. 'Perhaps I shall get lodging in that house to-

128

night.' She went in, and there was no one in it but an old woman, who was getting her supper ready. 'I am asking for lodging till morning.'

'I will give you no lodging,' said the old woman.

'Before I go farther, there is a boat there below, and it is better for you to take it into your hands.'

'Come in,' said the old woman, 'and I will give you lodging for the night.'

The old woman was always praying by night and day. Margaret asked her, 'Why are you always saying your prayers?'

'I and my mother were living a long while ago in the place they call the White Doon, and a giant came and killed my mother, and I had to come away for fear he would kill myself; and I am praying every night and every day that some one may come and kill the giant.'

The next morning there came a gentleman and a beautiful woman into the house, and he gave the old woman the full of a quart of money to say paters for them till morning. The old woman opened a chest and took out a handsome ring, and tried to place it on his finger, but it would not go on. 'Perhaps it would fit you,' said she to the lady. But her finger was too big.

When they went out Margaret asked the old woman who were the man and woman. 'That is the son of a king of the Eastern World, and the name that is on him is Stephen, and he and the woman are going to the White Doon to fight the giant, and I am afraid they will never come back; for the ring did not fit either of them; and it was told to the people that no one would kill the giant but he whom the ring would fit.'

The two of them remained during the night praying for him, for fear the giant should kill him; and early in the morning they went out to see what had happened to Stephen and the lady that was with him, and they found them dead near the White Doon.

'I knew,' said the old woman, 'this is what would happen to them. It is better for us to take them with us and bury them in the churchyard.' When they were buried, 'Come home,' said the old woman, 'and we'll know who is the first person comes the same way again.'

About a month after a man came into the house, and no sooner was he inside the door than Margaret recognised him.

'How have you been ever since, Simon?'

'I am very well,' said he; 'it can't be that you are Margaret?'

'It is I,' said she.

'I thought that billow that rose after you, when you got into the boat, drowned you.'

'It only left me on dry land,' said Margaret.

'I went to the Eastern World, and my father said to me that he sent my brother to go and fight with the giant, who was doing great damage to the people near the White Doon, and that my wife went to carry his sword.'

'If that was your brother and your wife,' said Margaret, 'the giant killed them.'

'I will go on the spot and kill the giant, if I am able.'

'Wait till I try the ring on your finger,' said the old woman.

'It is too small to go on my finger,' said he.

'It will go on mine,' said Margaret.

'It will fit you,' said the old woman.

Simon gave the full of a quart of money to the old woman, that she might pray for him till he came back. When he was about to go, Margaret said, 'Will you let me go with you?'

'I will not,' said Simon, 'for I don't know that the giant won't kill myself, and I think it too much that one of us should be in this danger.'

'I don't care,' said Margaret. 'In the place where you die, there am I content to die.'

'Come with me,' said he.

When they were on the way to the White Doon, a man came before them.

'Do you see that house near the castle?' said the man.

'I see,' said Simon.

'You must go into it and keep a candle lighted till morning in it.'

'Where is the giant?' said Simon.

'He will come to fight you there,' said the man.

They went in and kindled a light, and they were not long there when Margaret said to Simon, —

'Come, and let us see the giants.'

'I cannot,' said the king, 'for the light will go out if I leave the house.'

'It will not go out,' said Margaret; 'I will keep it lighted till we come back.'

And they went together and got into the castle, to the giant's house, and they saw no one there but an old woman cooking; and it was not long till she opened an iron chest and took out the young giants and gave them boiled blood to eat.

'Come,' said Margaret, 'and let us go to the house we left.'

They were not long in it when the king's son was falling asleep.

Margaret said to him, 'If you fall asleep, it will not be long till the giants come and kill us.'

'I cannot help it,' he said. 'I am falling asleep in spite of me.'

He fell asleep, and it was not long till Margaret heard a noise approaching, and the giant cried from outside to the king's son to come out to him.

'Fum, faw, faysogue! I feel the smell of a lying churl of an Irishman. You are too great for one bite and too little for two, and I don't know whether it is better for me to send you into the Eastern World with a breath or put you under my feet in the puddle. Which would you rather have — striking with knives in your ribs or fighting on the grey stones?'

'Great, dirty giant, not with right or rule did I come in, but by rule and by right to cut your head off in spite of you, when my fine, silken feet go up and your big, dirty feet go down.'

They wrestled till they brought the wells of fresh water up through the grey stones with fighting and breaking of bones, till the night was all but gone. Margaret squeezed him, and the first squeeze she put him down to his knees, the second squeeze to his waist, and the third squeeze to his armpits.

'You are the best woman I have ever met. I will give you my court and my sword of light and the half of my estate for my life, and spare to slay me.'

'Where shall I try your sword of light?'

'Try it on the ugliest block in the wood.'

'I see no block at all that is uglier than your own great block.'

She struck him at the joining of the head and the neck, and cut the head off him.

In the morning when she wakened the king's son, 'Was not that a good proof I gave of myself last night?' said he to Margaret. 'That is the head outside, and we shall try to bring it home.'

He went out, and was not able to stir it from the ground. He went in and told Margaret he could not take it with him, that there was a pound's weight in the head. She went out and took the head with her.

'Come with me,' said he.

'Where are you going?'

'I will go to the Eastern World; and come with me till you see the place.'

When they got home Simon took Margaret with him to his father the king.

'What has happened to your brother and your wife?' said the king.

'They have both been killed by the giants. And it is Margaret, this woman here, who has killed them.'

The king gave Margaret a hundred thousand welcomes, and she and Simon were married, and how they are since then I do not know.

(from *West Irish Folk Tales and Romances* by William Larminie, who was told the story by Michael Flaherty, of Renvyle, Co. Galway)

Fair, Brown and Trembling

by JEREMIAH CURTIN

King Aedh Cúrucha lived in Tir Conal, and he had three daughters, whose names were Fair, Brown, and Trembling.

Fair and Brown had new dresses, and went to church every Sunday. Trembling was kept at home to do the cooking and work. They would not let her go out of the house at all; for she was more beautiful than the other two, and they were in dread she might marry before themselves.

They carried on in this way for seven years. At the end of seven years the son of the king of Emania fell in love with the eldest sister.

One Sunday morning, after the other two had gone to church, the old henwife came into the kitchen to Trembling, and said: 'It's at church you ought to be this day, instead of working here at home.'

'How could I go?' said Trembling. 'I have no clothes good enough to wear at church; and if my sisters were to see me there, they'd kill me for going out of the house.'

'I'll give you,' said the henwife, 'a finer dress than either of them has ever seen. And now tell me what dress will you have?'

'I'll have,' said Trembling, 'a dress as white as snow, and green shoes for my feet.'

Then the henwife put on the cloak of darkness, clipped a piece from the old clothes the young woman had on, and asked for the

135

whitest robes in the world and the most beautiful that could be found, and a pair of green shoes.

That moment she had the robe and the shoes, and she brought them to Trembling, who put them on. When Trembling was dressed and ready, the hen-wife said: 'I have a honey-bird here to sit on your right shoulder, and a honey-finger to put on your left. At the door stands a milk-white mare, with a golden saddle to sit on, and a golden bridle to hold in your hands.'

Trembling sat on the golden saddle; and when she was ready to start, the henwife said: 'You must not go inside the door of the church, and the minute the people rise up at the end of Mass, do you make off, and ride home as fast as the mare will carry you.'

When Trembling came to the door of the church there was no one inside who could get a glimpse of her but was striving to know who she was; and when they saw her hurrying away at the end of Mass, they ran out to overtake her. But no use in their running; she was away before any man could come near her. From the minute she left the church till she got home, she overtook the wind before her, and outstripped the wind behind.

She came down at the door, went in, and found the henwife had dinner ready. She put off the white robes, and had on her old dress in a twinkling.

When the two sisters came home the henwife asked: 'Have you any news today from the church?'

'We have great news,' said they.
'We saw a wonderful, grand lady
at the church-door. The like of
the robes she had we have never
seen on a woman before. It's
little that was thought of our
dresses beside what she had on;
and there wasn't a man at the
church, from the king to the
beggar, but was trying to look
at her and know who she was.'

The sisters would give no peace till they had two dresses like
the robes of the strange lady; but honey-birds and honey-fingers
were not to be found.

Next Sunday the two sisters went to church again, and left the
youngest at home to cook the dinner.

After they had gone, the henwife came in and asked: 'Will you
go to church today?'

'I would go,' said Trembling, 'if I could get the going.'

'What robe will you wear?' asked the henwife.

'The finest black satin that can be found, and red shoes for my
feet.'

'What colour do you want the mare to be?'

'I want her to be so black and so glossy that I can see myself in
her body.'

The henwife put on the cloak of darkness, and asked for the
robes and the mare. That moment she had them. When Trembling
was dressed, the henwife put the honey-bird on her right shoulder
and the honey-finger on her left. The saddle on the mare was silver,
and so was the bridle.

When Trembling sat in the saddle and was going away, the henwife ordered her strictly not to go inside the door of the church,

but to rush away as soon as the people rose at the end of Mass, and hurry home on the mare before any man could stop her.

That Sunday the people were more astonished than ever, and gazed at her more than the first time; and all they were thinking of was to know who she was. But they had no chance; for the moment the people rose at the end of Mass she slipped from the church, was in the silver saddle, and home before a man could stop her or talk to her.

The henwife had the dinner ready. Trembling took off her satin robe, and had on her old clothes before her sisters got home.

'What news have you today?' asked the henwife of the sisters when they came from the church.

'Oh, we saw the grand strange lady again! And it's little that

any man could think of our dresses after looking at the robes of satin that she had on! And all at church, from high to low, had their mouths open, gazing at her, and no man was looking at us.'

The two sisters gave neither rest nor peace till they got dresses as nearly like the strange lady's robes as they could find. Of course they were not so good; for their like could not be found in Erin.

When the third Sunday came, Fair and Brown went to church dressed in black satin. They left Trembling at home to work in the kitchen, and told her to be sure and have dinner ready when they came back.

After they had gone and were out of sight, the henwife came to the kitchen and said: 'Well, my dear, are you for church today?'

'I would go if I had a new dress to wear.'

'I'll get you any dress you ask for. What dress would you like?' asked the henwife.

'A dress red as a rose from the waist down, and white as snow from the waist up; a cape of green on my shoulders; and a hat on my head with a red, a white, and a green feather in it; and shoes for my feet with the toes red, the middle white, and the backs and heels green.'

The henwife put on the cloak of darkness, wished for all these things, and had them. When Trembling was dressed, the henwife put the honey-bird on her right shoulder and the honey-finger on her left, and placing the hat on her head, clipped a few hairs from one lock and a few from another with her scissors, and that moment the most beautiful golden hair was flowing down over the girl's shoulders. Then the henwife asked what kind of a mare she would ride. She said white, with blue and gold-coloured diamond-shaped spots all over her body, on her back a saddle of gold, and on her head a golden bridle.

The mare stood there before the door, and a bird sitting between her ears, which began to sing as soon as Trembling was in the saddle, and never stopped till she came home from the church.

The fame of the beautiful strange lady had gone out through the world, and all the princes and great men that were in it came to church that Sunday, each one hoping that it was himself would have her home with him after Mass.

The son of the king of Emania forgot all about the eldest sister, and remained outside the church, so as to catch the strange lady before she could hurry away.

The church was more crowded than ever before, and there were three times as many outside. There was such a throng before the church that Trembling could only come inside the gate.

As soon as the people were rising at the end of Mass, the lady slipped out through the gate, was in the golden saddle in an instant, and sweeping away ahead of the wind. But if she was, the prince of Emania was at her side, and, seizing her by the foot, he ran with the mare for thirty perches, and never let go of the beautiful lady till the shoe was pulled from her foot, and he was left behind with it in his hand. She came home as fast as the mare could carry her, and was thinking all the time that the henwife would kill her for losing the shoe.

Seeing her so vexed and so changed in the face, the old woman asked: 'What's the trouble that's on you now?'

'Oh! I've lost one of the shoes off my feet,' said Trembling.

'Don't mind that; don't be vexed,' said the henwife; 'maybe it's the best thing that ever happened to you.'

Then Trembling gave up all the things she had to the henwife, put on her old clothes, and went to work in the kitchen. When the sisters came home, the henwife asked: 'Have you any news from the church?'

'We have indeed,' said they; 'for we saw the grandest sight today. The strange lady came again, in grander array than before. On herself and the horse she rode were the finest colours of the world, and between the ears of the horse was a bird which never stopped singing from the time she came till she went away. The lady herself is the most beautiful woman ever seen by man in Erin.'

After Trembling had disappeared from the church, the son of the king of Emania said to the other kings' sons: 'I will have that lady for my own.'

They all said: 'You didn't win her just by taking the shoe off her foot, you'll have to win her by the point of the sword; you'll have to fight for her with us before you can call her your own.'

'Well,' said the son of the king of Emania, 'when I find the lady that shoe will fit, I'll fight for her, never fear, before I leave her to any of you.'

Then all the kings' sons were uneasy, and anxious to know who was she that lost the shoe; and they began to travel all over Erin to know could they find her. The prince of Emania and all the others went in a great company together, and made the round of Erin;  they went everywhere, — north, south, east, and west. They visited every place where a woman was to be found, and left not a house in the kingdom they did not search, to know could they find the woman the shoe would fit, not caring whether she was rich or poor, of high or low degree.

The prince of Emania always kept the shoe; and when the young women saw it, they had great hopes, for it was of proper size, neither large nor small, and it would beat any man to know of what material it was made. One thought it would fit her if she cut a little from her great toe; and another, with too short a foot, put something in the tip of her stocking. But no use, they only spoiled their feet, and were curing them for months afterwards.

The two sisters, Fair and Brown, heard that the princes of the world were looking all over Erin for the woman that could wear the shoe, and every day they were talking of trying it on; and one day Trembling spoke up and said: 'Maybe it's my foot that the shoe will fit.'

'Oh, the breaking of the dog's foot on you! Why say so when you were at home every Sunday?'

They were that way waiting, and scolding the younger sister, till the princes were near the place. The day they were to come, the sisters put Trembling in a closet, and locked the door on her. When the company came to the house, the prince of Emania gave the shoe to the sisters. But though they tried and tried, it would fit neither of them.

'Is there any other young woman in the house?' asked the prince.

'There is,' said Trembling, speaking up in the closet; 'I'm here.'

'Oh! we have her for nothing but to put out the ashes,' said the sisters.

But the prince and the others wouldn't leave the house till they had seen her; so the two sisters had to open the door. When Trembling came out, the shoe was given to her, and it fitted exactly.

The prince of Emania looked at her and said: 'You are the woman the shoe fits, and you are the woman I took the shoe from.'

Then Trembling spoke up, and said: 'Stay here till I return.'

Then she went to the henwife's house. The old woman put on the cloak of darkness, got everything for her she had the first Sunday at church, and put her on the white mare in the same fashion. Then Trembling rode along the highway to the front of the house. All who saw her the first time said: 'This is the lady we saw at church.'

Then she went away a second time, and a second time came back on the black mare in the second dress which the henwife gave her. All who saw her the second Sunday said: 'That is the lady we saw at church.'

A third time she asked for a short absence, and soon came back on the third mare and in the third dress. All who saw her the third time said: 'That is the lady we saw at church.' Every man was satisfied, and knew that she was the woman.

Then all the princes and great men spoke up, and said to the son of the king of Emania: 'You'll have to fight now for her before we let her go with you.'

'I'm here before you, ready for combat,' answered the prince.

Then the son of the king of Lochlin stepped forth. The struggle began, and a terrible struggle it was. They fought for nine hours; and then the son of the king of Lochlin stopped, gave up his claim, and left the field. Next day the son of the king of Spain fought six hours, and yielded his claim. On the third day the son of the king of Nyerfói fought eight hours, and stopped. The fourth day the son of the king of Greece fought six hours, and stopped. On the fifth day no more strange princes wanted to fight; and all the sons of kings in Erin said they would not fight with a man of their own land, that the strangers had had their chance, and as no others came to claim the woman, she belonged of right to the son of the king of Emania.

The marriage-day was fixed, and the invitations were sent out. The wedding lasted for a year and a day. When the wedding was over, the king's son brought home the bride, and when the time came a son was born. The young woman sent for her eldest sister, Fair, to be with her and care for her. One day, when Trembling was well, and when her husband was away hunting, the two sisters went out to walk; and when they came to the seaside, the eldest pushed the youngest sister in. A great whale came and swallowed her.

The eldest sister came home alone, and the husband asked, 'Where is your sister?'

'She has gone home to her father in Ballyshannon; now that I am well, I don't need her.'

'Well,' said the husband, looking at her, 'I'm in dread it's my wife that has gone.'

'Oh! no,' said she; 'it's my sister Fair that's gone.'

Since the sisters were very much alike, the prince was in doubt.

That night he put his sword between them, and said: 'If you are my wife, this sword will get warm; if not, it will stay cold.'

In the morning when he rose up, the sword was as cold as when he put it there.

It happened when the two sisters were walking by the seashore, that a little cowboy was down by the water minding cattle, and saw Fair push Trembling into the sea; and next day, when the tide came in, he saw the whale swim up and throw her out on the sand. When she was on the sand she said to the cowboy: 'When you go home in the evening with the cows, tell the master that my sister Fair pushed me into the sea yesterday; that a whale swallowed me, and then threw me out, but will come again and swallow me with the coming of the next tide; then he'll go out with the tide, and come again with tomorrow's tide, and throw me again on the strand. The whale will cast me out three times. I'm under the enchantment of this whale, and cannot leave the beach or escape myself. Unless my husband saves me before I'm swallowed the fourth time, I shall be lost. He must come and shoot the whale with a silver bullet when he turns on the broad of his back. Under the breast-fin of the whale is a reddish-brown spot. My husband must hit him in that spot, for it is the only place in which he can be killed.'

When the cowboy got home, the eldest sister gave him a draught of oblivion, and he did not tell.

Next day he went again to the sea. The whale came and cast Trembling on shore again. She asked the boy: 'Did you tell the master what I told you to tell him?'

'I did not,' said he; 'I forgot.'

'How did you forget?' asked she.

'The woman of the house gave me a drink that made me forget.'

'Well, don't forget telling him this night; and if she gives you a drink, don't take it from her.'

As soon as the cowboy came home, the eldest sister offered him a drink. He refused to take it till he had delivered his message and told all to the master. The third day the prince went down with his gun and a silver bullet in it. He was not long down before the whale

came and threw Trembling upon the beach as the two days before. She had no power to speak to her husband till he had killed the whale. Then the whale went out, turned over once on the broad of his back, and showed the spot for a moment only. That moment the prince fired. He had but the one chance, and a short one at that; but he took it, and hit the spot, and the whale, mad with pain, made the sea all around red with blood, and died.

That minute Trembling was able to speak, and went home with her husband, who sent word to her father what the eldest sister had done. The father came, and told him any death he chose to give her to give it. The prince told the father he would leave her life and death with himself. The father had her put out then on the sea in a barrel, with provisions in it for seven years.

In time Trembling had a second child, a daughter. The prince and she sent the cowboy to school, and trained him up as one of their own children, and said: 'If the little girl that is born to us now lives, no other man in the world will get her but him.'

The cowboy and the prince's daughter lived on till they were married. The mother said to her husband: 'You could not have saved me from the whale but for the little cowboy; on that account I don't grudge him my daughter.'

The son of the king of Emania and Trembling had fourteen children, and they lived happily till the two died of old age.

(from *Myths and Folk-lore of Ireland*)

The
Birth of Bran

by JAMES STEPHENS

There are people who do not like dogs a bit — they are usually women — but in this story there is a man who did not like dogs. In fact, he hated them. When he saw one he used to go black in the face, and he threw rocks at it until it got out of sight. But the Power that protects all creatures had put a squint into this man's eye, so that he always threw crooked.

This gentleman's name was Fergus Fionnliath, and his stronghold was near the harbour of Galway. Whenever a dog barked he would leap out of his seat, and he would throw everything that he owned out of the window in the direction of the bark. He gave prizes to servants who disliked dogs, and when he heard a man had drowned a litter of pups he used to visit that person and try to marry his daughter.

Now Fionn, the son of Uail, was the reverse of Fergus Fionnliath in this matter, for he delighted in dogs, and he knew everything about them from the setting of the first little white tooth to the rocking of the last long yellow one. He knew the affections and antipathies which are proper in a dog; the degree of obedience to which dogs may be trained without losing their honourable qualities or becoming servile and suspicious; he knew the hopes that animate them, the apprehensions which tingle in their blood, and all that is to be demanded from, or forgiven in, a paw, an ear, a nose, an

147

eye, or a tooth; and he understood these things because he loved dogs, for it is by love alone that we understand anything.

Among the three hundred dogs which Fionn owned there were two to whom he gave an especial tenderness, and who were his daily and nightly companions. These two were Bran and Sceólan, but if a person were to guess for twenty years he would not find out why Fionn loved these two dogs and why he would never be separated from them.

Fionn's mother, Muirne, went to wide Allen of Leinster to visit her son, and she brought her young sister Tuiren with her. The mother and aunt of the great captain were well treated among the Fianna, first, because they were parents to Fionn, and second, because they were beautiful and noble women.

No words can describe how delightful Muirne was — she took the branch; and as to Tuiren, a man could not look at her without becoming angry or dejected. Her face was fresh as a spring morning; her voice more cheerful than the cuckoo calling from the branch that is highest in the hedge; and her form swayed like a reed and flowed like a river, so that each person thought she would surely flow to him.

Men who had wives of their own grew moody and downcast because they could not hope to marry her, while the bachelors of the Fianna stared at each other with truculent, bloodshot eyes, and then they gazed on Tuiren so gently that she may have imagined she was being beamed on by the mild eyes of the dawn.

It was to an Ulster gentleman, Iollan Eachtach, that she gave her love, and this chief stated his rights and qualities and asked for her in marriage.

Now Fionn did not dislike the men of Ulster, but either he did not know them well or else he knew them too well, for he made a curious stipulation before consenting to the marriage. He bound Iollan to return the lady if there should be occasion to think her unhappy, and Iollan agreed to do so. The sureties to this bargain were Caelte mac Ronan, Goll mac Morna, and Lugaidh. Lugaidh himself gave the bride away, but it was not a pleasant ceremony for him, because he also was in love with the lady, and he would have preferred keeping her to giving her away. When she had gone he made a poem about her, beginning:

> There is no more light in the sky

And hundreds of sad people learned the poem by heart.

When Iollan and Tuiren were married they went to Ulster, and they lived together very happily. But the law of life is change; nothing continues in the same way for any length of time; happiness must become unhappiness, and will be succeeded again by the joy it had displaced. The past also must be reckoned with; it is seldom as far behind us as we could wish: it is more often in front, blocking the way, and the future trips over it just when we think that the road is clear and joy our own.

Iollan had a past. He was not ashamed of it; he merely thought it was finished, although in truth it was only beginning, for it is that perpetual beginning of the past that we call the future.

Before he joined the Fianna he had been in love with a lady of the Shí, named Uct Dealv (Fair Breast), and they had been sweethearts for years. How often he had visited his sweetheart in Faery! With what eagerness and anticipation he had gone there; the lover's whistle that he used to give was known to every person in that Shí, and he had been discussed by more than one of

the delicate sweet ladies of Faery.

'That is your whistle, Fair Breast,' her sister of the Shí would say.

And Uct Dealv would reply:

'Yes, that is my mortal, my lover, my pulse, and my one treasure.'

She laid her spinning aside, or her embroidery if she was at that, or if she were baking a cake of fine wheaten bread mixed with honey she would leave the cake to bake itself and fly to Iollan. Then they went hand in hand in the country that smells of apple-blossom and honey, looking on heavy-boughed trees and on dancing and beaming clouds. Or they stood dreaming together, locked in a clasping of arms and eyes, gazing up and down on each other, Iollan staring down into sweet grey wells that peeped and flickered under thin brows, and Uct Dealv looking up into great black ones that went dreamy and went hot in endless alternation.

Then Iollan would go back to the world of men, and Uct Dealv would return to her occupations in the Land of the Ever Young.

'What did he say?' her sister of the Shí would ask.

'He said I was the Berry of the Mountain, the Star of Knowledge, and the Blossom of the Raspberry.'

'They always say the same thing,' her sister pouted.

'But they look other things,' Uct Dealv insisted. 'They feel other things,' she murmured; and an endless conversation recommenced.

Then for some time Iollan did not come to Faery, and Uct Dealv marvelled at that, while her sister made an hundred surmises, each one worse than the last.

'He is not dead or he would be here,' she said. 'He has forgotten you, my darling.'

News was brought to Tir na n-Óg of the marriage of Iollan and Tuiren, and when Uct Dealv heard that news her heart ceased to beat for a moment, and she closed her eyes.

'Now!' said her sister of the Shí. 'That is how long the love of a mortal lasts,' she added, in the voice of sad triumph which is proper to sisters.

But on Uct Dealv there came a rage of jealousy and despair such as no person in the Shí had ever heard of, and from that moment she became capable of every ill deed; for there are two things not easily controlled, and they are hunger and jealousy. She determined that the woman who had supplanted her in Iollan's affections should rue the day she did it. She pondered and brooded revenge in her heart, sitting in thoughtful solitude and bitter collectedness until at last she had a plan.

She understood the arts of magic and shape-changing, so she changed her shape into that of Fionn's female runner, the best-known woman in Ireland; then she set out from Faery and appeared in the world. She travelled in the direction of Iollan's stronghold.

Iollan knew the appearance of Fionn's messenger, but he was surprised to see her.

She saluted him.

'Health and long life, my master.'

'Health and good days,' he replied. 'What brings you here, dear heart?'

'I come from Fionn.'

'And your message?' said he.

'The royal captain intends to visit you.'

'He will be welcome,' said Iollan. 'We shall give him an Ulster feast.'

'The world knows what that is,' said the messenger courteously. 'And now,' she continued, 'I have messages for your queen.'

Tuiren then walked from the house with the messenger, but when they had gone a short distance Uct Dealv drew a hazel rod from beneath her cloak and struck it on the queen's shoulder, and on the instant Tuiren's figure trembled and quivered, and it began to whirl inwards and downwards, and she changed into the appearance of a hound.

It was sad to see the beautiful, slender dog standing shivering and astonished, and sad to see the lovely eyes that looked out pitifully in terror and amazement. But Uct Dealv did not feel sad. She clasped a chain about the hound's neck, and they set off westward towards the house of Fergus Fionnliath, who was reputed to be the unfriendliest man in the world to a dog. It was because of his reputation that Uct Dealv was bringing the hound to him. She did not want a good home for this dog: she wanted the worst home that could be found in the world, and she thought that Fergus would revenge for her the rage and jealousy which she felt towards Tuiren.

As they paced along Uct Dealv railed bitterly against the hound, and shook and jerked her chain. Many a sharp cry the hound gave in that journey, many a mild lament.

'Ah, supplanter! Ah, taker of another girl's sweetheart!' said Uct Dealv fiercely. 'How would your lover take it if he could see you now? How would he look if he saw your pointy ears, your long thin snout, your shivering, skinny legs, and your long grey tail? He would not love you now, bad girl!'

'Have you heard of Fergus Fionnliath,' she said again, 'the man who does not like dogs?'

Tuiren had indeed heard of him.

'It is to Fergus I shall bring you,' cried Uct Dealv. 'He will throw stones at you. You have never had a stone thrown at you. Ah, bad girl! You do not know how a stone sounds as it nips the ear with

a whirling buzz, nor how jagged and heavy it feels as it thumps against a skinny leg. Robber! Mortal! Bad girl! You have never been whipped, but you will be whipped now. You shall hear the song of a lash as it curls forward and bites inward and drags backward. You shall dig up old bones stealthily at night, and chew them against famine. You shall whine and squeal at the moon, and shiver in the cold, and you will never take another girl's sweetheart again.'

And it was in those terms and in that tone that she spoke to Tuiren as they journeyed forward, so that the hound trembled and shrank, and whined pitifully and in despair.

They came to Fergus Fionnliath's stronghold, and Uct Dealv demanded admittance.

'Leave that dog outside,' said the servant.

'I will not do so,' said the pretended messenger.

'You can come in without the dog, or you can stay out with the dog,' said the surly guardian.

'By my hand,' cried Uct Dealv, 'I will come in with this dog, or your master shall answer for it to Fionn.'

At the name of Fionn the servant almost fell out of his standing. He flew to acquaint his master, and Fergus himself came to the great door of the stronghold.

'By my faith,' he cried in amazement, 'it is a dog.'

'A dog it is,' growled the glum servant.

'Go you away,' said Fergus to Uct Dealv, 'and when you have killed the dog come back to me and I will give you a present.'

'Life and health, my good master, from Fionn, the son of Uail, the son of Baiscne,' said she to Fergus.

'Life and health back to Fionn,' he replied. 'Come into the house and give your message, but leave the dog outside, for I don't like dogs.'

'The dog comes in,' the messenger replied.

'How is that?' cried Fergus angrily.

'Fionn sends you this hound to take care of until he comes for her,' said the messenger.

'I wonder at that,' Fergus growled, 'for Fionn knows well that there is not a man in the world has less of a liking for dogs than I have.'

'However that may be, master, I have given Fionn's message, and here at my heel is the dog. Do you take her or refuse her?'

'If I could refuse anything to Fionn it would be a dog,' said Fergus, 'but I could not refuse anything to Fionn, so give me the hound.'

Uct Dealv put the chain in his hand.

'Ah, bad dog!' said she.

And then she went away well satisfied with her revenge, and

returned to her own people in the Shí.

On the following day Fergus called his servant:

'Has that dog stopped shivering yet?' he asked.

'It has not, sir,' said the servant.

'Bring the beast here,' said his master, 'for whoever else is dissatisfied Fionn must be satisfied.'

The dog was brought, and he examined it with a jaundiced and bitter eye.

'It has the shivers indeed,' he said.

'The shivers it has,' said the servant.

'How do you cure the shivers?' his master demanded, for he thought that if the animal's legs dropped off Fionn would not be satisfied.

'There is a way,' said the servant doubtfully.

'If there is a way, tell it to me,' cried his master angrily.

'If you were to take the beast up in your arms and hug it and kiss it, the shivers would stop,' said the man.

'Do you mean —?' his master thundered, and he stretched his hand for a club.

'I heard that,' said the servant humbly.

'Take that dog up,' Fergus commanded, 'and hug it and kiss it, and if I find a single shiver left in the beast I'll break your head.'

The man bent to the hound, but it snapped a piece out of his hand, and nearly bit his nose off as well.

'That dog doesn't like me,' said the man.

'Nor do I,' roared Fergus; 'get out of my sight.'

The man went away and Fergus was left alone with the hound, but the poor creature was so terrified that it began to tremble ten times worse than before.

'Its legs will drop off,' said Fergus. 'Fionn will blame me,' he cried in despair.

He walked to the hound.

'If you snap at my nose, or if you put as much as the start of a tooth into the beginning of a finger!' he growled.

He picked up the dog, but it did not snap, it only trembled. He held it gingerly for a few moments.

'If it has to be hugged,' he said, 'I'll hug it. I'd do more than that for Fionn.'

He tucked and tightened the animal into his breast, and marched moodily up and down the room. The dog's nose lay along his breast under his chin, and as he gave it dutiful hugs, one hug to every five paces, the dog put out its tongue and licked him timidly under the chin.

'Stop,' roared Fergus, 'stop that for ever,' and he grew very red in the face, and stared truculently down along his nose. A soft brown eye looked up at him and the shy tongue touched again on his chin.

'If it has to be kissed,' said Fergus gloomily, 'I'll kiss it. I'd do more than that for Fionn,' he groaned.

He bent his head, shut his eyes, and brought the dog's jaw against his lips. And at that the dog gave little wriggles in his arms, and

little barks, and little licks, so that he could scarcely hold her. He put the hound down at last.

'There is not a single shiver left in her,' he said.

And that was true.

Everywhere he walked the dog followed him, giving little prances and little pats against him, and keeping her eyes fixed on his with such eagerness and intelligence that he marvelled.

'That dog likes me,' he murmured in amazement.

'By my hand,' he cried next day, 'I like that dog.'

The day after that he was calling her 'My One Treasure, My Little Branch.' And within a week he could not bear her to be out of his sight for an instant.

He was tormented by the idea that some evil person might throw a stone at the hound, so he assembled his servants and retainers and addressed them.

He told them that the hound was the Queen of Creatures, the Pulse of his Heart, and the Apple of his Eye, and he warned them that the person who as much as looked sideways on her, or knocked one shiver out of her, would answer for the deed with pains and indignities. He recited a list of calamities which would befall such a miscreant, and these woes began with flaying and ended with dismemberment, and had inside bits of such complicated and ingenious torment that the blood of the men who heard it ran chill in their veins, and the women of the household fainted where they stood.

In course of time the news came to Fionn that his mother's sister was not living with Iollan. He at once sent a messenger calling for fulfilment of the pledge that had been given to the Fianna, and demanding the instant return of Tuiren. Iollan was in a sad condition when this demand was made. He guessed that Uct Dealv had a hand in the disappearance of his queen, and he begged that time should be given him in which to find the lost girl. He promised if he could not discover her within a certain period that he would deliver his body into Fionn's hands, and would abide by whatever judgement Fionn might pronounce. The great captain agreed to that.

'Tell the wife-loser that I will have the girl or I will have his head,' said Fionn.

Iollan set out then for Faery. He knew the way, and in no great time he came to the hill where Uct Dealv was.

It was hard to get Uct Dealv to meet him, but at last she consented, and they met under the apple boughs of Faery.

'Well!' said Uct Dealv. 'Ah! Breaker of Vows and Traitor to Love,' said she.

'Hail and a blessing,' said Iollan humbly.

'By my hand,' she cried, 'I will give you no blessing, for it was no blessing you left with me when we parted.'

'I am in danger,' said Iollan.

'What is that to me?' she replied fiercely.

'Fionn may claim my head,' he murmured.

'Let him claim what he can take,' said she.

'No,' said Iollan proudly, 'he will claim what I can give.'

'Tell me your tale,' said she coldly.

Iollan told his story then, and, he concluded, 'I am certain that you have hidden the girl.'

'If I save your head from Fionn,' the woman of the Shí replied, 'then your head will belong to me.'

'That is true,' said Iollan.

'And if your head is mine, the body that goes under it is mine. Do you agree to that?'

'I do,' said Iollan.

'Give me your pledge,' said Uct Dealv, 'that if I save you from this danger you will keep me as your sweetheart until the end of life and time.'

'I give that pledge,' said Iollan.

Uct Dealv went then to the house of Fergus Fionnliath, and she broke the enchantment that was on the hound, so that Tuiren's own shape came back to her; but in the matter of two small whelps, to which the hound had given birth, the enchantment could not be broken, so they had to remain as they were. These two whelps were Bran and Sceólan. They were sent to Fionn, and he loved them for ever after, for they were loyal and affectionate, as only dogs can be, and they were as intelligent as human beings. Besides that, they were Fionn's own cousins.

Tuiren was then asked in marriage by Lugaidh who had loved her so long. He had to prove to her that he was not any other woman's sweetheart, and when he proved that they were married, and they lived happily ever after, which is the proper way to live.

He wrote a poem beginning:

> Lovely the day. Dear is the eye of the dawn

And a thousand merry people learned it after him.

But as to Fergus Fionnliath, he took to his bed, and he stayed there for a year and a day suffering from blighted affection, and he would have died in the bed only that Fionn sent him a special pup, and in a week that young hound became the Star of Fortune and the very Pulse of his Heart, so that he got well again, and he also lived happily ever after.

(from *Irish Fairy Tales*)

FUNDAMENTALS OF CHINESE CULTURE

中国文化 ABC

Compiled by : Zhu Fayuan, David Wu, Xia Hanning, Brad Goldhorn

主　编：朱法元　吴琦幸　夏汉宁（美）高　汉

Translators : Wu Ke, Yuan Zhimei, Lin Ying, Yuan Zhen, You Jiajuan, Li Jian

翻　译：吴　可　袁志美　林　颖　袁　真　尤佳娟　李　健

Jiangxi People's Publishing House

江西人民出版社

Introduction

    As one of the world's oldest civilized nation with 5000-years culture, China is a great nation given with two spectacular mother rivers—the Yangtze River and the Yellow River. It's also a magical land pregnant with amazing tourist attractions like the Great Wall and Huangshan Mountain. And fifty-five minority ethnic groups such as Zhuang and Manchu are officially recognized besides the Han majority.

    To understand China, feasting your eyes on beautiful sceneries of great mountains and grand rivers is necessary and important . However, if you want to have best knowledge about China, you should step into the gorgeous palace of Chinese culture and explore her rich and time-honored history because you can't expect an acute insight into China before you have a good understanding of Chinese civilization.

    Therefore, scholars from China and America join their hands in planning and compiling this book as the supplementary reading material to bilingual teaching of Chinese culture on the basis of deliberation. Since this reading is designed for college students who're intended to learn Chinese in America, we establish three guidelines for the compilation of the book as follows. Firstly, we put an emphasis on its comprehensiveness. We try to offer a panoramic view of Chinese five thousand years culture within limited chapters. Secondly, we make our great effort to guarantee its representativeness, to introduce the most typical part of Chinese civilization. Thirdly, accuracy is another great concern for us. We strive to make this book accessible to its readers with spot-on information illustrated within it. To this end, we've invested more than three years' time hosting multiple conferences for the project. Meanwhile, much effort has been spent on frequent reviewing and rewriting. Furthermore, in order to guarantee this publication's readability and authenticity, we've invited Mr. Gao Han, a prominent American sinologist, to take responsibility to examine and revise the English version. Hence, this reading arises and evolves through the concerted efforts of people from China and U.S. academia, educational circles and the publishing company.

This book is dubbed *Fundamentals of Chinese Culture* due to, at least, the following two factors. In the first place, it contains the fundamental elements of Chinese civilization which, we believe, are some common sense necessary for any Chinese learner, although so many former compilers always overlook it. In the second, this is a popularization of Chinese culture and the Chinese academic community has achieved consensus on the validity of its content.

According to the time setting of Chinese language teaching in American universities, and the principle of gradual and orderly progress, the book is divided into four chapters with each chapter consisting of five units.

Chapter One covers the hallmarks of Chinese Character and Chinese language and related knowledge. In addition, it includes common sense of Chinese names, family appellation, greeting modes. At the same time, it introduces some appealing subjects about traditional Chinese festivals, calendar, solar terms, myths and legends. You can begin your travel into Chinese culture if you would like to equip yourself with above fundamental information.

Chapter Two is designed to lead you further into Chinese civilization and its time-honored history. It provides information for 5000-years historical vicissitude and the shifts between dynasties. It also introduces 56 Chinese ethnic groups, various wedding customs and Chinese people's conception of family. Besides, you can obtain an insight into China's four great ancient inventions, abacus and its usage, dak, post road, palanquin and horse-drawn trolley. Still, this chapter can guide you to take a cultural travel to the Great Wall, Terra-cotta Warriors and Horses, Yellow River (the birthplace of Chinese civilization), the old Silk Road, the Five Sacred Mountains and big rivers and lakes. Of course, you may be carried away either by the historic celebrities who made enormous contributions to Chinese culture, such as Lao Tzu, Confucius and Chuangtse, or by the immortal masterpieces like *The Book of Songs, Lyrics of Chu, Han Prosodies, Records of the Grand Historian of China, and History of the Han Dynasty*, etc.

Chapter Three continues to engage unique cultural China. Your mind will wander among Yangtze River Culture, eight great ancient capitals of China, palace and temple architecture. We believe you'd also admire tea and wine culture and eight cuisines because they're so typical of China. Moreover, this part provides a kaleidoscope of Han Chinese costume, cheongsam, Chinese folding fans, and folk handcraft. If you wish, you can probe into Chinese medicine, Chinese chess, Kungfu and so on. Apart from all these, you can immerse yourself into the sea of charismatic Chinese classics by reading Four Books and Five Classics, Tang Dynasty poetry, Song Dynasty poetry, Yuan Dynasty Opera and sundry dramas, novels of the Ming and Qing Dynasties...

Chapter Four unfolds a fun world in front of you. Everything presented here, including Chinese gardens, residence, the imperial mausoleums, porcelain wares, I-go, Bejing Opera, Kunqu Opera, Yue

Opera, Huang Mei Opera and Dun Huang Murals, is so special and fresh to you. Some other glittering gems of the cultural treasure house in China are the scholarly Confucian study, the study of Taoism, the Buddhist study, the ancient book-collecting culture, the imperial examination culture. In the end, you can not only enjoy a cultural feast on "China's Four Famous Classical (i.e. *The Dreams in Red Mansion, Heroes of the Marshes, The Romance of Three Kingdom, Journey to the West*), but also walk in the literature wonderland full of prevailing masterworks produced by eminent modern Chinese writers, such as Lu Xun, Guo Mo-ruo, Hu Shi, Mao Dun, Ba Jin, Lao She, Cao Yu.

Dear readers, if this book can offer you a happy reading and enkindle your interest in Chinese civilization; if it can catalyze an unquenchable interest for your exploring China, we will feel very happy and honored, because this shows that our original intention of composing already achieved.

And we're looking forward to your enthusiasm about Chinese culture.

Editorial Board of *Fundamentals of Chinese Culture*

March.1, 2010

导　言

中国是一个伟大的国家,中国又是一个神奇的国家。因为,在这片国土上,有长江、长城,有黄山,黄河,有汉族、壮族、满族等 56 个民族,更有历经五千年至今仍绵延不绝的华夏文化。

要了解中国,饱览她那充满魅力的名山大川和旖旎风光,这毫无疑问是非常重要的。但是,要想真正了解中国,更应该步入她那绚丽多彩的文化殿堂,去解读她那丰厚而又悠久的历史。因为,只有读懂中国文化,才能真正读懂中国!

正是基于这样的思考,中美两国的学者共同策划和编写了这部关于中国文化的双语教学辅助读物。由于这部读物是写给美国学习汉语的大学生阅读的,所以在编写时,我们确立了三个原则:第一,全面性。力图以有限的篇幅对五千年的中国文化作一个全景式的勾勒。第二,代表性。力图把最具代表性的中国文化介绍给读者。第三,准确性。力图做到所介绍的知识准确无误,语言通俗易懂。为此,我们付出了两年的时间,多次商讨,多次审稿、改稿。而且,为了保证英文翻译的准确与地道,我们还特别邀请了美国著名汉学家高汉先生对全书英文翻译进行修改和审定。可以说,这部读物是中美两国学术界、教育界、出版界共同努力的结晶。

这部读物之所以取名为《中国文化 ABC》,至少出于这样两个考虑:第一,书中所介绍的都是中国文化的基本常识。我们认为,这些常识应该是汉语学习者必须了解的,但遗憾的是,它又往往容易被编写者所忽视。第二,这是一部中国文化的普及读物,因此书中介绍的都是为学术界所认定的并达成共识的内容。

根据美国大学汉语教学的时间设置,同时也是本着循序渐进的原则,我们在编写时把这部读物分为四大部分,每个部分又分为五个单元。

第一部分,主要介绍了汉字、汉语及其相关的知识;介绍了中国人的姓名、问候语、称谓等常识;介绍了中国的节日、历法、节气和神话传说等饶有趣味的话题。可以说,掌握了这些知识,你就迈开了了解中国文化的第一步。

第二部分,我们开始试图引领你向中国文化的纵深迈进,以了解中国悠久的历史。在这个部分,你可以看到中国五千年的历史变迁和朝代更替;你可以了解为泱泱中华作出贡献的56个民族;你可以熟悉中国人的婚俗和家的观念;你可以知道中国的四大发明以及中国的算盘、珠算、驿站、驿道、轿子、马车;你可以领略神奇的长城、兵马俑、黄河文化;你可以踏上古老的丝绸之路、游览五岳和湖泊;你可以和那些为中国文化作出巨大贡献的历史名人老子、孔子、庄子等亲密接触;你还可以欣赏到流传千古的名篇巨制——《诗经》《楚辞》《汉赋》《史记》《汉书》……

第三部分,你仍将徜徉在中国历史文化的殿堂中,在寻访长江文化、八大古都、宫廷建筑、寺庙建筑之后,你还可品味到独具中国特色的茶文化、酒文化和八大菜系;在观赏汉服、旗袍、折扇及各地民间工艺之余,你还能探秘中医中药、中国象棋、武术等等;你还可以品读魅力无穷的中国经典——四书五经、唐诗宋词、元曲杂剧、明清小说……

第四部分,一个新奇的世界在你面前打开:中国园林、民居、皇陵、陶瓷、围棋、京剧、昆曲、越剧、黄梅戏、敦煌壁画等等,一定会带给你耳目一新的感觉;儒学、道学、佛学、中国藏书文化、科举文化等等,让你尽享中国文化的博大与精深;中国古代小说四大名著《红楼梦》《水浒传》《三国演义》《西游记》,中国现代作家鲁迅、郭沫若、胡适、茅盾、巴金、老舍、曹禺等人的佳作名篇,带着你在文学的天空中尽情地翱翔。

亲爱的读者朋友,当你读完这部书,你能将对中国文化的兴趣,化作对中国的向往,化作你走进中国的行动,那么,我们将感到万分荣幸,因为这证明了我们编写这部读物的初衷得到了实现。

为此,我们期盼着!

《中国文化 ABC》编委会

2010 年 3 月 1 日

Unit 1 第一单元

Unit 2 第二单元

Unit 3 第三单元

Chapter 2 第二章

Unit 1 第一单元

Unit 2 第二单元

Unit 3 第三单元

Chapter 3　第三章

Unit 1　第一单元

Unit 2　第二单元

Unit 3　第三单元

Unit 4　第四单元

Unit 5　第五单元

Chapter 4　第四章

Unit 1　第一单元

Unit 2　第二单元

Unit 3　第三单元

Chapter 1

第一章

Unit 1

The Origins of Chinese Characters

Chinese is the world's oldest written language, being used by the greatest number of people. According to records, Chinese writing emerges in the 14th century B.C. during the later part of the Yin Shang Dynasty. This period gives rise to the preliminary form of written Chinese—Oracle Bone Script. The invention and application of Chinese writing not only stimulated the development of Chinese culture, but also has had the far-reaching influence in the development of world civilization. At present, many countries use written phonetic alphabets, but Chinese writing has retained the property of ideograms. Therefore, from the form and structure of the writing, we can examine the life, society, customs, and the culture of originators. The writing is unique to China; most other

Oracle Bone Script

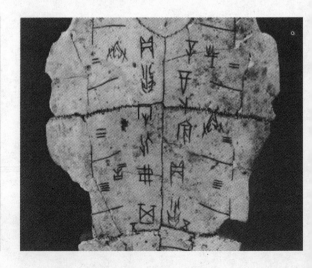

countries' script does not display this relationship in their writing.

Since ancient times, there have been numerous explanations regarding the birth of Chinese characters. The formation of characters by Cangjie is the widest spread one, with pervasive recordation in the ancient books. It is said that Cangjie was the historiographer of the Yellow Emperor. As legend has it, one day Cangjie saw a deity, his appearance was odd and his face looked like a picture with some writing on it. Consequently, Cangjie drew the god's imagery, creating the first Chinese characters. Ancient manuscripts state that as Cangjie created the words, nature's mysteries were revealed, millet (grain) fell from the heavens, and ghosts and gods cried and wailed during the night. Yet still another legend reveals that Cangjie observed the tracks of birds and animals, thus inspiring his script.

These certainly are beautiful legends, yet scientific evidence reveals the true origin of Chinese characters was ancient drawings. Modern scholars agree that figures engraved on excavated artifacts in all probability have the relation to the origin of writing. Dating over six thousand years, the Banpo archaeological site exhibits more than fifty written symbols. They are simple, trim, and orderly, containing the essence of writing. Experts agree that these are most likely the early shoots of Chinese writing. It is also believed that one person could not possibly conceive the entire system of Chinese writing. Ancient texts state in general that Cangjie is the architect of Chinese writing. If in fact there was a man named Cangjie, it may have been he who cataloged and promulgated the characters.

Besides the theories of Cangjie originating Chinese writing and early pictographs, there are still other explanations to its creation, such as the theory of knotted string, the Eight Trigrams, and many others. Some scholars believe words were created by the inspiration of knotted string, a method ancient Chinese used to record matters. Moreover, others state that it relates to the Eight Trigrams from the Book of Changes. Generally speaking, the writing of Chinese is a product of history, requiring interior and exterior conditions. The character itself and writing syntax are all inclusive. The emergence of Chinese writing indicates the necessities of people when facing practicality of life and resolving to long-term community practice. They began to remember things, engrave or draw figures to record events, eventually contributing to the foundation of language development, forming a civilized era, as a great leap forward in human evolution.

The Lengend of Cangjie Creating Chinese Character

When linguists explain the structure of the word, they follow the criterion of the Six Methods, dividing the words into six categories: pictogram, ideogram, ideogrammic compound, phono-semantic, derivative cognates, and phonetic loan.

The pictogram is the earliest example of character formation, consequently resulting in the first written words. These characters usually name material objects, their shapes indicating what they represent. For example, sun was originally written as "☉".

The method of forming ideograms uses an abstract symbol in iconic form to create a word with added intent to the pictogram. Therefore one is required to experience and observe carefully in order to comprehend it. There are two ways in which ideograms are formed. One way uses a pictogram as the basis with combined directive symbolism. For example, "本"(root) comes from the word of "木" (tree); a horizontal line added at the bottom indicates where lies the roots of a tree. The roots or the trunk of the tree, referring the foundation, or basis, symbolizes the literal meaning. The second is adopting pure symbols to indicate a symbol of something or some kind of meaning.

The second method of ideograms—ideogrammic compound joins two words together resulting in a new one. For example "明"(light) formerly written as "☽", stems from the "日" (sun) and the "月" (moon) that bring us light. Another guideline is the relation of position of the symbols, as indicated in "旦"(dawn) originally written as "Ō", signifying the sun rising over the horizon.

The phono-semantic method involves combining a character's phonetic aspect with a semantic element (radical), resulting is a significantly new word. For example, "爸"(father), contains "巴" (bā) the phonetic element, and the radical "父" (hand and axe), forming the word. According statistics, radical-phonetic characters account for about 90% of all Chinese characters, becoming the most facilitative way of producing new words.

Derivative cognates still retain the same etymological root yet the phonetics change among dialects. Later generations employed the symbols and dialects for their own purpose in different ways, adapting character synonyms yet with different phonetics. For example, the character "豕" (shǐ: pig) later in other regions as "豬"(zhū), as well as other places known as "彘"(zhì), transfers the pictogram "豕" to indicate pig. The addition of the phonetic symbols zhě and shǐ, new words, or mutually explanatory characters are formed. In this case, the meaning remains the same, while the pronunciation and character are slightly different.

The phonetic loan method uses homophones to create new words, which means one spoken word has two different meanings (rebus). This way of word formation is very important in the history of Chinese writing, the changing from ideograph to phonogram is a key tendency of development, reflecting the transformation of the character's quality.

Chinese Writing and Chinese Language

Written Chinese is the symbolic recordation of spoken Chinese, becoming the tools of literary works. Chinese writing and the Han Dialect are closely related and have a strong sense of space and time. It not only displays the similarities of ancient and modern Chinese, but also inter-

weaves many other different dialects. From the ancient Han Dialect to
the modern Chinese, the phonetics have changed considerably. The vocabulary and
grammar have also evolved immensely, yet the squared shape of the character has remained the
same.

Chinese writing is the unity of form, sound and meaning. Words supply the vocabulary, in turn
forming the syntax. One character has three aspects: initials, finals, and intonation. Altogether, the
Han Dialect contains 21 initials, 39 finals, and four tones. The Han Dialect has many homophones
(about 3755 words are in common usage, yet there are only 400 sounds). Over many hundreds of
years, common people have created numerous insightful allegorical expressions, using the same or
similar sounds of different characters. This has become one of the Chinese language's greatest
characteristics.

A distinct two-part allegorical expression, xiehouyu, is a distinct language usage created by
people with regards to their life experience. It is commonly composed of two phrases—the first half
being a vivid description and the second half containing a meaning which must be deciphered. The
expression contains references to nature or daily life. In certain social environments, usually the first
half is said, but the second half is omitted intentionally so that others must infer the intended
expression. Xiehouyu is a short, witty and vivid sentence. For example, in the expression "the stool of
paper—cannot work", work and sit sound similar in Mandarin. In the expression "The Buddhists'
house—wonderful", the Mandarin word "temple" has the same sound as "wonderful". Some
allegorical sayings have affiliations with Chinese traditional culture or historical figures, as in
"Songjiang's military advisor—worthless". Because of the counselor's name, "Wu Yong", sounds
like the word "worthless", yet the characters are quite different.

Idioms and proverbs are another defining characteristic of the Chinese language. An idiom is a
phrase with a fixed format having been used throughout time, attributing to the descriptiveness of
the written language. It commonly consists of four words, such as "胸有成竹". This idiom literally
translates to bamboo grows from the chest, but its figurative meaning is to have a well-thought-out
plan. Unlike idioms, proverbs have no limitation on the number of words. They are created and
popularized by common people, while remaining concise and comprehensive. It is a formed artistic
language, and its discipline demonstrates the people's wisdom and experience, as shown in the
example, With rain brightens all four directions, without rain shines the tip of the heavens. English
proverbs such as, a fall into a pit, a gain in your wit, and Rome was not built in a day, do not have
strict rules of framework while Chinese idioms are compelled to the four-word format.

Chinese Characters and Calligraphy

Calligraphy is the art of handwriting Chinese characters. It is distinctive art of China. Calligraphy includes the techniques and rules of writing, such as how to hold the brush, brushstrokes,
dotting, framing and layout (i.e. distribution, order, and composition). Along with the development of

culture, calligraphy evolved from the use of brush pens to write to include many more aspects of handwriting. For instance, it added many different kinds of pens and colored paints, not solely using black ink.

Chinese calligraphy emphasizes brush technique. This art is comprised of four parts: brush movement, the vigor of the strokes, the momentum of writing, and the intended concept. The brush movement is the controlling of the brush. The brushstroke is the force of the writing. The momentum of the writing is the tendency and the kinetics of the line. The intended concept suggests sentiment as implied, revealing the inner spirit. Traditional calligraphy makes use of the character "永" to show the eight distinct types of strokes in regular script. The Yongzi Eight Ways refers to the eight different strokes of the character "永," every stroke representing a type of action. The strokes are affiliated with a movement, such as a bird flying, reining in a horse, drawing a bow, kicking, whipping a horse, combing the hair, pecking for food, and hanging meat, as well as other common movements.

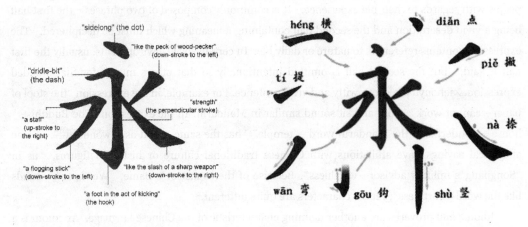

The Eight Ways of the Character "永"

The Oracle Bone Script is the first treasure in the history of Chinese writing. The script has variations of thickness, strength, and speed. The stroke begins light and fast, there is thickness and heaviness in the movement, and the end is quick. Such is the rhythm of calligraphy. Inscriptions on bronzes and seals depict other styles of Chinese calligraphy. Compared to the Oracle Bone Script, the inscriptions on bronzes are much more robust and impressive, reaching high standards.

The period of prosperity for calligraphy began in Eastern Han Dynasty. During this time emerging the specialist Cai Yi as the delegate of Li Shu calligraphy (clerical style), and Zhang Zi being the Cao Shu (grass style) delegate. Li Shu calligraphy reached the benchmark of perfection. It was distinguished by the squared nature of the characters, the strict rules, and the tendency of the writing of characters to slant downward towards the right direction. During the period of the

Wang Xizhi's Calligraphy

Three Kingdoms, the popularity of Li Shu calligraphy declined, thus giving rise to Kai Shu calligraphy, which became a standard form of the art. During the Jin Dynasty, a great number of master calligraphers emerged, the most important in this history is the influence of Wang Xizhi, known as the Sage of Calligraphy. His work *Preface to the Poems Composed at the Orchid Pavilion* is praised as the greatest calligraphy book under heaven.

The Sui Dynasty brought together the warring states of the north and south, unifying China, allowing the latter Tang Dynasty to enjoy a comparatively peaceful and stable era. Kai Shu calligraphy had fully developed its style, thus serving an important function of the past and ushering in the future of literary development.

Civilization in the Tang Dynasty was deep and profound, as China reached the highest peak of feudal culture. Calligraphy entered a new era of splendor. Kai Shu, Xing Shu, and Cao Shu calligraphy made rigorous strides in the new circumstances. The great masters of Kai Shu calligraphy include Ou Yangxun, Yu Shinan, and Chu Suiliang. The Cao Shu masters, such as Zhang Xu, Huai Su, Yan Zhenqing, and Liu Gongquan, were the most famous calligraphers of that period. Song Dynasty calligraphy kept the pace, simultaneously developing a particular technique of writing, bringing forth a new attitude, and giving people a new appreciation for the art. Calligraphers in this era include Su Shi, Huang Tingjian, Mi Fu, and Cai Xiang. During the Yuan Dynasty, circumstances advocated a return to the ancients. The style imitated the calligraphy of the Jin and Tang Dynasties, with almost no innovation. The core figure of calligraphy in Yuan Dynasty was Zhao Mengfu.

During the Ming Dynasty, the expert Cao Shu calligrapher was Liu-ji, while Song Sui was the master of Xiao Kai calligraphy. The preeminent calligraphers at that time were Zhu Ke, as well as Zhu Yunming, Wen Zhengming, and Wang Chong, known as The Three. By the late Ming Dynasty, calligraphy was romantic, free, and unrestrained. This movement took one step further during the Qing Dynasty, notably in the calligraphy of Zhu-fushan's Eight Eccentrics of Yangzhou, a collection of various works. The vivid and resplendent techniques in this work capture the eye, and offer great insight into the culture of Chinese calligraphy.

Using the Same Character, the Same Track Gauge

Before 221 B.C., there were many vassal states in China that often launched wars. Their inhabitants lived in chaos as the states fell apart. The Seven Warring States were the Han, Zhao, Wei, Chu, Yan, Qi, and Qin dynasties. Of the seven, the Qin State was eventually declared the victor with Ying Zheng as their leader. Ying Zheng became the first emperor of China, and was given the title of First Emperor. From 230 to 221 B.C., Ying Zheng launched a massive war, destroying the other six states. This time in Chinese history is known as the Qin Eradicate the Six States period. Following 221 B.C., one country was established for the first time in China's history and was ruled by a uniform, multinational, and centralized power called the Qin Dynasty (221-206 B.C.). Ying Zheng believed that his contributions exceeded more than the ancient Three Sovereigns & Five Emperors, so he proclaimed himself First Emperor. He wanted the position to be hereditary, therefore declared he as first in the succession.

After first unifying China, he implemented a series of laws and changes to society in order to maintain the unification of the Qin Empire where much power was entrenched in feudal systems of various areas. The First Emperor abolished feudalism and imposed a new national government. In order to avoid the insurgence of civilians, he ordered all weapons confiscated by the empire to be destroyed by melting or burning. To withstand invasions from minority factions, the First Emperor implemented a great deal of manpower, material, and financial resources to build the Great Wall, not to mention the great deal of time it took. Currently the Great Wall still rests on its original foundation, and the subsequent repairs were made on top of the original wall. The Great Wall is an extraordinary feat of human beings and a symbol of China. To control the thought of the citizenry, the First Emperor executed the policy of burning the books, burying the Confucians. In addition, the laws were nationalized, weights and measures mandated, and currency standardized.

The First Emperor of China—Ying Zheng

Among the Emperor's laws, one important regulation was implementing the same characters, the same road width policy. Before the unification, each state used different styles with which to write, making it very inconvenient to communicate. Therefore after the unification, the First Emperor Qin ordered the states to use the same character and same track gauge. Under the so-called same road width policy a government standard was created for the width of roadways, and relay stations for post horses were constructed throughout the country along the roadways in order to allow for better communication between states. The roads built before unification varied in size, making it difficult for vehicles to pass.

As a result the emperor decreed that the same width roads are to be built all over the country, limiting the axle length of carriages to six feet wide. In this way, the vehicles could travel on every road. One could say that this is China's oldest form of a postal service.

In short, the policies of Qin Emperor First, especially the same characters, same road width policy, established a firm foundation, main-

The Mausoleum of the First Emperor and the Terracotta

taining a unified China for over 2000 years. The unification mindset shines bright deep within the spirit of every Chinese person.

Crossbow Archer

Arcient Roads

Four Treasures of the Study

Cultural Study as it is called, emerges from the South and North Dynasty of China (420–589 A.D.), emphasizing scholarly study with regards to the brush, ink stick, paper, and ink stone, which are the four treasures of the study. Since most of the ancient literates could either write or paint, while some excelled at both, the inseparable brush, ink stick, paper, and ink stone are the essential tools of the four treasures.

The pen is the essential tool of writing. Among the myriad of pens, the writing brush is considered to be an innovation of China. Traditional writing brushes were not only the necessary writing tools for ancient literates, but also used to create a Chinese calligraphy that stands out as a unique form of writing. However, to see an ancient writing brush today is a rarity because the writing brush is delicate and difficult to maintain.

Black ink gave people the feeling of simplicity, and was indispensible. These original writing tools allowed the marvelous artistic conception of Chinese painting to manifest. The world of black ink is not tedious, but rather richly nuanced. This art form is very rarely used in modern times.

Paper is one of the four great inventions of ancient China and has made an outstanding contribution to the dissemination of Chinese culture and history. Even machine-made paper that is prevalent today evolved from the traditional methods, which produced the high quality paper of ancient paintings and calligraphy work.

The ink stone, also called an ink slab, was praised as the hand of

Four Treasures of the Study

the four treasures. In order to produce ink, water was poured into the ink stone, and the ink stick was ground on the ink stone. Ink stones are made of clay, mud, tile, metal, lacquer, porcelain, and stone, among other things, the most common being stone. The great demand for ink gave rise to many ink stone mines in every part of the country.

The Lake brush, Anhui ink, Duan ink stone, and fine Xuan paper are the finest examples of the four treasures of the study. Developed over the millennia, the four treasures of the study represent the innovation and artistic capacity of the ancient artisans and the numerous aspects of literacy development. They have become a gem of the Chinese culture.

In addition to the four treasures, other literary tools included brush pots, brush racks, ink beds, ink cartridges, armrests, pen washers, book presses, water bearers, water spoons, ink drippers, ink stone boxes, seal pastes, seal cases, paperknives, seals, canisters. These tools, together with the four treasures, composed the essentials of literary study.

The Dialects

China is a multiracial, multilingual country with numerous dialects. Generally speaking, modern Chinese has seven major dialects.

The North Dialect is spoken in the central plains, and vast parts of the northeast, northwest, and southwest areas of China. This dialect also has four secondary dialects that are spoken in northeast China—the North River dialect (Beifang Hua), Northwest dialect (Northwest Mandarin), Southwest dialect (Southwest Mandarin), and the Jianhuai dialect (South River Mandarin).

The Wu dialect, also known as the Jiangzhe dialect, is spoken in the area south of the Yangtze River, which is made of the Jiangsu province and the majority of Zhejiang province. Shanghainese is the primary subdialect of the Wu dialect.

The Xiang dialect, also called Hunan dialect, is spoken in the greater part of Hunan province. The Hunan and Changsha dialects are the main subdialects.

The Gan dialect, also called Jiangxi dialect, is spoken throughout the Jiangxi province, in the northwest Fujiang province, the eastern part of Hunan province, and southeast part of Hubei province. The Nangchang subdialect is the most widely spoken Jiangxi dialect.

The Hakka dialect, also known as Kejia Hua or Ke Hua, is widely scattered but rather concentrated in the areas it is spoken. Hakka is spoken in northeast region of Guangdong, the northwestern part of Fujian, Jiangxi, Hubei, Guangdong and Fujian, as well as Sichuan, Guangxi, and Taiwan. Among all the Chinese that live in Southeast Asia, most of them speak the Hakka dialect. The primary subdialect is the Meizhou dialect.

The Min dialect (northern and southern Min dialect) is spoken widely including most of Fujian province, the eastern part of Guandong, Chaoshan area, the western part of Leizhou Peninsula, Hainan province, the greater part of Taiwan province, the southern part of Zhejiang. It is also widely dispersed throughout Southeast Asia by way of the Chinese communities in the regions.

The Yue dialect, also called Yueyu, Cantonese, Guang Fu dialect, or Bai dialect, is spoken largely in the Guangdong province, the southeast part of the Guanxi autonomous region, as well as parts of Hong Kong, Macao, and North American communities. Guangzhou dialect is the primary subdialect.

These seven dialects are a rough division of modern Mandarin dialects (not including the minority dialects). In reality, the dialects are much more complex than this. Not only do the northerners not understand the Cantonese and Fujian people's language, even people in Guangzhou within the Guandong province, the Meizhou people and the Shantou people do not understand each other. The people of the Fuzhou district in Fujian province, the Putian people and Amoy people, all do not understand each other's language.

The difference among the dialects nowadays is mainly in the sound, yet the diversity of the vocabulary is immense. Although the Jing, Jun, and Tong districts are all neighbors, Beijing people say sweet potato (bái shǔ), while the people of Tongshan say red potato (hóng shǔ) to refer to the same thing. If you ask a young lady from Tiangjing, "Do you like to eat 'báishǔ?" she will be confused and think, "How can people eat a white mouse? Quite disgusting!"(In Tiangjin dialect bái shǔ'means white mouse.) So you see, there are great differences amongst the Chinese dialects.

Unit 2

Names

As recorded in *Explaining Simple and Analyzing Compound Characters* (a 2nd century Han dictionary), the word "surname" (姓) literally means people give birth, but also means from woman comes birth. Birth creates sound. It can be said that the word "surname" (姓) is a compound ideogram. The "woman" (女) radical is part of the character, in addition to "birth" (生), delegating a sound. Therefore, "surname" (姓) is a product of maternal clan society, the character symbolizing a family's bloodline. Chinese surnames helped usher in the maternal clan society.

Chinese surnames originated in many different ways. Firstly, in maternal clan society, descendants took a mother's maiden name; therefore, many ancient surnames contain the radical woman (女), such as "姜, 姚, 姬".Secondly, in the age of antiquity, people's fondness of nature influenced naming. Common names included horse, ox, and dragon. Thirdly, surnames were created according to the nation of a person's ancestry, like Zhao, Song, and Qin, among others. Fourthly, some people were named after an official, such as Shangguan, Sima, or Situ. Fifthly, people took on their ancestors' titles of nobility, including the rank of king, marquis, or official. Sixthly, some people were issued a name with regards to the area of residence and scenery. Examples of such names are Dongguo (East Wall), Ximen (West Gate), and Liu (Willow Tree). Seventhly, some people inherited surnames by occupation. For example, people who made ceramics are appropriately named Ceramic (Tao).

Eighthly, others acquired the surnames from the famous ancients. For example, the Yellow Emperor's name was Xuanyuan, which later became a surname.

One or two characters, sometimes three, generally form a Chinese surname. A one-character name is called a single surname, while a two-character name is called a compound surname. Although there is no exact figure about how many surnames there are in China, according to statistics, more than five thousand surnames appear in Chinese historical documents. Today, there are about 200 commonly used surnames. Zhang, Wang, Li, Zhao, Liu, are the most commonly seen single surnames. Zhuge, Ouyang, and Situ are examples of compound surnames. Influenced by Confucian teachings that we should respect our ancestors, Chinese pay close regard to surnames. Changing the surname means changing your ancestor, and this of utmost humiliation. In modern Chinese novels, particularly in heroic war novels, a man will vindicate his own pride. In a daring act, the character will often say, "A great man will never change his surname—I am indeed so-and-so!"

Chinese names have their own tradition and characteristics. Quite different from English names, Chinese surnames are placed before the given name—the opposite of English names. "姓" is similar to an English speaker's family name, passed down from generation to generation. "名" is the equivalent of an English first name, comprised of one or two characters. A Chinese name often has a specific meaning, expressing a certain aspiration. Some names include the place and time of birth, or natural phenomena, such as Capital, Morning, and Snow. Some Chinese names reveal hope or some kind of virtue, such as Loyalty, Righteousness, and Belief. Still other names reveal a yearning for health, long life, and happiness, such as Jian (health), Shou (long life), and Fu (fortune). Male names and female names are different. Male names express prestige and fierceness, as in Hu (tiger), Xiong (hero), and Gang (strength). Female names are expressed by warm and beautiful characters, such as Feng (phoenix), Yu (Jade), and Juan (graceful).

When Chinese give names, they often represent a person's place in the hierarchy of the family. For example, a name can include a character that represents seniority, while another character expresses the family name. In some names, a radical indicates family seniority in the clan. This is quite different from that in English. Chinese also avoid as much as possible giving the name of an elder family member to a junior member, which has been a taboo since ancient times.

Greeting Styles

Greeting is the most common etiquette of every day social intercourse. When people meet each other, it begins by paying one's respects, but there are great differences in greetings between nationalities. Chinese greetings have their own classification, content, ways of showing appellation, basic courtesy, and concrete meaning, while each having their own characteristics.

Firstly, Chinese greeting styles to send one's regards, to inquire, or to discuss are much like English. Nevertheless, the Chinese ways of expressing greetings are different from the West. For example, in English there is good morning, good afternoon, and good evening. Chinese oral language does not contain such reciprocal greetings. Instead, often used is "zao" (早) or "ni zao" (你早), meaning you got up quite early. Many greetings follow this simple syntax. At present, Chinese people more and more use "ni hao!" to greet each other, particularly intellects and cultured people in a crowd. There are also formal greetings showing honor and great respect. In Mandarin there also phrases such as "Where are you going?" and "Did you eat?" among other greetings of inquiry, revealing concern for the other person's well being.

Secondly, cultural discrepancies and restrictions in language behavior regard societal norms, the subject of conversation also different. English greetings use simple phrases, contain no specific information, and show great respect, but they lack feeling and expression. In Chinese, many greetings are in the form of a question, and most questions inquire about the other person's struggles of daily life, giving people the feeling of amiable concern. Chinese people often ask each other questions regarding age, income, martial status, health, and popular topics of conversation, in addition to more specific items, in order to show consideration for the individual.

The language of respectful greeting is a cultural characteristic, but each nationality has its own societal norms, standards of behavior, and guidelines for social interaction. The differences in cultural backgrounds may bring about different standards, which are reflected in the nature of the questions. When Chinese people greet, they often use respectful speech and modest words, expressing respect and honor towards their counterpart. This is a distinct characteristic of the Chinese language.

Besides verbal greeting styles, Chinese people also have style of body language that has its own distinctions. The body language of China and English speaking countries show some commonality. Chinese, especially youthful men, will often nod amongst one another, or perhaps wave as a form of greeting. Yet in former times when people met, one might bow or perhaps bow with the hands outstretched in greeting. Chinese greeting styles are generally rather implicit and reserved, even if there has been a long time of separation. There is also a pat on the shoulder for comfort, or perhaps a handshake, but absolutely no kissing. Generally, men and women hugging each other are rarely seen. At most they shake hands, but nothing more.

Kinship Appellation

Chinese people reside in their nationality, reflecting a language of complicated kinship appellation. The bloodline is taken very seriously. According to statistics, there are more than 230 words in Chinese regarding family appellation. In modern Chinese, there are just over 60 names, dating back three generations. Following the collapse of feudalism, many titles of hierarchy also vanished. In modern Chinese, the titles of appellation have been greatly simplified, but we still can see an obvious correlation to the ancestors' language of hierarchy.

The language of kinship status shows much respect towards elders, and reflects the ideas of honor, humbleness, and order. The paternal grandfather is called yé yé , and the paternal grandmother is called nǎi nǎi. For each generation, the word old (lǎo) is added in front of the title to distinguish generations. Consequently, great-grandfather is called old grandfather (lǎo yé yé), and great-great grandfather being old-old grandfather (lǎo lǎo yé yé). Regarding the younger generation, there is "grandson" and "granddaughter," adding "double" before the title expresses each generation as in double granddaughter, and double-double granddaughter. With respect to peers, the difference in age is extremely emphasized. In one's own family, there are the titles "older brother", "younger brother", "older sister" and "younger sister", so as not to confuse status and rank. Titles such as father's older brother, father's younger brother, sister-in-law, and brother-in-law, indicate one's rank in the hierarchy. This is completely different in English speaking countries, the titles of siblings and other relatives are the same regardless of age difference.

Many more forms of address exist to refer to distant relatives, and distinguish clan bloodlines. These appellations have the particular characteristics. One's title of rank corresponds to the mother or father's side of the family, showing strict distinction. For example, the parents of the father are called zǔ fù and zǔ mǔ (paternal grandfather and paternal grandmother), while the parents of the mother are called wài zǔ fù and wài zǔ mǔ (maternal grandfather and maternal grandmother). The brothers of the father are respectfully called bó bo and shū shu (father's older brother and father's younger brother). Uncles on the mother's side of the family are all called jiù jiu (maternal uncle), the order is denoted by adding a character to the beginning of the title as in big uncle (dà jiù), second uncle (èr jiù), or small uncle (xiǎo jiù) meaning brother-in-law, literally. In modern society the importance of ancestral relations has grown weaker, yet the extremely complex honorific language of the past has not completely dissolved. In villages located in vast areas of China, the diverse titles of nobility are still in use.

Chinese Zodiac

The ancient Chinese correlated the time in which certain animals are active with the time in their own daily lives, Thus, twelve animals make up the twelve signs of the zodiac. In ranked sequence they are rat, ox, tiger, rabbit, dragon, snake, horse, ram, monkey, rooster, dog, and pig.

Rat: 11pm—1am (called zishi). At this time, the nerves of the rat are strongest and it is most active.

Ox: 1am—3am (called choushi). At this time, the ox has finished eating grass and is ruminating the vegetation, it is slow and cozy.

Tiger: 3am—5am (called yinshi). Ancient records reveal that at this time, tigers are the most active and fierce, killing many people.

Rabbit: 5am—7am (called maoshi). At this time the sun is not yet exposed, the moon's radiance not yet vanished. In mythology, the Jade Hare is the only animal allowed in the Moon Palace.

Dragon: 7am—9am (called chenshi). As legend has it, dragons congregate and make the rain at this time. In folklore, dragons are the main animals, therefore this time belongs to the dragon.

Snake: 9am—11am (called sishi). It is believed that at this time, snakes cannot harm people and are not traversing the walking paths. Rather they are believed to remain concealed in the underbrush.

Horse: 11am—1pm (called wushi). According to Taoist teachings, when the midday sun is at the apex the yang energy reaches the extreme, as the yin energy gradually increasing, representing the pillar of yin and yang exchange. Generally at this time, all animals lie down to rest. Only the horse has the habit of remaining standing and never lying down to rest even when sleeping.

Ram: 1pm—3pm (called weishi). It is said that at this time rams urinate frequently, and in this way cures itself of mental illness.

Monkey: 3pm—5pm (called shenshi). At this time, the monkey likes to cry out in a most drawn out and resonating sound.

Rooster: 5pm—7pm (called youshi). At this time, the sun sets in the mountains, and the rooster returns to his nest for the evening.

Dog: 7pm—9pm (called xushi). Dark night approaches and the dog guards the house. The dog watches with great vigilance with the sharpest vision and hearing. At this time the dog can see things at great distances and hear very clearly.

Pig: 9pm—11pm (called haishi). At this time the pig is intoxicated with sleep. Its snoring resounds, the muscles of its body twitch fiercely, producing meat the fastest.

Chinese Zodiac

Not only do these twelve animals represent time periods throughout the day, but also they eventually came to represent a person's age.

There are many beautiful legends about the zodiac animals. According to one legend, in antiquity a person's memory was not great. He or she often forgot his or her name, producing much confusion. Upon seeing this, the Jade Emperor's heart could not bear this, so he thought of a simple way of using the zodiac to determine one's age. One must only remember the twelve-year cycle as a definite way of calculating a person's age. Consequently, he issued a proclamation to all animals to come to his Heavenly Courtyard so that he could select the animals of the zodiac in order of their arrival. The dragon, tiger, rabbit, and horse, animals of extraordinary ability and talent, often stopped as they traveled although they were not late in departing. Yet slow but sure was the ox, plodding along at its own pace, day and night, not daring to stop for rest. Meanwhile the rat quietly cunning jumped on the ox's horn and slept. The ox was to be the first to arrive in the Heavenly Court. However, the rat, seeing an opportunity, jumped from the ox's horn, becoming the first in rank of the zodiac animals. Thus the ox became second in the hierarchy. Due to the pig's extremely slow walk, it was naturally last in line.

Unit 3

The Traditional Calendar—
The Agricultural Calendar

The agricultural calendar is China's traditional calendar. It is divided into 24 solar terms and serves as a guide to agricultural activities. This calendar used in vast areas of China, and is known as the farming calendar. It is also referred to as the summer calendar, old calendar, and Chinese calendar, but it is most commonly referred to as the lunar calendar. The calendar uses strict guidelines, following the waxing and waning of the moon. It also employs an intercalary month, to average the lengths of the solar years. The lunar and solar calendars make note of the relation between yin and yang. Until now, many Chinese all over the world, as well as North Koreans, South Koreans, and Vietnamese, still use the agricultural calendar to calculate traditional festivals such as the Spring Festival, Mid-Autumn Festival, the Dragon Boat Festival, and the Pure Brightness (tomb-sweeping) Festival.

The agricultural calendar month and lunar calendar month share commonalities. The agricultural calendar month is 29.5366 days (29 days, 12 hours, 44 minutes, and 3 seconds), while the lunar calendar has full months of 30 days and shortened months of 29 days. There are, however, differences between the calendars. In the lunar calendar the full months and shortened months are arranged in specific order, yet the agricultural calendar requires rigorous calculations. As a result, in the agricultural calendar, there may be two consecutive full months as well as two consecutive shortened months. The first day of every agricultural month begins on the new moon (i.e. the moon is between the sun and the earth, the dark side of the moon facing the earth). Since the lunar cycle is somewhat greater than 29 days, for every one hundred months, there are approximately 53 full months and 47 shortened months.

The length of the agricultural calendar compared to the solar calendar is similar. A twelve-month solar year has more days than a lunar year, but lacks the thirteenth intercalary month. Ancient astronomers compiled the agricultural calendar such that specific days of the month mark the various phases of the moon. For example, on first day of the month the moon is dark, and then in about 15 days the moon becomes full, completing its cycle. At the same time, the agricultural calendar, noting the seasons, adopted a metonic system of 19 years and 7 leap months in this way. For every

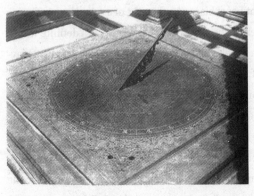

Sundial in Yuan Dynasty

19 agricultural calendar years, there are 12 common years, each of which has 12 months, as well as seven leap years, each containing 13 months. The months of the agricultural calendar are composed of the same number of days as regular months, 29 or 30, but a leap month is added depending upon the circumstances of the solar term.

The agricultural calendar is a substantial contribution of ancient China. Its main features are that any one-day of the month embodies significant phases of the moon and that it is comprised of a-gricultural dates, including calculations of the tide (the tide being an effect of the moon's gravity). This calendar, called shixianli (the state calendar), was instituted in 1645 and was officially used by the late Ming and early Qing dynasties.

The Twenty-Four Solar Terms

The twenty-four solar terms is the special creation of the Chinese. It reflects the changes of seasons, guides farming activity, and affects the daily life of thousands. The twenty-four solar terms are measured off by the position of the sun on the ecliptic (the orbit that the earth runs around the sun). The sun starts from the vernal equinox point (at this point, the sun's rays are perpendicular with the equator), and advances 15 degrees during one solar term, circulating one cycle and returning back to the vernal equinox point. This is called one tropical year, adding up to 360 degrees, exactly 24 solar terms.

The twenty-four solar term calendar and the Gregorian calendar dates are approximately the same year—the first half of the year occurs around the date of 6 or 21 of every month (summer solstice), and the next half on about 8 and 23. But in the agricultural calendar, solar term dates are difficult to ascertain. As the beginning of spring, for example, could begin one year as early as December 15, and the latest date could be January 15.

From the name twenty-four solar terms, one can speculate the division in the solar terms gives sufficient consideration to the seasons, climate, seasonal vegetation, and other changes of natural phenomena. The beginnings of spring, summer, autumn, and winter, as well as the vernal and autumnal equinoxes and the summer and winter solstices meflect the seasons' change. These are determined by divisions on the ecliptic, astronomical angles, the reflecting and turning point of the sun's altitude variation; differentiating the four seasons. With astronomical angles, the first four are the starts of seasons, and the later four are the turning points of the sun's altitude variation. Due to China occupying vast regions, possessing extremely distinct monsoon characteristics, and having various continental factors, those result in great differences in the climate. Consequently, the various regions' four seasons are different. Minor heat, great heat, limit of heat, minor cold, and major cold are five solar terms reflecting degrees of temperature. Rain, grain rain, minor snow, and major snow are four solar terms indicating rain and snow precipitation, the time periods, and the severity. Cold dew, white dew, and descending frost are the three solar terms regarding water vapor condensation and appearance. Yet this essentially reflects the process gradual temperature decline—when the air temperature drops to a certain degree, water vapor emerges and forms dew.

As the temperature continues to decline, the condensation increases as it gets colder and colder. When the temperature drops below zero degrees Celsius, water vapor turns to frost. Full grain and grain in the husk are two solar terms indicating the maturing of domestic crops and harvest time. The terms awakening of insects and clear and bright reflect the occurrence of natural phenomena. In particular, the awakening of insects indicates the first thunderstorm from the heavens stirring the underground insects from hibernation, indicating the return of spring.

To help people to remember, this simple poem is often recited:

Spring rain brightens the valleys and the heavens,

The summer's grain in the husk reflects the heat,

Autumn's dew and cold, as frost descends,

Winter snow brings the major cold,

Every month, two terms are constantly changing,

At most differing one or two days.

The first half of the year arrives on the sixth and the twenty-first day each month,

The last half occurs on the eighth and the twenty-third day.

The Spring Festival

The Spring Festival is the first day of the agricultural calendar, also called Lunar New Year, and commonly referred to as the Chinese New Year. It is among China's most ceremonious and most bustling holiday, equivalent to the western tradition of Christmas. Traditionally, the significance of the Spring Festival points to the beginning of the eighth day of the 12th lunar month (Layue), marking the Laji (ceremonial sacrifices). It is also held on the 23rd day of the 12th lunar month's Gizhao (worship of the kitchen god), and continues until the 15th day of the first month, including New Years Eve and New Year's Day as the climaxes. The last day of Layue is called New Year's Eve, the Eve of the Lunar New Year, and Year 30 (refer to the 30th of December in lunar calendar). New year's eve serves as a watershed for two years. A common saying is, "One night connects two years, as the double hour separates two years".

Regarding the origin of the year, Chinese tradition has produced this interesting story:

In remote antiquity, there was a fierce and hideous beast called Year. When winter arrived, food in the mountains became scarce, prompting the beast to run down from the mountains, invade villages, and injure people and domestic animals. Therefore, when winter would arrive, everybody was fearful, for the villages were not safe. Consequently, many people moved to remote locations to evade harm. As time passed, people discovered that, although Year was ferocious, it was afraid of three things: bright red color, fire, and loud noises. Thereupon the people devised a clever counter tactic. As winter arrived, indicating the time at which the beast came from the mountains to enter the village, the villagers mutually agreed to protect themselves in various ways. The door to every house was to be donned with a large board painted red. At the village gate would burn many fires. Nobody was to sleep at night and in the house they must beat gongs and play drums. Firecrackers were to be lit, and loud noises were to be made. Deep in the night, Year approached the village only to see bright fire and red everywhere and hear extremely loud noises. This frightened the beast and caused it to immediately return to the mountains. Since then, it has never dared to reappear. The next day at sunrise, the whole village gathered, congratulating each other and wishing happiness. Afterwards, every year on this day, on each household door a red board was hung, fires were burned, gongs and drums were played throughout the night, and firecrackers were lit. The next day, everybody wished each other happiness, celebrating his and her safety. Passed down from generations, these customs reflect the celebration of the Chinese New Year.

Bringing in the New Year

On New Year's Eve, everybody reunites with his or her family, eating a traditional dinner. This meal is eaten slowly by candle light, beginning at shien (one of the twelve hour periods), and lasting deep into the night with the family members coming and going at leisure. When the meal is finished, everyone sits in a circle under a lantern of beside a stove, sharing stories of the passing old year and discussing the new one forthcoming. The New Year's Eve overnight vigil signifies the driving away of evil, plague, sickness, and epidemic, and also expresses good fortune in the New Year. Ancient New Year's eve celebrations signify two meanings: the elders bring in the new year with the memory of years passed, cherishing the thoughts and the remaining time in their lives, as the younger generation brings in the new year as to prolong the parents bloodline.

Dust Sweep

According to an ancient Chinese idiom, "On the 24th day of the 12th lunar month (Layue), brush off the dust and sweep the house." In Mandarin, the words "dust" and "old" are homophones, meaning the Spring Festival's Dust Sweep attempts to rid the old and bring in the new by sweeping everything old and unlucky out the door. Therefore, as the Spring Festival approaches, every family thoroughly cleans the house, washes all of the utensils, washes the bedding and curtains, and sweeps to the six gates of the courtyard. Furthermore, they brush away the dust, dirt and spider webs, and dredge the irrigation ditches.

New Year Scrolls with the Character "福"

New Year Scrolls, also called Spring Festival Couplets, Double Characters, and Peach Symbols, are pasted on the doorways in the spring. They are fine works of art that are concise, convey dualism, and contain elaborate characters that portray this period of expressing happy wishes and desires. This has given rise to a distinct form of Chinese literature. Every Spring Festival, whether in a city or rural areas, every household has a big red scroll pasted to their door, in efforts to heighten the festive atmo-

New Year Scrolls with the Character "福" and Laterns Pasted on "福"

sphere. Some family members also paste on the gates, walls, and lintels, the character "fu" (福) in various sizes. "Fu" refers to good fortune, good fate, protection, and to look forward to a happy future and granted wishes. Embodying this spirit even more, some people will bluntly tear down scrolls, expressing they have already achieved happiness and good fortune.

Lighting Firecrackers

Chinese people have a saying, "open the door and light a firecracker". This indicates as the first day of the New Year arrives, the first thing every household commonly does is open its door and lights a firecracker, hoping the explosions removing the old and welcoming the new. Firecrackers are a specialty of China. Also called bao zhang, pao zhang, or bian pao. Fireworks occupy over two thousand years of Chinese history. In the course of time the applications of fireworks have become more and more extensive, increasing in variety and color. Every major holiday and festive celebrations such as weddings, building a house, and opening a business, all may use fireworks to express congratulations and to wish good fortune.

New Year's Greetings

On New Year's Day, everybody gets up early, puts on new clothes and a new hat, and decorates him or herself beautifully. They then go out and visit friends and relatives with regards to wishing them happiness and good fortune in the forthcoming year. When expressing New Year's wishes, the younger generation must first pay their respects to the older generation by bidding them longevity and good health. In advance, the elders may prepare New Year's money by wrapping it in red paper and giving it to the children. It is said that this money can subdue evil spirits. The meaning is derived from the words year (sui) and evil spirit (sui) are homophones. Receiving the money allows the younger generation to pass safely through another year.

The Pure Brightness Day

The Pure Brightness Day is a tradition in China, beginning approximately during the period of the Zhou Dynasty, with a history of over 2,500 years. Its origin, according to legend, is from ancient times when the emperors, generals, and ministers offered sacrifices at tombs and left gifts. Later, this was later was eagerly imitated by the commoners. On this day, offerings are made to ancestors and the tombs are swept in much of the same way as the previous generations, becoming a fixed regular custom of the Chinese nationality.

Pure Brightness Day (also called Walking amid Greenery Day), according to the Gregorian calendar, takes place every year on April 4 to April 6. At this time, radiant spring sun and lush grasslands and fonests constitute an opportune time to take a tour of spring (in ancient times called Stroll on the Grass). Consequently, the ancients correlated the Pure Brightness Walking amid Greenery Day with traditional sporting activities.

Another famous yet still long lost ancient tradition of the Pure Brightness Day is Cold Food Day.

Cold Food Day, as the name implies, constitutes refraining from using fire to cook meals, eating only cold food. The original date is only one or two days difference from the Pure Brightness Day, so eventually the two days merged into one. But as Cold Food Day in the present is referred to as Pure Brightness Day, the custom of eating unheated food still resides.

Local traditions of Pure Brightness Day are extremely abundant, including tomb sweeping, the planting of willows, hiking in the wilderness, and tree planting. Other various social customs exist, such as flying kites, swinging, cuju (ancient Chinese soccer), polo, and a series of sporting activities. Therefore, this day encompasses offerings of sacrifice, sorrow and tears for parted relatives while sweeping the tombs, as well as an amusing tone that demonstrates an appreciation for nature, making it an important festival.

Sweeping the Tomb

Commonly referred to as shang fen, it is a way to offer sacrifices to deceased ancestors. Many people of the Han ethnic group, as well as a few minority groups, sweep their family's tombs on the Pure Brightness Festival. According to old customs, on this day before noon, people bring the three lives (chicken, fish, and meat), wine, tea, rice, and paper scrolls, to the front of their ancestor's grave. In advance, they arrange the papers above of the grave, using green and red paper cut into tassels. The tassels placed above the grave flutter in the wind, letting it be known to other people that the tomb's occupant has a later generation. At this time, prepared food, steamed wine, and tea are placed in front of the tombs of close relatives. They also burn ritual money and light firecrackers, ultimately kneeling with one's head to the ground (kowtow) in respect. In some places on Pure Brightness Day, the family will repair the tomb or symbolically add earth to the head of the grave.

Sweeping the Tomb

Tree planting

Around the time of Pure Brightness Day, the spring's yang energy is quite prevalent, rain showers the earth, newly planted trees sprout tall and quickly mature in growth. Therefore, since ancient times, China has practiced the custom of planting trees on this festival. In 1979, the National People's Congress Standing Committee designated every March 12 as China's Arbor Day. This encourages every citizen of the country to take an active role in the reforestation of his or her motherland, and has become an extremely significant activity.

Flying Kites

During the Pure Brightness Festival, not only do people fly kites during the day, but also at night. During the night, attached to the bottom of the kite or the string are small multi-colored lanterns that glimmer like stars, thus being named divine lanterns. In ancient times, people would let their kite go into sky by cutting the string and allow it to fly to the ends of the earth. It is said that this removes sickness and calamity while bringing the person good luck.

Swinging

Swinging refers to grabbing a piece of leather rope with which to sway on. In ancient times, people tied the rope to a branch on a tree, then on to a wooden peg and colored ribbon, thus making a swing. They differ from modern swings that are made of two ropes attached to a seat. Swinging not only promotes health, but can also foster bravery and consciousness. Presently, many people are quite fond of the activity, especially young children.

The Dragon Boat Festival

In the Chinese traditional calendar, May 5 is a traditional day—The Dragon Boat Festival. Also called Duan Wu, or Duan Yang, it began during the Spring and Autumn or Warring States periods, containing a history of over two thousand years. There are many legends of it's origin, such as to remember Wu Zixu, to commemorate the filial daughter Cao Er, and the practice of the Yue people offering sacrifice to their ancient totems. Among this folklore, with the greatest impression is the commemoration of Qu Yuan.

Qu Yuan was a chancellor to Emperor Huai of Chu during the Spring and Autumn period. He pressed the worthy people to make the military stronger and the country wealthier, and advocated strongly to ally with the state of Qi in opposition to the state of Qin, yet Lord Zi Lan and others strongly opposed him, banishing him from the capital city and sending him into exile along the Yuan River in the Xiang valley. While in exile, he wrote, *Sorrow at Parting, Asking Heaven, and Nine Songs* to express the concern for his country and people. These immortal poems have exhibited great influence (the Dragon Boat Festival is also called Poets Day). In 278 B.C., the Qin army breached the capital of the state of Chu. Witnessing his motherland being invaded was like a knife in his heart. This produced the literary work "Embracing the Sand". Afterwards, he committed suicide by throwing himself into the Miluo River, ending his life as a magnificent writer of patriotic poetry.

Zongzi

Legend has it that after the death of Qu Yuan, the commoners in the state of Chu expressed deep sorrow. One by one they went to the banks of the Miluo River to pay homage to the great Qu Yuan. Fishermen rowed their boats to the river, surrounding the body of Qu Yuan to protect it. Some fishermen took out rice balls, eggs, and other food, and dropped them into the water for the fish, lobster, and

crabs to eat in so that they would not bite their beloved Minister Qu's body. As people saw this, they imitated them in succession. An old doctor brought a bottle of yellow wine, pouring it into the river as to intoxicate the dragon fish, in efforts to preserve the remains of Minister Qu. Fearing that the dragon fish would eat all of the food in the river, people wrapped rice in azalea leaves and tied them with a silk thread to feed the serpent. Later this developed into the modern day's zongzi. As a result, each year on May 5, dragon boat rowing competitions, eating zong zi and drinking yellow wine are social customs in commemoration of Qu Yuan.

Dragon Boat Race

China's observance of the Dragon Boat Festival is a grand celebration with activities of all sorts. A common custom is the dragon boat race. To the pulsing rhythm drums, boats in the shape of dragons are rowed, racing each other, in order to amuse the gods and people. This festival displays the characteristics of half religion and half entertainment. Now, it has broken the barrier of time and borders, becoming an international sporting competition.

Wearing Fragrant Pouches

It is said that the kids wearing the fragrant pouch during Dragon Boat Festival Day with the intention of avoiding evil spirits and pestilence. The pouch is filled with cinnabar, realgar (arsenic sulfide), and fragrant herbs, bound together by a five colored silk ribbon and button. The ornate pouches come in many shapes and sizes and may be strung together.

Dragon Boat Race

Hanging Mugwort and Calamus Leaves

A Chinese proverb states, "On the Pure Brightness Day insert a willow branch, on the Dragon Boat Festival insert a mugwort branch". On the Dragon Boat Festival, every family sweeps their rooms and courtyard and hangs the leaves of calamus and wormwood, traditional Chinese medicinal plants, on the gate lintel or in the main hall, marking significance to ancient China customs.

The Mid-Autumn Festival

The Mid-Autumn Festival is the most important festival in China, second only to the Spring Festival. The festival takes place on the 15th day of the eighth month on the Chinese traditional calendar, marking the middle of autumn, thus receiving the name. The traditional calendar contains four seasons, each season divided into three parts: meng, zhong, and ji. Therefore mid-autumn is also called Zhong Qiu Day. On the 15th day of the eighth month, the moon is much fuller and brighter than in other times of the year. In addition to the social custom to showing appreciation for the moon, people also eat moon cakes resembling to the moon. Therefore the festival is also called the

Moon Evening. On this night, people look into the sky at the moon for guidance, reuniting with one's family. By means of the moon, people traveling in a distant place send their thoughts and feeling to their relatives. Therefore, the Mid-Autumn Festival is also called the Festival of Reunion.

The legends regarding the Mid-Autumn Festival are rich and abundant, such as the myths of Chang'e flying to the moon, Wu Gan cutting down the laurel tree, and the Jade Rabbit pounding the medicine. The Mid-Autumn Festival's custom of paying homage to the moon, comes from the story Chang'e Flies to the Moon. According to ancient folklore, in the heavens ten suns appeared simultaneously, drying up and killing the crops, devastating the people. A hero named Hou Yi drew his divine bow and shot down nine of the suns, leaving one sun to rise and fall for the benefit of the people.

Therefore, Hou Yi earned the respect and the admiration of the people. And many warriors yearned to learn his skills. But his disciple Peng Meng harbored evil intentions. One day, Hou Yi went to Mount Kunlun to seek a friend's guidance, coincidently meeting the Queen Mother of the West, thus asking her for a packet of immortal medicine. It is said that once this medicine is taken, one instantly ascends to heaven and becomes an immortal. He accepted the medicine, but he did not wish to leave his beautiful wife Chang'e. Upon returning home, Hou Yi gave his wife the elixir and told her to hide it in a jewelry box on her dressing table, unaware of the watching eyes of the deceitful Peng Meng.

Three days later, Hou Yi led disciples on a hunt, but Peng Meng pretended to be ill and stayed behind. Soon after Hou Yi left, Peng Meng drew his sword and threatened Chang'e to hand over the immortal elixir. Knowing she was no match for Peng Meng, Chang'e desperately turned around, opened the box, and swallowed it. Immediately her body began to levitate as she rushed out the window towards the heavens. In concern for her husband, she flew to the moon, the closest thing to the earth, and become immortal.

As night descended, Hou Yi returned. Upon discovering this incident, he indignantly drew his sword with the intention of murdering Peng Meng, who had already fled. Hou Yi angrily beat his chest in sorrow and despair, looking towards the night sky, calling out his beloved wife's name. At this time, he noticed that the moon on this particular night shone especially bright, containing a silhouette resembling Chang'e. Then with all his intent he pursued the moon, but to no avail.

Hou Yi desperately missed his wife. But at the end of his wits, without any other option, he ordered her favorite fresh fruit, pomelos, to be placed on the incense table as an offering in the rear of the garden. When common people learned of this, they decorated their altars under the moon too, praying for the safety of the kind hearted Chang'e.

As well as paying homage to the moon during the Mid-Autumn Festival, a widespread custom is to eat moon cakes. As the proverb states, "On the 15th day of the 8th

Moon Cakes

month, as the moon is full, mid-autumn moon cakes are savory and sweet". Initially, moon cakes were used as an offering to the moon goddess. But people combined this practice and eating the cakes, with the implications of reuniting with the family. At first, these cakes were made within the household. But in modern times, they are commonly produced in a specialized bakery. Not only is the filling delicious, but the moon cake is quite pleasing to the eye, boasting characters and intricate designs sayings such as "Chang'e Flies to the Moon", "The Silver River's (Milky Way's) Night Moon", and "Three Pools Reflecting the Moon".

The Double Yang Festival

The traditional calendar's 9th day of the 9th month, signifies a festival of Chinese antiquity—the Double Yang Festival. On account of *the Book of Changes*, six is a yin number, as nine is a yang number. Consequently, on this day, the sun and the moon both embody the number nine, thus being named the Double Yang Festival, also known as the Double Ninth Festival.

The origin of the Double Yang Festival can be traced back to before the Qin Dynasty. At that time, the 9th month was a time to harvest the bumper crops, with offerings to the Celestial Emperor connected with activities of honoring ancestors. Arrived the Han Dynasty, owing to the influence of an ancient Taoist priest who beseeched medicine for immortality, people on this day began the customs of wearing dogwood (a kind of herb), eating herbal cakes, and drinking chrysanthemum wine, in efforts to seek a long life. During the Tang Dynasty, the Double Yang Festival was officially made a state holiday.

Today, the Double Yang Festival has been assigned a new meaning. In 1989, the Chinese government decided to make this date Elder's Day. Combining modern tradition with the ancient Double Yang Festival, people show honor, respect, and love towards elders, as well as offer assistance.

The celebration of Double Yang Festival contains rich and colorful activities. Commonly practiced are outings, ascending an overlook to admire the chrysanthemums, wearing dogwood, eating double yang cakes, and drinking chrysanthemum wine.

The Festival of Ascending Heights

Since antiquity, the Double Yang Festival is customary to climb to high places, referred to as the Festival of Ascending Heights. The origin of climbing to high places bears much importance, especially with regards to the elderly. High, takes on the meaning of longevity. Hence people believe that the Festival of Ascending Heights can increase longevity. There are no provisions regarding where to climb, a mountain being the same as a lofty pagoda.

Climbing to High Places at Double Yang Festival

Eating Double Yang Cakes

According to historical records, double yang cakes, also called flower cakes, chrysanthemum cakes, and five colored cakes, have no particular way to make them, just as one wishes. At dawn on the 9th month on the 9th day, parents place a cake on foreheads of their children, wishing their children one hundred things high, with the original idea derived from the ancients. Exquisite double yang cakes made on the 9th month have nine layers, resembling a pagoda. On top of the cakes are two rams in accordance with Double Yang (yang also means ram, a symbol of righteousness). In addition, some people place a little red flag and a candle on top of the cake with the writings "light the candle", "eat the cake", meaning "ascend to heights". The flag is a substitute for the dogwood twig.

Appreciation for Chrysanthemums, Drinking Chrysanthemum Wine

The Double Yang Festival occurs every year in the golden autumn, as the chrysanthemums are blooming. Following the tradition of the Double Yang Festival, it is customary to show appreciation for chrysanthemums, and drink chrysanthemum wine, originating from the Jin Dynasty poet, Tao Yuanming. Tao Yuanming is famous for living in seclusion, his poems, wine, and love for chrysanthemums. Later generations imitated this, thereupon customarily showing admiration for chrysanthemums.

Wearing Dogwood, Placing Chrysanthemums in the Hair

Ancients believed that wearing dogwood deters disaster and calamity. They wore dogwood twigs on their arms, put them in fragrant pouches, or stuck them in their hair, especially women and children, but in some places men did this also. Besides wearing dogwood, in some places it was customary to put chrysanthemums in one's hair.

The Temple Fair

The Temple Fair, also called Temple Market, or Festival Place, is a custom related to the activities at Buddhist and Taoist temples. At the same time, it also reflects the people's widespread belief in development. In early times, the Temple Fair not only included many ritual offerings, but followed economic development and the exchange of goods and services. As bazaars gradually assimilated with the religious activities, it was called Temple Market, showing great importance to townships. Some Temple Fair Festivals are held yearly, but some others may be a few days every month, with no particular guidelines regarding the dates. Wandering about the Temple Fair on New Years Day is an indispensible custom of the Chinese. But each region's bazaar is somewhat different with its own allure. The dragon dance, lion dance, and riddles written on lanterns, are a few of the Temple Fair's traditional forms of entertainment.

The Dragon Dance is also called the Swing the Lantern Dance, or Dragon Lantern Dance. From the Spring Festival to the Lantern Festival, many regions exhibit the custom of the Dragon Dance. The dragon is China's symbol for luck, respect, bravery, and power. On these festive days, people perform the Dragon Dance, praying to the dragon for protection, favorable weather, and an abundant harvest. The Lion Dance is another form of Chinese traditional folk art. During every Lantern Festival, or perhaps other festive celebration, the Dragon Dance is quite popular. This custom originated from the time period of the Three Kingdoms and spread during the Northern and Southern Dynasties, occupying over one thousand years of history. Performers dress accordingly as lions and mimic the movements of the animal to the music of gongs and percussion instruments. The traditional belief is that the Lion Dance can drive away evil spirits.

Riddles written on lanterns are a distinct feature of the Lantern Festival with an interesting story regarding its origin. As recalled in folklore, in early times, there lived a rich foreigner. Although his family was extremely wealthy, he was very rude. Everybody called him Smiling Tiger. He flattered those who were dressed in fine garments as he, and was autocratic and irrational to poor people. One of the commoners was named Wang Shao. In order to cajole Smiling Tiger, one year during the Lantern Festival as people were hanging lanterns, on his own lantern he wrote the riddle: "The head is pointed, the body white as silver, having nothing nice to say. With eyes on the rear end, recognizing the clothes, but not the person." Upon understanding this, Smiling Tiger became very angry and ordered his men to steal Wang Shao's lantern, but the men hurriedly came to his lantern, secretly smiling. Laughingly, Wang Shao said, "Master, how can you say I offend you?" The irritated Smiling Tiger replied, "If this isn't to offend me, then whom?" Still laughing, Wang Shao replied, "Oh, my lord is suspect! My poem is simply a riddle, the answer being a needle. Don't you think so?" Smiling Tiger thought for a minute and said, "No, it is not!" Glaring and with nothing to say, he turned around and embarrassingly slipped away, as the people in the surrounding area laughed heartily. Afterward, news of this matter spread far and wide. On the next Lantern Festival many people prepared riddles of their own to amuse onlookers. Therefore they are called lantern riddles. Following this well-established custom, various regions hold lantern riddle activities, still continuing today.

The Dragon Dance

The Lion Dance

Unit 4

The Emperors Yan and Huang

Throughout Chinese history, two people are believed the primogenitors of the Chinese nationality, Emperors Yan Di (Fiery Emperor) and Huang Di (Yellow Emperor). According to legend, in ancient times Yan Di was the chief of the Jiang tribe. It is said that when the mother of Yan Di was visiting Mt. Hua, she saw a divine dragon and by him became impregnated. Upon returning home, she gave birth to Yan Di. As soon as he was born, Yan Di showed great intelligence. At three days old he could talk, and after five days he could walk. Upon growing up, he became a prominent leader of the tribe with outstanding ability. Folklore states that he taught the people how to cultivate grains, becoming the founder of agriculture and earning the honorable title of the God of Agriculture. He would personally taste various kinds of plants, determining their medicinal properties and how to use them to treat illnesses, initiating the system of traditional Chinese medicine. Moreover, he constructed musical instruments, established markets, and taught people how to weave. These activities, among many other things, gradually transformed the uncultured humans into a civil society. Due to steady increase in the might of the tribe, Yan Di guided the tribe towards outward expansion, greatly influencing each region one by one. During the course of expansion, the tribe of Yan Di clashed with the equally powerful tribe of Huang Di. Until finally, at a place called Hillside Spring, Yan Di acknowledged the tribe of Huang Di as the victor.

In ancient times, Huang Di was the head of the Ji tribe, born on the second day of the second month of the Chinese traditional calendar. It is said, one night the mother of Huang Di unexpectedly saw the aurora borealis, thereupon she become pregnant, consequently giving birth to Huang Di. After ten days he could speak, as a juvenile he was quick witted, and kind hearted, and as an adult eventually become the leader of the tribe. Throughout Chinese cultural history, Huang Di plays an extremely significant role. He encouraged Cangjie to produce a character script that has formed into China's modern written language. His wife raised silkworms to make thread and manufacture clothes. He taught people how to construct boats, vehicles, and houses, making the lives of his people much more convenient. He composed the Ten Heavenly Stems and the Twelve Earthly Branches with which to measure time. Under the leadership of Huang Di, the tribe became the most powerful tribe in the central plains of China, thus acquiring the entire region and unifying other tribes, establishing the basis of Chinese civilized culture. Yan Di and Huang Di are Chinese culture's most illustrious people. They are continuously revered by Chinese people as the founders of the humanities. Even today, Chinese people still refer to themselves as Descendants of Yan-Huang, expressing gratitude for their substantial contributions. People commemorate them in many ways, in numerous places, people commonly have built mausoleums and temples to show their great respect.

Completed in 2006, in Henan province's Zhengzhou prefecture's famous scenic area, stands and enormous statue towering on the banks of the Yellow River. This statue's height is 106 meters, 8 meters higher than the Statue of Liberty in the United States, and two meters higher than Russia's The Motherland Calls, making it the highest statue in the world. This statue attracts Chinese people, or descendants of the Fiery and Yellow Emperors from various places domestic and international, to admire and pay their respects. The two emperors are contained in the essence of the Chinese nationality, as significant mark and symbol, each person being descendants of the Fiery and Yellow Emperors.

The Enormous Statue of Emperors Yan and Huang

Da Yu Controls the Water

As legend has it, a very long time ago, during rule of Emperor Yao, the people often met disaster and harm with the rising floodwaters. Emperor Yao quickly convened with the leader of every tribe about how to manage the floods, until finally it was Gun whom was unanimously elected to govern the floods. Upon accepting the task, he decided to create mounds of earth to make a dam with which resist the rising floodwaters. In the end, the completed dam often burst from the flood, and the suffering and calamity were still as grave as before. Thereupon Gun's project to control the water was deemed a failure. When Emperor Yao learned of this event, he ordered Gun to be executed.

Decades later, Yu Shun inherited the kingship of Yao. Once he ascended the throne, he was determined to find a way to control the floods. At this time, the son of Gun, Da Yu, was already an adult. Therefore Emperor Shun appointed Dayu to continue the project of controlling the floods. Initially, like his father, he built similar levees to govern the water. But not long after he finished the construction, the floodwaters rose, breaching the levees. After countless times of being defeated and learning the factors which cause the floods, Dayu Eventually realized that the floodwaters cannot invariably be blocked, but rather knowing the right time to fortify the levees when canals ought to be dredged is the solution. After understanding this reasoning, Dayu immediately changed his strategy of governing the water.

To begin with, Dayu surveyed every part of the country, taking note of the tendency of the rivers. When these routes became clear, Dayu led his people to construct a drainage canal, clearing a pathway for the river, drawing it towards the ocean. In managing the floodwaters, Dayu worked together with the common people. It is said that he was so busy managing the waters, that once Dayu passed his house three times, but did not go in at any time. This story has been eulogized to the saying "passing the house three times and not entering". With unremitting effort, at last Dayu managed to divert the floodwaters from all over the country to the ocean, as his method finally achieved success. Consequently, people once again could cultivate their land with ease, not worrying about the threat of rising waters.

Yu Mausoleum

In virtue of the accomplishment of controlling the flood and benefiting the people, in his old age, Emperor Shun passed on the kingship to Da Yu. As a famous emperor in ancient times, after his death he still receives much praise and merit from the Chinese people for contributing to the country's posterity. In Zhejiang province's Shaoxing prefecture, at the foot of Mt. Huiji, people have built a tomb called Yu Mausoleum to commemorate his glorious achievements. Still to this day, many people visit the Yu Mausoleum expressing great reverence for this famous emperor.

Pangu Creates the Universe

How did the universe come into being? In China, there is a legend that has been traditionally passed down of how Pangu split the heavens and the earth, forming the cosmos. Legend has it, long ago the earth had no sky and lacked the ground, as the entire universe existed as a gigantic egg. In this formless mass, was a being that resembles humans named Pangu. Pangu slept soundly in the egg for 18,000 years. Until one day, he awoke in pitch black, not being able to see anything. Making every effort to get out, he broke open the egg. At this time a substance resembling egg whites began to float upward, forming the sky; while the part resembling the yolk descended, creating the vast earth.

Having separated heaven and earth, Pangu was much more comfortable. But the recently formed heavens frequently sank down, reconnecting itself to the earth. Not wanting to return to the primal chaos of the large egg, with all his might, Pangu held up the heavens with his hands and the crown of his head, his feet touching the ground as to avert the heavens and he earth rejoining with each other. Pangu supported the heavens in this way every day, as his body continuously grew, causing heaven and earth to become increasingly distant, until finally separating forever. With this, Pangu grew extremely tired, thereupon reclining to rest for a while.

After lying down, Pangu would never rise again. His head became the eastern mountain, Tai Mountain; the abdomen formed the central Heng Mountain; his left arm in the south became what is also known as Heng Mountain (similar tones yet different characters). His right arm transformed into north Song Mountain, as his foot formed the prominent western mountain, Mt. Hua. The breath from his mouth also changed, becoming the spring wind, clouds, and mist, as the thunder became his voice that shook the heavens. His left eye turned into the burning sun, warming the earth every day. The right eye became the brilliant moonlight that illuminates the people. His blood filled the rivers and lakes, the flesh becoming fertile land. The teeth, bones, and marrow became the shining gold, silver, copper, and iron, as well as hard stone, smooth and full pearls, precious stones and jade. His skin and hair formed the countless flowers, plants, and trees, as the sweat of his body the dew and continuous rains. His hair and eyebrows transformed into all the stars in the celestial sky, his muscles forming intersecting paths. Every kind of bird, beast, fish, or insect embodied his spirit, as away of offering his entire body to the cosmos. The sun, moon, and stars in the heavens, as well as the flora and fauna of the mountains and valleys, embody the orderly dynamic universe.

Pangu Creats the Universe

Sacrificing his life to form the radiant universe, Pangu is revered by China's early ancestors as a god who brought us the cosmos as we know it. Later generations of Chinese people often worshiped him and offered him sacrifices. Since ancient times, many regions have built temples in honor of Pangu. For example Hunan province's Xiangxiang boasts the Pangu Ancestral Hall. Every traditional calendar year, on the third day of the third month, masses of people congregate to the Pangu Ancestral Hall to pay their respects, displaying much gratitude to the unbounded cosmos and nature, thanking the universe for everything it has bestowed, and cherishing its innate qualities.

Nüwa Goddess Makes Human Beings

What is the origin of human beings on earth? From remote antiquity, there exists a legend about Goddess Nuwa who created human beings. After the death of Pangu, in the cosmos there already existed a countless number of living things. But unfortunately, humankind had not appeared on earth. After tens of thousands of years, a celestial goddess, Nüwa, appeared and created humanity. Her appearance was extremely odd, with the head of a human and the body of a snake.

Upon coming to earth, Nuwa discovered all around her only the beasts of the land and the birds in the air, but no humans. Initially, these small creatures provided her with boundless happiness, making her feel exceptionally blessed. However, a long time passed and due to the fact that the animals could not talk, when Nuwa wanted to express herself, she could never find a partner, becoming lonely and depressed. On day as she was feeling bored, Nuwa used a twig to stir the moist clay that lay by her side. At will of her hands, she formed the earth into the likeness of a human. Nüwa blew one breath into the clay figure and give it life. Forming not only a woman that could speak, but also one who understands her intentions. Nüwa thought this was very interesting, but at the same time did not want the woman to feel lonely like her. Consequently, she made a man and allowed them to be mutual partners. To see these two people side by side made Nüwa extremely happy and content, thereupon she continued to form many more people, until finally becoming tired, dipped the twig into the mud and threw it into the sky. The mud fell to earth, creating many more humans. In order for the humans to reproduce offspring for later generations, Nüwa allowed the men and women to marry, thus creating the human race. It is said that the humans formed by Nüwa's hands became the upper class society of later generations, and the humans she created with the twig became the lower class peasants. No matter the case, since the time Nüwa created humans, the earth's humankind is allowed to have abundant opportunity and vitality.

But the joyous live of the humans did not last long. One day, the earth and humanity abruptly suffered a great catastrophe. The sky cracked, the earth split open, fires raged, and unceasing floods threatened human beings to extinction. Nüwa had not the heart to witness the suffering and destruction of her beloved creations. Therefore she refined a kind of five colored stone and used it to repair the hole in the sky. At the same time, she used the muds of reeds to hinder the inundating floods. Under the great effort of Nüwa, the peace and tranquility of humanity of the past was reinstated.

In order to express gratitude towards Nüwa's benevolence towards humanity, humans bestowed the title Mother Goddess Nüwa, honoring her as the creator of the human race, as all nations offered her sacrifices. Moreover, due to this myth, Chinese people have a deep profound sense about their land. In traveling great distances people will often take with them a bit of soil from their native place as a long lasting memory.

Nüwa Goddess Repairs the Hole in the Sky

Houyi Shoots the Suns

As it is said, in remote antiquity, there were ten suns in the sky. In these suns lived ten birds named Crow, all were the sons of the Celestial Emperor. Each day, one of the ten birds would emerge to do his task of providing light and radiant heat, while the other nine birds were elsewhere enjoying themselves and resting. Therefore, as daybreak approached, people on earth could witness the suns' ascents from the east, as one of the Crows appeared over the horizon to do his work.

For a long time, even though there were ten Crows and ten suns in the sky, people on earth only saw one. Under their grace the people scheduled work and rest, at sunrise tending the fields and at sundown sleeping, living contently. But one day, when the ten suns' mother was out for a period of time, the mischievous suns committed a horrible act. At dawn, the ten suns all came out together in the sky. The Crows thought this was amusing, but the people on earth and all living things suffered a calamity. The ten suns hung in the sky, releasing immense heat, quickly drying up seawater, and killing scores of fishes. Furthermore, this invoked a sea monster to come ashore, and plunder the crops of the people. All of the forests on earth were set ablaze, scorching many animals to death. The animals that did not die fled to the homes of people, wantonly seeking food, so the people and live-stock became the food of the animals. Day by day, the people remained hungry, and at the same time unable to endure the blistering hot weather, burning them to death.

At this time, existed a young and handsome divine archer named Houyi, with arrows of astounding accuracy. Upon seeing the devastation of human lives, he resolved to use his arrows to shoot down the troublesome Crows in the heavens. One day Houyi grabbed his weapon, packed his rations, and set off on a journey. He climbed 99 alpine mountains, forged 99 rivers, passed through 99 canyons, and suffered untold hardships, finally reaching the East China Sea where he climbed a supremely lofty mountain. On the peak, Houyi drew his bow and arrow and aimed at the Crow in the middle of one of the suns, shooting it down into the East China Sea, thereupon eliminating one sun from the heavens. In this way, he felled nine Crows, leaving one sun in the sky. At this time Houyi, put down his bow, allowing the sun to prevail in the sky to benefit humanity.

Since then, this sun rises every day from the eastern China seaboard, suspends in the sky, warms the world of the people, and allows

Houyi Shoots the Sun

the seedlings to grow and all living things to survive. To express the virtue of Houyi's achievements, the story of Hoyi Shoots the Suns is unfailingly passed on through successive generations, making this hero forever engrained in the minds of the people.

Unit 5

The Cowherd and the Weaving Maid

In China, there is an ancient beautiful story of romance, reflecting the love of Zhinü and Niulang.

As legend has it, in the heavens there existed a beautiful fairy named Zhinü (the Weaving Maid). She was the daughter of the heavenly courtyard's Queen Mother of the West. One day, Zhinü and a few companions furtively left the Heavenly Court and arrived to the world of the mortals, selecting a jade lotus pond in which to bathe. Since they lacked freedom in the Heavenly Court, this brought them joy beyond comparison.

Near the green lotus pool lived a handsome young man called the Niulang (the Cowherd). Shortly after being born into a peasant family, his parents had passed away. Therefore, Niulang lived with his elder brother and his sister-in-law on a section of land. But soon after, the sister-in-law expelled him from the family, giving him an old ox and a broken cart. They became mutually dependent upon each other for survival, but in reality, this old ox was a celestial immortal. To compensate Niulang for his truthfulness and benevolence, one day the old ox suddenly spoke like a person. It said, "Niulang, today you will go to the Jade Lotus Pond. There you will see a group of fairies bathing. Grab a set of red clothing and conceal it. Those red clothes of the fairy you take will become your wife." Upon hearing this, he became overjoyed and arrived at the Jade Lotus Pond shortly after.

The Cowherd and the Weaving Maid

Like the old ox had said, the in the Jade Lotus Pond frolicked a group of fairies. As they amused themselves, they paid no attention to Niulang snatching the red clothes and fleeing. As they happily played in the pond, they suddenly saw a human. One after another, they put their clothes and ascended into the heavens. But Zhinü could not find her clothes, so she had to stay. At this moment, Niulang walked to her and returned the clothes, and requesting her to be his wife. Zhinü saw that the cowherd was handsome and kind-hearted, thus she acknowledged his request and become his wife.

After getting married, the cowherd and his new wife, the weaving maid, were bounded by deep emotions and lived a fortunate blissful life together. Several years later they had a son and a daughter, both of them being very lovely. One day, Niulang returned home and said to Zhinü, "The old ox has just died. While it was dying, it ordered me to skin it, and said the skin can be used to fly to the heavens." Upon hearing this, her heart sprang an ominous premonition. At this time, a mighty wind blew darks clouds and densely covered the sky. Immortals then appeared from the heavens, to escort Zhinü back to the Heavenly Court. As Niulang saw the deities arrest her, anxiety filled his heart. Thereupon he donned the ox skin, grabbed his children, and left to purse Zhinü. Using the ox skin to fly, the distance between he and Zhinü were rapidly edging continuously closer. At this time the Queen Mother of the West pulled a gold hairpin from her head and drew a boundary between Niulang and Zhinü, thus forming the Celestial River (Milky Way). This heavenly river was unusually broad, and regardless of the great efforts of Niulang, there was no way to cross. The Celestial River forever separates them from meeting. Today we can still see them on either sides of the Milky Way, where there are two relatively large stars. Zhinü became Vega (in the constellation Lyra), and Niulang became the star Altair (in the constellation Aquila), remaining side by side. Near Altair you can see two smaller stars, one son and one daughter of Niulang and Zhinü.

Zhinü could not see her husband and children. Thus throughout the day, her face was washed in tears, until finally the Queen Mother of the West promised that every year on the seventh day of the seventh month, Zhinü is allowed to meet with her husband and children one time. On that day, a multitude of celestial magpies form a bridge in the heavens, connecting the two sides of the river. People call this the Magpie Bridge. On this bridge Niulang, Zhinü, and the children are allowed to meet. It is said that, on the seventh night of the seventh month, in the event that a person is under a vine of grapes, if you listen closely you will hear the faint sound of Niulang and Zhinü speaking to each other.

In China, people with regards to this story traditionally call the lunar calendar's seventh day of the seventh month Magpie Bridge Day, or Night of Sevens, honoring the faithfulness and romance of Niulang and Zhinü.

Night of Sevens is similar to the Western culture's February 14 holiday, becoming Chinese Valentine's Day.

Meng Jiangnü

Today, most people are familiar with the Great Wall of China, but among the Chinese there exists a story of Meng Jiangnü Weeps at the Great Wall. According to legend, during the period of the Qin Dynasty, the Meng household planted a melon in their garden. The vine grew to the neighboring Jiang house, producing a fruit. When the melon ripened, suddenly from the inside came forth a stout white young lady. Therefore they named her Meng Jiangnü, eventually becoming the mutual daughter of the two families. Meng Jiangnü grew up to become extraordinarily intelligent, with an honest character, the neighbors adoring her.

At that time, the First Emperor Qin was conscripting men into build the Great Wall. There was a scholar named Fan Xiliang, who constantly dodged east and west in order to evade the compulsory service. One day he was utterly parched and set out to look for water, thereupon arriving at the home of Meng Jiangnü. After her family understood the circumstances of Fan Xiliang, they expressed their sympathy, deciding to harbor him in their house. Not long after, Meng Jiangnü's parents had thought Fan Xiliang to be extremely honest, handsome, and well learned, thus resolving to allow their daughter Meng Jiangnü to marry him. Consequently they became a married couple with exceptional mutual love for each other.

But after only three days of the two being married, the authorities found out on the matter of Fan Xiliang avoiding his obligatory service, and arrested him, taking him away for forced labor. Seeing her husband apprehended, Meng Jiangnü felt great agony. Every day tears flowed from her eyes, as she longed for her husband. A year passed of Meng Jiangnü waiting in vain for her husband to return home, as there was not one bit of information about him. Consequently, she decided to personally go to the site of the Great Wall construction project to seek her husband. On the journey of five hundred kilometers, she met many trials and tribulations, but alas, reached the base of the Great Wall. She saw large numbers of servant workers, some carrying heavy bricks on their backs, while others were lifting large stones, and climbing up a high mountain with great difficulty. Their clothes were old and tattered, as sweat soaked their backs. After several days of searching and making inquires, she learned that her husband had already died, and furthermore his body was buried within the massive wall. Hearing this depressing news was like a thunderbolt from a clear blue sky. And she was overcome with sorrow, weeping at the foot of the Great Wall for three days and three nights. As she cried, the clouds obscured the sky, the sun and the moon failed to shine. Then, there was the sound of rumbling, and as section of the wall collapsed to the ground, her tears toppling over 400 kilometers of the Great Wall.

The story Meng Jiannü Weeps Down the Great Wall is very moving. It denounces the cruel and unjust compulsory service in the era of Emperor Qin Shi Huang, as well as sings praises of Meng Jiangnü's sincere romance. In order to commemorate her, at the base of the Great Wall, later generations built Meng Jiangnü Temple with a statue of her inside. Next to the temple is Waiting for Husband Rock, in which legend states that Meng Jiangnü climbed to search for her love.

Liang Shanbo and Zhu Yingtai

In China, there is a widely known legend, understood by everyone through the ages as a tragic romance known as the legend of Liang Shanbo and Zhu Yingtai (The Butterfly Lovers).

During the Eastern Jin Dynasty, in the Zhejiang province of Shangyu prefecture, there existed a family named Zhu. Their daughter, Zhu Yingtai, was exceptionally beautiful and intelligent. As a child she took interest in studying and furthermore wished to go to Hangzhou to learn from the masters. Unfortunately, at that time, girls were not allowed to attend school, so her parents refused this request. Determined to receive an education, she set off for Hangzhou disguised as a man. En route, Zhu Yingtai met by chance an intellect from Kuaiji (present day Zhejiang province, Shaoxing prefecture) named Liang Shanbo. It was like old souls meeting, as they admired each other, until at last on the Thatched Bridge Pavilion, pledged an oath as brothers. Soon after arriving Hangzhou, the two of them found themselves at Wan Song Academy as classmates. They studied together, as form and shadow. They attended school for three years with each other, developing a deep sea of emotions. Zhu Yingtai already profoundly loved Liang Shangbo, but from the beginning he was unaware that she was a woman. As their schooling ended, each of them had to return to his and her families. During this time of separation, the two were reluctant to part. On part of their journey home, Zhu Yingtai unceasingly suggested her love for Liang Shangbo, but honest and considerate, he still did not know that Zhu Yingtai was a woman, much less her falling in love with him. Finally, with no better option, she lies that in her family there is a young sister that looks like him and would be willing to marry Liang Shanbo. She greatly desired him to come to her family's manor, when in fact this younger sister was herself.

The two separated along the way, each returning home. Due to being impoverished, Liang Shanbo was unable to go to the Zhu family in a timely manner to propose marriage. By the time he came to the manor, he had realized that the younger sister she spoke of was none other than herself. But her father had already betrothed her to another man. When Liang Shanbo learned of this, he felt great remorse and became gravely ill. Before meeting death, he requested that his family bury him next to the road that Zhu Yingtai will pass on when she gets married, allowing him to see her as she is wed. Zhu Yingtai caught wind of his plea. On the day of the wedding, as the wedding procession passed and approached the tomb of Liang Shangbo, Zhu Yintai went to the grave and offered sacrifices. She wept in affection for this man, her heart shattered. At this time, the sky offered the wind and the rain, as an impressive flash of lightning struck accord, splitting open the tomb. Zhu Yingtai then leapt into the grave, the tomb closing, she uniting with her lover together in death. Afterwards, Liang Shanbo and Zhu Yingtai morph into butterflies, becoming a pair throughout time. Over a thousand years has passed, their tale of romance forever

Liang Shanbo and Zhu Yingtai Morph into Butterflies

enduring. This classic romance is considered the Romeo and Juliet of the Orient. There exists a violin concerto named Liang Zhu, was written with regards to the story, becoming popular in the past several years at home as well as abroad.

The Legend of the White Snake

The Legend of the White Snake is a story that emerged during the Song Dynasty. It is said, long ago a white snake was captured in the claws of a black falcon. When the black falcon prepared to eat the white snake, an old man named Xu saved its life. A millennia passed and the white snake became a demon, as the generation of the old man Xu continued as a handsome young scholar named Xu Xian.

From the Left in the Picture are Bai Suzhen, Xiaoqing and Xu Xian

In efforts to requite the old man for his life saving grace, the white snake transfigured into the appearance of a human and named herself Bai Suzhen and looked everywhere for the later generation of the Xu family, wishing to help them. In the course of events, she met a similar green snake named Xiaoqing, and as two proceeded together. In a prophecy, Bai Suzhen envisaged this Xu Xian from the later generation of the old man Xu, moreover foreseeing that on one particular day he will go to West Lake in Hangzhou.

Thereupon, on that day, at the Broken Bridge, Bai Suzheng arrived West Lake and had a chance encounter with Xu Xian, both feeling mutual affection for each other. Before long, they were gaily married and in love, as Xiaoqing became their servant. Bai Suzhen assisted Xu Xian in opening an herbal shop to treat the illnesses of the common people. Their treatments were exceptionally effective. In addition to not charging the destitute ill commoners, thus she became greatly loved by the local masses. As their blessed life continued, Bai Suzhen became pregnant, the whole family becoming even more grateful. As gradually forgetting she was actually a white snake, a disaster slowly descended upon the household.

One day, a monk from Jinshan Temple named Fahai arrived and informed Xu Xian that Bai Suzhen was actually a demonic snake, but he refused to believe him. Later, Fahai told him to allow her to drink some yellow wine on the day of the Dragon Boat Festival, in efforts to turn her back to her original form. This time, Xu Xian listened to his words, and secretly allowed her to drink the yellow wine. That night, Bai Suzhen morphed back into a snake, frightening Xu Xian to his death. In efforts to save him, she went to the Celestial Courtyard to steal the plant of the immortals, ultimately bringing him back to life. Even after learning his wife was actually a demonic snake he still profoundly loved her.

But Fahai had been ordered to capture Bai Suzhen. Therefore he placed Xu Xian under detention at Jinshan Temple. In love for her husband, Bai Suzhen and Xiaoqing traveled to the Jinshan Temple to contend with Fahai, who commanded the waters to inundate the Jinhan Temple, thus drowning the souls of many innocent people. Then Bai Suzhen, in violation of the heavens, gave birth to Xu Shilin. Yet Fahai caught up with them and imprisoned Bai Suzhen in the Thunder Peak Pagoda in efforts to separate her and Xu Xian for eternity.

Eighteen years later, their son Xu Shilin, grew up to become a high level scholar. He came before the Thunder Peak Pagoda and offered sacrifices to his mother. While he kneeled, the Thunder Peak Pagoda collapsed, thus reuniting the entire family.

The Legend of the White Snake is a truly touching romantic story. It was not only circulated as a novel in China, but also adapted to many Chinese operas and television programs. In 1958, The Legend of the White Serpent was adapted into a Japanese animation film. The influence also reached France, as noted by French scholar Ru Lian's translation of the novel.

Today's Thunder Peak Pagoda and West Lake

Hua Mu-lan

Legends spread that a girl named Hua Mu-lan was born in a Chinese family during war times long long ago. At that time, the imperial edict ordered that each household should send a man to the battlefield to protect the country. In order to prevent her aged father and very young brother from going to the frontline, Hua Mu-Lan determined to disguise herself as a man to take her elderly father's place in the army. Therefore, she bought a cavalry horse and packed her luggage in secret, then joined the emperor's troops marching on to the frontline.

Hua Mu-lan

For 12 years on the battlefield, she lived and fought as a man without her true identity being discovered. Thanks for her bravery at the front lines and extraordinary fighting ability, she distinguished herself many times in battles. Because of her outstanding achievements, she was offered a government post by the emperor himself when the war was ended. She turned down the position, returned to her family and lived with her parents.

Later, when her former comrades visited her at home, they were shocked to see her dressed as a girl.

Hua Mu-lan has been deeply respected as a courageous, witty and honest heroine for hundreds of years. In Tang Dynasty, she was deified as a goddess and an emperor conferred upon her the posthumous title of "Filial and Valiant General". The story of her maintains its popularity for thousands of years until today. In Song Dynasty, the famous *Collection of Music Bureau Poems* compiled by Guo Mao-qian includes *Ballad of Mu-lan*, which is a folklore unfolding a legend about Hua Mu-lan. With 300 Chinese characters in it, Ode to Mu-lan consists of very concise language and it ranks among excellent narrative poems in the ancient Chinese folk literature. Since then, her story has been produced into plays, movies and TV series. In particular, the influence of movie fabrication has extended to America and the rest part of the world.

Under the direction of Tony Bancroft and Barry Cook, Walt Disney Pictures released Mu-lan in 1998 America, with the story adapted into a quality legendary cartoon for modern audiences. A small fire-breathing dragon called Mu-shu was added to the animation pictures. It helped Mu-lan win the war with his insightful remarks and amazing superpower. Then in 2004, Mu-lan II was shot and directed by Darrell Rooney as a sequel to the 1998 one. It features that when Mu-lan and her fiancé General Li Xiang was going to get married, they suddenly received a secret mission: escorting the

Emperor's three daughters across the country to marry Xiongnu king for
the sake of border peace. They set out without delay; Mushu dragon and cricket went
along with them. However, the three princesses found themselves upset by their arranged marriages
and actually they loved somebody else. As an advocator of female freedom, Hua Mu-lan decided to
take a risk to help the girls escape from their forced marriage. In fact, Disney versions of the story
don't exist in traditional Chinese legends because the directors transfigured Mu-lan with American
ideology. In spite of image transformations, China-American Hua Mu-lan shares similar risky spirit
of pursuing freedom.

Animated film Mu-lan and its sequel aroused so extensive attention in the U.S. that the American media extolled Disney for producing the Chinese-based story Mu-lan by a poem, and it says:

Hua Mu-lan rose to fame in ancient China
because of taking her elderly father's place in the army
and outstanding service in warfare,
while Disney cartoon Mu-lan II
the triumph of American and Chinese imagination.

The character Mu-lan has become one of the most recognizable symbols of Chinese culture worldwide and it will sweep the globe with its unique charm.

汉字的起源

汉字是世界上使用时间最久、使用人数最多的文字之一,汉字的产生,有据可查的,是在约公元前 14 世纪的殷商中后期,这时形成了初步的定型文字,即甲骨文。汉字的创制和应用不仅推进了中华文化的发展,而且对世界文化的发展产生了深远的影响。目前,世界各国基本上都使用拼音文字,中国汉字则保留了表意文字的性质。从中国文字的形体结构,还可以追寻远古造字时代先民的生活、社会、风俗以及文化等等,这是中国文字所独有,其他任何文字都不具备的。

关于汉字的起源,自古以来流传多种说法,其中"仓颉造字"说流传最广。这是古书上最为普遍的记载。仓颉,传说是黄帝的史官。据说有一天,仓颉看见一名天神,相貌奇特,面孔长得好像是一幅绘有文字的画,仓颉便描摹他的形象,创造了文字。有的古书说,仓颉创造出文字后,由于泄漏了天机,天落下了小米,鬼神夜夜啼哭。还有一种传说,说仓颉观察了鸟兽印在泥土上的脚印,启发了他发明文字的灵感。

当然这些只是美丽的传说,关于汉字的起源,有一种比较科学的说法,即汉字真正起源于原始图画。现代学者认为,一些出土文物上刻画的图形,很可能与文字有渊源关系。在距今约 6000 年的半坡遗址等地方,已经出现刻画符号,共达 50 多种。它们整齐规范,并且有一定的规律性,具备了简单文字的特征,学者们认为这可能是汉字的萌芽。他们还认为,成系统的文字工具不可能完全由个人创造出来，古书普遍记载仓颉造字，仓颉如果确有其人，应该是文字整理者或颁布者。

关于汉字起源的说法，除了以上“仓颉造字”说和图画说外，还有结绳说、八卦说等多种说法。有的认为汉字在结绳记事的启示下创制而成，有的认为汉字起源于八卦。总的来说，文字是历史的产物，需要内部与外部的诸多条件，汉字的产生也一样。汉字是广大劳动人民根据实际生活的需要，经过长期的社会实践，在实物记事、契刻记事以及绘画记事的基础上慢慢丰富和发展起来的，它创造了一个文明的时代，是人类进化的一次飞跃。

文字学者在讲汉字构造的时候，一般都遵循“六书”的说法，把汉字分成象形、指事、会意、形声、转注、假借六类。

象形法，这是形成汉字的最早方法，因此创造了最原始的文字。这类字一般是表示实物的名词字，以形示意，如“日”写成。

指事法，这是用抽象的形符造字，所代表的词不是“物”的名称，而是“事”的名称，因此我们要仔细体察才可领会其意思。指事造字主要有两种方法，一是在象形的基础上加上指示性符号，如“本”，从“木”，下面的一横是加上的符号，指明树根之所在，其本义就是指草木的根或靠根的茎干。二是用纯粹的符号来指明或象征某种事物，某种意义。

会意法，这是由两个以上的独体表意字组合后的新意来体现所标语词的意义，或组合两个以上已造现成字所含的意义表意（以义会意）。如“明”字写成，意为“日”和“月”带来光明；或必合具体物类形象之间的关系表意（以形会意），如“旦”字写成，意为太阳出地平线而升起。

形声法，这是把表示声音的声旁和表示意义的形旁搭配起来而组成新字的造字法。如：“爸”字是表音的“巴”字和表形的“父”字的结合。据统计，形声字占汉字的90%左右，为汉字最能产的造字方法。

转注法，所谓转注，一般认为，指由于古今、方言的变化，后人根据汉字已有的表音表意符号部件和结构方式，转用标注异音同义词。如本有一个象形字“豕”，后来有的地方叫“豬”，还有的地方叫“彘”，所以又把“豕”作为表意符号，把“者”、“矢”作为表音符号新造了两个字：“豬”、“彘”。“豕”是本字，“豬”、“彘”是转注字。可见它们的意思是相同的，而语音称谓不同。

假借法，是指本来没有某字，根据音同、音近借一个字来托记要表达的事物的词，而不别造形体。在文字发展史上，假借造字法具有十分重要的意义，它的发展趋向是文字由表意到表音的关键，使文字符号的性质发生本质的变化。（刘双琴编著）

汉字与汉语

汉字是记录汉语的符号，是汉语的书面语工具，汉字和汉语有着密切的联系。汉字具有较强的超时空性，起着联系古今汉语、沟通各地方言的作用。从古代汉语到现代汉语，语音面貌发生了很大变化，词汇、语法也发生了较大变化，但是方块汉字没有变。

汉字是形音义的统一体,汉字组成汉语词汇,词汇组成汉语句子。一个汉字其语音包括声母和韵母、声调三个部分,汉字由这三部分拼读而成。汉语共有 21 个声母、39 个韵母、4 个声调。由于汉语同音字较多(汉字常用字有约 3755 个字,但只有 400 个字音),千百年来民间利用音同或音近的不同汉字,造出了许多有趣的歇后语,成为汉语的一大特色。

歇后语是中国人在生活实践中创造的一种特殊语言形式。它一般由两个部分构成,前半截是形象的比喻,后半截是解释、说明,十分自然贴切。在一定的语言环境中,通常说出前半截,"歇"去后半截,就可以领会和猜想出它的本意,所以称它为歇后语。歇后语是一种短小、风趣、形象的语句。例如:纸糊的凳子——不能做(坐),和尚的房子——妙(庙)。有的歇后语还与中国传统文化或历史人物相联系,如:宋江的军师——无用(吴用),孔夫子搬家——净是输(净是书)。

成语和谚语是汉语使用的又一大特色。成语是汉语中经过长期使用、锤炼而形成的固定短语,一般由四个汉字组成,如"粗枝大叶"、"不自量力"、"臭味相投"。使用成语要特别留神,中国成语具有比喻义,如"胸有成竹"并不是说"胸腔里有根竹子",而是比喻做事之先已有成算在胸。谚语则没有字数的限制,是民间集体创造、广为流传、言简意赅并较为定型的艺术语句,是民众丰富智慧和普遍经验的规律性总结,如"有雨四方亮,无雨顶上光"。英语也有一些谚语,如:A fall into a pit, a gain in your wit.——吃一堑,长一智。Rome was not built in a day.——冰冻三尺,非一日之寒。相比而言,在英语中,成语和谚语没有严格的区分,而且在形式上,不像汉语成语,有比较严格的四字格要求。(刘双琴编著)

汉字与书法

书法是汉字的书写艺术,是中国特有的一种传统艺术。从狭义讲,书法是指用毛笔书写汉字的方法和规律,包括执笔、运笔、点画、结构、布局(分布、行次、章法)等内容。随着文化事业的发展,书法已不仅仅限于使用毛笔书写汉字,其内涵已大大增加。例如,从使用工具上讲,仅笔这一项就五花八门,种类繁多;颜料也无奇不有,不单是使用黑墨块。

中国书法强调用笔。用笔包括笔法、笔力、笔势、笔意四个方面。笔法指用笔的方法与法度;笔力就是笔画力量感;笔势指线条的势态、运动感,以及与其他笔画的呼应、顾盼和走向的连接;笔意指点画的情趣意味,它能表现人的精神状态。书法传统是把"永字八法"作为楷书用笔的基本法则。"永字八法"其实就是"永"这个字的八个笔画,每一划都是事物特点的形象化,与鸟飞、勒马、挽弓、踢脚、策马、梳发、啄食、划肉等相联系,无一不显出动势。

甲骨文是中国书法史上的第一块瑰宝,其笔法已有粗细、轻重、疾徐的变化,下笔轻而疾,行笔粗而重,收笔快而捷,具有一定的节奏感。金文为中国书法史上的又一丰碑,较之于甲骨文,刻于青铜器上的金文更为粗壮有力,艺术成就也很高。

书法艺术的繁荣期,是从东汉开始的。东汉时期出现了以蔡邕为代表的隶书家,以张芝为代表的草书家。此时期隶书已登峰造极,字形方正,法度谨严、波磔分明。三国时期,隶书开始由汉代的高峰地位降落衍变出楷书,楷书成为书法艺术的又一主体。晋代,书法大家辈出,在书法史上最具影响力的书法家当属王羲之,人称"书圣"。王羲之的行书《兰亭序》被誉为"天下第一行书"。隋结束南北朝的混乱局面,统一中国,统一之后的唐都是较为安定的时期,楷书的形式正式完成,在书法史上具有承前启后的重要作用。

唐代文化博大精深、辉煌灿烂,达到了中国封建文化的最高峰,书法艺术进入了新的鼎盛时期。楷书、行书、草书发展到唐代都跨入了一个新的境地。楷书大家有欧阳询、虞世南、褚遂良,草书代表则有张旭、怀素。颜真卿、柳公权也是这一时期著名的书法大家。宋朝书法尚意,同时介导书法创作中个性化和独创性,凸显出一种标新立异的姿态,并给人以一种新的审美意境,代表人物是苏轼、黄庭坚、米芾、蔡襄。到了元代,书法总的情况是崇尚复古,宗法晋、唐而少创新,元朝书坛的核心人物是赵孟頫。

明代书法家有擅草书的刘基、工小楷的宋濂、精篆隶的宋遂和名满天下的章草名家朱克,以及祝允明、文征明、王宠"三子"。明末书坛则放浪笔墨,狂放不羁,这种风气在清代进一步延伸,如朱傅山、"扬州八怪"等人的书法创作,他们的作品璀璨夺目,可谓是中国书法文化的又一大景观。(刘双琴编著)

书同文,车同轨

公元前221年之前,在中国存在许多诸侯国。这些诸侯国之间经常互相发动战争,常使人民处于战乱之中,整个国家也四分五裂。这些诸侯国主要为:韩、赵、魏、楚、燕、齐、秦等七个国家。

在这七个诸侯国中,有一个诸侯国在战争中逐渐强大起来,这就是秦国。秦国当时君主叫嬴政,他就是后来的秦始皇。自公元前230年到公元前221年,嬴政发动了消灭六国的战争,这就是中国历史上所说的"秦灭六国"。嬴政消灭六国以后,在公元前221年建立了中国历史上第一个统一的、多民族的、中央集权制度的国家——秦朝(前221—前206)。嬴政认为自己的功劳可以胜过远古时代的三皇五帝,因此自称为"皇帝"。嬴政为了让自己的皇帝之位子子孙孙永远继承下去,因此将自己称为"秦始皇"。

秦始皇统一中国以后,实行了一系列的社会政治变革,以维护秦帝国的统一。例如,为了改变统一前分封制所造成的地方势力过于强大的现状,秦始皇废除了分封制,推行郡县制;为避免老百姓造反,秦始皇下令将各地的武器都收归中央,进行统一的销毁;为了抵御少数民族的入侵,秦始皇还动用了大量人力、物力和财力,并花费大量时间修筑长城。现在的长城就是在秦始皇修筑的基础之上不断增加并修复的。万里长城是人类一项伟大的奇迹,它已经成为了中国的标志;为了统治全国人民的思想,秦始皇还实行了"焚书坑儒"的政策;此外,秦始皇还统一了国家的法律、度量衡和货币等等。

在秦始皇的统一政策中,有一项影响很大的政策就是"书同文,车同轨。"所谓的"书同文",就是统一全国文字,在全国上下统一使用一种文字。在秦始皇统一中国前,各诸侯国使用不同的文字和书写方式,这极不方便人们的交流,所以在政权统一后,秦始皇便开始统一全国文字。所谓的"车同轨",就是修建全国统一标准的官方道路。

由于当时在全国建立了郡县制度,为了让政令上通下达,秦始皇决定在各地修建驿站,以便快速传递自己的命令。但是由于统一前各国修建的道路宽度不一,车辆要在不同宽度的车道上行走,非常不方便。于是秦始皇统一全国以后,便决定统一各地通往驿站道路的宽度,同时也规定车辆上两个轮子的距离一律改为六尺,这样马车就能在各地顺利的通行了。这可以说是中国最古老的邮递方式了。

总之,秦始皇所推行的许多政策,特别是"书同文,车同轨"的政策,为维护 2000 多年中国的统一局面奠定了坚实的基础,保证了中国长期以来的统一与繁荣。在此后的历史过程中,统一的思想深入到每个中国人的心灵深处。(黎清编著)

文房四宝

"文房"之名,起于中国历史上南北朝时期(420—589 年),专指文人书房而言,其中,笔、墨、纸、砚是文人书房中必备的四件宝贝,从而被人们誉为"文房四宝",因为中国古代文人基本上能书、能画,或既能书又能画,是离不开"笔、墨、纸、砚"这四件宝贝的。

笔是文房必不可缺的书写工具。在林林总总的笔类制品中,毛笔可算是中国独有的品类了。传统的毛笔不但是古人必备的文房用具,而且在表达中华书法、绘画的特殊韵味上具有与众不同的魅力。不过由于毛笔易损,不好保存,故留传至今的古笔实属凤毛麟角。

墨给人的印象似稍嫌单一,但却是古代书写中必不可缺的用品。借助于这种独创的材料,中国书画奇幻美妙的艺术意境才能得以实现。墨的世界并不乏味,而是内涵丰富。作为一种消耗品,墨能完好如初地呈现于今者,当十分珍贵。

纸是中国古代四大发明之一,曾经为历史上的文化传播立下了卓著功勋。即使在机制纸盛行的今天,某些传统的手工纸依然体现着它不可替代的作用,焕发着独有的光彩。古纸在留传下来的古书画中尚能一窥其貌。

砚,也称"砚台",被古人誉为"文房四宝之手"。因为墨须加水发磨始能调用,而发墨之石刑则是砚。其中有陶、泥、砖瓦、金属、漆、瓷、石等,最常见的还是石砚。可以作砚的石头极多,我国地大物博,到处是名山大川,自然有多种石头。产石之处,必然有石工,所以产砚的地方遍布全国各地。

湖笔、徽墨、端砚、宣纸为文房四宝之上品,代表了中国数千年来文房用具的发展水平和能工巧匠们的创造智慧与艺术才能,是文房用具中的瑰宝。

文房用具除四宝以外,还有笔筒、笔架、墨床、墨盒、臂搁、笔洗、书镇、水丞、水勺、砚滴、砚匣、印泥、印盒、裁刀、图章、卷筒等等,也都是书房中的必备之品。(刘双琴编著)

地方方言

中国是多民族、多语言、多方言的人口大国。一般说来，现代汉语有七大方言：

北方方言（广义的官话）：流通在中国中原、东北、西北和西南的广大地区。还可再分为华北东北次方言（狭义的北方话）、西北次方言（西北官话）、西南次方言（西南官话）、江淮次方言（下江官话）4大次方言。

吴方言：即江浙话，分布在江苏省的江南地区和浙江省大部。江浙话以上海话为主要代表。

湘方言：即湖南话，分布在湖南省大部。湖南话以长沙话为主要代表。

赣方言：即江西话，分布在江西省、福建省西北部和湖南省的东部以及湖北省的东南部。江西话以南昌话为主要代表。

客家方言：又叫客家话、客话。客家话分布比较分散，比较集中的地方是广东省东北部、福建省西北部、江西省与湖北、广东、福建接壤的地区，以及四川、广西和台湾等地。东南亚各国的华人中有很多说客家话的。客家话以梅州话为主要代表。

闽方言（分闽北方言和闽南方言）：即闽语，分布很广，包括福建省大部、广东省东部的潮汕地区和西部的雷州半岛、海南省、台湾省大部、浙江省南部，闽方言在东南亚华人社区流行很广。

粤方言：又叫粤语、广东话、广府话、白话，分布在广东省大部、广西壮族自治区的东南部，以及港澳地区和北美华人社区。粤方言以广州话为主要代表。

这七大方言乃是现代汉语方言的粗略划分（不包括少数民族的语言），实际上的方言情况还要复杂得多。不但北方人听不懂广东人、福建人说话，就连广东省内部的广州人、梅州人和汕头人之间，福建省内部的福州人、莆田人、厦门人也互相听不懂对方的话。

方言之间的分歧主要体现在语音差异，但是词汇之间的差异也十分明显，京津唐三地互为邻居，但是北京人所说的"白薯"，唐山人叫"红薯"。若问一个天津小姑娘："你爱吃白薯吗？"她可能就会很奇怪："白鼠怎么能吃？多恶心哪！"因为天津人管"白薯"叫"山芋"，所以跟她说"白薯"，小姑娘就以为是说"白鼠"。你看，汉语的方言分歧有多大！（刘双琴编著）

第二单元

姓名

《说文解字》记载"姓，人所生也"，又说"从女从生，生亦声"，可见"姓"是一个会意兼形声字，"女"为形符，"生"既为形符，又为声符。"姓"是一个产生于母系氏族社会的、标志家族血缘系统的字，因此，中国人的姓产生在母系氏族社会。

中国姓的来源，大概有以下几种情况：一、母系氏族社会，以母亲的名为姓，所以，很多古姓从"女"旁，如姜、姚、姬等；二、以远古时代人们崇拜的生物为姓，如马、牛、龙等；三、以祖先的国家为姓，如赵、宋、秦等；四、以祖先的官职为姓，如上官、司马、司徒等；五、以祖先的爵位为姓，如王、侯、公孙等；六、以住地的方位和景物为姓，如东郭、西门、柳等；七、以职业为姓，如做陶器的姓陶；八、以祖先的名号为姓，如中国人的祖先黄帝名叫轩辕，后来，轩辕就成了一个姓。

中国人的姓有一个字的，也有两个字和两个字以上的。一个字的姓叫单姓，两个字或两个以上的姓叫复姓。中国到底有多少姓，到现在也没有准确的统计数字。据统计，在中国的历史文献中出现过的中国姓有五千多个，现在常见的不过二百多个。张、王、李、赵、刘是中国最常见的单姓，诸葛、欧阳、司徒等是中国最常见的复姓。

受儒家的敬宗法祖的思想影响，中国人特别看重自己的姓氏。改了姓就意味着换了祖宗，这是莫大的耻辱。在中国近代的白话小说里，尤其是武侠小说中，当一个人表白自己光明磊落、敢作敢当的时候，就常说："大丈夫行不改姓，坐不更名——我就是某某人！"

中国人的名具有自己的传统和特点。与英语国家人的姓名不同，中国人的姓名都是姓在前，名在后，姓就相对于英语姓名中的 Family name，是家族一代一代传承下来的；名相当于英语姓名中的 First name。有一个字的，也有两个字的。中国人的名字往往有一定的含义，表示一定的愿望。有的名字包含着出生时的地点、时间或自然现象，如"京、晨、雪"等；有的名字人示希望具有某种美德，如"忠、义、信"等；有的名字表示希望健康、长寿、幸福，如"健、寿、福"等。男人的名字和女人的名字也不一样，男人的名字多用表示威武勇猛的字，如"虎、雄、刚"等，女人的名字常用表示温柔美丽的字，如"凤、玉、娟"等。

中国人在取名时，还经常会在名字中用一些方法来区别同一个家族的不同辈分。比如在名字中用一个字表示辈分，而用另一个字表示取名所标示的含义；也有的在名字中用相同的偏旁来表示同一辈分。另外，与英语国家不同，中国人在取名时，会尽量避免与长辈同名。这与中国古代的避讳制度也是密切相关的。(刘双琴编著)

问候方式

问候是人交际中最常用的日常礼节,人与人之间的交际都是以互致问候开始的。由于民族习俗不同,同样是互致问候,各个民族差异很大。中国人的问候方式在类别、内容、称谓方式、礼貌原则、具体含义等方面都有自己的特点。

首先,在问候类别上,与使用英语的民族一样,中国人的问候方式包括问好型、询问型,也存在评论型问候语。但在具体表达方式上中国人则与西方人不同。例如,英语中有"Good morning,Good afternoon,Good evening",汉语口头语中没有上述问候语的对应用语,常用的是"早"、"你(您)早"等,可能是"你起(来)得真早"等用语的简化。中国人现在也越来越多用"您(你)好!"来打招呼,尤其是在知识分子和有文化修养的人群中使用较多。这种问候比较正式,含有尊重、尊敬的色彩。汉语中还有"干吗去啊""吃了吗"等询问型问候语,以示对他人的关心,而英语国家的人可能认为这是不宜打探的隐私。

其次,文化差异和制约言语行为的社会规范不同,问候语涉及的话题也不同。英语问候语内容简单,不包含具体信息,重在礼貌而非情感表达。汉语问候语多由包含信息的问句组成,且大多涉及别人的起居寒暖,给人以亲切关心之感。中国人往往会互相问起对方的年龄、收入、婚姻和健康等非常大众化的话题,并且问得越细越具体,越能体现对别人的关心。

此外,问候语涉及礼貌是语言文化的特征,但由于每个民族都有自己的社会习惯、行为准则和社交方式,不同民族的文化背景差异可导致不同的衡量事物的标准,反映在礼貌问题上也是如此。中国人在问候时常用敬语和谦词表示对对方的尊重和礼貌,这是汉语文化所特有的。

除了以上语言问候方式,中国人的非语言问候方式即体态式问候也有自己的特点。体态式问候在中国和英语国家均是一种常见方式。中国人尤其是年青人之间通常会点头或挥手以示问候,而在旧时,人们见面还要鞠躬或作揖以示问候。中国人的问候方式一般比较含蓄、矜持,即使是久别重逢,也仅是抚拍肩膀,或握握手,但绝不会亲吻,一般男女之间连拥抱都很少有,至多握握手而已。(刘双琴编著)

亲属称谓

汉民族大多习惯于同族聚居,对血缘关系极为重视。反映在语言方面,便是创造出了繁复细密的亲属称谓语。据有关资料统计,汉语中主要亲属称谓词高达230个之多,现代汉语中仅三代以内的称谓词语就有60多个。随着封建社会的瓦解,许多与宗法等封建制度相关的称谓语也消失了,现代汉语中称谓语大大的简化了,然而,即使到了现代汉语,我们还是能看出汉语亲属称谓语具有的明显的宗法特征。

首先,亲属称谓语明长幼、重尊卑,体现了"尊卑有序、长幼有别"的观念。汉语对长辈和对晚辈的称谓,非常强调突出辈分,注重尊卑之序。如对父母以上的长辈,祖父为"爷爷",祖母为"奶奶";其上每长一辈,前加一"老"字以示区别:称曾祖父为"老爷爷",高祖父为"老老爷爷";对晚辈,子之子为"孙子"、"孙女";其下每低一辈,加一"重"字以示区别,如"重孙女"、"重重孙女"。在对同辈的称谓上,则非常注重长幼之别。如对父母的兄、弟、姐、妹的称谓因长幼不同而有伯、叔、大姑、小舅等不同的称谓,对自己的兄、弟、姐、妹的称谓更是不能混淆长幼。这与英语国家将自己的兄与弟统称为"brother",姐和妹统称为"sister",父母的兄、弟统称为"uncle",父母的姐、妹统称"aunt"完全不同。

其次,亲属称谓语分亲疏、别内外,体现了"家族血统"的意识,宗亲与外亲的称谓有着严格区别。如对父亲的父母称祖父、祖母,对母亲的父母则称外祖父、外祖母,对父亲的兄、弟分别称伯伯、叔叔,母亲的兄、弟则都以"舅舅"相称,若"舅舅"较多,为以示区别,则在"舅舅"前加上基数词,称"大舅"、"二舅"、"小舅"等。随着中国从传统社会向现代社会转变,宗法制度的影响相对变弱。但汉语中庞大复杂的亲属称谓语并没有随着社会的发展而消失。至少在中国广大农村,这些复杂的称谓语依然具有强大的生命力。

中国人称谓还有一个特点就是社会交往广泛使用亲属称谓语。在社会人际交往中广泛使用亲属称谓语。如对陌生人最常用的表示友好和亲热的方法就是以亲属称谓称呼对方,根据其年龄、性别特征,称之为"大爷"、"大娘"、"大哥"、"大嫂"、"大兄弟"、"小妹妹",而孩子则普遍把不相识的成年人统称之为"叔叔"、"阿姨"。这样,被称呼者与称呼者之间显现出一种和谐友好的气氛。(刘双琴编著)

生肖

中国古代根据动物出没时间和生活特征,将十二种动物作为十二生肖,其排行次序为:鼠、牛、虎、兔、龙、蛇、马、羊、猴、鸡、狗、猪。

鼠:晚上 11 时到第二天 1 时(即"子时"),这时候,老鼠胆量最大,活动最频繁。

牛:凌晨 1—3 时(即"丑时"),这时候牛吃足了草,"倒嚼"最细、最慢、最舒适。

虎:凌晨 3—5 时(即"寅时"),据古书载,这时候,老虎最活跃、最凶猛、伤人最多。

兔:清晨 5—7(即"卯时"),这时,太阳还没露出脸面,月亮的光辉还未隐退完全。玉兔是月亮代称,是月宫神话中唯一的动物。

龙:早晨 7—9 时(即"辰时"),传说这是群龙行雨的时候,龙是神话中的动物,于是辰时属龙。

蛇:上午 9—11 时(即"巳时"),据说这时候的蛇不会伤人,也不在人行走的路上游荡,多隐蔽在草丛中,这样巳时就属于蛇了。

马:上午 11 时至下午 1 时(即"午时"),依据道士的说法,中午太阳当顶,阳气达到达极点,阴气渐渐增加,在阴阳换柱之时,一般动物都躺着休息,只有马还习惯地站着,甚至睡觉也站着,从不躺着。

羊:下午 1—3 时(即"未时"),据说羊在这时候撒尿最勤,撒出的尿可治愈自身一种惊疯病。

猴:下午 3—5 时(即"申时"),这时候,猴子最喜欢啼叫,声音拉得最长,最洪亮。

鸡:下午 5—7 时(即"酉时"),这时候,日落山冈,鸡开始进笼归窝、夜宿。

狗:晚上 7—9 时(即"戌时"),黑夜来临,狗看家,守夜的警惕性最高,并产生一种特殊的视力和听力,看得最远,听得最清楚。

猪:晚上 9—11 时(即"亥时"),这时候猪睡得最酣,发出的鼾声最洪亮,全身肌肉抖动得最厉害、长肉最快。

后来,这十二种动物不仅成为时辰的代表,还成为年岁的代表。

关于十二生肖的来历,还有许多美丽的传说。传说在古时,人类的记忆力太差,往往记不住自己的年龄,因此产生很多烦恼,玉皇大帝见到这般情景,于心不忍,想出一个简易的办法,以十二生肖作为年岁的代表,只要记住十二生肖的循环更替,就可以轻易地推算年龄,万无一失了。于是传令天地间的飞禽走兽按时前往天庭,以报到的先后依序选出十二种生肖。百兽之中,龙、虎、兔、马诸兽都自以为身手不凡,不是迟迟动身,就是上路时走走停停,只有老牛自知步伐缓慢,日夜赶路,不敢稍作停留。老鼠狡猾,悄悄跳上老牛角上休息,当老牛第一个赶到天庭的时候,投机取巧的老鼠立刻由牛角一跃而下拔得头筹,受封为十二生肖的首领,老牛屈居第二。猪由于走得最慢,就排在了最后。(刘双琴编著)

第三单元

传统历法——农历

农历是中国的传统历法。这种历法中安排有二十四节气以指导农事活动,而且主要在广大农村使用,因此称为"农历",又名夏历、旧历、中历,民间也有称为阴历的。它用严格的朔、望周期来定月,又用设置闰月的办法使年的平均长度与回归年相近,兼有阴历月和阳历年的性质,因此它实质上是一种阴阳两历并用的历法。至今几乎全世界所有华人及朝鲜、韩国和越南等国家,仍使用农历来推算传统节日如春节、中秋节、端午节、清明节等。

农历的历月以朔望月为依据。朔望月的时间是 29.5366 日(即 29 日 12 小时 44 分 3 秒),因此农历和阴历一样,也是大月 30 天,小月 29 天,但两者又有所不同,阴历大小月是交替编排的,而农历年大小月则是经过推算决定的,所以有时可能连续出现两个大月,也可能连续出现两个小月。农历每个月的初一都正好是"朔"(即月亮在太阳地球中间,且以黑暗的半面对着地球的时候)。由于朔望月稍大于 29 天半,所以在农历的每 100 个历月里,约有 53 个大月和 47 个小月。

农历的历年长度以回归年为准,但一个回归年比 12 个朔望月的日数多,而比 13 个朔望月短。古代天文学家在编制农历时,为使一个月中任何一天都含有月相的意义,即初一是无月的夜晚,十五左右都是圆月,就以朔望月为主,同时兼顾季节时令,采用十九年七闰的方法:在农历十九年中,有十二个平年,每一平年十二个月;有七个闰年,每一闰年十三个月。闰月天数与正常月份天数一样,为 29 或 30 天。至于闰哪个月则由节气情况决定。

农历是中国古代的伟大创造之一,它的特点是:任何一日都含有月相的意义;利用农历日期可以推算潮汐（潮水是月亮的吸引力造成的）。现行中国农历的版本，是 1645 年正式使用的明末清初的《时宪历》。（倪爱珍编著）

二十四节气

二十四节气是中国劳动人民的独特创造，它反映季节的变化，指导农事活动，影响着千家万户的衣食住行。二十四节气是根据太阳在黄道（即地球绕太阳公转的轨道）上的位置来划分的。它视太阳从春分点（黄经零度，此刻太阳垂直照射赤道）出发，每前进 15 度为一个节气，运行一周又回到春分点，为一回归年，合 360 度，刚好是 24 个节气。

二十四节气的公历日期每年大致相同：上半年在 6 日、21 日前后，下半年在 8 日、23 日前后。但在农历中，节气的日期却不大好确定，以立春为例，它最早可在上一年的农历 12 月 15 日，最晚可在正月 15 日。

从二十四节气的命名可以看出，节气的划分充分考虑了季节、气候、物候等自然现象的变化。其中，立春、立夏、立秋、立冬、春分、秋分、夏至、冬至是用来反映季节变化的。春分、秋分、夏至、冬至是从天文角度来划分的，反映了太阳高度变化的转折点。而立春、立夏、立秋、立冬则反映了四季的开始。由于中国地域辽阔，具有非常明显的季风性和大陆性气候，各地天气气候差异巨大，因此不同地区的四季变化也会有所不同。小暑、大暑、处暑、小寒、大寒等五个节气反映气温的变化，用来表示一年中不同时期寒热程度；雨水、谷雨、小雪、大雪四个节气反映降水现象，表明降雨、降雪的时间和强度；白露、寒露、霜降三个节气表面上反映的是水汽凝结、凝华现象，但实质上反映的是气温逐渐下降的过程和程度：气温下降到一定程度，水汽出现凝露现象；气温继续下降，不仅凝露增多，而且越来越凉；当温度降至摄氏零度以下，水汽凝华为霜。小满、芒种这两个节气反映的是有关农作物的成熟和收成情况；惊蛰、清明反映的则是自然物候现象，尤其是惊蛰，它用天上初雷和地下蛰虫的复苏来预示春天的回归。

为了方便记忆，人们把它编成易读易诵的诗歌：

> 春雨惊春清谷天，夏满芒夏暑相连，
> 秋处露秋寒霜降，冬雪雪冬小大寒。
> 每月两节不变更，最多相差一两天。
> 上半年来六廿一，下半年是八廿三。

（倪爱珍编著）

春节

春节，是农历正月初一，又叫阴历年，俗称"过年"。它是中国民间最隆重、最热闹的节日，相当于西方的圣诞节。传统意义上的春节是指从腊月初八的腊祭或腊月二十三的祭灶，一直到正月十五,其中以除夕和正月初一为高潮。腊月的最后一天为除日,除日晚上叫除夕,也叫大年夜,民间称年三十。除夕零点为两年的分水岭,俗语说:"一夜连双岁,五更分二年。"

关于"年"的由来,民间流传着这样一个有趣的故事:

太古时期,有一种叫"年"的凶猛怪兽。到了冬天山中食物稀少时,便跑出山来,闯进村子,见人伤人,见畜伤畜。因此一到冬天,人人惊恐,村村不安。大伙儿都搬到远远的地方以逃避年的伤害。时间长了,人们发现年虽凶猛,却也害怕三样东西:一是鲜红的颜色,二是明亮的火光,三是巨大的声响。于是人们商量出了一个对策:到了这年的冬天,在年快要出山进村时,村里人相互约定,家家户户的门上都挂上用红色涂抹的大木板,门口烧着旺旺的火堆,夜里大家都不睡觉,在家里敲锣打鼓,燃放爆竹,发出巨大的声响。夜深了,年窜到村口,只见处处红色,处处光亮,还有声声巨响,吓得赶快掉头躲进山里,从此再也不敢出来了。第二天清早,全村的人聚在一起,互相祝贺道喜。以后每年的这个日子,家家户户都挂上红色木板,点着火堆,通宵敲锣打鼓,燃放爆竹。第二天相互道喜,欢庆平安。如此代代相传,过年的习俗就形成了。

守岁

除夕之夜,全家团聚在一起吃年夜饭。这顿饭要慢慢地吃,从点灯时分入席,有的人家一直要吃到深夜才散去。吃过年夜饭,大家围坐在灯下或火炉旁闲聊,等着辞旧迎新时刻的到来。除夕通宵守夜,象征着把一切邪瘟病疫照跑、驱走,新的一年吉祥如意。古时除夕守岁有两种含义:年长者守岁为辞旧岁,有珍爱光阴的意思;年轻人守岁,是为延长父母寿命。

扫尘

"腊月二十四,掸尘扫房子。"按民间的说法,"尘"与"陈"谐音,新春扫尘有"除陈布新"的含义,其用意是要把一切穷运、晦气统统扫出门。所以,每逢春节来临,家家户户都要打扫环境,清洗各种器具,拆洗被褥窗帘,洒扫六闾庭院,掸拂尘垢蛛网,疏浚明渠暗沟。

贴春联、倒贴"福"字

春联也叫门对、春贴、对联、对子、桃符等,它以工整、对偶、简洁、精巧的文字描绘时代背景,抒发美好愿望,是中国特有的文学形式。每逢春节,无论城市还是农村,家家户户都要精选一幅大红春联贴在门上,为节日增加喜庆气氛。有一些人家还要在屋门上、墙壁上、门楣上贴上大大小小的"福"字。"福"指福气、福运,寄托了人们对幸福生活的向往,对美好未来的祝愿。为了更充分地体现这种向往和祝愿,有的人干脆将"福"字倒过来贴,表示"幸福已到"、"福气已到"。

放爆竹

中国民间有"开门爆竹"一说,即在新的一年到来之际,家家户户开门的第一件事就是燃放爆竹,以"哔哔叭叭"的爆竹声除旧迎新。爆竹是中国特产,亦称"爆仗"、"炮仗"、"鞭炮"。起源很早,至今已有两千多年的历史。放爆竹可以营造喜庆热闹的气氛,是节日的一种娱乐活动。随着时间的推移,爆竹的应用越来越广泛,品种花色也日见增多,每逢重大节日及喜事庆典,如婚嫁、建房、开业等,都要燃放爆竹表示庆贺,图个吉利。

拜年

新年的初一,人们都早早起来,穿上新衣,戴上新帽,打扮得漂漂亮亮,出门走亲访友,相互拜年,恭祝来年大吉大利。拜年时,晚辈要先给长辈拜年,祝长辈长寿安康,长辈可将事先准备好的压岁钱用红纸包裹好分给晚辈。据说压岁钱可以压住邪祟,因为"岁"与"祟"谐音,晚辈得到压岁钱可以平平安安度过一岁。(倪爱珍编著)

清明节

清明节是中国的传统节日,大约始于周代,已有 2500 多年历史。它的起源,据传始于古代帝王将相"墓祭"之礼,后来民间也竞相仿效,在这一天祭祖扫墓,历代沿袭便成为中华民族一种固定的风俗。

清明节,又叫踏青节,按阳历来说,它是在每年的 4 月 4 日至 6 日之间,此时春光明媚,草木吐绿,正是春游(古代叫踏青)的好季节,所以古人有清明踏青并开展一系列体育活动的习俗。

谈清明节,还须从古代一个非常有名现在已失传的节日——寒食节说起。寒食节,顾名思义,就是不生火做饭,吃冷食。它的日期距清明不过一两天,由于日期接近,渐渐的两者就合二为一了,寒食既成为清明的别称,也成为清明时节的一个习俗。

清明节的习俗非常丰富,既有扫墓、插柳、踏青、植树等风俗,又有放风筝、荡秋千、蹴鞠、打马球等一系列体育活动。因此,这个节日既有祭扫新坟生离死别的悲酸泪,又有踏青游玩的欢笑声,是一个很特别的节日。

扫墓

俗称上坟,是祭祀死者的一种活动。汉族和一些少数民族大多都在清明节扫墓。按照旧的习俗,清明这天中午以前,人们携带"三牲"(鸡、鱼、肉)、酒、茶、饭和纸标(锁钱)到祖先的坟茔前。先在坟头上插上纸标,纸标是用红绿彩纸剪成的彩纸穗。彩纸穗在坟头上随风飘扬,让别人很远就能看见,知道此坟尚有后人。再将食物供祭在亲人墓前,蒸上酒、茶,焚烧纸钱,燃放爆竹。最后叩头行礼祭拜。有的地方还在清明这天修整坟墓,或象征性地给坟头添土。

踏青、植树

清明前后,春阳照临,春雨飞洒,种植树苗成活率高,成长快。因此,自古以来,中国就有清明植树的习惯。1979 年,人大常委会规定,每年 3 月 12 日为中国的植树节。这对动员全国各族人民积极开展绿化祖国活动有着十分重要的意义。

放风筝

每逢清明时节,人们不仅白天放风筝,夜间也放。夜里在风筝下或风稳拉线上挂上一串串彩色的小灯笼,像闪烁的明星,被称为"神灯"。过去,有的人把风筝放上蓝天后,便剪断牵线,任凭清风把它们送往天涯海角,据说这样能除病消灾,给自己带来好运。

荡秋千

秋千,意即揪着皮绳而迁移。古时候,人们以树丫枝为架,再栓上彩带,就做成了一个秋千。现在的秋千多用两根绳索加上踏板做成。荡秋千不仅可以增进健康,还可以培养勇敢精神,至今为人们特别是儿童所喜爱。(倪爱珍编著)

端午节

农历五月初五，是中国民间的传统节日——端午节。端午也称端五、端阳，它始于春秋战国时期，至今已有2000多年历史。关于它的由来有很多传说，如纪念伍子胥说、纪念孝女曹娥说、古越民族图腾祭说等，其中影响较大的是纪念屈原说。

屈原是春秋时期楚怀王的大臣。他倡导举贤任能，富国强兵，力主联齐抗秦，遭到贵族子兰等人的强烈反对，后被陷害赶出都城，流放到沅、湘流域。他在流放中，写下了忧国忧民的《离骚》《天问》《九歌》等不朽诗篇，影响深远（因而，端午节也称诗人节）。公元前278年，秦军攻破楚国京都。屈原看到自己的祖国被侵略，心如刀割，在五月五日这天写下了绝笔之作《怀沙》后，投汨罗江而死，以自己的生命谱写了一曲壮丽的爱国主义诗篇。

传说屈原死后，楚国百姓异常哀痛，纷纷涌到汨罗江边凭吊屈原。渔夫们划起船只，在江上来回打捞他的尸体。有位渔夫拿出为屈原准备的饭团、鸡蛋等食物，"扑通、扑通"地丢进江里，说是让鱼龙虾蟹吃饱了，就不会去咬屈大夫的身体。人们见后纷纷仿效。一位老医师则拿来一坛雄黄酒倒进江里，说是要药晕蛟龙水兽，以免伤害屈大夫。为怕饭团为蛟龙所食，人们想出用楝树叶包饭，外缠彩丝，后来发展成今天的粽子。以后，每年的五月初五，就有了龙舟竞渡、吃粽子、喝雄黄酒等风俗，人们以此来纪念屈原。

中国民间过端午节是较为隆重的，庆祝活动也多种多样，比较普遍的有：

赛龙舟

赛龙舟，是端午节的主要习俗。在急鼓声中划着龙形的独木舟做竞渡游戏，以娱神与乐人，是古代祭仪中半宗教性、半娱乐性的节目。现在它已突破时间、地域界线，成了一项国际性的体育赛事。

佩香囊

端午节小孩佩香囊，传说有避邪驱瘟之意。香囊内装有朱砂、雄黄、香药，外用丝布包住，再以五色丝线弦扣成索，做成各种不同形状，结成一串，形形色色，玲珑可爱。

悬艾叶、菖蒲

民谚说："清明插柳，端午插艾。"端午节这天，家家洒扫庭院，把菖蒲、艾条插在门楣或悬在堂中。艾和菖蒲都是良好的中药材，古人插艾和菖蒲是有一定道理的。（倪爱珍编著）

中秋节

中秋节是中国仅次于春节的第二大传统节日，节期为农历八月十五。这时正是一年秋季的中期，所以称为中秋。在中国的农历里，一年分为四季，每季又分为孟、仲、季三个部分，因而中秋也称仲秋。八月十五的月亮比其他几个月的满月更圆，更明亮，而且中秋节的主要风俗是赏月、吃月饼，这些都与月有关，所以中秋又叫"月夕"。

此夜，人们仰望天空的圆月，自然期盼家人团聚。远在他乡的游子，也借圆月寄托对故乡和亲人的思念之情。所以，中秋又称"团圆节"。

中秋节的传说非常丰富，嫦娥奔月、吴刚伐桂、玉兔捣药之类的神话故事流传甚广。中秋拜月的风俗就来自于嫦娥奔月的故事。

相传，远古时候天上有十日同时出现，晒得庄稼枯死，民不聊生。一个名叫后羿的英雄，拉开神弓，一气射下九个太阳，并严令最后一个太阳按时起落，为民造福。后羿因此受到百姓的尊敬和爱戴，不少志士慕名前来投师学艺，心术不正的蓬蒙也混了进来。

一天，后羿到昆仑山访友求道，巧遇由此经过的王母娘娘，便向王母求得一包不死药。据说，服下此药，能即刻升天成仙。然而，后羿舍不得撇下美丽善良的妻子嫦娥，回家后便把不死药交给嫦娥珍藏。嫦娥将药藏进梳妆台的百宝匣里，不料被小人蓬蒙看见。

三天后，后羿率众徒外出狩猎，心怀鬼胎的蓬蒙假装生病，留了下来。待后羿率众人走后不久，蓬蒙用宝剑威逼嫦娥交出不死药。嫦娥知道自己不是蓬蒙的对手，危急之时当机立断，转身打开百宝匣，拿出不死药一口吞了下去。她的身子立刻飘离地面，冲出窗口，向天上飞去。由于嫦娥牵挂着丈夫，便飞落到离人间最近的月亮上成了仙。

傍晚，后羿回家知道此事后既惊又怒，抽剑去杀蓬蒙，可是他早已逃走。后羿气得捶胸顿足，悲痛欲绝，仰望着夜空呼唤爱妻的名字。这时他惊奇地发现，今晚的月亮格外皎洁明亮，而且里面有个晃动的身影酷似嫦娥。他便拼命地朝月亮追去，可是怎样也追不上。

后羿思念妻子又无计可施，只好派人到嫦娥喜爱的后花园里，摆上香案，放上她平时最爱吃的蜜食鲜果，遥祭嫦娥。百姓们闻知嫦娥奔月成仙的消息，纷纷在月下摆设香案，向善良的嫦娥祈求吉祥平安。

中秋节除拜月、赏月外，还有一个普遍的风俗，就是吃月饼。俗话说，"八月十五月正圆，中秋月饼香又甜"。月饼最初是用来祭奉月神的祭品，后来人们逐渐把中秋赏月与品尝月饼结合在一起，寓意家人团圆。月饼最初是家庭制作，到了近代，出现了专门制作月饼的作坊，制作出的月饼不仅馅料考究，外形也十分美观，月饼的外表印有各种精美的图案，如"嫦娥奔月"、"银河夜月"、"三潭印月"等。(倪爱珍编著)

重阳节

农历九月九日，是中国一个古老的传统佳节——重阳节。因为《易经》中把"六"定为阴数，把"九"定为阳数，九月九日，日月并阳，两九相重，故而叫重阳，也叫重九。

重阳节的源头，可以追溯到先秦之前。那时已有在九月农作物丰收之时祭飨天帝和祖宗以谢其恩德的活动。到了汉代，由于受古代巫师(后为道士)采集药物服用以求长生不老的影响，开始有了九月九日佩茱萸、吃蓬饵、饮菊花酒求寿的风俗。唐代时，重阳被正式定为民间的节日。

今天，重阳节被赋予了新的含义。1989 年，中国把每年的九月九日定为老人节，传统与现代巧妙地结合,重阳节成为尊老、敬老、爱老、助老的老年人节日。

庆祝重阳节的活动丰富多彩,一般包括出游赏景、登高远眺、观赏菊花、遍插茱萸、吃重阳糕、饮菊花酒等活动。

登高

在古代,民间有重阳登高的风俗,故重阳节又叫"登高节"。登高受人重视,特别是受老年人重视的一个原因,是"高"有高寿的意思,因此人们认为"登高"可以长寿。登高所到之处,没有统一规定,一般是登高山、登高塔。

吃重阳糕

据史料记载,重阳糕又称花糕、菊糕、五色糕,制无定法,较为随意。九月九日天明时,以片糕搭儿女头额,口中念念有词,祝愿子女百事俱高,是古人九月做糕的本意。讲究的重阳糕要做成九层,像座宝塔,上面还做成两只小羊,以符合重阳(羊)之义。有的还在重阳糕上插一个小红纸旗,并点蜡烛灯。这大概是用"点灯"、"吃糕"代替"登高"的意思,小红纸旗是用来代替茱萸的。

赏菊花、饮菊花酒

重阳节正是一年的金秋时节,菊花盛开。据传重阳赏菊、饮菊花酒等风俗,起源于晋朝大诗人陶渊明。陶渊明以隐居出名,以诗出名,以酒出名,也以爱菊出名,后人效之,遂有重阳赏菊之俗。

插茱萸、簪菊花

古人认为在重阳节这一天插茱萸可以避难消灾。他们把茱萸或佩带于臂,或放在特制的香袋里,或插在头上。佩带者以妇女、儿童居多,有些地方男子也佩带。除了佩带茱萸,有的地方还也有头戴菊花的风俗。(倪爱珍编著)

庙会

庙会,又称"庙市"或"节场"。庙会风俗则与佛教寺院以及道教庙观的宗教活动有着密切的关系,同时它又是伴随着民间信仰活动而发展、完善和普及起来的。早期庙会仅是一种隆重的祭祀活动,随着经济的发展和人们交流的需要,庙会就在保持祭祀活动的同时,逐渐融入集市交易活动。这时的庙会又得名为"庙市",成为中国市集的一种重要形式,货物种类齐全,锅盆碗筷,日用百货,衣帽鞋袜等应有尽有,成为老百姓的购货市场。随着人们的需要,又在庙会上增加娱乐性活动。庙会有的是一年一度,有的一个月内就有数天,会期除固定的,还有不定天数。过年逛庙会是中国人不可缺少的过年内容。但各地区庙会的具体内容稍有不同,各具特色。舞龙、舞狮、灯谜是庙会传统的娱乐节目。

舞龙也叫"耍龙灯"、"龙灯舞",从春节到元宵灯节,许多地方都有舞龙的习俗。龙在中华民族代表了吉祥、尊贵、勇猛,更是权力的象征。人们在喜庆日子里用舞龙来祈祷龙的保佑,以求得风调雨顺,五谷丰登。舞狮也是中国传统的民间艺术,每逢元宵佳节或集会庆典,民间都以舞狮前来助兴。这一习俗起源于三国时期,南北朝时开始流行,至今已有一千多年的历史。表演者在锣鼓音乐下,装扮成狮子的样子,作出狮子的各种形态动作。中国民俗传统,认为舞狮可以驱邪辟鬼。

灯谜是元宵佳节的特色节目。关于灯谜的起源,有个有趣的传说。据传,很早的时候,有个姓胡的财主,家财万贯,横行乡里,人们都叫他"笑面虎"。这笑面虎对那些比自己穿得好的人拼命巴结,对那些粗衣烂衫的穷人则蛮横无理。有个叫王少的穷人,为了斗斗这个笑面虎,就在某年元宵节挂花灯之时,在自家的花灯上写了一首诗:"头尖身细白如银,论秤没有半毫分。眼睛长到屁股上,光认衣裳不认人。"笑面虎知道了,非常生气,就吩咐家丁来抢王少的花灯,王少忙挑起花灯,笑嘻嘻地说:"老爷,咋见得是骂你呢?"笑面虎恨声说:"这不是骂我骂谁?"王少仍笑嘻嘻地说:"噢,老爷是犯了猜疑。我这四句诗是个谜,谜底就是'针',你想想是不是?"笑面虎一想:可不哩!只气得干瞪眼,没啥说,转身狼狈地溜走了。周围的人见了,只乐得哈哈大笑。这事后来越传越远。第二年灯节,不少人都将谜语写在花灯上,供观灯的人猜测取乐,所以就叫"灯谜"。以后相沿成习,每逢元宵灯节,各地都举行灯谜活动,一直传到现在。(刘双琴编著)

第四单元

炎黄二帝

在中国历史上,有两位被认为是中华民族共同的人文始祖,那就是炎黄二帝。

炎帝,传说为上古时期姜姓部落的首领。据说炎帝的母亲在游览华山时,看见一条神龙,并因此而怀有身孕,回家后便生下炎帝。炎帝一出生便非常聪颖,三天能说话,五天能走路。长大后,炎帝以其突出的才能成为部落的首领。传说中,他教老百姓学会了耕种谷物,是农耕文化的创始人,因此人们也敬称其为"神农";他亲自品尝各种植物,确定它们的药性,以便为人们治病,开创了中药之先河;此外,他还制造乐器,设立市场,教人织布等等,使人类逐渐由蒙昧走向文明。由于部落的逐渐强大,炎帝带领部落不断向外扩张,周围的部落纷纷归顺炎帝。后来,炎帝部落在扩张的过程中与同样强大的黄帝部落发生冲突。最后,在一个名叫"阪泉"的地方发生战争,炎帝被黄帝战败,最终炎帝部落臣服于黄帝部落。

黄帝,传说为上古时期姬姓部落的首领。他出生于农历二月初二,据说黄帝的母亲在一天傍晚突然看见北极光,于是怀孕生下了黄帝。黄帝出生几十天就会说话,少年时思维敏捷,为人敦厚能干,后来成为部落的首领。黄帝在中华文明史上有着重要的贡献,他令仓颉制造文字,使中国文字一直沿用至今;他让自己的妻子养蚕取丝,以丝制成衣服;他教人们制造舟车、房屋,方便老百姓的生活;他作干支用来计时等等。在黄帝的带领下,其部落文明程度得到了提升,实力也大大增强,并最终在与炎帝部落的战争中取得了胜利。

黄帝部落合并炎帝部落之后,成为中原最为强大的部落。随后,黄帝部落与炎帝部落一道,兼并了中原地区其他各个部落,统一了中原,奠定了中华民族文明的基础。炎帝和黄帝作为中华文明的杰出开创者,一直被中国人尊奉为中华民族的人文始祖,至今每个中国人仍将自己称为"炎黄子孙"。为感激炎黄二帝在中国文化史上所作出的巨大贡献,人们以各种形式来纪念他们,例如在许多地方便建有他们的陵庙,以表达对他们的崇敬之情。

2006年,在河南省郑州市郑州黄河风景名胜区内,炎黄二帝的巨型塑像屹立在黄河岸边。这个雕像高106米,比美国自由女神像高8米,比俄罗斯母亲像高2米,是"地球第一雕"。这一巨型雕像吸引着来自海内外不同地方的华人以"炎黄子孙"的身份前来瞻仰和祭拜。炎黄二帝已经成为凝聚全球华人的一个重要标志和象征,每一位华人都以是"炎黄子孙"而感到自豪。(黎清编著)

大禹治水

据说,在很久很久以前,尧统治中国的时代,人们经常遭受到洪水灾难的危害。君王尧非常焦急,立即召集各个部落的首领商量如何治理水患。最后,大家一致推举鲧去治理洪水。鲧接受任务后,便决定用土堆筑堤坝的方式来阻挡洪水,结果筑好的堤坝往往被洪水冲垮,洪水之患依然很严重,鲧治水的工作于是宣告失败。君王尧得知这一结果后,便将鲧处死了。

几十年以后,舜继承了尧的王位。舜一登上王位便下决心要治理好洪水。这时,鲧的儿子大禹已经成人,于是舜就任命大禹继续治理洪水。刚开始,大禹也和他的父亲一样,采用修筑堤坝的方式来治水,可是,当大禹将堤坝修筑好之后,不久堤坝便会被洪水冲垮。经过无数次的失败和教训之后,大禹逐渐地明白:洪水不能一味地去堵,而应该是该堵的时候堵,该疏通的时候疏通。明白这个道理以后,大禹立刻改变了自己的治水策略。

首先,大禹走遍全国各地,考察河水的走势。弄清楚这些之后,大禹带领人们开渠排水,疏通河道,把河水引到大海去。在治理洪水时,大禹也和老百姓一起参加劳动。据说,由于忙着治水,有一次大禹三次经过自己的家门,他都没有进去。这就是人们所传颂的"三过家门而不入"的故事。经过不懈努力,大禹终于把全国各地的洪水引到了大海,他的治水也最终获得了成功。人们又可以在土地上安安心心的耕种了,再也不用担心洪水的危害了。

由于大禹治水有功,造福了人民,舜年老时便将王位传给了他。作为远古中国的一位明君,大禹死后,一直受到华夏子孙的称颂和怀念。在今天浙江省绍兴市的会稽山下,人们修建了一座大禹的陵墓——"禹陵",用来纪念他的丰功伟绩。就是在今天,还有许多人来到"禹陵",缅怀大禹,以表达对这位明君的崇敬之情。(黎清编著)

盘古开天

宇宙到底是怎样形成的? 在中国,自古以来一直流传着盘古开天辟地形成宇宙的传说。据说,很久以前,世界上没有天也没有地,整个宇宙就像一个"大鸡蛋"。在这个混沌的"大鸡蛋"中孕育着一个像人的生命,这就是盘古。盘古在"大鸡蛋"里熟睡了18000年之后,一天,当盘古醒来的时候,他看见周围一片漆黑,什么也看不见。于是,他便奋力将"大鸡蛋"撑破。这时,"大鸡蛋"中的一些像蛋清一样轻的东西便飘浮起来,最后形成了天空;而"鸡蛋"中一些像蛋黄一样重的东西则渐渐沉下去,结果形成了厚实的大地。

盘古将天地一分开,便觉得非常舒服。但是,刚刚形成的天却不时地往下沉,想与大地连在一起。为了不回到混沌的"大鸡蛋"中去,盘古只得用双手和头拼命地顶着天,用脚踏着地,避免天与地连在一起。盘古每天都这样地撑着,随着他身体的不断增长,天和地之间的距离也随之变得越来越遥远了。最终,天地永久分开,但盘古也感到非常累了,于是他便躺下去休息会儿。

躺下之后,盘古就再也没有起来过了。他的头变成了东岳,也就是泰山;他的腹部变成中岳,也就是恒山;他的左臂变成了南岳,也就是衡山;他的右臂变成了北岳,也就是嵩山;他的脚变成了西岳,也就是华山;他从嘴里呼出的气,也变成了春风和云雾;他的声音变成了下雨时的雷鸣;他的左眼变成了炙热的太阳,每天给大地传送温暖;他的右眼变成了皎洁的明月,给黑夜的人们以照明;他的血液变成了江河湖泊;他的肌肉变成了无数的田地;他的牙齿、骨头和骨髓变成了闪光的金银铜铁、坚硬的石头、圆润的珍珠、精美的玉石;他身上的皮肤和汗毛则变成了无数的花草、树木;而身上的汗水则变成了雨露和甘霖;他的头发和眉毛变成了天上满天的繁星;他的筋脉变成了地上纵横交错的道路;他的精灵变成了各种鸟兽鱼虫。就这样,盘古将他的整个身体献给了宇宙。也正因为如此,从此天上才有了日月星辰,地上才有了山川树木、鸟兽虫鱼,宇宙变得丰富多彩起来。

盘古以自己的生命创造了丰富多彩的宇宙世界,他被中国的先民看做是创造宇宙的一位大神,并接受后世中国人的崇拜和祭祀。自古以来,在许多地方都建有纪念盘古的庙,如湖南省湘乡的"盘古祠"。每年农历的三月初三这一天,都有大批的人聚集到"盘古庙"去祭拜盘古。所以,中国人一直对宇宙自然怀着无限的敬畏与感恩,他们感谢宇宙所赐予的一切,并倍加珍惜!(黎清编著)

女娲造人

地球上的人类是如何出现的? 在中国,流传着一个远古时代女娲造人的神话故事。

盘古死后,宇宙万事万物都已经比较齐备了,但遗憾的是,在当时,地球上还没有出现人类。后来,不知过了多少万年,地球上终于出现了一个人类的始祖,她便是女娲。女娲是天上的女神,她长相非常奇怪,长着人的脑袋、蛇的身子。女娲来到地球之后,发现在她周围只有一些飞禽走兽,而没有人类。起初,这些小动物给女娲带来了无穷的快乐,她也感觉自己非常幸福。但是时间久了以后,由于动物们都不能说话,女娲想要交流的时候总是找不到对象,她开始感到了孤独与寂寞。一天,女娲感到无聊,于是用树枝搅和着身边的湿泥,并用手随意地捏着,捏着捏着,手中的泥土便变成了人的模样。女娲朝泥人吹了一口气,泥人便活了,变成了一个不仅能说话,而且还能够懂得她想法的女人。女娲觉得非常有趣,同时为了不

使女人像自己以前那样孤单,于是她再捏了一个男人,让他们互相
为伴。有了这样两个人在身边,女娲觉得开心快乐了许多,于是继续捏了好多
对人,最后实在是累了,她就用树枝蘸着湿泥在空中一划,地球上便有了许多的人。为了让这
些人繁衍子孙后代,女娲便让男女进行婚配。就这样,地球上出现了人类。并且有人认为,女
娲捏的人及其后代后来变成了上流社会,而她用树枝创造出的人则成了下层劳动人民。不管
如何,自从女娲造了人以后,地球因为有了人类变得更加富有生机和活力了。

但是,人类的美好生活没过多久,突然有一天地球和人类遭受了一场浩劫,天破了,地裂
了,大火熊熊,洪水泛滥,人类面临覆亡的危险。这时,女娲目睹了人类所遭受到的一切,她不
忍心人类遭受灭亡,于是,她炼了一种五色石,并用它去修补天上破了的缺口,同时又用芦灰
去堵住了泛滥的洪水。在女娲的努力下,人类最终才得以恢复了往昔平静的生活。

为了感谢女娲对人类的恩德,人们将其称为"女娲娘娘",尊其为人类的始祖,全国许多
地方都有关于她的祭祀活动。此外,由于传说中人是由女娲用泥土造的,所以中华民族与土
地之间有着非常深厚的情感。远走他乡的游子,也常常不忘带上一把故乡的泥土,作为永远
的思念。(黎清编著)

后羿射日

据说,在遥远的古代,那时的天空一共有十个太阳。在这十个太阳里面住着十只名叫
"乌"的鸟,他们都是东方天帝的儿子。每一天,都由十只"乌"中的一只出来工作,为
大地提供阳光和热量,而其他九只则在别的地方玩耍和睡觉。所以,当黎明来临的时候,地球
上的人们便可以看见太阳从东方升起来,一只"乌"已经起来开始工作了。

长久以来,虽然天空有十只"乌",也就是有十个太阳,但是人们所看到的太阳还只是一
个。地球上的人们在太阳的恩惠下,按时作息,日出而耕,日落而息,生活得非常美满。可是有
一天,由于十个太阳的母亲要外出一段时间,于是这十个太阳便做出了一个非常糟糕的举
动,在黎明来临的时候,这十个顽皮的太阳一起出现在天空中。这一下,十个太阳自己是玩得
很开心了,但是大地上的人们和万物就遭殃了。十个太阳一出来,释放出来的热量非常巨大,
很快,海水干涸了,许多鱼类也死了,水中的怪物爬上岸来,抢夺人类的食物;地球上的森林
着了火,好多动物被烧死,那些没有被烧死的动物纷纷跑到人类居住的地方,大肆地寻找食
物,许多家畜和人成了动物的食物;地里的庄稼也都干枯了,人们经常饿着肚子,没有食物
吃,同时还要忍受炎热的天气,许多人被晒死了。

这时,有个年轻英俊的神箭手名叫后羿,他箭法超群,百发百中。当他看到人们生活在苦
难中时,便决定用箭去射掉天上那些讨厌的太阳。一天,后羿拿着弓和箭,带着干粮便出发
了。他爬过了九十九座高山,迈过了九十九条大河,穿过了九十九个峡谷,历经千辛万苦,终
于来到了东海边。他登上一座非常高的山,在山顶上,后羿拉开弓,搭上箭,瞄准天上的太阳,
朝太阳中的"乌"射去,一只"乌"被射中了,落入了东海,于是天上便少了一个太阳。就这
样,后羿一连射下了九只"乌",天空中只剩下了一个太阳了。这时,后羿便收起了弓箭,留下

了最后一个太阳，让他造福于人类。从此，这个太阳每天从东方的海边升起，悬挂在天空，温暖着人间，禾苗得生长，万物得生存。

为了感谢后羿对人类的功德，"后羿射日"的故事在中国历代相传，经久不衰。人们永远铭记着这位英雄！（黎清编著）

第五单元

牛郎织女

在中国，有一个古老而美丽的爱情传说，那就是牛郎和织女的爱情故事。

传说天庭上有一位非常漂亮的仙女，名字叫织女，她是天庭王母娘娘的孙女。一天，织女和几个伙伴偷偷从天庭来到人间，她们选择在一个叫"碧莲池"的地方洗澡。由于在天庭她们很少有自由，所以在池水中洗澡时她们感到无比快乐。

在"碧莲池"的附近，有位英俊的小伙子，名字叫做牛郎。他出生在一个农民家中，刚出生不久，他的父母便都离开了人世。牛郎开始和他的哥与嫂子住在一块，不久后他嫂子把他赶出了家门，并且只给了牛郎一头老牛和一辆破车。从此，牛郎便与他的这头老牛相依为命。实际上，这头老牛是天上的神仙。为了报答诚实而又善良的牛郎，一天，老牛突然像人一样说话了。它对牛郎说："牛郎，今天你去'碧莲池'，你将会看见一群仙女在'碧莲池'中洗澡，你将那件红色的衣服藏起来，那穿红衣服的仙女就会成为你的妻子。"牛郎听说后非常高兴，一会儿就来到了"碧莲池"。

果然如老牛所说，"碧莲池"里真的有一群非常漂亮的仙女，她们在尽情地嬉戏、游玩。趁仙女们不注意，牛郎拿起那红色的衣服就跑。仙女们在池水中正玩得高兴，突然看见有人来，便纷纷穿上衣服飞向天空。而织女由于找不到衣服，便只能待在原地。这时，牛郎走过来将衣服还给织女，并请求织女做他的妻子。织女看见牛郎既英俊又善良，便答应了牛郎的请求，成为他的妻子。

牛郎和织女结婚以后，相亲相爱，生活过得幸福美满。数年后，他们便有了一儿一女，他们活泼可爱。一天，牛郎突然跑回家告诉织女："老牛死了。老牛临死的时候，它叫我将它的皮剥下来，以后披上它可以飞到天上去。"织女一听，心里便有一种不祥的预感。正在这时，天空刮起了大风，乌云密布。天上的神仙从天而降，押解着织女飞向天庭。牛郎一看织女被天神抓走，心里非常焦急，他披上牛皮，带着两个儿女，去追赶织女。牛郎披着牛皮飞了起来，眼看牛郎和织女的距离也越来越近了。就在这时候，王母娘娘拔下头上的金簪，往牛郎和织女中间一划，于是在他们中间就出现了一条天河。这条天河非常宽，并且无论牛郎怎么努力都飞不过去。就这样，天河将牛郎和织女分隔在两边，永远不能相见了。至今，我们还可以看见在银河的两边，有两颗比较大的星星，那就是织女和牛郎，他们成了天空中的织女星和牵牛星。在牵牛星的旁边，还有两颗比较小的星星，那就是牛郎织女的一儿一女。

织女不能与自己的丈夫和儿女相见，整天以泪洗面。最后，王
母娘娘向织女承诺：每年的七月初七，织女可以与自己的丈夫和孩子相会一
次。在那一天，天上无数的喜鹊会飞来为他们在河面上架起一座桥梁，人们称它为"鹊桥"。
在鹊桥上，牛郎和织女还有他们的孩子在那里团聚。据说每年的七月初七夜晚，如果人们在
葡萄架下静静地倾听，还能隐隐听到牛郎和织女的谈话呢！

在中国民间，人们将传说中牛郎和织女"鹊桥相会"的日子，也就是每年的农历七月初
七，称为"七夕节"，以此来纪念牛郎和织女之间纯洁坚贞的爱情。

七夕节，就像西方每年 2 月 14 日情人节一样，被称为是中国的"情人节"。（黎清编著）

孟姜女

今天，许多人都知道中国的长城。在中国民间，关于长城，还有一个"孟姜女哭长城"的
故事。

相传在秦朝的时候，有一个姓孟的人家，种了一棵瓜，瓜藤长到隔壁的姜家并结了瓜。瓜
熟的时候里面突然出来了一个又白又胖的小姑娘，于是两家人就叫她孟姜女，孟姜女最后成
为两家人共同的女儿。孟姜女长大后非常聪明伶俐，心地又善良，周围的邻居都喜欢她。

当时，秦始皇正在到处抓人去修长城。有一个叫范喜良的读书人，为了躲避服役，到处东
躲西藏。一天，他感到十分口渴，想找点水喝，于是来到了孟姜女家。孟姜女的家人知道了范
喜良的情况后，觉得他非常可怜，于是决定让他藏在自己家里。不久后，孟姜女的父母觉得范
喜良非常老实，人长得也英俊，并且很有学问，于是决定将女儿孟姜女嫁给他。很快，孟姜女
便和范喜良结婚了，彼此都非常相爱。

但是，就在两人结婚后的三天，官府便知道了范喜良逃避服役的事情，于是将他抓去服
劳役了。看到自己的丈夫被抓走了，孟姜女非常痛苦，她每天都流着眼泪，思念着她的丈夫。
孟姜女天天盼着她的丈夫回家，但是一年过去了，还是没有一点丈夫的消息。于是，孟姜女决
定亲自去修筑长城的地方寻找丈夫。一路上，孟姜女千里迢迢，历尽千辛万苦，终于来到了长
城脚下。只见成群结队的役工，有的背着又大又重的城砖，有的抬着石块，向高山上艰难地爬
着。他们衣衫破旧，汗流浃背。经过几天的寻找和打听，孟姜女才知道，自己的丈夫范喜良，已
被累死了！并且他的尸首还被埋在了城墙中。孟姜女听到这一噩耗，真如晴天的霹雳。她悲
痛万分，一直在长城脚下哭了三天三夜，直哭得天昏地暗，日月无光。这时，只听"轰隆隆"一
声响，城墙坍塌下来，修好的长城被孟姜女哭倒了 800 里。

孟姜女哭倒长城的故事非常动人。它既是对秦始皇时代残酷徭役的控诉，又是对孟姜女
真挚爱情的歌颂。为了纪念这位孟姜女，后人在长城脚下修建了"孟姜女庙"。在庙里有孟姜
女的塑像，庙旁还有传说孟姜女寻夫时登高眺望的"望夫石"。（黎清编著）

梁山伯与祝英台

在中国,流传着一个家喻户晓、被誉为千古绝唱的爱情故事,这便是梁山伯与祝英台之间的爱情传说。

东晋时期,在浙江省上虞县的祝家庄,有户姓祝的人家,他们有个女儿叫做祝英台。祝英台长得美丽聪颖,从小爱好读书,并且一心想去杭州拜师求学。在当时女孩是不允许上学的,所以祝英台的父母拒绝了这个请求。但是祝英台坚决想出去求学,于是她就乔装成男子,来到杭州求学。在途中,祝英台邂逅了同样来杭州求学的会稽(今浙江省绍兴市)书生梁山伯。两人一见如故,相互欣赏,最后在一个叫"草桥亭"上地方结拜为兄弟。不久,二人来到杭州城的"万松书院",一起学习。从此,两人同窗共读,形影不离。梁山伯和祝英台同学三年,情深似海。祝英台已经深深地爱上了梁山伯,而梁山伯却始终不知她是女子。三年后,祝英台和梁山伯各自要回到自己家,分别时,两人依依不舍。在相送途中,祝英台不断暗示自己对梁山泊的爱情。但梁山伯忠厚淳朴,他并不知道祝英台是位女孩,并且她已经爱上了自己。最后,祝英台无奈,谎称家中有个妹妹,长得跟自己很相似,愿意将妹妹嫁给梁山伯。她希望梁山伯到时候能来自己家里娶自己的妹妹。实际上,祝英台所说的妹妹就是她自己。

两人分别后,由于贫穷,梁山伯未能如期去祝英台家提亲。等到后来梁山伯去祝英台家求婚时,才知道祝英台所说的妹妹就是祝英台自己,并且祝英台的父亲已经将祝英台许配给了别人。梁山伯知道这些后,非常懊悔,并且一病不起。临死前,他要求家人把自己葬在祝英台结婚要经过的路边,让自己看到祝英台出嫁。祝英台得知这些以后,结婚那天,当经过梁山伯的坟墓时,她特意来到梁山伯墓前祭奠。祝英台为她深爱的人哭得非常伤心。这时,天空风雨雷电大作,坟墓裂开,祝英台跃入坟中,墓坟又合拢,梁山伯和祝英台这对相爱的人便死在了一起。后来梁山伯和祝英台都变成了蝴蝶,成双成对整天待在了一起。

一千多年来,梁山伯和祝英台的爱情故事久传不衰。这一东方版的《罗密欧与朱丽叶》一直被认为是一个经典爱情题材。小提琴协奏曲《梁祝》就是根据这一故事创作的,多年来一直蜚声海内外。(黎清编著)

白蛇传

白蛇传的故事发生在中国的宋朝。据说,很久以前有一条白蛇被一只黑鹰抓住,正当黑鹰准备吃白蛇的时候,有一位姓许的老人救了这条白蛇。经过了千年之后,这条白蛇成了千年蛇妖,而那位姓许的老人则有一个后代,他是一位年轻英俊的书生,名叫许仙。

为了报答姓许老人的救命之恩,白蛇变为人的模样,并取名叫白素贞。白素贞到处寻找姓许老人的后人,希望能够帮助他们。在寻找的过程中,白素贞遇到一条名叫小青的蛇精,于是两人结伴而行。通过法术,白素贞知道姓许老人有个后代名叫许仙,并且知道许仙在某一天一定会去杭州的西湖。

于是，在那一天，白素贞特意来到西湖，最后在断桥与许仙邂逅。两人一见便互相爱上了对方。后来，白素贞与许仙结婚，小青也成了他们的女仆。婚后两人非常相爱，并且白素贞帮助许仙开了一家药店，为附近的老百姓治病。他们医术非常高明，而且还经常免费为穷人治病。这样，白素贞深受当地老百姓喜欢。两人就这样幸福的生活着，不久，白素贞怀孕了，一家人更是高兴。白素贞慢慢忘记了自己是一条白蛇。但是，一场灾难也在慢慢地降临这个家庭。

一天，金山寺一个名叫法海的和尚来到这里，他告诉许仙白素贞是一个蛇妖。许仙开始并不相信。后来，法海教许仙在端午节那天让白素贞喝雄黄酒，那她就会现出原形。许仙真的听从了法海的话，偷偷让白素贞喝下了雄黄酒。结果晚上白素贞真的变成了一条白蛇，许仙自己也被吓死了。白素贞为了救许仙，到天庭盗取仙草，最终将许仙救活。知道自己的妻子是蛇妖以后，许仙还是非常爱着白素贞。但是，法海却一直想将白素贞抓起来，于是他将许仙骗至金山寺并软禁了许仙。白素贞爱丈夫心切，便和小青一起来到金山寺与法海斗法，并且让水淹没了金山寺，因此伤害了许多无辜的生灵。白素贞触犯天条，在生下孩子许仕麟后被法海镇压在西湖的雷峰塔下。这样，白素贞和许仙便永久不能相见。

18年后，白素贞的儿子许仕麟长大了，并考取了状元。他来到雷峰塔前祭拜母亲，在他跪下去的时候，雷峰塔倒了，白素贞获救了，全家因此团聚。

白蛇传这一动人的爱情故事不但在中国广为流传，被改编成许多戏曲和电视。在日本，1958年白蛇传也被拍成了动画电影。此外，其影响也波及法国，法国汉学家儒莲也曾将白蛇传翻译成法文。（黎清编著）

花木兰

传说，在很久以前的中国，有个女孩名叫花木兰。那时候由于经常发生战争，所以朝廷就规定：每一户人家必须派一名男子去参军打仗。按规定，花木兰家也要派一名男子上战场，但是，她的父亲年纪已经很大了，而弟弟年纪还很小。为了不让年迈的父亲上战场，花木兰决定自己扮成男人的模样，代替父亲去参军。于是，花木兰偷偷买好了战马，准备好了行李，加入了开赴前线的军队。

在军队，花木兰一待就是12年。这期间，她和其他男性战友一起生活，一起战斗，但是他们都没有发现木兰是女性。在战场上，花木兰凭借着自己的机智和勇敢，建立了许多战功。最后，战争取得了胜利，皇帝因为她卓越的功绩，想请她做官，但是被她拒绝了，而是回到了故乡陪伴父母。一回到家，花木兰就又打扮成女孩模样，这时，她以前在军队里的伙伴才发现她是女孩，都感到非常惊讶。

花木兰一直是深受中国人尊敬的一位女性，她勇敢、机智而又淳朴。在唐代，花木兰被人们当做神来祭祀，她也被皇帝封为了"孝烈将军"。千百年来，花木兰的故事一直被人们所传诵。宋代郭茂倩编的《乐府诗集》中便有一首《木兰诗》，以叙事诗的形式表现了花木兰的传奇故事。《木兰诗》长300余字，非常凝练，是中国古代民间文学中的一篇优秀叙事诗。此后，其故事也被多种文艺作品所表现,如戏剧、电影、电视剧等等。尤其是电影,其影响甚至波及美国乃至全世界。

1998年,由美国导演 Tony Bancroft 和 Barry Cook 拍摄了迪斯尼动画片《Mu-lan》。这部影片对中国传说中的花木兰进行了一些改造,使其具有了神话与现代色彩。比如,影片中多了一只会说话而且具有超能力的木须龙,它一直陪伴在花木兰身边,并帮助花木兰最终取得了胜利。2004 年,美国导演 Darrell Rooney 拍摄了喜剧片《Mu-lan II》。故事讲述的是,当花木兰和李翔准备结婚时,他们突然接到一项秘密任务。为了抵抗强大的匈奴,皇帝决定派他们护送三位公主嫁给匈奴国王,希望能维持边疆的和平。于是他们立刻出发,木须龙和蟋蟀也跟随在一起。但是,在途中花木兰却发现公主其实不愿嫁给匈奴国王,更糟糕的是公主居然还爱上了别人。崇尚女性自由的花木兰,因此决定冒险帮助公主逃跑。影片中讲述的花木兰故事,在中国传说中并不存在,那是经过了导演的艺术改编。但是,影片中花木兰敢于冒险和追求自由的精神,与中国传说中的花木兰是相似的。

影片《花木兰》在美国引起了广泛的关注,美国新闻媒体赋诗称赞:"古有神州花木兰,替父从军英名响;今有卡通'洋木兰',融中贯西四海扬。"具有东方神韵的花木兰传奇,它一定会以自己独特的魅力传遍全世界!(倪爱珍编著)

Chapter 2

第二章

Unit 1

Chinese Dragon Culture

L ong (the dragon) is held in high esteem and plays a significant role in Chinese culture. From the Neolithic Age back 7000 years, the dragon germinated as a totem of primitive human. Even nowadays, people regard it as an auspicious creature and there are a variety of idioms and allusions related with dragon. The dragon has firmly embedded in Chinese culture during thousands of years in history and become the one that is encountered across all aspects of Chinese society and in the minds of its people. Thus, the Chinese dragon is comparable as the symbol of Chinese nation, the emblem of Chinese race as well as the token of Chinese civilization. Such terms as "posterity or descendents of the dragon" may always catalyze excitement, aspiration or pride in Chinese people's minds.

Then, what was the dragon's original form? How is the concept of it created? How the image of the dragon and its cultural connotations are evolved and what kind of role does it play in Chinese culture?

Various sources abound in ancient interpretations of Chinese dragon. Some have suggested that it is a flying dragon without legs, looking like a soaring python. An alternative view is that it has the appearance of a horse's head and a python's tail. Others have proposed that its shape is the merger of the following: its horns resemble those of a stag, his ears those of an ox, his head that of a camel, his eyes those of a rabbit, his neck that of a python, his belly that of a clam, his scales those of a carp,

his soles those of a deer, his claws those of an hawk. Later depictions of
the dragon reveal that its image has undergone a series of complex changes over the
original ones. It has been constantly enriched and gradually developed, as increasing totems are incorporated into it. Many scholars have made numerous further researches of its prototype and
brought about a list of theories. Some advocate that the early dragon is described as a species of
crocodile, while others maintain that it resembles lizard. And a part of the researchers propose that it
has characteristics of a horse. However, the theory of pythons as the origin of the Chinese dragon is
the widely accepted keynote. The system of this view was initially put forward by Wen Yi-duo in his
famous work *An Examination of Fuxi* (a legendary ruler). He notes that every time after the python
clan annexed another species, "they integrated his defeated enemy's emblem into their own. Such a
myth explains why the dragon appears to have attributes of various animals: legs of fierce animals,
the head of a horse, a hyena's tail, a stag's horns, a dog's claws, a carp's scales and tentacles."

Although the original image of the dragon was very simple, the ancient Chinese began to paint
their totem with more association and imagination as their links to other tribes grew stronger and
stronger. Such a figure was evolved into a completely different dragon or totem after a long period of
time. The dragon can be classified into different varieties according to their types or postures. It falls
into the following categories: scaly flood dragon, horned dragon, hornless dragon, winged dragon,
one-footed dragon, ichthyosaurus, one-head two-body dragon, double-headed dragon, firedrake and
etc. In addition, its gestures are as rich and varied as below: sitting dragon, walking dragon, flying
dragon, diving dragon, two dragons playing with a pearl of fire, and dragon amidst clouds, etc.

As a common totem for all of the Chinese, the dragon is traditionally regarded as the god of
wind, snow, rainfall, and floods. From the geographical point of view, most Chinese regions feature a
vast hinterland which is situated in a temperate climatic zone. Therefore, such advantages greatly facilitate the formation of a society that is founded upon agriculture and animal husbandry totally reliant upon its natural environment and in particular the climate. Timely wind and rain can bring
good harvest, thus each family is well-fed and well-clothed. On the contrary, drought or flooding may

Two Dragons Playing With A Pearl of Fire

cause the farmers to miss harvest and leave the land strewn with corpses of hunger victims. As a result, the python-like dragons are worshipped as rulers of water-related weather phenomenon who are the source of all that was beneficial to communal well being. For one thing, pythons are often found in deep wet valleys, pools or swamps. For another, they like sporting in water in rainy or hazy days and shuttling between forest and grassland. Therefore, they're deified as governors of water who have the capacity to summon wind and rain and to mount the clouds and ride the mist. In the beginning, the dragon originated as a totem of an ancient tribe. With the advance of history, culture of various nationalities blended together during the process of inter-tribal wars, population migration, mixed residence and intermarriage. Different tribes came to be united under a common banner and the dragon was adopted as a national totem.

With the establishment of a feudal society, emperors compared themselves to the dragon, thereby making it the exclusive symbol of imperial majesty. Chinese emperors thought they were the real dragons and the sons of the heaven. Thus the emperor's ceremonial dresses were called the dragon robes, the imperial cap the dragon crown, the throne the dragon seat, and the boats they took were named the dragon boats. Chinese dragon is used as an emblem of imperatorial authority in many terms, for example: "the dragon is indisposed (i.e. the king is sick)", "The dragon is in great rage (i.e. the reigning sovereign turn angry), and "the Majesty has a descendant of the dragon" (means the throne has a newly-born son). As a result, uniquely designed dragons can be seen on royal buildings such as the Imperial Palace, as well as in decoration and ornament.In modern times, belief in the dragon as the saint patron of the feudal rulers has faded without a trace. However, among people, dragon-related recreation customs has been passed down from remote times. The dragon is developed into a symbol of the spirit of the Chinese nation and has an important influence on all aspects of

Dragon Robes

China's cultural traditions and social lives. The dragon is widely used in denominating family names, pavilions, and even rivers and lakes. The dragon also plays an important part in Chinese festivals, such as dragon lantern show on festival of lanterns and dragon boat races on dragon boat festival. Chinese dragon seems omnipresent with dragon star hanging high above the sky, dragon vein lying deep under the ground, dragon-horse being a beast, dragon juniper being a plant, even the dragon appearing in China's twelve zodiacs (or symbolic animals which are used to designate years in the Chinese calendar). In addition, countless proverbs and idioms are labeled with the dragon, for example, "dragons rising and tigers leaping (i.e. a scene of bustling activity)", "like the flight of the dragon and the dance of the phoenix (i.e. lively and vigorous in calligraphy)", "doughty as a dragon and lively as a tiger (i.e. full of vim and vigor)", "moaning of dragons and howling of tigers", "crouching tiger, hidden dragon (i.e. undiscovered or concealed talents or experts)", "as energetic as a dragon and a horse" , and so on. In short, cultural phenomena associated with the dragon are beyond count.

It is worth mentioning that Chinese Long (dragon) has distinct features, comparing with the western dragon. In Chinese art, dragons are typically portrayed as an embodiment of massive virtues and unmatched qualities. They are fearless, staunch, and chivalrous warriors. Much deification has been bestowed upon the dragon ranging from prophecy and miraculous changing powers. Chinese dragon (Long) is a god-like creature and Dragon Palace is a treasure house and a symbol of imperial authority. Meanwhile, since it is righteous and benevolent, it would take any risk to bring rainfalls to the arid areas. In contrast to Chinese dragons, European dragons are considered as an incarnation of demon of evil.

Chinese dragon civilization prospers not only on the land of China, but also in many other regions and countries. The most compelling and biggest numbers of decorations are still dragon ornaments in Chinese residential sectors or Chinese communities around the globe. Chinese dragon is often utilized for decorative purpose on most of the eye-catching decorated archways standing at the entrance of Chinatowns. For example, 270 Chinese dragons painted on the arch (a Chinese gate) built at the 7th Street in Chinatown of Washington D.C. look spectacular. Walking in Chinatown, one cannot fail to notice a variety of dragon-style advertisements designed to attract customers and to discover dragon lanterns hanging around everywhere. Overseas Chinese traditional architectures have an unique style, partly due to the dragons adorned on them. For example, dragon carvings can be seen on every part of the Confucian Shrine in Nagasaki City of Japan , even the entire building is almost made with dragon carving, even the ramp in front of the temple were paved with dragon designs stairs. At overseas, a lot of places are named after Long (the dragon), such as Dragon City in Australia, granite dragon gate in Malaysia, Dragon-Spring Cave in Iwate county of Japan. Besides, you can catch a trace of the dragon if you're careful enough. For example, commemorative stamps with dragon patterns were ever issued in some nations like Italy and Japan.

In fact, Chinese dragon (Long) has participated, undergone and witnessed the formation process of the Chinese nation, a course of harmonious integration. Chinese people call themselves "descendants of the dragon", because they believe they've inherited the dragon-related cultural spirit in the same strain, which instead, doesn't mean that they bear genetic similarities to the dragon species. Cultural ideology produced in the evolution of the earliest Chinese ancestors is similar with the essence that derived from the development of the dragon families. Both types of spirit put an emphasis on harmony and tolerance, benevolence, nature abidance, and progress. Therefore, Chinese people can only be called offspring of the dragon. Such concepts as "descendants of the dragon" and "land of the dragon" have won world-wide recognition with the extensive spread of Chinese dragon culture.

The Vicissitudes of the Dynasties

In the time-honored traditions of China, variations in dynasties are fragmentary and complicated. The first order of business for each dynasty's founder was to establish a guohao or official name.

The earliest dynasty dates back to the 21st century B.C., with the establishment of the Xia Dynasty. Due to the brutal reign of Emperor Jie, he was overthrown by the military of Emperor Shangtang, thus creating the second dynasty, the Shang Dynasty.

The last monarch of the Shang Dynasty was Emperor Zhou. His tyranny induced seething discontent. Especially in Xiqi, where Ji Chang and his son Ji Fa, led a revolt against Emperor Zhou and established the Zhou Dynasty (the dynasty Zhōu and the Emperor Zhòu are different characters).

In the Late Zhou Dynasty came the Spring and Autumn and the Warring States periods (770-221 B.C.), as all of China was divided into vassal states, large and small. It wasn't until 221 B.C. that Emperor Qin conquered and annexed the six major states, establishing China's first feudal dynasty, The Qin Dynasty.

Emperor Qin ordering the masses to build the Great Wall and to dig irrigation channels, in brief, exploiting the labor of the people for wealth, met these practices with popular grievances. Coupled with the corrupt politics of the Qin Dynasty, this resulted in Liu Bang to lead a takeover and defeat Xiang Yu in 206 B.C., instituting the Han Dynasty. Ruling over 400 years, it was composed of the Western Han and the Eastern Han.

By the late period, there was an increase of vying for supremacy known as the famous Three Kingdoms period. During this time, war raged throughout involving struggle for authority by the war lords Cao Cao, Sun Quan, and Liu Bei. Zhuge Liang and Zhou Yu each competed with courage and prominent ability, filling brilliant chapters in Chinese history books.

The wars among the Three Kingdoms lasted over a half-century. Ultimately the Wu and the Shu states were overthrown by the Wei state. Yet these circumstances led to Sima Yan to seize power, establishing the Jin Dynasty, ruling for over 150 years.In 420 A.D, once again China entered a period of disunity during the Northern and Southern Dynasties.

The Southern Dynasty experienced four smaller dynasties in succession, the Song, Qi, Liang and Chen, while the Northern Dynasty was occupied and ruled by the Wei, Qi and Zhou.

In 581 A.D., a man named Yang Jian concluded China's current situation of division, unifying the north and the south, and establishing the Sui Dynasty, lasting only for a brief period. The Second Emperor Yang Guang, Whose reign was extremely brutal and corrupt, formed seething unpopular opinion. Consequently, Li Yuan with the help of his son, Li Shimin led the masses to topple the Sui Dynasty, establishing the Tang Dynasty in 618 A.D.

The Tang Dynasty was the most prosperous dynasty in the history of China. With great economic gains and a developing culture, they emerged as a great influence on the entire world. This continues today, as foreigners still refer to overseas Chinese as people of the Tang.

Due to the An Shi Rebellion, the decay of the Tang Dynasty that already was unable to reform itself was finally crushed, consecutively giving rise to the five smaller states of the Later Liang, the Later Tang, the Later Jin, the Later Han, and the Later Zhou, then continuing with ten small kindoms, which were the Former Shu, the Later Shu, Wu, the Southern Tang, Wu Yue, Min, Chu, the Southern Han, the Southern Ping and the Northern Han. This period is historically called "The Five Dynasties and Ten Kingdoms".

In 960 A.D. of the Later Zhou period, a general emerged, Zhao Kuangyin, wearing the robe of the emperor, thus founding the Song Dynasty.

The Song Dynasty frequently clashed with the Khitans, Nüzhen and Mongolias. Highly regarding literature before warfare, the Song wished to reside in peace. Later, treacherous court officials that held power faced substantial corruption. Ultimately, incapable of withstanding the increasing attacks of the Mongolias and having been conquered by the Kublai Khan in 1279, China entered a new era, the Yuan Dynasty.

Regardless any one particular feudal dynasty, the rise and fall of power all show a regular pattern in which exemplifies the corrupt politics in its later stages. As seen in the later period of the Yuan Dynasty, not only did the corruption cause its fall, but also the Han people resented their country being ruled by foreigners, resulting in many military insurrections. Once such revolt succeed under the leadership of Zhu Yuanzhang.

With the assistance of the writer Liu Ji and the military expertise of Xu Da, Zhu Yuanzhang overthrew the Yuan Dynasty in 1368, initiating the Ming Dynasty, which ruled nearly 300 years. But again with corruption in the courts, they were eventually defeated by Manchu, giving rise to the Qing Dynasty.

In the history of China, the Qing Dynasty marks a period of great prosperity, particularly under the reigns of emperors Kangxi, Yongzheng, and Qianlong. The areas of politics, economics, culture, and academics reached unprecedented heights.

The latter period of the Qing Dynasty followed the set pattern of corruption, allowing vulnerability. Foreign aggressors took advantage of this void and entered China, instilling wars of both foreign and domestic factions, signaling a period of suffering and misfortune. Sun Yat-sen had persuaded the people to oppose the emperor, resulting in the overthrow of the last feudal dynasty in the history of China, establishing the Republic of China in 1911. After that, through a long period of struggle against aggression and civil war, the People's Republic of China (brief for PRC) was eastablished led by Mao Zedong, in 1949.

Regarding the vicissitudes of the various Chinese dynasties, this popular poem has been passed down through the generations:

The Xia and the Shang, the Western Zhou

The Eastern Zhou contains two factions

The Spring and Autumn and the Warring States periods

Emperor Qin's unification, the two Han dynasties

The Three Kingdoms of the Wei, Shu, and Wu

Followed by the Jin Dynasty

Northern and Southern Dynasties existing side by side

The Sui, Tang, and the Five Dynasties

The Song, Yuan, Ming, and Qing arriving later

Completing the rule of the imperial court

Minority Ethnic Groups

China has been a united multi-ethnic country since ancient times. After the PRC was established, the central government confirmed altogether 56 ethnic groups within the country. Due to the overwhelming population of the Han nationality, the other 55 are considered to be ethnic minority groups. The various groups are: the Mongol, Hui, Tibetan, Uighur, Hmong, Yi, Zhuang, Bu, Korean, Manchu, Dong, Yao, Bai, Tujia, Hani, Kazakh, Dai, Li, Lisu, Kawa, She, Gaoshan, Lahu, Shui, Dongxiang, Nakhi, Jingpo, Kyrghiz, Tu, Daur, Mulao, Qiang, Blang, Salar, Maonan, Gelao, Xibo, Achang, Pumi, Tajik, Nu, Uzbek, Russian, Ewenki, De'ang, Baoan, Yugur, Vietanmese, Tatar, Drung, Elunchun, Hezhen, Menba, Luoba and the Jinuo.

According to the fifth national census compiled in 2000, the ethnic minorities ranking in the top five in terms of population are the Zhuang with the population of 17 million, the Manchu of 10.68 million, the Hui of 9.8 million, the Hmong of 8.94 million and the Uighur of 8.4 million people.

Each of China's ethnic groups are distributed throughout the country, mutually coinhabiting small as well as larger regions. The minorities live in regions of the Han, while the Han inhabit regions of ethnic minorities. Over the course of history, this pattern of diffusion has developed as each ethnic group associates with each other, making mutual exchanges. The minority population, although few, are distributed widely, mainly throughout Inner Mongolia, the Uighur, Ningxia Hui, Guangxi Zhuang and Tibetan autonomous regions; and the Yunnan, Guizhou, Qinghai, Sichuan, Gansu, Liaoning, Jilin, Hunan, Hubei, and Hainan, and Taiwan provinces, Yunnan being the most diverse with 25 different ethnicities.

China's ethnic minority areas are extensive regions abundant in natural resources. The surface area of grassland in China's minority regions amounts to over 300 million hectares, accounting for over 75% of the entire country's grassland. China is well known for its five distinct regions of grasslands and grazing pastures. The forested area occupies roughly 5.648 million hectares, consisting of 43.6% of the country, and the volume of available timber reaches 5.249 billion cubic meters accounting for over 55.9% of the nations reserve. Hydroelectricity reserves amount to 446 million kilowatts, accounting for approximately 65.9% of China's power consumption. Moreover, there are still vast amounts of mineral resources, plentiful flora and fauna, as well as the benefits of tourism.

The regional autonomy of ethnic minority regions reflects the government policy that links

them together. This was a major decision in politics. On May 5, 1945, under the leadership of the established Chinese Communist Party, the first provincial
level autonomous region was designated—Inner Mongolia. Later, the People's Republic of China established in succession: the Xinjiang, Uighur, Guangxi Zhuang, Ningxia Hui, and Tibetan autonomous regions. Currently, of the 55 ethnic minority groups, there has been established 44 autonomous regions, occupying an area of about 64% of China's total land mass. The Chinese government continues to implement policies of equality with regards to the ethnic groups' languages, systems of writing, and religious beliefs. All are respected and protected by law.

In the long history of the spread
of ethnic minority groups, a unique
culture has been formed. As social
customs, for example, every ethnic
group has a distinct mode of production and way of life reflecting many
modern aspects such as clothing, food
and drink, residences, marriage, etiquette, and funerary practices. With
regards to diet, China has about ten
ethnic minority groups that eat halal
foods in accordance with Islamic tradition. Funerary practices that honor

Songkrang Festival of the Dai Group

the deceased include traditions such as cremation, earth burial, water burial, and sky burial. Also a-
mong the various groups, the New Years Festival tradition is richly colorful. For example, the Tibetan
regional calendar includes the Lasha Shonton Festival. Groups such as the Hui and the Uighurs observe the Ramadan and Eid al-Azha festivals. While the Mongolians celebrate Nadam, the Dai maintain the Songkrang Festival, and the Yi ethnic group has the Torch Festival.

Family Ideology

The notion of family to the Chinese holds special meaning, as the concepts of a warm safe household, united as one. The family consists of a loving mother and a strict father, a virtuous wife,
and cosseted son. Everyone is familiar with the mountains and rivers, edible delicacies, and the beautiful historical legends of their native hometowns. From this love for the family and one's birthplace,
a feeling of pride of the country is invoked. Chinese living at home and returning from abroad are truly the descendents of the Yellow and Fiery Emperors, with great respect for their motherland.

China is an extremely affectionate country, placing much emphasis on the family, making them
a very homebound nationality. Home, family affection, and reunion weigh heavily in the hearts and
minds of the Chinese. The reunification of the whole family continues to be a core tradition of Chi-

nese culture. There are sayings such as "blood is thicker than water" and "every festival, and I miss my relatives twice as much". When the Spring Festival, Pure Brightness Festival, Mid-Autumn Festival, and the Double Yang Festival arrive, on these days Chinese people will all miss their relatives twice as much.

The Spring Festival is China's most celebrated annual holiday. Every year on this day family members that work or study away from home will make every effort to return home. Despite the distance of travel or economic hardships, much importance is placed on returning home to reunite with their families. Reunion is in fact the essence of the Spring Festival.Each family member sits next to each other around a steaming dining table, with festive happiness and excitement. This could be said that this is the greatest characteristic of the New Year and exhibits deep love and affection for one's family.

The 15th day of the eighth month is the Mid-Autumn Festival, which also holds the tradition of family reunion. Making use of the full moon, the entire family, old and young, sit at the table, and listen the words of their grandparents, as the children laugh. Bathed in the moonlight, everyone shares in this domestic bliss. This continues to be in the psyche of every Chinese person. Therefore the Mid-Autumn Festival has a special place in the hearts of the Chinese, the reunion being a profound symbol of sentiment.

Chinese people have been influenced by Confucianism for thousands of years, "孝"(filial piety), is regarded as the Chinese household's most important virtue. The Chinese will often say, "Of one hundred things, to be filial is the first", and "A filial son is a worthy grandson." Also commonly said is, "Be forever filial". The notion of being filial is representative of Chinese culture and is a core concept in the hearts and minds of individuals. China has always been know as a country of etiquette, emphasizing love and affection for their relatives, friends, life, and their birthplace, as well as advocating respect for their elders and cherishing their young as a standard of ethics. Confucian ideology encompasses eight concepts to live by: filial piety, duty, loyalty, faith, courtesy, righteousness, honesty, and humility. Among these, filial piety is the most virtuous. It is often said, "A Loving father and filial son is brotherly friendship and respect." This exemplifies an embodiment of the thousands of years of cultural moral principals used to rear younger generations.

In a Chinese household, the opinions of the elders are greatly respected. It is often quoted, "The elder of the family is the treasure." and "A deaf ear to the elder's speech results in nothing to eat before the eyes." The latter phrase is particularly used, reflecting the elder's guidance of the younger generation. The Chinese family also stresses the importance of a child's education and character development. Many proverbs demonstrate these ethics, such as "An unlearned son is the workings of the father." and "A child stealing a needle as an adult will steal gold."

For a Chinese person, there is great importance of reunion, love, the virtue of filial piety, and the emphasis of peace within the family. The most sought after expectation is a peaceful happy home while working contently, family and all things flourishing. People who cause too much inter-family strife create the most regret. A Chinese poem says, "If the stem is born of the root, why should one prosper at the expense of the other?" When there is a conflict in the management of household affairs, it is a taboo to discuss these problems in the presence of others. Therefore it is often said, "If the house is disgraced, one should not scatter gossip to the wind." Also said is, "Harmony is precious." and "Amiability makes you wealthy."These are very important to Chinese individuals as well as greatly influential to social prosperity.

Due to the great influence of the feudal patriarchal system, the notion of the clanastic family is emphasized and advocates, "rightly treat the respectable and the humble, the elder and the young", paying attention to "the different ways one gets along with the respectable the humble, and the elder and the young". Also addressed is the position within the family's hierarchy. It will be regarded as impolite if a Chinese addressed the elder by name directly. In the Chinese feudalistic society, the strict concept caused the formation of the system of the feudal ethical code of the Three Cardinal Guides (ruler guides subject, father guides son, and husband guides wife) and the Five Constant Virtues (benevolence, righteousness, propriety, wisdom, and fidelity).

To reiterate the concept of family, the household clan symbol is simply the family name. These have systematically been recorded since before the Han Dynasty. The culture formed by the family name exemplifies the prosperity and stability of the family. Recording genealogy is thus a continuing activity within the Chinese culture and is an important medium for the importance on the notion of kinship. Seeking the root of one's ancestry is the basis and discovering the relations of the parents lets the individual know that they are not at all alone in the world. At the same time, knowing that one's actions will not disrespect their ancestors, the success of oneself depends on the preservation of one's ancestry. Thus one understands humbleness, and knows how to better deal with personal relationships. Therefore, Chinese people believe that their genealogy is an extremely important matter.

In the time-honored tradition of Chinese history, there has continued a pursuance of prosperity and unification. Thus in the eyes of a Chinese person, his or her family, although very important, is equally important with one's country, especially in the eras of wars. During this times of crisis, larger numbers of gentleman display benevolence by defending the country, and show love for one's country as one's family, abandoning a small family, to look after everyone. For their country's safety they offer their life, being very proud people. In China, family and country are interwoven. As this civilization continues for over five thousand years united as one, the feeling of sentiment for family and one's nation have remained constant.

Marriage Customs

Chinese people regard marriage as one of the top priorities of life, bringing much happiness to the clan, as the family's incense continues to burn, maintaining a stable society. Therefore there are many distinct kinds of marriage customs, the ceremonies having many complicated aesthetics.

Traditional Chinese wedding is comprised of Three Letters and Six Etiquettes.

The Three Letters includes a request letter, gift letter, and the welcoming letter.

The request letter is used as a formal agreement of the parents to allow the marriage.

The gift letter is a detailed list of prepared gifts, including a larger gift. The welcoming letter is the letter for welcoming the bride, which is used by groom on the day of the marriage when he goes to his bride's household to take her into his home.

The Six Etiquettes refers to the six protocols of traditional Chinese marriage—na cai, wen ming, naji, na zheng, qing qi, and qin ying.

Na cai is referred to nowadays as a marriage proposal. In ancient Chinese marriages, the strongly emphasized is the fate of the parents and the words of the matchmaker. Therefore, for a man and woman to get married, the man must employ a matchmaker to go to the house of the intended bride to propose marriage.

Wen ming is usually called he bazi. The man inquires about the woman's surname, birthday, and time of day she was born to foresee good or ill luck.

With regards to na ji, also called guo wending or xiao ding, if each other's name and birth data is compatible, the matchmaker will be sent to the woman's family to offer small gifts.

Na Zheng, or guo dali, means the man's family formally sends betrothal gifts such as money, bride cake presents, and pastries.

Qing qi is what we say today as selection day, it is the day of the wedding chosen by a fortuneteller as asked by the man's family.

Afterwards, on the day of the marriage, the groom takes a four-wheeled carriage to greet the bride. This is called qin ying (welcoming the relatives).

The traditional Chinese marriage ceremony mainly contains the following customs:

1.Exchanging age charts. If the each other's name and birth data is shown to be compatible after the proposal of the matchmaker, the two families will exchange each other's birth information as initial proof of engagement.

2. Guo wending (meaning sending small gifts). It is as a prelude to guo dali (sending large gifts). This usually takes place one month before the wedding ceremony. The man's family chooses a propitious day to offer three things: domestic animals, wine, and gifts with the formal letter of engagement.

3. Guo dali (meaning sending large gifts). This is the grandest ceremony, which takes place 15 or 20 days before the marriage. The man selects a fortunate day to offer a bestowal money and many other gifts.

4.An chuang (meaning installing the bed). Several days before the wedding, a particularly fortunate day is chosen, because a long and happy life requires a new bed to be moved to a suitable place. Later, before the wedding day, to ensure a long and happy life, the grandmother of the bride makes up the bed, readies the mattress and lays the sheets of the dragon and phoenix, and spreads on the bed delicacies they are fond of such as jujube, cinnamon sticks, dried lychee, as well as red and mung beans.

After installing the bed, no one is allowed enter the new bridal chamber or touch the new bed until the new couple have entered the room on the wedding night. After the newly weds enter the room, they can allow the children to sit on the bed and eat the fruits. This is called ya chuang (meaning pressing the bed), and allows one to obtain one hundred sons and one thousand grandsons. The bride's peer brothers are then allowed to make loud noises in the bridal chamber. From antiquity, it is believed if the new people are not noisy they will not expel, the more noise, the more expelling, signifying the noise driving away evil and bringing luck to the marriage.

5. Sending the dowry. After the guo dali, the bride's family must send a box (dowry) to the bridegroom's family no later than one day before the wedding ceremony. This box, large or small, indicates the status and wealth of the bride's family. Beside precious stones and jewelry, the box may contain symbols of prosperity, such as scissors (symbolizing a pair of flying butterflies), candy (indicating sweetness), a wallet and belt (meaning wealth), a flower vase (indicating blooming riches and honor), a copper basin and shoes (meaning a happy and long life), quilts with embroidered dragons and phoenixes, bed sheets, and pillows.

6. Shang Tou. One the eve before the wedding, the bride and groom's families mutually select a good date and time (the man's family beginning an hour earlier) to conduct the shang tou ceremony. This ceremony must have a man from a good life, and a woman from a good life (the families independently choose people from an older generation or friends and relatives with healthy children and a happy marriage) to preside over the ceremony. The newly wed couple puts on pajamas. The bride's family selects a table near a window that the moon shines through, lighting dragon and phoenix candles, and incense, together with lotus seeds and jujubes, making three bowls of soup, putting six or nine in each bowl. Fresh fruit, roasted meat, and a chicken heart, are included to pay homage to the heavens. The families of the man and the woman will also prepare a measuring tape, mirror, scissors, a so-called dragon head mirror and cuts the measuring tape with the scissors. In order for their brightness to last, the chosen good man and woman by the families then comb the couple's hair saying, "One brush for the hair, two brushes for mutual respect in old age, three brushes for many descendents, and four brushes for the four strips of silver on the upmost branches of the tree." The shang tou symbolizes the new couple's transition into adulthood.

The Couple Bow to Each Other

7. Ying qin (meaning escorting the bride). In China, escorting the bride is the climax of the wedding ceremony. Accompanied by the families, relatives and friends, the bridegroom greets the bride with a bouquet of flowers. Upon arriving her house, the groom first must enter the door, in order to receive the bride. During this process he must subject himself to a series of intelligence and physical stamina tests, as well as reciting terms of endearment or love songs. Also a key for entering the door is to give the older and younger sisters of the bride gifts or red envelopes with money, often 10 or 20 yuan each. When the sisters are satisfied, the groom is allowed to enter. Upon entering, the sisters give the brothers of the groom tea and cake, receiving the guests. After entering the door, the bride follows her older sister, or bridesmaid, as she is presented her to the father. The parents then present the bride to the groom as a formal rite of a man and woman meeting.

The new couple will first kneel, express their gratitude toward the heavens, and then offer their parents tea as they bow (kowtow). The bride then prepares two envelopes of li shi (money), representing prestige prosperity, and benefit. After passing through the door, she presents them to her bridegroom's sister.

8. Chu men (meaning exiting the door). When going outdoors, the bride's elder sister or the maid of honor shields the bride from the sun with a red parasol, symbolizing a flourishing branch with leaves. The elder sister and the younger sisters walk side by side, facing the sky. Rice (red and mung beans may be included) is then sprinkled by them over the parasol head or tossed in the air used to feed the Golden Rooster, so that the Golden Rooster will eat the food and not peck at the bride. The elder sister then carries the bride on her back to the marriage sedan. It is said that the bride's feet should not touch the ground for fear of bad luck. Before entering the sedan, the bride bows to the friends and relatives as a show of respect.

9. Guo men (meaning crossing the entrance). After the bride exits her house, she pays a formal visit the groom's household, paying respects to the paternal aunt, the parents, and the elders of his family.

10. Sanzhao huimen (meaning in three days returning to the entrance). On the third day after the wedding ceremony, the new couple returns to visit the bride's parents, bringing roasted pork and other gifts as offerings to their ancestors. Sometimes, they even live with them for a day before returning to the man's home.

Modern Chinese wedding ceremonies still retain some aspects of traditional customs, but are much more simplified. Even as new styles of wedding ceremonies emerge, generally, the wedding ceremony of the Chinese embodies grandness, happiness and liveliness. Friends, family, and the community continue to compliment them and wish them well. There are proverbs such as, "live to old age in conjugal bliss" and "give birth to a child soon" in congratulating the newly weds.

Unit 2

The Four Great Inventions

China is an ancient country that has established a brilliant history of civilization. The four great inventions: papermaking, printing, gunpowder and the compass are China's substantial contributions to science and technology, having had much influence in the history of human development. Karl Marx has insightfully indicated that the three inventions of gunpowder, the compass, and printing indicate the arrival of the bourgeoisie society. Gunpowder literally exploded on society, crushing the knights of cavalry. The compass not only opened the world market, but also allowed for colonization. Printing became the new tool of learning and recording scientific methods, as well as having great leverage in psychological development.

Papermaking

In the Eastern Han Dynasty (105 A.D.), using the basis of the current technology, Cai Lun invented and popularized a new method of papermaking. Forever altering the oracle bone script of the Shang Dynasty, the Western Zhou's bronze inscriptions, and the bamboo writing slips, wood documents, and thick writing silks of the Spring and Autumn period used to record history. This important contribution allowed the Han Dynasty to suddenly flourish in economics and cultural development.

Cai Lun Invented Papermaking Method

Cai Lun used tree bark, hemp fiber, rags, and fishing nets. Employing a series of artistic and scientific procedures, he pressed them together, duplicated them, and baked the material to create a plant fiber based product, thus allowing the manufacture of a significant amount of paper. Cai Lun presented the paper to the Han Emperor. Upon receiving it, the emperor expressed great recognition for his methods, thus making it be known under the heavens and on earth. Paper made by Cai Lun was officially called Caihou paper in 105 A.D., which is considered by some to be the year in which modern paper was invented.

Printing Technology

Around the period of the Tang Dynasty, people invented a method of block printing. Its concrete procedures are: cutting and shaping wood blocks, then writing the character in reverse on tissue paper and pasting it to the wood block, doing this for every character according to the number of strokes. Later, a chisel is used to carefully carve the block as to create a raised character block with each stroke being visible. After the entire wood block is carved, a document can then be printed. When printing, first brush ink on the surface of the carving, then use white paper to cover the block. Using a clean brush, lightly brush the back of the paper. Finally pulling off the paper as a completed page. After printing several pages consecutively, the pages are then bound into a volume, eventually becoming a book. Since this method of printing uses carved wood, it is also called "woodblock printing."

Bi Sheng Created Clay Movable Type of Printing

Printing during the time of the Northern Song Dynasty period was improved by common inventor Bi Sheng. With generations of experience and through trial and error, during the reign of Emperor Ren Zong (1041-1048 A.D.), he created clay movable type. This implemented typesetting, greatly increasing printing efficiency, achieving a momentous revolution in the history of printing.

Gunpowder

In the process of ancient Chinese alchemists concocting pills of immortality, gunpowder was invented. In the course of events, they incidentally discovered that a mixture of the appropriate amount of sulfur, saltpeter, and charcoal would quickly burn and even explode as it is ignited. This in fact is the earliest known formula for gunpowder.

Arrow with Gunpowder

At that time, people had little interest in using gunpowder for military applications. Until the late Tang Dynasty and during the period of the Five Dynasties, the whole country was in rebellion. The originators of gunpowder, from rich and honorable scholars of wealthy families, became destitute and homeless, thus enlisting in the army, gradually developing a string of weaponry that employed gunpowder. As the Song Dynasty arrived, most major cities had weapons manufacturing industries involving gunpowder. The military employed generous amounts of gunpowder by use of fire canisters and exploding arrows. In the early period of gunpowder weaponry, the formidable power was limited, it could not replace the cold arms of the knife and sword. But after the middle of the Southern Song dynasty, outstanding improvements were made with regards to gunpowder artillery. From that time on, and throughout the wars between the Song, the Jin, the Yuan, the advantage of gunpowder became more frequently used.

Compass

The compass is a scientific instrument that uses a magnet and the polarity of the earth's magnetic field to indicate direction. The earliest compass that emerged was called a si nan (south pointer). It was commonly used during the Warring States Period. It is carved natural magnetic stone resembling a spoon that was balanced on a smooth chassis, surrounded by intervals of 24 directions. Pushed slightly, the needle would and spin around. After the rotations stopped, longer end of the needle would point towards south.

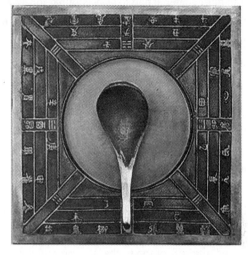

The Former Compass—Sinan

The south-pointing compasses that were made with natural magnets were with weak magnetism. Until the Song dynasty arrived, people invented a method of artificial magnetization, producing a north pointing fish-shaped compass and the much more practical north-pointing needle compass. By rubbing magnetite on a steel needle and using the magnetism created to point to north. Later a pan indication direction was installed, thus being called "luo pan" (compass), marking a significant stride the history of compass development.

By the 11th century A.D., the compass had become a commonly used instrument of direction, greatly contributing to the development of ocean navigation.

The Abacus and Calculation

The abacus, a traditional Chinese calculating tool, is a significant invention of ancient China. It has been widely used in the world before the emergence of Arabic numerals. The abacus has a history of more than 600 years, the basis of the invention being the counting rods, which already had long been used by the Chinese. In ancient times, people used these small sticks to calculate, the small sticks were called "suan chou", and the method of calculation was called "chou suan" (rod calculation). Due to the increase of development and production, using small sticks for calculation was limited. Consequently, a more advanced tool of calculation was invented—the abacus.

There are many different forms the abacus, and the materials vary as well. Generally, they are made of wood or plastic, with a rectangular frame and an array of equal number of counting beads. A horizontal beam in the middle divides the abacus into upper and lower sections with straight pillars through the middle of the beads. Each rod containing the beads is commonly called a "dang". Abacuses may have nine, eleven, or fifteen rods. There are two beads above the horizontal bridge, each bead represents the number five. Below the bridge on each rod are five beads abacus used in finance has four beads below the bridge, each bead representing the number one.

There exists a beautiful story regarding the history of abacus. According to legend, during the reign of the Yellow Emperor there were no accountants. After uniting the tribes, more and more material had to be accounted for. Every family and every household continuously had more things to count, creating much confusion with numbers, thus aggravating the emperor. Consequently, a scribe in the emperor's palace discovered a way to use wild fruits to keep record of who killed what prey. But who expects such brightness for long—the various wild fruits were deposited and after some time they all became rotten, sending the accounts into chaos. Thereupon the scribe once again discovered a way of using different colored stones to keep track of the prey, this way, he did not fear of rot or change in color. At this, the scribe was happy, but the accounts were not rightfully safeguarded. One day, as he went out on business, his son arrived with a group of children. They were drawn to the scribe's pan with the beautifully colored stones inside, taking great interest. The curious children carelessly quarreled over the stones, causing the plate to fall and shatter, the stones scattering everywhere. Once again, the scribe's accounts were ruined.

Having no alternative, he crouched down to the floor and gathered the stones. As this happened, the wife of the scribe, Huanü came over to him, giving instructions, "You should bore an eye through each stone and bind them with string, that way it won't be so confusing!" The scribe at once took out a dagger and carved a hole in each stone, and one by one strung them together. Each time a thread obtained ten or one hundred stones, a different colored stone was placed in between. This made it much easier to handle the financial records, allowing the scribe to know in his heart the workings of the numbers. Since then, there were no fraudulent claims made from outside the palace doors.

In the wake of continuous production and forward development, the various types of prey increased, the skins were more and more, and there was more variety, thus requiring more stones and again becoming very troublesome. This made the scribe quite vexed. When Empress Feng learned of this, she said to him, "To figure the accounts you need not use so many stones, just one hundred stones will be sufficient". Even though the scribe did not understand, Empress Feng continued to say, "For example, today's hunters brought back only five deer, and so you would push five stones on a bamboo rod. Tomorrow if they return with six deer, five plus six is 11, then move one bead on the next rod. The number of beads will only be two, but in fact they represent the number 11. Each time it exceeds the number ten or one hundred, simply advance one more place." The scribe then asked, "How do you record the number after advancing to the next place?" Empress Feng replied, "That's easy, simply make a mark after advancing to the next place. For example, after adding up to the number ten, make a circle, after one hundred add two circles. After one thousand add three circles, and after ten thousand add four circles. These can be called tens, hundreds, thousands, and ten thousands." Therefore the scribe returned home and made a large clay plate, and in gathering pearls form the belly of a tortoise, he bore a hole through each one. Every strand represented ten, as numbers 1 to 100 could be represented, calling it the abacus. After this, it became much easier to record the numbers, giving rise to the tens, hundreds, thousands, and ten thousands place values. Therefore to handle the accounts, one did not need so many stones.

The abacus is China's calculator, having been invented 5000 years ago. In the progressing times, constant changes have been made to the abacus, forming today's methods of calculation. This invention was fundamental particularly in times of illiteracy. As long as people could understand the simple principals and operating rules of the abacus, everyone in society could use it. Therefore, in ancient times, the abacus quickly diffused to a wide range in China.

Abacus

With continued use of the abacus, people summarized many computations as mnemonic devices, greatly increasing the speed of calculations. This method of calculation is called "zhu suan", corresponding to four mathematical operations, collectively known as the laws of "zhu suan". With regards to general calculation, the abacus is much faster than the calculator, especially in the areas of addition and subtraction. When employed, the mnemonic devices determine which way to move the beads in relation to the problem. Calculations with the abacus are quick and convenient. Chinese stores have commonly employed the use of this of computation instrument. As the Ming Dynasty arrived, not only could the abacus perform the four basic rules of arithmetic (addition, subtraction, multiplication, and division), but also it could calculate land surface area and dimensions of various sized objects.

Due to the simple manufacture of the abacus, the low cost, easy mnemonic rules to remember, and convenience of computation, it has been used throughout China, in addition to circulating to Japan, Korea, the United States, and regions in Southeast Asian countries.

Today we have already entered the age of modern computers, yet the ancient abacus still plays and important function. In China, every type of industry has an abacus computation expert. In using the abacus to calculate, not only is it convenient to use for math, but it also develops hand and eye coordination and is an exercise for the brain.

Post Roads and Relay Stations

There are many types of Ancient Chinese roads such as galloping road, post road, and plank road. Among these the post horse road was the most important in ancient times as a passage for horse and carriage, opening up many innovations of transportation and exchange. Ancient post roads have many names, such as government road, plank road, and salt road. The greatest difference between the post roads and the small inter-mountain roads, was the lack of necessary maintenance, they were more level, and accessible by horses and people. Rulers of successive dynasties used the post roads to transmit documents, transport tribute, and for official inspections, as the use of the post roads become extremely prominent. In ancient times, communication was undeveloped and information difficult to acquire. The post road assumed the responsibility of the transportation of goods, people traveling from afar, and the delivery of products and services, helping to maintain the livelihood of the people. On the wayside of the road, relay stations for post horses were implemented. Passing carriages could stop there for reserve horses and vehicles. Post roads are ancient China's primary form of dry land communication and transport, also serving as military outposts, such as the famous Silk Road, the ancient Huguang post road, the Nanyang and Xiangyang roads, the Qinghao Passage, and the ancient Mei Pass.

Post City of Jiming Mountain

Post roads and relay stations, they were mainly used to transmit orders, military intelligence, documents, government officials, provisions, weapons, equipment, tribute, services, and other goods. In addition, the relay stations provided much needed repairs for the carriages, feed and fodder for the horses, and lodging. When sending official documents and military intelligence, or possibly a government official en route, these stations provided a place of rest and as a means to exchange horses. China is one of the first countries to establish efficient lines of communication and transportation. Although the history of the relay stations date over 3000 years, not many of the cultural relics remain. Among these is the famous Jiming Mountain in Hubei province's Huailai county. Also, a widely known structure in the Yicheng district exists as completely intact.

Post stations were used in surveying the land and as checkpoints. Feudal officials used these stations when traveling on inspections. As goods and services were delivered, the direction of travel would depend on the postmark. The Minister of War employed these postmarks with extremely strict regulation. In particular, these were reserved for specific purposes such as dispatching troops and delivering documents, all required by the Ministry of War to display their pass to continue travel past the stations. Delivery letters by horseback also required the proper documents for the post stations. In case one needed to reach the capital of the country, or perhaps an outside area quickly, there was a form to fill in. The bound document called ma shang fei di (lit. on a horse flying) would then travel 300 li (600 km) in a day. Documents marked as urgent traveled 400, or perhaps 600 li in a day, the postmark indicating the time limit for delivery, but this way was not excessively used. In the Qing Dynasty the regulation of relay stations had reached perfection, with set punishable violations by law. By the end of this period of rule, the relay stations began to be linked closely to offices of information, becoming one of the same.

Post stations in ancient China played a significant role and function in ancient times. Communi-

cations under these methods were greatly expanded. The stations involved every aspect of politics, the economy, culture, the military, and the transmis-
sion of official decrees, leading to a high level of increase in the exchange of information. Relay stations of each dynasty in ancient times had their own characteristics. The official seal was different,
but the strict regulation and legal formalities were similar. Feudal monarchs used these stations to
gather intelligence, collect harvest, issue commands, and relay information, reaching a high plateau
of feudal government control. At that time the level of science and technology was restricted compared to the speed and the amount of goods transported, but its strict level of organization and coverage compare to modern day communications and transport. It can be said that that time allowed for a
basis of our modern system. Today, postal systems, highways, trade routes, and logistics of distribution have replaced relay stations. In the periphery of relay stations, there was frequently an endless
stream of horses and carriages, exceptionally bustling with activity, and taking shape as busy cities.
China has several major cities, for example, Shenyang, the capital of Liaoning province, that owes its
development to the presence of ancient relay stations.

The Sedan and Horse Carriage

The sedan, formerly called the emperor's carriage, shoulder carriage, or Yan zi, was in ancient
times a unique means of transportation. According to historical documents, the fledgling stages
of the sedan chair were already prevalent in the Xia Dynasty. From the pre-Qin to the Jin dynasties,
the ruling social class began using sedans for outings. Even though at that time their use was not very
widespread, a small section of royalty increasingly employed them. In the Jin dynasty, Gu Kaizhi's
painting Admonitions of the Instructress to the Palace Ladies vividly portrays a scene of Emperor
Cheng of the Western Dynasty and imperial concubine Ban Jieyu on the same sedan chair. Up until
the Tang Dynasty, the use of sedan chairs were generally reserved for regal purposes, women, the elderly and sick, and government officials. During the Song Dynasty, sedan use received widespread
popularity, producing many new complex designs. The well-known painting *Along the River During the
Qingming Festival* depicts main street in the Song Dynasty capital city Bianliang, revealing many sedan
chairs being used. Even though they look very similar to the ones carried by two people of the Han
and Tang eras, the essence of the material was different. For example, hardwood was heavily relied
upon and there were artistic decorative carvings, making them quite pleasing to the eye. During the
Northern Song period, sedan chairs advanced another step in popularity. As the later stages of the
Ming Dynasty arrived, even the small landlords, as it was commonly said, preferred sedans to horseback. In the Ming and Qing dynasties, the sedan chair developed to be carried by four or eight people.
More and more aristocrats preferred the sedan as a means of transportation because there was less
fatigue as opposed to riding in horse carriages, as it was smooth, steady, and comfortable. During this
period, sedan chairs became the principal means of transportation.

Generally there are two types of ancient sedan chairs. One type has no curtain and is called the cool sedan, also called bright sedan or xian sedan. The warm sedan was equipped with a curtain, thus also called a dark sedan. There were different government sedans manufactured with curtains of brightly colored cloth and with strict regulations. For example, in the period of the Ming and Qing dynasties, a common official would use blue or green wool to make the sedan curtain. Therefore appropriately called, the blue government sedan, or the green government sedan. As the sedans played different roles, they were named differently. The one used by the royal family was called a carriage sedan, sedans used by high government officials were called official sedans, and ones used to escort the bride to a wedding are called wedding sedans.

Wedding Sedan

There can be few or many porters, generally two to eight people. Among the common people, two people carried the sedan. Government officials were allowed four to eight porters. Moreover, regulations set during the Qing dynasty stated that officials of the third rank or higher were permitted to ride in a sedan with a pointed silver top and black curtains. Within the capital, four porters were provided and in leaving the capital, eight men were used. Officials of fourth rank and below were only allowed to ride in a small sedan with a tin roof carried by two people. The landlords and members of gentry were obliged to ride in darkly painted sedans with flat roofs and black curtains. Furthermore, there were other strict regulations regarding litters that reflected the hierarchy of feudal society.

The horse and carriage was another imperative mode of transportation in ancient China, with a history of at least 3,000 years. Archeological evidence implies that during the Shang Dynasty, two horses drove most carriages. Towards the end of the Shang and the beginning of the Zhou Dynasty, a carriage driven by four horses emerged. Evidence shows the Shang Dynasty, technology used for manufacturing ancient horse carriages was relatively advanced. Carriages in the Zhou Dynasty were fundamentally the same as in the Shang period, but the structure was greatly improved upon. For example, the shaft and the crosspiece became curved, more spokes were added to the wheels, and a roof was installed on top. The reigns and mountings for the horses also developed. Leaving nothing to be desired, the Shang carriages increased the production of ornamentation, copper bells, copper spurs, and various other parts. In efforts to make the carriages stronger, there was a number of crucial copper components added. Wood linchpins were upgraded to ones made of copper and the yolk carried copper reinforcement. In addition, also used in manufacturing the carriages were lead, gold, silver, bone, shell, and animal skins to produce a multitude of fine detail.

Carriages of the Shang Dynasty were originally pulled by two horses and then gradually increased to three, four or six. The two-horse cart was called "pian" and the three-horse carriage was referred to as "can". Carriages pulled by four horses were called "si". The Western Zhou, Spring and

Autumn, and the Warring States periods were a flourishing eras for the
ancient Chinese chariot, lasting over a millennium. During this time, the construction and ornamentation were far stronger and more luxurious than the carriages of the Shang Dynasty, reaching a new stage of perfection. Ancient chariots were not only employed for military purposes, but also to escort royalty, being a clear indicator of power and status. This tradition continued
until the final years of the Qing Dynasty where in some northern cities, commoners would not dare
ride in a carriage without proper authority.

Interestingly enough, if we compare the spoke wheel of the war chariot from the Zhou Dynasty
period with that of the Eurasian grasslands, Egypt, and Southwest Asia, many similarities and even
minor details are prevalent. For example, the East and the West both used spoke wheels, adopting
the technology to shape wood in a circle. The Pelham bit, the whip, and other components, are similar in manufacture, as technology diffused to different regions. Methods of use and cultural restrictions are also interlinked, as all are built by the jurisdiction of the ruling social elite, as the various degrees of chariots were viewed as an instrument of wielding power. There were also a few discrepancies between the eastern and western regions' chariot. These were mainly in the dimensions of the
body, the quality of the components, and the decoration, this in part due to the separation of geography and differences in cultural traditions.

Unit 3

Yellow River Culture

The Yellow River is the second longest river in China and the fifth longest in the world. The
headwaters originate in lake Qinghai in the Kunlun Mountains, as it flows through nine
provinces and autonomous regions: Qinghai, Sichuan, Gansu, Ningxia, Inner Mongolia, Shaanxi,
Shanxi, Henan, and Shandong. With a total length of 5464 kilometers and a drainage area of 750,000
square kilometers, the Yellow River is the mother river of China, producing one of the world's oldest
and brilliant civilizations that would shape Chinese history.

The Yellow River culture occupies an extensive history. At the Xi Hongdu ruins found on the
eastern bank of the Yellow River in Ruicheng county of Shanxi province, there have been discovered
stone tools that date to over 1.8 million years. This convinces us of early human activity before that
time. The Xi Hongdu site unearthed more than 30 stone artifacts. Up to now, this is the earliest representation of humankind in China. Whether existing during the time of the Three Sovereigns, the
Xia, Shang, or Western Zhou Dynasties, all civilizations emerged from the Yellow River basin, the
cradle of ancient Chinese civilization.

In 4,000 years of history, beginning of the Xia Dynasty in the 21st century B.C., several successive dynasties have established their capitals in the Yellow River basin continuously for over 3,000

years. These are known in Chinese history as the Seven Ancient Capitals of China, examples of these city centers are Anyang, Xi'an, Luoyang, and Kaifeng.

As the capital of the Shang Dynasty, Anyang (at that time under the jurisdiction of Yellow River basin) contains numerous oracle bone inscriptions. Some have been excavated, revealing the precursor of Chinese characters. Xi'an (containing Xianyang) is a well-known ancient capital encompassing a 1,000 year period of history, serving since the times of the Western Zhou, Qin, Han, and continuing to the Sui and Tang, totaling thirteen dynasties altogether. After the Eastern Zhou Dynasty moved their capital to Luoyang, the Eastern Han, Wei, Sui, Tang, the later Liang, and the later Zhou dynasties all once formerly had established Luoyang as their capital, occupying a history over 900 years. Thus it is known as the Ancient Capital of Nine Dynasties.

Hukou Waterfall in Yellow River

Located on the southern bank of the Yellow River, Kaifeng established as the capital of the Northern Song Dynasty for over 200 years. In this stretch of history, the political, economic, and cultural centre continued to be located in the Yellow River basin. The middle and lower reaches of the Yellow River reveals the country's earliest development of science, technology, literature, and art.

Around 2000 B.C., bronze wares had already emerged in the Yellow River basin. As the Shang Dynasty arrived, bronze-smelting technology reached a high plateau. Simultaneously, the smelting of iron began to develop, indicating a new level of productivity and development.China's four great inventions are all products of the Yellow River basin. From The Book of Songs to Tang poetry, Song prose, literary classics, as well as large amounts of cultural canonical texts, much literature has been produced in this region.

After the Northern Song Dynasty, although the economic center of the country gradually shifted from Yellow River area to the Yangtze River valley, the Yellow River basin and its lower plains still retained an important status in course of economic and cultural development. The long cultural history of the Yellow River basin has left a rare and precious legacy for the Chinese nationality. Not only is the Yellow River culture a jewel to China, but it has also made an indelible contribution to human civilization.

But in the wake of the glorious culture of the Yellow River, it has increasingly faced major challenges, especially in the modern era. Due to excessive development and environmental factors, the destruction of the ecology has been quite severe. Of all the major rivers in the country, the Yellow River is the most difficult to manage. The northwest region's barren Gobi Desert faces severe drought as large part of the river basin experiences semi-arid to arid conditions. The northern reaches contain vast desert, sandstorms, continuing damage to the water, as well as poor soil drainage.

These factors have created an extremely frail ecosystem, thus obstructing the economic and social development of the Yellow River basin.

Currently, management and proper development on Yellow River is a top priority to keep sustainable social and economic development in the Yellow River valley, in efforts to reinvigorate the once glorious Yellow River culture.

The Silk Road

The term Silk Road originates from German geographer Ferdinand von Richthofen's book *China—My Traveling Achievements*, written in 1877. The Silk Road was initiated by Zhang Qiang to open the doors to the Western Regions during the Western Han period (202-138 B.C.). The starting point is in Chang'an (the modern city of Xi'an), continuing by way of Gansu, Xinjiang, to central and southwest Asia, and reaching the Mediterranean Sea, linking several countries (this route is also called the Northwest Silk Road, differing from two other routes also known as the Silk Road). Renowned for the westward transportation of goods, among which silk was the most influential, the route was called The Silk Road. The fundamental push was during the two Han Dynasties, consisting of three passages: southern, central, and northern routes.

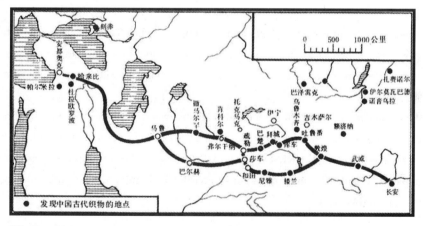

Silk Road Map

The opening and maintaining of the Silk Road has played a significant role in the exchange of both material and spiritual culture between China and the West. On this route, many cultural stories were exchanged between the East and West. Long before Zhang Qian's route the West, a great deal of silk had already been transported to the western world. In ancient Rome, silk clothing became fashionable attire of the aristocracy. Since it came from the East, it was quite expensive. Rome spent massive amounts of gold on importing silk. Due to its transparency, the Roman senate believed it offended public decency, thus issued many orders forbidding the wearing of silk clothes because of its transparency. Yet the laws proved to be invalid, as beauty is irresistible. Today on the Goddess Statue in the Pantheon and on the Druidess of Bacchus in the Naples Museum in Italy, one can see the elegant and beautiful silk clothing of the Greek and Roman periods.

Classic storytellers in the Roman Empire spoke of the silk-producing country of Seres, referring to China, being greatly intrigued by Chinese silk. For quite some time, the people of Rome, and even western scholars, remained perplexed about how it was actually produced. They believed erroneously that it was derived from trees, as raising silkworms and silk weaving technology did not reach the west until much later.

Cultural exchange is mutually exclusive. As China has bestowed exquisite and practical silk fabric to the western world, each country in Europe has returned the favor. In reference to ancient documents, the walnut, cucumber, shallot, coriander, pepper, poplar fruit, carrot and many other plant species have come from western regions.(These things in China begin with the word "胡"—hú, which refers to something coming from the north and the west minority groups. Later on, it is widely used to represent something brought in from abroad.) Furthermore, the documents credit the envoy Zhang Qian of transplanting of the different species of plants from this region. Beginning in the Han Dynasty, not only were plants imported from the west, but also arriving were Roman glassworks, western music, dance, and acrobatics.

With the exchange of material culture, the diffusion of spiritual culture continued along the Silk Road. One of the world's three major religions, Buddhism, entered China as early as the final years of the Western Han Dynasty. Along the Silk road lie many Buddhist grottos such as the famous Uch-Turpan Monastery in Kucha, the Mogao Caves in Dunhuang county, the Anxi Yulin caves, the Wuwei prefecture's Tianti mountain, Yongjing county's Bingling Temple, Maiji Mountain in the Tianshui prefecture, Cloud Ridge in the Datong prefecture, and Luoyang's Longmen (Dragon Gate). These sites reveal an integration of eastern and western art styles, the Silk Road being a witness to the cultural exchange.

With its long history, the Silk Road has helped foster friendly relations, but the iron hoof of warfare has also trampled it. Today people are forgetting the suffering and looking to link the East-West cultures. For the past few years, UNESCO has initiated a Silk Road research project, claiming the Silk road is the path to dialogue. This project aims to positively promote the exchange and cooperation between the East and West.

The Great Wall

The Great Wall is an outstanding building achievement of the ancient Chinese and is listed as one of the seven wonders in the world. Located in the northern part of China, the Great Wall reaches from Shanhai Pass in Hebei Province in the east, traversing to Jiayu Pass in Gansu province in the west. It runs a length of 6,700 kilometers (about 13,300 Chinese li) through seven provinces and several cities and autonomous regions such as Hebei, Beijing, Inner Mongolia, Shaanxi, Shanxi, Ningxia, and Gansu. It's called the Ten Thousand Li Great Wall, which winds like a dragon across lofty mountains, passes through boundless grasslands and vast deserts, until it faces the horizon of the endless sea.

According to historic documents, since the beginning of the Warring States Period, the construction of the Great Wall had been a tremendous undertaking. Over twenty vassal states and feudal dynasties have contributed their own parts to the structure. Currently, one can see the ruins of the Great Wall in many provinces, cities, and autonomous regions such as Xinjiang, Gansu, Ningxia, Shaanxi, Inner Mongolia, Shanxi, Hebei, Beijing, Tianjin, Liaoning, Jilin, Heilongjiang, Henan, Shandong, Hubei and Hunan. Among these areas, the Inner Mongolia section of the great Wall occupies over 30,000 li (about 15,000 km). In the history of its construction, the Qin and Ming dynasties are especially noted.

After unifying the Six States, the First Emperor Qin began building the Great Wall. The millions of people who were employed to construct the wall accounted for one-twentieth of the country's population. The lack of machines during this period resulted in vast amounts of human power working under extremely arduous conditions. As a result, many people continuously died during construction. This led to great resentment of the First Emperor's building project, as exemplified in the traditional story of Meng Jiangnü Weeps at the Great Wall.

The Great Wall

During the Ming Dynasty, northern invaders unceasingly threatened the safety of the borders. Thus, throughout the two hundred years of reign, the Ming Dynasty scarcely ceased. Of all the dynasties they spent the most time, initiated the largest engineering projects, and built the largest defense systems. The Great Wall embodies China's ancient technology and building accomplishments, as well as the wisdom and talent of the working people.

In ancient times, the various states in power continued the construction of the Great Wall, mainly to deter military intrusions of the minority groups of bordering regions. In theory, the Great Wall was complex defense engineering project of ancient China, protecting the people of the central plains and their economic and cultural development.

Presently, there still exist several sections of the Great Wall. Badaling is located in Yanqing of the Beijing municipality. This particular section is the best-preserved and complete section of the Ming Dynasty era, being a typical representation of its construction. It was a significant mountain pass used for military affairs during the Ming Dynasty, in addition to being a major protective screen for the capital of Beijing. Ascending the Badaling section of the Great Wall, it is possible to "live high and look down" (idiom). One sees the upmost views of precipitous mountains and majestic beauty. Over 300 major public figures have visited this section including Richard Nixon and Margaret Thatcher. Shanhai Pass is the world famous section of the Great Wall known as the entrance to the sea. Its overall length within the Great Wall occupies 26 kilometers. Included in this old twisting dragon is the soul of China's flourishing reputation. The Jiayu Pass section of the Great Wall is the western most starting point of the Ming Dynasty building project. Built in 1372, during the five-year reign of Ming Emperor Hongwu, it is the best-preserved section outside of city gates and has served as an important stop on the Silk Road.

The Jiayu Pass

When compared with the other engineering projects in the ancient world, the Great Wall is unparalleled in the time it took to complete, its tremendous size, difficulty level of construction, and its cultural and historical significance.

The great democratic revolution pioneer of modern China, Dr. Sun Yat-sen, once commented on the Great Wall, "The most well-known project in China is the Great Wall...which is also a spectacle of the world." After visiting the Great Wall, former US president Richard Nixon, gave his high praise, saying, "None but a great nation could make such a great wall."

As a marvel of human history, in 1987 the Great Wall was listed in the *World Heritages Records*, without any reservations. Not only does is embody a rich cultural heritage, it also provides a unique feature to the landscape. Nowadays, tourists from home and aboard are eager to climb the Great Wall for themselves, experiencing the culture, and obtaining a view of the majestic mountains and rivers. Often said with sentiment is the proverb, "One who does not visit the Great Wall is not a worthy person." The former British Prime Minister Howard Heath once said of his visit to the Great Wall, "China's past and future both have equal charisma...when I arrived at the Great Wall, I personally felt it to be far more spectacular than what I had previously seen in pictures, embroideries, and paintings. To see the Great Wall is a spectacular sight."

As a symbol of China, the Great Wall stands forever on the ground of Shenzhou (old name for China) and world civilization.

The Terracotta Warriors

In spring of 1974, in the Lintong district of Xi'an City, Shaanxi Province, a local farmer was digging a well 1.5 kilometers east of the of Emperor Qin Shi Huang's Mausoleum, when he accidently unearthed a ceramic head of a warrior. After further archeological excavation, the tomb of the First Emperor and the Terracotta Warriors had been discovered, shocking the world.

The First Emperor's Terracotta Warriors are buried in an array of three pits, at the request of the Emperor. One pit contains only foot soldiers, and from east to west the pit measures 230 meters. The north to south width is 62 meters, with a depth of 5 meters, occupying a surface era of 14,260 square meters. The second pit includes the cavalry, war chariots, and soldiers (also including archers). These special branches of the military are spread out over 6,000 square meters. The third pit was reserved for the high-ranking officers, occupying 520 square meters. All inclusive there are over 7,000 terracotta figurines, 100 war chariots, 400 horses, and over 100,000 weapons. The Terracotta Warriors of the First Emperor is a grand scene, awe-inspiring, orderly in formation, and displays the strength of the Qin army and its formidable weaponry.

These terracotta warriors and horses are exact imitations of actual horses and figures in size. The heights of the terracotta figures varies from 1.75 meters to 1.95 meters with well-proportioned physiques, made of molds of the actual officers of high rank of the Qin military. As with the different branches of the military, the warriors are categorized as foot soldiers, cavalry, crossbow archers, and high-ranking officers. Foot soldiers in uniform carry a bow and arrows on their backs. Most of the earth-made cavalry have one hand holding a halter and another hand grasping a bow and arrow, wearing a short piece of armor, tight breeches, and with riding boots, prepared to mount the horse and go into battle at any moment. The crossbow archers are combat-ready, gazing ahead, some standing, some on one's knee. The appearance of the face of the officer is calm and composed, showing no fear, expressing the demeanor of a great general. The terracotta horses stand roughly 1.5 meters high with a length of 2 meters. They reflect large healthy bodies, well developed muscles, their heads high with facial expressions depicting their astuteness, as a quick battlefield steed. The Terracotta Warriors convey the First Emperor's great influence and the uniting of the powerful militaries of the six states. The Emperor posthumously ordered the construction of these figurines at the expense of large amounts of labor power and financial resources, emphasizing his awesome influence during his lifetime and his absolute rule even after death.

The ruling Emperor Qin Shi Huang's posthumous status initiated the construction of the terracotta warriors and horses, yet they also possess high artistic value. The figurines were produced based on molds of actual warriors and horses, expressing meticulous artistic skill. Their clothing and mannerisms, gestures, and facial expressions are all unique. From these attributes one can determine if the statue is of an official or infantry, or if is the likeness of a foot soldier or of the cavalry. Here you will find the long-bearded veteran of the battlefield and the beginning youthful warriors. In conclusion, the First Emperor's Terracotta Army captures distinct and intense characteristics of that era, not only enriching ancient Chinese culture but it also holds an important status in the world's history of art.

Terrocotta Warrior and Horse

In 1961, China's State Council as a major cultural relic under the state protection designated the Mausoleum of Emperor Qin Shi Huang. In 1987 UNESCO listed the site on the *World Heritage Records*. An exhibition hall has been built over Pit No. 1, and the Museum of the Emperor Qin Shi Huang's Terracotta Warriors and Horses have been constructed to serve from travelers home and aboard.

The Terracotta Warriors has an allure that attracts people worldwide. Over 100 international government leaders have come here as visitors. The first one was Lee Kuan Yew, the founding Prime Minister of Singapore. Visiting on May 14 of 1976, he gave praise, "This is an astonishment of the world and the pride of Chinese nation." In 1985, while visiting the terracotta warriors and horses for the second time, he left his written words, "This magnificent historical cultural relic implies a magnificent future." The Former Secretary of State Henry Kissinger of the United States visited the site and remarked, "This is an unparalleled marvel of the world." Walter Mondale, former United States vice-president observed, "This is a genuine miracle and all people of the world should come here to see for themselves."

In 1978, then mayor of Paris, former French President Jacques Chirac upon visiting had these words, "There are 7 miracles in the world. The pits of terracotta warriors and horses are the eighth wonder of the world. As you would not visit Egypt without visiting the pyramids, you would not be regarded as visiting China without seeing the terracotta warriors and horses." Since then, the international media has embraced his words of praise for the First Emperor's Tomb and Terracotta Warriors, they are now commonly regarded by the international press as the eighth wonder of the world.

The Museum of Emperor Qin Shi Huang's Terracotta Warriors and Horses can be compared to the pyramids in Egypt and the sculptures of ancient Greece, as they are all cultural treasures to the world.

The Five Sacred Mountains in China

In ancient China, people referred to the central plains areas of the east, south, west, north and central area of having the "Five Sacred Mountains," namely, Eastern Sacred Mount—Mt.Tai in Shandong Province rising 1524 meters above sea level, Southern Sacred Mount—Mt. Heng in Hunan Province with its summit of 1290 meters, Western Sacred Mount—Mt. Hua in Shaanxi Province with 2154.9 meters, Northern Sacred Mount—Mt. Heng in Shanxi province, with an elevation of 2017 meters, and the Central Sacred Mount—Mount Song in Henan Province rising 1440 meters above sea level.

Mount Tai, the first of Five Sacred Mountains, also referred to as the first mountain under heaven, is located in the center of Shandong Province, in the eastern part of China. Therefore it is also referred to as the Eastern Sacred Mountain. Rich cultural connotation of the Ming and Qing Dynasties is deeply rooted in various styles of architecture at Mount Tai. In ancient times, Mount Tai was thought to be the Mountain of the Gods, it was one of the only mountains where emperors held grand-scale sacrificial ceremonies. Many emperors through the ages paid personal visits to Mount Tai, where Buddhism and Taoism flourished. Throughout history, these royal visits contributed to the construction of statues, temples, and steles with inscriptions, leaving behind numerous cultural relics and historical sites. Personages of successive dynasties have come to Mount Tai, praising the verses here that compose over one thousand poems. To enter Mount Tai is to step into a profound moment of Chinese history. The optimum time of year to visit Mount Tai is on March 11. Sightseeing there largely depends on four main spectacles—the sunrise, the jade sea of clouds, the glow of the sunset,

Sunrise at Mount Tai

and the golden shores of the Yellow River.

The Western Sacred Mountain, Mount Hua, lies within the boundaries of Huayin in Shaanxi Province, about 120 kilometers from Xi'an. The mountain consists of five main peaks: the Central Peak, the East Peak, the West Peak, the South Peak, and the North Peak. From a distance, these five peaks resemble a lotus flower at the top of the mountain, giving it its name (in ancient China Lian hua referred to lotus). It is also known as the strangest and most rugged mountain under heaven. In ancient times, many dignitaries came to Mount Hua to perform rites of sacrifice. These include Emperor Qin Shi Huang, Emperor Wu of the Han Dynasty, Empress Wu Zetian, and Emperor Xuan Zong of the Tang Dynasty, came to Mount Hua to conduct grand-scale sacrificial ceremonies. At the same time, Mount Hua is also a well-known Taoist mountain that seats more than 20 Taoist temples. Since the Sui and Tang Dynasties, poets such as Li Bai and Du Fu have written over a thousand works related to Mount Hua. April 10 is the ideal time of year to visit. On the fifteenth day of the third month on the traditional calendar, large gatherings and celebrations take place in the temples as the sunrises over the mountain. The four seasons on Mount Hua produce a mystical and variable landscape. The different seasons can all be admired, and are often referred to as Mount Hua clouds, Mount Hua rain, Mount Hua fog and Mount Hua snow.

The Southern Sacred Mountain, Mount Heng, stands in Nanyue District of Hengyang city in Hunan Province. Due to its favorable climate conditions in comparison to the other four sacred mountains, the terrain is composed of deep forests and lofty bamboos. Throughout the year it remains emerald green, displaying exquisite natural beauty, thus receiving the honorific title of the "Great South Mountain". Mount Heng produces Clouds and Mist Tea, from a famous type of tealeaf known as Tribute Tea by the Tang Dynasty.

North Mount Heng of the Five Sacred Mountains is known as the second mountain under heaven. It lies 10 kilometers south of Hunyuan county seat of Shanxi province and 62 kilometers from Datong prefecture. This particular Mount Heng is the luxuriant mountain of modern Hebei province. After the second reign of the Qing Emperor, the jurisdiction shifted to the Shanxi province. Throughout history, successive emperors have come here to bestow their titles, such as Qin Shi Huang, Emperor Wu of the Han, emperors Taizong and Xuanzong of the Tang Dynasty, and Emperor Zhenzong of the Song. Emperor Ming Taizu also came here to experience its divine essence. Mount Heng has also supported the long-standing tradition of Taoism. It is believed that here Zhang Guolao, a legendary Taoist sage, practiced the austerities to become immortal. Mount Heng contains many bizarre natural landscapes. Among them are the Bitter and Sweet Wells, located halfway up the mountain. The two wells are one meter apart from each other, yet the water quality in each are poles apart. The water in one of the wells is sweet and cool, but in the other well, the water is bitter and unfit to drink.

Center Mount Song stands in the northwest of Dengfeng City in Henan Province. On Feb 13th of 2004, UNESCO listed the mountain as an International Geological Park, due to its undulating hills and oddly steep summits. In addition to the elegant nature and scenery, there are also numerous places of historical interest. For example, a famous Buddhist monastery situated in Mount Song known is Mount Song Shaolin Temple. Mount Song is also a place where kings and emperors through the ages bestowed sacrifices. Of the Five Sacred Mountains, Mount Song has the most historical sites and cultural relics. Here we can appreciate the process of China's 8,000-year history. Historic relics of the Yangshao and Longshan cultures, the Three Sovereigns and Five Kings, and the Xia Dynasty capital of Yangcheng are located here.

Ancient emperors believed that on all Five Sacred Mountains lived immortals. Upon being enthroned, they paid regal visits to the mountains, conducting impressive sacrificial ceremonies. Therefore, the five mountains in ancient China were more than just famous summits and conveyed rich historical and cultural implications.

Shaolin Temple at Mount Song

Lakes

China is a country with many lakes, among the many bodies of water, more than 2,800 have areas of over one square kilometer. The total area of the lakes reaches 80,000 square kilometers. The freshwater lakes occupy roughly 36,000 square kilometers, accounting for about 45% of the total area. The overwhelming majority of them categorized as lakes of small scale. There are 11 famous lakes with a total area of over 1000 square kilometers. The largest fresh water lake is Poyang Lake, the largest saltwater lake is Qinghai Lake, and the greatest hyper saline is body of water is Qarhan Lake. Frog Lake in northern Tibet lies at an altitude of 5,644 meters above seal level and is the highest saltwater lake in the world. It is in the vicinity of the highest fresh water lake in the world, Siling Co Lake, which has an altitude of 5,386 meters. The Turpan Depression in Xinjiang holds world's lowest lake, Lake Aydingkol, located at an altitude of 155 meters below sea level. Located on the border between China and North Korea, Tianchi Lake lies atop Baitou Mountain, the highest peak in the Changbai mountain range. Its depth reaches 312.7 meters, the deepest of its kind in China.

China's most famous lakes include Poyang Lake and Dongting Lake along the middle and lower reaches of the Yangtze River, Taihu Lake along the Yangtze River Delta, and the Huaihe River basin's Hongze Lake and Chaohu Lake. These lakes make up the five largest freshwater lakes in China. There are also many salt lakes; the five largest in China are the well-known Qinghai Lake, Namtso Lake, Siling Co Lake, Lake Ulungur, and Yamdrok Lake.

Poyang Lake, the most sizable freshwater lake in China, is located in the northern regions of Jiangxi. It empties itself into the Yangtze River by way of Hukou Falls, and has inflows of the Gan River, Xiu River, Rao River, Xin River, and Fu River. As a wetland of international importance, Poyang Lake is the main reservoir of the Yangtze River and plays a crucial role in adjusting and retaining immense amounts of floodwater, protecting the biodiversity. As one of the 10 ecological protection areas in China, it is also an ecological area of global importance. It has been appointed by the World Wildlife Fund and plays a key role in protecting regional and national ecological concerns. Moreover, the environment, water quality, and climate make it a suitable place for migratory birds to pass the winter, gradually leaving in the spring during the month of April. Today, the conservation district is home to over 300 species and approximately one million birds. Among these species, fifty are rare breeds, making it the world's largest bird conservation district. Furthermore, the largest

flock of white cranes has been found living here. In 2002, the number of white cranes living through winter in Poyang Lake was up to 4000, accounting for 95% of the world's white cranes. Accordingly, Poyang Lake is called the World of the White Crane and the Kingdom of Rare Birds.

Dongting Lake was originally the largest freshwater lake in China, but in the last century, the volume of the lake has decreased considerably,

Poyang Lake Becomes the World of the White Crane

becoming China's second largest lake. Stretching over Hunan and Hubei provinces, the lake covers a total area of 18,780 square kilometers, of which 2,740 square kilometers are of natural lake, and embankments form 1,200 square kilometers are of an inner lake. In 1954, 1964, and 1970s, three stages of construction to the lake's infrastructure allowed for water management and the creation of farmland. Since then, Dongting Lake has become one of China's most important regions of grain production and freshwater fisheries.

Taihu Lake, the third largest freshwater lake, is located in southern Jiangsu province and the northern region of Zhejiang province. It consists of a system of 180 inter-connected lakes of various sizes. Together with the tributaries and out-flow of rivers, the lakes form an integrated waterway, making it quite useful for shipping, irrigation, and water level adjustment.

Hongze Lake is China's fourth largest freshwater lake, located at the lower reaches of the Haihe River in the western region of Jiangsu province. It is a suspended lake in that the bottom is four to eight meters above the Subei Plain in the east. The main tributary of Hongze Lake is the Haihe River, which has suffered from great floods since ancient times. Therefore, the history of humankind contending with rising waters is colorfully portrayed in local stories and legends. Hongze Lake incorporates the Dujiangyan irrigation project, with a history of over two millennia, was constructed almost entirely of columnar basalt. Maintained by successive dynasties, it spans a length of 67 kilometers as it twists and turns over the landscape as the aquatic version of the Great Wall.

Chao Lake is located in the central part of Anhui province. Covering an area of 769.5 square kilometers, it is the largest lake in the province as well as the fifth largest freshwater lake in China. The major tributary rivers are the Hangbu River, Fengle River, Shangpai River, Nanfei River, and Zhegao River, and by way of the Yuxi River influxes to the Yangtze River. The lake is beneficial as a reservoir and is used for irrigation purposes. In addition, the lake's whitebait (similar to herring) is widely popular.

Qinghai Lake is not only China's largest inland lake, but also the largest saltwater lake. Located in the northeast part of Qinghai province, roughly 30 rivers surround the region. On the eastern shore of the lake lie two smaller lakes—Gahai Lake, a saltwater lake with an area of 10 square kilometers, and Erhai Lake, a freshwater body occupying 4 square kilometers. In December of each year, the surface of Qinghai Lake freezes over with ice half a meter thick, lasting for 6 months. Five small is-

The Pure and Beautiful Qinghai Lake

lands rest in the center of the lake, of which Haixin Mountain Island is the most sizable. Bird Island, located in western part of the lake, covers an area of 110 square meters, creating an ideal place for the habitat and breeding of over 10 varieties of migratory birds such as the bar-headed wild goose, fish gull, and the brown-headed gull, accounting for over 100,000 birds. Presently, an environmental projection reserve area is being established on Bird Island.

Namtso Lake in Tibetan means Lake of Heaven. It is the second largest saltwater lake next to Qinghai Lake. The lake's water turns a deep azure color under a clear cloudless blue sky, thus receiving its name. Located at north of Lhasa in Tibet, it borders the two districts of Damxung and Baingoin. As the largest closed lake in Tibet, the primary water sources of are precipitation and snowmelt.

In Tibetan, Reflecting Demon Lake refers to Siling Co Lake. As the second largest lake in Tibet, it is located in the bordering regions between Baingoin county and Shenzha county. With an area of 1,640 square kilometers, the lake lies 4,530 meters above sea level, its greatest depth being 33 meters. The drainage basin occupies an area of over 45,530 square kilometers.

The Xinjiang Uighur Autonomous Region contains Ulungur Lake is located in the northern part of Junggar Basin. Existing as a triangular shape, the width measures 30 kilometers from south to north, with a length of 35 kilometers from east to west and occupying an area of 827 square kilometers. With an average water depth of eight meters, it has long been known as the Gobi Sea and for its delicious Fuhai fish.

Yamdrok Lake

Lake Yamdrok is situated on the southern bank of the Yarlung Tsangbo River in Nagarzê county of Lhokha prefecture. Covering an area of over 700 square kilometeres at 4,441 meters above sea level, the average depth is over 30 meters, and in some places reaches 60 meters. The lake is fed by the surrounding snow-capped mountains and has no outlet. A dynamic balance is found between the melting snow and the evaporation of lake water, making Yamdrok Lake world famous for its beautiful waters.

Unit 4

Lao Tzu

Lao Tzu, is native to Ku county (modern day Henan province's Lu city) in the State of Chu during the end of the Spring and Autumn Period. His given name is Er and his surname is Li. As the legend states, he was born with white eyebrows and a beard, therefore people called him Lao Tzu (meaning old master). Lao Tzu assumed the responsibility of Keeper of the Archives for the royal court of Zhou. During this period, Confucius often consulted Lao Tzu about the rites. Later, when recognized the gradual decay of the kingdom, nobody knew of his whereabouts.

Lao Tzu

Lao Tzu is traditionally regarded as the founder the Taoist school of thought, his theory later developed by Chuang Tzu. His book Lao Tzu also called *The Book of Tao*, was compiled and written in the early and middle stages of the Warring States Period, which inaugurated the ancient Chinese philosophy, exerting an important influence from ancient times to the modern day on China's ideology and culture.

Lao Tzu's thought mainly includes:

(1)Tao (the way) is the basis of all living things.

Lao Tzu created the philosophy of Tao. He is regarded as the founder of the ontology of ancient Chinese philosophy in seeking a creator and the origins of the structure of existing world. The Tao is the foremost ideological concept of Lao Tzu. The character Tao emerges 73 times in the book *The Way of Lao Tzu*, continually indicating profound meanings.

Tao is described as the myriad of all nature under the sky. "Tao gave birth to the one, from one came two, two birthed three, forming a multitude of all living things." Without form and content, Tao is independent beyond all the things, moving in cycles and by no means ceasing. Tao refers to not only the essence that is the material basis of the universe, but also the general laws and fundamental principles. Lao Tzu believed all things are in the process of changing, and that it is impossible to perceive and acknowledge the Tao eternally or invariably. Lao Tzu's thought embodies an unadorned dialectic. His beliefs state that all living things are changing, contradicting, integrating, and mutually transforming. Furthermore he says, "All things are of birth, birth itself is of from nothing," he continues, "As all people recognize beauty under the heavens the idea of ugliness exists. As virtue is recognized as virtue, this gives rise to wickedness. Existence mirrors non-existence, difficultly achieves success, long and short test each other, as high determines low. Sound becomes harmony, back follows front." He is also quoted as saying "Calamity is dependent on fortune, in fortune lurks calamity".

(2) Nature's laws of wuwei (inaction and action)

On the basis of Tao, Lao Tzu proposes two key principles. The Tao of heaven, and the Tao of humans. The Tao of heaven follows the laws of wuwei, or nature's inaction and action. The Tao of humans relates to people allowing nature take its course. These theories of natural law (sometimes referred to as heavenly law) and wuwei are the foundations of Taoist thought.

Tao is the root of all things in nature, therefore humans, the earth, and the heavens must follow the way of Tao. But Tao itself is not governed and acts on its own will, following the laws of nature. Here nature does not refer to nature in a physical sense, but indicates involuntary action, which opposes human effort. Lao Tzu believed the heavens, earth, and humanity, follow a common law of the Tao of nature, emphasizing everything should accord with nature and obey the common code of humankind and all matters of the universe.

Since the Tao of the heavens, nature, and humankind follow this natural law, Taoism pursues the principal of nature without action (wuwei). Lao Tzu said, "Tao never acts; yet through it, all things are accomplished." Wuwei does not mean nothing being done, but rather indicates natures unfaltering will to transform all living things in the course of time, so as to achieve action without action.

The notion of wuwei of nature is demonstrated in modern political ideology, emphasizing altruism. In relation to human philosophy, wuwei indicates selflessness and humbleness. Therefore it leads one not to desire to know contentment. To be humble makes one capable of modesty. Lao Tzu advocated conduct to be modest and prudent, as well as yielding and weak. But yielding and weak are simply means of using the weak to overcome the strong.

(3) Political ideology of a small country with a small population

Lao Tzu lived during the Spring and Autumn Period, and witnessed the degeneration of feudal religious rights. His political ideology reflects his dissatisfaction and resentment of social reality. He opposed violence and theft, and objected to justice by rule of law. He believed that the Confucian doctrines of righteousness, courtesy, and knowledge could not resolve society's current dilemmas. Therefore, to reinstate Tao as the ruler was his fundamental policy. Lao Tzu opposed the endless catastrophes of war, demonstrating a praiseworthy belief in human ideology. He surmised that a small number of greedy rulers with inadequate resources are the leading factor of war; therefore to overcome the disaster of war, people must avert their appetite for expansion to fundamentally improve humanity. Certainly, he was not apposed to a righteous war, yet reminded the monarchs to not allow them to go to extremes. Even though one may stand as righteous, one must not admire conflict and allow their character to become warlike. This, in his views, would be a dreadful matter. Thus, although the war may prevail, there must be sympathy for the victims at the funerals.

While criticizing social reality, Lao Tzu frames an ideal society of a small country with a small population. Given this principle, one needs not use people as tools, but rather allow them to die in defense of their homes, instead of relocating to another region. He believes despite the fact that sedans exist, one needs not ride on them; there may still be weapons, but they need not be brandished; and one should return to tying the rope for its intended use. People should be content with their food, pleased with their clothing, satisfied with their homes, and take pleasure in their daily tasks. The neighboring countries may hear each other's roosters and the dogs until death without ever associating with them. In Chinese intellectual history, Lao Tzu is the first thinker to overall criticize and demonstrate unreasonable politics, and at the same time offering a conception of an ideal society.

Lao Tzu and his Taoist thought exerted great influence on China afterwards, becoming an important philosophy existing simultaneously with Confucianism. In Ancient China, when a literati or minister of the state were in low tide in their career or personal life, they often would seek guidance and comfort from Lao Tzu's principles. The philosophy of Lao Tzu not only still exists in China, but has also had extensive influence throughout the world. With the passage of time, people increasingly recognize his concepts of non-action and respect for natural law.

Chuang Tzu

Chuang Tzu (369-286 B.C.) was given the name Zhou and was native of the State of Song in Warring States Period. As a well-known thinker, philosopher, and writer, he was a chief representative of Taoism. He promulgated and developed the philosophical thought of Lao Tzu, becoming the founder of the Chuang Tzu School of Thought during the pre-Qin Dynasty era. His theory encompassed almost every aspect of social life of that period, but its fundamental aspects still reverted to the philosophy of Lao Tzu. Successive generations have entitled them together as "Lao Chuang," their credos are collectively known as Lao Chuang Philosophy.

Chuang Tzu

Chuang Tzu inherited and continued to develop the knowledge of Lao Tzu and Taoist thought, forming his own distinctive philosophical ideology system that possessed an unique style of study and writing. He considers Tao as surpassing all space and time and of an infinite noumenon, existing in all living things, and is omnipresent. Its current form is within all things, it is the origin of the myriad of the heavens and natural law. On the politics of wuwei, in order for humanity to survive, he advocated a return to a plain and simple coexistence. He writes, "The heavens, the earth, and myself are born of the same, thus all living things and myself are one", as he contemplated spiritual boundaries, and advocated an unfettered peaceful consciousness.

In Chuang Tzu's opinion, the real essence of life is involuntary nature. Therefore one needs not to instruct and regulate, but rather delete the matters, disregard the measures, neglect intention, and resist opportunity and distinction. Such being the case, there is no use of politics to disseminate the idea of propriety and righteousness. This governed advice and education created a phony person, therefore we need to abandon it.

Chuang Tzu maintained that benevolence and righteousness, as well as differentiation of right and wrong, were punishment upon the people, attacking the ruler's righteousness and rule of law. He sharply criticized propriety, law, authority, and power. His incisive view suggests concise criticism as in the quote, "As long as the sage never dies, the bandits will excessively plunder", and "A small thief is put to death, but he who steals a country is a monarch."

With regard humankind's way of life, he upholds nature and advocates a spiritual condition of "coexistence with the heavens and the earth and myself as all living things." Furthermore, he believed that utmost boundary in human life is to be free and content, with unconditional spiritual liberty, placing blame on material goods and hypocritical fame. The thoughts and allegations of Chuang Tzu exert a profound influence on later generations, becoming a precious spiritual wealth of information in the history of human intellect.

Lao Chuang philosophy, on the foundation of the school of Taoist thought, is the only philosophical ideology that can compare as equals to Confucianism and Buddhism as great theoretical frameworks of ancient China.

Chuang Tzu's influence on later generations is not only present in today's philosophy, but also in modern literature. His political claims and philosophical thoughts are by no means dull and dry preaching; they contain vivid images and wit in humorous fables, which he makes alluring by throwing off the restraint in the sea of literature. His book reads like a collection of folkloric tales. With great imagination, these fables create vivacious images and strong artistic intent.

The structure of his articles is quite idiosyncratic. In general, it's loose and always gives you unexpected feelings. The style of his writing has his own way, full of change and without limit. At times sections of his works are arranged as he wishes, seemingly not related to each other, but the idea is embodied from the beginning to the end. The syntax is quite pliable, written in sequence or in reverse, perhaps long or short, using vivid words and minuscule details. In addition to irregular rhyme, the writing style appears full of lavish expression and innovation.

Chuang Tzu preserved his moral integrity during his lifetime and lived a poor reclusive life, inheriting and developing the Taoist ideology of Lao Tzu. He was not only a philosophical master but also a talented literary virtuoso. In his Butterfly Dream, he fails to separate dream from reality. He once had a wonderful debate with Huizi, asking him, "How do you know whether the fish is happy or not?" It's said that, upon the death of his wife, Chuang Tzu sang songs accompanied by drumming on a bowl.

With a fluent and free writing style, a unique imagination, use of vivid images, and a broad-minded temperament, his words give readers a feeling of transcending worldliness and lofty sweetness. He develops a school of his own in the history of Chinese literature. His syntax structure breaks away from the style of quotations and signifies the development of pre-Qin prose to a mature phase. It is often said that the Book of Chuang Tzu represents the highest achievement of pre-Qin Dynasty prose.

During his lifetime, he wrote a book using over 10,000 words called The Book of Chuang Tzu, which symbolized the philosophical ideology and literature in China had prospered to a profoundly high level during the Warring States Period. The work is a treasure among the Chinese classics. Therefore, Chuang Tzu is not only a famous thinker in the history of philosophy, but also a brilliant litté rateur of China. Whether of philosophical ideology or have literary language, he has exerted a deep and profound influence on thinkers and writers of past dynasties in China, enjoying a great status among them.

Confucius

During the Spring and Autumn and Warring States periods, in China emerged a well-known philosopher and educator named Confucius.

Confucius, whose surname was Qiu and given name was Zhongni, was native to the State of Lu (now part of Shandong Province). When he was three years old, his father died of illness. His mother then relocated, bringing him to the imperial city of Qufu, the capital of the state. Both of them mutually depended on each other, yet experienced a life of poverty. At about 30 years old, Confucius began operating a private school. Confucius is said to have risen to the position of Justice Minister of the State of Lu

Confucius

around the age of 50. But before long, due to the political turbulence in Lu, he was forced to leave the state after three months in his position. This prompted him to travel with his students to other states, living 14 years in exile. In his later years, he returned to the State of Lu, spending the remainder of his life in lecturing and compiling ancient texts.

Confucius spent most of his lifetime in the field of education as a famous teacher in ancient China. It's been said that Confucius once had over 3,000 students, among whom 72 were men of prominent achievement. Confucius initiated private schools, changing the government standard and having great significance to the history of education in China. He compiled six books, including *The Book of Poetry, The Book of History, The Book of Rites, The Book of Changes, The Book of Music, and The Spring and Autumn Annals.* These classics were used as his teaching materials, preserving and developing Chinese culture.

In 40 years of being and educator, Confucius accumulated profuse experiences in teaching. He expressed many thoughts and principles on education and instruction, which still have great significance today. For example, his belief of teaching students in line with their ability implies adopting different methods of teaching in light of the various dispositions of the students. Teaching without discrimination explains that regardless of if the student is rich or poor, a sage or a simpleton, the individuals should be treated equally, irrespective of backgrounds. Also expected of teachers is to be insatiable in learning and instructing with tireless zeal, meaning one should never feel content in learning or fatigued in teaching. He earnestly practiced what he advocated—when his students encountered misunderstandings, he always patiently explained it to them until they could fully comprehend. Another conviction of his is if three walk together, then one should be my teacher. Confucius advised people to be modest and erudite to others, believing that when a group of people is walking together, one can most certainly learn from the others.

Confucius was not only a great educator, but also a great philosopher, his thoughts reflected in *The Analects of Confucius*. Most likely completed during the initial stage of the Warring States Period after his death, the book was arranged and compiled by the recollection of his disciples and students of them. The contents touch upon many aspects such as philosophy, politics, economy, education, literature, and art, becoming a classic text among Confucian doctrine.

The core of Confucianism is benevolence, which appears 108 times in *The Analects of Confucius*, and was often mentioned by his followers. The benevolent love for others—to love a person is the origin of benevolent thought—is the nucleus as well as the ultimate goal.

Benevolence in today's politics is embodied as moral behavior. From within his heart, the ruler must love the people and establish a benevolent government that is in the best interests of his subjects. Teaching without discrimination, ensures anyone, despite financial status, has the right to an education. In modern times, benevolence also refers to zhong (loyalty), shu (kind-heartedness), xiao (filial piety), and ti (fraternal love). Loyalty is to be faithful and honest. Kind-heartedness is the doctrine of tolerance and forgiveness stemming from *The Analects of Confucius*. They are exemplified in the following thoughts: putting oneself in the place of another; wishing to establish oneself while seeking also to establish others; and do not do to others what you would not have them do to you. All of these proverbs instruct people to stand in someone else's shoes, to consider, show compassion, understand, and help others. Filial piety refers to respecting one's parents and the elders. Fraternal love relates to the love and respect of brothers and fathers. Confucius believed that filial piety and fraternal love are the foundations of benevolence, asking, "How can a person who doesn't love his or her family love others?" Thus it can be seen that the benevolence Confucius spoke of is a kind of altruism towards the masses, in the realm of ethics of putting others before oneself. Confucian thoughts are revealed in *The Record of Rites, Commonwealth of the State*:

All men love and respect their own parents and children, there is caring for the old, duties for adults, and education for the youth. There is means of support for the widows and widowers, the disabled, and all who find themselves alone in the world. Every man and woman has a distinct role in society.

Then how can we achieve benevolence? Confucius preached, "Restrain yourself and return to the rites, do not look at what is contrary to propriety, do not listen to what is contrary to propriety, do not speak about what is contrary to propriety, and do not act in any way that is contrary to propriety." This propriety is not of the such as we know in modern times, but rather etiquette, a general criterion of the way people regard others, their actions and speech, diet, dress, and living conditions, as to establish oneself with the norm in society. Propriety has the ability to get to the root of the problem and allows people to comprehend right and wrong, disgrace and honor, the heart filling with virtue. Furthermore, propriety is pliable and does not rely on enforcement, but rather strict self-regulation of one's own heart.

The whole of society could be in harmony under the condition that everyone, from monarchy to ordinary people, abide by the law and behave discreetly. Therefore, the core of propriety is using proper titles, namely, clarifying the ranks of person's status, privilege, responsibility, and accepted code of behavior.

Confucius further said, "Let the ruler be the ruler, the minister be the minister, the father be the father, and the son be the son." In other words, every title contains certain implications that constitute the essence of the duties of each. The ruler, minister, father, and son should follow their specific ways respectively, thus being the key social order of Chinese feudal society. Confucius always judged people's thoughts and behaviors by yi (righteousness), which in essence means conforming to propriety, if not, one's actions are unjust.

After Confucius passed away, every dynasty held memorial ceremonies and constructed temples of Confucius throughout the land. During the Western Han Dynasty, Emperor Gaozu Liu Bang held for the first time the Tai Lao (grand sacrifice), an enormous ceremony that offered sacrifices to Confucius, the heavens, and the Yellow Emperor. In feudal times, this became known as the Three Kingdoms Sacrifice.

Beginning in the Western Han Dynasty, Confucianism became the orthodox of culture, occupying over two thousand years of feudal society in China and greatly influencing the ideology, lifestyle, and values of Chinese citizens.

In recent years, we've witnessed a fever of cultural development of Confucianism, Chinese nationalism, and tradition. There are over 140 Confucius Institutes in 50 countries thus far. During the International Culture of Confucius Festival in 2005, a grand memorial ceremony was globally held in unison. On June 23, 2006, the Confucius Educational Award, set up by UNESCO and in the name of Chinese government, was offered in the city of Qufu in Shangdong Province, the hometown of Confucius. It was the first time that an international award had been named after a person of Chinese nationality.

Mencius

Mencius (372-289 B.C.), whose given name was Ke and his courtesy name was Zi Che or Zi Ju, was a great thinker in ancient China as one of the main representatives of Confucianism during the Warring States Period. *The Book of Mencius* is the expression his opinions compiled and edited by Mencius and his students. The work focused on his words, political opinions, and actions with regards to Confucianism. Mencius continued and developed Confucian thoughts, becoming a master and after Confucius was titled the Second Saint. Confucius and Mencius were jointly titled Kong-Meng. The theory of Mencius was based on *The Analects of Confucius*, and conveyed the thought of benevolent governance while advocating moral rule of a country. In the Southern Song Dynasty, Zhu Xi combined *The Book of Mencius*, *The Analects of Confucius*, *The Great Learning*, and *The Doctrine of the Mean* into what is known as *The Four Books*. From then until the Qing Dynasty, the *contents of The Four Books* were imperative with regard to the imperial examination.

Mencius

When Mencius was three years old, his father passed away, leaving his mother to raise him through many hardships. She was very strict with her son. Still many interesting stories have been passed down over thousands of years about how she moved their household three times to provide him a better environment in which he could learn. Her weaving talents are also a subject of folklore. In later generations, through these stories she became a paragon for mothers rearing their children.

The thought of Mencius can be summarized in the following aspects:

(1) The concept of the citizen

"The citizen is most precious, the state is second, and the monarch is of least importance." His ideals insist the ruler ought to protect the populous and ensure people's rights. He also endorsed the overthrow of tyrannical regimes.

(2) The theory of benevolent governance

Mencius inherited and further progressed the Confucian thought of moral governance, developing the doctrine of benevolent governance, which became the core of his political ideology. In order to ease the tension of social contradiction and safeguard the long-term benefits of the feudal governing class, he applied the principles of qin-qin (amiability) and zhang-zhang (eldership) to the political field.

In some aspects, Mencius strictly differentiates the ruler from the class that is ruled, believing "Those who labor with the mind rule, those who work with physical strength are ruled." He lays out a fixed system of hierarchy from the rightful emperor to the common people, in accordance with the doctrines of the Zhou Dynasty. He compares the relationship between the ruler and the ruled to that of parents and their children, proposing that the ruler should care for the people's suffering and people should respect the ruler as their parents. Mencius believed this to be an ideal political spectrum. If the ruler governs the state by benevolence, he is fully supported by people. On the contrary, if the ruler neglects the life and death of his subjects, or imposes oppressive rule, he must be overthrown. The concrete substance of benevolent governance is quite comprehensive; it includes economics, politics, education, and the unification of the country, becoming one thread in the framework of the citizen.

Mencius maintained that the treatment of a populous is extremely important and bears the weight of the rise and fall of a nation. Mencius attached great importance to the ambition as well as the opposition of the people, by use of many historical events as examples. This elaborated the crucial importance to a country's gains and losses. He implies, "Benevolent government must first create geographic boundaries." Mencius advocated the dividing of cropland and implementing an equal-field system, which was based on a feudalistic natural economy. Each family of every household is given a small agricultural basis, forming a system of serfdom labor and taxation. A family was given a plot of five mu (1/5 of an acre), with one hundred mu completing a field, allowing for self-sufficiency of food and clothing. Mencius believed that "The way of the people is this: if they have a certain livelihood, they will have a fixed heart. If they have not a certain livelihood, they have not a fixed heart. As long as people have permanent property and land designated to live on, they will live in peace and work happily, only then will they not offend criminal law or perpetuate outrages".

In his own opinion, once the material lives of people are guaranteed, the government is able to establish schools, educate people using filial piety, civic duty, and just conduct, guiding them to be kind-hearted. Thus, the favorable moral fashion of qin-qin and zhang-zhang is exemplified in his words, "The work of one's duty lies in what is easy, while people seek for what is difficult."

He also advocated benevolent governance by the ruler to obtain a realm of support by his people, this way giving him the advantage of unparalleled rule. The benevolent governance should be based on the rulers who possess a heart of mercy. Mencius said, "Ancient kings were merciful, therefore the governments were also merciful." The believed they should consist of a commiserating mind of great sympathy and kindheartedness. He maintained one should be affectionate to parents and benevolent to people and to "Honor the elderly as one's own aged parents and care for other's children as we do our own." The policy of benevolence is an embodiment of kindheartedness in politics.

Mencius weaves an inseparable knot of ethics and politics, emphasizing virtue and accomplishment as the fundamentals of just governing. Also saying, "The root of the kingdom is in the State, the root of the State is in the family, root of the family being the individual." The theory of "Self-cultivation, Family Harmony, State Governing and world Peace " in the work the Great Learning was developed from the thought of Mencius.

(3) Moral ethics

Mencius generalizes ethics into the four categories of benevolence, righteousness, propriety, and knowledge. He points to human relationships of five kinds, stating, "Between father and son there should be affection, between ruler and subject, righteousness. There should be allowance for differences between husband and wife, a proper order among old and young, and of friends, fidelity." He believed among the concepts of benevolence, righteousness, propriety, and knowledge, the former two are most important and are the foundation of filial piety and fraternal love. Filial piety and fraternal love are the fundamental ethics in building relationships between father and son, as well as among brothers. He considers that if each person in society is tolerant of each other through benevolence and righteousness, a credible guarantee will be provided to keep the feudal system stable and the country unified.

In order to clarify the origin of these moral ethics, Mencius brought forth the notion of innate goodness of the individual, believing that although there exists different divisions of social classes, the human characteristics remains the same. He adds, "Thus all things which are the same in kind are like one another; why should we doubt man to be the solitary exception? The sage and we are of the same in kind." While discussing general human nature, he equates the status of the ruler and the ruled, keeping up with the historical trends of slave emancipation and the social transformations of the era. It is an in-depth understanding of the intensity of human thought and a tremendous boost to the development of ethical ideology.

Mo Tzu

Mo Tzu

Mo Tzu (ca. 468–376 B.C.), whose given name was Di, was a native of Tengzhou in Shangdong province. As a well-known thinker during the Warring States Period, he was the founder of a system of education labeled after his name—Mohist School. He expressed the thoughts of indiscriminate love, non-aggression, esteem, and frugalness. His thoughts were handed down in the book bearing his name, *Mo Tzu*. The book consists of two sections. One part combines the words and actions of Mo Tzu with the statements of his thoughts, representing an earlier stage of Mohist School. The other section is composed of six chapters, generally known as the Six Teachings or the Six Disciplines, stressing epistemology and logic, as well as a great deal of natural science, representing a later stage of Mohist School. The influence of Mohist School was as great as that of Confucius at that time, regarded an orthodox school together with Confucianism.

The main ideology of Mo Tzu includes the following:

(1) Indiscriminate love and non-aggression.

Indiscriminate love embodies equality and humanity. Mo Tzu requires that the ruler and subjects, father and son, and mutual brothers get along with each other equally. "One should love others as love oneself." He believed that the existence of torment, insult, and arrogance between the strong and week, rich and poor, noble and humble is because they do not mutually love each other.

(2) The will of the heavens and sprits.

Advocating the will of the heavens and the existence of sprits is another distinguishing feature of Mohist thought. Mo Tzu believed that one aspiration of the heavens is to love people unconditionally. He states, "No matter young or old, noble or humble, all are subject of the heavens.""The heavens love the people deeply." Mo Tzu also points out, if a ruler disobeys the will of the heavens, he will be punished, whereas, if he is in compliance, he will be rewarded. Not only does he firmly believe in the existence of spirits, but also thinks that spirits will punish or reward rulers and aristocrats who are benevolent or deceptive. Mohism embraces the concept of human rights and places restrictions on monarchy, which is a main point in this philosophy.

(3) Identification with the Superior and the Virtuous

Identification with the superior means that common and the ruler should respect the intention of the heavens, employing a righteous government. Identification with the virtuous requires the selection of virtuous people as officials and rulers. Mo Tzu proposes that a king should choose people of high moral standards and common people should obey to administration of king. Furthermore, he suggests that rulers understand the conditions or feelings of ordinary people so that kindness will be awarded and violation will be punished. He requires rulers to pay more attention to the virtuous people and place the talented in important positions, neglecting the unworthy. Mo Tzu pays much attention to identification of the virtuous, which is considered as the core of governing. He strongly opposes the ruler appointing people of kin and asserts nominating ethical people without prejudice. He suggests, "Officials will not likely always be noble and people will not likely be forever humble."

(4) The Economy of Expenditures and Funeral Rites

The economy of expenditures is an opinion greatly emphasized by Mohists who strongly opposed the extravagance of rulers and aristocrats. In particular, especially they were against the custom of ceremonious funerals favored by Confucians. They believed rulers and aristocrats should live a thrifty and simple life like that of Yu the Great (Da Yu) of ancient times. Mo Tzu required his adherents to earnestly practice what they advocated in this regard.

A key contribution to Mohist philosophy is epistemology. He maintains that cognition is base on what one sees and hears. In his views, judgments of the existence or non-existence of things should not depend on individual assumptions or merely the perception of others. He emphasizes taking indirect or direct experiences and social effect as a guide, while striving for removing personal subjective prejudice. With relation to the proper names of things, they should be not just in name, but also in reality. He also suggests that the validity of epistemology is still full of limitations. Mo Tzu believes the existence of spirits and demons is based on the conclusions that some people have perceived them.

As an important pioneer in the framework of logic in ancient China, Mo Tzu consciously adopted deductive methods to establish and demonstrate one's own ideas of politics and ethics. He is the first person who employs the concepts of debate, classification, and reason in the history of Chinese philosophy, demanding that debating be used as a specialized knowledge to study. Although the notion of argument proposed by Mo Tzu refers to the techniques of debate, it is also established on the basis of understanding the classification and reason of objects and ideas. Therefore, it belongs to a category of logical analogy and argumentation. He is also apt at applying analogical methods to reveal the opponents' self-contradiction. Owing to the proposals of enlightenment by Mo Tzu, Mohism has established a tradition of respecting reason and developed the first complex system of logic in ancient China.

Moreover, Mo Tzu contributed a great deal to scientific and technological fields. For example, with regard to the theory of the cosmos, he believed that the universe is a continuous macrocosm and any individual or part is an integral component. He proposed the concept of space and time existing as continuous and endless, consisting of the smallest units. Among them, the infinite embodies the nonfinite, and continuation embodies non-succession.

In the field of mathematics, Mo Tzu is the first scientist in Chinese history that uses a high level of rationally in the treatment of mathematical computation. He presents a series of propositions and definitions in mathematical concepts with great abstraction and preciseness, such as the definitions of multiplication, equivalence and squares.

With regard to physics, his research involved the subdivisions of mechanics, optics and acoustics, giving rise to the concept of inertia. He made many important discoveries and summarized some of the main theories of physics.

In the field of mechanical engineering, Mo Tzu is a master machinist, spending three years meticulously manufacturing a type of wooden bird capable of flying. As an expert in fabricating carts, he could finish building a cart in one day with a load capacity of 30 dans (1,500 kilograms) of stones.

Sun Tzu

Sun Tzu

Sun Tzu, a well-known military expert in Chinese history, is titled as the forefather of military strategy. His surname was Sun and his given name Wu, his courtesy name being Changqin. Later generations addressed him respectfully as Sun Tzu, or Sun Wu Tzu. His father was an aristocrat and well-known general of the state of Qi during the Spring and Autumn Period. He composed *The Art of War* by Sun Tzu which is known as the earliest military book in the world, laying the foundation of Chinese military science.

The Art of War by Sun Tzu consists of 13 chapters composed of 5,000 words. Every chapter has a different theme but they are all interconnected, revealing a series of patterns in military affairs, forming a complete theory of military strategy. With separate and inter-related themes for each chapter, the book expounded a series of general military rule, forming a comprehensive study of military affairs.

The chapter "Laying Plans" is devoted addressing the possibility of going to war. Sun Tzu postulated that war is a matter of life and death to a country. Moral law (Tao), heaven, earth, the commander and method and discipline are the essential deciding factors of battle.

The chapter "Waging War" stresses how to advance in conflict, advocating a rapid victory. Even more praiseworthy is his assertion of preferential treatment of the captives, believing in this way even more quickly defeats the enemy.

The chapter "Attack by Stratagem" emphasizes the plot of assault to achieve victory in battle, stating, "Knowing the enemy and yourself will get you unscathed through a hundred battles."

"Tactical Dispositions" relates to achieving complete victory by taking advantage of material conditions. He asserted that the advantages of material conditions are based on military expenditure, the amount of supplies, number of soldiers, as well as the balance of power.

"Use of Energy" stresses defeating the enemy by combined efforts. Sun Tzu advocated using advantageous situations to defeat the enemy, such as a surprise attack or ambush.

The chapter "Weak and Strong Points" stresses how to be flexible in time and knowing when to initiate the attack. He maintained that it is vital to gain dominance by enticing the enemy and understanding the situation in the enemy camp, as well as concealing one's own situation while noting the regular patterns of troop movement. Sun Tzu advocated exploiting the enemy's weaknesses and errors to crush the enemy. Avoiding the strong and attacking the weak can thus achieve victory.

The chapter "Maneuvering an Army" deals with the importance of taking advantage of certain situations to achieve a favorable position. Sun Tzu stated one must refrain from hasty decisions of advancement and should understand the trends of the country, be familiar with the roads and the topography, employ adept guides, thus deceiving the enemy. Also, the fortification and the dispersal of troops in light of different conditions and the enemy's position, morale, and military strength.

"Variation of Tactics," the next chapter, elaborates on the importance of flexibility in commanding. Sun Tzu believed this to be the basis of determining the comprehensive pros and cons of conducting movement. This approach has the capacity to threaten, subdue, and perplex the enemy, as to entice them.

The following chapter is "The Army on the March", dealing with the importance of organizing and deploying an army, observing and gathering enemy intelligence, as well as rallying the officers and soldiers.

The chapter "Classification of Terrain" stresses the relationship of various terrains to military course of action.

The chapter "Nine Situations" deals with nine distinct battlefields and the corresponding requisite.

The chapter "Attack by Fire" relates to the targets, category, combustible materials, and atmospheric conditions needed to carry out the assault.

"The Use of Spies" is a chapter that indicates the importance of the underlying principles of espionage.

The Art of War by Sun Tzu not only has had a great influence in China, but has also been successfully translated into several languages and widely spread throughout in the world. The famous French statesman and military expert Napoleon Bonaparte, after being defeated in Waterloo, incidentally sees *The Art of War* by Sun Tzu and with unbounded lament sighs, "If I would have seen *The Art of War* by Sun Tzu twenty years ago, history would have a separate ending." Now, in Vietnam, Korea, Japan, Israel, as well as the United Kingdom, Germany and Russia, the military experts all welcome the manual. In the preface of English version, the well-known British strategist Sir Basil Liddell Henry Hart states, the ancient Chinese military strategy of 2,500 years ago is very beneficial to war in the modern era.

Besides its importance placed on military affairs, *The Art of War* by Sun Tzu has expanded to influence other affairs, especially in the field of business administration, as the financial market itself is a war without a smoking guns. Japanese entrepreneur points out in his book, *A Complete Collection of Military Tactics Management*, "Adopting thoughts of Chinese military science to instruct the management of enterprises is still far more reasonable and effective than the method of business management in the United States." Furthermore, an American economist also indicates that "Many principles and theories uncovered in *The Art of War* by Sun Tzu thus far are indisputable and full of value."

Han Fei Tzu

Han Fei Tzu

Han Fei (ca. 280- 233 B.C.), also called Han Fei Tzu, was native of the State of Han in the late Warring States period, as a well-known philosopher, thinker, and writer, as well as a great contributor of the Legalist school of philosophy. Although he often stuttered, he was quite adept in writing. Moreover, he continued to develop the legalist ideology of Xun Tzu and at the same time adopted the theories of previous Legalist doctrincs. By comparing experiences of success and failure of political reform in different states, he presented a combined theory of law, method, and the wielding of power. In succeeding in compiling a large portion of Legalist thought, Han Fei Tzu wrote to the king of the state of Han several times to make suggestions on political reform. However, his suggestions were never adopted, therefore he determined to write books to expand his theory in an attempt to be reputable and famous.

Yingzheng, the emperor of the state of Qin, attached great importance to Han Fei's thoughts and admired his ideas. Thus, Emperor Yingzheng wrote a letter to the emperor of the state of Han, requesting him to send Han Fei on a diplomatic mission to the state of Qin. The theory of Legalist doctrine, served as theoretical basis for the birth of the first unified and centralized state power in the history of China. But while in the state of Qin, he met by misfortune Prime Minister Li Si, who arranged to have him imprisoned, resulting in his death. 55 articles were passed down in his works *Han Fei Tzu*.

During the pre-Qin era, the legalist school attached great importance to law, opposing the rites of Confucianism. They were famous for advocating rule by law in governance, proposing a series of theories and methods, which contributed immensely to the study. They made fruitful achievements in probing the relationships of basic themes such as origin, nature, and the effect of law with the social economy. Also discussed were the demands of the era, the power of a nation, the virtue of ethics, social customs, the natural environment, and the population and personal relationships.

Legalist School philosophers believe that good prevails and evil does harm, or undertaking advantages to avoid calamity is of human nature. Moral standard means nothing when people face such kinds of choices. Therefore, ruler should guide people with benefits and honors. For example, large rewards such as official positions should be offered to anyone who distinguishes themselves in action so that to inspire soldiers and generals to take courage in battle. This is one of the reasons why the Qin army was so powerful. The ideology of humanity in the Legalist school of thought plays a significant role in the Qin state's process of unifying China.

The Legalist School opposed the conservative ideal of returning to ancient times, and proposed vigorous reform. They claimed that as the trends of history moved forward, all laws and social systems should develop with the times. Maintaining that reverting to neither ancient times, nor diehard conservative attitudes can be accepted. Shang Yang(a famous reformer in Warring States Period) explicitly stated, "The ancient laws do not adhere to modern society's standards." Han Fei further developed Shang Yang's opinion in stating "The society would be led to chaos if the government didn't change with the times." He even satirized the conservative Confucians as fools guarding a tree stump to wait for rabbits (to wait idly for opportunities).

As three representatives of Legalist School, Shang Yang, Shen Dao, and Shen Buhai respectively advocated attaching great importance to law, the wielding of power, and method, forming inseparable concepts, each with different features. Han Fei, by means of ancient fables, combined the three concepts, summarizing the success and failure of monarchs in ancient times. He clarified the theory of governing by law systematically, expressing his ambition and opinion. Law indicates the robust legal system, the wielding of power points to the authority and influence of a monarch as the sole leader of the military. Method, in these terms, is the act of propagating law and maintaining rule by the issuance of tactics and strategy as to preserve the hierarchy, importance was also stressed on political awareness and preventing rebellion.

But the Legalist school of philosophy also has disadvantages, such as exaggerating the impact of law and advocating harsh tactics to govern the state by using punishment to remove punishment, not only administering harsh sentencing for petty crimes, but also employing superstitious laws. The neglect of benevolence and righteousness, which were strongly advocated by Confucianism, is considered to be one of the leading causes to collapse of the Qin Dynasty.

Unit 5

The Book of Songs

*T*he *Book of Songs* is the first collection of ancient musical works in China, composed of 305 poems collected from various parts of the country. Dating back to early Western Zhou Dynasty (11th century B.C.) to the middle of the Spring and Autumn Period (6th century B.C.), sometimes more than five hundred years separate some of the poems. Originally called *Poems*, or *Three Hundred Poems* in the pre-Qin Dynasty, it was listed as the first of the *Five Classics* by Confucius and has been called by the honorific title of *The Book of Songs* by Confucians since the Han Dynasty.

The Book of Poems was originally a collection on song lyrics, adjoined with musical composition, divided by three categories, *Airs of the States*, *Courtly* Songs, and Hymns.

The ballads of different regions, compromising fifteen distinct folkloric songs, namely Airs of the States, consists of 160 entries, occupying over half the book. In the sections, Courtly Songs, and Hymns when compared Airs of the States, seem to take a deep breath of fresh air and exhibit a vivacious manner, as in the opening ballad *The Crying Ospreys* is written with a stream of passion and youthfulness. *Meng* is a poem that describes the grief of a woman after being abandoned by her husband. Jing Nü is another work that conversely writes about subtle romantic love.

Courtly Songs is a collection of music beginning from the State of Zhou period. They are orthodox songs and formal music sung by the nobles in the court or at banquets. According to the type of music, Courtly Songs is divided into 31 *Greater Courtly Songs* and 74 *Lesser Courtly Songs*, occupying over 105 songs. In *Lesser Courtly Songs*, a few entries are folk songs but for the most part are the works of aristocratic scholars; and performed in common celebrations. *Greater Courtly Songs* are used in grand ceremonies and large banquets.

Hymns is a collection of anthems used as prayer offerings during imperial sacrifices to ancestors and gods. It is divided by the sections, 31 *Zhou Praises*, 4 *Lu Praises*, and 5 *Shang Praises*, totaling 40, which all are works of the literate aristocracy.

The Book of Songs marks a splendid origin in the history of Chinese poetry. Its rich and plentiful content includes epic sagas, poems of sarcasm, narratives, love songs, songs of war, carols, as well as various songs from the laborers. They reflect many aspects of the Zhou Dynasty era such as labor and love, military conflict, oppression, customs, marriage; including every aspect of life. For example, in *Greater Courtly Songs* the poem *Sheng Min* embodies the birth if Hou Ji to King Wu of Zhou overthrowing tyrant Zhou of Shang. The book is a reflection of the Zhou Dynasty culture and aided to develop the literary history of other states.

In the technique of expression, the selections *The Book of Songs* are mostly four-character based, with structural repetition of phrases and stanzas rhyming at the end of every line or every other line to strengthen the expression of emotions. A great artistic effect is achieved with only several changes of words in each chapter. In addition, three literary devices, fu, bi and xing, are frequently employed in *The Book of Songs*. Fu indicates directly expressing one's emotions in great detail; it is the most basic way of expression. Bi is the English equivalent of metaphors. There are many poems in the book using metaphors with various methods. For example, in the poem *Meng* (common people), the flourishing and withering of the mulberry tree is used to compare to vicissitudes of love between husband and wife. Xing is used at the commencement of a poem by invoking images other than the subject matter. Xing is often used at the beginning of a poem or the first paragraph of a poem.

The Book of Songs marked a brilliant beginning of Chinese literature. Owning to its rich content and high achievements in ideology and art, the book holds an important status in Chinese and world cultural history. It sets the precedent of brilliant traditional Chinese poems, which exerts an indelible influence on literature in later times. As early as the Spring and Autumn Period, *The Book of Poem* was already widely spread and generally used as teaching materials by aristocrats in China for thousands of years. In the *Analects*, Confucius says: "a person who doesn't learn *The Book of Songs* will not know how to speak." Also teaching his students by quoting knowledge from the book.

Of *The Five Classics*, namely, *The Book of Songs*, *The Book of History*, *The Book of Changes*, *The Book of Rites*, and *The Spring and Autumn Annals*, Confucius and his disciples used *The Book of Poems* as a textbook for their students. Even when the First Emperor of the Qin Dynasty issued a decree to burn all the volumes, the book continues to be spread by scholars by word of mouth. It has also had great influence outside China. The book has been introduced to Japan, Korea, and Vietnam in an early time. From the beginning of the 18th century, versions of French, German, English and Russian come emerged.

Poetry of the South

Poetry of the south, also called Songs of Chu, was one of the folk style songs of Chu State created by representative poet Qu Yuan of the late Warring States Period. At the end of the Western Han Dynasty, Liu Xiang compiled 16 pieces of works by Qu Yuan, Shong Yu, and writings by Huainan Xiaoshan, Dong Fangsuo, Wang Bao and Liu Xiang, who followed Qu Yuan and Song Yu in writing style, completing great works. Liu Xiang named it *Songs of Chu* and later, Wang Yi added his works *Nine Thoughts*, which finally became 17 pieces of works with the name of *Poetry of the South*. Due to the of the representative work *Sorrow for Departure* of Qu Yuan, *Songs of Chu* set the style of the that region. As the first collection of romantic poems, it has exerted deep influence on literature afterwards, which not only marked a beginning of subsequent rhymed prose but also exerted an effect on prose writing of the past dynasties. *Songs of Chu* initiated a positively romantic poetry style in China.

The existent *Songs of Chu* mainly covers the works by Qu Yuan and Song Yu, encompassing a rich flavor of the local culture, literary style, dialects and rhymes of the Chu area. *Songs of Chu* reflects history and custom, natural landscape, and the stories of local people. In *Songs of Chu*, Historical stories, fairy tales, customs, as well as artistic style, ways of emotional expression, and the fustian style used by the poems, all contain lively cultural features from the Chu area, which consists of the basic foundation of the Poetry of South. Songs of Chu is a vital part of Chu culture, combining the local features and traits of central China.

One of main authors of *Songs of Chu* is Qu Yuan, who created the immortal masterpieces *Sorrow for Departure*, *Asking Heaven*, *Nine Songs*, *Nine Elegizes*, among many others, Qu Yuan (ca. 339–278 B.C.), whose given name is Ping, is the earliest patriotic poet in the history of Chi-

Qu Yuan

nese literature. In view of the threat to Chu from the powerful State of Qin, Qu Yuan argued for reform in the government and alliance with the wealthy state of Qi in the east against the State of Qin in the west to ensure the safety of Chu. Yet the King of Chu was surrounded by the self-absorbed, whom having accepted bribes from Qin's envoy, not only dissuaded the King from taking Qu Yuan's advice, but also had him removed from office. Moreover, when King Chu Xiang succeeded to the throne, Qu Yuan was banished in exile. Helpless in saving his own country and viewing his ambitions to reality, he drowned himself in the Miluo River. As a major work by Qu Yuan, in *Sorrow for Departure*, the political lyric reflects his advanced ideal, his unremitting striving for reality and ambition coupled with his frustration and depression. Full of passion and imagination, the lyric embodies his unswerving loyalty to his homeland and his firm determination to seek a higher conscious.

With a rich flavor of local characteristic, *Songs of Chu* was developed on the basis of folk songs of Chu area by re-creation and compiling. Owning to the difference of geography and language environment, the Chu area developed a unique style of music and singing called the Southern Feng since the ancient times. It has a long history characterized by popularity of sortilege and local people paying sacrifice to the heavens by hymns and dances. Volumes of mythology have been preserved in the list of songs, developing quickly the first grand religious atmosphere. The songs all have the distinctive high pitch, yet emerges is a deep profound color to the style. Therefore, the rise of *Songs of Chu* is closely connected with edification of folk music and local culture in the Chu area.

Songs of Chu is also the product of the combination of the northern Chu culture and northern central Chinese culture. After the Spring and Autumn and Warring States Periods, the State Chu, which has long been considered barren state, becomes increasingly stronger. In the process of frequent contacts with northern states in communication with central China and contending for hegemony, extensive exchanging of culture had been promoted between the south and the north, as well as central China. Due to this adjoining of southern and northern culture, the great poet, Qu Yuan, and his extraordinary poems of splendor *Songs of Chu* was able to blossom.

With an important role in Chinese poetry history, the appearance of *Songs of Chu* begins another volume of Chinese songs after *the Book of Songs*. Later generations equally entitled the *Book of Songs* and *Songs of Chu* respectively Feng and Sao. Feng refers to the culture of the fifteen vassal states, represented in the *Book of Songs* with realism and spirit. Sao refers to Li Sao (*Sorrow for Departure*), which magnifies the true romanticism of Chu poetry. Feng and Sao became the two schools of thought embodying the realism and romanticism of Chinese classic poetry.

Han Fu and Han Yue Fu

Han Fu(Han Phapsody) refers to the Han Dynasty era rhymed prose of combining elements of poetry and style, focusing on elaborating the theme. In its literary form, the vivid description of objects and the diverse content, expresses great aspiration. Han Fu mainly covers 5 varieties of

contents: the rendering of palaces and cities, description of king's hunting expeditions, narration of travel experience, expressing emotions, and various animals, birds, grasslands and forests. The two former QUOTES are the representative works of Han Fu,
becoming another new literary form in Chinese literature after *the Book of Songs* and *Songs of Chu* and
become the most popular literary form of that time. During the 400 years of the two Han dynasties,
scribes generally adapted to this literary form, becoming the fashion of the times, and is a key component of Han literature.

Han Fu consists of Greater Han Fu and Lesser Han Fu. Greater Han Rhapsody is also called
Lisao style rhapsody. It is grand in scale, with an extensive framework, containing majestic vigor and
flowing diction, forming masterpieces of extensive length. Jia Yi, Mei Cheng, Sima Xiangru, and
Yang Xiong were the masters in the Western Han Dynasty; and Ban Gu, Zhang Heng were representatives of Han Fu in the Eastern Han Dynasty. Among these artists, Sima Xiangru, Yang Xiong, Ban
Gu and Zhang Heng are known as the four masters of Han Fu. Developing the useful and discarding
the useless of Greater Han Fu, Lesser Han Fu with its shorter length and comely literary grace, focuses mainly on the reality of society and the natural surroundings. Zhao Yi, Cai Yong, Mi Heng are the
experts of Lesser Han Fu.

Han Fu, especially Greater Han Fu, enjoys a high status in Chinese literature history, despite the
shortcomings of the ornate rhetoric, attends to trifling things and neglects the essentials, lacks emotion; it still occupies a significant status in Chinese literary history. To begin with, Greater Han Fu describes palace courtyards, the king's hunting grounds, and great cities, depicting and eulogizing vast
areas of land, rich products, prosperous cities, and governing achievements made by State Han.
Moreover, the ruler is endowed with positive significance, indicating the cultural and military
achievements. Also, although Greater Han Fu boasts strange flowery rhetoric, certain achievements
had been made in terms of a rich vocabulary, the exercise of the language, and structure of the sentence; improving means of depicting the image. Furthermore, in the historical context, the prosperity
of Rhapsody in the two Han Dynasties promotes the formation of distinct ideas in Chinese literature.
From the beginning of *the Book of Songs* and *Songs of Chu*, to the Han Dynasty and the development of
Han Fu, literature and general learning begin to separate from each other. As there is more recognition of the literary characteristics, the ideology on becomes increasingly more transparent.

Han Yue Fu, a form of Chinese poetry of the Han Dynasty, is poetry collected by Yue Fu officials. Parts of the poetry are songs and their musical scores for the purpose of ceremonial court occasions by the rulers to their ancestors, similar to Hymns in *the Book of Songs*. Another characteristic is
the music passed down by generations, which are called Yue Fu ballads.

Yue Fu poetry is classified according to different form of music. In 100 volumes of *Collection of
Yue Fu Poetry* by Guo Maoqian of the Song Dynasty, which is so far the most integrated poetry collection from the Han Dynasty to the Five Dynasties. This sorts Yue Fu into 12 categories. Most prevalent
are the following 4 kinds: (1) songs in temple, which are used by aristocratic literati for sacrifice ceremony; (2) songs by drum and pipe, which are also called cymbals songs, were introduced from northern minority groups at the beginning of the Han Dynasty and mainly used as the military music of

that time.

Xianghe Ballads are for the most part folk songs and ballads passes on freely among commoners. Xianghe refers to a way of singing, including the use of a combination of silk and bamboo instruments with voices. (4) various songs is another form, yet the musical scores have been for the most part lost and can not be traced back to their origins. Most Han Yue Fu songs are preserved within the styles of xianghe, songs by drum and pipe, and various songs; among them, xianghe is the most prevalent.

Most of the over 40 ballads of Han Yue Fu are works of the Eastern Han Dynasty which have been kept in the *Collection of Yue Fu Poetry*, reflecting the social reality and people's life at that time. With sharp language to express feelings of love and hatred, the ballads tends to be realistic style, exposing resistance against class exploitation and oppression, criticizes war and compulsory service, protests feudal Confucian ethics and marriage, and sings praises of great love towards the common people.

Han Yue Fu is another collection of ballads of ancient times after *the Book of Songs*. Different from the romanticism of *the Book of Songs*, Han Yue Fu marks the beginning of realist style. The subject matter of women began to hold an important position in Han Yue Fu. Using common language to form a work of art relating to everyday life, there were adopted five emphasized topics. Among these are adopting a narrative, portraying the character to the finest detail, bringing about the character's temperament, the complete interwoven plot, as well as vivid description of particulars reaching a higher plane of thought and meaning. These are five distinct languages of poetry that play an important role in the development of Chinese writing styles.

The Roadside Mulberry and *The Peacock Flies Southeast* are examples of Han Yue Fu ballads. The latter is the longest narrative of ancient China and accompanied with *The Ballad of Mulan*, they are known as the two pearls of Yue Fu.

The Record of the Grand Historian,
The History of the Western Han

*T*he Record of the Grand Historian is China's first comprehensive history book written in biographical style, praised by later generations as "great works of historians without the rhyme of *Sorrow for Departure*". It records 3,000 years of Chinese history of from Emperor Huang to Emperor Han Wu, including 130 pieces, with 526,500 words. The book is composed of 5 parts including 12 Basic Annals, 8 Treatises, 10 Tables, 30 Genealogies and 70 Biographies. The Basic Annals depicts the reigns of various emperors, recording the emperors' words, deeds, and achievement while in power by succession. Biao is a brief timeline of events with regards to personages and history. Treatises records and narrates system development, laws of astronomy, music, military science, social economy, and aspects of the delta culture. Genealogies is a descriptive record of the succession of feudal offspring and inheritance in the dynastic aristocracies. Biographies is a collection of essays outlining important figures in history. *The Record of the Grand Historian* was complied from 104–91 B.C. and

was much admired by a great scholar, Dongfang Suo. In the book he
refers to himself with three characters as the Grand Scribe or Tai Shi Gong (太史公).
Tai Shi simply refers to his official position and Gong is an honorific term. *The Record of the Grand Historian* at first has no fixed title; it is also called *The Record of the Grand Scribe* or *The Book of the Grand Scribe*. The Record of the Grand Historian was the generic term used since the beginning of the Three Kingdoms, eventually becoming the famous Book of the Grand Scribe.

Sima Qian

The author of *The Record of the Grand Historian* is Sima Qian (145–90 B.C.), also called Tzu Chang, a well-known historiographer and literary master of the Han Dynasty. Each time before writing on a historical character or event, he would first conduct a full research within historical documents. It is with the precise and earnest writing style that he creates history. In his 20s he left Chang'an, capital of the Western Han and began his traveling and investigative experience of historical relics. He crossed numerous great mountains and rivers, broadening his vision and opening his mind while learning many anecdotes of historical figures and the local folk customs and economy. Ban Gu, a historian in the Han Dynasty, ever highly appraised Sima Qian's anthropologic approach and his full and accurate recording of historical events, eulogizing his objectivity, use of reliable historical facts, and practical realistic recording. This is a golden achievement for Sima Qian in that what he wanted to reflect was true history and providing historical reference for feudal rulers. He would select historical figures according to his or her practical conduction rather than social status or official position. For instance, he wrote great volumes of biographies regarding the wandering of knight's, merchants, doctors, and introduced extremely worthy people of the lower class. In his heart, these people have noble desirable attributes.

The Record of the Grand Historian marks a beginning of historical works written in the style of biography and interweaving ways by combining various knowledge of politics, economics, nationality, and culture; while carrying on age-old historical tradition of precise realistic writing. It casts an extensive influence on fiction, drama, biographical literature, and prose of the ancient times. It is a great monument, both in Chinese historic and literary history.

Following *The Record of the Grand Historian*, another historical classic, *The Book of Han* was written by Ban Gu (32–92 A.D). Born in Fufeng Anlin (the northeast part of Xianyang City in Shanxi province), he was a genius from a child and could compose writings as early as 9 years old, studying extensively as he grew up the Nine Schools of Thought. *The Record of the Grand Historian* records the history until the early years of Emperor Wu of the Han Dynasty. Therefore, at that time many people attempted to continue in this manner of writing. Yet Ban Gu's father, Ban Biao, was not satisfied with these continuations thus writing 65 articles in Post Biography with for *The Record of the Grand*

Historian. After his father passed away when in his 20's, Ban Gu set about collecting and settling his father's posthumous manuscript with a determination of succeeding his father's cause and finishing a continuation of *The Records*—compiling *The Record of the Grand Historian Post Biography*. Not long after his publishing his work *The Book of Han*, somebody in the court lodged an accusation against him of "conspiring to alter national history" and he was put into jail, all the books in his home confiscated. Later, Ban Chao, his younger brother, reported to Emperor Ming of the Han stating the intention of his brother in compiling and writing the book. Local officials also presented Ban Gu's manuscript for the emperor. After understanding the situation, the emperor appreciated talents of Ban Gu and summoned him to the division of records and appointed him as an official in charge of proofreading historical documents.

The style of *the Book of Han*, compared with *The Record of the Grand Historian*, developed in change. *The Record of the Grand Historian* is a general history, while the Book of Han writes of dynastic history. Basic Annals in the former was simply titled Annals in The Book of Han, Treatises was changed into Records, and the content on the meritorious ministers in Genealogy was combined into the Biographies section. Other historical books hereafter followed these changes in style. *The Book of Han* includes 12 pieces of the Annals of emperors, 8 Tables, 10 Records, 70 Biographies, altogether 100 pieces, which were divided into 120 volumes by later generations mainly recording a history of 230 years from the First Year (206 B.C) of Emperor Gao Zu of the Han Dynasty to the Fourth Year of Di Huang of Wang Mang (23 A.D). It is another milestone of historical classics after The Record of the Grand Historian.

Discussing and comparing imperial edicts were the main point in *The Book of Han*. In addition, biographies on minority groups across frontiers were many. It adds the new contents as *The Record of Criminal Law*, *The Record of the Five Phases of Philosophy*, *The Record of Geography*, and *The Record of Art and Literature*. Evolution of law system and some concrete law regulations were systematically recited for the first time in *The Record of Criminal Law*. *The Record of the Five Phases of Philosophy* systematically recorded the natural calamity phenomenas from the *Spring and Autumn* to the end of Western Han dynasty. In *The Record of Geography*, county and district partition, history evolution and registered permanent residence of that time were recorded. Moreover, records on local products, the situation of economic development and folk customs were especially attractive. Textual research on origins of various academic schools can be found in *The Record of Art and Literature*, in which a catalogue of books has been preserved that were recorded as the earliest existing in China.In addition, *The Record on Agriculture and Commerce*, with more detailed content, was evolved from *Pingzhun Shu*. It consisted of two volumes. The first volume was on the agricultural and economic situation, the second regarding commerce and the monetary situation, which was the specialized economy of that time.

Although *the Book of Han* contains orthodox feudal ideology, it marks a new compilation style of employing the history of dynasties while sequentially recording biography. It embodies a wealth of material as many important historical documents have been preserved, playing an important role in Chinese historiography.

第一单元

龙文化

中国文化中,龙有着重要的地位和影响。从距今7000多年的新石器时代,先民们对原始龙的图腾崇拜,到今天人们仍然多以带有"龙"字的成语或典故来形容生活中的美好事物。上下数千年,龙已渗透到中国社会的各个方面,成为一种文化的凝聚和积淀。龙成了中国的象征、中华民族的象征、中国文化的象征。"龙的子孙"、"龙的传人"这些称谓,常令中国人激动、奋发、自豪。

那么,龙的原形是什么?龙的概念是怎样形成的?它的形象与文化含意又是如何发展变化的? 龙在中国文化中有何影响?

古人对龙有种种解释。有人说龙是蛇没有脚而能飞,有人说龙的形象是马首蛇尾,还有人说龙的形状是鹿的角、牛的耳朵、驼的头、兔的眼、蛇的颈、蜃的腹、鱼的鳞、鹿的脚掌、鹰的爪子。这显然是晚期发展了龙的形象,比最初的龙越来越复杂,被综合进去的图腾也越来越多,说明它在不断丰富发展。对于龙的主体原形的探讨,后世学者们作过许多有益的研究。有鳄鱼说、蜥蜴说、马说等等,但普遍认同龙的基调是蛇。最初系统提出这一见解的是闻一多的名篇《伏羲考》。闻一多认为,蛇氏族兼并别的氏族以后,"吸收了许多别的形形色色的图腾团族(氏族),大蛇这才接受了兽类的四脚、马的头、鬣的尾、鹿的角、狗的爪、鱼的鳞和须",而成为后来的龙。

虽然第一条龙只有一种单一的形象,但随着中国古人彼此间的联系越来越多,人们开始把他们的图腾描绘得更具有想象力。经过很长一段时间,这种图像就演化成了一种性质完全不同的龙或图腾。龙的种类开始丰富多样,有鳞的叫蛟龙,有角的叫虬龙,无角的叫螭龙,有翅膀的叫应龙,一只脚的叫夔龙,龙头鱼身的叫鱼龙,一头双身的叫肥翼龙,一身双头的叫窃由龙,可喷火的叫火龙等等;龙的姿态也逐渐变化多端,正襟危坐的是坐龙,缓缓行走的是行龙,头向上而飞升的是升龙,头向下而俯降的是降龙,两条龙戏耍一颗火珠的是双龙戏珠,奔腾在云雾中的是云龙等等。

龙成为中华民族共同的图腾,首先是因为龙包含着自然崇拜的因素,也就是说,人们把龙当做主宰风雪雨露的神来敬重。从地理环境角度来看,中国基本处在温带气候带,又有着广阔的内陆腹地,非常适宜农耕文明的生息繁衍,自古以来,就一直以农业立国,而雨水又是农业生产的命脉,只有风调雨顺,才能五谷丰登,家给人足,否则就会颗粒无收,饿殍遍野。正是基于这一利害关系,古人对以蛇为基调的龙的威力产生了敬畏,形成了龙的图腾崇拜。因为蛇类尤其是大型蛇类往往存在于幽谷深潭或沼泽之中,这些地带终年不涸,再者蛇类又喜欢在阴雨雾霭的天气里溯游戏水,还能在森林草树间游弋如飞,似能呼风唤雨、腾云驾雾,从而古人就将其同主宰风雨的神相附会了。龙作为图腾最初源于远古的个别部落,后来,随着历史的向前推进,各部落间因战争、迁徙、杂居、通婚等因素,彼此间文化相互渗透融合,就逐渐形成了中国历史上广泛的龙图腾崇拜。

在封建社会,龙的神威则长期被历代帝王利用以树立个人权威,并成为皇室的标志。皇帝是"真龙天子",穿龙袍、戴龙冠、坐龙椅、乘龙舟。皇帝生病说是龙体欠安,生气要说龙颜大怒,生了儿子称作龙种,皇帝的一切都因为跟龙扯上关系而显示出他的至尊地位。因此,那些代表统治者至高权力的宫廷建筑,如故宫,雕梁画栋必要有龙。如今,作为封建统治者守护神的龙早已不知去向,而在民间,从远古以来就一脉相承的游艺风俗则代代相传,积淀成为中华民族精神的象征,龙逐渐渗透到文化传统和社会生活的各个方面。人物姓氏、亭台楼阁、乃至江河湖水,往往以龙为名,元宵节看龙灯,端午节赛龙舟,天上有龙星,地下有龙脉,动物有龙马、植物有龙柏,十二生肖中也少不了龙。此外,冠以龙字的词语、成语也不计其数,如龙腾虎跃、龙飞凤舞、生龙活虎、龙吟虎啸、藏龙卧虎、龙马精神等。总之,与龙有联系的文化现象数不胜数。

值得一提的是,中国的"龙"与西方的"dragon"不同,中国的龙的形象是正面的,人们把各种美德和优秀的品质集中到龙的身上,龙是英勇善战的,它不畏强暴;龙是聪明多智的,它能预测未来;龙是本领高强的,它能大能小,变化多端;龙是富裕神气的,龙宫成为权威的象征,宝藏的集中地;龙又是正直善良的,它解救人们的干旱之苦。而"dragon"常常是作为魔鬼的化身,是恶的、消极的形象。

中国龙的文化除了在中华大地上传播承继外,还被远渡海外的华人带到了世界各地,在世界各国的华人居住区或中国城内,最多和最引人注目的饰物仍然是龙。遍布世界各地称之为唐人街的华人聚居区,大多数的入口处,都建有一座引人注目的中国式牌楼,牌楼上的一个重要装饰就是龙。例如美国首都华盛顿第七街口的中国城,一座饰有 270 条金龙的大型牌楼矗立在城端,蔚为奇观。漫步唐人街上,各种以龙形招徕顾客的广告比比皆是,街头到处挂着龙灯。海外的中国传统建筑,龙形的各种装饰,几乎成为独特的建筑风格。如日本长崎的孔庙,整座建筑几乎是用龙雕饰而成,连殿前的御道也铺设有雕刻精美的龙阶。海外以龙命名的地方也不少,如澳大利亚的龙城,马来西亚的石龙门和日本岩手县的龙泉洞等。甚至连一些并不引人注意的地方,也能发现关于龙的印记。如意大利、日本等国,都曾发行过设计精美的龙图案的纪念邮票。

中华民族的形成过程是一个融合的过程,龙参与、伴随、见证、标志了这个过程。龙的传人主要指文化精神的一脉相承,而非血缘意义上的基因遗传。中华始祖的文化精神与龙融合、福生、谐天、奋进的精神同一。因此,中华民族只能是龙的传人。随着龙文化的广远流传,"龙的传人"、"龙的国度"也获得了世界的认同。(倪爱珍编著)

朝代变迁

中国历史悠久,朝代更零星纷繁。每朝的创建者第一件事就是确立国号(朝代名称)。国号就是一个国家的称号。

中国最早的朝代是公元前21世纪建立的夏朝,由于最后一位君王桀残暴,商汤起兵推翻了他的政权,而商汤建立的就是第二个朝代,即商朝。

商朝的最后一位君主是纣,纣王残暴,导致民怨沸腾,西岐崛起,姬昌和他的儿子姬发领导人民起兵伐纣,他们建立了周朝。

周朝后期就是春秋战国,这一时期中国处于分裂时期,大小诸侯国并存,直到公元前221年,秦王嬴政并吞六国,建立中国历史上第一个封建王朝——秦朝。

由于秦始皇命万人修长城,挖渠道,劳民伤财,加上秦朝后期朝政腐败,民怨沸腾,刘邦率众推翻秦朝、打败项羽,于公元前206年建立了汉王朝。刘汉王朝又分为西汉、东汉两朝,统治了中国四百多年。

到了东汉后期,群雄崛起,著名的三国鼎立便形成于此时。这一时期,群雄混战,曹操、孙权、刘备争权,诸葛亮、周瑜斗勇,各显神通,在中国历史上写下了精彩的篇章。

三国争战达半个世纪之久,最终吴、蜀为魏所灭。但好景不长,265年,魏司马炎篡权,建立了晋。晋代统治中国150余年,于420年灭亡,中国又进入一个四分五裂的时期,这就是南北朝时期。

其中,南朝先后经历了宋、齐、梁、陈四个小朝代,北朝则经历了魏、齐、周等国的统治。

公元581年,一个叫杨坚的人结束了中国分裂的局面,统一了南北,建立了隋朝。隋朝是个短暂的王朝,隋朝的第二个皇帝,隋炀帝杨广荒淫无道,民怨沸腾,因此李渊携子李世民率众推翻了隋朝,于618年建立了唐朝。

唐朝是中国历史上最繁盛的朝代之一,经济发达、文化繁荣,在当时世界上产生了很大的影响,因此直到今天,不少外国人还称中国人为"唐人"。

唐朝后期,由于安史之乱,衰败已经无法挽回,最终灭亡,继之而起的先后为后梁、后唐、后晋、后汉、后周五个朝代。在这五朝之外,还相继出现了前蜀、后蜀、吴、南唐、吴越、闽、楚、南汉、南平、北汉等"十国",史称"五代十国"。

公元960年,后周将军赵匡胤,黄袍加身当上了皇帝,建立了宋朝。

宋朝时常受到周边契丹、女真族、蒙古族等外族的骚扰。宋朝崇文抑武,居安求和,后期奸臣当权,朝政腐败,最终无法和日渐强大的蒙古族对抗,于 1279 年为忽必烈所灭。中国进入了新的时期——元朝。

任何一个封建王朝从建立到灭亡都有一个规律,就是后期朝政腐败,元朝后期,被推翻不仅仅因为衰败,还有当时的汉人不满于被蒙古人统治等原因,当时起义军非常之多,最后成功的只有朱元璋。

朱元璋文有刘基,武有徐达,推翻了元朝,于 1368 年建立了明朝。明朝统治了中国近三百年,后期朝廷腐败,被崛起于中国东北的满族打败,清朝建立。

清朝是中国历史上又一个繁盛的朝代,尤其是经过康熙、雍正、乾隆的治理,政治、经济、文化、学术等方面都达到了空前的高度。

清朝后期,朝政走向腐败,外国侵略者更是乘虚而入,国内军阀鹊起,外忧内患之时,孙中山领导人民反帝反封,推翻了中国历史上最后一个封建王朝,于 1911 年建立了中华民国。之后又经历了长期的反侵略斗争及国内战争,在毛泽东的率领下,于 1949 年建立了中华人民共和国,简称中国。

关于中国朝代的变迁,流传较广的有这样一首歌谣:

夏商与西周,
东周分两段。
春秋和战国,
一统秦两汉。
三分魏蜀吴,
二晋前后沿。
南北朝并立,
隋唐五代传。
宋元明清后,
皇朝至此完。

(刘双琴编著)

少数民族

中国自古以来就是一个统一的多民族国家。新中国成立后,通过识别并经中央政府确认的民族共有 56 个。

由于汉族以外的 55 个民族人口较少,习惯上称之为"少数民族"。他们是:蒙古族、回族、藏族、维吾尔族、苗族、彝族、壮族、布依族、朝鲜族、满族、侗族、瑶族、白族、土家族、哈尼族、哈萨克族、傣族、黎族、傈僳族、佤族、畲族、高山族、拉祜族、水族、东乡族、纳西族、景颇族、柯尔克孜族、土族、达斡尔族、仫佬族、羌族、布朗族、撒拉族、毛南族、仡佬族、锡伯族、阿昌族、普米族、塔吉克族、怒族、乌兹别克族、俄罗斯族、鄂温克族、德昂族、保安族、裕固族、京族、塔塔尔族、独龙族、鄂伦春族、赫哲族、门巴族、珞巴族、基诺族。

依照 2000 年第五次全国人口普查统计的结果，人口数排在前五位的少数民族依次是壮族、满族、回族、苗族、维吾尔族，依次为 1700 万、1068 万、980 万、894 万、840 万。

中国各民族分布的特点是大杂居、小聚居，相互交错居住。汉族地区有少数民族聚居，少数民族地区也有汉族居住。这种分布格局是长期历史发展过程中各民族间相互交往、流动而形成的。少数民族人口虽少，但分布很广。主要分布在内蒙古、新疆、宁夏、广西、西藏、云南、贵州、青海、四川、甘肃、辽宁、吉林、湖南、湖北、海南、台湾等省、自治区。民族成分最多的是云南省，有 25 个民族。

中国少数民族地区地域辽阔，资源丰富。草原面积 30000 万公顷，占全国草原面积的 75%，中国著名的 5 大天然牧区，都在少数民族地区；森林面积 5648 万公顷，占全国的 43.6%；林木蓄积量 52.49 亿立方米，占全国的 55.9%；水力资源蕴藏量 4.46 亿千瓦，占全国总量的 65.9%。此外，还有大量的矿藏资源，以及丰富的动植物资源和旅游资源。

民族区域自治制度是中国政府结合中国实际情况采取的一项基本政策，也是中国的一项重要政治制度。1945 年 5 月，中国建立了中国共产党领导下的第一个相当于省一级的民族自治地区内蒙古自治区。中华人民共和国成立以后，又相继建立了新疆维吾尔自治区、广西壮族自治区、宁夏回族自治区和西藏自治区。截至目前，全国 55 个少数民族中，有 44 个民族建立了自治地方，自治面积占全国国土总面积的 64% 左右。中国共产党和政府坚持贯彻执行民族平等政策，少数民族的语言文字、宗教信仰等都得到了应有的尊重和法律的保障。

少数民族在长期的历史发展过程中，形成了独具特色的文化。以风俗习惯为例，各个民族具有不同的生产方式和生活方式，表现在服饰、饮食、居住、婚姻、礼仪、丧葬等多方面。饮食上，中国约有十个少数民族有食用清真食品的传统习惯。丧葬上，有火葬、土葬、水葬、天葬等不同葬法。年节习俗更是丰富多彩。如：藏族的藏历新年、"雪顿节"，回族、维吾尔等民族的"开斋节"、"古尔邦节"，蒙古族的"那达慕"、傣族的"泼水节"、彝族的"火把节"等等。(倪爱珍编著)

家的观念

家对中国人有着特殊的含义：家意味着温暖，家意味着安全，家意味着团聚；家有慈母严父，家有贤妻娇子，家有亲朋好友；家乡有熟悉的山水，家乡有珍馐美味小吃，家乡有美丽的历史传说……由家而衍生出来的家乡恋情和国家情怀，游子归故，成为海内外炎黄子孙对祖国的一种浓浓的思乡情怀。

中国是一个非常重亲情的国度，中华民族是一个非常恋家的民族，家、亲情、团圆在中国人心目中一直有着非同一般的分量，团团圆圆也一直是中华传统文化里非常核心的理念。因此中国人有一句俗语，"血浓于水"。"每逢佳节倍思亲"，春节、清明、中秋、重阳等传统节日到来时，中国人都会加倍思念家人。

春节是中国一年一度最盛大的传统节日，每年这一天，在外工作或学习的人都会力破万难，不顾路途的遥远与艰辛，回到家中与亲人团聚。中国的春节，其实只有一个主题，那就是团圆。一家人围坐在热气腾腾的饭桌旁，就是透着那么一股喜庆热闹劲儿，这可以算是中国民间过年的最大特点了，而这里面深含的却是浓浓的亲情。

八月十五"中秋节"也是一个家家盼团圆的传统节日。利用这样的一个月圆之夜，全家老老小小围坐桌旁，听着爷爷奶奶的唠叨，伴着孩子们的欢笑，沐浴着柔和的月光，一家人共享天伦之乐，这一直是中国人心的一个情结。所以中秋佳节在中国人心中有着别样的地位，"中秋"已经成为了团圆的一个符号，深深地印在每一个中国人的心里。

中国人受儒家思想的影响几千年，"孝"是中国家庭最看重的美德，中国人常说："百行孝为先"、"孝子贤孙"、"孝思不匮"。孝文化是中国人伦理文化的代表，是中国人家庭观念的核心之一。中国素来有"礼仪之邦"之称，强调亲情、友情、世情、乡情等，倡导尊老爱幼的伦理道德标准。中国儒家文化，以孝、悌、忠、信、礼、义、廉、耻等"八字"来代表，其首位是"孝"，核心为"仁"。中国人常说的"父慈子孝，兄友弟恭"，正是几千年来养老育幼、代际互动的伦理文化。

中国人在家庭中还特别重视父母、长辈的意见，常说："家有一老，如有一宝"；"不听老人言，吃亏在眼前"，特别是后一句谚语，正是在强调长辈的经验对于年轻人的指导作用。中国人还强调家庭教育对孩子人格形成的重要影响，常说"子不教，父之过"，"上梁不正下梁歪"，"小时偷针，长大偷金"，等等。

中国人重团圆、重亲情、讲孝道，并强调家庭的和睦。中国人最期望的就是"安家乐业"、"家和万事兴"。而最令人遗憾莫过于同室操戈，古诗云："本是同根生，相煎何太急"。当家庭中出现了矛盾的时候，中国人最忌讳把这些矛盾暴露在外人面前，所以中国人常说"家丑不可外扬"。"和为贵"、"和气生财"，这对于中国人来说非常重要，对于社会的繁荣也极为重要。

由于封建宗法制度的影响，古代中国人家族观念中有强烈的"重尊卑、别长幼"思想，非常讲求"尊卑有序、长幼有别"，说话做事不能"没大没小"、"没老没少"，对长者不能直呼其名，否则就是没有礼貌。在中国封建社会，这种"重尊卑、别长幼"思想非常严格，并形成了"三纲五常"等系统的制度。

中国人重家族，家族的一个标志就是"姓氏"，中国在汉代已有了关于姓氏的系统性著作。姓氏文化的成熟标志着家族的稳定，续写家谱因此成为中华民族特有的一种文化活动。家谱是家族人伦观念及传统文化的重要载体，是寻根问祖的最重要依据，有睦宗族、正风俗、明教化等作用。家谱让中国人知道自己的父母子女关系，知道自己是有根的，自己并不孤独；同时知道自己的行为要对得起祖宗，自己的成功有赖祖德荫庇，从而懂得谦卑，更好地处理好各种人伦关系。因而，修家谱对于中国人来说是一件具有重大意义的事情。

中国历史悠久，且一直追求强盛统一，因此在中国人眼里，家虽然非常重要，国也同样重要，甚至国要大于家，特别是战争年代，涌现了一大批仁人志士，保家卫国，爱国如家，国而忘家，舍小家顾大家，为了国家的安危献出自己的生命，他们是中华民族的骄傲。在中国，家，总是与国连在一起的，才有了这个文明绵延五千年的"国家"，也有了中国人亘古不变的家国情怀。（刘双琴编著）

婚俗

中国人把婚姻看做人生中非常重要的一件事情,关涉到家庭幸福、家族香火的延续和社会的安定,因此有关婚姻的习俗也就特别繁多,结婚的仪式有很多讲究,十分复杂。

传统的中国婚礼包括"三书六礼"。

"三书"包括聘书、礼书、迎亲书。

聘书是定亲之书,男女双方正式缔结婚约,纳吉(过文定)时用。礼书是过礼之书,即礼物清单,详尽列明礼物种类及数量,纳征(过大礼)时用。迎亲书是迎娶新娘之书,结婚当日(亲迎)接新娘过门时用。

"六礼"指纳采、问名、纳吉、纳征、请期、亲迎。

纳采就是今天所说的提亲,古代婚礼,强调"父母之命,媒妁之言",因此男女结婚,男方一定要延请媒人到女方家提亲。

问名通常也叫做"合八字",男方探问女方的姓名及生日时辰,以卜吉兆。

纳吉也称"过文定"或"小定",问名若属吉兆,遣媒人致赠薄礼,谓之纳吉。

纳征也叫"过大礼",即正式送聘礼奉送礼金、礼饼、礼物及祭品等。

请期今称"择日",由男家请算命先生选择结婚日期。

择日之后,新郎乘礼车,于结婚之日赴女家迎接新娘,谓之亲迎。

传统的中国婚礼仪式主要包括以下步骤:

1. 换庚谱。媒人提亲后,若男女双方八字相合,没有相冲,便互相交换两家的庚谱,作为定亲的最初凭据。

2. 过文定。为"过大礼"的前奏,通常在婚礼前一个月举行。男家择定良辰吉日,携备三牲酒礼至女家,正式奉上聘书。

3. 过大礼。定亲之最隆重仪式,约在婚前十五至二十天进行。男家择定良辰吉日,携带礼金和多种礼品送到女家。

4. 安床。择定良辰吉日,在婚礼前数天由好命佬将新床搬至适当位置。然后,在婚礼之前,再由好命婆负责铺床,将床褥、床单及龙凤被等铺在床上,并撒上各式喜果,如红枣、桂圆、荔枝干、红绿豆。

安床后任何人皆不得进入新房及触碰新床,直至新人于结婚当晚进房为止。结婚当晚,新人进新房后可让小孩在床上食喜果,称为"压床",取其百子千孙之意。新郎的同辈兄弟可以闹新房,古时认为"新人不闹不发,越闹越发",并能为新人驱邪避凶,婚后如意吉祥。

5. 送嫁妆。收到大礼后,女家的妆套须最迟于结婚前一天送到男家。这批大箱小箱的嫁妆,为女家身份与财富的象征。嫁妆除珍贵的珠宝首饰外,主要是一些象征好兆头的东西,如:剪刀(蝴蝶双飞)、片糖(甜甜蜜蜜)、银包皮带(腰缠万贯)、花瓶(花开富贵)、铜盆及鞋(同偕到老)、龙凤被、床单、枕头等。

6. 上头。男女双方在婚礼前夕,择定良辰(男方要比女方早一个小时),进行上头仪式。这种仪式须由"好命佬"及"好命婆"(分别是男女双方的长辈或亲友,择父母子女健在,婚姻和睦者)在男女双方各自家中举行。一对新人均要穿上睡衣,女方应选择一个能看见月亮的窗口案上,燃起龙凤烛,点起清香一炷,连同莲子、红枣、汤丸三碗,每碗六个或九个,生果、烧肉及鸡心向天参拜。男女双方并要准备尺、镜、剪刀,即所谓"龙头镜、较剪尺",取其光明继后之意,让"好命佬"及"好命婆"替新人梳头,一面梳,一面说:"一梳梳到尾,二梳梳到白发齐眉,三梳梳到儿孙满地,四梳梳到四条银笋尽标齐。"上头象征一对新人已步入"成人"阶段。

7. 迎亲。在中国,接新娘是整个婚礼的一大高潮。新郎在众人陪同下,携着花球迎接新娘。当抵达女家后,第一关便是"入门"。若要顺利接得美人归,必须经过一连串智力及体能测试,必要时还加上唱情歌,但最重要的还是丰厚的"开门利是",即打点女方众姊妹的茶点礼物等,众姊妹满意后才开门。新郎顺利入门后,姊妹应以茶点招待兄弟。开门后,新娘应由大姐或伴娘带领出来交给其父亲,再由父亲交给新郎,正式行夫妻见面礼。新人先拜天地,再向双亲奉茶跪拜,最后新人对拜。新娘准备两封红包,分别为威旺金及满堂利是,过门后交予家姑。

8. 出门。在露天地方,由大姐或伴娘撑起红伞护着新娘,意指开枝散叶。大姐及众姊妹一边行,一边向上空、伞顶及花车顶撒米(可加红绿豆),用来"喂金鸡",意思指鸡啄米后便不会啄新娘。吉时,女子出门时须由大姐背着上花轿,据说新娘双足是不可沾地的,否则便会带来麻烦。上花车前,新娘子应向送行的亲友鞠躬,以示谢意。

9. 过门。过门指新娘由女家出门后正式踏入男家,拜见翁姑及男家其他长辈。

10. 三朝回门。在婚后第三天,新妇在夫婿陪同下,带备烧猪及礼品回娘家祭祖,甚至小住一段日子,然后再随夫婿回家。

现代的婚礼仍然保留一部分传统的习俗,但已经简化很多,而且有许多新式婚礼不断出现,但总体来讲,中国人的婚礼讲究隆重、喜庆、热闹。亲朋好友都会道贺,祝愿新人白头偕老,早生贵子等。(刘双琴编著)

第二单元

四大发明

中国是世界文明古国,有着悠久的历史和灿烂的文化。中国的四大发明——造纸术、印刷术、火药、指南针是中华民族奉献给世界的伟大科技成果,对人类历史的进程产生过巨大的影响。马克思精辟地指出:"火药、指南针、印刷术——这是预告资产阶级社会到来的三大发明。火药把骑士阶层炸得粉碎,指南针打开了世界市场并建立了殖民地,而印刷术则变成了新教的工具,总的来说变成了科学复兴的手段,变成对精神发展创造必要前提的最强大的杠杆。"

造纸术

东汉时期（105 年），蔡伦在前人造纸术的基础上，发明和推广了新的造纸技术，改变了商代用甲骨，西周用青铜器，春秋用竹简、木牍、缣帛作为书写材料的历史，适应了汉代经济社会繁荣发展的新形势，为汉代文明的勃兴作出了重大贡献。

蔡伦用树皮、麻头、破布、渔网，经过挫、捣、抄、烘等一系列的工艺加工，制成植物纤维纸，这也是真正意义上的纸。105 年，蔡伦向汉和帝献纸，受到和帝赞誉，造纸术因此广为天下知。蔡伦造的纸被称为"蔡侯纸"，105 年则被认为是造纸术的发明年。

印刷术

大约在唐朝时，人们发明了雕版印刷术。它的具体操作程序是：把木材锯成一块块木板，把要印的字写在薄纸上，反贴在木板上，再根据每个字的笔画，用刀一笔一笔雕刻成阳文（凸出来的文字），使每个字的笔画突出在板上。木板雕好以后，就可以印书了。印书的时候，先用一把刷子蘸了墨，在雕好的板上刷一下，接着，用白纸覆盖在板上，另外拿一把干净的刷子在纸背上轻轻刷一下，把纸拿下来，一页书就印好了。一页一页印好以后，装订成册，一本书也就成功了。这种印刷方法，是在木板上雕好字再印的，所以被称作"雕版印刷"。

北宋时期，平民发明家毕昇总结历代雕版印刷经验，经过反复试验，在宋仁宗庆历年间（1041—1048）制成胶泥活字，实行排版印刷，大大提高了印刷的效率，完成了印刷史上一项重大的革命。

火药

火药是中国古代炼丹家在炼丹过程中发明的。他们在炼制丹药过程中，偶然发现将适量的硫黄与硝石混合再加上木炭会着火甚至爆炸。这其实就是最早的火药配方。

但那时人们对火药在军事上的应用并没有过多的兴趣，直到唐末五代时期，天下大乱，烽烟四起，许多原先寄食于豪门贵族家中的方士流离失所，有的投身军旅，从而逐渐将火药配方引用至军事方面，相继出现了一系列火药武器。到了宋代，许多城市都设有火药兵器制造业，军队也已大量配备火药弓箭、火药火炮箭等。早期的火药兵器威力有限，不可能取代刀剑等冷兵器。但自南宋中期以后，火药兵器在兵器中的比重显著增大。在此后的宋、金、元之间的战争中，火药的使用愈益频繁。

指南针

指南针是利用磁铁在地球磁场中的南北指极性而制成的一种指向仪器。最早出现的指南工具叫司南，战国时已普遍使用。它是利用天然磁石琢磨而成，样子像一只勺，重心位于底部正中，底盘光滑，四周刻二十四向。使用时把长勺放在底盘上，用手轻拨，使它转动，停下后长柄就指向南方。

用天然磁石制成的司南，成品较低，磁性较弱。到了宋代，人们发明了人工磁化方法，制造了指南鱼和指南针。特别是指南针，使用起来非常方便。它是以天然磁石摩擦钢针制成，在地磁作用下保持指南性能。后来人们把它装置在方位盘上，就称为罗盘。这是指南针发展史上的一大飞跃。

指南针在公元 11 世纪时已是常用的定向仪器。指南针的最大贡献，是大大地促进了航海事业的发展。（倪爱珍编著）

算盘和珠算

算盘是中国传统的计算工具。中国古代的一项重要发明,在阿拉伯数字出现前是世界广为使用的计算工具。算盘是中国人在长期使用算筹的基础上发明的,迄今已有 600 多年的历史。古时候,人们用小木棍进行计算,这些小木棍叫"算筹",用算筹作为工具进行的计算叫"筹算"。后来,随着生产的发展,用小木棍进行计算受到了限制,于是,人们又发明了更先进的计算器——算盘。

现存的算盘形状不一、材质各异。一般的算盘多为木制(或塑料制品),算盘由矩形木框内排列一串串等数目的算珠组成,中有一道横梁把珠统分为上下两部分,算珠内贯直柱,俗称"档",一般为 9 档、11 档或 15 档。档中横以梁,梁上 2 珠(财会用为 1 珠,每珠代表 5;梁下 5 珠(财会用为 4 珠),每珠代表 1。

关于算盘的来历,有一个美丽的传说。相传黄帝时代有没有算账先生,黄帝统一部落后,物质越来越多,算账、管账成为每家每户每个人经常碰到的事,出出进进的实物数目越多越乱,黄帝为此事大为恼火。黄帝宫里的隶首于是想出了一个办法,就是用不同的野果给交上来的不同猎物记账,这样上交猎物的人谁也别想赖账。谁料,好景不长。各种野果存放时间一长,全都腐烂了,账目也全混乱了。隶首于是又想出一种办法,用不同颜色的石头片给不同的猎物记账,这下记账再也不怕变色腐烂了。由于隶首一时高兴没有严格保管。有一天,他外出有事,他的孩子引来一群顽童,一见隶首家放着很多盘盘,里边放着不同颜色的美丽石片,孩子们觉得好奇,你争我看一不小心,盘子掉地打碎,石头片全散了。隶首的账目又乱了。他一人蹲在地上只得一个个往回捡。隶首妻子花女走过来,指点:"你给石片上穿一个眼,用绳子串起来就不会乱了!"隶首顿时茅塞大开,便给每块不同颜色石片都打上眼,用细绳逐个穿起来。每穿够十个数或 100 个数,中间穿一个不同颜色的石片。这样清算起来就省事多了。隶首自己也经常心中有数。从此,宫里宫外,上上下下,再没有发生虚报冒领的事了。

随着生产不断向前发展,获得的各种猎物、皮张、数字越来越大,品种越来越多,要穿的石片越来越多,非常麻烦。隶首为此很苦恼。风后知道了,便告诉隶首说:"算账不需要用那么多的石片。只用 100 个石片就够了。"隶首还是不明白,风后继续解释说:"比如,今天猎队交回 5 只鹿,就从竹棒上往上推 5 个石片;明天再交回 6 只鹿,5 个加 6 个是 11 个,就向前进一位。从颗数上看,只有两个,实际上是 11 个数。就是说,每够十个数,每够 100 个数,都要向前进一位。"隶首又问:"进位后,怎么能记得下!"风后接着说:"这好办,进位后,应划个记号。比如,十个数后边划个圈(10);100 个数后边划两个圈(100);1000 个数后边划三个圈(1000);10000 个数后边划四个圈(10000)。这就叫个、十、百、千、万。"隶首于是回家做了一个大泥盘,把人们从龟肚子挖出来白色珍珠拣回来,给每颗上边打成眼。每 10 颗一穿,穿成 100 个数的"算盘"。然后在上边写清位数;如十位、百位、千位、万位。从此,记数、算账再也用不着那么多的石片了。

算盘,中华民族当代"计算机"的前身,5000 年前就这样诞生了。随着时代不断前进,算盘不断得到改进,成为今天的"珠算"。特别是民间,当初认字人不多,但只要懂得了算盘的基本原理和操作规程,人人都会应用,所以,算盘在古老中国民间很快广泛流传和被应用。

随着算盘的使用,人们总结出许多计算口诀,使计算的速度更快了。这种用算盘计算的方法,叫珠算。珠算有对应四则运算的相应法则,统称珠算法则。相对一般运算来看,熟练的珠算不逊于计算器,尤其在加减法方面。用时,可依口诀,上下拨动算珠,进行计算。珠算计算简便迅捷,为中国商店普遍使用的计算工具。到了明代,珠算不但能进行加减乘除的运算,还能计算土地面积和各种形状东西的大小。

由于算盘制作简单,价格便宜,珠算口诀便于记忆,运算又简便,所以在中国被普遍使用,并且陆续流传到了日本、朝鲜、美国和东南亚等国家和地区。

现在,已经进入了电子计算机时代,但是古老的算盘仍然发挥着重要的作用。在中国,各行各业都有一批打算盘的高手。使用算盘和珠算,除了运算方便以外,还有锻炼思维能力的作用,因为打算盘需要脑、眼、手的密切配合,是锻炼大脑的一种好方法。(刘双琴编著)

驿道和驿站

中国古代道路可以分为驰道、驿道和栈道等种类,驿道是其中最重要的一种。驿道是中国古代为传车、驿马通行而开辟的交通大道。古驿道的叫法有多种,如"官道"、"栈道"、"盐道"等。驿道和山间小道最大的不同是经过人工修整、较为平坦、人马可行。历代统治者要传递公文、贡品运输、官员视察等,驿道的作用显得十分突出。古代交通不发达,信息闭塞,驿道又承担着商品运输、平民出行、物产交易的职责,驿道又维系着民众的生计。沿途按一定距离设置驿站。传车、驿马即是驿站备用的车辆和马。驿道是中国古代陆地交通主通道,同时也是属于重要的军事设施之一,如著名的丝绸之路,古代的湖广驿道、南阳—襄阳驿道、青蒿驿道、梅关古驿道等。

古代驿道的开辟,驿站的设置,主要是为了传递谕令、军情、文书,运送官差、粮秣、武器、装备、贡品和赏赐等物资,并为之提供运输工具和供应食宿。驿站是古代供传递官府文书和军事情报的人或来往官员途中食宿、换马的场所。中国是世界上最早建立组织传递信息的国家之一,邮驿历史虽长达3000多年,但留存的遗址、文物并不多。其中,鸡鸣山驿在河北怀来,是中国仅存的一座较完整的驿城。

驿站使用的凭证是勘合和火牌。凡需要向驿站要车、马、人夫运送公文和物品都要看"邮符",官府使用时凭勘合,兵部使用时凭火牌。使用"邮符"有极为严格的规定。对过境有特定任务的,派兵保护。马递公文,都加兵部火票,另沿途各驿站的接递如果要从外到达京城或者外部之间相互传递的,就要填写连排单。公文限"马上飞递"的需要日行三百里。紧急公文则标明四百里或者五百里、六百里字样,按要求时限送到。但不得滥填这种字样。驿站管理至清代已臻于完善,并且管理极严,若违反规定,均要治罪。到了清代末期由于有文报局的设立,开始与驿站相辅而行,继而驿站被废除。

驿站在中国古代运输中有着重要的地位和作用,在通讯手段十分原始的情况下,驿站担负着各种政治、经济、文化、军事等方面的信息传递任务,在一定程度上也是物流信息的一部分。中国古代驿站在各朝代虽形式有别,名称有异,但是组织严密、等级分明、手续完备是相近的。封建君主是依靠这些驿站维持着信息采集、指令发布与反馈,以达到封建统治控制目标的实现。由于当时历史条件的限制,科学技术发展的水平局限,其速度与数量与今无法相比,但就其组织的严密程度,运输信息系统的覆盖水平也不亚于现代通讯运输。可以说那时的成就也是我们现代文明的基础的一部分。驿站与当今的邮政系统、高速公路的服务区、货物中转站、物流中心等等,颇有异曲同工之处。驿站周边往往车水马龙、熙熙攘攘,热闹异常,并形成一些热闹的城市。现在中国的一些大城市,如辽宁省会沈阳,就是以古代驿站起家而发展起来的。(刘双琴编著)

轿子和马车

轿子,古代也称步辇、肩舆、檐子,是中国古代的一种特殊的交通工具。据史书记载,轿子的雏形远在夏朝时期就已经存在。从先秦到两晋时期,统治阶级主要是乘车外出。虽说当时轿子还不流行,但是在皇室贵族的一小部分人中还是越来越喜欢用轿子的。晋朝顾恺之在他所画的《女史箴图》中,就生动地描绘了西汉成帝与班婕妤同乘一架轿子的情景。但是直到唐朝,轿子除了帝王乘坐之外,一般还仅仅为妇女和老弱有病的官员所享用。轿子作为一种交通工具,得到较大普及的是在宋朝,这一时期的轿子种类繁多,式样繁新。在著名的《清明上河图》中,繁华的北宋京城汴梁大街上有许多轿子出游。这些轿子虽然同汉唐时期的轿子大同小异,仍两人抬杠,但选材精良,以硬木为主,上雕花纹飞龙,造型美观。南宋时,轿子的使用进一步推广。到明朝中后期,连中小地主也"人人皆小肩舆,无一骑马者"。明清时期,轿子发展为四人抬或八人抬。王公贵族之所以越来越宠爱轿子,是因为坐在这种特殊的交通工具上,无车马劳顿之苦,安稳舒适。这时,轿子已成为一种比较普遍的重要交通工具。

古代的轿子,大致有两种形制或类型,一种是不上帷子的凉轿,也叫亮轿或显轿,一种是上帷子的暖轿,又称暗轿。不同的官品,在轿子的形制类型、帷子的用料颜色等方面都有严格的区分。如明清时期的一般官吏,得用蓝呢或绿呢作轿帷,所以有"蓝呢官轿"、"绿呢官轿"之称。另外,轿子按其用途的不同,也有种种不同的名字:皇室王公所用的,称为舆轿;达官贵人所乘的,叫做官轿;人们娶亲所用的那种装饰华丽的轿子,则称为花轿。抬轿子的人有多有少,一般二至八人,民间多为二人抬便轿,官员所乘的轿子,有四人抬和八人抬之分。如清朝规定,三品以上大官可用银顶,皂色盖帏,在京城内四个人抬,出京用八人。四品以下只准乘锡顶、两人抬的小轿。至于一般的地主豪绅,只能乘黑油齐头、平顶皂幔的轿子。此外,乘轿还有一些其他方面的规定,处处显示着封建社会里森严的等级制度。

马车是中国古代的又一重要交通工具,在中国起码已有 3000 多年的历史。出土资料表明,商代的车大多为两马驾辕,至商末周初始见四马驾车。可见至商代,中国古代造车技术已相当成熟。周代的车与商车基本相同,但在结构上却有所改进,如直辕变曲辀,直衡改曲衡,辐数增多,舆上安装车盖。在车马的配件上也更加完备,增加了许多商车上所没有的零部件。如车轙、铜銮、铜、铜辖。为求坚固,在许多关键部位都采用了青铜构件,如变木辖为铜辖,轭上包铜饰,并有一套用铜、铅、金、银、骨、贝和兽皮条等材料制成的饰件和鞁具,制作精美,名目繁多。

驾车的马也由商车的二匹增加到三匹、四匹、甚至六匹。车驾二马的叫"骈",车驾三马的称"骖",车驾四马的名"驷"。西周至春秋战国时期可以说是中国古代独辀车发展的鼎盛时期,流行了上下近千年。这一时期的车,在构造和装饰方面远比商代车坚固、豪华,可以说已达到完美阶段。古代马车除作为战争工具外,主要为王公贵族出门乘坐,是权力与身份的象征。这种传统一直延续到清末,北方一些城市普通人家仍然不敢擅自乘用马车。

实际上,如果我们把中国商周时期的轮辐战车与欧亚草原、埃及和西亚的马车相比,会发现它们有许多相似之处,甚至一些细微的地方也一样。例如东西方战车都使用辐式车轮,采用的技术都是揉木为轮,马衔、马鞭、弓形器的形制相似,都采用了同样的技术制造马车,对马车的维护方法也有相通之处,而且都是由上层统治阶级控制着马车的生产,都是统治阶级炫耀权力的工具,马车的使用具有等级等等。当然,东西方的马车也存在着一些差异,主要体现在马车的大小、车马器的质地、装饰上,这种差异是由东西方不同的地理环境、文化传统等因素造成的。(刘双琴编著)

第三单元

黄河文化

黄河是中国第二长河,世界第五长河,源于青海巴颜喀拉山。干流贯穿九个省、自治区,流经青海、四川、甘肃、宁夏、内蒙古、陕西、山西、河南、山东,全长 5464 公里,流域面积 75 万平方公里。黄河是中华民族的母亲河,经过亘古不息的流淌,孕育出世界最古老、最灿烂的文明,形成中国历史上特有的黄河文化。

黄河文化具有悠久的历史。根据山西省芮城县境内黄河东岸西侯度遗址发现的 180 万年前远古人类用过的石器,我们可以相信,早在 180 万年以前,黄河流域便已有了人类。西侯度出土了 30 余件石制品,是迄今为止中国内地发现的人类文化遗存中最早的代表。中国古代无论是三皇五帝传说,还是夏商西周等朝代,都从黄河流域兴起的。所以中华文明源于黄河流域,黄河是"中国古代文化的发祥地"或"中国古文化的摇篮"。

从公元前 21 世纪夏朝开始,迄今 4000 多年的历史中,历代王朝在黄河流域建都的时间延绵 3000 多年。中国历史上的"七大古都",在黄河流域和近邻地区的就有:安阳、西安、洛阳、开封。

作为商朝的国都安阳(当时属黄河流域),在那里遗存有大量的甲骨文,开创了中国文字记载的先河。西安(含咸阳),自西周、秦、汉至隋、唐,先后有 13 个朝代在此建都,历史长达千年,是著名的古都。东周迁都洛阳以后,东汉、魏、隋、唐、后梁、后周等朝代都曾在洛阳建都,历时也有 900 多年,被誉为"九朝古都"。

位于黄河南岸的开封,北宋王朝在此建都,先后历时约 200 多年。在相当长的历史时期,中国的政治、经济、文化中心一直在黄河流域。黄河中下游地区是全国科学技术和文学艺术发展最早的地区。

公元前 2000 年左右,流域内已出现青铜器,到商代青铜冶炼技术已达到相当高的水平,同时开始出现铁器冶炼,标志着生产力发展到了一个新的阶段。中国古代的 "四大发明"——造纸、活字印刷、指南针、火药,都产生在黄河流域。从《诗经》到唐诗、宋词等大量文学经典,以及大量的文化典籍,也大多都产生在黄河流域。

北宋以后,虽然全国的经济重心逐渐向长江流域转移,但是在中国政治、经济、文化发展的进程中,黄河流域及黄河下游平原地区仍处于重要地位。黄河流域悠久的历史,以及它所形成的黄河文化为中华民族留下了十分珍贵的遗产。黄河文化不仅是中华文明宝库中的瑰宝,而且对人类文明的发展做出了不可磨灭的贡献。在中国文化中占有着极其重要的地位。

但是,黄河文化在辉煌之后,面临着越来越大的挑战,特别是在当代。由于过去过度开发和自然地理等原因,黄河流域生态破坏比较严重。在全国的大江大河中,黄河的治理最难。黄河流域西北紧临干旱的戈壁荒漠,流域内大部分地区也属干旱、半干旱地区,北部有大片沙漠和风沙区,西部是高寒地带,中部是世界著名的黄土高原,干旱、风沙、水土流失灾害严重,生态环境脆弱。这严重阻碍了黄河流域经济社会的发展,从而影响到了黄河文化的继续发展。

当前,治理和开发好黄河,是保证黄河流域经济和社会持续发展的一件头等大事,是古老而灿烂的黄河文化重新获得生机与活力的前提条件。(黎清编著)

丝绸之路

丝绸之路的名字来源于 1877 年德国地理学家费迪南·冯·李希霍芬(F. von Richthofen)的著作《中国——我的旅行成果》。它是指西汉(前 202—前 138 年)时,由张骞出使西域开辟的以长安(今西安)为起点,经甘肃、新疆,到中亚、西亚,并联结地中海各国的陆上通道(这条道路也被称为"西北丝绸之路"以区别于日后另外两条冠以"丝绸之路"名称的交通路线)。因为由这条路西运的货物中以丝绸制品的影响最大,故称作"丝绸之路",简称丝路。其基本走向定于两汉时期,包括南道、中道、北道三条路线。

丝绸之路的开通与维持,为中西物质文化和精神文化的交流作出了重要贡献。在这条路上,流传着许多东西方文化交往的故事。早在张骞通西域之前,丝绸已经大量转运到西方世界。在古代罗马,丝绸制的服装成为当时贵族们的高雅时髦装束。因为来自遥远的东方,所以造价昂贵。罗马为了进口丝绸,流失了大量黄金。丝绸比较透明,罗马元老院认为有伤风化,曾多次下令禁止穿用,可并没有起到多大作用。美丽的力量是挡不住的。人们今天在雅典卫城巴台农神庙的女神像身上,在意大利那不勒斯博物馆收藏的酒神巴克科斯的女祭司像上,都可以看到希腊罗马时代的人所穿着的丝绸服装,轻柔飘逸,美丽动人。

罗马帝国的古典作家们把产丝之国称为"赛里斯"(Seres),而赛里斯就是指中国,可见中国丝绸在罗马的影响之大。罗马人,甚至包括西方的学者们在相当长的一段时间内并不清楚丝绸是如何制成的,他们以为是从树上采摘下来的。中国的养蚕和缫丝技术很晚才传到西方。

文化的交流总是双向的。中国奉献给西方世界以精美实用的丝绸,欧亚各国人民也给我们以丰厚的回报。胡桃、胡瓜、胡葱、胡荽、胡椒、胡桐泪、胡萝卜等古代文献中记载的一批带有"胡"字的植物十有八九是来自西方(因为"胡"是古代对来自北方和西方少数民族东西的称呼,后来泛指来自国外的东西)。而且,古代文献中往往把这些植物的移植中国,归功于第一位中西交通的美好使者——张骞。汉初以来,西来的不仅有植物,还有罗马的玻璃器,西域的乐舞、杂技等。

在物质文化交流的同时,通过丝绸之路开展的精神文化交流也在不断地进行。作为世界三大宗教之一的佛教,早在西汉末年就传入中国。沿着丝绸之路留存下来的佛教石窟,著名的如龟兹的克孜尔、吐鲁番柏孜克里克、敦煌莫高窟、安西榆林窟、武威天梯山石窟、永靖炳灵寺、天水麦积山、大同云冈石窟、洛阳龙门石窟等等,大多融会了东西方的艺术风格,是丝绸之路上中西文化交流的见证。

丝绸之路的历史漫长而久远。它传播了友谊,也饱受了战争铁蹄的践踏。今天,人们已经忘却昔日的苦难,把它看做是联结东西方文明的纽带。近年来,联合国教科文组织发起了"丝绸之路研究计划",把丝绸之路称作"对话之路",这将为东西方的交流与合作起到积极地推动作用。(倪爱珍编著)

长城

长城是中国古代劳动人民创造的奇迹,现为世界七大奇迹之一。长城位于中国的北部,它东起河北省的山海关,西至内陆地区甘肃省的嘉峪关。横贯河北、北京、内蒙古、山西、陕西、宁夏、甘肃等七个省、市、自治区,全长约6700公里,约13300里,有"万里长城"之誉。它好像一条巨龙,翻越巍巍群山,穿过茫茫草原,跨过浩瀚的沙漠,奔向苍茫的大海。

根据历史文献记载,自战国时期开始,修筑长城一直是一项大工程。历史上有20多个诸侯国家和封建王朝修筑过长城,若把各个时代修筑的长城加起来,总共有10万里以上。现在中国新疆、甘肃、宁夏、陕西、内蒙古、山西、河北、北京、天津、辽宁、吉林、黑龙江、河南、山东、湖北、湖南等省、市、自治区都有古长城的遗迹。其中仅内蒙古自治区的长城就达3万多里。在历代修筑长城的国家中,尤其以秦朝和明朝最为著名。

在秦朝,秦始皇在灭亡六国以后,便开始修筑长城。在修筑长城的过程中,他使用了近百万劳动力,占全国人口的1/20!当时没有任何机械,全部劳动都得靠人力,而工作环境又非常艰苦。许多人在修筑长城的过程中纷纷死亡,这导致了人们对秦始皇修筑长城的怨恨。正因为如此,才出现了"孟姜女哭长城"的民间传说。

明朝，北方少数民族不断威胁边境安全，为了巩固北方的边防，在明朝的 200 多年统治中，修筑长城几乎没有停止过。明长城是中国历史上费时最久，工程量最大，防御体系和结构最为完善的长城工程。它充分体现了中国古代建筑工程的高度成就和古代劳动人民的聪明才智。

中国古代各个国家不断修筑长城，其主要原因是为了防御北方少数民族对中原地区的军事侵扰。实际上，长城就是古代中国的一个完整的防御工程体系。它保护着中原地区的人民和经济，有利于中原地区经济和文明的发展与积累。

目前现存几段长城主要有：八达岭长城、山海关长城、嘉峪关长城。位于北京延庆的八达岭长城是明长城中保存最完好，最具代表性的一段。它是明朝重要的军事关隘和首都北京的重要屏障。登上八达岭长城，可以居高临下，尽览崇山峻岭的壮丽景色。迄今为止，已有包括尼克松、撒切尔夫人在内的三百多位知名人士到此游览。山海关长城是举世闻名的万里长城的入海处。现属山海关境内的长城全长 26 公里。其中的老龙头长城有"中华之魂"的盛誉。嘉峪关长城则是明代长城最西端的起点，建于明洪武五年（1372 年），是目前保存最完整的一座城关，是丝绸之路上的重要一站。

长城连续修筑时间之长，工程量之大，施工之艰巨，历史文化内涵之丰富，这是世界其他古代工程所难以相比的。中国近代伟大的民主革命先驱孙中山评论长城时说："中国最有名之工程者，万里长城也。……为世界独一之奇观。"美国前总统尼克松在参观长城后说："只有一个伟大的民族，才能造得出这样一座伟大的长城。"

作为人类历史的奇迹，1987 年长城被列入《世界遗产名录》，当之无愧。它既是具有丰富文化内涵的文化遗产，又是独具特色的自然景观。今天国内外游人以"不到长城非好汉"这一诗句来表达一定要亲自登上长城，一览中华悠久文明、壮丽河山的心情。英国前首相希思在参观长城时说："中国的过去与将来都同样具有魅力。……抵达长城时，我觉得比以往从照片上、刺绣上和绘画上见到的长城，更为壮观了。"

万里长城作为中国的标志，将与神州大地长存，将与世界文明永在。（黎清编著）

兵马俑

1974 年春，在陕西省西安市临潼区的秦始皇陵坟丘东侧 1.5 公里处，当地农民打井时，无意中挖出一个陶制武士头。后经考古人员发掘，终于发现了令全世界都为之震惊的秦始皇陵兵马俑。

秦始皇陵兵马俑共有 3 个兵马俑坑，呈品字形排列，它是秦始皇陵的陪葬坑。一号坑为步兵部队，东西长 230 米，南北宽 62 米，深约 5 米，面积为 14260 平方米。二号坑是由骑兵、战车和步兵（包括弩兵）组成的多兵种特殊部队，面积约为 6000 平方米。三号坑为统帅一、二号坑的指挥机关，面积为 520 平方米。三个坑共有 7000 余件陶俑、100 余乘战车、400 余匹陶马和数十万件兵器。

秦始皇陵兵马俑场面宏大，威风凛凛，队列整齐，展现了秦军的编制、武器的装备等。秦始皇陵兵马俑皆仿真人、真马制成。陶俑身高 1.75—1.95 米，多按秦军将士的形象塑造，体格魁伟，体态匀称。陶俑又按兵种的不同分为步兵俑、骑兵俑、弓弩手、将军俑等。步兵俑身着战袍，背挎弓箭；骑兵俑大多一手执缰绳，一手持弓箭，身着短甲、紧口裤，足蹬长筒马靴，准备随时上马参加战斗；弓弩手张弓搭箭，凝视前方，或立姿，或跪姿；将军俑神态自若，表现出毫不畏惧的大将风度。陶马高 1.5 米，长 2 米，体形健硕，肌肉丰满，昂首伫立，表情机警敏捷，匹匹都像是奔驰战场的骏马。这些都显示了秦始皇威震四海、统一六国的雄伟军容。秦始皇花费大量人力和财力建造这些兵马俑，就是希望他死后能够像他生前那样威风凛凛，依然保持着绝对的统治地位。

这批为维持秦始皇死后统治地位而建的兵马俑在今天看来，却具有另外的价值，那就是它具有很高的艺术价值。兵马俑的塑造，是以现实生活为基础而创作，艺术手法细腻、明快。陶俑装束、神态都不一样。光是发式就有许多种，手势也各不相同，脸部的表情更是神态各异。从它们的装束、表情和手势就可以判断出是官还是兵，是步兵还是骑兵。这里有长了胡子的久经沙场的老兵，也有初上战场的青年。总之，秦始皇陵兵马俑具有鲜明的个性和强烈的时代特征。这批兵马俑是雕塑艺术的宝库，为中华民族灿烂的古老文化增添了光彩，在世界艺术史上也具有重要的地位。

1961 年，中华人民共和国国务院将秦始皇陵定为全国文物重点保护单位。1987 年，秦始皇陵及兵马俑坑被联合国教科文组织批准列入《世界遗产名录》。在兵马俑一号坑址上建成了展览厅，设立了"秦始皇陵兵马俑博物馆"，向中外广大旅游者开放。

秦始皇陵兵马俑以其独特的魅力吸引着世界各国的人们，它曾先后迎接了一百多位外国国家领导人。1976 年 5 月 14 日，兵马俑迎来的第一位外国领导人，他是新加坡总理李光耀。他对兵马俑评价说："这是世界的奇迹，民族的骄傲。"1985 年，李光耀总理第二次访问秦始皇陵兵马俑博物馆，题字留言："这一伟大的历史文物，寓意着伟大的未来。"前美国国务卿基辛格看过秦始皇陵兵马俑之后，赞叹说："这是世界上独一无二的奇迹！"前美国副总统蒙代尔则说："这才是真正的奇迹，全世界人民都应当到这里看一看。"而 1978 年，时任巴黎市长希拉克参观后也说："世界上有了七大奇迹，秦始皇陵兵马俑的发现，可以说是八大奇迹了。不看金字塔，不算到埃及；不看秦始皇陵兵马俑，不算到中国。"从此秦始皇陵兵马俑被誉为"世界第八大奇迹"。希拉克的评价被国际媒体广为引用，这对中国秦始皇陵兵马俑走向世界发挥了重要作用。秦始皇陵兵马俑是可以同埃及金字塔和古希腊雕塑相媲美的世界人类文化的宝贵财富。（黎清编著）

五岳

在中国古代，人们把位于中原地区的东、南、西、北方和中央的五座高山定为"五岳"。即东岳泰山（在山东省，海拔 1,524 公尺）、南岳衡山（在湖南省，海拔 1,290 公尺）、西岳华山（在陕西省，海拔 2154.9 公尺）、北岳恒山（在山西省，海拔 2,017 公尺）、中岳嵩山（在河南省，海拔 1,440 公尺）。

东岳泰山,为中国五岳之首,号称"天下第一山"。泰山地处山东省中部,因位于东部,所以称为东岳。泰山有着深厚的文化内涵,其古建筑主要为明清的风格。泰山被尊为华夏神山。它是中国历史上唯一受过皇帝封禅的名山。同时泰山也是佛、道两教兴盛之地,是历代帝王朝拜之山。历代帝王所到之处,建庙塑像,刻石题字,留下了众多文物古迹。历代名人对泰山亦仰慕备至,纷纷到此游览,历代赞颂泰山的诗词多达一千余首。走进泰山,就如同走进了深厚的中国历史。游览泰山的最佳时间为每年的3月到11月。游泰山时要看四个奇观:泰山日出、云海玉盘、晚霞夕照、黄河金带。

西岳华山,是著名的五岳之一,位于陕西省华阴市境内,距西安120公里。它由中、东、西、南、北五个山峰组成,远望状如莲花,故称"华山"。华山素有"奇险天下第一山"之称。在历史上,秦始皇、汉武帝、武则天、唐玄宗等十几位帝王曾到华山进行过大规模祭祀活动。同时,华山还是道教名山,山上现存有道观20余座。此外,华山还留下了无数名人的足迹。自隋唐以来,李白、杜甫等作家有关华山的作品有一千余篇。华山的最佳旅游时间是每年的4月到10月。农历三月十五日是朝山日,会有盛大的庙会和庆祝活动。华山四季景色神奇多变,不同的季节可以欣赏到"云华山"、"雨华山"、"雾华山"、"雪华山"。

南岳衡山,是著名的五岳之一,位于湖南省衡阳市南岳区。由于气候条件较其他四岳好,处处是茂林修竹,终年翠绿,自然景色十分秀丽,因此又有"南岳独秀"的美称。南岳产的云雾茶,是一种著名的茶叶,在唐代就被列为"贡茶"。

北岳恒山,著名的五岳之一,被称为是"天下第二山"。位于山西省浑源县城南10公里处,距大同市62公里。古北岳恒山为今河北省大茂山,自清朝顺治以后转移到山西。历史上,先后有秦始皇、汉武帝、唐太宗、唐玄宗、宋真宗封北岳为王、为帝,明太祖又尊北岳为神。同时,恒山作为道教的活动场所也由来已久。相传,神话中的古代道教神仙张果老就是在恒山修炼成仙的。在恒山,有许多奇异的自然景观,其中的苦甜井便是自然景观中的奇迹。苦甜井在恒山半腰,两井相隔一米,水质却截然不同。一井水甜美清凉,被称为甜井,另一井水却苦涩难饮。

中岳嵩山,著名的五岳之一,地处河南省登封市西北面。2004年2月13日被联合国教科文组织地学部评选为"世界地质公园"。这里山峦起伏,峻峰奇异。嵩山除优美的自然风光外,还有众多的名胜古迹。例如少林寺就位于嵩山,所以又称"嵩山少林寺"。嵩山也是历代帝王将相封禅祭祀的地方。山上名胜古迹众多,居五岳之冠,被誉为文物荟萃之地。在嵩山可以领略中华八千年历史的进程。仰韶文化、龙山文化、三皇五帝、夏朝国都阳城在这里都有遗址。

古代帝王相信五岳上都有神仙居住,许多帝王便在五岳上举行封禅和祭祀盛典。因此,在古代中国,五岳就不仅仅是著名的高山,它还具有更为丰富的历史文化内涵。(黎清编著)

湖泊

中国是一个多湖泊国家,面积在 1 平方公里以上的天然湖泊即达 2800 多个,总面积约 8 万平方公里,其中淡水湖泊面积为 3.6 万平方公里,占总面积的 45% 左右。中国绝大部分湖泊属中、小型湖泊。面积大于 1000 平方公里的共 11 个,最大淡水湖泊为鄱阳湖,最大咸水湖是青海湖,最大盐湖是察尔汗盐湖。藏北的青蛙湖湖面海拔 5644 米,是世界上海拔最高的咸水湖,海拔 5386 米的森里错,则为世界海拔最高的淡水湖。海拔最低的湖泊是新疆吐鲁番盆地的艾丁湖,湖底海拔 –155 米。中国最深湖泊是位于长白山主峰白头山上的天池,湖水深度最大达 312.7 米,它也是中、朝两国的界湖。

在中国,比较著名的湖泊主要有:长江中下游的鄱阳湖、洞庭湖,长江三角洲的太湖,淮河流域的洪泽湖、巢湖,被称为中国五大淡水湖;中国的咸水湖也很多,其中最著名的有青海湖、纳木错湖、色林错湖、乌伦古湖、羊卓雍错湖,被称为中国五大咸水湖。

鄱阳湖,中国最大的淡水湖,位于江西省北部。它汇集了赣江、修河、饶河、信江、抚河等江河水经湖口注入长江。鄱阳湖是国际重要湿地,是长江干流重要的调蓄性湖泊,在中国长江流域中发挥着巨大的调蓄洪水和保护生物多样性等特殊生态功能,是中国十大生态功能保护区之一,也是世界自然基金会划定的全球重要生态区之一,对维系区域和国家生态安全具有重要作用。此外,鄱阳湖的环境、水质和气候条件都比较适合候鸟越冬,直到第二年春(4月)逐渐离去。如今,保护区内鸟类已达 300 多种,近百万只,其中珍禽 50 多种,已是世界上最大的鸟类保护区。并且在这里发现了当代世界上最大的白鹤群,2002 年白鹤越冬种群总数达 4000 只以上,占全世界白鹤总数的百分之九十五以上。因此,鄱阳湖被称为"白鹤世界","珍禽王国"。

洞庭湖,原为中国第一大淡水湖,近百年来由于湖盆显著缩小,因此现为中国第二大淡水湖。湖区横跨湖南、湖北两省。湖区面积 1.878 万平方公里,天然湖面 2740 平方公里,另有内湖 1200 平方公里。洞庭湖区经 1954 年、1964 年和 20 世纪 70 年代三阶段以治水为中心的农田基本建设,已成为中国重要的商品粮基地之一,重点淡水渔区之一。

太湖,中国第三大淡水湖,在江苏省南部,浙江省北部。整个太湖水系共有大小湖泊 180 多个,连同进出湖泊的大小河道组成一个密如蛛网的水系。对航运、灌溉和调节河湖水位都十分有利。

洪泽湖,中国第四大淡水湖,在江苏省西部淮河下游。洪泽湖是一个"悬湖",湖底高出东部苏北平原 4~8 米。洪泽湖的主要水源是淮河,淮河是中国自古以来水患最多的河流之一。因此洪泽湖的历史也就是一部人类与洪水的抗争史,并留下许多美丽的传说。洪泽湖的千年古堤就是历代为治水而建的,与都江堰齐名,全长 67 公里,几乎全用玄武岩的条石砌成,蜿蜒曲折,远远望去,宛如一座水上长城。

巢湖,中国第五大淡水湖。位于安徽省中部,是安徽境内最大的湖泊,面积 769.5 平方千米。有杭埠河、丰乐河、上派河、南淝河、柘皋河等注入,湖水经裕溪河流入长江。有蓄水、灌溉的功能。此外,巢湖出产的银鱼非常著名。

青海湖,既是中国最大的内陆湖泊,也是中国最大的咸水湖,位于青海省东北部。湖区有大小河流近 30 条。湖东岸有两个子湖,一名尕海,面积 10 余平方公里,是咸水;一名耳海,面积 4 平方公里,为淡水。青海湖每年 12 月封冻,冰期 6 个月,冰厚半公尺以上。湖中有 5 个小岛,其中海心山最大。鸟岛位于湖的西部,面积 0.11 平方千米,是斑头雁、鱼鸥、棕头鸥等 10 多种候鸟繁殖生息的场所,数量多达 100,000 只以上。现已建立鸟岛自然保护区。

纳木错湖,是藏语"天湖"的意思,它是仅次于青海湖的第二大咸水湖。因为湖水湛蓝明净如无云的蓝天,所以称为纳木错湖。它位于西藏拉萨市以北当雄、班戈两县之间。纳木错的湖水来源主要是天然降水和高山融冰化雪补给,湖水不能外流,是西藏第一大内陆湖。

色林错湖,西藏自治区第二大湖,藏语意为"威光映复的魔鬼湖"。位于班戈县与申扎县交界处,面积 1640 平方千米,湖面海拔 4530 米最大水深超过 33 米。流域面积 4.553 万平方千米。

乌伦古湖,位于新疆维吾尔自治区准噶尔盆地北部。湖形似三角形,南北宽约 30 千米,东西长 35 千米,湖水面积 827 平方千米,湖水平均深度为八米。乌伦古湖素以"戈壁大海"和鲜美"福海鱼"而著称。

羊卓雍错湖,位于雅鲁藏布江南岸、山南地区浪卡子县境内,湖面海拔 4441 米,有 700 多平方公里的水面,平均水深 30 多米,最深处有 60 米。它的水源来自周围的雪山,但却没有出水口,雪水的融化与湖水的蒸发达到一种动态的平衡。羊卓雍错被誉为世界上最美丽的水。(黎清编著)

第四单元

老子

老子,春秋末期楚国苦县(今河南鹿邑)人,姓李,名耳,字伯阳,谥曰聃。传说他一生下来,就有白色的眉毛和胡子,所以人称"老子"。老子曾任周王室的柱下史,掌管王室图籍。孔子到周时曾向他请教有关"礼"的问题。后来,老子见周王室逐渐衰败便离去,以后就没有人知道他的情况了。

老子是道家学派的创始人,其学说后来被庄子发展。他所撰述的《老子》(又名《道德经》),大约成书于战国中前期,开创了中国古代哲学思想的先河,对中国古代以至现在的思想文化的发展,都有着重要的影响。

老子的思想主要包括:

(一)以"道"为本的宇宙观

老子创立了以"道"为中心的哲学体系,被认为是中国古代哲学本体论的创造者,因为他探讨的是有关世界的起源、结构及存在的问题。"道"是老子哲学中最重要的概念,在《老子》一书中共出现 73 次,其内涵丰富深刻。

"道"是天地万物的本原,"道生一,一生二,二生三,三生万物"。道没有形状和内容,独立于万物之外,周而复始,循环运行,绝不止息。"道"不仅指"道"之质,即化生为万物的原物质,还指"道"之性,即这种原物质化生万物时所遵循的普遍规律、基本法则。老子认为一切事物都处在变化之中,所以人们对"道"的把握与认识不可能是永恒的,一成不变的。老子思想中包含着朴素的辩证法。他认为,世间万事万物都是变化的,对立统一的,它们相辅相成,相互转化。如,"天下万物生于有,有生于无","天下皆知美之为美,斯恶已;皆知善之为善,斯不善已。有无相生,难易相成,长短相形,高下相倾,音声相和,前后相随","祸兮福之所倚,福兮祸之所伏"等。

（二）自然无为的天道观

在"道"论的基础上,老子提出天道与人道两大法则。天道自然无为,人道顺其自然,前者即道家的自然论,后者即道家的无为论。这两论构成道家的基本理论。

"道"是宇宙万物创生的根源,所以人、地、天都要法"道",但"道"并不是毫无规律,为所欲为,它还必须以"自然"为法。这里的"自然"不是自然界的意思,而是指自然而然,与"人为"相对。老子以天道作为天、地、人的共同法则,主张"道法自然",强调一切要合乎自然,顺从人与万物的自然本性。

既然天道自然,人道取法天道,所以道家奉行"自然无为"的行为原则。老子说:"道常无为而无不为。""无为"并非指什么都不做,而是指不能以自己的主观意志改变万物的自然本性,要顺其自然,从而达到"无不为"的效果。

"自然无为"表现在政治思想方面,就是"无私"、"无为";表现在人生哲学方面,就是"无欲"、"不争"。因为无欲,所以能够知足;因为不争,所以能够谦下。老子主张为人处事应谦下谨慎,甘居柔弱。但柔弱只是手段,以弱胜强、以柔克刚才是目的。

（三）小国寡民的政治观

老子处在礼崩乐坏的春秋时代,其政治思想突出表现了对社会现实的不满和愤懑。老子反对强暴和掠夺,反对礼义和法治,认为儒家的"仁义礼智"不能解决社会问题,恢复"大道"才是根本之策。老子反对战争,因为它给人民带来无穷灾难,表现出可贵的民本主义思想。老子认为少数当权者的贪心和不足是战争的起因。所以,人类要避免战争的灾祸,就必须克服占有欲和扩张欲,从根本上改善人性。当然,对于反侵略的正义战争,老子是不反对的。但他提醒人们正义战争不要走过了头,变成非正义战争。老子认为,即使站在正义一边,也不要赞美战争,不能让好战成为人的习性,那将是很可怕的事。所以即使战胜了,也应"以丧礼处之",对战争怀有悲哀之情。

老子在批判社会现实的同时,为人们设计了一个"小国寡民"的理想社会。"小国寡民,使有什伯之器而不用,使民重死而不远徙。虽有舟舆,无所乘之;虽有甲兵,无所陈之,使人复结绳而用之。甘其食,美其服,安其居,乐其俗。邻国相望,鸡犬之声相闻,民至老死,不相往来。"在中国思想史上,老子是第一个在全面批判和论证当时制度不合理的同时,又为人们构想出一幅理想社会图景的思想家。

老子及其道家思想对后世中国影响非常大,成为与儒家思想并立的一个哲学流派。中国古代的文人士大夫,每当在仕途和人生失意的时候,往往都会在老子的思想中寻求心灵的救助和安慰。老子及其思想不仅在中国，而且在世界上都有着广泛的影响。我们相信，随着时间的推移，老子"道法自然"、尊重自然规律的思想一定会被越来越多的人所重视。（倪爱珍编著）

庄子

庄子（约前369—前286年），名周，战国时期宋国人，著名思想家、哲学家、文学家，是道家学派的代表人物，老子哲学思想的继承者和发展者，先秦庄子学派的创始人。他的学说涵盖着当时社会生活的方方面面，但根本精神还是归依于老子的哲学。后世将他与老子并称为"老庄"，他们的哲学为"老庄哲学"。

庄子在哲学上继承发扬了老子的道家思想，形成了自己独特的哲学思想体系和独特的学风、文风。他认为"道"是超越时空的无限本体，它生于天地万物之间，而又无所不包，无所不在，表现在一切事物之中，是宇宙万物的本源，天道自然无为。在政治上主张无为而治，在人类生存方式上主张返璞归真，追求一种"天地与我并生，万物与我为一"的主观精神境界，主张精神上的安时处顺，逍遥自在。

在庄子看来，真正的生活是自然而然的，因此不需要去教导什么，规定什么，而是要去掉什么，忘掉什么，忘掉成心、机心、分别心。既然如此，就用不着政治宣传、礼乐教化、仁义劝导，这些宣传、教化、劝导，庄子认为都是人性中的"伪"，所以要摒弃它。

庄子把提倡仁义和是非看做是加在人身上的刑罚，对当时统治者的"仁义"和"法治"进行抨击，他对世俗社会的礼、法、权、势进行了尖锐的批判，提出了"圣人不死，大盗不止"，"窃钩者诛，窃国者为诸侯"的精辟见解。

在人类生存方式上，他崇尚自然，提倡"天地与我并生，万物与我为一"的精神境界，并且认为，人生的最高境界是逍遥自得，是绝对的精神自由，而不是物质享受与虚伪的名誉。庄子这些思想和主张，对后世影响深远，是人类思想史上一笔宝贵的精神财富。

作为道家学派始祖的老庄哲学是在中国的哲学思想中唯一能与儒家以及后来的佛家学说分庭抗礼的古代最伟大的学说。

庄子对后世的影响，不仅表现在他独特的哲学思想上，而且表现在文学上。他的政治主张、哲学思想不是干巴巴的说教，相反，都是通过一个个生动形象、幽默机智的寓言故事，通过恣肆汪洋、仪态万方的语言文字，巧妙活泼、引人入胜地表达出来，全书仿佛是一部寓言故事集，这些寓言表现出超常的想象力，构成了奇特的形象，具有强烈的艺术感染力。

庄子的文章结构，很奇特。看起来并不严密，常常突兀而来，行所欲行，止所欲止，变化无端，有时似乎不相关，任意跳宕起落，但思想却能一线贯穿。句式也富于变化，或顺或倒，或长或短，更加之词汇丰富，描写细致，又常常不规则地押韵，显得极富表现力，极有独创性。

庄子一生洁身自爱始终过着清贫的隐居生活，他继承并发扬了老子的道家思想，是惊世骇俗的哲学大家，也是才华横溢的文学奇葩。曾经"庄周梦蝶"，他分不清梦境和现实的差距；他与时人惠子有"安知鱼乐"的精彩辩论；相传，庄子妻子过世时，他鼓盆而歌。

庄子文字的恣肆洒脱,意象的雄浑飞越,想象的奇特丰富,情致的滋润旷达,给人以超凡脱俗与崇高美妙的感受,在中国的文学史上独树一帜,他的文章体制已脱离语录体形式,标志着先秦散文已经发展到成熟的阶段,可以说,《庄子》代表了先秦散文的最高成就。

庄周一生著书十余万言,书名《庄子》。这部文献的出现,标志着在战国时代,中国的哲学思想和文学语言,已经发展到非常玄远、高深的水平,是中国古代典籍中的瑰宝。因此,庄子不但是中国哲学史上一位著名的思想家,同时也是中国文学史上一位杰出的文学家。无论在哲学思想方面,还是文学语言方面,他都给予了中国历代的思想家和文学家以深刻的、巨大的影响,在中国思想史、文学史上都有极重要的地位。(刘双琴编著)

孔子

春秋战国时期,中国出现了一个著名的思想家、教育家,那便是孔子。

孔子,名丘,字仲尼,鲁国人。三岁时,父亲病故,母亲带着他迁居到鲁国国都曲阜城里的阙里居住。两人相依为命,过着清贫的生活。大约 30 岁时,孔子开始私人讲学,50 岁左右,当上了鲁国的"中都宰",不久升为"司寇"。但鲁国的政局动荡不安,他只做了 3 个月的司寇便被迫离开,带着学生周游列国,度过了 14 年的流亡生活。晚年时重返鲁国,专门从事讲学和整理古代文献的工作,一直到去世。

孔子一生大部分时间都从事教育,是我国古代著名的教育家。相传他所收的学生多达 3000,取得突出成就的有 72 人。孔子首创私人办学,改变了"学在官府"的局面,在中国教育史上影响甚大。他整理编订了《诗》《书》《礼》《易》《乐》《春秋》,并把它作为教材,保存和传播了中国文化。

孔子从教 40 余年,积累了丰富的教育教学经验,提出了许多教育教学的思想和原则,至今仍有积极意义。如:"因材施教",即根据个人的禀性不同实施不同的教育方式;"有教无类",即不管学生是富贵还是贫寒,是贤能还是愚笨,孔子都一视同仁;"学而不厌,诲人不倦",即学习永不满足,教导别人不知疲倦,孔子身体力行,学生遇到不懂的问题,孔子总是耐心地为他们讲解,直到弄明白为止;"三人行,必有我师",孔子认为几个人一起走路,里面一定有一个人可以做我的老师,他以此规劝人们要虚心好学。

孔子不仅是伟大的教育家,也是伟大的思想家。他的思想比较集中地反映在《论语》一书中。《论语》大约成书于战国初期,是孔子死后由其弟子和再传弟子根据笔记和回忆加以整理汇编而成的一部书,内容涉及哲学、政治、经济、教育、文艺等诸多方面,是儒家学说最主要的经典。

儒家思想的核心是"仁",《论语》中共出现一百零八次"仁"字,而且又多出自孔子及其弟子之口。"仁者爱人","爱人"是"仁学"思想的出发点、核心内涵,同时也是终极目标。

"仁"体现在政治上就是"德治"。统治者要有爱民之心,实施仁政和德政,为老百姓谋利益。"仁"体现在教育上就是"有教无类",不问贵贱贫富,都可以平等地接受教育。"仁"体现在生活中,就是"忠"、"恕"、"孝"、"悌"等。"忠"是忠诚老实,"恕"是宽容待人。《论语》中的"推己及人","己欲立而立人,己欲达而达人","己所不欲,勿施于人",都是教导人们凡事要设身处地为别人着想,关心别人,理解别人,帮助别人。"孝"是尊敬父母长辈,"悌"是敬爱兄长。孔子认为"孝"、"悌"是仁的基础,因为一个连父母兄弟都不爱的人是不可能爱其他人的。由此可见,孔子所说的"仁"是一种泛爱众的利他主义,一种先人后己的道德伦理境界。孔子所追求的是"人不独亲其亲,不独子其子,使老有所终,壮有所用,幼有所长,鳏寡孤独废疾者皆有所养,男有分,女有归"(《礼记·礼运篇》)的理想国。

那么,怎样才能做到"仁"呢?孔子认为,"克己复礼为仁","非礼勿视,非礼勿听,非礼勿言,非礼勿动"。这里的"礼"不是指我们现在所说的"礼节"、"礼貌",而是指人们视听言行、吃喝穿住、立身处世的一切规范。在孔子看来,政令刑罚只能治标,"礼"才能治本,才能让人从根本上明白是非荣辱,在内心形成道德堤防。"礼"是一种柔性的法,它不是靠外力强制执行,而是靠内心严格的自律。

上至国君,下至子民,各安其位,各守其分,全社会才能和谐有序。所以,"礼"的核心是"正名"。所谓"正名",也就是明确人的等级名分、权利责任以及礼制所确认的行为规范。

孔子提出"君君,臣臣,父父,子子"作为"正名"的具体内容,就是说,为君者要符合君道,为臣者要符合臣道,为父者要符合父道,为子者要符合子道,从而奠定了中国封建社会的主要社会秩序。孔子经常用"义"来评判人们的思想行为,所谓"义",也就是符合"礼",不符合则"不义"。

孔子逝世后,各个朝代都举行祭孔活动,各地都建有孔庙。西汉时,汉高祖刘邦首次以"太牢"(即皇帝祭天大典)祭祀孔子,"祭孔"也从此与"祭天"、"祭黄(即祭祀黄帝)"一起成为封建时代的"三大国祭"。自西汉始,孔子学说成为中国 2000 余年封建社会的正统文化,它对中国人的思想观念、思维方式、价值取向具有极深的影响。

近年来,孔子热、国学热、传统文化热不断升温。中国在国外开设的孔子学院目前已达 140 多所,遍布全球 50 个国家。2005 年国际孔子文化节期间,"全球联合祭孔"盛会隆重举行。2006 年 6 月 23 日,以中国政府名义在联合国教科文组织设立的"孔子教育奖"在孔子故里——山东曲阜颁发,这是首次以中国人命名的国际奖项。(倪爱珍编著)

孟子

孟子(前 372—前 289 年),名轲,字子舆,又字子车、子居,中国古代伟大的思想家,战国时期儒家代表人物之一,著有《孟子》一书。《孟子》一书是孟子的言论汇编,由孟子及其弟子共同编写而成,记录了孟子的语言、政治观点和政治行动的儒家经典著作。孟子继承并发扬了孔子的思想,成为仅次于孔子的一代儒家宗师,有"亚圣"之称,与孔子并称为"孔孟"。其学说出发点为性善论,提出"仁政"、"王道",主张德治。南宋时朱熹将《孟子》与

《论语》《大学》《中庸》合在一起称"四书"。从此直到清末,"四书"一直是科举必考内容。孟子三岁丧父,孟母艰辛地将他抚养成人,孟母管束甚严,其"孟母三迁"、"孟母断织"等故事,成为千古美谈,是后世母教之典范。

孟子的思想可以概括为以下几个方面:

（1）民本思想

"民为贵,社稷次之,君为轻。"意思是说,人民放在第一位,国家其次,君在最后。孟子认为君主应以爱护人民为先,为政者要保障人民权利。孟子赞同若君主无道,人民有权推翻政权。

（2）仁政学说

孟子继承和发展了孔子的德治思想,发展为仁政学说,并成为其政治思想的核心。他把"亲亲"、"长长"的原则运用于政治,以缓和阶级矛盾,维护封建统治阶级的长远利益。

孟子一方面严格区分了统治者与被统治者的阶级地位,认为"劳心者治人,劳力者治于人",并且模仿周制拟定了一套从天子到庶人的等级制度;另一方面,又把统治者和被统治者的关系比作父母对子女的关系,主张统治者应该像父母一样关心人民的疾苦,人民应该像对待父母一样去亲近、服侍统治者。孟子认为,这是一种最理想的政治,如果统治者实行仁政,可以得到人民的衷心拥护;反之,如果不顾人民死活,推行虐政,将会失去民心而变成独夫民贼,被人民推翻。仁政的具体内容很广泛,包括经济、政治、教育以及统一天下的途径等,其中贯穿着一条民本思想的线索。

孟子认为,如何对待人民这一问题,对于国家的治乱兴亡,具有极端的重要性。孟子十分重视民心的向背,通过大量历史事例反复阐述这是关乎得天下与失天下的关键问题。孟子说:"夫仁政,必自经界始"。所谓"经界",就是划分整理田界,实行井田制。孟子所设想的井田制,是一种封建性的自然经济,以一家一户的小农为基础,采取劳役地租的剥削形式。每家农户有五亩之宅,百亩之田,吃穿自给自足。孟子认为,"民之为道也,有恒产者有恒心,无恒产者无恒心",只有使人民拥有"恒产",固定在土地上,安居乐业,他们才不去触犯刑律,为非作歹。

孟子认为,人民的物质生活有了保障,统治者再兴办学校,用孝悌的道理进行教化,引导他们向善,这就可以造成一种"亲亲"、"长长"的良好道德风尚,即"人人亲其亲、长其长,而天下平"。

孟子认为,统治者实行仁政,可以得到天下人民的衷心拥护,这样便可以无敌于天下。孟子所说的仁政要建立在统治者的"不忍人之心"的基础上。孟子说:"先王有不忍人之心,斯有不忍人之政矣。""不忍人之心"是一种同情仁爱之心。孟子主张,"亲亲而仁民","老吾老以及人之老,幼吾幼以及人之幼"。仁政就是这种不忍人之心在政治上的体现。

孟子把伦理和政治紧密结合起来,强调道德修养是搞好政治的根本。他说:"天下之本在国,国之本在家,家之本在身。"后来《大学》提出的"修齐治平"就是根据孟子的这种思想发展而来的。

（3）道德伦理

孟子把道德规范概括为四种,即仁、义、礼、智。同时把人伦关系概括为五种,即"父子有亲,君臣有义,夫妇有别,长幼有序,朋友有信"。孟子认为,仁、义、礼、智四者之中,仁、义最为重要。仁、义的基础是孝、悌,而孝、悌是处理父子和兄弟血缘关系的基本的道德规范。他认为如果每个社会成员都用仁义来处理各种人与人的关系,封建秩序的稳定和天下的统一就有了可靠保证。

为了说明这些道德规范的起源,孟子提出了性善论的思想。他认为,尽管各个社会成员之间有分工的不同和阶级的差别,但是他们的人性却是同一的。他说:"故凡同类者,举相似也,何独至于人而疑之?圣人与我同类者。"这里,孟子把统治者和被统治者摆在平等的地位,探讨他们所具有的普遍的人性。这种探讨适应于当时奴隶解放和社会变革的历史潮流,标志着人类认识的深化,对伦理思想的发展是一个巨大的推进。(刘双琴编著)

墨子

墨子(约前468—前376年),名翟,山东滕州人,战国时期著名的思想家,墨家学派的创始人。他曾提出"兼爱""非攻""尚贤""节用"等观点,创立墨家学说,并有《墨子》一书传世。《墨子》分两大部分:一部分是记载墨子言行,阐述墨子思想,主要反映了前期墨家的思想;另一部分是《经上》《经下》《经说上》《经说下》《大取》《小取》等 6 篇,一般称作墨辩或墨经,着重阐述墨家的认识论和逻辑思想,还包含许多自然科学的内容,反映了后期墨家的思想。墨学在当时影响很大,与儒家并称"显学"。

墨子的学说思想主要包括以下几点:

(1)兼爱、非攻。

所谓兼爱,包含平等与博爱的意思。墨子要求君臣、父子、兄弟都要在平等的基础上相互友爱,"爱人若爱其身",并认为社会上出现强执弱、富侮贫、贵傲贱的现象,是因天下人不相爱所致。

(2)天志、明鬼。

宣扬天志鬼神是墨子思想的一大特点。墨子认为天之有志——兼爱天下之百姓。因"人不分幼长贵贱,皆天之臣也","天之爱民之厚",君主若违天意就要受天之罚,反之,则会得天之赏。墨子不仅坚信鬼神其有,而且尤其认为它们对于人间君主或贵族会赏善罚暴。墨子宗教哲学中的天赋人权与制约君主的思想,是墨子哲学中的一大亮点。

(3)尚同、尚贤。

尚同是要求百姓与天子皆上同于天志,上下一心,实行义政。尚贤则包括选举贤者为官吏,选举贤者为天子国君。墨子认为,国君必须选举国中贤者,而百姓理应在公共行政上对国君有所服从。墨子要求上面了解下情,因为只有这样才能赏善罚暴。墨子要求君上能尚贤使能,即任用贤者而废抑不肖者。墨子把尚贤看得很重,以为是政事之本。他特别反对君主用骨肉之亲,对于贤者则不拘出身,提出"官无常贵,民无终贱"的主张。

(4)节用、节葬。

节用是墨家非常强调的一种观点,他们抨击君主、贵族的奢侈浪费,尤其反对儒家看重的久丧厚葬之俗。认为君主、贵族都应像古代大禹一样,过着清廉俭朴的生活。墨子要求墨者在这方面也能身体力行。

墨子哲学思想的主要贡献是在认识论方面。他以"耳目之实"的直接感觉经验为认识的唯一来源,他认为,判断事物的有与无,不能凭个人的臆想,而要以大家所看到的和所听到的为依据,强调以间接经验、直接经验和社会效果为准绳,努力排除个人的主观成见。在名实关系上,主张以实正名,名副其实。墨子强调感觉经验的真实性的认识论也有很大的局限性,他曾以有人"尝见鬼神之物,闻鬼神之声"为理由,得出"鬼神之有"的结论。

墨子也是中国古代逻辑思想的重要开拓者之一。他比较自觉地、大量地运用了逻辑推论的方法,以建立或论证自己的政治、伦理思想。他还在中国逻辑史上第一次提出了辩、类、故等逻辑概念。并要求将"辩"作为一种专门知识来学习。墨子的"辩"虽然统指辩论技术,但却是建立在知类(事物之类)明故(根据、理由)基础上的,因而属于逻辑类推或论证的范畴。墨子还善于运用类推的方法揭露论敌的自相矛盾。由于墨子的倡导和启蒙,墨家养成了重逻辑的传统,并由后期墨家建立了第一个中国古代逻辑学的体系。

另外,墨子在科学技术领域中的成就和贡献是多方面的。如宇宙论方面,墨子认为,宇宙是一个连续的整体,个体或局部都是由这个统一的整体分出来的,都是这个统一整体的组成部分。并提出了时空是连续无穷的,这连续无穷的时空又是由最小的单元所构成,在无穷中包含着有穷,在连续中包含着不连续的时空理论。

在数学方面,墨子是中国历史上第一个从理性高度对待数学问题的科学家,他给出了一系列数学概念的命题和定义,这些命题和定义都具有高度的抽象性和严密性,如"倍"、"同长"、正方形等的定义。

在物理学方面,墨子的研究涉及力学、光学、声学等分支,给出了"力"、"动"、"止"等不少物理学概念的定义,并有不少重大的发现,总结出了一些重要的物理学定理。

机械制造方面,墨子是一个精通机械制造的大家,他曾花费了3年的时间,精心研制出一种能够飞行的木鸟。他又是一个制造车辆的能手,可以在不到一日的时间内造出载重30石的车子。(刘双琴编著)

孙子

孙子是中国历史上著名的军事家,被尊崇为"兵家之祖"。他姓孙名武,字长卿,后人尊称其为孙子、孙武子,是春秋时期齐国贵族和名将的后裔。他所撰写的《孙子兵法》,是世界上最早的兵书,也是中国兵学的奠基之作。

《孙子兵法》共13篇,约5000字,各篇均有主题,但又互相联系,揭示了一系列具有普遍意义的军事规律,构成了一套完整的军事理论体系。

《计》篇论述的是能否进行战争的问题。孙子指出,战争是关系到国家生死存亡的大事。"道"、"天"、"地"、"将"、"法"是决定战争胜负的五项基本要素。

《作战》篇主要论述的是如何进行战争。孙子主张速战速胜,更为可贵的是,孙子还主张优待俘虏，认为只有这样，才能更为迅速地战胜敌人。

《谋攻》篇主要论述如何进攻敌国的问题。孙子强调以谋略取胜，提出了"知彼知己，百战不殆"的著名军事思想。

《形》篇主要讲如何利用物质之"形"来保全自己，取得完全的胜利。孙子认为能使自己立于不败之地的物质之"形"，是由国土的大小所产生的物产、军资、士卒的多少，以及军事实力对比的强弱。

《势》篇主要论述如何造成有利的态势来压倒敌方。孙子提出了出奇制胜的战略，即以正兵当敌，以奇兵取胜。

《虚实》篇主要论述指挥作战时如何争取主动权，灵活地打击敌人。孙子认为，要取得主动，就要善于诱敌以利，善于了解敌情和隐瞒自己军队的意图、行动和用兵规律，要充分利用敌军的弱点和错误，以众击寡，避实击虚，因敌而制胜。

《军争》篇论述的是如何通过机动掌握主动先于敌人造成有利态势和取得制胜的条件。孙子指出，要先敌取得制胜的条件，必须避免轻率冒进，要把握各国的动向，了解道路、地形，重视向导，善于欺骗敌人，根据情况分散或集中使用兵力，擅长指挥军队，根据军队的士气、军心和军力因敌而变。

《九变》篇主要论述如何发挥指挥上的灵活性。孙子认为，灵活性的基础在于对利弊进行全面的衡量。只有认识这一点，才能设法威胁、挫折和困扰敌国，以利诱敌。

《行军》篇主要论述如何配置组织军队、观察判断敌情和团结将士。

《地形》篇主要论述在不同的地形条件下如何指挥军队的行动。

《九地》篇论述在九种不同的作战地区指挥作战的原则。

《火攻》篇论述火攻的目标、种类、发火的物质、气象条件以及实施方法。

《用间》篇论述使用间谍的重要性及其方法。

《孙子兵法》不仅在中国产生积极影响，而且先后被译成多种语言，在世界上广泛流传。法国著名政治家、军事家拿破仑，在兵败滑铁卢之后，偶然得见《孙子兵法》，无限感慨地说："如果20年前能见到《孙子兵法》，历史将会是另外一个结局。"如今，在越南、朝鲜、日本、以色列乃至英、德、俄等国，《孙子兵法》都很受军事家们的欢迎。英国著名的战略家利德尔·哈特在《孙子兵法》英译本的序言中说："2500多年前，中国这位古代兵法家的思想对于研究核时代的战争是很有帮助的。"

《孙子兵法》除了在军事上有着重要的影响力之外，还被推广运用到其他领域，尤其是企业经营管理，因为市场竞争本身就是一场没有硝烟的战争。日本企业家大桥武夫所著《兵法经营全书》中就指出："采用中国的兵法思想指导企业经营管理，比美国的企业管理方式更合理、更有效。"一位美国经济学家曾指出："《孙子兵法》一书中揭示的许多原理原则，迄今犹颠扑不破，仍有其运用价值。"（倪爱珍编著）

韩非子

韩非（约前 280—前 233 年），战国晚期韩国人，是中国古代著名的哲学家、思想家和散文家，法家思想的集大成者，世称"韩非子"。韩非口吃，但他善于写作，且继承和发展了荀子的法术思想，同时又吸取了他以前的法家学说，比较各国变法得失，提出"以法为主"，法、术、势结合的理论，集法家思想大成。韩非多次上书韩王变法图强，未被采用，于是发愤著书立说，以求闻达。

秦王嬴政慕其名，写信给韩王强邀其出使秦国。韩非的思想被秦始皇所重用，他创立的法家学说，为中国第一个统一专制的中央集权制国家的诞生提供了理论依据。韩非在秦遭李斯、姚贾诬害，死于狱中。今存《韩非子》55 篇。

法家是先秦诸子中对法律最为重视的一派，而反对儒家的"礼"。他们以主张"以法治国"的"法治"而闻名，而且提出了一整套的理论和方法，在法理学方面作出了贡献，对于法律的起源、本质、作用以及法律同社会经济、时代要求、国家政权、伦理道德、风俗习惯、自然环境以及人口、人性的关系等基本的问题都做了探讨，而且卓有成效。

法家认为人都有"好利恶害"或者"就利避害"的本性，没有什么道德的标准可言，所以，就要用利益、荣誉来诱导人民去做。比如战争，如果立下战功就给予很高的赏赐，包括官职，这样来激励士兵与将领奋勇作战。这也是秦国军队战斗力强大的原因之一。灭六国统一中国，法家的人性论思想具有一定的积极意义。

法家反对保守的复古思想，主张锐意改革。他们认为历史是向前发展的，一切的法律和制度都要随历史的发展而发展，既不能复古倒退，也不能因循守旧。商鞅（战国时著名的改革家）明确地提出了"不法古，不循今"的主张。韩非则更进一步发展了商鞅的主张，提出"时移而治不易者乱"，他把守旧的儒家讽刺为守株待兔的愚蠢之人。

法家代表人物商鞅、慎到、申不害三人分别提倡重法、重势、重术，各有特点。到了法家思想的集大成者韩非时，则提出了将三者紧密结合的思想。韩非通过许多寓言故事，系统地阐明法、术、势的法治理论，总结了古代国君的得失，表达了自己的抱负和主张。法是指健全法制，势指的是君主的权势，要独掌军政大权，术是指的驾驭群臣、掌握政权、推行法令的策略和手段，主要是察觉、防止犯上作乱，维护君主地位。

但是法家也有其不足的地方。如极力夸大法律的作用，强调用重刑来治理国家，"以刑去刑"，而且是对轻罪实行重罚，迷信法律的作用，忽视了仁、义等儒家所倡导的思想，这也是导致秦朝灭亡的一个重要原因。（刘双琴编著）

第五单元

《诗经》

《诗经》是中国第一部诗歌总集。它汇集了从西周初年到春秋中叶,也就是前 1100 年到前 600 年,约 500 多年间的诗歌 305 篇。《诗经》在先秦叫做《诗》,或者取诗的数目整数叫《诗三百》,本来只是一本诗集。但是,从汉代起,儒家学者把《诗》当做经典,尊称为《诗经》,列入"五经"之首。

《诗经》中的诗当初都是配乐的歌词,按当初所配乐曲的性质,分成"风、雅、颂"三类。"风"的意思是土风、风谣,也就是各地方的民歌民谣。"风"包括了 15 个诸侯国的民歌,即"十五国风",共 160 篇。占了诗经的一半以上。与《雅》《颂》相比,《风》显得活泼,生活气息更浓,如开篇《关雎》写初涉爱河的青年;《氓》写被丈夫抛弃的女子的哀怨;《静女》写恋爱时的微妙心理。

"雅"是周王朝直辖地区的音乐,即所谓正声雅乐,是正统的宫廷乐歌。《雅》诗是宫廷宴享或朝会时的乐歌,按音乐的不同又分为《大雅》31 篇,《小雅》74 篇,共 105 篇。除《小雅》中有少量民歌外,大部分是贵族文人的作品。《大雅》是用于隆重盛大宴会的典礼;《小雅》则是用于一般宴会的典礼。

"颂"是祭祀乐歌,用于宫廷宗庙祭祀祖先,祈祷赞颂神明,《颂》诗分为《周颂》31 篇,《鲁颂》4 篇,《商颂》5 篇,共 40 篇,全部是贵族文人的作品。

《诗经》是中国韵文的源头,是中国诗史的光辉起点。它形式多样:史诗、讽刺诗、叙事诗、恋歌、战歌、颂歌、节令歌以及劳动歌谣样样都有,内容丰富,对周代社会生活的各个方面,如劳动与爱情、战争与徭役、压迫与反抗、风俗与婚姻等各个方面都有所反映。其中有些诗,如《大雅》中的《生民》等,记载了后稷降生到武王伐纣,是周部族起源、发展和立国的历史叙事诗。

在表现手法上,《诗经》以四言为主,兼有杂言,章节复沓,反复咏叹。在结构上多采用重章叠句的形式加强抒情效果。每一章只变换几个字,却能收到回旋跌宕的艺术效果。此外,《诗经》还大量运用赋、比、兴的表现手法。赋是指铺陈叙述,即直接表达自己的感情。赋是最基本的表现手法。比,就是比喻。《诗经》中用比喻的地方很多,手法也富于变化,如《氓》用桑树从繁茂到凋落的变化来比喻爱情的盛衰。兴就是借助其他事物为所咏之内容作铺垫,它往往用于一首诗或一章诗的开头。

《诗经》是中国现实主义文学的光辉起点。由于其内容丰富、思想和艺术上的高度成就,在中国以至世界文化史上都占有重要地位。它开创了中国诗歌的优秀传统,对后世文学产生了不可磨灭的影响。早在春秋时期,《诗经》就已广泛流传,是中国几千年来贵族教育中普遍使用的文化教材。孔子在《论语》里也有"不学《诗》,无以言"的说法,并常用《诗》来教育自己的弟子。

此后,它与《尚书》《礼记》《周易》《春秋》并称"五经"。孔子以后的儒家学派人物,都

把《诗》当做教本,传授不绝。虽经秦始皇焚书,但《诗》由于学者
的口头传诵,得以流传下来。《诗经》的影响还越出中国的国界而走向全世界。
日本、朝鲜、越南等国很早就传入汉文版《诗经》。从 18 世纪开始,又出现了法文、德文、英文、
俄文等译本。(刘双琴编著)

楚辞

"楚辞"又称"楚词",它是战国后期以屈原为代表的诗人,在楚国民歌基础上开创的一种新诗体。西汉末年,刘向将屈原、宋玉的作品以及汉代淮南小山、东方朔、王褒、刘向等人承袭模仿屈原、宋玉的作品共 16 篇辑录成集,定名为《楚辞》,后来王逸又增入自己的作品《九思》,成 17 篇。《楚辞》遂又成为诗歌总集的名称。由于屈原的《离骚》是《楚辞》的代表作,故楚辞又称为"骚"或"骚体"。《楚辞》作为中国第一部浪漫主义诗歌总集,对后世文学影响深远,不仅开启了后来的赋体,而且影响历代散文创作,是中国积极浪漫主义诗歌创作的源头。

现存的《楚辞》总集中,主要是屈原及宋玉的作品。作品运用楚地(今两湖一带)的文学样式、方言声韵,叙写楚地的山川人物、历史风情,具有浓厚的地方特色。除此而外,《楚辞》中屈、宋作品所涉及的历史传说、神话故事、风俗习尚以及所使用的艺术手段、浓郁的抒情风格、铺排夸饰的诗风,无不带有鲜明楚文化色彩。这是楚辞的基本特征,它们是与中原文化交相辉映的楚文化的重要组成部分。

楚辞的主要作者是屈原。他创作了《离骚》《九歌》《九章》《天问》等不朽作品。屈原(约前 339—前 278 年),名平,是中国文学史上最早出现的爱国诗人。因主张彰明法度,举贤授能,联齐抗秦,受楚怀王之子子兰及靳尚等人潜毁,被革去官职。楚襄王时,屈原被放逐,他无力挽救楚之危亡,又无法实现政治理想,遂投汨罗江而死。《离骚》是屈原的代表作。这篇宏伟的政治抒情诗表现了作者的进步理想,为实现理想而进行的不懈斗争,以及斗争中所遇到的挫折及自己的苦闷。全诗充满了浓烈的激情和奇幻的想象,集中表现了诗人忠贞不渝的故国情感和追求崇高理想九死不悔的精神。

楚辞是在楚国民歌的基础上经过加工、提炼而发展起来的,有着浓郁的地方特色。由于地理、语言环境的差异,楚国一带自古就有它独特的地方音乐,古称南风、南音,也有它独特的土风歌谣。更重要的是楚国有悠久的历史,楚地巫风盛行,楚人以歌舞娱神,使神话大量保存,诗歌音乐迅速发展,使楚地民歌中充满了原始的宗教气氛。所有这些影响使得楚辞具有楚国特有的音调音韵,同时具有深厚的浪漫主义色彩和浓厚的巫文化色彩。可以说,楚辞的产生是和楚国地方民歌以及楚地文化传统的熏陶分不开的。

同时,楚辞又是南方楚国文化和北方中原文化相结合的产物。春秋战国以后,一向被称为荆蛮的楚国日益强大。它在问鼎中原、争霸诸侯的过程中与北方各国频繁接触,促进了南北文化的广泛交流,楚国也受到北方中原文化的深刻影响。正是这种南北文化的汇合,孕育了屈原这样伟大的诗人和《楚辞》这样异彩纷呈的伟大诗篇。

《楚辞》在中国诗史上占有重要的地位。它的出现,打破了《诗经》以后两三个世纪的沉

寂而在诗坛上大放异彩。后人也因此将《诗经》与《楚辞》并称为风、骚。风指十五国风,代表《诗经》,充满着现实主义精神;骚指《离骚》,代表《楚辞》,充满着浪漫主义气息。风、骚成为中国古典诗歌现实主义和浪漫主义的创作的两大流派。(刘双琴编著)

汉赋和汉乐府

汉赋是在汉代涌现出的一种有韵的散文,它的特点是散韵结合,专事铺叙。从赋的形式上看,在于"铺采擒文";从赋的内容上说,侧重"体物写志"。汉赋的内容可分为 5 类:一是渲染宫殿城市;二是描写帝王游猎;三是叙述旅行经历;四是抒发不遇之情;五是杂谈禽兽草木。前两者是汉赋中的代表,赋是继《诗经》《楚辞》之后,在中国文坛上兴起的一种新的文体,是最流行的文体。在两汉 400 年间,一般文人多致力于这种文体的写作,因而盛极一时,后世往往把它看成是汉代文学的代表。

汉赋分为大赋和小赋。大赋又叫散体大赋,规模巨大,结构恢宏,气势磅礴,语汇华丽,往往是成千上万言的鸿篇巨制。西汉时的贾谊、枚乘、司马相如、扬雄,东汉时的班固、张衡等,都是大赋的行家。司马相如、扬雄、班固、张衡被誉为"汉赋四大家"。小赋扬弃了大赋篇幅冗长、辞藻堆砌、舍本逐末、缺乏情感的缺陷,在保留汉赋基本文采的基础上,创造出篇幅较小、文采清丽、讥讽时事、抒情咏物的短篇小赋,赵壹、蔡邕、祢衡等都是小赋的高手。

汉赋,特别是那些大赋,尽管有着辞藻堆砌、舍本逐末、缺乏情感等缺点,在文学史上仍然有其一定的地位。首先,那些描写宫苑、田猎、都邑的大赋大都是对广阔的国土、丰盛的物产、繁荣的都市,以及汉帝国的文治武功的描写和颂扬,这对当时的统治具有一定意义。而赋中对统治者的劝谕之词,也具有一定的积极意义。其次,汉大赋虽然炫博耀奇,堆垛辞藻,但在丰富文学作品的词汇、锻炼语言词句、描写技巧等方面,都取得了一定的成就。最后,从文学发展史上看,两汉辞赋的繁兴,对中国文学观念的形成,也起到一定促进作用。中国的韵文从《诗经》《楚辞》开始,中间经过西汉以来辞赋的发展,到东汉开始初步把文学与一般学术区分开来。对文学基本特征的探讨和认识,促进文学观念日益走向明晰化。

汉乐府是指汉时乐府官署所采制的诗歌,是汉代的又一大文学样式。汉乐府掌管的诗歌一部分是供执政者祭祀先祖神明使用的效庙歌辞,其性质与《诗经》中"颂"相同;另一部分则是采集民间流传的无主名的俗乐,世称之为乐府民歌。

乐府诗历来根据所用音乐不同来分类。宋人郭茂倩所编《乐府诗集》100 卷,是收罗汉迄五代乐府最为完备的一部诗集,将乐府分为 12 类,但主要是以下 4 类:(1)郊庙歌辞,主要是贵族文人为祭祀而作的乐歌。(2)鼓吹曲辞,又称短箫铙歌,是汉初从北方民族传入的北狄乐,当时主要用作军乐。(3)相和歌辞,音乐多为各地俗乐,歌辞也多时街巷陌上的民间之谣。所谓"相和",是一种演唱方式,含有"丝竹更相和"与"人声相和"两种。(4)杂曲歌辞,乐调多已失传,不知所起,因无可归类,就自成一类。汉乐府民歌主要保存在"相和"、"鼓吹"、"杂曲"三类中,相和歌辞中尤多。

《乐府诗集》现存汉乐府民歌 40 余篇,多为东汉时期作品,反映当时的社会现实与人民生活,包括对阶级剥削和压迫的揭露与反抗,对战争和徭役的控诉与揭露,对封建礼教和婚姻的抗议,对劳动人民坚贞爱情的歌颂等,用犀利的言辞表现爱恨情感,较为倾向现实主义风格。

汉乐府是继《诗经》之后,古代民歌的又一次大汇集,不同《诗经》的浪漫主义手法,它开诗歌现实主义新风。汉乐府民歌中女性题材作品占重要位置,它用通俗的语言构造贴近生活的作品,由杂言渐趋向五言,采用叙事写法,刻画人物细致入微,创造人物性格鲜明,故事情节较为完整,而且能突出思想内涵着重描绘典型细节,开拓叙事诗发展成熟的新阶段,是中国诗史五言诗体发展的一个重要阶段。

《陌上桑》和《孔雀东南飞》都是汉乐府民歌,后者是中国古代最长的叙事诗,与《木兰诗》合称"乐府双璧"。(刘双琴编著)

《史记》《汉书》

《史记》是中国历史上第一部纪传体通史,被后人誉为"史家之绝唱,无韵之离骚",记载了中国 3000 多年的历史 (黄帝至汉武帝),《史记》全书共 130 篇,共 526500 字,分为 12 本纪、8 书、10 表、30 世家、70 列传五大部分。"本纪"就是帝王的传记,按年月记述帝王的言行政绩。"表""用表格来简列世系、人物和史事。"书"则记述制度发展,涉及礼乐制度、天文兵律、社会经济、河渠地理等诸方面内容。"世家"记述子孙世袭的王侯封国史迹。"列传"是重要人物传记。其中的本纪和列传是主体。《史记》约成书于公元前 104 年至公元前 91 年,本来是没有书名的,司马迁完成这部巨著后曾给当时的大学者东方朔看过,东方朔非常钦佩,就在书上加了"太史公"三字。"太史"是司马迁的官职,"公"是美称,"太史公"也只是表明谁的著作而已。《史记》最初没有固定书名,一般称为《太史公书》,或称《太史公记》,也省称《太史公》。《史记》本来是古代史书的通称,从三国开始,《史记》由通称逐渐成为《太史公书》的专名。

《史记》之作者司马迁(前 145—前 90 年),字子长,中国西汉伟大的史学家、文学家。司马迁撰写史记,态度非常严谨认真。他写的每一个历史人物或历史事件,都经过了大量的调查研究,并对史实反复作了核对。司马迁早在 20 岁时,便离开首都长安遍踏名山大川,实地考察历史遗迹,了解到许多历史人物的遗闻轶事以及许多地方的民情风俗和经济生活,开阔了眼界,扩大了胸襟。汉朝的历史学家班固称赞司马迁文章公正,史实可靠,不空讲好话,不隐瞒坏事。这便高度评价了司马迁的科学态度和史记的记事翔实。司马迁想为封建统治者提供历史的借鉴作用,反映的是真实的历史,这是非常可贵的。本着实录的精神,司马迁在选取人物时,并不是根据其官职或社会地位,而是以其实际行为表现为标准。比如,他写了许多诸如游侠、商人、医生、倡优等下层人物的传记。在司马迁心目中,这些人都有可取之处。

《史记》开创了"纪传体"体例,开创了政治、经济、民族、文化等各种知识的综合纂史方法,秉承了秉笔直书的宝贵史学传统。同时,对古代的小说、戏剧、传记文学、散文,都有广泛而深远的影响。《史记》无论在中国史学史还是在中国文学史上，都堪称是一座伟大的丰碑。

继司马迁撰写《史记》之后，班固撰写了《汉书》。班固（32—92年），扶风安陵（今陕西咸阳东北）人，自幼聪敏，九岁就能写文章，诵诗赋，成年后博览群书，"九流百家之言，无不穷究"。由于《史记》只写到汉武帝的太初间，因此，当时有不少人为它编写续篇。班固的父亲班彪对这些续篇感到很不满意，因此为《史记》作《后传》65篇。班彪死后，年仅二十几岁的班固，动手整理父亲的遗稿，决心继承父业，完成这部接续《史记》的巨作——《史记后传》。就在班固着手编撰《汉书》不久，有人向朝廷上书，告发班固"私改作国史"。皇帝下诏收捕，班固被关进了监狱，家中的书籍也被查抄。其弟班超便上书在汉明帝面前申说班固著述的本意，地方官也将其书稿送到朝廷。汉明帝了解情况后，很欣赏班固的才学，召他到校书部，任命他为兰台令史。

《汉书》的体例与《史记》相比，已经发生了变化。《史记》是一部通史，《汉书》则是一部断代史。《汉书》把《史记》的"本纪"省称"纪"，"列传"省称"传"，"书"改曰"志"，取消了"世家"，汉代勋臣世家一律编入传。这些变化，被后来的一些史书沿袭下来。《汉书》包括帝纪12篇，表8篇，志10篇，列传70篇，共100篇，后人划分为120卷。主要记述汉高祖元年（前206年）至王莽地皇四年（23年）共230年的史事，是继《史记》之后中国古代又一部重要史书。

《汉书》比较完整地引用诏书、奏议，成为《汉书》的重要特点。此外，边疆诸少数民族传的内容也相当丰富。《汉书》新增加了《刑法志》《五行志》《地理志》《艺文志》。《刑法志》第一次系统地叙述了法律制度的沿革和一些具体的律令规定。《五行志》系统地记载了《春秋》记事起至西汉末年间的自然灾异现象和其间历代学者的相关解释。《地理志》记录了当时的郡国行政区划、历史沿革和户口数字，有关各地物产、经济发展状况、民情风俗的记载更加引人注目。《艺文志》考证了各种学术别派的源流，记录了存世的书籍，它是中国现存最早的图书目录。此外，《食货志》是由《平准书》演变来的，但内容更加丰富了。它有上下两卷，上卷谈"食"，即农业经济状况；下卷论"货"，即商业和货币的情况，是当时的经济专篇。

《汉书》虽然具有浓厚的封建正宗思想，但它开创了断代为史和整齐纪传史的编纂体例，且资料丰富，保存许多重要的历史文献，在中国史学史上具有重要的地位。（刘双琴编著）

Chapter 3

第三章

Unit 1

Yangtze River Culture

The Yangtze River Valley and Yellow River Basin are the birthplaces of Chinese ancestry. Stretching back to ancient times, they form the cradle of Chinese culture and civilization, embodying material and spiritual civilization.

The Yangtze River is the longest river in China and third longest in the world, shorter than only the Amazon and Nile Rivers. Originating from the north of Tanggula Mountain Range on the Qinghai Tibetan Plateau, and the southwest side of Shaanxi the snow-capped mountain of Geladandong, the Yangtze River spans three major regions of China. Stretching across the southwest, central, and eastern regions of China, it pushes its way through 11 provinces, cities, and autonomous regions of Qinghai, Tibet, Yunnan, Sichuan, Chongqing, Hubei, Hunan, Jiangxi, Anhui, Jiangsu, and finally merges into the East Sea in Shanghai. The extent of the Yangtze River is more than 6,300 kilometers long, approximately 1,000 kilometers longer than the Yellow River. The area of the entire valley is 1.802 million square kilometers, accounting for 18.75% of the nation's land. Its drainage area is 1.002 million square kilometers larger than that of the Yellow River. In this region, generations of Chinese people gradually shaped a unique culture through diligence and wisdom.

In the past, only Yellow River valley and its culture were regarded as the cradle of Chinese civilization. In fact, however, history has shown that Yangtze River is also the origin of Chinese cultural development. Just as

the Euphrates and Tigris gave birth to Babylonian culture and the Indian
and Ganges Rivers produced India's culture, both the Yangtze and Yellow River cultures should be considered as the root of Chinese heritage.

The Yangtze River culture has a long history. In the Yangtze River Basin, a fossil known as Yuanmou Man was unearthed in Yuanmou county of Yunnan Province in May 1929. According to the scientific evaluation, Yuanmou Man lived roughly 1.7 million years ago, becoming the earliest primitive human discovered thus far in China, existing about one million years earlier than the better-known Peking Man fossils uncovered in the Yellow River valley. In addition, the excavation of historical ruins of the Yangshao culture, which can be traced back 5,000 to 7,000 years ago, reveals the earliest culture in the Yellow River Valley. Correspondingly, the Hemudu culture, representing the civilization of Yangtze River Valley, originated about 5,300 to 7,000 years ago. The splendid primitive culture discovered in Yangshao and Hemudu provides strong evidence that both the Yangtze River Valley and Yellow River Valley are the cradles of the Chinese civilization.

The discovery of the Sanxingdui (Three Star Mounds) has significant meaning in the history and culture of the Yangtze River Valley. Sanxingdui is located in Nanxing Town, west of Guanghan city, in the upper reaches of the Yangtze River. The name of Sanxingdui refers to three earth mounds on the site on the Chengdu plain. The three mounds have been described as three gold stars; hence as the name Sanxingdui (Three Star Mounds). In the spring of 1929, a peasant named Yan Daocheng found a piece of bright-colored jade while digging a ditch. That was the catalyst to the discovery of a mysterious ancient kingdom. Eventually, the two sacrificial pits of Shang Dynasty were unearthed in 1986. Archaeologists brought to light thousands of cultural relics including bronze wares, jade articles, ivory, cowry shells, pottery, and gold plates. Many of the mysterious ancient Shu treasures are of bizarre and impressive shapes. The following are some of the striking finds. First, the world's earliest and largest bronze holy tree was uncovered. The 3.84 meter bronze tree is constructed in sections, and is divided into three parts from root to top with three branches in each section. Fruit grows on the nine branches, and nine birds perch exquisitely on the tips of the branches; an uncanny dragon twists downward on the trunk. The second piece is a bronze human figure. The striking statue is 2.62 meters tall and 180 kilogram in weight. It is the oldest and most complete life-size standing human statue in the world. The most overwhelming find is that of a large bronze head 64.5 centimeters in height with giant protruding eyes and ears spaced at 138.5 centimeters, also being the world's largest bronze bust. These treasures are unprecedented rarities in the spiritual realm. Besides these artifacts, there are many other invaluable gems, such as lustrous gold staffs and jade articles carved with mysterious patterns. According to experts, Sanxingdui was built at latest in the beginning of the Shang Dynasty. The archeological discovery aroused worldwide attention and was hailed the world's ninth wonder. Meanwhile, the historical site is of great archaeological significance in determining the age and the stage of development of ancient society. Traditionally, historians regarded the Yellow River as the

Yangtzu River

mother river where Chinese culture began and gradually diffused throughout China. Yet, the discovery of Sanxingdui provides important factual evidence that civilizations in western China of the ancient state of Shu go back at least 5,000 years. Such evidence defies the traditional theory that the Yellow River was the sole "cradle of Chinese civilization," adjoining both the Yangtze River and the Yellow River cultures as the origins of Chinese civilization.

However, Yellow River culture flourished in human progress as Yangtze River culture was on the fringe of a marginal status. The Yangtze River civilization eventually achieved the same vital position as Yellow River culture after the era of the Wei Jin and Southern and Northern Dynasties.

During this period, residents of the Yellow River Basin were forced to migrate to the Yangtze River area because of natural disasters and frequent warfare. Yangtze Valley, especially areas of the middle and lower reaches, experienced rapid economic development in the Sui and Tang dynasties. The second expansive growth in the southern region occurred after the An Shi Rebellion as large amount of refugee Northerners fled to the south. Immigrant communities cropped up in present-day Jiangsu, Anhui, Jiangxi, Hubei and Sichuan provinces. The third tide of population migration occurred in the Song, Yuan and Ming dynasties. Northerners settled in almost every town of the central and lower reaches of the Yangtze River.

In the process of several population influxcs, thc Yellow River culture gradually merged into the Yangtze River society, taking a giant leaps forward in the development of Yangtze civilization. The beautiful and rustic countryside of the south inspired many northern scholars to create prose of spiritual influence. At the same time, northern style architecture and decoration fashions began to spread throughout the south. Cultural fusion contributed immensely to the improvement of the Yangtze River culture, which made a positive impact on Chinese civilization.

In modern times, the social transformation in the Yangtze River Valley is more progressive than that of Yellow River Basin.

It is said that the Yellow River is the traditional region of government politics; correspondingly the Yangtze River region is the model of vigorous commerce.

The Yangtze River Valley in Southeast Asia is the origin of China's early development, of which Shanghai is a modern metropolis.

Yangtze River culture still displays ever-increasing vigor and vitality in modern times. The regions cover only one-fifth of total land, yet the agriculture yields can feed nearly one-third of the population and accounts for one-half of the industrial and agricultural sectors capital. In modern times, the Yangtze River civilization will be playing an increasingly prominent role.

Yangtze River culture has sparked much enthusiasm among academic circles at home and abroad in recent years.

"The First International Symposium on Yangtze Culture and Chu Culture" was held in Hubei province at the end of 20th century, preceding the "International Symposium on Sanxingdui Culture and Yangtze Civilization" hosted in Sichuan in October of 2003. In addition the publication of the Research Library of Changjiang Culture, undoubtedly stimulated intense interest among people around the globe.

Tea Culture

The Chinese always have the seven necessities: firewood, rice, oil, salt, soy sauce, vinegar, and tea. Among these, tea holds great importance in daily life.

China is the birthplace of tea, thus it was the first country to produce and drink tea.

According to several sources, the discovery of tea can be traced to approximately 2737 B.C. to 2697 B.C., the period of the Three Sovereigns and Five Emperors. However, tea was used as an herbal medicine when it was first discovered.

During the late Western Han dynasty, tea was a high quality beverage revered by monks, royalty, and dignitaries.

From the period of the Three States, drinking tea in the royal court became common practice.

Chinese tea evolved from a palace delicacy to a common beverage during the Jin and Sui Dynasties.

However, it was not until the early Tang Dynasty that the custom of drinking tea spread all over the country. During this era, the art of tea drinking gradually shifted from a crude style of quenching the thirst to a refined fashion, giving way to enjoying small sips to appreciate the subtle allure of tea. The Sage of Tea Lu Yu was the great contributor to the transition, which marked a great event in the history of tea culture. His book *The Classic of Tea* is a symbol of the creation of the Chinese tea society. *The Classic of Tea* is a historical integration of the natural connotation and human value of partaking in tea before the Tang Dynasty. Lu Yu, the initiator of the science of tea, incorporated Confucian, Taoist, and Buddhist philosophy into his works. In the Tang Dynasty, another factor in the formation of the art lies in the rise of Zen meditation. Because drinking tea was known to improve one's mental performance and quench the thirst of the spirit, the monasteries advocated tea drinking. Tea ceremony in the Tang Dynasty fell into three variations: tea ceremonies of the royal court, monastery tea ceremonies, and literati tea rites.

In the Song Dynasty, professional tea-tasting associations emerged, such as the official Social Soup and the Buddhist component Thousand Beings Society. Emperor Zhao Kuangyin of the Song dynasty was extremely fond of tea. At that time, an office was established in the royal court to manage the different grades of tea and develop system of etiquette for drinking tea. Tea was listed as the prime gift for the emperor to prompt the ministers, manifest his love and care for relatives, and to strengthen relations with foreign countries. Tea drinking customs were particularly lively among common people. Neighbors would offer tea to express their best wishes to a family who planned to move. Yuanbao Tea was commonly offered to a guest upon entering a home. Moreover, tea was considered as an important betrothal gift. On the wedding day, it was customary that the couple serves their parents tea. The newlyweds would then share a cup of tea before they entered the bridal chamber. Common people's interest in tea initiated the tea selectors culture, holding competitions of great importance, with subjects ranging from the quality, color, and fragrance of the leaves, to the participants' art of tea selection. Tea manufacturing technology, such as steaming, pan drying, and a baking technique, achieved great strides. Tea sets were characterized by their diverse styles, varying textures, and fascinating designs.

The art of tea experienced significant changes in tea types and drinking methods during the Ming and Qing Dynasties. From the time of the Tang dynasty, loose tea became the foundation for development, thus becoming the norm in the Ming and the Qing dynasties. It was passed down through the generations and is the primary form of tea served today. The Ming dynasty's loose-leaf pan-fired method was primarily used for green tea, but also included teas of flowers. Tea types were greatly expanded in the Qing Dynasty. Besides the green tea and flower teas, Oolong, red, black, white, and many other types of teas emerged, thereby establishing China's comprehensive categories of tea.

All the world's extensive tea trees, brewing methods, and tea drinking customs have all emerged from China. It is estimated that Chinese tea spread overseas approximately 2,000 years ago. In the 5th century (Northern and Southern Dynasties), Chinese tea was gradually exported to neighboring countries in Southeast Asia and other parts of Asia. In the 9th century, a Japanese monk brought tea seeds to Japan, which initiated the Japanese custom of tea drinking. In the 10th century, Mongolian trade caravans brought Chinese brick tea via Siberia to remote areas of central Asia.

In the beginning of the 15th century, the tea trade further spread when Portuguese merchants came to China for commerce. In 1610, Chinese tea went to West Europe in a Dutch merchant ship, reaching Eastern Europe after 1650, then to Russia and France; and by the 17th century, tea arrived the Americas. In the early period of the 18th century, Chinese tea was adopted by the upper class in Britain as a gift of luxury. Meanwhile, drinking red tea became the fashion there. British East India Company has reaped huge profits from its large-scale sales of Chinese tea since the 18th century. In 1880, the export of Chinese tea to England amounted to 1.45 million piculs (29,000 kg), accounting for 60~70% of the total tea export volume. By the 19th century, Chinese tea reached around the globe with its unique charm. It is now consumed by many people all over the world.

A modern Chinese tea plantation covers an area of nine 1.1 million hectares. Tea regions spread from the eastern coast of Taiwan Province (Longitude 122° E) to Yulin city of Hainan province in the south (Latitude 18° N). These regions end in the west in Yigong of the Autonomous Tibet Region (Longitude 95° E) and to the north in Rongcheng County of Shandong province (Latitude 37° N), which spars over 27° in longtitude and 19° in Latitude. There are 21 provinces (autonomous regions, municipalities) and 967 counties large tea productions. There are four main tea areas in China: the southwest region, southern region, and areas south and north of the Yangtze River. There are ten immensely popular teas, namely West Lake's Dragon Well Tea, Spring Snail, Wuyi Stone Tea, Anxi's Iron Goddess, Tunxi Green Tea, Qi Men Red, Xinyang's Fur Tip, Silver Needle Tea, Pu'er Tea, and Yunnan Black Tea.

Tea–planting Area in Zhejiang Province

Wine Culture

Chinese tea culture is famous for its time-honored history, but the wine culture in no way pales by comparison. In the thousands of years since the development of civilization, alcohol has penetrated nearly every aspect of Chinese social life.

Throughout China in ancient times, cereal grains were primarily used in the process of fermentation. The base of the nation's economy is agriculture. The prosperity of the wine business, therefore, depended on the bounty of the grain harvest, the state of society, political economic activity, and the intimate bonds of cultural traditions. In ancient Chinese books a legend of Ape Wine, has been recorded. Of course, it doesn't state that apes brewed wine themselves, but rather tells of apes and monkeys fruit collecting fruit. The fruit that was not eaten then fer-

Wine Workshop of Old Times

mented and produced cider. Therefore, China's earliest "wine" imitated nature's masterpieces of fruit cider, and fermented milk (animal milk will naturally ferment, becoming sour).

In Chinese antiquity, cereal grains were used to produce yellow wine. Also called rice wine, it belongs to a category occupying an important position in the world's three major brewages: yellow wine, grape wine, and beer. With unique brewing techniques, it has become the model and representative of oriental wine making. Yellow wine received its name due to its yellow coloration, thus the literal translation. In fact, there are certainly other distinct hues of yellow wine such as black and red, thus one cannot comprehend it only by name. Yellow wine is produced with the raw materials of grains, using a wheat or barley starter, or possibly rice and sugar to initiate fermentation. In Northern China, millet is the major ingredient, while in South China rice is preferred. In modern times, rice wine is commonly used in translation to refer to Yellow Wine.

In ancient times, wine was perceived as divine, thus the process of making it a serious matter. As classical antiquity arrived, wine was a necessity in ceremonial sacrifices. Ancient rulers viewed wine as an "important matter of the state, for sacrifice and military affairs" as they are inseparable to ceremony used as a libation to heaven, deities, and their ancestors to express reverence. In times of conflict, wine was adopted to boost the warriors' morale before they entered into battle.

Wine is not only related to state affairs, but is also an unalienable part of human life, thereby creating great diversity in the customs of drinking wine.

In China, there exists the custom of drinking wine at weddings. Joyful Wine or Xijiu, is often synonymous with the wedding ceremony, therefore the partaking of the Xijiu may be considered as attending the wedding. Almost every step in a wedding is related with wine. Specifically, wine plays an inseparable role on many occasions, such as daughter wine, union wine cups, welcoming wine, send-off wine, banquet of relatives wine, and homecoming wine.

The important festivals of each year are accompanied by their corresponding social customs of drinking, such as the calamus wine on Dragon Boat Festival and the chrysanthemum wine on the Double Ninth Festival and the New Year's Wine on the New Years Eve.

Full Moon Wine or Hundred Days Wine is presented during a full moon and shortly after the birth of a child. Banquet tables are arranged with wine, inviting friends and family to jointly congratulate the family. Normally those joining the feast will bring some gifts or a red envelope to show their regards.

Generally the 50th, 60th, and 70th birthdays are called the elders' grand birthdays, for which a feast is held by the children or grandchildren of the elder and attended by many friends and relatives, serving shoujiu.

In rural areas of China, on the day when construction is completed, such as building a new house or major event in a citizen's life, a banquet is commonly held where Shangliang Wine is offered. On the day when a family moves to a new location, they will also prepare a feast with Housewarming Wine to celebrate and to praise deities and ancestors to avoid misfortunes.

Opening business wine or bonus wine is served when a common store is opened, when the boss of a workshop treats the employees to a feast, or perhaps at the end of the fiscal year as stock dividends are awarded.

Robust wine, also called farewell wine is used at a banquet honoring a friend about to embark on a long journey. In periods of war, before the troops were to execute a dangerous and life threatening mission, military officials would commonly offer a cup of robust wine.

Confucianism, the core of Chinese traditional civilization, is embodied by drinking manner, which focused on people's etiquette of self-restraint and compliance.

Chinese people are very hospitable and at banquets will commonly offer Quan wine. Not only is it accompanied by a variety of entertainment, but a series of wine games and songs that provoke interest.

Over millennia of development of wine culture, many amusing anecdotes evolved out of wine. Long-standing tales are of lakes of wine and forests of meat, describing unbridled debauchery; and The Wine Master, Lu Wine of Handan, The Feast of Hongmen, The First Han Emperor Beheads the White Serpent, Wenjun Danglu, Steamed Hero Wine, The Seven Sages of the Bamboo Grove, Pure Wine Makes the Sage, The Eight Drinking Immortals, and Dismissing the Military Hierarchy using Wine Cups.

Since ancient times, wine has enjoyed an affinity with literature and art and it has spurred massive invaluable creations in painting, opera, music and richly colorful classical narratives.

The Eight Cuisines

Cuisine is a central part of the Chinese food culture. Regional cuisines have taken shape after long-history evolution under the influence of geographical environment, climate, local products, eating habits and other factors. With several thousand years of creative and accumulative efforts, the Chinese cuisine has stood out unequaled in the world. The most influential and representative regional variations are Lu, Chuan, Yue, Min, Su, Zhe, Xiang and Hui Cuisines, which are commonly known as the Eight Great Cuisines.

Lu (Shandong) Cuisine ranks the first of the Eight Great Cuisines. Since the Song Dynasty, Shandong cuisine has developed into a representative of northern Chinese cooking. During Ming and Qing dynasties, Lu cuisine entered the imperial court as rare royal delicacies. In the modern era, it has evolved to the local flavor of Jinan and Jiaodong regions. Characteristics of Shandong cuisine are noted by a distinct aroma, fresh and tender, and simple tasting; with special attention to broth and milk soup. Clear soup is rather thin, while the milk soup is creamy and white. Jinan cuisine masters the cooking techniques of popping, roasting, deep fry, stir fry, among other famous methods. Typical courses in Shandong cuisine include Nine-turned Large Intestine, Crackling Soup, Roasted Oysters, and Bird's Nest Soup. Jiaodong dishes are mainly made of seafood, featuring delicious, refreshing, pure and light tastes. Braised Whelk with Brown Sauce and Steamed Red Porgy (fish) are highly recommended.

As one of the eight Chinese cuisines, Sichuan cuisine has a long history. It is recorded in historical books that Sichuan cuisine dates back to the States of Shu and Ba in ancient times. Sichuan style dishes took shape during the late Qin Dynasty to the early Han period, experiencing rapid development in Tang and Song dynasties. It evolved into one of the major cuisines with the native flavors of China's Ming and Qing dynasties as Sichuan restaurants emerge around the world today. Traditional Sichuan cuisine is exemplified in the dishes of the cities Chengdu and Chongqing. It features the properties of sour, sweet, tingling, spicy, savory, oily, and a concentrated taste with particular attention to seasonings. Inseparable in the style are the Three Peppers (chili pepper, black pepper, and Chinese prickly ash), fresh ginger root, and the universally accepted spicy and tingling flavor, give rise to the saying, "One dish exhibits one flavor, one hundred dishes offer one hundred different tastes." Sichuan culinary art boasts numerous cooking techniques, such as roasting, baking, dry frying, and steaming. Famous dishes are typified by Braised Dry Bead Curd Shreds, Stewed Eel, Chicken with Special Hot Sauce, and Mapo Tofu.

Yue Cuisine, short for Guangdong Cuisine and one of the main cuisine styles in China, is composed of

Mapo Tofu

Guangzhou, Chaozhou and Dongjiang cooking styles. Guangdong Cuisine has gradually formed its own three distinct characteristics. Firstly, a wide variety of ingredients are used for cooking. Animals that fly in the sky, crawl on land, and swim in the water; and all in attendance at banquets. Secondly, special attention is paid to the intensive selection of ingredients, elaborate techniques, and substantial variety of dishes. The chefs excel at fusing the appeal of delicacies from all over the country, making innovations in the culinary arts. Thirdly, emphasis is placed on quality and taste. The flavor is rather light, with an emphasis on fresh, tender, crisp, smooth, and aromatic qualities. Famous dishes are Roasted Suckling Pig, The Dragon and Tiger Battle, Taiye Chicken, Stewed Grain Worms, Boiled Dog Meat, Five-Colored Shrimp, and Stewed Snake and Cat with Chrysthemum Flowers.

Fujian cuisine originates from Minhou County of Fujian province. It is comprised of three branches—Fuzhou, South Fujian and West Fujian, with slight differences among them. Fujian cuisine has four individual qualities. One is the emphasis on fine slicing techniques so that it is reputed as thin as paper and shredded as slender as hairs. The second is that the Fujian people are peculiar about soup, which is full of alterations. The third main aspect of Fujian cuisine is the clear, refreshing, delicious and light flavors embodying a slightly sweet and sour taste. Fourth are the exquisite culinary techniques that include stir-frying, steaming and stewing. Some of the appealing dishes are: Buddha Jumping Over the Wall, Chicken with Bamboo Shoots, Three Stewed Sea Cucumbers, Fried Scallops, Sliced Chicken in Bird's Nest Soup, and Lychee Pulp.

Jiangsu Cuisine originated from Southern and Northern Dynasties, became as famous as Zhejiang Cuisine after Tang and Song Dynasties, and was recognized as a distinct regional style during the Ming and Qing dynasties, enjoying the same status as Sichuan and Guangdong cuisines at that time. Huai Yang cuisine, one branch of Jiangsu cooking, was once common in the imperial courts and is now commonly served at Chinese state banquets. Jiangsu cuisine consists of the styles of Jiangsu-Yangzhou, Suzhou-Wuxi, Nanjing-Xuzhou dishes. Its slicing techniques are delicate and much attention is paid to the heating temperature. The flavor of Huaiyang Cuisine is well-known for its not-too-spicy, not-too-bland taste. And the cuisine is light, fresh and sweet and with delicate elegance. Cooking techniques consist of stewing, roasting, baking, simmering, and stir frying. When preparing food, strict attention is paid to the color and shape of the food, as well as the four seasons. Famous dishes are Clear Fire Soup, Shark Fin Stuffed Duck, Squirrel with Mandarin Fish, Watermelon Chicken, and Salted Duck.

West Lake Fish in Vinegar Sauce

Zhejiang cuisine is comprises of the specialties of Hangzhou, Ningbo and Shaoxing. As a whole, Zhejiang Cuisine tradition is noted for its own local characteristics. The four main signatures of the style are the meticulous selection of small, fresh and unique ingredients. Secondly, Zhejiang cuisine specializes in stir-frying, deep-frying, braising, quick fry, steaming, and roasting. The third quality is the preserving of the color and the texture and allowing the inherit qualities of the food emerge. Fourthly, special attention is paid to the cuisine's meticulous shape and elaborate designs, obtaining the natural flavor and taste. The dishes are not only delicious in taste but also extremely elegant in appearance. The culinary art is noted for its West Lake Fish in Vinegar Sauce, Dongpo Pork, Fried Shrimp with Dragon Well Tea, Beggar's Chicken, Dachang Fish Soup, and Popping Cuttlefish Rolls.

Hunan cuisine consists of a variety of local dishes from the Xiangjiang River valley, Dongting Lake area and Western Hunan mountain area. Hunan people are quite fond of hot pepper. As mirrored by the saying, "Jiangxi natives do not fear hot peppers, Sichuan locals fear them even less, and Hunan people fear to be without them." Hunan Cuisine is characterized by thick and pungent flavor, including hot spicy, numbing and spicy, fresh spicy, hot and sour, and bitter spicy tastes. And "General Tso's Chicken" is the hottest item on the menu of Hunan Cuisine. Hunan food has five characteristics: (1) wide selection of materials; (2) abundant tastes and flavor; (3) fine workmanship in cutting; (4) various kinds of seasonings; (5) a wide variety of techniques. Typical courses include: Dong'an Chicken, Spicy Chicken, Stewed Shark Fins and Brown Sauce, Puffed Tripe Soup, Lotus Seeds in Rock Sugar Sauce, and Spotted Butter Fish.

Anhui Cuisine is mainly composed of local flavors of Huizhou and other areas along the Yangtze River and the Huai River. Chefs in Anhui province are experts especially in cooking delicacies of mountains and seas. The highly distinctive characteristics of Anhui cuisine rely on several factors. One is the strict selection of ingredients that draws from local resources. With the changing of the four seasons, Anhui's abundant mountains support many treasures of wild game. The second characteristic is the control of the cooking flame, achieving the desired texture, aroma, and rare style. Thirdly, the prevalence of popular cooking methods such as roasting, stewing, smoking, and steaming also makes this style distinct. Fourth, particular attention is paid to the supplemental value of food, using food as medicine, focusing on raising a healthy body and simultaneously retaining the local flavor, while dividing the dishes among their nutritional values. Popular dishes include Braised Masked Civet, Fuliji Roasted Chicken, Stewed Ham and Bamboo Shoots, Braised Pheasant with Snow Vegetables, Gourd Duck, Salted Mandarin Fish, Stewed Soft Shell Turtle with Ham, and Maofeng Anchovies.

Unit 2

Han Attire

Han attire, or Hanfu, refers to the clothing worn by the Han ethnic people before the Qing Dynasty. This type of dress was designed and made popular by the Han Dynasty, hence the name. Han attire is easily identifiable because of its unique characteristics, such as the Y-shaped cross collar (left one over the right), no buttons, and a string or a belt for fastening which gave it a relaxed yet elegant feel.

Han attire includes formal dress and common clothing. Generally the formal outfit consists of an upper garment and a lower garment (the lower garment in ancient times was a skirt). Shenyi (informal wear) was made by stitching the upper and lower sections together, but also included a shorter jacket. Among them, the court dress with upper and lower garment became the most formal attire which was reserved for emperors and officials of the highest rank. The closed full-body garment was an informal dress for various other officials and scholars. The short coat, shirt,

and skirt were favorites of women, while ordinary laboring people wore short upper garment and trousers. Accessories and hair ornaments are also important components of Hanfu. In ancient times, men and women of the Han nationality would wear their hair in a bun and hold it in place with a hairpin. Men traditionally donned their heads with coronets, turbans and caps. Women would comb their hair in various styles and wear all kinds of hair ornaments such as pearls, flowers and hairpins with pendants. Also in vogue was stylized hair in the area of the temples and the use of veils. Jade girdle ornaments were a unique feature of Han attire. Han attire for men falls into two categories according their features. One type of dress is representative of the clothing during the ancient Qin and Han Dynasties. It includes a large

Shenyi (informal wear)   Ruqun (short jacket)

over-lapping lapel, crossed collar, wide sleeves, and extensive wraps. Such attire persisted through the Shang, Zhou, Spring and Autumn and Warring States Periods, the period of the Three Kingdoms, the two Jin dynasties, the Southern and Northern dynasties, the Sui, Tang, the Five Dynasties, Song, Yuan, and Ming dynasties; influencing countries such as Japan and Korea. The kimono in Japan was modeled after this style. The other style of Hanfu is the closed, round collared robe which was worn during Sui and Tang Dynasties. It was also prevalent during the Five Dynasties, as well as the Song, Yuan, and Ming dynasties. Such clothing also greatly affected the garments of Japan and Korea. In the early styles of Hanfu, the one-piece clothing style (shenyi) of women and men were similar, but later incorporated styles of shorter in length. For millennia, Han Chinese clothing has retained its simple and elegant style despite the changes in dynasties. The fashion of the Ming Dynasty was a long coat and was basically the same as that of Western Han Dynasty except for some minor details. The styles of garments during the Spring Autumn and Warring States Periods were still the continuation of the Shang Dynasty with only slight alterations. Garments of the Spring Autumn and Warring States Periods embodied a more relaxed style than those of the Shang period. The sleeves were flared, and the collars were of varied sizes. There were no buttons as a belt cinched the clothing at the waist, and some belts had jade ornamentation. People in following Qin Dynasty adored the color black, so black became a common hue for the clothing of that time, but the style of the overlapping lapel (from left to right) was retained.

Informal wear for men in the Han Dynasty falls into two categories: diagonal body wrapping robes (quju) and garments with straight lapels (zhiju). Quju robes evolved from the long coat that was popular during the Warring States Period and into the Han Dynasty. Yet as the Eastern Han period arrived, few people wore full body garments. Straight-lapel gowns could be worn in everyday life, but they were not suitable for formal occasions. During the Qin and Han Dynasties the styles of quju robes were similar for men and women. They consisted of a long one-piece slender robe that would often drag and had a diagonal lapel. The lower section flared out and concealed the feet as one walked. The sleeves were flared and the cuffs were commonly decorated with trim. The collar was low-set so as to expose the underlying garments. As every layer of clothing is being worn, at most three layers, each portion must be revealed. These three layers are known as the three main garments. Straight-lapel garments for men and women emerged in and persisted through the Western Han Dynasty. They could not serve as formal attire; the reason being ancient trousers had no crotch, therefore trouser legs reached only to the knees. Also a belt was worn around the waist. This style of crotchless pants was worn in the household, but long robes covering the entire body were worn in public in the belief that exposing one's trousers in important situations was disrespectful. Later improvements of undergarments led to the emergence of crotched trousers. The fashion of the Eastern Han Dynasty and thereafter regarded the traditional long robe as superfluous and the style was abandoned.

Men's Quju   Women's Quju

By and large, men's coats were distinctive for their broad sleeves during Wei and Jin Periods and the Southern and Northern Dynasties. This type of layered men's clothing was greatly loved and admired even into the Southern Dynasty. Dresses for ordinary women inherited the style from the Qin and Han Dynasties. The fashion of the time consisted mainly of slender and form-fitting blouses or short jackets with loose sleeves accompanied by long pleated floor skirts completing the elegance of the women. Round-collared robes with narrow sleeves was the uniform for officials throughout the Tang Dynasty, but ceremonial clothing would still be donned on significant occasions. The styles of ceremonial dress were adopted from the former Sui Dynasty, consisting of conical or flat cap, wide-buttoned sleeves, a petticoat, and a jade-adorned belt. Ruqun (short jacket) was the major style for women in Tang Dynasty. Beginning in the Sui period, women wore short jackets that featured narrow sleeves and tight, long skirts. The waistband was set very high, sometimes up to the underarm area, with a ribbon connected to the back to compliment the beauty of the female shape. Compared to the early Tang era, runqun styles were broader and more relaxed in the mid-Tang Dynasty, but it was fundamentally the same fashion.

Since ancient times China has been renowned as a country of formal dress and etiquette because of its rich culture of attire. Hanfu (hat and clothes) has gradually become a cultural symbol of the long and rich culture of China.

Under the rule of the Manchurian Qing dynasty, an order was issued to have all the men shave the front of their heads in order to strike a blow to the self-respect of the Han nationality. Moreover, the entire system of attire was changed, altering the appearance and politics of dress of the Han people and burying the Han traditional attire for the next three millennia. Traditional Han attire has a distinct appeal that has written a brilliant chapter in the history of China. Even today, the unique style is admired worldwide.

Cheongsam

The cheongsam is a style of clothing which developed from Manchurian attire. During the Manchurian period of minority rule, women wore a traditional long gown, modeled after the garb of the Manchu women. The cheongsam was labeled qipao after the Manchurian social group named qiren (referring to the eight banners). Chinese dress Due to improvements to the cheongsam in the early 20th century, it reached the height of popularity in the 1930s when it became known worldwide as the Chinese dress. This was in fact the golden age of the qipao. From its birthplace in Shanghai, it rapidly became the fashion in almost every part of the country and the standard of dress for all Chinese women. The female socialites of Shanghai experienced a high level of social interaction. During the 1930s, they embraced luxury and the modern waves of fashion. Soon afterwards, the whole country was inundated by the qipao as the choice attire of Chinese women. Shanghai revered the Western lifestyle to such an extent that a Western-influenced cheongsam emerged on the scene. This style broke the mold of the traditional aesthetic creating a more slender, voluptuous look, emphasizing the beauty of women and becoming a fresh distinguishing fashion among Chinese women. After several years of modification and improvements, the cheongsam has become a fashion complimentary to American women. The traditional dress of China, qipao, is constructed using traditional materials such as silk and brocade. Commonly worn with the hair wrapped in a tall bun, the dress compliments the flowing, melodic beauty of the Chinese woman, like a natural, unrestrained painting accompanied by poetry. This emerges in modern times as a warm and virtuous, attractive, lucid and elegant, matching the temperament and standard of fashion of the first half of the 20th century, as the East-West esthetic conceptions were exchanged and interwoven. The breathtaking charm of the Orient propelled a popular classic style into today's iconic fashion.

There are a wide range of qipao styles. There are styles of button lapels, pipa-style lapels, slanting lapels, double lapels, high-collared, low-collared, no collared, long, short, with or without sleeves, possibly a slit on the side of various lengths, as well as custom fitting for the height of the individual, making each one unique. The changes in the style of cheongsams that occurred during the first half of the 20th century were of mainly the sleeves and the lapels, yet the fundamental pattern and certain distinct features endured. Qipao is now recognized as the epitome of classic Chinese women's attire. Despite thousands of fashion trends, fashion designers still look towards this classical treasure for incessant inspiration.

Diversified Styles of Cheongsam in 1930s' China

The exterior appearance of the qipao most commonly has a large lapel which overlaps from left to right, with either a full-buttoned or half-buttoned style, a standing collar with a button, a slit on one side, and the pattern is generally cut from one piece of material. The opening on the side is a distinct trait of the cheongsam, but is not a required feature. There are slits on both sides and the upper and lower sections of the dress are approximately the same size. The collar and the cuffs are adorned with meticulous decoration, which are fine examples of the complex handicrafts of embroidery, embedding, inlay, and coiling. In modern times, the cheongsam has entered an era of three-dimensional design. It has become more form fitting in the waist and back with added western style sleeves, or sleeves with great curtail. The fine embroidery patterns are even more exquisite, which replaces hours of meticulous handmade embroidery.

Cheongsam reached the peak of its popularity in the 1930s and 1940s. However, in the wake of the Communist Revolution, the general populous regarded elegant clothing in a completely different manner. The leisure and wise virtuous woman image represented by Cheongsam gradually lost its status in that atmosphere. During the 1980s and 1990s, the uniform cheongsam emerged. Women began wearing cheongsams as greeters of businesses promotions, in ceremonies, as greeters and entertainers, and as waitresses in restaurants. Since the 1990s, people began to turn their eyes to the cheongsam after society's aesthetic conceptions about ideal female images underwent drastic changes. Cheongsam was fitting for the fashionably tall, slender feminine physique, once again attracting new attention.

Qipao is the traditional dress for Chinese women of modern times, but the true traditional Chinese clothing is the Han attire. It has undergone several changes over time, but more importantly, it has diffused throughout the modern world. The cheongsam embodies a definite historical value. Moreover, it has retained its value as elegant fashion. Even though some of the modern styles may lack content, some regions still have preserved their elegant folk art and are bound to increase in worth as they are greatly admired.

Chinese Folding Fans

In ancient times the folding fan was called jutou fan, san fan, or zhedie fan. The names refer to the two ends of the fan folding together. The slats of the fan were typically constructed of bamboo or ivory, with a paper or silk covering them. Three components of a folding fan are: the slats, the leaves, and the face. Generally, the slats of an ordinary fan were made of bamboo with paper annealed to the face. In addition, more elaborate fans were adorned with famous paintings and calligraphy. Extremely high-quality folding fan slats and leaves were generally made of ivory, and many featured extremely intricate carvings. Rare masterpieces such as these invariably were painted or etched by a famous artist.

The folding fan emerged before the Song Dynasty, but was sot widespread. As the Song Dynasty arrived, the production of folding fans reached a considerable scale. This trend continued throughout the Ming Dynasty, as the emperor issued an edict that all artisans should replicate the gaoli fan of Korea, drawing from foreign influence to develop a Chinese version. The Ming and Qing eras were the golden age for the folding fan. Using fine, rare materials and exquisite techniques, various artistic forms were expressed on the on the slats, creating a unique style admired by many. Every inch of the fan embodies the heart and soul of the artist and incorporates an elaborate overall arrangement. The face is adorned with scenic mountains and rivers, as well as birds, flowers, or a scene of activity with people, expressing an elegant, classical rhetoric and spiritual intensity.

The Folding Fan with Birds and Flowers

In the early stages of fan making, nobles of the Ming dynasty used folding fans commonly made of bamboo and silk. Later, the imperial court issued an edict that every year numerous exquisite fans were to be manufactured and presented as tribute to the emperor. This practice gained increasing momentum among the palace of the Ming dynasty day by day. The selection of materials used to produce the fans became more and more refined and skillfully innovative. Fans slats are made of ivory, hawksbill tortoise shell, fragrant sandalwood, agar wood, Lady Palm, as well as various other types of wood. Refined techniques of fan making included spiral gold inlaying, etched lacquer ware, and lustrous stain. Various designs and patterns are carved on the slats, exhibiting exceptional and wonderful artisanship. During the Yongle period of the Ming Dynasty, Emperor Zhudi prompted a tide of fan manufacturing, ordering great amounts of fans to be made. On the face of the fan was inscribed classical poetry, and these fans were given as gifts to his ministers. At one time the folding fan was quite rare, but later became typical fashion. Literary and refined scholars wrote verses expressing friendly analogies and metaphors in calligraphy on the fan. Carrying a fan in hand was an indication of nobility and refinement. The folding fan continued to e-

volve, reaching the pinnacle of perfection during the period of the Qing
Dynasty. During the Ming and Qing dynasties, the production of masterpieces of the
Jiangnan region emerged, wherein scholars expressed their romantic passion with intricate design.
Their classical works depicted the scenic beauty of the Jiangnan region and the heavy romantic atmosphere of river culture. They incorporated poetry and landscape paintings. By means of the folding
fan, these talented works were and continued to be displayed in imperial palaces, official residences,
boudoirs, common households, and overseas, thereby retaining their intrinsic worth and receiving a
tremendous boost in prestige.

Various types fans are produced using different materials, and the fans are named accordingly.
The spring fan or autumn fan is composed of many light slats. The fragrant fan is a kind of fan doused
with perfume. Travelers made use of the boot fan as it was easy to concealed in the boots for later use.
Another type of fan is the qiaolang fan whose face is made of a transparent muslin and allows one to
see through it. There is also a type of fan called a three-faced fan that is opened from the left and the
right because the face was made of three distinct panels. In the middle of one of the panels is a painting of the Spring Palace.

In addition, fans produced by particular manufacturers and different artists are named accordingly, such as Huang shan, Cao shan, Pan shan, Chuan shan, and Qingyang shan. The folding fan varied in its ornamentation and practical use; the material and craftsmanship determined its use.

It is recorded that the earliest fan business was Hangzhou's Fangfeng establishment. This family grew wealthy from generations of producing and selling fans. Within the walls of Hangzhou city,
they purchased established a villa, secluded by flowers, trees, bamboo, and rocks. Their 100-slat fan
is one of the ancient classical fans still produced today. Although its slats surpass 100 pieces, it looks
small and dainty with antique color tones. In addition, Chengdu, Nanjing and other regions are also
well-known for their fan manufacturing.

The folding fan is far less practical than the cattail leaf fan in its cooling effect. Yet the Chinese
folding fan has grown beyond the realm of functionality, with distinguishing art representing the
beauty of life. It is commonly believed that the folding fan was brought to China from Japan. After
this Japanese fan arrived to China during the Song Dynasty, it quickly generated widespread interest
in imperial households and amongst scholars, gaining the favor of literary artists. After their early
contact with the Japanese fan, artisans in Zhejiang province absorbed its merits promptly. They
adopted Lady Palm, mottled bamboo, ivory, boxwood, and sandalwood to produce the fan ribs. Artisans also carved poems, pictures of figures, landscapes, flowers, and birds on the slats. They adorned
the fans with such pendants as jade accessory and fringe, offering rich treasures to the artistic world.
Today, China is the world's largest producer and exporter of folding fans, allowing the fans to find
their ways to several countries.

Folk Arts and Crafts

Folk arts and crafts play a significant role in China's five thousand year history, and retain a strong essence of life and distinguishing features. A great variety of art forms enrich the scope of folk crafts, such as paper-cuttings, embroidery, printed cloth, batik dyes, kites, ceramics, wood-cut, shadow theater, clay sculpture, and New Year paintings. Often, the various skilled techniques are employed to create daily commodities which have a high practical value. Still other craftsmen put an emphasis on ornamental value as they produce artwork used on marriage ceremony and festivals. Paper-cutting and embroidery are widely acknowledged as excellent examples of Chinese artistry.

Paper-cuts refer to traditional handicrafts made by cutting paper with scissors to form different patterns. Material utilized for this popular art range from common paper, gold and silver foil, tree bark and leaves, to cloth and leather. Paper-cutting is one of the oldest handicrafts of China, having close relationship with Chinese festivals and marriage ceremonies. At these times, people paste paper-cuts on walls, windows, pillars, and mirrors to enhance the festive atmosphere and pray for good

Rats Marrying off Their Daughters

luck and fortune. Regional styles with distinct local character have emerged all over China. In particular, paper-cuts in Gaomi of Shandong province and Foshan of Guandong province are unique for their outstanding characteristics. Generally speaking, the artistic style of the northern Chinese paper-cut is straightforward, bold, honest, simple, and concise. In the south, it's more exquisite, refined, and delicate, and often incorporates humorous subject matter. As a reflection of cultural folklore, such subjects include Eight Immortals Crossing the Sea, One Hundred Years of Lotuses, The Qilin (unicorn) Carrying its Son, and Rats Marrying Off Their Daughters.

The art form of paper-cut emerged in the 6th century A.D. During the Tang Dynasty, paper-cut evoked the soul of the social customs of that time and circulated among the common people, reaching high levels of achievement as complete intricate works of art were created. The technology of making paper experienced great improvement in Song Dynasty, as different colors of paper were introduced, thus stimulating the popularity of paper cutting. Paper-cut designs were commonly used as decoration on gifts, or placed on windows, lanterns, and tea cups. Among the masses during the Song Dynasty, the popularity of paper-cut greatly expanded. In the Jizhou district of Jiangxi province, artists discovered a method of incorporating a type of paper-cut and a ceramic kiln, using a delicate glaze and firing process to form a type of ceramic. Common images popular among the people included a donkey, an ox, a horse, a ram, and other shadow puppet animals. Furthermore, carved human images completed the shadow theater cast. During the Ming and Qing dynasties, the art of papercutting

was immensely popular as it reached its peak. The public expanded the
use of paper-cut patterns as bright floral designs on lanterns and fans, as decorative
motifs, as well as integrated with embroidery. The use of machinery to cut the patterns also began to
be incorporated. Even more common, the art form has been extensively applied as household decor
to create an appealing social environment. People adorn wooden gates, windows, cabinets, as well as
on canopies and at festive events. Besides the professional male artisans that emerged during the
Northern Song dynasty, among the common people in rural villages, many highly-skilled women excelled at this art. Paper-cut is also a traditional skill in China typically shared by the women in the
past. Similarly, the art of papercutting has also commonly been studied by women from an early age.
They commonly learn the crafts from their elders or older sisters. There are the methods of the face
cut, double cut, and drawn cut, and portray a self-reflexive love and appreciation of nature's birds,
beasts, flora, and fauna. The skill travels from one's heart, as great expression is revealed with scissors. Like ivy on a tree, the art of papercutting, retains its vigor and vitality from ancient times until
today, bearing symbolic meaning with discreet mannerisms, including practical and esthetic intentions.

Embroidery of ancient times was known as zhenxiu. It involved using brightly colored thread to
stitch decorative designs on textile, evolving as a pioneer in the field of visual arts. Traditionally practiced by women, is was referred to in the past a nühong (female needlework). Excellent examples of
surviving Chinese handmade embroidery exemplifying exquisite balance have been excavated in
Hubei and Hunan Provinces. These artifacts date to the Warring States Period and the periods of the
two Han eras. Embroidery of the Tang and Song dynasties is characterized by the fine and even distribution of thread and vivid colors. Also prevalent at that time was embroidered calligraphy and precise decorative patterns. The works commissioned by the Ming and Qing royal palaces are quite u-
nique. Simultaneously, there was further development in the skills among the common artisans, giving rise to four distinct regional styles—Su, Yue, Xiang, Shu—all having their own specific style and
ever-lasting charm, with their techniques passed down from one generation to another.

Su embroidery has a long history, made popular during the Song era. During this time, in the
city of Suzhou in Jiangsu province emerged an embroidery and clothing district that produced great
amounts of artistic works. During the Ming dynasty, Su embroidery continued to develop its distinct
attributes, expanding its influence even more. The Qing dynasty allowed for a mature phase—embroidery for the royal courts was mainly from the hands of Su needle workers, as styles among the
masses also became abundantly colorful. Suzhou embroidery has widely been regarded as fine, distinct, and elegant. Beautiful designs, quiet colors, brilliant luster, agile stitching, and meticulous work
give birth to life-like images. The criteria can be summarized briefly as balance, luster, orderliness,
distribution, harmony, arrangement, thinness, and density in 8 words.

Numerous stitching methods were developed, but mainly employed were the straight stitch,
backstitch, crouching and laid work, the cross stitch, and the satin stitch. Su embroidered arts fall into two major categories. One type includes commonly used items such as quilts, pillow-cases, clothes,
theater costumes, floor rugs, and cushions. The second style strives for aesthetics, and includes works

such as wood framed designs, hanging scrolls, and standing screens. Embedded in the work are a wide range of subjects such as flowers, plants, animals, human personas, landscape, and calligraphy.

Su Embroidery

Yue embroidery, also called Guang embroidery contains complex and arranged compositions with dazzling rich colors, well distributed materials, numerous types of stitching, and continuous flowing lines. Yue embroidery encompasses many brilliant works. Greatly admired are the famous wall scrolls, as well as hanging and standing screens. Items of everyday use include decorate quilts, pillowcases, bed covers, shawls, scarves, valances, and embroidered garments. The works typically include images of birds and flowers and are full of ornamental design. Frequently depicted are the phoenix, peony flowers, cranes, apes, and deer. Chickens, geese, and things of these matters are also often seen blending together within the frame.

Xiang embroidery comes from areas around the Changsha prefecture of Hunan Province. Early works of Xiang embroidery gives prominence to the decoration of articles of daily use. Later it developed into subject matter that created brilliant works of art. Distinctive qualities of Xiang embroidery include the use of velvet thread (without wool) and delicate weaving patterns, which produce a genuine work of art. Frequently used was the popular blue tint of traditional Chinese paintings and deep multicolored thread, with an emphasis on contrast, intensely life-like imagery, and a bold unconstrained style.

Also called Chuan embroidery, Shu embroidery is the general term for embroidery products originating from the areas surrounding Chengdu in the Sichuan Province. Shu needlework is made of soft satin and brightly colored silk as raw materials. Designs on Shu embroidery include landscapes, personages, fish, birds, and flowers of all sorts. Various methods include the crotch stitch, yun stitch, slanted stitch, rotating stitch, chain stitch, tent stitch, and the plaited stitch—reaching over one hundred varieties. The works are found on such items as quilts, pillow-cases, clothing, and shoes. Shu embroidery is characterized by its distinctly vivid qualities, bright colors, use of three dimensions, and meticulous flat and even stitches that are densely appropriated.

Unit 3

The Eight Great Ancient Capitals of China

The capital cities that emerged in the early wake of nation building are numerous, it is estimated about two hundred have existed since ancient times. Among the capitals of various dynasties, Beijing, Xi'an, Luoyang, Kaifeng, Nanjing, Hangzhou, Anyang, and Zhengzhou are the most famous—known as the Eight Great Ancient Capitals. The capitals are noted for their capability of governing vast regions. The years occupied by the dynasty are a determining factor of its overall impact on the historical record.

Beijing, the capital of The People's Republic of China, is the center of the China's politics, economics, culture, transportation, and tourism. It is one of the world's greatest historical and cultural cities, as well an ancient capital. Beijing was a strategic city during the slave-owning society of the Yan and Ji periods. It was the provincial capital of the Liao Dynasty, and was also the seat of the government of the Jin, Yuan, Ming, and Qing. At ground level as well as subterranean, it is abundant in preserved cultural relics, and is known around the globe as a significant ancient city in the course of history. This ancient city has a time-honored tradition, representing a history of over 3000 years. Currently existing are: Tiananmen Square, the Monument to the People's Heroes, The Memorial Hall of Chairman Mao, The Forbidden City, North Sea Park, The Temple of Heaven, The Summer Palace, The Thirteen Tombs of the Ming, The Great Wall, as well as ruins of early humans, and numerous relics of revolutionary and cultural significance.

Xi'an, in ancient times called Chang'an, is located in the Guanzhong Plain, in the southern regions of the Weihe River. As the capital of many dynasties that boasts the longest history, former regimes that chose Xi'an their capital, include the Zhou, Qin, Han, the Western Jin Dynasty, pre-Zhao Dynasty, pre-Qin, Late Qin, the Western Wei Dynasty, Northern Zhou Dynasty, the Sui, and Tang Dynasty. As a world renowned ancient capital, it is plentiful in cultural relics located in various places. Among these, the following sites are the most famous: Fenggao of the Western Zhou, Epang Palace of the Qin Dynasty, Chang'an City of Han Dynasty, Palace of Tang, Giant Wild Goose Pagoda, Small Wild Goose Pagoda, in addition to the bell and drum towers of Ming Dynasty and The Stele Forest. The surrounding area also holds Emperor Qin Shihuang's Mausoleum, The Terracotta Warriors, the ancient walls of Xianyang, and the ruins of the Banpo

Hall of Supreme Harmony in Forbidden City

Neolithic Village. In 139 B.C., the well-renowned ambassador and traveler, Zhang Qian, led a detachment of troops on a diplomatic mission. For the first time, they traveled from Chang'an to the Western Regions, visiting Loulan, Guizi, and Yutian regions, establishing what history recognizes as the Silk Road. This road passes through Central Asia, reaching the lofty Pamir Plateau and connecting to Southwest Asia. For several centuries, the route has played an important role in promoting the cultural communication between China, India, Rome, and Persia. The great inventions of the Chinese such as silk, gunpowder, paper, and printing, were spread to the West via this route. Simultaneously, Buddhism, Nestorian Christianity, and Islam were introduced to China, as the Silk Road had always served as a bridge in the form of amiable communication between China and the outside world.

Luoyang, formerly called Yi Luo, used to be part of Yuzhou in ancient times, received its name due to its location on the ardent slope of the ancient Luoshui River. The eastern portion is connected by the Zhengzhou prefecture, the Pingdingshan, and Nayang prefectures to its south; Sanmenxia in west, and the Jiaozuo prefecture to its north, and separated by the Yellow River. Luoyang was a famous capital city for nine dynasties, therefore full of historical sites such as the most famous in the southern region of the city—The Longmen Grottoes. In the eastern portion lies White Horse Temple, the first Buddhist temple in China. In addition, this area boasts ruins of the ancient cities of the Han, Wei, Western Zhou, Sui, and Tang periods, as well as the numerous ancient Tombs of Guanlin. Luoyang is a famous historical and cultural relic as one of the four largest capitals on ancient China, with tourism being important to its development. Thirteen dynasties and regimes chose Luoyang as their capitals in succession: the Xia, Shang, Western Zhou and Eastern Zhou Periods, Eastern Han, Cao Wei Dynasty, Western Jin Dynasty, Northern Wei, Sui, Tang, Late Liang, Late Tang, as well as the Late Jin periods. It is remarkable for its one thousand year history as a capital city, second only to Xi'an.

Kaifeng, as an ancient capital called Bianliang, is located in the central region of China. Settled on the banks of the Yellow River, it occupies an extrodinary role in Chinese history, and is considered the cradle of Chinese civilization. To date, the city has an established tradition of over 2,700 years. Kaifeng served for a period as the Capital of Seven Dynasties, including the Wei State of the Warring States Period, the Late Liang Period of the Five Dynasties, Later Jin Dynasty, Later Han Period, Later Zhou, Northern Song, and Jin dynasties. A great number of cultural relics and historic sites occupy the area, including the Iron Pagoda, Fan Tower, Dragon Pavilion, The Terrace of King Yu, Daxiangguo Temple, and the Northern Song's Bianliang City Ruins. Kaifeng city enjoys a superior geographic location, temperate climate, bountiful resources, and convenient transportation. It has experienced remarkable development in education, advancement in technology, and a prospering economy, thus becoming a major city of tourism and opening its walls to the outside.

As one of the eight celebrated capitals, Nanjing has been described as where tigers crouch and dragons coil—in reference to its strategic location. Known as the Jingling ancient imperial state, Nanjing has been a regal state since former times, leaving behind a brilliant cultural heritage. From ancient times until today, it has been occupied in succession by the Wu dynasty, Eastern Jin, Song, Qi,

Liang, Chen, Northern Tang, Ming, and the Taiping Heavenly Kingdom.
It was also the seat of the Republic of China. Encompassing over 455 years of history,
it is commonly referred to as the Capital of the Ten Dynasties. Within its borders contain a variety of
historical and cultural heritage such as Yuecheng, the Ruins of Jilin, Tomb Carvings of the Six Dynasties, The Two Imperial Mausoleums of Southern Tang Dynasty, The Ming Dynasty City Wall Ruins,
The Mansion of the Prince of the Taiping Heavenly Kingdom, Dr. Sun Yat-sen's Office, as well as his
memorial at Zhong Shan Mausoleum. The scenery of the city is exquisite, with undulating hills in the
southeast, the flowing rivers in the northwest, and the lush trees within the city walls, totaling over
48 scenic wonders. The culture of the area also is fascinating. To
imagine of ancient times, and the sight of the numerous fluttering flags in the Qinhuai district of the city convinces one of the
gracefulness and beauty of the inhabitants of Nanjing. This reveals a sense of fascination of the regal state of Jiling.

Dr.Sun Yat-sen's Office

Hangzhou is also one of China's ancient capitals. The Qin
Dynasty invested in establishing Qiantang county, which became
the city of Hangzhou in the Sui Dynasty. It was the capital city of
the Wu and Yue States during the period of the Five Dynasties,
therefore also becoming the temporary capital of the Southern
Song Dynasty. Hangzhou is a world-renowned city of tourism
with numerous ancient cultural relics, such as the West Lake Lingyin Temple, the Temple of Yuefei,
the Six Harmonies Pagoda, among many others. The West Lake is undoubtedly the most renowned
feature of Hangzhou. Often quoted is, "In heaven there is paradise, on earth there is Suzhou and
Hangzhou," expressing sincere praise for such a brilliant city throughout the ages. Su Dongpo, a talented writer of the Song Dynasty writes, "Among the thirty-six western lakes under the heavens,
Hangzhou contains the greatest one." West Lake is surrounded by cloud-capped hills on three sides,
creating a landscape of beautiful mountains and rivers bordering the city walls on one side. It is said
its natural beauty can match that of a beautiful woman with or without makeup, as it connects the
natural beauty of the landscape and all living things.

Hangzhou's scenic beauty blends naturally with the cultural traditions. In this scenic area are:
ancient gardens, pavilions, pagodas, springs and gullies, grottoes, inscriptions carved on a stele cliff
faces, bead curtains, jade belts, willow trees and bridges, the West Lake Lingyin Temple, the Six Harmonies Pagoda, Feilai Peak, the Temple of Yuefei, the Xiling Pass, Dragon Well, and Tiger-running
Spring, as the most frequently visited attractions. These marvelous scenes of myriad posture, lush
mountains, and clear waters, have attracted generations of scholars, as once quoted, "Among all the
sights to remember in Jiangnan, Hangzhou is the most memorable!"

Anyang is native to the famous oracle bone inscriptions and the birthplace of *The Book of
Changes*. Anyang's history as a capital city dates from Shang Dynasty when King Pan'gen moved the
seat of the government to Anyang in 1300 B.C. (today's suburbs of Anyang). It had served as the capital city of Shang Dynasty for 254 years, supporting eight dynasties and twelve emperors. Excavation

of this area has uncovered the earliest evidence of writing in China—the oracle bone script—in addition to the world's largest bronze tripod vessel—Simuwu. It is closely related to many tales of ancient folklore, such as Dayu Controls the Water, King Wen Consults the Changes, Fuhao's Request, Su Qin Pays his Respects, Xi Menbao Governs the Ye District, and The Mother-in-law Gives a Tattoo. Anyang's numerous cultural relics are currently under efforts of preservation. Within its borders there are eight major sites under state-level protection, with thirty-two cultural relic sites under provincial-level protection. A long history and resplendent culture has left invaluable historical and cultural heritage in Anyang.

Zhengzhou used to be one of the capitals in the Xia and Shang Dynasties, as well as the capital of the Guan, Zheng, and Han vassal states. Research of this area has revealed the 8,000 year old Peiligang culture, the Dahe village dating over 5,000 years, numerous relics of Prince Qin, as well as the Dragon Mountain historical site. A long history has left a rich cultural heritage in Zhengzhou. The entire city possesses over 1,400 cultural places of interest; among these 26 are national heritage conservation sites. The Songshan Scenic Area is one of 44 key scenic areas and a national model of scenic interest and tourism. Shaolin Temple, honored as the grandest temple under the heavens, is located at the base of the Songshan Mountain. The world-renowned Shaolin kung fu originated at this temple. There are also many distinct structures here, such as China's earliest astronomical construction—Zhougong's Observation Deck and The Star Observation Terrace of the Yuan Dynasty. Also included are one of China's four ancient academies—The Songyang Academy of the Song Dynasty, and the Zhongyue Temple, China's largest existing Taoist structures. Zhengzhou and its surrounding areas are also scattered with sites of ancient cities, civilizations, tombs, ancient architecture, old mountain passes, and ruins of battlefields. It is the birthplace of many great historical figures, such as Lie Zi, Zi Chan, Du Fu, Bai Juyi, and Gao Gong. Located in the hinterland of the central plains, Zhengzhou is an important city and a major transportation hub along the newly established Eurasian Continental Bridge.

Palace Architecture

From the construction of the royal palace of the Qin Dynasty, architecture has become an important part of Chinese society. The palace is where the monarch and regal family resided. To exemplify the emperor's prestige and rule over all things under the heavens, the design of ancient palace architecture imposed such dignity in its awe inspiring beauty. Generally designed as two sections—front and back—the front portion was the place for emperor to deal with the politics of the dynasty, and the back parts were the living quarters for his concubines and wives. In the middle lays the main palace, built on a north and south central axis, symmetrical with two sides of the building. Courtyards existed one after another, and the royal halls of the palace were endless, revealing vast amounts of the precise stately architecture.

The middle of the palace was covered by a large roof of gold and jade in glorious splendor (idiom), lined with pillars of vermillion wood, grand entrances, windows, and broad white marble floors.

The great roofs of the palaces are not only very beautiful but also function to safeguard the building. Layer upon layer of eaves and roof horns are intelligently curved as to divert the rainwater from the palace, thus protecting the wooden structures. The birds and beasts decorated on the roof not only are shrouded in mystery, but they also serve as pivoted fastening point and also prevented corrosion from precipitation. The roof of the palace is commonly decked with gold tinted glazed tiles. The color resembles imperial power, thus was reserved exclusively for the royal family.

Using large amounts of timber to build the palace is a fundamental characteristic of Chinese architecture. The roof beams, pillars, doors, and windows were made by wood and painted a rich vermillion color, symbolizing happiness and wealth. In some places, paintings portrayed dragons, phoenixes, flowers, plants, and seas of clouds. The bright colors not only incarnate the palace splendor, but also have the function of waterrproofing and resistance to termites. The Hall of Supreme Harmony in Beijing is the largest wooden palace in China.

Pure thick white marble is the basis of the flooring and foundation of the imperial palace. The Palace Museum in The Hall of Supreme Harmony is constructed of three floors of white marble, the stele and the steps carved with exquisite dragons and various kinds of decorative designs. The main routes of the emperor were carved of immense stones as waves of the sea, flowing clouds, and raging dragons, forming an extremely spectacular sight.

For thousands of years, the emperors did not hesitate to use the kingdom's labor, material, and financial resources to construct their expansive royal palaces. However, the pity is that most of this splendid architecture was destroyed by fire in the wars. Also, many palaces were set fire in conjunction with their emperor's passing. The Forbidden City in Beijing is today's most preserved and intact royal structures.

The Beijing Imperial Palace also called The Forbidden City, originating during the Ming and Qing dynasties and acting as the residence of 24 emperors. There are numerous grandiose halls. It is one of the largest and the most intact ancient constructions and it is ranked number one of the world's Five Great Palaces (Beijing's Imperial Palace, France's Versailles Palace, Buckingham Palace in London, the United States' White House, and the Kremlin in Russia). The palace incorporates Chinese traditional classic styles and Eastern patterns, existing as an indispensible site of heritage in China. Furthermore, it was ranked as a national historic cultural relic in 1961.

The Temple of Heaven occupies an area of 2.72 millon square kilometers, larger than that of The Forbidden City. Double walls form inside and outside altars, surrounding the area. The main parts are The Hall of Prayer for Good Harvests, The Imperial Vault of Heaven, and The Earthly Mount. The altar's wall is square in the southern portion and round in the northern part. This symbolizes the roundness of the heavens and the squared nature of the earth.

The Temple of Heaven

The Earthly Mount altar is in the south, The Hall of Prayer for Good Harvests altar in the north. Both of them rest on a north/south axis line, but separated by a wall. In the area of the Earthly Mount Altar, there are the Earthly Mount and the Imperial Vault of Heaven. At the Altar of Prayer for Grain, there is the Hall of Prayer for Good Harvests, The Hall of Imperial Zenith, and the Gate to the Hall of Annual Prayer. The Temple of Heaven's rational layout and beautiful meticulous construction has become famous in China and abroad. It was the palace of the Ming and Qing dynasties emperors to offer sacrifices to heaven and pray for the grain production in the region. It is the largest group of ancient sacrificial structures in modern China and also a treasured heritage of world architecture.

The Summer Palace

Besides the Imperial Palace and the Temple of Heaven, the Summer Palace and the Old Summer Palace are very famous royal court architecture styles of Chinese history. The Summer Palace is the most well-known landscape garden in China, displaying green mountains and spark-ling rivers. Also present are lofty pavilions and wandering corridors, all of them resplendent and magnificent. It enjoys a high reputation among Chinese and foreign countries in the history of landscape. Here lays the Long Corridor, the most extensive corridor in the whole country, connecting the distant mountains and close waters, possessing an extremely high artistic value.

Temple Architecture

China is a country with many religions. There is the native-born Taoism, as well as foreign beliefs such as Buddhism, Islam, and Christianity. These various religions have their own distinct architecture. The Taoists constructed what are called palaces or monasteries. The Buddhism religion in housed temples, pagodas, and grottos. The Islam has the mosque, and Christianity has the church, the religions determining their particular styles. Yet after fusing with the foreign religious architecture styles, the religious structures built have retained much Chinese influence. The following is a primary introduction of Buddhist temple architecture.

Buddhist temples are generally constructed in the mountains, far from the racket of the city. Most scenic area in China adorned with a monastery, the most famous are the Four Sacred Mountains of Buddhism. Namely, Mt. Wutai, Emei Mountain, Mt. Jiuhua, and Mt. Potala; each exhibiting celebrated temples.

Buddhism arrived from India, but Chinese Buddhist structures are quite different than their Indian counterparts. India's temples base the minaret as the center. China adopted this building practice, placing the palace hall in the middle. The overall arrangement of the temple, the structure of the hall, and the construction of the roof, all imitated the palace of the emperor, displaying distinct attributes of Chinese Buddhist architecture.

Chinese temples are commonly built on a south and north central axis, with symmetrical construction. Generally, the shrine built on this axis includes the monastery gate, the Emperor's Heavenly Palace, the Hall of Great Strength, the Preaching Hall, and the Hall of Buddhist Scriptures. Also included on either side of the main hall are drum towers, adjoining palace halls, and living quarters for the monks. The entire architecture of the temple is splendid and grandeur, imposing a magnificent stately feeling. The Luoyang White Horse Temple and Heng Mountain's Suspended Temple are typical representatives of this type of construction.

The White Horse Temple is situated nine kilometers east of the city of Luoyang. The north is backed by Qi Mountain, as the Lou River flanks the south. Ample evergreen and cypress trees reflect a solemn environment, and shadow lush vegetation and vermillion walls. Housed in the rectangular courtyard are the Hall of the Heavenly Emperor, Hall of the Great Heroes, Hall of One Thousand Buddhas, Guanyin Pavilion, and the Pilu Pavilion. Among these, the main structure is the Hall of the Great Heroes. As well as tourists visiting the temple, many Buddhists make the journey from within the country as well as from abroad to pay respects.

As the first official Buddhist temple in China, White Horse Temple was commissioned by the Han Emperor Liu zhuang, in accordance with the demand of Buddhism and admiration of traditional architecture. After the establishment of the temple, Buddhist influence developed greatly, deeply influencing the thoughts and lives of people. Later, Buddhism spread from China to foreign countries such as Vietnam, Korea, and Japan, influenced by factors from China and other countries. Therefore, White Horse Temple is referred to as Buddhism's Ancestral Courtyard.

Within the borders of Shanxi province lays the Suspended Temple on the lofty northern sacred mount, Mt. Heng. Seemingly hanging among the clouds, this temple represents the great wisdom and techniques of ancient artisans. The Suspended Temple leans against a precarious cliff, over-looking a deep ravine. The temple has a distinct design with building methods rarely seen. The Suspended Temple was built in the halfway up the mountain on the west side of the Golden Dragon Valley, 35 kilometers south of Huanyuan County. Presently, it is the only wooden temple in China situated on an overhanging cliff. It

The Suspended Temple at Mount Heng

was first constructed during the Northern Wei period, and consecutively restored during the Tang, Jin, Ming, and Qing dynasties. The entire temple faces Mt. Heng, as a screen of jade-green vegetation backs the rear side. The endless stone stairs lead to the spectacle of Mt. Heng.

Wutai Mountain in Shanxi province is one of the most famous holy lands of Buddhism in China. There are many Buddhist structures on Wutai Mountain. Currently, 58 ancient buildings have been preserved.　Among them are the most famous South Meditation Temple and the Light of the Buddha Temple. The area of the South Meditation Temple is not large,　from north to south it measures 60 meters,　and the east-west length is 51.3 meters,　and was constructed during the Tang Dynasty within three years (beginning in 782 A.D.). Due to the four distinct wonders of the temple are statues, murals, calligraphy, and architecture, which have been called a gem of the world.　The Light of the Buddha Temple has been continuously renovated throughout various dynastic periods. Situated at the waist of the mountain, it contains three levels of courtyards, each area enclosing a palace hall, main chamber, residences, and structures of all sorts. The Light of the Buddha Temple has an earthly configuration, the pillars, arches, gateways, and walls leave nothing but a flowery green tint, and as prescribed are painted vermillion.

Chinese temple architecture differs from region to region, as each nationality possesses a distinct style.　For example,　the Lamasim temples contain the Great Buddha Palace,　and a Hall of Buddhist Scriptures, built in relation to each particular mountain. The Tibetan temples were built of earth, timber, and stone, with timber being the main material. The Hall of Buddhist Scriptures has three floors. The thick walls are built of brick and stone mortar, with extremely small windows, portraying a steadfast tone. The Potala Palace in Lhasa, Tibet is one of the most prominent temples of China. It has the typical architecture style of the Tang Dynasty and absorbs the artistic building methods of Nepal and India, and has become a major the tourist attraction of Chinese as well as foreigners.

The Great Buddha Palace in Tibet

Unit 4

Currency

China ranks among the first countries in the world to use money, as currency has been used in China for at least 4,000 years.

Before the advent of currency, people mainly used the barter system, but this proved to be difficult, thus a form of monetary exchange emerged on the market. China's earliest currency was introduced during the Shang Dynasty (17th century to 11th century B.C.), at first existing mainly as cowry shells. In the later period of the Shang Dynasty, the bronze shell-shaped coins heralded the beginning of the mintage of Chinese coins. Although used as currency for the Shang, they were not widely circulated. As the Spring and Autumn Period arrived (770-476 B.C.), minted bronze coins become common currency. Throughout the Spring Autumn & the Warring States periods (770-221 B.C.), every state issued a different type of coin. Among them, the state of Chu issued the ying yuan, China's earliest form of gold currency. This evidence suggests China to be among the earliest nations to adopt gold as a form of exchange.

In 221 B.C., Emperor Qin Shi Huang unified China and standardized the currency, stipulating gold to be the unit of highest value, and the lesser valued bronze coins to be used for daily circulation. Furthermore, bronze coin manufacturing was regulated to produce circular coins with a hole in the middle, henceforth giving China's currency a fundamental shape. This style continued over 2,000 years, until the final days of the Qing Dynasty.

In the first year of the reign of the Han Dynasty (338 A.D.), minted coins first began to bear the name of the emperor's reign. This type of currency is called Han Xing, as it clearly indicated the first year of the reign of Emperor Li Shou, being the earliest of such coin.

The Tang Dynasty (618 –907 A.D.) is ancient Chinese society at its peak of perfection. Continued development of politics, economy, and culture stimulated significant changes to currency. The Tang Dynasty currency separated from the process of naming the coin by weight, made of precious metals, the value was not calculated by mass, and was renamed the Tong Bao. Among these coins was the Kai Yuan Tong Bao, and it persisted to be the main coin in circulation for over three hundred years during the Tang period. Also during the Tang era, emerged a type of paper money called Fei currency. Merchants gained massive coins from trade, but it was inconvenient and not secure for them to the money back to their homes, therefore a different mechanism of exchange was developed. This institution, along with wealthy individuals, each kept half a receipt to indicate a withdrawal or deposit. Merchants could then return home with financial records. Fei currency was quite similar to the exchange of personal checks in modern times.

Coins minted during Song Dynasty surpassed those made in former dynasties in both quantity and quality. The dominant form of coinage of Northern Song period was copper. During the Southern Song Dynasty, iron was prevalent as currency. At the same time, silver also played an important role in monetary circulation. One of the most significant events was the birth of jiaozi, the earli-

Kai Yan Tong Bao Coin

est paper note in the world. Paper currency became increasingly useful and it was also known by a variety of names such as kuaizi or guanzi. The paper bills first emerged in Sichuan during the Northern Dynasty, and was named using the local dialect. Jiaozi was first issued among few merchants, but eventually replaced the circulation of copper and iron coins. People welcomed paper notes because it was easy and safe to carry. Afterwards, the government of the Northern Song established offices to handle the issuance of jiaozi. During the Southern Song Dynasty, state-issued kuaizi and guanzi, similar to jiaozi were put into circulation and became the dominant forms of currency at that time.

The pinnacle of ancient Chinese paper money came during the Yuan Dynasty, but silver remained a standard form of exchange. Silver ingot, collectively called yuan bao originated from the Yuan Dynasty. In the early period of the Yuan government, at one time the use of copper coins was prohibited. Although later in that period, a few types of copper coins were minted, but still far less than in previous times. The paper note became the dominant form of currency, while silver money remained and accounted for a large proportion of the wealth.

The Ming Dynasty vigorously issued paper currency named chao. In the early period of its history, only chao was used as exchange, copper coins were not in circulation. Later it became a mixture of the copper coins and chao, and eventually led to the printing of only one kind of paper bank note, the Great Ming Bao Chao. Silver issued by the Ming Dynasty became legal tender and was used for large business transactions, while the paper chao notes were utilized for smaller exchanges. All currency in circulation at that time was collectively called tong bao.

The Qing dynasty maintained the use of small volumes of silver for frequent business transactions. At the onset of the Qing Dynasty, the over two thousand year tradition of minting coins, developed a process of casting to make the coins. During the later period, they emulated the machine processes of coinage of foreign countries.

Furthermore, imported silver coins were made popular during the Qing Dynasty and the Republic of China. They was imported from Spain during Wanli Period of the Ming Dynasty (1573–1620 A.D.), but were not extensively circulated until the Qing era. In 1793, during the fifty-eighth year of the reign of Qing Emperor Qianlong, throughout the Tibetan region a type of silver coinage called Qianlong Baozang was issued. During the reign of Dao Guang (1821–1850 A.D.), the Taiwan and Fuzhou regions mimicked coins of foreign origin, producing the Yin Bing. The Guangdong area minted silver coins called Guangxu Yuanbao in the fifteenth year of the reign of Guangxu (1889 A.D.).

Other regional mints were consequently established, producing similar coins. In the second year of the reign of Xuan Tong (1910 A.D.), the Qing government issued regulations on the monetary system, establishing silver as the standard coin. But the Xinhai Revolution erupted and the system was not officially adopted.

In 1912, the first year of the Republic of China, souvenir coins were issued in honor of the founding father Dr. Sun Yat-sen. In 1914, silver coins were minted with the head of former Emperor Yuan Shikai on the one side. Among ordinary people it was referred to as Yuan Datou. In 1935, the Nationalist Government enacted currency reforms prohibiting the circulation of silver coinage.

After the People's Republic of China was established, the People's Bank of China collected and exchanged the remaining silver at a fixed rate, as the circulation of silver was deemed to be illegal.

Chinese currency takes pride in its time-honored history, particularly of the paper money that emerged during the Song Dynasty, ushering in a new era of currency production in the whole world. The Chinese paper jiaozi outdates the earliest Western paper currency by five hundred years, referring to the Swiss Bank notes issued in 1661.

Traditional Chinese Medicine and Chinese Herbs

Traditional Chinese medicine is referred to as Zhong Yi, and has thousands of years of history. During the Warring States Period (221 B.C.), a systematic work of medical theory appeared entitled The Yellow Emperor's Internal Classic. Chinese medicine is the only medical system that has survived without interruption, as today it still plays a vital role in treating diseases.

The medical theory of Chinese medicine is focused on human body, but it also views the human body as part of nature, instead of studying anatomy in isolation. Therefore, in its pathology, Chinese medicine attaches great importance to the relationship of diseases and human state of mind, living conditions, and environmental factors, especially with regard to changes in weather. In clinical treatment, Chinese medicine opposes the simple thought of treating the head for a headache and treating the foot for foot pain, emphasizing the complete understanding of the root causes of disease and treating them accordingly. Simultaneously, Chinese medicine regards human body itself as an organic whole. It does not study symptoms of diseases independently on the surface. Instead, it closely inspects and makes correlations to internal organs, meridians (energy channels), the blood, and bodily fluids. In the field of pharmacology, it places emphasis on the compatibility of medicines in the prescription. This is exemplified by prescribing different medicines according to the traits of each patient. Close attention is also paid to the properties of the medicines and the proper ratios in formula mixtures. This theory and doctrine uses modern scientific observation and methods that creates a profound understanding.

During the continual development of Chinese medicine, a series of unique diagnosis and treatments have been gradually summarized. These are commonly referred to as observation, listening, questioning the patient, and feeling the pulse. The diagnosis by observation refers to examining patient's body, complexion of the skin, and the shape and coating of the tongue. In this way, the location and nature of the disease can be diagnosed in accordance with the changes of the above-mentioned considerations. This method is also referred to as inspection diagnosis. Listening implies that the doctor should identify the sounds and smells of the patient, in addition to the condition and changes of the voice as a means of diagnosis. Thus it is also referred to as listening and smelling. Questioning is simply interviewing the patient and family regarding the outbreak and the development of the disease, as well as understanding current symptoms and conditions which are relevant to the diseases. Feeling the pulse, also called touching, refers to observing the patient's pulse, probing the skin, hands, abdomen, limbs, and other parts of the body in order to diagnose disease. Among these four observations feeling the pulse and probing are unique ways of diagnosing diseases in the practice of Chinese medicine. The observance of the pulse reveals that doctors in ancient China had mastered pulse conditions and their relations to various parts of the human body, such as the relationship of heart, blood and blood vessels, the rate of circulation of the blood, breathing, and pulse frequency. All of these aspects require great knowledge of anatomical physiology. The method of diagnosing the pulse and probing the body was introduced overseas long ago. Besides neighboring countries such as Japan and Korea, it has disseminated to Arab regions in the 10th century, reaching Europe during the 17th century.

In attempt to remedy a disease, acupuncture therapy is a primary treatment in traditional Chinese medicine. Acupuncture is an in-depth methodological system of Chinese medicine. Its advantages lie in curing disease without taking medicine, as the patient is pierced with needles corresponding certain parts of the body. Heat may also be used to stimulate particular regions, thus combating the illness. These methods are collectively known as acupuncture and moxibustion. According to ancient medicine and meridian theory, each part of human body is covered with main and collat-

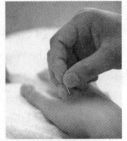
Acupuncture Therapy

eral channels of blood vessels and energy channels, which regulate the flow of qi (气) and blood (血). These relate to functions of the organs and blood, and connect the upper and lower parts of the body, in addition to and its internal and external functions. Acupuncture points serve to monitor meridian networks. Stimulating acupuncture points plays a significant role in the regulation meridian systems. Acupuncture therapy has a clear and obvious effect in treating illness. Many foreign scholars regard China as the motherland of acupuncture therapy.

With regard to pharmacology, Chinese pharmacists through the ages have studied and recorded more than 3,000 plants, animals, and properties of minerals, as well as the efficacy and usages of them. With these materials as ingredients, different types of curative decoctions, pills, powders, ointments, and pellets are made. Chinese traditional therapeutic formulas are referred to as Zhongyao.

Throughout the continual evolution of Chinese medicine, many famous medical works have been preserved. One such book is *Shennong's Herbal Classic*, completed in Eastern Han Dynasty. It's the first specialized work in the world on the study of medicine, outdating European books regarding this subject by at least 16 centuries. *The Treatments for Typhoid and Other Complicated Diseases*, written by Zhang Zhongjing during Eastern Han Dynasty, is one of the earliest specialized classics on pharmacology in the world, emerging hundreds of years earlier than *The Cannon of Medicine* by the Persian medical scientist, Avicenna. A groundbreaking text emerged during the Song dynasty entitled *Record of Washed Grievances*, compiled by Song Ci. It is the world's first specialized compilation of forensic science. During the Ming dynasty, Li Shizheng published a work entitled *Compendium of Materia Medica*, and is celebrated as Oriental medicine's dictionary. It has consequently been successively translated and published into several foreign languages. These famous indispensible works have enabled the science of Chinese medicine to be handed down from generation to generation.

Throughout the history of Chinese medicine, there appeared many famous doctors such as Hua Tuo, Bian Que, and Zhang Zhongjing. Among them, Hua Tuo of the Eastern Han dynasty was the first to administer a general anesthesia. It was not until 1805 did Japanese surgeon Hanaoka Seishu use datura flowers as an anesthetic, which is acclaimed as a pioneering achievement in the history of anesthesia. However, this great undertaking occurred much later than the practices of Hua Tuo.

As a unique medical system in China, Chinese traditional medicine has made significant contributions to medical science. Some even call it the fifth great invention, referring to the four great inventions of China.

Chinese Chess

Xiangqi, referred to as Chinese Chess, is a unique invention of the Chinese for entertainment. Its long history originates from the Warring States Period. After a long period of development, the modern form of Chinese Chess appeared during the Northern Song Dynasty, consisting of thirty-two pieces and a chessboard containing a river boundary. The pastime received much attention in the following Southern Song Dynasty.

Xiangqi is played by two opponents, with the object of killing or capturing the enemy's general (checkmate). Generally, the player with the red pieces moves first. Both opponents move in response to the other on separate lines, lasting until victory, defeat, or a draw. Each player in turn moves one piece from the point it occupies to another intersection point of lines. A piece can be moved onto a point occupied by an opponent's piece, in which case the enemy piece is captured and removed from the board. A move and a response made respectively are called a round. Chinese Chess an ideal game to enrich people's cultural life, cultivate personality and perseverance, boost intelligence, and improve one's capacity of dialectical analysis.

There are a total of 32 pieces of red and black, with one person accounting for 16 red pieces and the opponent controlling 16 black pieces. The two opponents have similar pieces, divided into seven categories on each side, The red side has one king and two of each of the following pieces: guards, ministers, chariots, knights, and cannons, in addition to five soldiers (pawns). The black opponent has a general, two pieces each of advisors, elephants, knights, chariots, and cannons, as well as five soldiers. On both sides, the general and the king, guards and advisors, ministers and elephants, and foot soldiers have the same functions. The chess pieces are played on a distinct Chinese chessboard. The board is a rectangular plane, consisting of nine parallel lines wide by ten lines long, with a total of ninety intersecting points on which the pieces are placed, forming a square grid. The middle is divided by a void between the fifth and sixth horizontal lines, called a river boundary. An area with two diagonal lines connecting opposite corners and intersecting at a center point, forms a matrix is called the nine points of the palace. The entire board is divided by the river boundary that establishes the two opposing sides. In order to record competitions and study strategy, people have implemented a system that uses a notation to describe absolute positional references. The positions of the board are numbered one to ten from closest to farthest away, followed by a digit from one to nine for the files from right to left. Both values are relative to movement of each player. The black and red pieces are placed on the appropriate intersections before commencing a game. Each movement towards the opponent is recorded as an advance, a withdrawal is written as retreat. If the forces are equal, it is called balanced.

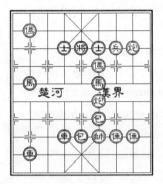

Chinese Chess

Soon after People's Republic of China was founded in 1956, Chinese Chess was listed as a national sport. Statewide chess competitions are presently divided into the categories of men's singles, men's team, women's singles, and women's team competitions. The best players are awarded specific titles by the Chinese National Sport Committee, such as Chess Grandmaster and Distinguished Grand-master.

In November 1978, the Asian Chinese Chess Federation was launched under the concerted efforts of overseas gentry and inhabitants of various regions of Southeast Asia. Its membership has expanded to include the Philippines, Malaysia, Thailand, Singapore, Indonesia, China, Brunei, Hong Kong and Macao of China. Hong Kong business tycoon Huo Yingdong was once appointed as president. The Preparatory Committee of Chinese Chess Federation was set up in Beijing in 1988, encouraging the development of traditional Chinese chess. The first World Chinese Chess Championship was held in Singapore in 1990.

In western countries, what is referred to as international chess is similar to Chinese chess. International chess is a strategic board game between two respective players using black and white game pieces. White always moves first, as the object of the game is to similarly checkmate the opponent's king. The game is played on a checkered board with sixty-four squares, arranged in an eight by eight array of spaces. The colors of the sixty-four squares alternate and are referred to as white squares and black squares. Each color having thirty-two squares, the game is set up with sixteen pieces places on the corresponding place and color. These consist of one king, one queen, two rooks, two bishops, two knights, and eight pawns. When a king is under immediate attack by one or more of the opponent's pieces, it is said to be in check. If opponent has no counter moves, the king is captured (checkmate). Besides ending in checkmate, a player may resign if the situation looks hopeless, thus ending the game. If it is a timed game, a player may run out of time and forfeit, even with a much superior position in the game. Games also may end in a draw, and may occur in several situations including draw by agreement, stalemate, a three-fold repetition of a position, the fifty-move rule, or a draw by impossibility of checkmate (usually because of insufficient pieces).

In recent years, there has been vigorous development of Chinese chess. Chess leagues and clubs are distributed widely throughout the world and Chinese Chess Associations have been established in many countries such as the United States and France. Chinese chess, along with international chess, enjoy immense popularity as pastimes among many countries in Europe and the Americas.

Martial Arts

Martial Arts or Wushu, also known as kung fu, consists of a number of fighting styles that were developed over the centuries in China. Martial arts are one of the chief representatives of traditional Chinese culture. The movements in martial arts include the kick, punch, throw, hold, and thrust. Among these, the thrust is greatly emphasized. By mastering these techniques, one learns self-defense with his or her bare hands, or by use of specialized weapons through restricted movements. Two main components of kung fu are hand-to-hand combat and a series of skills and techniques. These methods are arranged as a series of predetermined combined movements practiced in linear form. The combinations of attack and defense movements are greatly admired and are a spectacle to witness. Wushu can be practiced so-lo, paired, or as a group, and barehanded or armed with ancient Chinese weapons. Among the many styles are Changquan (Longfist), Nanquan (Southern Fist), Tai Chi Chuan, Xingyiquan (shadowboxing), and Baguazhang. The use of weaponry includes many categories such as the knife, sword, staff, spear, double broadsword, double rapier, nine-section whip, and three-section truncheon. There are three distinct types of sparring—hand-to-hand, the use of weapons, and a barehanded opponent versus a weaponed opponent. Group exercise involves an assembly of practitioners performing hand-to-hand sparring or weapons combat. The abundant forms of routine and movement not only display combative and defensive skills, but carry an aesthetic value. Wushu is a popular form of barehanded fighting technique.

After thousands of years evolution, some unique features gradually developed within Chinese martial arts. For one, it gives prominence to physical and mental harmony. Chinese kung fu practitioners follow the philosophical ideal that both the body and mind are an inseparable integral system. They believe wushu is by no means limited to the external movement, but also emphasizes the full display of the internal temperament, mental attitude, and potential of the human being. As well as exercising the body, the spirit is also trained. The three fundamentals of wushu are the practice of thought, the flow of qi, and the body's capacity of strength. Also, much attention attached to harmonious social relations. Traditional Chinese schools of martial arts often deal with the study of martial arts not just as a means of self-defense and mental training, but also as a system of ethics. Although different sects of martial arts have their own distinct characteristics and practices, the moral character and etiquette are held in great esteem by all schools of wushu masters. The values stress cultivating generosity and tolerance for the sake of a stable and orderly society. Every school has a set of precepts to preserve the dignity of the teacher, to propagate goodwill, and to avenge evil. The master will test the virtue of the potential pupils before he accepts them as his disciples. Within Chinese wushu, there exists a martial morality that is a criterion to evaluate wushu competitions and related events. Another characteristic of wushu is the importance of the harmony of humans and nature, and has been recognized by various martial arts masters. In their views, humans have an intrinsic relationship with the universe, and are able to draw inspiration from the laws of change in nature to create different styles of fighting. For example, martial artists have developed the Snake Fist style by imitating the movements of snakes.

Among the Chinese martial arts communities, the Shaolin Monastery holds a prominent status. Situated at Mount Shaoshi (belongs to Song Mountain), west of the city of Zhengzhou, Henan Province in Dengfeng district, the Shaolin Temple has a long history. It was constructed during the Northern Wei Dynasty in the 19th calendar year of the reign of Emperor Taihe. During the early period of the Tang Dynasty, the 30 monks of the Shaolin Temple fought on behalf of Li Shiming, the king of the state of Qin, as they defeated the selfappointed emperor Wang Shichong. After Li Shimin was enthroned as emperor, he awarded the Shaolin Temple with large grants of land and money to expand the temple complex. During the period, the Shaolin temple witnessed explosive growth and Shaolin kungfu was greatly improved upon and developed due to the substantial support from the imperial court. In China, people firmly believe that all kung fu under the heavens originates from the *Shaolin Temple*. In 1982, the film Shaolin Temple starring Jet Li attracted thousands of wushu fans from within China as well as abroad, resulting in scores of individuals visiting the Shaolin Temple and practicing Shaolin martial arts. Moreover, Shaolin kungfu has captivated the attention of more and more people in other nations. There are Shaolin Kung Fu Associations prevalent in over 40 countries worldwide. In countries such as the United States and Germany, *Shaolin Temples* have been established in accordance of traditional training and skills of the Shaolin monks, and is warmly received the people with deep respect and admiration.

Another traditional martial art popular in China is Tai Chi Chuan (Supreme Ultimate Fist). Originating in China, Tai Chi Chuan is a collection of motions that tempers force with mercy, and is conducive to health and self-defense, owing to its perfect balance of forcing and yielding. Tai Chi Chuan training exemplifies great efficacy to clear away obstructions in the body, synchronize the heart and blood, nourish the viscera, strengthen the muscles and bones, as well as

Shaolin Monks are Praticing Kung Fu

many other beneficial aspects.

Most modern styles of Tai Chi Chuan trace their development to at least one of the five traditional schools—Chen, Yang, Wu Hao, Wu, and Sun styles. Tai Chi Chuan is quite common in China. In public spaces, one can often see people practicing the martial art. In other parts of the world such as Europe, the Americas, Southeast Asia, and Japan, it has been greatly received and accepted as form of exercise and is enjoyed by many. Rough statistics indicate that in the United States alone more than 30 books on Tai Chi Chuan have been published. Furthermore, several countries from around the world have established Tai Chi Chuan Associations and groups.

Chinese martial arts have also greatly influenced motion picture films. The displays of kung fu by stars such as Bruce Lee, Jackie Chan and Jet Li, have been widely accepted and admired by Hollywood. Many foreign countries continue to appreciate Chinese kungfu on the silver screen.

Folk Musical Theater

Folk musical theater (quyi) is a general term to describe the performances of speaking and singing, it is the tradition of oral literature and song. Over time, these art forms have greatly evolved, developing into distinct styles. Oration and song are the major artistic devices of folk musical theater. According to survey, there are approximately 400 varieties of theater that are still performed by people all over the country. Among the various types folk musical theater that have been passed down, the widely popular and influential forms include comic dialogue, short sketch, storytelling, ballad singing, monologue storytelling, kuai ban and duet performances.

Chinese comic dialogues originated in Beijing and became popular in all parts of the country. It is generally believed that comic dialogues originated during the Qing dynasty. As an artistic form which amuses the audience by means of telling jokes or comic questions and answers, they are mainly performed in the Beijing dialect, but in different parts of China local dialects are also used. As to the forms of performance of Chinese comic dialogues, there are mainly three types: monologues, cross talk, and group banter. In the monologue form of comic dialogue, one actor performs and tells jokes. In cross-talk comic dialogue, there are two performers, and three or more actors perform in group banter style, also called qun huo. The artistic devices employed in cross talk mainly include speaking, imitating, teasing, and singing. Speaking refers to telling jokes, guessing lantern riddles, and performing tongue twisters. Imitating points to emulating the sounds of birds and animals, as well as the actions, speech, and facial expressions of peddlers, opera singers, and various other characters. Teasing involves the actors mutually joking with each other. Singing means the vocalizing of traditional peaceful songs. Over its long development, there appears a list of famous actors in the art of Chinese comic dialogue, including Hou Baolin, Ma Sanli, Ma Ji, and Jiang Kun. Chinese comic dialogues enjoy great popularity not only in China, but abroad as well, especially the form of imitation. At the end of 1989, Canadian Mark Rowswell (Chinese name Dashan) honored the famous performing artist Jiangkun as his teacher of the art of comic dialogue. Later, he continued to perform on many stages in various parts of China as well as on television, leading him to become a household name.

Short sketch refers to brief dialogues and performances. Using the foundation of distinct spoken languages, it is often improvised, and includes a complete understanding and precise representations of the characters and their particular language. As a type of impromptu performance, shorts require that actors embody everyday life experiences and express them using a common language. Comedic scenes are the most common forms of short sketches. One genre of Chinese comedy originated from the early 1980s. Based on the inheritance and development of the merits of drama, cross talk, dance duets, and short plays, Chinese comedy has broadened its horizons. There have been several famous actors who have performed humorous acts, most notably Zhao Benshan and Chen Peisi.

Storytelling, also called pingci, is the popular term used in the north, northeastern, and north-western parts of China. In southern China, the popular form of oration is called pinghua. It is an oral form of literature. Cveated by Chinese folk people. In the early days of storytelling, one person sat behind a table, accompanied by the props of a fan and a wooden gavel. The gavel was used to strike a wooden block, indicating the beginning of the performance or the intermission. It was also used to remind the audience to remain quiet or to get their attention, thus reinforcing the theatrical effect. Usually the performers wore traditional gowns as they recited and commented on ancient folklore. Development during the middle of 20th century led to an abandonment of the props of tables, folding fans, and gavels. Actors began to stand during the performance and routinely did not wear gowns. Monologue storytelling is mainly performed with the northern dialect as the basis, as the Beijing dialect of Mandarin serves as its standard tone. Since monologue storytelling is performed in an oral language, the third-person narrative is mainly used in the presentation of the story. Shan Tianfang is a prime example of a famous performer of monologues.

Ballad singing, also referred to as Suzhou pingtan, is the general name for Suzhou storytelling performed using lyrics of the Suzhou dialect. It's an ancient and graceful artistic form of describing and singing. In this form of storytelling, one actor performs on stage, describing historical romance and chivalrous heroes. Another lyrical aspect involves two actors singing with the accompaniment of the pipa (lute), or perhaps one person playing an instrument and vocalizing. The ballads often depict love stories of legendary novels and folk tales. As ballad singing is mainly performed in Suzhou dialect, it is a flexible artistic form of speaking and singing. The art is celebrated by many as the most beautiful vocals in China and is quite pleasant to the ears.

Monologue storytelling, developed in Beijing and Tianjin, involves oration mainly in the Beijing dialect with drum accompaniment. Before 1946, there were many different names for the performance art. After folk musical theater guilds were established in Beijing in 1946, Jingyun Dagu became the official unifying name. The accompaniment instruments involved are mainly the three-stringed sanxian and the four-stringed sihu. In certain situations, the pipa (lute) is also played. Performers create rhythms by beating drums and wooden percussion instruments. This form of theater emphasizes singing songs of short duration in the Beijing dialect.

Kuai ban, was originally a type of singing and performing from beggars among the streets. Lat-

er, it has gradually developed into a special form of musical theater
through the continual creation of the thespians. Common performances of kuai ban
consist of actors standing on stage while keeping rhythm with a bamboo clapper and singing rhyming
lyrics. Kuai ban places an emphasis on composing improvisational lines. The actor must be well
versed in impromptu and articulate thoughts without hesitation. These demands require performers
to be quite talented in forms of expression.

Duets, also called bengbeng, originated and has been made popular in Three Northeast
Provinces of China. People in these regions, especially rural farmers, are quite fond of such performances. It is a form of theater that involves speaking, singing, dynamic music, and lively dance. At
present, it has a history of about two hundred years. Duets are mainly presented in the following way:
a man and a woman are both clad in brightly colored clothing, holding folding fans and handkerchiefs
in their hands. They step, sing, and dance side by side, as a story is revealed. The singing is uninhibit-
ed and humorous, with the opera libretto easily understood in the language. There is a fine sense of
humor and breath of fresh air full of the vivid colors of life. Of the many famous duet song and dance
performers, Zhao Benshang is one of the most famous.

There are many forms of Chinese folk musical theater that greatly enrich the lives of the people.
Moreover, with its abundant cultural connotations, these forms of musical performances are also appealing to foreigners.

Traditional Folk Musical Instruments

In ancient times, Chinese people invented a great number of musical instruments of distinct nationality. With varying designs and traits, all of the musical instruments produce beautiful and
rich melodies. They and are pleasing to both the eye and mind, thus are greatly admired by people.
Chinese musical instruments are able to express subtle feelings as well as complicated changes of e-
motions. There are a great number of Chinese folk instruments. Those still existing and popular today
include the reed pipes, bamboo flutes, the zither, a long zither, and the two-stringed erhu.

The reed pipes, also called bamboo xiao, is a very ancient musical instrument. They are manufactured of bamboo to be directly blown into. Along with the bamboo flute, they share a long history
and belong to the same family of musical instruments. The timbre of the reed pipes has a gentle and
round tone with the illusion of seclusion. When played in the night, the warm and beautiful sound
moves people. In China, performers are commonly referred to as chuixiao or pinxiao. These names
reflect the belief that only individuals of high moral sentiment are able to play the lovely melodies
through the reed pipes. Therefore, ancient scholars greatly admired this musical art form. Much later,
reed pipes were introduced abroad where such music was also well received. At the International Ex-
position in London in 1896, and in Panama in 1913, the Chinese yuping reed pipes was respectively
awarded with gold and silver medals, for the first time establishing a Chinese musical instrument to
win world prize.

Bamboo flutes, also called dizi, are made from a single section of bamboo and are blown by holding it horizontal. Bamboo flutes have a fairly long history in China. Sima Qian's Record of the Grand Historian from the Han dynasty has mention of bamboo flutes. Bamboo flutes have distinct ethnic features and produce a bright warm sound that is enjoyed by many. Thus, they are celebrated by foreigners as amazing musical instruments with irreplaceable ethnic qualities. Bamboo flutes very common throughout China, in rural villages live many musicians that are able to play the bamboo flute.

Zither

The guzheng or zither is an extremely ancient Chinese stringed instrument. According to *The Record of the Grand Historian* by Sima Qian, the guzheng was fairly popular in the state of Qin during the Warring States Period. In 1979, in the city of Xianyan in Guixi County of Jiangxi province, an archeological discovery was made of a guzheng in a group of tombs, proving it's test of time. During the periods if the Tang and the Song dynasties, the guzheng typically had thirteen strings, later developing into variations of sixteen, eighteen, twenty-one, and twenty-five stringed instruments. Today the guzheng in general composed of twenty-one strings.The general technique of playing the guzheng is to use the thumb, index finger, and middle finger of the right hand to pluck the strings and play the melody. The left hand is manipulated to control the variation of tone and pitch of the strings. The range in sound of the guzheng is extremely wide, allowing for a beautifully colored tone, therefore it has been regarded as the king of musical instruments and the piano of the Orient.

The guqin, also called the heptachord or long zither, is one of the most ancient plucked string instruments of China. The guqin enjoyed great popularity during the period of Confucianism, and since then has continued to influence the Chinese upper class for the last 3,000 years. The name guqin, literally meaning ancient stringed instrument, was coined in the early 20th century. It is generally made to be a length of three chi and six and five tenths cun (about 120~125 centimeters), symbolizing the three hundred and sixty-five days in a year. The guqin originally only had five strings. Later, the number of strings increased to seven, therefore it was called the seven-stringed qin. The temperament of the tone of the guqing is peaceful and elegant. In order to achieve an ideal mood for artistic conception, performers are required to fuse together the outdoor surroundings of the environment and a peaceful state of mind. In ancient Chinese society, the guzheng, Chinese chess, classic literature, and painting were traditionally regarded as essential means to cultivate the personality of literati and scholars. Moreover, people of such stature have traditionally favored the guzheng as an instrument of great subtlety and refinement for thousands of years. Continuing today, sounds produced by the guzheng are a symbol of the soul and essence of Chinese music. One particular piece of guzheng music has been recorded and pressed on a gold plated record that is aboard the United States spacecraft Voyager. The music unceasingly echoes day and night through boundless space, yearning to make intimate acquaintances throughout the universe. On November 7, 2003, UNESCO

headquarters in Paris issued the second list of representative works of o-
ral and non-material human inheritance, the traditional Chinese guzheng was respectively mentioned on the list.

Beginning during the Tang Dynasty and continuing until today, the two-stringed erhu occupies a history of over one thousand years. It first emerged with the ancient nomads of northern China, and was known throughout the regions as the huqin. It is one of the most common bowed string instruments. The tradition of the huqin continued throughout China during the Ming and Qing dynasties, becoming a main instrument of accompaniment during theater performances. As the modern era arrived, it was renamed erhu. With elegant and mellow timbre, the erhu can be used to express secluded, exquisite, and almost lyrical emotional tones, much like the human voice. Throughout China, famous erhu music includes a well-known composition by Abing (Hua Yanjun) entitled *The Moon's Reflection on the Two Springs*. This work embodies deep emotion with a unique timbre and expressive force, as the strings sing to the hearts of millions. Not only has the composition fascinated Chinese people, but it has earned a great reputation in international music circles. The world-famous Japanese conductor Seiji Ozawa commented, "I should kneel down upon listening."

For their unique regional characteristics and ethnic flavor, Chinese musical instruments offer the world a unique aesthetic enjoyment of music, which is rich in Chinese cultural connotation.

Chinese Painting

The art of Chinese classical paintings in ancient times had no established name. They were generally called danqing, mainly referring to paintings on loosely woven silk and fine paper. The finished work was then mounted on scrolls that were hung or rolled up. As the modern era arrived, in efforts to differentiate between Western paintings and the traditional Chinese styles, the former style was referred to as Western oceanic paintings as the latter were called Chinese paintings or National paintings. The tools used in traditional Chinese painting are the paintbrush, ink, traditional water-based paint, and special paper or silk. On the basis of traditional artistic styles and techniques, the painters create outstanding visual works.

Chinese paintings can be categorized by the use of materials and the means of expression. Ink and wash painting embodies the subjects of people. So-called landscape paintings are of mountains and rivers, and bird and flower style paintings are appropriately of animals. With its deep rooted ideological implications, Chinese paintings reflect social ideologies and aesthetic tastes of Chinese people. They also represent the artists' understanding of nature, society, politics, philosophy, religion, moral, literature, and art.

Ink and wash painting, is a distinct form of traditional Chinese painting. It makes use of water-based ink (shuimo) to produce the painting. The style developed in China during the Tang Dynasty and continued during the period of the Five Dynasties, also enjoying great popularity among the Song and Yuan. Throughout the Ming and Qing dynasties and followed by the modern era, the style became even more refined. In the mastering of the brush, the artist has the capability of producing rich strokes with abundant layers of saturation and a wide arrangement of colors. Wang Wei of the Tang Dynasty believed these painting to be divine, and later generations were also of his opinion. Ink and wash paintings have long occupied an important position in the history of Chinese art.

Renwu hua are paintings that are fundamentally of human portrayal. These figure paintings, called in short renwu, are a major form of Chinese art, as they emerged earlier than landscape art and paintings of birds and flowers. They generally include Taoist and Buddhist art, paintings of official women, portraits, and paintings of social customs and historical events. The paintings make every effort to portray the distinct characteristics of the individual, with a vivid life-like appearance of both the body and the spirit. Often depicted in the washes of ink is the environment of a residence, the embodiment of the social atmosphere, or a gracefully moving physique. The object of ancient Chinese caricature paintings is to depict an image that is spiritually vivid. Gu Kaizhi was a master of this style during Eastern Jin Dynasty.

As another type of Chinese painting, landscape painting, is also called mountains and waters. Landscape paintings refer to paintings that primarily illustrate natural scenery such as mountains and rivers. They were gradually developed during the Wei and Jin Dynasties, as well as during the Northern and Southern dynasties. But figure paintings were still popular in those times, therefore this style predominately served as a background. Distinct styles emerged on a grand scale during the Sui and Tang dynasties, the period of the Five Dynasties, and the era of the Northern Song. Many famous painters existed during these times such the well-known father and son, Mi Fu and Mi Youren.

Painting of Mi Fu

The Yuan dynasty turned towards writing to convey meaning, letting correct ideology guide practical work, placing emphasis on the technique and beauty of the brush and ink, opening doors to innovation. During the Ming and Qing dynasties, and continuing to this day, the genre of landscape paintings has witnessed further development by the use of contemporary features.

Bird and flower paintings is a kind of Chinese painting named after its subject matter of plants and animals. The birds and flowers genre is focused on expressing the aesthetic relationship between human and nature in a romantic way. Through their depictions of plants and animals, the artists reflect their own thoughts and feelings on the spirit of the times and the state of society. Paintings of this sort resemble distinctive features of foreign paintings with similar themes. Famous painters in this style range from Zhu Da of the Qing Dynasty to the artist Wu Changshuo of modern times.

Chinese national paintings possess distinct characteristics particular to China, showing a great contrasts between Chinese paintings and Western paintings. Chinese paintings place an emphasis on romantic charm, whereas western paintings attach much importance to the representation of form. In comparison, differences between Chinese and Western paintings can be described as followed.

One, brushstrokes distinctive of Chinese paintings are used throughout, while such strokes are not common Western paintings. In Chinese paintings, painters use these brushstrokes to represent objects and motion, while Western painting is primarily concerned with representational and classical modes of production. As seen at a glance, the Western styles of painting pays close attention to material objects, while in the Chinese tradition, this is not necessarily the case.

Two, Chinese paintings do not emphasize perspective as much as the Western paintings. Typical of Western paintings are stereoscopic objects represented on the plane, as the style strives to resemble real objects. Therefore, to achieve this, perspective must be greatly emphasized. Chinese paintings are typically not in this vain and are not constrained by perspective. Painters paint as far as their imagination will take them.

Three, classical Chinese paintings do not fully express anatomy, while Western paintings of figurines are greatly associated with bodily physique. Western portraits typically strive to portray a genuine anatomy of the human body. Figures depicted in traditional Chinese paintings focus on representing the posture and traits of the subject, instead of the sizes and dimensions. Therefore, this genre of symbolic art as opposed to realism was adopted to achieve a sense of spirit, rather than the likeness of common appearance.

Four, Western paintings place much emphasis on the background, whereas with Chinese paintings this is not always the case. Chinese paintings typically do not reach to the boundary of the canvass. For example, a plum blossom may be painted in the middle of the piece, seemingly suspended in midair, as large blank white margins remain on the sides. This is by no means the way Western realist paintings are created, as every object requires setting. For example, fruits are portrayed with desks as a background. Figures are depicted indoors or in open fields as the settings. Commonly, there is no blank space left on the canvass of a Western style painting. Also, emphasis placed on true resemblance and vivid qualities of the subjects is also a disparity. The portrayal of a setting is systematic in classical Western paintings, due to the theory of outward appearance and resemblance. Conversely, Chinese paintings strive to capture the spirit of the subject and choose to leave out trivial matters, as the theme is high-lighted.

Five, most of themes of Chinese paintings are of nature, while human subjects are usually the major themes in classical Western paintings. Before the Han Dynasty, this was also the case, but landscape paintings began to take center stage during the Tang Dynasty. Continuing until today, landscape painting has been the most impressive style of Chinese painting. Since Greek era, portraits have been the major theme in the West. During the medieval age, generally paintings of portraits focused on religious figures.

The style of Chinese classical painting exhibits a distinct art form, especially as it develops in modern times and inherits the traditional skills and methods of classical artistic works.

Unit 5

The Four Books and Five Classics

The Four Books and Five Classics is are set of representative Confucian essays. The Four Books include *The Analects of Confucius*, *Mencius*, *The Great Learning*, and *The Doctrine of the Mean*. The Five Classics refer to *The Book of Songs*, *The Book of History*, *The Book of Rites*, *The Book of Changes*, and *The Spring and Autumn Annals*.

The Analects of Confucius records the words and deeds of the great ideologist Confucius and his disciples. Confucius, whose given name was Qiu and courtesy name Zhong Ni, lived between 551 B.C. and 479 B.C. in the State of Lu—present day Qufu of Shandong province—during the Spring and Autumn Period of China. He was a great thinker, statesman, educator, and founder of Confucianism, having waived significant influence on Chinese culture and ethics.

The Four Books and Five Classics

Finished during the early period of the Warring States era by his disciples, *The Analects of Confucius* is one of the classic works of the Confucian school, involving philosophical, political, economical, educational, and literary aspects.

Mencius is a written account of the thoughts and actions of the philosopher Mencius and his students. Mencius (372–289 B.C.), also known by his birth name Meng and courtesy name Ziyu. He was from Zou County (present day southeastern city of Zoucheng in Shandong province) during the middle of the Warring States Period. He was a great ideologist, politician, educator, and advocator of Confucian ideology.

Prior to the Southern Song Dynasty, *The Great Learning* was originally one chapter in *The Book of Rites*, it had not been published separately. The work was said to be authored by Zeng Can (505 ‑ 434 B.C.), a disciple of Confucius. During the Southern Song Dynasty, Confucian scholar Zhu Xi took the chapter of "The Great Learning" from *The Book of Rites*, rearranging the work as an integral masterpiece among The Four Books, along with *The Analects of Confucius*, *Mencius*, and *The Doctrine of the Mean*. Furthermore, Zhu Xi ranked *The Great Learning* as most significant of The Four Books.

The Doctrine of the Mean was also originally part of *The Book of Rites*, and was not published independently before the Southern Song Dynasty. It is said that the grandson of Confucius, Zisi (483—402B.C.), compiled the work. During the Southern Song Dynasty, Zhu Xi withdrew the section from The Book of Rites including it into The Four Books. *The Book of Songs*, in the early Qin dynasty period originally called *Poetry* or *Three Hundred Poems*, is the first anthology of Chinese poems. It is a collec-

tion of 305 poems written over a period of 500 years, spanning from the
onset of the Western Zhou dynasty to the middle of the Spring and Autumn Period.
Sources indicate the work was edited by Confucius. *The Book of Songs* can be divided into three parts:
Feng, Ya, and Song. Feng indicates the local music and collected folk songs. Ya is the music intended
for nobles, and Song is the accolade used during temple ceremonies. The book is commended as an
encyclopedia of ancient society, mirroring social reality with glimpses of ordinary life.

The Book of History, in ancient times called *The Book*, received its present title from the Han Dynasty. It is the earliest compilation of documented records that reveal events throughout China's ancient history. Recorded in this book are the periods of emperors Rao and Shun, continuing until the
Eastern Zhou era, and occupying a history of more than 1,500 years. The contents of this book are
mainly of ancient imperial proclamations and conversations between emperors and ministers. There
are two versions of *The Book of History*—the modern language format and the ancient Chinese version.

The Book of Rites is an anthology of articles written by Confucian scholars from the Warring
States Period until the Qin and Han Dynasties. The work regards their interpretations of the ancient
text *Etiquette* and *Ceremony*. However, *The Book of Rites* overshadows *Etiquette* and *Ceremony* in its influence because it is much more indepth with multiple aspects. There are two adaptations of *The Book
of Rites*. One version was written by Dai De and originally consisted of 85 chapters. Presently there
only remain 40 chapters, known as *The Classic Rites of Da Dai*. The nephew of Da Dai went on to
compile another version comparable to the modern Book of Rites, consisting of 49 chapters selected
by Dai Sheng, it known as *The Classic Rites of Xiao Dai*.

As one of the most important texts of ancient China, *The Book of Changes* is revered as an early
leader of classic literature. *The Book of Changes*, also referred to as *The Changes of the Zhou*, is a work
completed during the Zhou Dynasty that contains 24,070 Chinese characters. *The Book of Changes* is
comprised of two parts, the script and the commentary. Commentary is written to explain and expand on the meanings of the script. As a manual of divination, *The book of Changes* is a summary of
life experiences and development. It uses abstract symbolism to interpret the phenomena of the cosmos and laws of nature.

The Spring and Autumn Annals was originally a general term of the official chronicles of every
state during the pre-Qing Period. With the passage of time, only the official chronicle of the State of
Lu remained intact. The text was compiled by various scribes from the State of Lu. It is believed that
it was arranged, revised, and bestowed particular meaning by Confucius, becoming a classic scripture
of Confucianism. *The Spring and Autumn Annals* is the ancestor of Chinese chronological historical
texts, documenting the 242-year history of the State of Lu. The sentences are brief, with scarcely any
portrayal of composition, but voiced in a spoken language, it expresses a disciplined and prudent
quality. By careful employment of words and their intended allusions, Confucius—writing in the annuals style—expounded his political ideals and propositions by exemplifying historical figures and
events in *The Spring and Autumn Annals*. Therefore, it was classified by later generations as one classic
that delivers profound thought by use of sublime words. Moreover, The Spring and Autumn Annals

has had a great impact on the development of chronological historical records and literature of later times.

After the Southern Song Dynasty, The Four Books and Five Classics became a required textbooks of Confucianism in schools and became fundamental concepts in the imperial examinations. In particular, service exams of dynasties after the Southern Song Dynasty required scholars to have a good command of The Four Books, which led to the popularization of the Four Books. In ancient times The Four Books and Five Classics were held in extremely high regard, similar to the status of *The Holy Bible* and *The Koran*.

The classics have had extensive influence on several aspects of Chinese social norms, interpersonal communication, social civilization, and self-development. Continuing today, the contents of The Four Books and Five Classics convey great philosophical meaning and strong ethical values. The ever expanding authority of this classic literature on overseas countries enables it to be highly ranked among the world's heritage of human civilization.

The Eight Great Prose Masters of the Tang and Song Dynasty

The Eight Classical Chinese Prose Masters in Tang and Song Dynasties was a general term used to describe the eight main representatives of prose. They include Han Yu and Liu Zongyuan of Tang Dynasty. The Song period gave rise to the Three Su—the father Su Xun, the elder brother Su Shi, and the younger brother Su Zhe. Other prominent authors of the Song Dynasty include Ouyang Xiu, Wang Anshi, and Zeng Gong. At the on-set of the Ming Dynasty, Zhu You selected and edited the essays of these eight literary giants in *Works of the Eight Masters*. Shortly after, Mao Kun arranged and compiled their writings, and entitled the collection *Prose of the Eight Masters of the Tang and Song Dynasties*. From then on, later generations referred to them as the Eight Masters.

Han Yu(768–824 A.D.) was born in Heyang (today's western region of Mengzhou city, Henan province). The writer was also known as Han Changli because his ancestral home was the city of Changli in Hebei province. He was a litterateur, philosopher, and cultural leader of the Tang Dynasty.

Liu Zongyuan's Calligraphy

As one of China's finest essay writers, he ranks first among the Eight Great Prose Masters. Han Yu underwent a chain of setbacks in pursuance of passing the imperial examination and entering political life. This was due to his reverting to the old ways of thinking and advocating orthodox Confucian ideology. He initiated the Ancient Literature Movement of the Tang Dynasty, leading a revolution of prose against the popular formal style. He insisted that literature should be a carrier of ethics to serve as meaningful guidance to later generations. His works are compiled in *The Collected Works of Chang Li*.

Liu Zongyuan's (773–819A.D.) ancestral home was Hedong, hence his penname Liu Hedong. Born in the city of Changan during the reign of Zhenyuan, he was a renowned imperial graduate, eminent ideologist, and literary master of the Tang dynasty. As one of the Eight Great Masters, Liu Zongyuan opposed the former literary circles, bringing forth an ornate and intricate style, while advocating unadorned and fluent essays. His popular works are contained in *The Anthology of Liu Hedong*.

Ouyang Xiu (1007–1072 A.D.) was born in Mianyang of Sichuan province. As a statesman, writer, historian, and poet of the Northern Song Dynasty, he was self-titled The Drunkard. He was a reformer of both politics and literature, and was a strong supporter of the Qingli Reformation, spurred by Fan Zhongyan. During the Northern Song era, he was a leader of innovation in the classical prose movement. As a patron of later talents, Su Shi and his sons, Zeng Gong, and Wang Anshi, were all at one time his students. During his time as a writer, his poems, lyrics, and various essays were extremely popular. His influential ideological thinking and euphemistic expression makes him

Ouyang Xiu

one of the greatest masters of the Tang and Song era in the genre of reformed prose. His famous works are compiled in *Collected Works of Ouyang Xiu*. After his death, he was buried in the ancient capital of Kaifeng in Xinzheng county (modern Henan province).

Su Xun (1009–1066A.D.) was a famous essay writer born of a literary family. He, together with his sons Su Shi and Su Zhe, are known as The Three Su's of Meishan of the former State of Mei (modern day Meishan in Sichuan). Su Xun was an expert essayist, especially with regard political commentary. His prose is remarkable for its fluency and vigorous penmanship. Famous selected works of his are bounded in *The Collected Works of Jiayou*. Legend has it that Su Xun did not begin to study until he was 27 years old, yet achieved great strides in literature after decades of hard work.

Su Shi (1037–1101 A.D.) was a writer, poet, essayist, artist, and calligrapher of the Song Dynasty. He was often referred to as Su Dongpo. As the fifth son of Su Xun, he was born in Mei Shan, located in the Sichuan Province. During the second year of the reign of Jiayou, he and his younger brother, Su Zhe, both passed the highest level of the imperial examination. In second year of the Yuan Feng era (1079A.D.), Su Shi introduced the controversial and critical style of wutai poetry, leading the government to sentencing him to exile. He compiled famous masterpieces as exemplified by the anthology *Seven Works of Dongpo*. Su Shi's literary theory was in direct line with that of Ouyang Xiu, but the he emphasized originality, expressive force, and the artistic value of literature. The essays of Su Shi are comprehensible, fluent, unstrained, and passionately written. Following Ouyang Xiu, Su Shi was another leader among literary circles of the Northern Song Dynasty. He associated with and mentored many scholars during his lifetime, and had had a profound effect on the development of Chinese literature in his day as well as in years to come. Su Shi is a rare genius in the history of Chinese literature and art.

Su Zhe(1039–1112 A.D.), known as one of the Three Su's, was native to Meizhou, near Mount

Emei in what is now Sichuan province. He appealed to atone for his imprisoned brother, Shu Shi, who was found guilty of offensive writing. Thereby he offered to forfeit his official post. As a master writer, Su Zhe was greatly edified by his father and his brother. Su Zhe advocated cultivating and disciplining one's capacity for greatness, believing the efficacy of an article depends on the education the author has received. His most popular writings are represented in the *Collected Works of Luancheng*.

Wang Anshi

Wang Anshi (1021—1086A.D.), also known as Wang Jinggong, was a native of Linchuan (present day Fuzhou city of Jiangxi province). He was also referred to as Mr. Wang of Linchuan. He was a remarkable politician, philosopher, litterateur, and reformer during the Northern Song Dynasty. In the third term of the Xi Ning era (1069A.D.), Wang Anshi came to power as a prime minister and introduced and advocated his socioeconomic reform policies. He was not only a prominent politician and ideologist, but also a remarkable literati, placing great significance on the social function of literature, and writings aimed to serve society. As Wang Anshi regarded practicality as a fundamental discipline for literary creation. His works mirrored social abuse and contradiction, with an emphasis on politics. His essays and poems have been compiled in the *Wang Linchuan Anthology*.

Zeng Gong (1019–1083 A.D.), emerged from Nanfeng of Jiangxi province as a scholar of the Northern Song Dynasty. He is classified as one of the eight great literary masters of the Tang and Song Dynasties. His political performance would pale in comparison with his literary philosophy and development. As an advocate of moral values, he stressed the concepts of benevolence and honesty. He was one of the supporters of the Northern Song's new prose reform movement and is well-known for his outstanding essays. In his essays, he followed the examples of *Sima Qian*, Han Yu, and Ouyang Xiu, promoting literary works that illuminate ethics. His articles have exerted a deep impact on writers of later generations. Some essayists, such as Wang Shenzhong and Tang Shunzhi of the Ming Dynasty, and Fang Bao and Yao Nai of the Qing Dynasty, sanctify Zeng Gong's works to a great extent. Zeng Gong's most prolific writings can be found in the collected works entitled *Yuanfeng Leigao*.

Works of the eight great masters of prose are the epitome of literary achievement during the Tang and Song dynasties, as well as brilliant exam-ples of Chinese classic literature.

Tang Dynasty Poetry

Tang dynasty poetry refers to lyrics written during China's Tang dynasty, often considered as the Golden Age of Chinese poetry. Tang poetry is one of the brilliant literary heritages of China. It occupies a history of over one thousand years and is still widely known today. *Three Hundred Tang Poems*, compiled by Qing scholars, for numerous years was a household anthology of poems originating from the Chinese Tang Dynasty.

A splurge of poets emerged during the Tang Dynasty. Today's statistics indicate there have been 2,300 confirmed famous authors. Furthermore, there are still many yet to be discovered. Their works are preserved in the *Complete Poetry of the Tang*, containing more than 48,900 poems. The styles of Tang poetry are greatly diversified. The ancient style of verse basically includes five-character and seven-character poems, while the modern-style verse is divided into two categories—four-lined and eight-lined poems, both of which can be further divided into five-character and seven-character poems. The modern style of poetry has strict comprehensive rules and formats, henceforth it is also called metrical verse.

Tang Poetry can be classified into four main groups: early, flourishing, middle and late Tang poetry. During the onset of Tang poetry, the art of literature was reformed and became more vigorous, greatly due to influence of the Four Talents—Wang Bo, Yang Jiong, Lu Zhaolin, and Luo Binwang. Besides these writers, there were many more poets such as Chen Zi'ang, Shen Quanqi, and Song Zhiwen. The style and fundamentals of Tang poetry took shape in the early stages of its development. Poems of the period known as the flourishing Tang era enjoyed a golden age. This was in part due to the wise reign, prosperous economy, and the prevailing strength of the civilization. A large number of gifted poets emerged during this time, pushing the development of poetry to its pinnacle by producing a wide range of composition. At that time, descriptions of fields, rivers, and mountains, as well as wars admist borders, accounted for a large proportion of the subjects. Li Bai, entitled the Immortal of Poetry, and Du Fu, known as the Sage of Poetry, were also very active during this period. In the middle and late periods of the Tang Dynasty, though the splendid and height of society has passed, the creation of poetry persisted, with the emergence of numerous talented poets of various styles; including Han Yu, Liu Zongyuan, Li He, Bai Juyi, Yuan Zhen, Liu Yuxi, Du Mu, Li Shangyin, and Wen Tingyun. Their poems were artistic recounting of the decline in prosperity of the Tang, exemplifying a high artistic level and prominent status within the history of Chinese literature.

Li Bai and Du Fu, the two greatest poets of Tang Dynasty, were crowned by later generations as the Immortal of Poetry and the Sage of Poetry respectively. These two poets hold outstanding positions in the history of poetry and appeal greatly to poets of later ages.

Li Bai (701–762A.D.) was born in Longxi (now Gansu province). Being a celebrated romantic poet in the Tang Dynasty, he created many talented works. *Gazing at the Waterfall of Lu Mountain* was one of his classics. His poems are characterized by the following distinctive features: first, his poetry has a strong sense of passion. Li Bai had a broad sense of emotions, despising the concept of love and hate. He would drink and sing to his satisfaction and feel jubilant, laughing sardonically. But he would also vent his grief and indignation by his wild railing and wailing. Secondly, his poems brought forth his incredible imagination into full expression. The inspiration would hit him like lightning, but soon afterwards his drive would unexpectedly escape him like a gust of wind. The range of

The Immortal of Poetry—Li Bai

subjects of his poems was very wide, covering historical figures, astronomy, geography, and illusory myths. Lastly,Li Bai often expressed his unruly emotion in an extravagant way. For example, he used one line "my white hair streams back 30,00 feet long", to describe his deep grief. He, therefore, was bestowed the title of the Immortal of Poetry.

The Sage of Poetry—Du Fu

Du Fu (712–770A.D.) was born in Gong county of Henan province. He came from a family of scholars. His paternal grandfather was Du Shenyan, a well-noted poet. Epic works created by Du Fu were Three Officials and Three Separations. Du Fu is an exemplary realist poet in the history of Chinese literature, inventing multiple poems mirroring the social outlook of the once prosperous Tang Dynasty. Du Fu's ideological sentiment sparked the conscience of many outstanding ancient intellectuals. Despite his body's suffering, Du Fu offered great sympathy to common people and revealed the sharp line between exploiters and the exploited in his poems. His political inclination served as a model for traditional men of letters. Du Fu wrote heartfelt poems featuring rich social content, sincere enthusiasm, deep indignation, and solemnness. Du Fu's life-long effort to achieve the perfection of his distinct style is greatly admired by poets of later periods. He inherited and carried forward the tradition by opening and studying ten thousand scrolls (idiom). His endless language is everlasting, but at the same time, he never ceases to refine his own writing style. He was particularly skillful at composing both ancient-style and modernstyle verse. Therefore, he was honored as the Sage of Poetry His former residence, known as Du Fu's Thatched Cottage in Chengdu, Sichuan province is still well preserved by historians and serves as a place for people to visit and show respect.

Tang poetry is nearly synonymous with Tang literature due to its astonishing value. In the history of Chinese literature, Tang Poetry is an unparalleled style from which generations upon generations of poets draw from to enrich and improve their writing abilities. Furthermore, Tang Poetry has become a symbol and a fundamental element of traditional Chinese culture.

Song Dynasty Poetry

Song dynasty poetry represents the literary achievements of the Song Dynasty and is compared to in ancient literature with poetry of the Tang. As a liter-ary form that is accompanied by music, Song poetry is also called as Folk-song Poetry. The rise, development and prosperity of Song poetry bears a resemblance to music. It originated from the Sui Dynasty and took its form in Tang, reaching its summit in the Song era. More than 20,000 poems by 1,330 poets have been compiled in the *Complete Collection of Song Poems*. The sheer number of poems presents a scene of prosperity of Song artistic works. Song poetry contains distinct forms of verse. For example, man jiang hong, and xi jiang yue, which decides the format. Lyric writers must produce works in compliance with the rhythm and arrangement of the music.

There are many famous poets of the Song era including: Yan Shu, Yan Jidao, Liu Yong, Su Shi, Zhou Bangyan, Li Qingzhao, Xin Qiji, and Jiang Kui.

Yan Shu (991–1055A.D.), a former Song dynasty poet, was born in Linchuan of Jiangxi province. More than 130 works by him were compiled into *Pearl and Jade Verses*. Under the influence of Southern Tang poet Feng Yansi, Yan Shu's lyrical poems reflect the tastes of the affluent conservative literati with graceful language and sweet rhythms. A line from *The Silk–Washing Brook*, "The flower has no alternative but to fall, just like the return of the swallows..." has become a lasting sentence.

Yan Jidao(ca. 1040–1112 A.D.), the 7th son of Yan Shu, was also a celebrated poet. He compiled more than 200 pieces of work in *Poems of the Hills*. His verses have great artistic value because his poems are endowed with sincere and sorrowful sentiment, reaching the boundaries of high art. It is said that his poetry can sway the hearts of the people. In the art of poetry, Yan Jidao and his famous father are known as the Two Yans.

Liu Yong (987–1053 A.D.) is native the Wuyi Mountain region of Fujian province. One of the greatest writers of the Northern Song era, *Bells in Rain* is representative of his work. In his young adulthood, Liu Yong lived in large cities and brothels. Therefore his writings mainly revolve around his interaction and love affairs with female singers and prostitutes. His poetry fascinated people of all ranks, from the prostitutes to the emperor, due to its local and colloquial style. It was said that any place where there were inhabitants, there were singers who could sing Liu Yong's verses. Liu Yong's *Collection of Music and Songs* consists of more than two hundred poems.

Su Shi, (1037–1101 A.D.) native to Mei Shan in Sichuan Province, was an eminent poet of the Northern Song Dynasty. His 340 poems took on a broader social outlook than poems which formerly focused almost entirely on the sentimental feelings among men and women. Su Shi occupies a unique status in the history of Chinese poetry. He transformed the traditional styles of the late Tang and Five Dynasties, developing a bold and unrestrained style. He also made significant contributions in thematic extension and poetic innovation. His prominent works, *My Darling Slave* and *The Moon Festival*, are heralded as showcasing this unrestrained style. Together with the other great litterateur, Xin Qiji, they are collectively known as Su Xin.

Zhou Bangyan (1056–1121 A.D.) emerged in Hangzhou city of Zhejiang province as an excellent poet during the Northern Song Dynasty. He excelled at musical temperament and had a strict sense of combined poetry. His lyrics express the love between a man and a woman, with artistic and elegant language. Zhou Bangyan was extremely influential during the Song Dynasty period. In the final years of the Northern Song era, his unrestrained artistic works were immensely popular. His works are typified by the collection *Qingzhen Poetry*, also known as *Poems of Jade*.

Li Qingzhao (1084–1155 A.D.) is native to Jinan city in Shandong province. She emerged from a family known for literary talent, was a

Li Qingzhao

prime artist during the Northern and Southern Song eras and is one of the first great female poets in the history of Chinese literature. Her early lyrics mainly recount the lives of aristocratic girls and expresses their loneliness and longing for love, while the style of her later poetry expresses fallen destiny and deep melancholy. Li Qingzhao's lyrics are woven with a distinct female perspective. She claimed there was a great distinction between lyrical poetry creation and prose writing. One of her most prominent poems is *Sound, Sound, Slow*. The collection of her masterpieces is entitled *Poems of Washed Jade*. Moreover, Li Qingzhao is the only female poet in Chinese history to have a crater on the moon named after her.

Xin Qiji (1140–1207A.D.) was a talented and notable poet during the Southern Song Dynasty. His ancestral home is Jinan in Shandong province. Throughout history, he has been paired with the great litterateur Su Shi, known as Su Xin. Together with Li Qingzhao, they are collectively known as Two Greats of Jinan. Xin Qiji's poetry is brimming with enthusiasm, vehemence, solemnness, and e-motionality, and embodies a bold and unrestrained style. His stunning lyrics are regarded as the dragon of Song poetry. He further extended the themes of prose using the fundamentals of Su Shi, enhancing the status of poetry in literature.

Jiang Kui,(1155–1221A.D.) born in Poyang of Jiangxi province, was a famous poet and composer of Southern Song Dynasty. He was orphaned from childhood and was housed by his elder sister during his adolescent period. He greatly cherished music, literature, and calligraphy. His words were of a primarily desolate manner, forming an elegant style that differed from the traditional schools of writing. In addition, he labeled his lyrics with a type of ancient Chinese musical notation. These are the only well-preserved musical documents with Song lyrics, thus they have significant cultural value. The collection of his works is entitled *Songs of Jiang Baishi* (Jiang Kui's nickname).

The poetry of the Song Dynasty is a large brilliant diamond in the Chinese crown of ancient literature. The style is highly praised as the most beautiful of all Chinese poetry. Today it still catches the attention of people, giving them a great enjoyment and creating much appreciation for the art.

Yuan Dynasty Opera, Mixed Theater

Yuan Opera refers to Chinese opera of the Yuan Dynasty. It can be divided into Yuan opera and Yuan mixed theater, being the main body of literature of the Yuan Dynasty. Yuan opera, together with Tang poetry and Song lyrics, are the three most significant accomplishments of Chinese literature. However, Yuan mixed theater far exceeds Yuan opera in achievements and influence, therefore some include Yuan opera in mixed theater. The following section will mainly focus on mixed theater.

Yuan mixed theater reached its summit in the late half of the 13th century. As a new and complete form of drama, Yuan mixed theater has its own distinct sophistication and strict format. Chinese opera evolved by combining music, dialogue, and dance into one performance on stage. In addition, many scripts were produced featuring a perfect mixture of rhymed verse and prose, systematically integrating drama and literature.

Yuan mixed theater has integrity and meticulous composition. The performance generally consists of four acts and an interlude. Although each production always has four acts, another interlude may sometimes be included. The so-called zhe is similar to the modern act of a theater production. One script contains four acts with suites of music and the portrayal of the conflict and the natural resolution with the passage of time. Among the performances of Yuan mixed theater, in addition to the four acts, a zhe or prelude is often used to explain the circumstances of the plot and summarize the story. Frequently, a zhe is placed in between acts.

The division of roles includes dan (female character type in Chinese opera), mo (role of middle-aged man in classical opera), jing (actor with a painted face), and za (miscellaneous staff). Zheng dan refers to the leading female role and wai dan is the second lead. Mo includes the main male part zheng mo, and secondary role of fu mo. Jing are roles characterized by facial makeup and their ability to provide comic relief. Za is a collective term for all of the other actors. These include roles such as gu (official) and jia (emperor). In Yuan mixed theater, only major roles played by the lead male or lead female have librettos. In the latter case, dan ben is the term used to describe the libretto of zheng dan (lead female role). A prime example of this is the production of *The Injustice to Dou E*, consisting of the female leading role. The primary male character's libretto is called zheng mo, such as the lead male role in *Autumn in the Palace of the Han*.

Illustrations of *Autumn in the Palace of the Han*

In Yuan mixed theater, there also exists binbai and kejie. Binbai, also called binshuo, constitutes the additional stage dialogues and monologues. Kejie, also referred to as ke, includes the complimentary singing and actions of the other performers. In terms of Yuan opera, ke refers to four main aspects. Stage blocking, the performers facial expressions, acrobatic fighting, and dance. Oftentimes, stage effects will be included in the performance.

Many extraordinary playwrights and works of art arose in the prosperous age of Yuan opera. Included among them are Guan Hanqing, Ma Zhiyuan, Zhen Guangzu, and Bai Pu, whom are honored as the Four Great Yuan Playwrights.

Born at the end of the Jin Dynasty or the beginning of the Yuan Dynasty in Dadu (called Beijing today), Guan Hanqing is regarded as a leading playwright of Yuan dynasty. Much of his history is unknown. According to some relative material, he played an active role in theatre development from 1210 to 1300 in Dadu and had visited regions such as Hangzhou. Guan Hanqing was a productive writer with over 60 various operas. Only 18 of these operas still remain. His most famous work is *The Injustice to Dou E*. Guan Hanqing has had immense influence on later generations; on the planet Mercury lays a crater that was named after him.

Ma Zhiyuan (c.a. 1250–1323A.D.) was a celebrated playwright of Dadu (present day Beijing) during the Yuan Dynasty. His style of script was distinct in that he was adept at turning simple and natural words into fine-grained sentences to vividly delineate characters. His representative work,

Autumn in the Palace of the Han, is praised as one of the greatest classics of Yuan drama. Furthermore, Ma Zhiyuan was an expert composer of music as the authority of the Yuan period. Today, more than 130 of his lyrical works have been preserved. His best work, *Autumn Thoughts*, is poetic and picturesque, creating an everlasting impression.

Zheng Guangzu is native to Xiangfen county of Shanxi province. Although it is unclear exactly when he lived, he was a well-known playwright of the Yuan Dynasty He composed 18 theatrical scripts in his life. Among them, *A Young Lady's Departed Soul* is his masterpiece. His dramas mainly involved two subjects; love stories of young men and women, and historical legends.

Bai Pu, (his original given name was Heng), was born in 1226. By 1306, although still living, his whereabouts were unknown. He came from an official family, his father was a successful graduate of the imperial exam, becoming an office holder. His celebrated composition, *Rain on the Paulowina Tree*, depicts the romance between Emperor Li Longji and his consort Yang Yuhuan. The play exerted great influence on the Hong Sheng's *The Palace of Eternity*, a noted Qing Dynasty work.

The four great tragedies of Yuan drama include Guan Hanqing's *The Injustice to Dou E*, *Rain on the Paulowina Tree* by Bai Pu, Ma Zhiyuan's *Autumn in the Han Palace*, and *The Orphan of the Zhao Family* by Ji Junxiang. Meanwhile, the following plays are classified as the four greatest romance plays: *The Pavilion of Moon-Worship* by Guan Hanqing, *Romance of the West Chamber* by Wang Shifu, *Over the Wall on a Horse* by Bai Pu, and *A Young Girl's Departed Soul* by Zheng Guangzu.

Yuan Dynasty theater is an extremely dramatic artistic form with distinct traditional Chinese cultural traits. In his book *The History of Song and Yuan Drama*, Wang Guowei acclaims Yuan opera represents China's most natural literature.

Drama continues to move forward and later playwrights have scored enormous achievements following the peak of flourish in Yuan Dynasty. And Ming Dynasty witnesses the emergence of Tang Xianzu, who has gained immortality as the Ming Dynasty's most gifted playwright for four of his plays, including *Peony Pavilion*, the *Legend of Purple Hairpin*, *Handan Dream* and *Southern Branch Dream*. The quartet is dubbed Four Dreams at Linchuan because Tang Xianzu is a Linchuan native and he meets his characters from his major works in his dreams.

Tang Xianzu and his "Four Dreams" possess an outstanding position and have an enormous influence in the history of Chinese dramas. Particularly, *Peony Pavilion* has been performed for four centuries and is warmly received to the present. It was said that a female reader Yu Erniang from Loujiang city was moved very deeply, so she was in great sorrow everyday, at last she died for this tragic story. Even nowadays, as one of the popular repertoire, *Peony Pavilion* is frequently staged and the performances find their ways into many college campuses. From the beginning of the 20th century, Tang Xianzu's plays have been translated into different languages of many countries and well performed by overseas artists. He is praised as "Shakespeare of the East" for his renowned works reflects the significant role of Chinese opera in world stages of drama.

Novels of the Ming and Qing Dynasties

The Ming and Qing Dynasties were prosperous periods in the history of Chinese novels. From the beginning of the Ming Dynasty, novels served as literary forms, fully displaying social functions and academic values. Breaking the dominance of orthodox verses, it achieved an equal position in literary history with the poems of the Tang Dynasty, the lyrical works of the Song Dynasty, and musical scores of the Yuan Dynasty. In the Qing Dynasty period, classical Chinese novels reach their zenith and begin to descend, later transitioning into the era of modern novels.

Luo Guanzhong

A large number of varied collections of novels emerged during the Ming and Qing eras, typified by China's Four Great Classic Novels, including *Romance of the Three Kingdoms, Water Margin, Journey to the West,* and *Dream of Red Mansions.*

Romance of the Three Kingdoms authored by Luo Guanzhong, is one of the first ancient Chinese novels and has enormous historical influence. It is widely known in China as one of the four brilliant classic literary works. The novel is based on the history of the three kingdoms of Cao Cao, Liu Bei, and Sun Quan (respectively known as the states of Wei, Shu, and Wu), and their struggle to reunite the empire in the 3rd century. Using a broad historical background, it reveals a complex era of bitter politics and war. A major artistic component of Romance of the Three Kingdoms is the depiction of the human endeavors of military conflict. The novel presents graphic descriptions of large and small battles, with a fascinating plot line and superb writing, as it depicts blood on the gleaming knife. Among the stories of The Battle of Guandu and The Campaign of Redcliff are effective portrayals of the warfare that frightens the heart and moves the spirit.

At the same time, *Romance of the Three Kingdoms* contains more that two hundred vivid characters, the most notable being Zhuge Liang, Cao Cao, Guan Yu, and Liu Bei.Zhuge Liang is the embodiment of a "virtuous councilor" who is endowed by the novelist with incredible curiosity and impressive strategic insight. Cao Cao is considered to be a treacherous warlord who is an embodiment of an ambitious but cunning and cruel ruler. Guan Yu is revered by later generations for his loyalty and courage. Liu Bei is the author's model of an emperor who embraces universal benevolence, respect for the wise, and the skill to know his subordinates and assign them jobs commensurate with their abilities.

The military and political stratagem revealed in *the Romance of the Three Kingdoms* exerts an ever expanding influence on later generations. It is the greatest and most influential work among the historical novels, producing an immeasurable impact on the history of Chinese literature as well as the lives of the public due to its endless charm and everincreasing popularity. Today, it still sheds light on the study of human talent, military strategy and technology, and political science, The novel has also been well-received and admired among foreign readers. As early as 1569, *Romance of the Three Kingdoms* was introduced in Korea. By 1635, it was included in the collections of Oxford University in England. Since then, it has reached global proportions with versions in Japanese, English, French, and Russian.

Water Margin was written solely by Shi Nai'an in the Ming Dynasty, or possibly was completed under the concerted efforts of Shi Nai'an and Luo Guanzhong. In its brilliantly crafted writing, it depicts the full development of a peasant uprising from its inception, including the rise of a rebel group at Liangshan, and down to its defeat. Through descriptions of the darkness and corruption of the feudal society, Water Margin fully examines one of commonly cited themes regarding the authorities forcing the people to rebel. The novel is marked by its appealing plot and its effective revelation of the characters' personalities. Some of the literary images, such as Li Kui, Wu Song, Lin Chong, and Lu Zhishen, have become household names. Water Margin created a common, concise, vivid, and expressive literary dialogue, becoming one of China's first novels to use native folk dialect. In addition, the novel has extended its influence over Chinese literature and society, reaching other countries throughout the world. Among the many English translated versions, *All Men Are Brothers* by Pearl S. Buck in the mid to late 1920s is the first translation. It was published in 1933 as the first complete English translation, becoming an instant hit in the United States. So far, *Outlaws of the Marsh* is considered as a relatively good English version, translated by Sidney Shapiro, an American Jewish scholar of Chinese nationality.

Journey to the West was created by Wu Cheng'en of the Ming dynasty. It tells the story of Xuanzang, a Buddhist monk of the Tang Dynasty, and his disciples Sun Wukong (Monkey King), Zhu Bajie (Pigsy in some the English translations), Master Sha Wujing, and the White Dragon Horse. They endure eighty one trials and tribulations in the course of events to reach the Western Paradise to obtain the sought after Buddhist scriptures. The author creates a supernatural world of gods and demons, as readers experience his bold and free imagination. *Journey to the West* is the pinnacle of classic Chinese novels, and is also considered one of the masterpieces of romanticism among world literature. Encyclopedia Americana claims that it "renders an enchanting world where rich social contents and brilliant thinking are inseparably blended." Furthermore, French Encyclopedia lists it as a humorous and clever book that "is a pleasure to read." Since the beginning of the 19th century, the classic has been translated into over a dozen languages, including Japanese, English, French, German, and Russian.

A Dream of Red Mansions, completed during the Qianlong period of the Qing Dynasty, is the peak of Chinese classical realist novels. The modern work is comprised of 120 chapters, the first 80 of which were written by Cao Xueqin, the remaining 40 chapters were composed by Gao E. Using the characters Jia Baoyu, Lin Daiyu, and Xue Baochai, the novel depicts a tragic tale of romance and marriage in the times of declining fortunes of a large royal family. The story unfolds at the collapse of feudal society and the beginning trend towards democratic ideas. The great success of *A Dream of Red Mansions* is remarkably reflected by the creation of characters with distinctive personalities. The success of the masterpiece also lies in its intricate plot, detailed descriptions, and elegant language. The novel describes more than 480 characters, dozens of whom are highly individualized. At the same time, characters such as Jia Baoyu, Lin Daiyu, Xue Baochai, and Wang Xifeng, have become unforgettable stunning images. Cao Xueqin's flawless language provides convincing and vivid characterizations. Not only does each character have a unique appearance, they also possess distinct voices and emotions. In conclusion, *A Dream of Red Mansions* is highly applauded as an outstanding artistic achievement among novels of the Ming and Qing eras. *A Dream of Red Mansions* has had a great impact on Chinese literature and society. This influence has created international research and review, forming the subject of Redology, dedicated to commentary of the novel. The novel is not only a great artistic work of China, but also a rare gem of world literature. It not only enjoys high prestige in China with a circulation totaling more than one million, but has also spawned a large number of popular journals in various foreign countries. The novel has been translated into over ten languages, including English, French, and Russian. *A Dream of Red Mansions* has gradually become a spiritual wealth shared by all people from around the world.

Besides the Four Great Classic Novels, relatively famous stories of the Ming and Qing periods include the anonymously authored novel *The Golden Lotus*, the Qing Dynasty's *Strange Tales of a Lonely Studio* by Pu Songling, and *The Scholars* by Wu Jingzi.

Novels of the Ming and Qing periods play an indispensable role in the history of Chinese literature and culture. Specifically, The Four Great Classic Novels have all been adapted for television, which incorporate many aspects of traditional Chinese daily life, becoming an enduring spiritual treasure.

第一单元

长江文化

长江流域和黄河流域一样,是中华民族先民的诞生地。它源远流长,与黄河一起,成为中华民族文化和文明的摇篮。我们所说的长江文化,就是指长江流域的一切物质文化和精神文化的总和。

长江是中国的第一大江河,也是世界第三大河流,仅次于尼罗河与亚马逊河。它发源于青藏高原唐古拉山脉北面,格拉丹冬雪山西南侧。长江主要流经青海、西藏、云南、四川、重庆、湖北、湖南、江西、安徽、江苏、上海等 11 个省(市、区),横跨中国的西南、华中、华东三大区域,最后在上海流入东海。长江全长约6300 公里,流域面积约为 1802000 平方公里,占全国总面积的 18.75%。这比黄河长近千公里,流域面积要大约 1002000 平方公里。在如此广大的长江流域,历代中国人通过自己的勤劳智慧,逐渐创造出了一种特有的长江文化。

过去,一说中华文明的摇篮,人们只是说黄河流域及其所形成的黄河文化。实际上,长江文化也是中华民族的摇篮。这两条大河在中国文明史上应当相提并论,正如幼发拉底河、底格里斯河构成了巴比伦文化,印度河、恒河构成了印度文化一样,长江文化和黄河文化一道共同构成了中华文化。

长江文化有着悠久的历史。1929 年 5 月,在长江流域的云南省元谋县发现了"元谋直立人"化石。据科学家测定,"元谋直立人"生活距今约 170 万年前,这是目前中国境内已知最早的古人类。"元谋直立人"比黄河流域发现的"北京直立人"化石早约 100 万年。此外,从已挖掘的文化遗址看,黄河流域最早的是仰韶文化,距今约5000—7000年。与此相对应,长江流域则有河姆渡文化,距今约5300—7000年。由此可见,长江文化与黄河文化一样,有着悠久的历史。

另外,在长江文化中,三星堆遗址的发现也有着非常重要的意义和价值。三星堆位于长江上游的四川省广汉市南兴镇。因为有三座突兀在成都平原上的黄土堆而被称为"三星堆"。1929年春,当地农民燕道诚在住宅旁挖水沟时,发现了一坑精美的玉器,由此拉开三星堆文明的研究序幕。1986年,三星堆两个商代大型祭祀坑的发现,出土了大量的青铜器、玉石器、象牙、贝、陶器和金器等。在这批古蜀秘宝中,有许多光怪陆离奇异诡谲的青铜造型:有世界上最早、最高的青铜神树,它高384公分,三簇树枝,每簇三枝、共九枝,上有27果9鸟,树侧有一龙缘树逶迤而下;有世界上最大、最完整的青铜大立人像,通高262公分,重逾180公斤,被称为铜像之王;有世界上最大的青铜纵目人像,高64.5公分,两耳间相距138.5公分等等。这些均堪称独一无二的旷世神品。而以流光溢彩的金杖为代表的金器,以满饰图案的边璋为代表的玉石器,亦多属前所未见的稀世之宝。专家认为,三星堆的建造年代至迟为商代早期。这一考古发现轰动了世界,被誉为世界"第九大奇迹"。同时,三星堆古遗址被还称为20世纪人类最伟大的考古发现之一:以前历史学界认为,中华民族的发祥地是黄河流域,然后才渐渐传播到全中国。而三星堆的发现则将古蜀国的历史推前到5000年前,再一次证明了长江流域与黄河流域一样同是中华民族的发祥地,证明了长江流域地区存在过不亚于黄河流域地区的古文明。长江文明和黄河文明共同属中华文明的母体。

但是,随着历史的发展,黄河文化逐渐发展兴盛起来,一度成为中国的主导文化,而长江文化则长期处于边缘化的地位。魏晋南北朝以后,长江文化逐渐兴起,并最终取得与黄河文化同等重要的地位。

魏晋南北朝时期,由于自然灾害和频繁的战乱,黄河流域的人民被迫向长江流域迁移。隋唐时期,长江流域特别是中下游地区,经济发展很快。安史之乱后,北方人到南方避乱,这是中国历史上的第二次人口大迁移,使南方人口迅速增加。今天的江苏、安徽、江西、湖北、四川都出现了许多新的移民居住点。宋元明时期,北方人口第三次大规模向南迁移,长江流域中下游的城镇几乎无镇没有北方人前来定居。

经过几次大规模的人口迁移,黄河文化逐渐融入到长江文化中,促进了长江文化的飞速发展。南方恬静的乡村使北来的学者增添了赋诗作文的灵气。同时,北方的建筑样式、雕饰图案都得以在南方传播。经过融合改造后的长江文化对中国文化发挥着重要的贡献和影响。长江流域的南京和杭州便都曾是古代中国的首都。长江文化也一度成为中国文化的中心。

与黄河流域相比,长江流域在近代的社会转型中显得更有生机。

如果说黄河流域是传统型、政治型的区域,那么长江流域则是活跃型、商业型的区域。

长江流域的东南地区便是中国早期现代化的起源地,其中上海更是一个现代化的大都市。

长江文化在近代以来越来越充满着活力和生机,最终使得这一流域能以占全国五分之一的土地,养活近三分之一的人口,创造了二分之一的工农业产值。长江文化在现代正发挥着越来越重要的作用。

近年来,长江文化已成为海内外学术界关注的"热点"之一。

尤其是20世纪末在湖北举行的"首届长江文化暨楚文化国际学术讨论会"和2003年

10月在四川召开的"三星堆文化与长江文明国际学术研讨会"以及随着《长江文化研究文库》的推出,长江文化会越来越引起世人的瞩目。

(黎清编著)

茶文化

中国人向来有"关门七件事,柴、米、油、盐、酱、醋、茶"之说,由此可见茶在人们日常生活中的重要位置。

中国是茶树的原产地,因而也是茶叶的故乡,是世界上最早的饮茶制茶的国家。很多书籍把茶的发现时间定为公元前2737—前2697年,那是中国历史上的三皇五帝时期。不过,茶最初不是像现在这样作为饮料使用的,而是作为药使用。

西汉末年,茶是寺僧、皇室和贵族的高级饮料。三国时期,宫廷饮茶已很普遍。从晋到隋,饮茶逐渐普及开来,茶开始成为民间饮品。

但茶风的大盛却是在大唐帝国建立以后。唐以前的饮茶是粗放式的,多用于解渴。随着唐代饮茶的蔚然成风,饮茶方式也发生了显著变化,出现了细煎慢品式。这一变化在饮茶史上是一件大事,其功劳应归于茶圣陆羽。他所著《茶经》,是唐代茶文化形成的标志。《茶经》概括了茶的自然和人文双重内涵,探讨了饮茶艺术,把儒、道、佛三种文化融入饮茶中,首创中国茶道精神。唐代茶文化的形成还与禅教的兴起有关,因茶有提神益思、生精止渴功能,所以寺庙崇尚饮茶。唐代形成的茶道分宫廷茶道、寺院茶礼、文人茶道三种。

宋代时,文人中出现专业品茶社团,如由官员组成的"汤社",由佛教徒组成的"千人社"等。宋太祖赵匡胤是位嗜茶之士。当时的宫庭中设立了茶事机关,宫廷用茶已分等级,茶仪已成礼制,赐茶成为皇帝笼络大臣、眷怀亲族的重要手段,也成为向国外使节表达友谊的珍贵礼品。至于下层社会,茶文化更是生机勃勃,迁居时邻里要"献茶",客人来时要敬"元宝茶",定婚时要"下茶",结婚时要"定茶",同房时要"合茶"。民间兴起"斗茶"风,比赛茶叶的质量、茶汤的色香味、斗茶者的茶技茶艺。制茶方法多种多样,有蒸青、炒青、烘青等,茶具的款式、质地、花纹也千姿百态。

明清时代的饮茶,无论在茶叶类型上,还是在饮用方法上,都与前代差异显著。散茶在唐宋的基础上发展扩大,成为盛行明、清两代并且流传至今的主要茶类。明代炒青法所制的散茶大都是绿茶,兼有部分花茶。清代除了名目繁多的绿茶、花茶之外,还出现了乌龙茶、红茶、黑茶和白茶等类茶,从而奠定了中国茶叶结构的基本种类。

当今世界广泛流传的种茶、制茶和饮茶习俗,都是从中国传播出去的。据推测,中国茶叶传播到国外,已有2000多年的历史。约于公元5世纪南北朝时,中国的茶叶就开始陆续输出至东南亚邻国及亚洲其他地区。公元9世纪时,日本僧人将中国茶籽带回本国种植,从而使茶逐渐普及为大众化饮料。10世纪时,蒙古商队来华从事贸易时,将中国砖茶从中国经西伯利亚带至中亚以外。15世纪初,葡萄牙商船来中国进行通商贸易,茶叶贸易开始出现。荷兰人约在公元1610年左右将茶叶带至西欧,1650年后传至东欧,再传至俄、法等国,17世纪时传至美洲。18 世纪初，品饮红茶逐渐在英国流行，并成为一种高雅行为，茶叶成了英国上层社会人士相互馈赠的高级礼品。著名的英国东印度公司于 18 世纪开始大规模经销中国茶，并获得了巨额利润。1880 年，中国出口至英国的茶叶多达 145 万担，占中国茶叶出口量的百分之六十到七十。19 世纪，中国的茶叶终于走向全世界，成为世界性饮料。

中国现有茶园面积 110 万公顷。茶区分布辽阔，东起东经 122 度的台湾省东部海岸，西至东经 95 度的西藏自治区易贡，南自北纬 18 度的海南岛榆林，北到北纬 37 度的山东省荣城县，东西跨经度 27 度，南北跨纬度 19 度，共有 21 个省（区、市）967 个县、市生产茶叶。全国有四大茶区，即西南茶区、华南茶区、江南茶区和江北茶区；有十大名茶，即西湖龙井茶、洞庭碧螺春、武夷岩茶、铁观音、屯溪绿茶、祁门红茶、信阳毛尖、君山银针、普洱茶、滇红茶。（倪爱珍编著）

酒文化

中国的茶文化历史悠久，中国的酒文化也毫不逊色。在几千年的文明发展史中，酒几乎渗透到社会生活的各个领域。

中国的酒，绝大多数是以粮食酿造，而中国又是一个以农立国的国家，所以酒业的兴衰、粮食的丰歉与国家的社会发展状况、政治经济活动、文化生活习俗息息相关。

在中国古代史籍中，有所谓"猿酒"的记载。当然这并不是说猿猴自己会酿酒，而是猿猴采集的水果偶然地一次没吃完，水果自然发酵生成了果酒。所以，中国最早的酒是模仿大自然的杰作而制成的果酒和乳酒（动物乳汁自然发酵成酒）。

中国用粮食酿造的最古老的酒是黄酒。黄酒，也称米酒，在世界三大酿造酒（黄酒、葡萄酒和啤酒）中占有重要一席，其酿酒技术独树一帜，成为东方酿造界的典型代表。黄酒，顾名思义是黄颜色的酒。所以有的人将黄酒这一名称翻译成"Yellow Wine"，其实这并不恰当。黄酒的颜色并不总是黄色的，还有黑色、红色，所以不能光从字面上理解。黄酒是用谷物作原料，用麦曲或小曲做糖化发酵剂制成的酿造酒。中国北方用谷子作原料，南方则用稻米，现在翻译上通行用"Rice Wine"表示黄酒。

古时候，酒被视为神圣的物质。酒的使用，是一件很庄严的事。远古以来，酒都是祭祀时的必备用品之一。古代的统治者认为"国之大事，在祀在戎"，而无论是"祀"，还是"戎"，都离不开酒。祭祀时，酒作为美好的东西，首先要奉献给上天、神明和祖先享用。战争时，勇士在出征之前，要用酒来激励斗志。

酒不仅与国家大事密切相关，而且与人生大事不可分割，从而形成了多姿多彩的饮酒习俗。

婚姻饮酒习俗：在中国，"喜酒"往往是婚礼的代名词，办喜酒即办婚事，去喝喜酒，也就是去参加婚礼。

与婚姻相关的还有"女儿酒"、"交杯酒"、"接风酒"、"出门酒"、"会亲酒"、"回门酒"等。

节日饮酒习俗：中国人一年中的几个重大节日，都有相应的饮酒活动，如除夕夜饮"年酒"，端午节饮"菖蒲酒"，重阳节饮"菊花酒"。

"满月酒"或"百日酒"：生了孩子，满月时，摆上几桌酒席，邀请亲朋好友共同庆贺。亲朋好友一般都会带上礼物，也有的送上红包。

"寿酒"：中国人有给老人祝寿的习俗，一般50、60、70岁等生日被称为大寿，儿女或者孙子、孙女都要为老人举办酒宴，邀请亲朋好友参加。

"上梁酒"和"进屋酒"：在中国农村，盖房是件大事，盖房过程中，上梁又是最重要的一道工序，所以在上梁这天，要办"上梁酒"。房子造好了，举家迁入新居时，要办"进屋酒"，一是庆贺新屋落成，一是祭祀神仙祖宗，以求保佑。

"开业酒"和"分红酒"：举凡店铺开张、作坊开工之时，老板都会置办酒席，以志喜庆贺；店铺或作坊年终按股份分配红利时，也会办"分红酒"。

"壮行酒"（也叫"送行酒"）：有朋友远行，要为其举办酒宴，表达惜别之情。在战争年代，勇士们上战场执行重大且有生命危险的任务时，指挥官都会为他们斟上一杯"壮行酒"。

中国传统文化的核心是儒学，它在酒文化中的体现的是喝酒讲究"酒德"，也就是说喝酒者要有德行，遵守各种礼节。

中国人特别好客，酒席上喜欢"劝酒"，而且还会采用各种各样的方式助兴，如行酒令、唱酒歌等。

中国的酒文化绵延几千年，留下了很多关于酒的历史故事和异闻传说，如酒池肉林、箪醪劳师、鲁酒薄而邯郸围、鸿门宴、汉高祖醉斩白蛇、文君当垆、煮酒论英雄、竹林七贤、清圣浊贤、饮中八仙、杯酒释兵权等。

酒自古还与文学艺术结下了不解之缘，酒与诗、与画、与戏曲、与音乐的故事丰富多彩，数不胜数。（倪爱珍编著）

八大菜系

菜系是中华民族饮食文化的结晶。每一菜系的形成，都有它深远的历史背景和人文背景，同时也与各个地区的自然地理、气候条件、资源特产、饮食习惯等密切相关。中国各大菜系的形成，从萌芽到花繁果硕，已有千年以上的历史。其中最有影响、最具代表性的是鲁、川、粤、闽、苏、浙、湘、徽等菜系，也即人们常说的中国"八大菜系"。

鲁菜：鲁菜为八大菜系之首。在中国历史上，自宋代以后鲁菜即成为"北食"的代表。明、清两代，鲁菜已成为宫廷御膳的主体。现今鲁菜由济南和胶东两地的地方菜演化而成。其特点是清香、鲜嫩、味纯，十分讲究清汤和奶汤的调制，清汤色清而鲜，奶汤色白而醇。济南菜擅长爆、烧、炸、炒，其著名品种有"九转大肠"、"汤爆双脆"、"烧蛎蝗"、"清汤燕窝"等。胶东菜以烹制各种海鲜而驰名，口味以鲜为主，偏重清淡，其著名品种有"干蒸加吉鱼"、"油爆海螺"等。

川菜：川菜系也是一个历史悠久的菜系，其发源地是古代的巴国和蜀国。秦末汉初时初具规模,唐宋时发展迅速,明清时已富有名气,现今川菜馆遍布世界各地。正宗川菜以四川成都、重庆两地的菜肴为代表。川菜特点是酸、甜、麻、辣、香、油重、味浓,注重调味,离不开三椒(即辣椒、胡椒、花椒)和鲜姜,以辣、酸、麻脍炙人口,为其他地方菜所少有,享有"一菜一味,百菜百味"的美誉。烹调方法擅长于烤、烧、干煸、蒸。代表菜肴有"大煮干丝"、"黄焖鳗"、"怪味鸡块"、"麻婆豆腐"等。

粤菜:粤菜即广东菜的简称,由广州、潮州、东江客家菜三种地方菜构成,但又各有特色。总的说来,粤菜有三大特点:第一,选料广博奇异,品种花样繁多,令人眼花缭乱。天上飞的,地上爬的,水中游的,几乎都能上席。第二,用量精而细,配料多而巧,装饰美而艳,而且善于在模仿中创新,品种繁多。第三,注重质和味,口味比较清淡,讲究清、鲜、嫩、爽、滑、香。著名菜肴有"烤乳猪"、"龙虎斗"、"太爷鸡"、"炖禾虫"、"狗肉煲"、"五彩炒蛇丝"、"菊花龙虎凤蛇羹"等。

闽菜:闽菜起源于福建省闽侯县,又称福建菜,拥有福州、闽南、闽西三路不同的技术和风味。闽菜具有四大鲜明特征:一为刀工巧妙,素有"剖花如荔、切丝如发、片薄如纸"的美誉;二为汤菜众多,变化无穷,素有"一汤十变"之说;三为调味奇特,偏于甜、酸、淡;四为烹调细腻,以炒、蒸、煨技术最为突出。代表名菜有"佛跳墙"、"鸡茸金丝笋"、"三鲜焖海参"、"班指干贝"、"鸡丝燕窝"、"荔枝肉"等。

苏菜:苏菜始于南北朝时期,唐宋以后,与浙菜一起成为"南食"两大台柱。清代时,苏菜流行于全国,相当于现在川菜、粤菜的地位。苏菜中的一支——淮扬菜系曾为宫廷菜,目前国宴中的大多数菜肴仍属于淮扬菜。因此,淮扬菜又称国菜。苏菜主要由淮扬菜、苏锡菜、金陵菜、徐州菜组成。它以重视火候、讲究刀工而著称。其特点是浓中带淡,鲜香酥烂,原汁原汤,浓而不腻,口味平和,咸中带甜。其烹调技艺以擅长于炖、焖、烧、煨、炒而著称。烹调时用料严谨,注重配色,讲究造型,四季有别。著名菜品有"清汤火方"、"鸭包鱼翅"、"松鼠桂鱼"、"西瓜鸡"、"盐水鸭"等。

浙菜:浙菜由杭州、宁波、绍兴、温州等地的菜肴为代表发展而成。就整体而言,有比较明显的特色风格,概而言之有四:一为选料刻求"细、特、鲜、嫩";二为烹调擅长炒、炸、烩、熘、蒸、烧;三为注重清鲜脆嫩,保持主料本色和真味;四为形态精巧细腻,清秀雅致。久负盛名的菜肴有"西湖醋鱼"、"东坡肉"、"龙井虾仁"、"叫花童鸡"、"大汤黄鱼"、"爆墨鱼卷"等。

湘菜:湘菜即湖南菜,由湘江流域、洞庭湖区和湘西的地方菜组成。湖南人嗜辣如命,有一句话叫"江西人不怕辣,四川人辣不怕,湖南人怕不辣"。湖南湘菜的辣有香辣、麻辣、鲜辣、酸辣及苦辣。在湖南辣菜谱中,左宗棠鸡的辣度算是榜首。湘菜有其鲜明的特色:第一,选料广泛;第二,品味丰富,湖南现有不同风味的地方菜和风味名菜多达800多个;第三,刀功精妙,基本刀法有十几种之多;第四,擅长调味;第五,技法多样。著名菜品有"腊味合蒸"、"东安子鸡"、"麻辣子鸡"、"红煨鱼翅"、"汤泡肚"、"冰糖湘莲"、"金钱鱼"等。

徽菜:徽菜以沿江、沿淮、徽州三地区的地方菜为代表构成的。徽州菜素以烹制山珍野味著称。基本特点有:一、就地取材,选料严谨,四季有别,充分发挥安徽盛产山珍野味的优势;二、火功独到,使用不同控火技术,是徽菜形成酥、香、鲜独特风格的基本手段;三、烹调技法上以烧、炖、熏、蒸而闻名;四、讲究食补,以食补疗,药食并重,以食养身,在保持风味特色的同时，十分注意菜肴的滋补营养价值。著名菜品有"红烧果子狸"、"符离集烧鸡"、"火腿炖鞭笋"、"雪冬烧山鸡"、"葫芦鸭子"、"腌鲜桂鱼"、"火腿炖甲鱼"、"毛峰熏鲥鱼"等。

第二单元

汉服

汉服即汉族传统民族服饰的简称，又称为汉装、华服，主要是指清代以前，在文化发展和民族交融过程中形成的汉族服饰。这种服饰到了汉朝已全面完善并普及，汉人汉服由此得名。汉服的主要特点是交领、右衽、宽袖、束腰，用绳带系结，也兼用带钩等，给人洒脱飘逸的印象。这些特点都明显有别于其他民族的服饰。

汉服有礼服和常服之分。从形制上看，主要有"上衣下裳"制（裳在古代指下裙）、"深衣"制（把上衣下裳缝连起来）、"襦裙"制（襦，即短衣）等类型。其中，上衣下裳的冕服为帝王百官最隆重正式的礼服；袍服（深衣）为百官及士人常服，襦裙则为妇女喜爱的穿着。普通劳动人民一般上身着短衣，下穿长裤。配饰头饰是汉族服饰的重要部分之一。古代汉族男女成年之后都把头发绾成发髻盘在头上，以笄固定。男子常常戴冠、巾、帽等，形制多样。女子发髻也可梳成各种式样，并在发髻上佩带珠花、步摇等各种饰物。鬓发两侧饰博鬓，也有戴帷帽、盖头的。汉族人装饰还有一个重要特征就是喜欢饰玉佩玉。从朝代上看，汉服男装的式样基本有两种。一是自古传下来的大襟、右衽、交领、宽袍大袖、博衣裹带那种（秦汉服饰为代表），延续了商、周（春秋战国）、秦、汉、三国、两晋、南北朝、隋、唐、五代、宋、元、明，并影响了日本、朝鲜等国。日本和服最常见的式样就是这种。二是自隋唐开始盛行的圆领衫，延续了唐、五代、宋、元、明，也影响到日本、朝鲜等国。女装在早期和男装类似，也穿深衣，后来则以襦裙为主。汉族各朝服饰某些地方有些不同，但主体部分相同。西汉的深衣和明朝的汉服基本式样是相同的，只是在细枝末节上不同。春秋战国时期，服饰大致沿袭商代的服制，只是略有变化。衣服的样式比商代略宽松，衣袖有大小两式，领子通用矩领，没有钮扣，一般在腰间系带，有的在带上还挂有玉制的饰物。秦尚黑，所以秦的服饰标准色都是黑色，但式样依然是大襟右衽交领这种。

汉代的男子的服装样式，大致分为曲裾、直裾两种。曲裾，即为战国时期流行的深衣，汉代仍然沿用，但多见于西汉早期。到东汉，男子穿深衣者已经少见，一般多为直裾之衣，但并不能作为正式礼服。秦汉时期曲裾深衣不仅男子可穿，同时也是女服中最为常见的一种服式，这种服装通身紧窄、长可曳地，下摆一般呈喇叭状，行不露足。衣袖有宽窄两式，袖口大多镶边。衣领部分很有特色，通常用交领，领口很低，以便露出里衣。如穿几件衣服，每层领子必露于外，最多的达三层以上，时称"三重衣"。汉代的直裾男女均可穿着。这种服饰早在西汉时就已出现，但不能作为正式的礼服。原因是古代裤子皆无裤裆，仅有两条裤腿套到膝部，用带子系于腰间。这种无裆的裤子穿在里面，如果不用外衣掩住，裤子就会外露，这在当时被认为是不恭不敬的事情,所以外要穿着曲裾深衣。以后,随着服饰的日益完备,裤子的形式也得到改进,出现有裆的裤子,由于内衣的改进,曲裾绕襟深衣已属多余,所以至东汉以后,直裾逐渐普及,并替代了深衣。

魏晋南北朝时期,男子的服装有时代特色,一般都穿大袖翩翩的衫子。直到南朝时期,这种衫子仍为各阶层男子所爱好,成为一时的风尚。魏晋时期妇女服装承袭秦汉的遗俗,在传统基础上有所改进,一般上身穿衫、袄、襦,下身穿裙子,款式多为上俭下丰,衣身部分紧身合体,袖口肥大,裙为多折裥裙,裙长曳地,下摆宽松,从而达到俊俏、潇洒的效果。唐代官吏除穿圆领窄袖袍衫之外,在一些重要场合,如祭祀典礼时仍穿礼服。礼服的样式,多承袭隋朝旧制,头戴介帻或笼冠,身穿对襟大袖衫,下着围裳、玉佩等。襦裙是唐代妇女的主要形式。在隋代及初唐时期,妇女的短襦都用小袖,下着紧身长裙,裙腰高系,一般都在腰部以上,有的甚至系在腋下,并以丝带系扎,给人一种俏丽修长的感觉。中唐时期的襦裙的比初唐的较宽阔一些,其他无太大变化。

中国自古就被称为"衣冠上国、礼仪之邦",而"衣冠"便成了文明的代名词。

在漫长的历史中"汉服"逐渐成为汉人自我认同的文化象征。满族入主中国之后,为了在文化上打击汉族的民族自尊心,下令在全国推行剃头改服的制度,使汉族人的服装面貌产生了一个重大的变化,将延续了3000年的汉民族冠冕衣裳送进了坟墓。汉服文化以其独特的魅力,在中国服饰史上写下了灿烂的篇章,至今仍吸引着世人赞叹的目光。(刘双琴编著)

旗袍

旗袍起源于满族服饰,是民国时期中国妇女穿的一种带有传统风格的长衫,其式样从满族妇女的长袍演变而来,由于满族称为"旗人",因此称旗袍。改良后的旗袍诞生于20世纪初叶,30年代几乎发展到顶峰状态,全世界家喻户晓的旗袍,实际上正是指这一时期的旗袍,这是旗袍的黄金时代,旗袍很快从发源地上海风靡至全国各地,几乎成为中国女性的标准服装。当时上海是上流名媛、高级交际花的福地,她们热衷于奢华的社交生活和追赶时髦,引领了服饰风潮,使得旗袍很快流行全国。由于上海一直崇尚海派的西式生活方式,以致后来出现了"改良旗袍",从遮掩身体的曲线到显现玲珑突兀的女性曲线美,使旗袍彻底摆脱了旧有模式,成为中国女性独具民族特色的时装之一。经过多年的修正与改良,旗袍已经成为一种能很好体现女性曲线美的服装,用中国最传统的布料,丝绸、锦缎等,做成最中国的服装——旗袍,穿在发髻高挽身段窈窕的中国女子身上,以其流动的旋律、潇洒的画意与浓郁的诗情,表现出近代中国女性贤淑、典雅、性感、清丽,诠释着20世纪上半叶的中国城市女性特有的时尚性情与气质,那种东西方审美观的完美结合、东方的神韵,令人叹为观止,因此旗袍成为中国永恒的时装经典,被誉为近代中国女性时装的代表。

旗袍的样式很多,开襟有如意襟、琵琶襟、斜襟、双襟;领有高领、低领、无领;袖口有长袖、短袖、无袖;开衩有高开衩、低开衩;还有长旗袍、短旗袍、夹旗袍、单旗袍等。旗袍款式的变化主要是袖式、襟形的变化。经过20世纪上半叶的演变,旗袍的各种基本特征和组成元素慢慢稳定下来。旗袍成为一种经典女装。经典相对稳定,而时装千变万化。但时装设计师常从经典的宝库中寻找灵感,旗袍也是设计师灵感的来源之一。

旗袍的外观特征一般是右衽大襟的开襟或半开襟形式,立领盘纽、摆侧开衩,单片衣料、衣身连袖的平面裁剪等。开衩只是旗袍的很多特征之一,不是唯一的,也不是必要的。满族旗装大多采用平直的线条,衣身宽松,两边开叉,胸腰围度与衣裙的尺寸比例较为接近,在袖口领口有大量盘滚装饰,是精细的手工制作,适用各种刺绣、镶、嵌、滚等工艺。近代旗袍则进入了立体造型时代,衣片上出现了省道,腰部更为合体并配上了西式的装袖,旗袍的衣长、袖长大大缩短,腰身也越为合体,刺绣精细,式样简洁合体的线条结构代替精细的手工制作。

在经历了 20 世纪三四十年代的顶峰期后,随着新中国的建立,人们对衣着美的追求已完全转化成了对革命工作的狂热,旗袍所代表的悠闲、舒适的淑女形象在这种氛围里逐渐失去其生存空间,旗袍的鼎盛年代成为了历史。不过,在八、九十年代,却出现了一种具有职业象征意义的"制服旗袍"。为了宣传和促销等目的,礼仪小姐、迎宾小姐以及娱乐场合和宾馆餐厅的女性服务员都穿起了旗袍。随着九十年代以来女性理想形象的改变,高挑细长、平肩窄臀的身材为人们所向往,而作为最能衬托中国女性身材和气质的中国时装代表——旗袍,再一次吸引了人们注意的目光。

旗袍是近代兴起的中国妇女的传统时装,而并非正式的传统民族服装。它既有沧桑变幻的往昔,更拥有焕然一新的现在。旗袍本身就具有一定的历史意义,加之可欣赏度比较高,因而富有一定收藏价值。现代穿旗袍的女性虽然较少,但现代旗袍中不少地方仍保持了传统韵味,同时又能体现时尚之美,所以也具有一定的收藏价值。(刘双琴编著)

折扇

折扇,古称"聚头扇",或称为撒扇、折叠扇,以其收拢时能够二头合并归一而得名。是一种用竹木或象牙做扇骨、韧纸或绫绢做扇面的能折叠的扇子,用时须撒开,成半规形,聚头散尾。一把折扇主要由扇骨、扇页和扇面三部分构成。普通的折扇,一般用竹木做扇骨,韧纸做扇面。讲究一点的,扇面上还要题诗作画。高级的折扇,扇骨和扇叶往往要用象牙制作,有的还要雕刻出各种纹饰,扇面也大多带有名人的字画。

宋代之前,折扇就已经出现,但并不流行。到了宋代,折扇的生产已有相当规模。折扇盛行于明代,皇帝下诏命宫内工匠仿制高丽扇,吸取外来工艺制作,促进中国扇子发展。明清是折扇发展鼎盛期,用料贵重,制作精湛,扇骨上采用了各种艺术的表现手法,深得人们所爱。这种特殊的艺术形式,在不足盈尺的扇面上经丹青高手巧运匠心,精心布局,或山水花鸟,或人物动态,无不能小中见大,表现出美的情致和神韵。

最初,明宫中也不过使用竹骨茧纸薄面折扇而已。后来朝廷定制,每年多造重金折扇进献御前,这种习尚,在明代宫廷中,日盛一日。折扇选用材料,越选越精,极奇穷巧。扇骨有用象牙的,玳瑁的,檀香的,沉香的,棕竹的以及各种木料的。工艺则有螺钿的,雕漆的,漆上洒金的,退光洋漆的,等等。这些折扇骨,都刻有各种花样,备极奇巧。明永乐帝开始主导折扇潮流，他命人大量制作折扇，并在扇面上题诗赋词，分赠于大臣。一时折扇大贵，成为一种时尚。文人雅士学着互赠题诗词字折扇，表喻友情别意。手持折扇，成为当时生活中高雅的象征。折扇一旦流行，久盛不衰。在清代，折扇之随处可见，发展登峰造极。明清时，在折扇生产地——江南一带，出了很多名士，他们的风流才情，与折扇有着丝丝缕缕的关系。他们所营造出的江南如水的文化氛围，表现出柔情氤氲的诗画美境，通过以折扇为媒介，流传于皇宫、府第、闺室、民间、海外，而折扇也因为这些美画佳句而身价百倍。

根据制作材料和方法的不同，这些折扇命名也不一样。扇骨多而轻细的，叫春扇或者秋扇。以香料涂抹扇面的，叫香扇。可以藏在靴子中，以备行旅途中使用的，叫靴扇。更有一种以各色漏地纱为扇面，可以隔扇窥人的，叫瞧郎扇。还有一种左右可以打开，制成三层扇面，中间一层画着春宫画的，叫三面扇。

此外，根据制作式样各别，产地和制作人不同，而叫做黄扇、曹扇、潘扇、川扇、青阳扇等等。折扇的附属装饰品是扇坠，扇坠又往往根据材料质地分为不同品级。

相传制作折扇历史最久远的，是杭州的芳风馆。这家世代制售折扇为业，因此致富。在杭州城内购置一处别墅，花木竹石，十分精幽。其制作的小巧折扇，称"百骨扇"，扇骨可达一百之多，但一点儿不显得扇骨多而厚大。颜色古润苍细，是折扇中的传世古物。此外，成都、南京等地的折扇制造也很有名。

折扇在引风纳凉方面的作用，远不如蒲扇直截了当，但无论团扇，还是折扇，都是在实用基础上的进步，是对生活美化的装点。通常的说法认为，折扇是由日本传入中国的，来到中国的日本折扇，很快地在宋代的朝廷和文人学士中间广泛流传，博得了文学艺术家们众口一致的好评。最先接触到日本折扇的浙江匠师们很快地吸收了日本折扇艺术上的长处，并利用棕竹、湘妃竹、象牙、黄杨木、檀香木等为扇骨进行制作，在两边的扇柄上镌刻诗词字画、人物、花鸟、山水等，扇柄下还饰以玉坠或彩色丝绒编结而成的流苏，创造了具有中华民族独特艺术风格的折扇，给世界留下了宝贵的艺术财富。如今，中国成为世界上折扇最大的生产国和出口国，其生产的折扇销往许多国家。（刘双琴编著）

民间工艺

民间工艺在中国五千多年的文明中，占据着重要的位置，具有强大的生命力和鲜明的特色。民间工艺种类繁多，如剪纸、刺绣、印花布、蜡染、风筝、陶瓷、木刻、皮影、泥塑、年画等等。这些民间工艺有的是以日常生活用品为主，所以在设计制作的时候很注意其实用性；而结合婚嫁喜事和传统节令风俗的民间工艺品，则表现出强烈的装饰性。其中，剪纸和刺绣是中国民间工艺中的优秀代表。剪纸是一种镂空艺术和中国最为流行的民间艺术，用来裁减的材料可以是纸张、金银箔、树皮、树叶、布、皮、革等片状材料。剪纸是中国最古老的民间美术之一，许多地方逢年过节，婚丧嫁娶，乡民都会自备剪纸点缀墙壁、门窗、房柱、镜子等处，以表祈祷福寿，吉祥如意之意。全国各地都能见到剪纸，甚至形成了不同地方风格流派，比较著名的就有高密剪纸、佛山剪纸等等。总体而论，北方剪纸粗犷豪放、淳朴简练，南方剪纸则更倾于秀雅繁茂、精致和美。其中不乏群众喜闻乐见的题材，像八仙过海、百年好荷、麒麟送子、老鼠嫁女等。

剪纸手工艺术约在公元 6 世纪就已经出现。唐代，以剪纸招魂的风俗当时就已流传民间，剪纸手工艺术水平已极高，画面构图完整。宋代造纸业成熟，纸品名目繁多，为剪纸的普及提供了条件。如成为民间礼品的"礼花"，贴于窗上的"窗花"，或用于灯彩、茶盏的装饰。宋代民间剪纸的运用范围逐渐扩大，江西吉州窑将剪纸作为陶瓷的花样，通过上釉、烧制使陶瓷更加精美；民间还采用剪纸的形式，用驴、牛、马、羊等动物的皮，雕刻成皮影戏的人物造型。明、清时期剪纸手工艺术走向成熟，并达到鼎盛时期。民间剪纸手工艺术的运用范围更为广泛，举凡民间灯彩上的花饰，扇面上的纹饰，以及刺绣的花样等等，无一不是利用剪纸作为装饰再加工而成的。

中国民间常常将剪纸作为装饰家居的饰物，美化居家环境，如门栈、窗花、柜花、喜花、棚顶花等，都是用来装饰门窗、房间的剪纸。除南宋以后出现的纸扎花样工匠外，中国民间剪纸手工艺的最基本的队伍，还是那些农村妇女。女红是中国传统女性完美的一个重要标志，作为女红的必修技巧——剪纸，也就成了女孩子从小就要学习的手工艺。她们从前辈或姐妹那里要来学习剪纸的花样，通过临剪、重剪、画剪，描绘自己熟悉而热爱的自然景物，鱼虫鸟兽、花草树木、亭桥风景，以至最后达到随心所欲的境界，信手剪出新的花样来。中国民间剪纸手工艺术，犹如一株常春藤，古老而长青，它特有的普及性、实用性、审美性，具有了符合民众心理需要的象征意义。

刺绣，古称针绣，是用绣针引彩线，按设计的花纹在纺织品上刺绣运针，以绣迹构成花纹图案的一种工艺。因刺绣多为妇女所作，故又名"女红"。刺绣是中国古老的手工技艺之一，湖北和湖南出土的战国、两汉的绣品，水平都很高。唐宋刺绣施针匀细，设色丰富，盛行用刺绣作书画，饰件等。明清时封建王朝的宫廷绣工规模很大，民间刺绣也得到进一步发展，先后产了苏绣、粤绣、湘绣、蜀绣，号称"四大名绣"，各具风格，沿传迄今，历久不衰。

苏绣历史悠久，在宋代已具相当规模，在苏州就出现有绣衣坊等生产集中的坊巷。明代苏绣已逐步形成自己独特的风格，影响较广。清代为盛期，当时的皇室绣品，多出自苏绣艺人之手；民间刺绣更是丰富多彩。苏州刺绣，素以精细、雅洁著称。图案秀丽，色泽文静，针法灵活，绣工细致，形象传神。技巧特点可概括为"平、光、齐、匀、和、顺、细、密"八个字。针法有几十种，常用的有齐针、抢针、套针、网绣、纱绣等。绣品分两大类：一类是实用品，有被面、枕套、绣衣、戏衣、台毯、靠垫等；一类是欣赏品，有台屏、挂轴、屏风等。取材广泛，有花卉、动物、人物、山水、书法等。

粤绣，又称"广绣"。构图繁而不乱，色彩富丽夺目，针步均匀，针法多变，纹理分明，善留水路。粤绣品类繁多，欣赏品主要有条幅、挂屏、台屏；实用品有被面、枕套、床楣、披巾、头巾、台帷和绣服等。一般多作写生花鸟，富于装饰味，常以凤凰、牡丹、松鹤、猿、鹿以及鸡、鹅等为题材，混合组成画面。

湘绣，以湖南长沙为中心的刺绣品的总称。早期湘绣以绣制日用装饰品为主，以后逐渐增加绘画性题材的作品。湘绣的特点是用丝绒线（无拈绒线）绣花，劈丝细致，绣件绒面花型具有真实感，常以中国画为蓝本，色彩丰富鲜艳，十分强调颜色的阴阳浓淡，形态生动逼真，风格豪放。

蜀绣，又名"川绣"。是以四川成都为中心的刺绣品的总称。蜀绣以软缎和彩丝为主要原料。题材内容有山水、人物、花鸟、虫鱼等。针法经初步整理，有套针、晕针、斜滚针、旋流针、参针、棚参针、编织针等100多种。品种有被面、枕套、绣衣、鞋面等日用品和台屏、挂屏等欣赏品。蜀绣的特点是形象生动，色彩鲜艳，富有立体感，短针细密，针脚平齐，片线光亮，变化丰富，具有浓厚的地方特色。（刘双琴编著）

第三单元

八大古都

中国的都城是随着早期国家的建立而诞生的，古都数目众多，总数约在200处以上。在所有的王朝都城之中，特别著名的是北京、西安、洛阳、开封、南京、杭州、安阳以及郑州，称为"八大古都"。在历代古都之中，以八大古都所统治的地域最为广大，经历的年代最为悠久，在历史上所产生的影响最为重要。

北京是中华人民共和国的首都，是中国政治、经济、文化、交通和旅游中心，也是世界的历史文化名城和故都之一。北京在奴隶社会时期就是燕、蓟重镇，辽的陪都和金、元、明、清的故都，地上地下文物保存非常丰富，为世界闻名的历史文化古城。这座古城历史悠久，距今已有3000多年历史。现有天安门、人民英雄纪念碑、毛主席纪念堂、故宫、北海、天坛、颐和园、明十三陵、万里长城和中国猿人遗址等重要革命和历史文物。

西安位于关中平原渭河南部，原名长安，曾有周、秦、汉、西晋、前赵、前秦、后秦、西魏、北周、隋、唐各代建都于此，是中国历史上建都朝代最多、历时最久的城市。它是世界闻名的历史古城，遗存有大量地上地下文物，如西周的丰镐、秦阿房宫、汉长安城、唐大明宫遗址、大雁塔、小雁塔以及明钟楼、鼓楼、碑林等。周围还有秦俑博物馆、古咸阳城、半坡遗址等。公元前139年，西汉著名的外交家、旅行家张骞带领一支队伍，首次从长安出使西域，到达楼兰、龟兹、于田等地，开辟了中国历史上著名的"丝绸之路"。这条路穿越中亚、翻过帕米尔高原、直抵西亚。十几个世纪以来，它将中国的文化与印度、罗马及波斯文化联系起来，将中国的丝绸、火药、造纸及印刷术这些伟大的发明传到了西方，也将佛教、景教及伊斯兰教等及相关的艺术引入中国。自古以来，丝绸之路就一直是中外人民友好交往的纽带和桥梁。

洛阳古为豫州的一部分，地处洛河之阳而得名，因境内有伊、洛两水，也旧称伊洛。东与郑州市相连、南与平顶山市南阳市相邻、西与三门峡市相接，北隔黄河和焦作市相望。洛阳为中国著名的九朝故都，名胜古迹以市南龙门石窟最有名，城东白马寺是中国第一座佛寺，还有汉魏故城遗址、西周王城、隋唐故城遗址、关林以及大量的古墓葬。洛阳是中国著名的历史文化名城和重点旅游城市，是中国四大古都之一。先后有夏、商、西周、东周、东汉、曹魏、西晋、北魏、隋朝、唐朝、后梁、后唐、后晋共13个王朝在此建都。以洛阳城为都将近千年，仅次于西安,是中国历史上第二个建都时间最长的城市。

开封古称汴梁,位于中国版图的中部,地处中华民族历史文化摇篮的黄河之滨,是一座历史文化悠久的古城。自建城至今已有 2700 多年的历史。战国时期的魏国,五代时期的后梁、后晋、后汉、后周以及北宋和金七个王朝曾先后建国都于开封,故称"七朝都会"。文物古迹有铁塔、繁塔、龙亭、禹王台、大相国寺和北宋汴梁城遗址等。开封地理位置优越,气候温和,物产丰富,交通便利,文化教育发达,科技进步,经济繁荣,是中原地区的重要旅游城市和对外开放城市。

作为"八大名都"之一的南京,素有虎踞龙盘之称。"金陵自古帝王州",从中古到近现代,继孙吴之后,东晋、宋、齐、梁、陈、南唐、明朝、太平天国以及中华民国先后定都南京,共455 年,史称"十代故都",留下了丰富的文化遗产。境内文物古迹众多。越城、金陵邑遗址、六朝陵墓石刻、南唐二陵、明代城墙、太平天国天王府、孙中山临时大总统办公处和中山陵等大批历史遗迹,显示出强烈的古都特色。城市风景秀美。东南山峦起伏,西北江水环绕,城内绿树成荫,四十八景风光迷人,民俗风情引人入胜,想象当年秦淮河畔的旖旎风情,欣赏婉约可人的南京佳丽,相信你应该能彻底地体会到"江南佳丽地,金陵帝王州"意境。

杭州是中国古都之一。秦朝置钱塘县,隋朝为杭州治,五代时是吴越国都,南宋时以此为行都。杭州是世界著名的游览城市,名胜古迹很多,如西湖灵隐寺、岳庙、六和塔等。杭州以其美丽的西湖山水著称于世,"上有天堂、下有苏杭",表达了古往今来的人们对于这座美丽城市的由衷赞美。宋代大文豪苏东坡曾写道:"天下西湖三十六,就中最好是杭州"。西湖,她拥有三面云山,一水抱城的水光山色,她以"浓妆淡抹总相宜"的自然风光情系天下众生。杭州人文景观丰富多彩,古代庭园、楼阁、塔寺、泉壑、石窟、摩崖碑刻遍布,或珠帘玉带、烟柳画桥,或万千姿态、蔚然奇观,或山清水秀、风情万般,尤以灵隐寺、六和塔、飞来峰、岳王庙、西泠印社、龙井、虎跑等最为著名。因此古人说:"江南忆,最忆是杭州!"

安阳是甲骨文的故乡,《周易》的发源地。公元前 1300 年商王盘庚迁都于殷(今安阳市郊小屯一带),经八代十二王,历时 254 年。中华民族最早使用的文字——甲骨文、世界上最大的青铜器——司母戊大方鼎都在这里出土问世。著名的大禹治水、文王演易、妇好请缨、苏秦拜相、西门豹治邺、岳母刺字等历史故事都发生在这里。安阳文物古迹较多,境内共有国家级文物保护单位 8 处,省级文物保护单位 32 处。悠久的历史,灿烂的文化,为安阳留下了宝贵的历史文化遗产。

郑州曾为夏、商都城之一,为管、郑、韩等藩国的首府。辖区内发现有距今 8000 年的裴李岗文化,距今 5000 年的大河村、秦王寨等多种类型的仰韶文化与龙山文化遗址。悠久的历史给郑州留下了丰富的文化积淀,全市有各类文物古迹 1400 多处,其中国家级文物保护单位26 处。嵩山风景名胜区是全国 44 个重点风景名胜区之一和全国文明风景旅游区示范点,"天下第一名刹"少林寺就坐落在嵩山脚下,威震海内外的少林功夫从这里走向世界。这里还有中国最早的天文建筑周公测景台和元代观星台、中国宋代四大书院之一嵩阳书院、中国现存最大的道教建筑群中岳庙等。在郑州周围,还有星罗棋布的古城、古文化、古墓葬、古建筑、古关隘和古战场遗址,著名历史人物列子、子产、杜甫、白居易、高拱等出生在郑州。郑州地处中原腹地,为全国重要的交通枢纽,是新亚欧大陆桥上的重要城市。(刘双琴编著)

宫廷建筑

从秦始皇开始,宫廷建筑就成了中国建筑的重要组成部分。宫廷,是封建帝王居住的地方。为了显示皇家至高无上的地位和统领天下的威严,中国古代宫廷的设计、建筑都特别追求雄伟壮观和富丽华贵。古代宫廷的设计,一般分为前后两部分:前面是皇帝处理朝政的地方,后面是帝王、后妃们居住的地方。皇宫中的主要宫殿都建在一条南北中轴线上,两侧的建筑整齐而对称。重重院落,层层殿堂,展示了皇宫的齐整、庄严和浩大。

宫廷中的建筑,大都由金碧辉煌的大屋顶、朱红的木制廊柱、门窗和宽阔洁白的汉白玉台基组成。

宫廷建筑中的大屋顶不但华美壮丽,而且对建筑物起到了很好的保护作用。大屋顶层层飞翘的屋檐和屋角,使屋面形成了巧妙的曲线,这样,雨水从屋顶流下,会被排得更远,从而保护了木造的宫殿不受雨淋。大屋顶上装饰的鸟兽,不但给庄严的宫殿罩上了一层神秘的色彩,也对古建筑起到了固定和防止雨水腐蚀的作用。宫廷建筑的屋顶上,一般都铺设金黄色的琉璃瓦,因为金黄色象征皇权,所以只有王室才能使用这种颜色。

用木材建造房屋,是中国古代建筑的基本特点。宫廷建筑的梁柱、门窗等,都是用木材建造的,而且被漆成了象征喜、富的朱红色。有的地方,还描绘着龙凤、云海、花草等彩画。鲜艳的颜色,不但体现了帝王殿宇的华贵,也对木制的建筑起到了防潮、防蛀的保护作用。北京故宫的太和殿,就是中国最大的木结构大殿。

洁净宽阔的汉白玉台基,是雄伟宫殿的基座。北京故宫的太和殿就建在三层汉白玉台基上。台基四周的石柱和台阶上,雕刻着精美的石龙和各种花纹。中间皇帝专用的通道,用巨大的石料雕刻着海浪、流云和翻腾的巨龙,十分壮观。

几千年来,中国历代帝王都不惜人力、物力和财力,建造规模巨大的宫廷。可惜的是,这些辉煌的建筑大都在战火中毁坏了。许多宫廷建筑随着其主人离开历史舞台而烟飞灰灭,北京紫禁城是现今保存最好最完整的宫廷建筑。

北京故宫又称紫禁城,这里原为明、清两代的皇宫,住过 24 位皇帝,建造了许多宏伟壮丽的宫廷建筑,是世界现存最大、最完整的古建筑群,被誉为世界五大宫之首(北京故宫、法国凡尔赛宫、英国白金汉宫、美国白宫、俄罗斯克里姆林宫)。其建筑宏伟壮观,完美地体现了中国传统的古典风格和东方格调,是中国乃至全世界现存最大的宫殿,是中华民族宝贵的文化遗产,1961 年被列为全国重点文物保护单位。

天坛占地 272 万平方米,整个面积比紫禁城(故宫)还大些,有两重垣墙,形成内外坛,主要建筑祈年殿、皇穹宇、圜丘建造在南北纵轴上。坛墙南方北圆,象征天圆地方。圜丘坛在南,祈谷坛在北,二坛同在一条南北轴线上,中间有墙相隔。圜丘坛内主要建筑有圜丘坛、皇穹宇等,祈谷坛内主要建筑有祈年殿、皇乾殿、祈年门等。天坛以其布局合理、构筑精妙而扬名中外,它是明、清两代皇帝"祭天"和"祈谷"的地方,是中国现存最大的古代祭祀性建筑群,也是世界建筑艺术的宝贵遗产。

除了故宫、天坛外，颐和园、圆明园等也集中了中国历史上有名的宫廷建筑群。颐和园是中国最有名的园林，园中山清水绿，阁耸廊返，金碧辉煌，在中外园林史上享有盛誉，这里有全国最长的游廊——长廊，把远山近水连成一体，具有很高的艺术价值。（刘双琴编著）

寺庙建筑

中国是个多宗教的国家。既有土生土长的道教，又有从外国传入的佛教、伊斯兰教和基督教等。这些宗教各有各的建筑。道教的建筑称"宫"或"观"，佛教的建筑有寺、塔和石窟，伊斯兰教有清真寺，基督教有教堂。世界上不同宗教的建筑有不同的风格，但建立在中国大地上的宗教建筑，在融合了外国宗教建筑的特点后，都明显地"中国化"了。下面主要介绍遍布中国大地的佛教寺庙的建筑。

佛教的寺庙大都建在远离闹市的山中。中国各地许多景色秀美的山上，都建有寺庙，尤其是四大佛教名山五台山、峨眉山、九华山、普陀山，更是集中了中国历代著名的寺庙建筑。

佛教是由印度传入中国的，但中国的佛教建筑与印度的寺院大不相同。印度的寺院以塔为中心。中国的寺庙受古代建筑的影响，以佛殿为中心，整个寺庙的布局、殿堂的结构、屋顶的建造等，都仿照皇帝的宫殿，创造出了中国佛教建筑的特色。

中国寺庙的主要建筑都建在寺院南北的中轴线上，左右的建筑整齐对称。一般来说，中轴线从南往北的建筑有供奉着佛像的山门殿、天王殿、大雄宝殿、法堂以及藏经楼。建在这些大殿两侧的，有钟鼓楼和一些配殿、配屋及僧人们的生活区。整个寺院的建筑金碧辉煌，气势庄严。洛阳白马寺、恒山悬空寺、五台山佛教建筑是中国有代表性的寺庙建筑。

白马寺位于洛阳市城东 9 公里的地方。北靠邙山，南望洛水，绿树红墙，苍松翠柏，显得十分肃穆。白马寺占地面积大约 4 万平方米，是一个长方形的院落，院内主要有天王殿、大雄殿、千佛殿、观音阁、毗卢阁等。其中最主要的殿堂是大雄殿。白马寺不仅为中外旅游者游览、观赏，而且也是许多国家的佛教徒朝拜的圣地。

白马寺是中国官方营建的最早的佛寺，是汉明帝刘庄在洛阳按照佛教的要求和传统式样建造的。白马寺建成后，佛教在中国的势力大大发展起来，对人们的思想和生活都产生了很大的影响。此后，佛教又从中国传播到越南、朝鲜和日本等国，对中外文化起了推动作用。所以，白马寺被称为佛教的"祖庭"。

山西省境内北岳恒山悬空寺，这是一座凌空架起的寺院，表现了古代工匠高超的智慧和技巧。上靠危岩，下临深谷，造型独特，是极为罕见的建筑。悬空寺位于浑源县城南 3.5 公里处的金龙峡谷西侧绝壁的山腰上，是中国现存唯一的建于悬崖上的木构建筑。始建于北魏时期，唐、金、明、清历代均有修葺。整个建筑面对恒山，背依翠屏，壁岩无阶，高楼仰止，是北岳恒山第一奇观。

山西省的五台山是中国著名的佛教圣地之一。五台山上的佛教建筑非常多，保存至今的就有 58 处。其中南禅寺和佛光寺比较著名。南禅寺面积不大，南北长 60 米，东西宽 51.3 米。它建

于唐代建中三年（782 年），是中国现在保存下来的一座最早的木结
构寺院建筑。佛光寺建于唐代大中十一年（857 年），因为寺内有"四绝"：塑
像、壁画、墨迹和建筑，被称为"世间的瑰宝"。佛光寺在建筑上荟萃了中国各个时期的建筑形
式。这座寺院建筑在半山腰，上下共三个院落，各个院落都有殿、堂、房、舍等各种建筑。佛光寺
外形朴实，比如寺庙的柱子、斗拱、门窗、墙壁等没有什么花花绿绿的色彩，一律涂成土红色。

中国的寺庙建筑，各派、各地、各民族又有不同的风格。如喇嘛教寺庙建筑的特点是佛殿
大、经堂高，建筑多依山势而筑；藏族的寺庙建筑以土木石结构相结合，以木结构为主，大经
堂为三层建筑，墙体用块石砌成，厚而窗子小，给人非常浑厚稳定的感觉。位于西藏拉萨的布
达拉宫，是中国最著名的寺庙建筑之一，既具有典型的唐代建筑风格，也吸取了尼泊尔和印
度的建筑艺术特色，历来为中外旅游者所称道。（刘双琴编著）

第四单元

货币

中国是世界上使用货币最早的国家之一。中国的货币，至少已有 4000 多年的历史。

在货币出现以前，人们主要靠以物换物的形式来交易，这样非常不方便，于是货
币就出现了。中国最早的货币出现在商朝（前 17 世纪—前 11 世纪），起初的货币还主要是贝
壳。到了商代后期，出现了铜贝，这是我国最早的金属货币。铜贝，作为货币在商代还尚未广
泛使用。到了春秋时期（前 770—前 476 年），铜贝才被普遍使用。此外，在春秋战国时期（前
770—前 221 年），各个国家还流行着许多不同形态的货币。但其中楚国出现的一种"郢爰"，
那是我国最早的金币。这让中国成为最早使用贵金属——黄金作货币的国家。

公元前 221 年，秦始皇统一了中国，同时统一了当时的货币。当时规定黄金为上币，以铜
钱为下币，并且规定铜钱一律采用"圆形方孔"的外形。从此，我国的货币形态基本固定为
"圆形方孔"，并延续了 2000 多年，一直沿用到清末。

汉兴元年（338 年），在中国货币史上首次出现了年号钱。这种钱被称为"汉兴钱"，它是
昭文帝李寿于汉兴元年铸的，所以叫"汉兴钱"。"汉兴钱"是中国最早的年号钱。

唐朝(618—907 年)，是中国古代社会发展的高峰。政治、经济、文化空前发展。货币方面也
有重大的改革。唐代货币的名称与重量完全分离，钱币不再以重量来计算，而改称"通宝"，即
通行的宝货。其中"开元通宝"是唐朝三百年间最主要铸币。在唐代，还出现一种名叫"飞钱"
的票证。商人售货获得大量货币，如果将他们随身带回家，这样既不安全也不方便，于是他们
便将货币交当地相关机构和富人。这些机构和富人便会给商人半联票据，另外半联寄给商人
所在地的相关机构。商人回家后，便可凭票据去取款。飞钱有点类似于今天银行的汇票。

宋朝（960—1279 年）是铸币业比较发达的时期，从数量和质量上都超过了前代。北宋
（960—1127 年）货币以铜钱为主，南宋（1127—1279 年）货币以铁钱为主。同时，白银的流通

亦取得了重要的地位。最为重要的是,在北宋年间出现了世界上最早的纸币——"交子",其后陆续出现其他种类的纸币:"会子"和"关子",并且纸币占的地位越来越重要。北宋纸币"交子"首先在四川民间出现,是当地方言票券的意思。"交子"最初是一些商人发明的,用于代替铜、铁钱的流通。用纸币代替金属货币,既方便又安全,深受人们的欢迎。随后,北宋政府设立机构,发行官方纸币——"交子"。南宋出现的"会子"和"关子"与"交子"一样,也是一种纸币,只不过它们流通的范围更大。

元朝(1271—1368 年),那时主要行使纸币,同时确立了白银在货币流通中的重要地位。银锭统称"元宝"即来源于元朝。元初曾一度禁止使用铜钱,后来虽然铸过不少种类的铜钱,但数量较少。用以流通的主要是纸币,白银的流通量也占有较大比例。

明朝(1368—1644 年),大力推行纸币——钞,明初只用钞不用铜钱,后来改为铜钱和钞兼用,但明代只发行了一种纸币——大明宝钞。白银在明代成为了法定的流通货币,大交易多用银,小交易用钞或钱。明朝所有钱币统称"通宝"。

清朝主要以白银为主,小额交易往往用钱。清初铸钱沿袭 2000 多年前的传统,采用模具制钱,后期则仿效国外,用机器制钱。另外,清朝和民国还有一种外来货币形态比较流行,那就是银圆。虽然银圆最早在明朝万历年间(1573—1620 年)由西班牙流入中国,但是在清朝才使用的比较普遍。清乾隆五十八年(1793 年),清朝政府首次在西藏铸行"清乾隆宝藏"银币。道光年间(1821—1850 年),台湾、福建等地也曾仿制银圆,称为银饼。光绪十五年(1889 年),广东开铸"光绪元宝"银圆,从此各省纷纷效仿。宣统二年(1910 年),清朝政府颁布《币制则例》,规定银圆为本位币,但因辛亥革命爆发而未正式发行。

民国元年(1912 年),国民政府开铸孙中山开国纪念币。1914 年铸造袁世凯侧面一元银币,老百姓一般称之为"袁大头"。1935 年国民政府实行货币改革,禁止银圆流通。

中华人民共和国成立后,各种银圆均由中国人民银行按一定比价收兑,禁止流通。

货币在中国有着悠久的历史,而宋代出现的纸币则在世界货币发展史上具有重大的意义。在西方首次使用纸币的是在瑞士,由瑞士银行在 1661 年发行,这比中国宋朝出现的纸币——"交子"晚了约 500 年。

中医中药

中国传统医学简称为"中医"。中医有着几千年悠久的历史,早在战国时期(前 221 年)就出现了比较系统的医学理论著作《黄帝内经》。中医是世界上唯一没有中断过的医学体系,至今在治疗疾病方面仍发挥着重要的作用。

在医学理论上,中医虽然以人体为对象,但是它把人体看做是自然界整体的一部分,不是孤立地去研究人体。因此,在其病理学说中,非常重视疾病与人体自身精神状态、生活状态以及外部环境,特别是气候变化的关系。在临床治疗中,它反对单纯的"头痛医头,脚痛医脚",强调要掌握疾病出现的根本原因,针对不同的情况进行治疗。同时,它又把人体本身看做一个有机的整体,不是简单、孤立地研究疾病的症候,而是把各脏腑、经络、气血、津液等紧密地联系在一起,

进行全面的考察。在用药方面,它讲究药物配伍的原则,即根据每个
病人各自的特性,因人施药,并注意主治药物和辅助性药物的搭配。这些理
论和原则,即使用现代科学观点和方法来加以考察,也是非常深刻和具有积极意义的。

在中医不断发展的历程中,逐渐总结出来了一套独特的诊治方法,这就是"望、闻、问、
切"。望,就是观察病人形体、脸色、舌体、舌苔,根据形色变化确定病位、病性,也称为望诊。
闻,就是医生凭听觉和嗅觉辨别病人的声音和气味的变化测知病性的方法,也称为闻诊。问,
就是通过询问病人和家属,了解疾病的发生与发展过程,以及目前症状及其他与疾病有关的
情况,也称为问诊。切,就是切按病人的脉搏和触按病人的皮肤、手、腹部,四肢及其他部位以
诊断疾病的方法,也称为切诊。在四种诊断方法中,切脉诊断是中医药学上一项独特的诊断
方法。切脉诊断的应用表明,中国古代的医生已掌握了脉象与身体各部分关系的知识,也就
是关于心脏、血液与血管的关系,血流速度与人体健康的关系,呼吸和脉搏频率的关系等解
剖生理学的知识。这种诊断方法很早就传到国外,除邻近的日本、朝鲜等国外,大约在10世
纪时已传至阿拉伯,17世纪时传至欧洲。

在治疗方面,中医主要采用针灸疗法。针灸疗法是中医一种独特的医疗方法。其特点是
治病不靠吃药,只是在病人身体的某个部位用针刺入,或用火的温热刺激烧灼局部,以达到
治病的目的。前一种称作针法,后一种称作灸法,统称"针灸疗法"。根据古代医学经络学说,
经络遍布人体各个部位,有运送全身气血、沟通身体上下、内外的功能。穴位则是经络系统的
控制机关,刺激穴位可以起调节经络系统作用。针灸疗法非常神奇,其治疗效果也非常明显,
许多外国学者因此称中国为"针灸的祖国"。

在药物方面,中国历代的医学家对3000多种植物、动物、矿物的性能、功效、用法都有详
细的研究和记载,并将这些植物、动物、矿物作为原料,配制成汤剂和丸、散、膏、丹等不同类
型的成药。中国传统的药物,也被称为中药。

中医在不断地发展过程中,还保留了许多著名的医学著作。如成书于东汉时期的《神农
本草经》,世界上的第一部药学专著。这比欧洲出现的药学书至少要早16个世纪;东汉张仲
景所著的《伤寒杂病论》,是世界上的第一部临床医学专著,它比阿拉伯医学家阿维森纳所
著的《医典》要早数百年;宋朝宋慈所著的《洗冤集录》,是世界上第一部系统的法医学专
著;明朝李时珍所著的《本草纲目》,则被称誉为"东方医学巨典",先后被译成多种外文出
版。这些医学著作使得中医能够代代相传,从未中断过。

在中医历史上,还出现了一些著名的医生,比如华佗、扁鹊、张仲景等等。其中,东汉时期
的名医华佗,他第一次使用麻醉剂——麻沸散,进行全身麻醉。国外直至1805年,日本的华
冈青州才使用以曼陀罗花为主的麻醉剂,被誉为世界外科学麻醉史上的首创,但这比中国的
华佗要晚得多。

中医是中国独特的医学体系,它对医学有着重要的贡献,有人甚至称它为"中国四大发
明"之外的第五大发明。(黎清编著)

象棋

象棋，又称中国象棋，是中华民族发明的一种娱乐活动。象棋具有悠久的历史，它大约起源于战国时期。经过历代的发展，象棋于北宋末定型成近代模式：32 枚棋子，有河界的棋盘。

象棋是由两人轮流走子，以"将死"或"困毙"对方将（帅）为胜的一种棋类运动。对局时，由执红棋的一方先走，双方轮流各走一着，直至分出胜、负、和，对局即结束。轮到走棋的一方，将某个棋子从一个交叉点走到另一个交叉点，或者吃掉对方的棋子而占领其交叉点，都算走一着。双方各走一着，称为一个回合。象棋不仅能丰富文化生活，陶冶情操，更有助于开发智力，启迪思维，锻炼辩证分析能力和培养顽强的意志。

象棋共有 32 个棋子，分为红黑两组，各有 16 个，由对弈的双方各执一组。双方兵种都是一样的，分为 7 种：帅（将）、仕（相）、车、马、炮、兵（卒）。红方有：帅一个，仕、相、车、马、炮各两个，兵五个。黑方有将一个，士、象、车、马、炮各两个，卒五个。其中帅与将；仕与士；相与象；兵与卒的作用完全相同，仅仅是为了区别红棋和黑棋而已。棋子活动的场所，叫做"棋盘"。在长方形的平面上，绘有 9 条平行的竖线和 10 条平行的横线相交组成，共有 90 个交叉点，棋子就摆在交叉点上。中间部分，也就是棋盘的第五、第六两横线之间未画竖线的空白地带称为"河界"。两端的中间，也就是两端第四条到第六条竖线之间的正方形部位，以斜交叉线构成"米"字方格的地方，叫做"九宫"（它恰好有九个交叉点）。整个棋盘以"河界"分为相等的两部分。为了比赛记录和学习棋谱方便，人们规定：按九条竖线从右至左用中文数字一至九来表示红方的每条竖线，用阿拉伯数字 1—9 来表示黑方的每条竖线。比赛开始之前，红黑双方应该把棋子摆放在规定的位置。任何棋子每走一步，进就写"进"，退就写"退"，如果像车一样横着走，就写"平"。中华人民共和国成立以后，1956 年起象棋被列为我国国家体育项目，近年来，在全国性比赛中，除男子个人赛，又先后增加了男子团体、女子个人、女子团体等比赛项目。成绩优异的棋手由国家体委授予"象棋大师"和"特级大师"等称号。

1978 年 11 月间，在东南亚一些地区和国家的侨胞名流和棋界人士的发起与合作下，亚洲象棋联合会应运而生。现在，菲律宾、马来西亚、泰国、新加坡、印尼、中国、文莱、中国香港、澳门地区都是"亚洲象棋联合会"的成员。香港名流霍英东先生曾出任会长。为了推动象棋的国际化，在此基础上，"中国象棋联合会筹委会"于 1988 年在北京成立。第一届世界杯象棋锦标赛于 1990 年在新加坡举行。

在西方国家，有一种与中国象棋相似的棋类，称为国际象棋。国际象棋由黑白两棋组成，执白先行，国际象棋的对局目的是把对方的王将死。国际象棋棋盘是个正方形，由横纵各 8 格、颜色一深一浅交错排列的 64 个小方格组成。深色格称黑格，浅色格称白格，棋子就放在这些格子中移动。棋子共 32 个，分为黑白两组，各 16 个，由对弈双方各执一组，兵种是一样的，分为六种：国王（1 个）、皇后（1 个）、城堡（2 个）、主教（2 个）、骑士（2 个）、兵卒（8 个）。在比赛中，当一方的国王受到对方棋子攻击时，成为王被照将，攻击方称为"将军"，此时被攻击方必须立即"应将"，如果无法避开将军，王即被将死。除"将死"外，还有"超时判负"与"和局"。如果出现以下情况，就算和局：一方轮走时，提议作和，对方同意；双方都无法将死对方王时，判和；一方连续不断将军，对方王却无法避开将军时，成为"长将和"；轮到一方走棋，王没有被将军，但却无路可走，成为"逼和"；对局中同一局面出现三次，而且每次都是同一方走的，判为和局。

近年来，象棋在欧美有了可喜的发展。美国、法国等国纷纷成立象棋协会或象棋社。中国象棋与国际象棋一道，成为欧美国家一种比较流行的棋类活动。（黎清编著）

武术

武术，也叫中国功夫，是中国传统的技击术，同时也是一种独特的中国文化。它是以踢、打、摔、拿、击、刺等技击动作作为主要内容，通过徒手或借助于器械的身体运动表现攻防格斗的能力。武术主要包括套路和散手两种运动形式。武术套路，它由风格各异的技术动作组成，具有攻防内涵、蕴含哲理，有很高的观赏价值，给人以美的享受。武术套路形式有拳术、器械、对练和集体项目。拳术主要包括长拳、南拳、太极拳、形意拳、八卦掌等。器械有刀、剑、棍、枪、双刀、双剑、九节鞭、三节棍等。对练项目分为徒手对练、器械对练以及徒手对器械的三种类型。集体项目是多人进行拳术、器械演练的形式。这些不同的套路形式，不仅体现了武术的攻防格斗内涵，同时又具有优雅美观、节奏鲜明的风格特点。武术散手是徒手格斗运动的一种形式。

经过几千年的发展，中国武术逐渐形成了一些自己的特点，主要有：第一，重视"身心和谐"。中国武术将人体生命看做是一个大系统，心与身是统一的，将人作为一个整体来看待和训练。他们认为，人体是武功的载体，武功的强弱与武功载体的强弱密切相关。载体的强壮又可分为外部强壮和内部强壮，外部强壮固然重要，但更重要的还是内部强壮。以外练形体、内练精气神为训练对象，练意、练气、练力，是武术练功的三要素。第二，重视"人际和谐"，与人为善。在武术的形成和发展过程中，武术不仅逐渐形成一整套自己独特的理论、技术、功法，也形成了一套与武术密切相关的道德体系，这就是人们常说的武德。尽管中国武术门派众多，并且每个门派都有各自不同的风格特点，但是武术各家各派都非常注重武德，注意人与人之间的和谐，处理人际关系时都强调宽厚、容忍。还制定了各自的一套严格的尊师重道、扬善惩恶的戒律规范，如："习武先习德"，以求人际的和谐。在中国武术中，对武术人物和武术事件的评价，都是以武德作为衡量的标准和依据。第三，重视"天人和谐"，即宇宙自然与自身的统一，这是中国武术养练功法的核心内容之一。他们认为，作为武术运动对象的主体——人体自身，与宇宙自然的客体，二者有着内在的紧密联系，武术家们往往通过领悟宇宙的变化规律而用于拳法，创造出不同的拳法种类。例如通过观察蛇的生活习性，武术家们创造出了"蛇拳"、

在中国武术中，少林寺具有重要的地位。少林寺位于河南省登封城西的少室山（属嵩山），因此又叫做嵩山少林寺。少林寺有着悠久的历史，它始建于北魏太和十九年（495年）。唐朝初年，少林寺的13位武僧帮助秦王李世民在讨伐王世充的征战中取得了胜利。后

来，李世民当上了唐朝的皇帝，少林寺得到了李世民的赞誉和封赏。在此期间，由于朝廷的大力支持，少林寺发展非常快，获得了"天下第一名刹"的美称，少林功夫也从此美名远扬。在中国，人们都认为"天下功夫出少林"。特别是1982年李连杰主演的电影《少林寺》拍摄成功以后，少林寺和少林功夫更是风靡一时。同时，少林寺的巨大影响还传播到世界其他国家。许多外国人纷纷来到少林寺学习功夫。少林寺在40多个国家成立了少林功夫协会。在美国和德国等一些国家还建立了少林寺，由少林寺的武僧传授少林功夫，深受人们的欢迎和喜爱。

在中国，还有一种武术非常普及，那就是太极拳。极拳起源于中国，它是一种动作刚柔相济，既可技击防身，又能增强体质、防治疾病的传统拳术。太极拳在疏经活络、调和气血、营养腑脏、强筋壮骨等方面具有很好的功效。

太极拳经过长期流传，演变出许多流派，其中流传较广或特点较显著的有以下5派：陈式太极拳，杨式太极拳，吴式太极拳，武式太极拳，孙式太极拳。太极拳在中国非常普及，在许多公共场所，人们都可以看见有人在打太极拳。太极拳在国外，也受到普遍欢迎。欧美、东南亚、日本等国家和地区，都有太极拳活动。据不完全统计，仅美国就已有30多种太极拳书籍出版，许多国家也都成立了太极拳协会等团体。

中国武术还流行于电影，由李小龙、成龙、李连杰演的中国功夫电影在好莱坞深受欢迎，许多外国人也因此喜欢上了中国功夫。（黎清编著）

曲艺

曲艺是中华民族各种说唱艺术的统称，它是由民间口头文学和歌唱艺术经过长期发展而演变形成的一种独特的艺术形式。它以"说"或"唱"为主要的艺术表现手段。据调查统计，在中国仍活跃在民间的曲艺品种大概有400个左右，存在于全国各地。在众多曲艺中，流传较广、比较有影响的主要有：相声、小品、评书、评弹、京韵大鼓、快板和二人转等。

相声，起源于北京，流行于全国各地。一般认为相声形成于清朝。是以说笑话或滑稽问答引起观众发笑的曲艺形式。相声主要用北京话讲，各地也有以当地方言说的"方言相声"。相声的表演形式主要有单口、对口、群口三种。单口相声由一个演员表演，讲述笑话；对口相声由两个演员表演；群口相声又叫"群活"，由三个以上的演员表演。相声采用的艺术手段主要有：说、学、逗、唱。"说"，就是叙说笑话和打灯谜、绕口令等；"学"，就是模仿各种鸟兽叫声、叫卖声、唱腔和各种人物表情、语言等；"逗"，是互相逗笑；"唱"专指唱太平歌词。相声经过长时间的发展，出现了一批著名的相声演员，主要有：侯宝林、马三立、马季、姜昆等。相声不仅在中国非常受欢迎，外国人也非常喜欢相声，并且学习相声。加拿大人大山(Mark Rowswell)在1989年底，就拜著名相声表演艺术家姜昆为师。之后他不断在各地的舞台上和电视屏幕上进行演出。成了一位家喻户晓的"洋笑星"。

小品，指较短的关于说和演的艺术，它的基本要求是语言清晰，形态自然，能够充分理解和表现出各个角色的性格特征和语言特征。小品是一种即兴式的表演，但它需要演员具有丰

富的生活阅历和鲜活的生活语言。在小品中，最具代表性的是喜

剧小品。中国喜剧小品起源于20世纪80年代初，它是在继承和发展话剧、相声、二人转、小戏等优点的基础上发展起来。著名的喜剧小品演员有：赵本山、陈佩斯等。

评书，也叫评词，流行于华北、东北、西北一带；在南方则称为评话。它是中国人民创造的一种口头文学。评书的表演形式，早期为一人坐于桌子后面，以折扇和醒木为道具。醒木是一种敲击桌面的木块。常在开始表演或中间停歇时使用，用来提醒听众安静或警示听众注意力，以加强表演效果。演员一般身着传统长衫，说演讲评故事。发展至20世纪中叶，多为不用桌椅及折扇、醒木等道具，而是站立说演，衣着也不固定为专穿长衫。评书使用的语言以北方语音为基础，以北京语音为标准音调的普通话进行说演。因使用口头语言说演，所以在语言运用上，以第三人称的叙述和介绍为主。著名的评书演员有单田芳等。

评弹，又称苏州评弹，是苏州评话和弹词的总称。是一门古老、优美的说唱艺术。评话通常是一人登台表演，表演内容多为历史演义和侠义豪杰。弹词一般两人说唱，以琵琶为伴奏乐器，自弹自唱，内容多为儿女情长的传奇小说和民间故事。评弹主要以苏州方言来进行说唱。评弹是一种形式灵活，音乐优美动听的说唱艺术，被称为"中国最美的声音"。

京韵大鼓，主要形成于北京、天津两地。在1946以前，京韵大鼓有过许多种不同的称谓。1946年，北京成立曲艺公会后，正式统一名称为"京韵大鼓"。京韵大鼓主要伴奏乐器为大三弦与四胡，有时配以琵琶。演员自击鼓、板掌握节奏。京韵大鼓比较重视歌唱，主要唱一些短篇曲目。

快板，最初是乞丐沿街乞讨时的一种演唱活动，后来经过艺人不断的创造，逐渐形成一种特殊的曲艺形式。快板的表演形式一般由演员站着手持竹板敲出节奏，伴以押韵的语言。快板讲究口头即兴编词，看见什么就说什么，擅长随编随唱，表达自己的见解，抒发感情。这要求演员具备良好的语言能力。

二人转，也叫"蹦蹦"。它产生并盛行于东北三省(辽宁、吉林、黑龙江)，受到东北群众、特别是农民的喜爱。它是一种有说有唱、载歌载舞、生动活泼的走唱类曲艺形式，迄今大约已有200年的历史。二人转的主要表演形式为：一男一女，服饰鲜艳，手拿扇子、手绢，边走边唱边舞，表现一段故事，唱腔高亢粗犷，唱词诙谐风趣。它的唱本语言通俗易懂，幽默风趣，生活气息浓厚、富有地方特色。著名的二人转演员有赵本山等。

中国曲艺种类非常繁多，极大地丰富了人们地娱乐活动。同时，由于中国曲艺具有深厚的中国文化内涵，它也深受外国人的喜欢。(黎清编著)

民族乐器

在古代，中国人发明制造了许多具有民族特色的乐器。这些造型特色各异的乐器，演奏出美妙丰富的音律，悦耳动人的声音，非常受人们喜欢。中国乐器大都能够表达细微的感情及复杂的感情变化。中国的民族乐器非常多，至今存在并比较受人们青睐的主要有：箫、竹笛、古筝、古琴、二胡等。

箫，又名洞箫，是一种非常古老的乐器。它由竹子制成，为直吹乐器。箫历史悠久，与笛同源。箫的音色非常圆润轻柔，幽静典雅，在夜深人静的时候吹奏乐声更为幽美悦耳。在中国，演奏箫这种乐器时一般不叫"吹箫"，而尊称为"品箫"。那是因为，人们认为箫具有非常高的品位，只有道德情操非常高的人才能用箫吹奏出优美的音律。所以，中国古代读书人都非常喜欢箫这种乐器。后来，箫还传播到国外，其吹奏出来的音乐深受人们的欢迎。在1896和1913年的伦敦和巴拿马国际展赛会上，中国的玉屏箫分别获得金奖和银奖，这是中国在世界上首次获奖的乐器。

竹笛，也称笛子，由一根竹管做成的横吹乐器。竹笛在中国有着非常悠久的历史，在汉代著名史书司马迁的《史记》中就有笛子的记载。竹笛具有强烈的民族特色，发出的声音清脆、明亮，给人以美的享受。因此，竹笛被外国人称赞为"具有如此奇妙的音响及不可替代的民族性"。竹笛在中国非常普遍，即便在农村都有许多人会吹奏竹笛。

古筝，一种弦乐器。古筝是一种非常古老的民族乐器。据汉代历史学家司马迁在《史记》中记载，古筝在战国时期的秦国比较盛行。而在1979年，通过考古发现，在江西省贵溪县仙岩东周墓葬群中也发现了筝这种乐器。可见，古筝在中国有着非常悠久的历史。在唐宋时，古筝一般为13根弦，后来逐渐增加到16根弦、18根弦、21根弦、25根弦等，目前最常用的古筝为21根弦。演奏方法为右手大指、食指、中指三指拨弦，弹出旋律、掌握节奏，用左手控制弦音的变化。古筝的音域非常宽广，音色优美动听，被称为"众乐之王"，也被人称为是"东方钢琴"。

古琴，又称七弦琴，为中国最古老的弹拨乐器之一。古琴在孔子时期就已经非常盛行，它在中国历史上流传了3000余年不曾中断，在20世纪初才被称作"古琴"。琴一般长约三尺六寸五（约120~125公分），象征着一年365天。古琴最初只有五根弦，后增加为七根弦，所以又称七弦琴。古琴的音律虚静高雅，要达到这样的意境，则要求弹琴者必须将外在环境与平和的内在心境合而为一，才能达到很好的艺术境界。在中国古代社会，"琴、棋、书、画"历来被视为文人雅士修身养性的必由之径。因此，古琴千百年来一直是中国古代文人、士大夫手中爱不释手的乐器。直至今日，古琴音乐依然作为中国音乐的灵魂与精髓，铸刻在美国"旅行者"号太空飞船的镀金唱片里，昼夜不息地回响在茫茫的太空之中，寻觅着宇宙间的"知音"。2003年11月7日，联合国教科文组织在巴黎总部宣布了世界第二批"人类口头和非物质遗产代表作"，中国的古琴名列其中。

二胡，始于唐朝，至今已有1000多年的历史。它最早发源于中国古代北部地区的少数民族，所以又叫"胡琴"。它是一种拉弦乐器。明朝和清朝时期，胡琴已传遍全中国，成为民间戏曲伴奏和乐器合奏的主要演奏乐器。到了近代，胡琴才更名为二胡。二胡的音色具有柔美抒情的特点，发出的声音极富歌唱性，宛如人的歌声。在中国，著名的二胡乐曲有阿炳的《二泉映月》等。阿炳的《二泉映月》以它深沉、悠扬而又不失激昂的乐声，撼动着千百万人的心弦。它不仅在国内深得人民喜爱，在国际乐坛上也获得了很高的评价。世界著名指挥家小泽征尔对该曲的评价是："我应该跪下来听。"

中国乐器由于其独特的民族特色和民族风格，为世界音乐提供了各种独具特色的审美样式，富有中国文化内涵。（黎清编著）

中国画

中国画在古代没有确定的名称,一般称之为丹青,主要指的是画在绢、宣纸、帛上并加以装裱的卷轴画。近现代以来,为了区别西方的油画(又称西洋画)等外国绘画而称为中国画,简称"国画"。它是用中国所独有的毛笔、水墨和颜料,依照长期形成的表现形式及艺术法则而创作出的绘画。

中国画按其使用材料和表现方法,可分为水墨画等;按其题材又有人物画、山水画、花鸟画等。中国画在思想内容和艺术创作上,反映了中华民族的社会意识和审美情趣,体现了中国人对自然、社会及与之相关联的政治、哲学、宗教、道德、文艺等方面的认识。

水墨画,中国画的一种。指纯用水墨所作之画。相传始于唐代,成于五代,盛于宋元,明清及近代以来仍有发展。以笔法为主导,充分发挥墨的功能。认为墨的浓淡变化就是色的层次变化,色彩缤纷可以用多层次的水墨色度来代替。唐代王维认为画是"水墨为上",后人继承了这种观点。长期以来水墨画在中国绘画史上占着重要地位。

人物画,指以人物形象为主体的绘画。中国的人物画,简称"人物",是中国画中的一大画科,出现较山水画、花鸟画等为早;大体分为道释画、仕女画、肖像画、风俗画、历史故事画等。人物画力求人物个性刻画得逼真传神,形神兼备。其传神之法,常把对人物性格的表现,寓于环境、气氛、身段和动态的渲染之中。故中国画论上又称人物画为"传神"。著名人物画画家有东晋的顾恺之等。

山水画,简称"山水"。中国画的一种。指以描写山川自然景色为主体的绘画。在魏晋、南北朝已逐渐发展,但仍附属于人物画,作为背景的居多;隋唐开始独立;五代、北宋山水画大兴,出现了许多著名画家,如米芾、米友仁父子,成为中国画中的一大画科;元代山水画趋向写意,以虚带实,侧重笔墨神韵,开创新风;明清及近代,继续发展,并出现了一些新的面貌。

花鸟画,中国画的一种。它主要以动植物为主要描绘对象。中国花鸟画集中体现了中国人与自然生物之间的一种审美关系,具有较强的抒情性。它往往通过动植物抒写画家自己的思想感情,体现时代精神,间接反映社会生活,在世界各民族同类题材的绘画中表现出十分鲜明的特点。著名的画家有清代的朱耷,近代的吴昌硕等。

中国画具有鲜明的中国特色,与西方绘画存在着较大的差异。中国画重神韵,西洋画重形似。两者比较起来,主要有以下几个不同点:

第一,中国画常用线条,西方绘画线条都不显著。线条大都不是物象所原有的,而是画家用以代表两物象之间的境界。西方绘画则不是这样,只有各物的界,界上并不描线。所以西方的绘画很像实物,而中国画不像实物,一望而知其为画。

第二,中国画不注重透视法,西方绘画非常注重透视法。透视法,就是在平面上表现立体物。西方绘画力求肖似真物,故非常讲究透视法。而中国画就不如此,它不讲究透视法,想到哪里,画到哪里,不受透视法的拘束。

第三,中国人物画不讲解剖学,西方人物画很重解剖学。西方绘画中画人物画,必须描得同真的人体一样。但中国画中的人物画,目的只在表出人物的姿态和特点,却不讲人物各部分的尺寸与比例。故不用写实法而用象征法。不求形似,而求神似。

第四,中国画不重背景,西方绘画很重背景。中国画不重背景,例如写梅花,一支悬挂空中,四周都是白纸。所以中国画的画纸,留出空白的地方很多。西方绘画就不如此,凡物必有背景,例如果物,其背景为桌子。人物,其背景为室内或野外。故画面全部填涂,不留空白。中国画与西方绘画的这一差别,也是由于写实与传神的不同而产生的。西洋画重写实,所以必须描绘背景;中国画重传神,所以必须删除琐碎而特写其主题,以此增强画的主题。

第五,中国画题材以自然为主,西方绘画题材以人物为主。中国画在汉代以前,也以人物为主要题材。但到了唐代,山水画占了主要地位。一直到今日,山水常为中国画的正格。西方自希腊时代起,一直以人物为主要题材。中世纪的宗教画,大都以人物为题材。

中国画有着独特的艺术魅力,特别是近现代以来,在继承传统和吸收外来技法的基础上,中国画有了更进一步的发展。(黎清编著)

第五单元

四书五经

"四书五经"是"四书"和"五经"的合称,是中国儒家经典的书籍。"四书"指的是:《论语》《孟子》《大学》和《中庸》;而"五经"指的是《诗经》《尚书》《礼记》《周易》和《春秋》。

《论语》是记载孔子及其学生言行的一部书。孔子(前551—前479年),名丘,字仲尼,春秋时鲁国陬邑(今山东省曲阜)人,是儒家学派创始人,中国古代最著名的思想家、政治家、教育家,对中国思想文化的发展有极其深远的影响。《论语》成书于春秋战国之际,是孔子的学生及其再传学生所记录整理。《论语》涉及哲学、政治、经济,教育、文艺等诸多方面,内容非常丰富,是儒学最主要的经典。

《孟子》是记载孟子及其学生言行的一部书。孟子(约前372—前289年),名轲,字子舆,战国中期邹国(今山东省邹县东南人)。孟子是著名的思想家、政治家、教育家,孔子学说的继承者。

《大学》原本是《礼记》中一篇,在南宋以前从未单独刊印。《大学》相传为孔子学生曾参(前505—前434年)写作。南宋时,朱熹将《大学》从《礼记》中抽出来,与《论语》《孟子》《中庸》并列,成为四书之一。并且,朱熹还将它列为四书之首。

《中庸》原来也是《礼记》中一篇,在南宋前也从未单独刊印过。相传为孔子的孙子子思(前483—前402年)所作。南宋时,朱熹将《中庸》从《礼记》中抽出来,成为四书之一。

《诗经》在先秦称《诗》或《诗三百》,是中国第一本诗歌总集,汇集了从西周初年到春秋中期五百多年的诗歌305篇,是西周初至春秋中期的诗歌总集。传说为孔子编定。《诗经》分"风"、"雅"、"颂"三部分,"风"为地方歌谣,"雅"为西周王室雅乐,"颂"为上层社会祭祀的歌辞。此书广泛地反映了当时社会生活各个方面,被誉为古代社会的人生百科全书,对后世影响深远。

《尚书》古时称《书》《书经》,至汉称《尚书》。该书是古代最早的一部历史文献汇编。记载上起传说中的尧舜时代,下至东周,约1500多年时间的历史。基本内容是古代帝王的文告和君臣谈话内容的记录。《尚书》有两种版本,一种是《今文尚书》,一种是《古文尚书》。

《礼记》是战国到秦汉年间儒家学者解释说明经书《仪礼》的文章选集,是一部儒家思想的资料汇编。《礼记》虽只是解说《仪礼》之书,但由于涉及面广,其影响乃超出了《仪礼》。《礼记》有两种传本,一种是戴德所编,有85篇,现在存有40篇,称《大戴礼记》;另一种,也便是我们现在所见的《礼记》,是戴德的侄子戴圣选编的49篇,称《小戴礼记》。

《易经》在中国传统文化的经典著作中,被誉为诸经之首。《易经》也叫做《周易》,共有24,070字。《易经》分本经和大传两部分。本经是《易经》的主体,故称为经;大传为解释《易经》而作,故曰传。《易经》将总结出来的生活经验和生产经验,用抽象的符号记录下来,用来说明宇宙间的一切现象和规律。

《春秋》原是先秦时代各国史书的通称,后来仅有鲁国的《春秋》传世,便成为专称。这部原来由鲁国史官所编《春秋》,相传经过孔子整理、修订,赋予特殊的意义,因而也成为儒家重要的经典。《春秋》是我国编年体史书之祖,记载了242年间的历史。它的文句极简短,几乎没有描写的成分。但它的语言表达,具有严谨精炼的特点。《春秋》最突出的特点就是寓褒贬于记事的"春秋笔法"。相传孔子按照自己的观点对一些历史事件和人物作了评判,并选择他认为恰当的字眼来暗寓褒贬之意,因此《春秋》被后人看做是一部具有"微言大义"的经典。并且,在史书和文学作品的写作上,也对后人产生了很大的影响。

"四书五经"是南宋以后儒学的基本书目,儒生学子的必读之书。特别是其中的"四书",南宋以后各个朝代都以"四书"为科举考试的范围,因而使"四书"在中国古代非常普及。"四书五经"在古代中国具有重要的地位,几乎与《圣经》《古兰经》的地位相似。

"四书五经"在社会规范、人际交流,社会文化等方面对中国人产生不可估量的影响。时至今日,"四书五经"所载的内容及哲学思想仍对我们现代人具有积极的意义和极强的参考价值。"四书五经"对国外也有非常深的影响,已经成为人类文明的共同遗产。(黎清编著)

唐宋八大家

唐宋八大家是唐宋时期八位著名散文代表作家的合称,即唐代的韩愈、柳宗元和宋代的苏洵、苏轼、苏辙(苏洵是苏轼、苏辙的父亲,苏轼是苏辙的哥哥。又称"三苏")、欧阳修、王安石、曾巩。在明朝初年,朱右将以上八位散文家的文章编成《八先生文集》,八大家之名始于此。不久以后,茅坤又选了以上八位散文家的文章,编为《唐宋八大家文钞》,唐宋八大家的名称于是固定下来，为后人所沿用。

韩愈（768—824 年），又称韩昌黎，河阳（今河南省孟州市）人，祖籍河北昌黎，所以又称韩昌黎。他是唐代杰出的文学家、思想家，古文运动的领袖，"唐宋八大家"之首，在中国散文发展史上有着崇高的地位。他在科举和仕途上屡受挫折，思想倾向复古，提倡儒家正统思想。他领导了唐代的"古文运动"，反对华而不实的形式主义文风。他提出的文道合一的写作理论，对后人具有指导意义。他的作品都收集在《昌黎先生集》中。

柳宗元（773—819 年），祖籍河东（今山西省永济市），又称柳河东。柳宗元生于长安，贞元初年考取了进士。他是唐代著名的思想家和杰出的文学家。作为唐代古文运动倡导者和唐宋八大家之一，柳宗元反对过去文坛上出现的绮靡浮艳文风，提倡质朴流畅的散文。著有《柳河东集》。

欧阳修(1007—1072 年)，北宋时期政治家、文学家、史学家和诗人，又称醉翁。吉安永丰（今属江西）人出生于绵州（今四川绵阳）。欧阳修在政治和文学上都主张革新，既是范仲淹庆历新政的支持者，也是北宋诗文革新运动的领导者。他喜欢奖掖后进，苏轼父子及曾巩、王安石都是他的学生。他的诗、词、散文创作在当时都非常著名。他的散文说理畅达，抒情委婉，为"唐宋八大家"之一。他的著作为《欧阳文忠公文集》。欧阳修死后葬于开封新郑（今河南新郑）。

苏洵（1009—1066 年），著名散文家。他与他的儿子苏轼、苏辙合称"三苏"。眉州眉山（今四川眉山）人。苏洵擅长写作散文，特别擅长写议论政治的散文。他的散文议论明畅，笔势雄健。著有《嘉佑集》。据说苏洵 27 岁才开始发愤读书，经过十多年的努力学习，最终在文学上取得了很大的成就。

苏轼（1037—1101 年），在诗、词、散文、书画等方面都取得了杰出的成就，又称"苏东坡"。眉州眉山（即今四川眉山）人，是苏洵的第五个儿子。嘉祐二年（1057 年）与弟苏辙一起考取进士。元丰二年（1079 年），苏轼遭遇"乌台诗案"，被贬官流放。著作有《东坡七集》等。苏轼的文学主张与欧阳修一脉相承，但更强调文学的独创性、表现力和艺术价值。苏轼散文风格平易流畅，豪放自如。苏轼是继欧阳修之后主持北宋文坛的领袖人物，在当时的作家中间享有巨大的声誉，当时和他交往或接受他指导的人非常多。苏轼是中国历史上少有的文学和艺术天才。

苏辙(1039—1112 年)，眉州眉山(今属四川)人。与他的父苏洵、哥哥苏轼合称为"三苏"。当他的哥哥苏轼因为写诗被捕入狱时，他请求以自己的官职为哥哥赎罪。苏辙的学问深受他的父亲和哥哥影响。苏辙在古文写作上主张"养气"，认为"养气"既在于内心的修养，但更重要的是依靠广阔的生活阅历。苏辙著有《栾城集》。

王安石（1021—1086 年），又称王荆公，世称临川先生。抚州临川人（今江西抚州）。北宋杰出的政治家、思想家、文学家、改革家。熙宁三年（1069 年），王安石为宰相，开始大力推行改革。王安石不仅是一位杰出的政治家和思想家，同时也是一位卓越的文学家。他为强调文学的作用首先在于为社会服务。因为王安石以"适用"作为文学创作的根本，所以他的作品多揭露时弊、反映社会矛盾，具有较浓厚的政治色彩。著作有《王临川集》等。

曾巩(1019—1083 年)，南丰(今江西抚州南丰县)人。北宋文学家，"唐宋八大家"之一。曾巩在政治上表现得并不算是很出色，他的更大贡献在于学术思想和文学事业上。曾巩在思想上强调"仁"和"诚"。曾巩的散文创作成就很高，是北宋诗文革新运动的积极参加者。他的文章主要学习司马迁、韩愈和欧阳修，主张用文章来阐明道德。曾巩的文章对后世的影响很大。明代散文家王慎中、唐顺之等，清代散文家方苞、姚鼐等都非常尊崇他的文章。曾巩一生的著作非常丰富，主要著作有《元丰类稿》等。

唐宋八大家的散文代表了唐宋散文的最高成就，他们的文章也成为中国古代散文的优秀典范。（黎清编著）

唐诗

唐诗，即唐代诗歌。唐代是中国古典诗歌发展的全盛时期。唐诗是我国优秀的文学遗产之一，尽管离现在已经有 1000 多年了，但唐代的许多诗篇还是在今天广为流传。其中清代人选编的《唐诗三百首》，便是几百年来家喻户晓的唐诗选本。

唐代的诗人非常多，犹如天空中的星星，今天我们知道名字的诗人就有 2300 多人，此外还有许多不知道名字的。他们的作品，保存在《全唐诗》中的就有 48900 多首。唐诗的形式也是多种多样的，有古体诗，基本上是五言和七言两种，以及近体诗，包括绝句和律诗。绝句和律诗又各有五言和七言的差别。近体诗有严格的音律要求，所以有人又称它为格律诗。

唐代诗歌主要分为：初唐诗歌、盛唐诗歌、中晚唐诗歌。初唐诗歌，是唐诗繁荣的准备时期。在这一时期，重要诗人有被称为"初唐四杰"的王勃、杨炯、卢照邻、骆宾王。此外，还有陈子昂、沈佺期、宋之问等。在初唐阶段，唐代诗歌的样式已经基本形成。盛唐诗歌。到公元 8 世纪初，唐朝出现了所谓的"开元盛世"，经济、文化发展达到鼎盛。诗歌创作领域也出现了大批优秀诗人，创作了异常丰富的诗歌，成为唐代诗歌史上的鼎盛阶段。其中描写田园山水和边塞战争的诗占相当大的比重。"诗仙"李白和"诗圣"杜甫也出现在这一时期。中晚唐诗歌。唐代中后期，唐朝的鼎盛时期虽然已经过去，但当时的诗歌创作还是没有衰歇，先后出现了韩愈、柳宗元、李贺、白居易、元稹、刘禹锡、杜牧、李商隐、温庭筠等风格不一的杰出诗人。他们的诗从不同角度反映了唐朝从强盛走向衰落的过程，艺术性比较高，对后世影响也很大。

唐代诗歌，出现了两位非常重要的诗人，那就是"诗仙"李白和"诗圣"杜甫。这两位诗人在中国诗歌史上地位非常高，后世许多诗人都曾受到过他们的影响。

李白（701—762 年），祖籍陇西（今甘肃省）。李白创作了许多天才的诗歌，是浪漫主义诗歌的代表人物，其代表作品有《望庐山瀑布》等。他的诗歌主要特点是：第一，他的诗具有浓烈的激情。李白胸怀开阔，爱憎分明，高兴时喝酒唱歌，仰天大笑；悲愤时哭笑怒骂，无所避忌。第二，李白具有丰富的想象力。灵感来时有如闪电，灵感去时有如疾风，变幻莫测。古今历史人物，天文地理知识，虚幻的神话，常常成为他诗歌中的内容。第三，李白常用夸张的语言来抒发激情。如用"白发三千丈"来描写他的愁思。正因为如此，李白被人们称为"诗仙"。

杜甫（712—770 年），生于河南省巩县，杜甫出生于富有文化教养的家庭，祖父杜审言是一位著名的诗人。杜甫诗歌中的代表作品有"三吏"、"三别"等。杜甫是现实主义诗歌的代表人物,他创作了大量反映当时社会生活的诗歌。杜甫的诗歌主要体现了古代优秀知识分子的良心。虽然杜甫自身比较贫困,但是他能够与百姓同忧乐,在诗歌中书写人民悲惨的命运和遭受的不公平。在这方面,他是中国传统知识分子的典范。杜甫一生的心血都用在写诗上,其诗具有丰富的内容,纯真的热情,深沉的激愤,凝重的格调。在这方面,他又是诗人学习的榜样。他"读书破万卷",善于学习和继承传统;他"语不惊人死不休",写诗态度严肃认真,无论古体诗还是近体诗,都写得出神入化。因此,杜甫也被人们称作"诗圣"。在四川省成都市,至今还留有一处杜甫的遗迹,这就是"杜甫草堂"。"杜甫草堂"成为历代人们特别是诗人瞻仰和怀念杜甫的地方,吸引着无数人的到来。

唐诗,是唐代最具代表性的文学样式,几乎成为唐代文学的一个代名词。唐诗是中国诗歌史上的一座高峰,此后历代诗人都或多或少地从中汲取营养,丰富和提高自己的诗歌创作水平,但都难以达到与唐诗相同的高度。同时,唐诗也已经成为一个文化符号,成为中国传统文化中的一个基本要素。(黎清编著)

宋词

宋词,即宋代的词,是继唐诗之后在宋朝出现的又一种文学体裁,历来与唐诗并称双绝。词是一种音乐文学,所以又称为曲子词。它的产生、发展以及创作、流传都与音乐有关系。词起源于隋朝,形成于中晚唐,兴盛于宋朝。《全宋词》一共收录了宋朝词人有 1330 多人,将近有两万首词。从这一数字可以知道当时宋词创作的盛况。宋词都有词牌,例如满江红,西江月等等,它规定着词的格式。创作词时必须按照词牌所规定的格式来进行写作。宋词在发展过程中,出现了许多著名的词人。其中的代表人物主要有:晏殊、晏几道、柳永、苏轼、周邦彦、李清照、辛弃疾、姜夔等。

晏殊(991—1055 年),江西省临川人,北宋前期著名词人。他的词集为《珠玉词》,共收录词 130 余首。晏殊的词多表现他的诗酒生活和悠闲情致,语言含蓄婉丽,音韵和谐,颇受南唐冯延巳的影响。在晏殊词中有一首《浣溪沙》,其中的两句"无可奈何花落去,似曾相识燕归来",成为千古传诵的名句。

晏几道,是晏殊的第七个儿子,也是一位著名的词人。他的《小山词》收录词 200 多首。在词中,他怀念往事,抒写哀愁,饱含感伤,情感深沉真挚,具有极高的艺术境界。以致人们认为他的词"能动摇人心"。在词的成就上,晏几道与其父齐名,世称"二晏"。

柳永(约 987—1053 年),福建武夷山人。是北宋第一位专业写作词的词人,其代表作有《雨霖铃》。柳永年轻的时候有过一段都市和妓院生活的经历,所以他的词比较多的描绘了宋朝的都市生活,尤其是他与歌女和妓女间有交往和爱情。他的词具有通俗化和口语话的特点,词作流传极广。他的词不仅为妓女们所喜爱,而且皇帝也非常喜欢。据说,在当时,凡是有人的地方就会有人唱柳永的词。柳永的词集为《乐章集》,有词约 200 首。

苏轼(1037—1101 年),四川省眉山人,北宋著名词人。苏轼的词现存 340 多首,改变了过去专写男女恋情和离愁别绪的狭窄题材,具有广阔的社会内容。

苏轼在中国词史上具有重要而特殊的地位。他改革了晚唐、五代以来的传统词风,在词的创作中采用诗的创作方法,开创了与婉约词派并立的豪放词派,丰富了词的意境,对词的革新和发展做出了重大贡献。名作有《念奴娇》《水调歌头》等,开豪放词派的先河,与辛弃疾并称"苏辛"。

周邦彦(1056—1121 年),浙江杭州人,北宋著名词人。周邦彦精通音律,因此他的词在音律上非常严谨。周邦彦的词多表现男女恋情,语言精致典雅,极具艺术性。周邦彦在宋代影响非常大,是北宋末年婉约词派的"集大成"者。他的词集为《清真词》,又名《片玉词》。

李清照(1084—1155 年),山东省济南人。李清照出生于一个爱好文学艺术的家庭,是南北宋之交著名的词人,也是中国文学史上最伟大的女词人。李清照的词前期多写悠闲的生活和相思的情感;后期多抒发命运的飘零,情调非常感伤。她擅长以女性特有的视角,表达丰富、细腻的情感。她反对以写诗文的方法写作词。她代表词有《声声慢》等。她的词集有《漱玉词》。同时,李清照还是中国历史上唯一一位名字被用作月球环形山的女性。

辛弃疾(1140—1207 年),山东省济南人,南宋著名词人。在历史上,他与苏轼并称为"苏辛",与李清照并称"济南二安"。辛弃疾的词热情洋溢、慷慨悲壮,风格雄厚豪迈,形成一种以豪放为主的词风。他的词被称做是"词中之龙"。辛弃疾在苏轼的基础上,大大开拓了词的意境,提高了词在文学上的地位。

姜夔(约 1155—1221 年),江西鄱阳人,南宋著名的音乐家和著名词人。姜夔童年时便失去父母,在姐姐家度过了青少年时期。他爱好音乐、文学和书法。他的词以凄凉为主要风格,形成一种与婉约和豪放不同的"清雅"词风。另外,姜夔曾在自己创作的词旁,标注了一种中国古代使用的乐谱。这是现今唯一保留下来的有关宋词的音乐文献,具有重大价值。姜夔的词集为《白石道人歌曲》。

宋词是中国古代文学皇冠上一颗光辉夺目的钻石。它被称为是"中国诗中最美的诗"。它所具有的艺术感染力,至今陶冶着人们的情操,给人们带来很高的艺术享受。(黎清编著)

元曲、杂剧

元曲,即元代戏曲,它包括元散曲和元杂剧,是元代文学主体。元曲和唐诗、宋词并举,成为我国文学史上三座重要的里程碑。由于元杂剧的成就和影响远远超过散曲,因此元曲也经常单指元杂剧。现在,我们主要介绍元杂剧。

13世纪后半期是元杂剧最繁盛的时期。元杂剧作为一种新型的完整的戏剧形式,有其自身的特点和严格的体制。它形成了歌唱、说白、舞蹈等有机结合的戏曲艺术形式,并且产生了韵文和散文结合的,结构完整的文学剧本。

元杂剧具有完整、严密的结构,"四折一楔子"是元杂剧最常见的剧本结构形式。即每个剧本一般由四折戏组成,有时再加一个楔子。所谓的"折"相当于现在的"幕",是音乐单元,也是全剧矛盾冲突的自然段落;"四折"即是开端、发展、高潮、结尾四个阶段。元杂剧在四折戏外，为了交代情节或贯穿线索，往往在全剧之首或折与折之间，加上一小段独立的戏，称为"楔子"。

元杂剧的角色分为旦、末、净、杂。旦包括正旦、外旦等。正旦为杂剧中主要的女演员，外旦为杂剧中次要的女演员。末包括正末、副末等。正末是杂剧中主要的男演员，副末是杂剧中次要的男演员。净是地位低下的喜剧性人物。杂是除以上三类外的演员。有孤（官员）、驾（皇帝）等。元杂剧一般由一个人主唱或男、女主角唱，主唱的角色不是正末，就是正旦。正旦主唱称旦本，如《窦娥冤》。正末主唱的称为末本，如《汉宫秋》。

在元杂剧中还有宾白和科介。宾白，也称说白。它是除唱词以外演员说的话，包括人物的对白和独白。科介，也称为科，指唱、白以外的动作。一般来说，元杂剧剧本中的科表示四个方面的意思：一、表示人物一般的动作，二、表示人物的表情，三、表示武打动作和舞蹈，四、有时也表示剧中的舞台效果。

元杂剧在发展繁荣的过程中，出现了许多优秀的剧作家和作品。这其中有被称为"元曲四大家"的关汉卿、马致远、郑光祖和白朴。

关汉卿，大都人（今北京市人），元代著名的杂剧作家。关汉卿生平事迹不详，根据相关资料来看，他是金末元初人，活跃于约 1210 年至 1300 年间。主要在大都（今北京）附近活动，也曾到过杭州等地。他的成就主要是在杂剧创作方面，一生写了 60 多种杂剧，今存 18 种，最著名的有《窦娥冤》。关汉卿对后代影响非常巨大，水星上有一座环形山就是以他的名字命名的。

马致远（约 1250—1323 年），元代初期杂剧作家，大都人（今北京人）。他的杂剧特点是：语言清新，善于把比较朴实自然的语句变得精致而富有表现力。代表作有《汉宫秋》等。《汉宫秋》被后人称作元曲的最佳杰作。同时，马致远也是撰写散曲的高手，是元代散曲大家，今存散曲约 130 多首。他的写景作品《秋思》，如诗如画，余韵无穷。

郑光祖，山西襄汾县人，生卒年不详，元代著名的杂剧家。郑光祖一生写过 18 种杂剧剧本，其中以《倩女离魂》最为著名，描写的是王文举与倩女之间的爱情故事。在他的杂剧中，主要有两个主题：一个是青年男女的爱情故事，另一个是历史题材故事。

白朴，原名恒，后改名为朴。他生于 1226 年，1306 年还在世，此后行踪不详。白朴出身官员家庭，他的父亲是一个进士，也是一个官吏。他的著名杂剧作品有《梧桐雨》，描写唐朝皇帝李隆基和杨玉环之间的爱情故事。对清代洪升的戏曲《长生殿》有着重大影响。

在元杂剧中，还有所谓的"元曲四大悲剧"，即：关汉卿的《窦娥冤》，白朴的《梧桐雨》，马致远的《汉宫秋》，还有纪君祥的《赵氏孤儿》；以及"元曲四大爱情剧"，即：关汉卿的《拜月亭》，王实甫的《西厢记》，白朴的《墙头马上》，郑光祖的《倩女离魂》。

元杂剧是一种非常具有中国传统特色的戏曲艺术形式。在《宋元戏曲史》中，王国维先生高度称赞元杂剧为"中国最自然之文学"。

在元曲繁荣过后，戏剧继续向前发展，并取得了非常大的成就。明代出现了汤显祖的"临川四梦"——《牡丹亭》《紫钗记》《邯郸记》《南柯记》。之所以又称为"临川四梦"，是因为作者是临川人，并且四部戏剧中都涉及梦境。

汤显祖和他的"临川四梦"在中国戏剧史上具有重要的地位和影响，特别是《牡丹亭》，

在舞台上演出了 400 来年,非常受欢迎。据说,有一位娄江的女读

者俞二娘在读了《牡丹亭》以后,终日郁郁寡欢,最后忧愁而死。就是在今天,

《牡丹亭》依然在舞台上演出,并进入各个大学校园。在 20 世纪初期,汤显祖的剧作就不断

翻译成各国文字,在国外争相上演,并大受欢迎。正是由于汤显祖的杰出戏剧创作,他被人们

称为"东方的莎士比亚"。中国戏剧也因此在世界舞台上发挥着重要的影响。(黎清编著)

明清小说

明清是中国小说的繁荣时期。从明代始,小说这种文学形式就充分显示出了其社会作用和文学价值,打破了正统诗文的垄断地位。在文学史上,小说取得与唐诗、宋词、元曲并列的地位。清代则是中国古典小说盛极而衰并向近现代小说转变的重要时期。

明清时期,小说家创作的小说非常众多,其中就有后来人们所公认的"四大名著",即:《三国演义》《水浒传》《西游记》《红楼梦》。

《三国演义》,作者为明朝罗贯中。它是中国古代第一部长篇章回小说,是历史演义小说的经典之作。小说描写了公元 3 世纪以曹操、刘备、孙权为首的魏、蜀、吴三个政治、军事集团之间的矛盾和斗争。在广阔的社会历史背景上,展示了那个时代尖锐复杂又极具特色的政治军事冲突。《三国演义》的艺术成就最主要的是在战争描写和人物塑造上。《三国演义》描写了大大小小的战争,构思宏伟,手法多样,使我们清晰地看到了一场场刀光剑影的战争场面。其中官渡之战、赤壁之战等战争的描写波澜起伏、跌宕起伏,读来惊心动魄。

同时,《三国演义》刻画了近 200 个人物形象,其中最为成功的有诸葛亮、曹操、关羽、刘备等人。诸葛亮是作者心目中的"贤相"的化身,他被作者赋予了呼风唤雨、神机妙算的奇异本领;曹操是一位奸雄,他既有雄才大略,又残暴奸诈;关羽非常重义气;刘备被作者塑造成为仁民爱物、礼贤下士、知人善任的仁君典型。

《三国演义》在政治、军事谋略方面,对后世产生了深远的影响。《三国演义》是古代历史小说中成就最高、影响最大的一部作品,它广泛流传,魅力无穷,在中国文学史上和人民生活中都有着难以估量的深远影响。至今,人们还不断从中得到人才学、军事学、领导科学、商战技术等各个角度的启示。《三国演义》也深受外国读者欢迎。《三国演义》早在 1569 年就已经传入朝鲜。1635 年《三国演义》被英国牛津大学收藏。此后,日本、英国、法国、俄国等都使用本国文字翻译过《三国演义》。

《水浒传》为明朝施耐庵著,另说为施耐庵、罗贯中合著。《水浒传》以它杰出的艺术描写手段,揭示了中国封建社会中以宋江为首的农民起义的发生、发展和失败的过程。《水浒传》的社会意义在于它深刻揭露了封建社会的黑暗和腐朽以及统治阶级的罪恶,说明造成农民起义的根本原因是"官逼民反"。《水浒传》的故事情节非常曲折,故事性很强,善于在叙事中刻画人物,李逵、武松、林冲、鲁智深等成为妇孺皆知的文学形象。《水浒传》的语言以口语为主,无论是作者描述的语言,还是作品中人物的语言,都是惟妙惟肖,极具个性,是中国第一部用通俗口语写成的长篇小说。《水浒传》对中国文学和社会都有着巨大的影响。此外,

《水浒传》还传播到了国外。其中，在众多英译本中，最早的是赛珍珠女士在 1920 年代中后期翻译的 "All Men Are Brothers"（《四海之内皆兄弟》）。它于 1933 年出版，是《水浒传》的第一个英文全译本，当时在美国颇为畅销。迄今为止《水浒传》被认为比较好的英文版本，应该是中国籍的美国犹太裔学者沙博理先生（Sidney Shapiro）翻译的 "Outlaws of the Marsh"（水泊好汉）。这个译本，被认为更忠实于原著。

《西游记》，明朝吴承恩著。故事叙述唐僧与徒弟孙悟空、猪八戒、沙僧和他的坐骑白龙马，经过八十一次磨难，到西天取经的过程。《西游记》向人们展示了一个绚丽多彩的神魔世界，人们无不惊叹于作者丰富而大胆的艺术想象。《西游记》是古代长篇小说浪漫主义的高峰，在世界文学史上，它也是浪漫主义的杰作。《美国大百科全书》认为它是"一部具有丰富内容和光辉思想的神话小说"，《法国大百科全书》认为"全书故事的描写充满幽默和风趣，给读者以浓厚的兴味"。从 19 世纪开始，它被翻译为日、英、法、德、俄、等 10 多种文字流行于世。

《红楼梦》，成书于清朝乾隆年间，章回体古典长篇小说，是中国现实主义文学的经典之作。现在通行的《红楼梦》为 120 回，前 80 回的作者为曹雪芹，后 40 回的作者一般认为是高鹗。以贾宝玉与林黛玉、薛宝钗的爱情与婚姻悲剧为主要线索，描写了贾氏家族由盛而衰的历史，反映出进入末期的中国封建社会不可避免的崩溃结局和初步的民主主义思想倾向。《红楼梦》情节缜密，细节真实，语言优美。作者善于刻画人物，塑造出许多富有典型性格的艺术形象。小说中有名有姓的人物就多达 480 多人，其中能给人印象深刻的典型人物，至少也有几十个人。而贾宝玉、林黛玉、薛宝钗、王熙凤等，则成为千古不朽的典型形象。《红楼梦》中人物的语言也非常有特色，都能够准确地显示人物的身份和地位，能够形神兼备地表现出人物的个性特征。总之，《红楼梦》取得了卓越的艺术成就。在明清小说中，最为后人称道的莫过于《红楼梦》。《红楼梦》对中国文学和社会影响非常巨大，从而使学术界产生了以该书为研究对象的专门学问——"红学"。《红楼梦》这部伟大的作品不仅是属于中国的，同时也是属于世界的。它不仅在中国已有数百万的发行量，成为家喻户晓的名著。而且它还有英语、法语、俄语等十几种语种的翻译本，并且在国外也有不少人在对它进行研究，写出不少论著。《红楼梦》正日益成为世界人民共同的精神财富。

除四大名著外，在明清时期，比较著名的小说还有：明朝无名氏的《金瓶梅》，清朝蒲松龄的《聊斋志异》，清朝吴敬梓的《儒林外史》等等。

明清小说是中国文学史和文化史上一个重要重要的组成部分。特别是其中的"四大名著"（它们都被拍成电视剧或电影），影响到了中国人生活的方方面面，成为中国人永远的精神财富。（黎清编著）

Chapter 4

第四章

Unit 1

Gardens

China has a time-honored tradition of landscape gardens. As early as the Western Zhou Dynasty, the royalty and aristocracy had begun to construct gardens. During the Qin and Han periods, more and more country residences were constructed, such as the famous ancient Chinese gardens of Epang Palace (during the Qin Dynasty) and the Shanglin Garden of the Han. Chinese gardens serve as both entertainment facilities and residences. Most are distinguished by the integration of hills and forest within the residential areas of the city. These kinds of landscape parks do not simply present a natural setting; they reflect the artistic sensibilities of classical Chinese landscape paintings and poetry, creating a backdrop that summarizes the essence of the environment's innate beauty while using a slightly impressionistic approach. The structure of classical Chinese gardens are based mainly on the natural landscape, integrated with human-made structures that include palaces, pavilions, corridors, buildings, terraces, various multi-storied towers, as well as artificial interpretations of nature. All reflect the zeitgeist of the various historical periods, especially within the artistic realm of famous ancient Chinese classical poems, verses, and paintings.Chinese classical gardens are world renowned, the most famous being The Summer Palace, The Mountain Resort, The Humble Administrator's Garden and The Lingering Garden; also known as the four great classical gardens of China.

The Summer Palace

The Summer Palace lies 15 kilometers northwest of Beijing. It served as the imperial gardens of the Qing Dynasty, as place for royalty to escape the summer heat. The picturesque scenery is made up of springs, marshes, jade green mountains, and flowing rivers. The construction of the imperial gardens in this area began in the 11th century. In the 15th year of Emperor Qian Long's reign during the Qing Dynasty (1750 A.D.), it was expanded and became known as The Garden of Clear Ripples. The garden was unfortunately ransacked and burned by Anglo-French allied forces in 1860. In the year 1888, the Empress Dowager Cixi embezzled the military expenditure of the Chinese navy to rebuild the grounds, costing over 30 million ounces of silver and lasting over ten years. Upon the completion of the project, it was once again entitled The Summer Palace. By the end of the Qing Dynasty, the total area of the garden covered more than 1,000 hectares. Such a vast and exquisite royal garden is a rarity throughout the world.

The Summer Palace is home to Longevity Hill and Kunming Lake. Three quarters of the garden is water. There are more than 3,000 buildings such as palaces, pagodas, temples, corridors, and terraces surrounding the hills and lakes. These structures, mountains, and lakes reflect and balance one another. Each are placed in such a way that they are in harmony with the overall scene and the feeling of the garden. There are four major scenic areas in The Summer Palace. The most eastern part contains the Eastern Palace Gates. This part was used by the emperor for both his political activities and as a place of temporary residence. It houses The Hall of Benevolence and Longevity, home to elegant dormitories, theatrical stages, and courtyards. It was also used for meetings with ministers and officials from the north and the south. The Hall of Jade Ripples started off as Emperor Guangxu's living palace, but shortly after, it became his prison. Today one can still see the towering wall that was constructed to block the passage. Along the front face of the lofty Longevity Hill, lies most of the structures. The entire scenic area is based on two perpendicular lines with a central axis. The east/west axis contains the famous Long Corridor. Beginning in the middle promenade of The Long Corridor, in succession on the north/south axis lie The Gate of Dispelling Clouds, The Cloud Dispelling Hall, The Garden of Harmonious Virtue, and The Tower of Buddhist Incense. The Tower of Buddhist Incense is the centre of the garden. From here, the buildings are meticulously symmetrically distributed in grand synchronicity, to resemble a myriad of stars surrounding the moon. In the most northern part of the scenic landscape, behind the lakes and mountains, there are few structures amongst the plentiful trees and twisting pathways. The tranquil style is a sharp contrast to the luxurious area in front of the mountains. A group of Tibetan structures and buildings characteristic of the water villages of Suzhou in southern China are in a compact layout, each with its own wit and beauty. Three quarters of the total area of Summer Palace are water, no body of which is more visible than the front lake, with its infinite waves. Mountains occupy the west, while most of the structures are huddled together in the north. In the

The Tower of Buddhist

lake, there is a western causeway, lined with peach trees and willows.

There are also six distinct styles of arched bridges, along with three islands housing classic structures. The exquisite Seventeen Arch Bridge stretches over the lake. Not only is it a pathway to the middle of the lake, but it also makes for an unforgettably picturesque setting. The main building of The Summer Palace is the Tower of Buddhist Incense on Longevity Hill which is built on a foundation twenty-one meters height. The pavilion is 40 meters high, including eight faces, three floors, and four series of eaves. Inside the pavilion, there are eight huge Ceylon ironwood pillars. The structure is extremely complex and was built in the style of ancient classical architecture. Cloister and horn kiosk are used commonly in the garden. The Long Corridor of The Summer Palace, at 728 meters in length, is the longest of any throughout the world. More than 14,000 paintings line the corridors, vividly depicting traditional lore, flowers, birds, fishes, and insects. The splendid Kouru Pavilion with its eight series of eaves lies on the eastern shores of Kunming Lake, and is the largest of its kind in China. Also occupying the area is the richly carved and vividly ornamented Marble Boat with it's with immense size and matchless beauty.

The Summer Palace contains various kinds of garden styles from different regions. It is the quintessence of classical Chinese architecture and is often referred to as the museum of Chinese gardens.

The Mountain Resort

The Mountain Resort is also named Chengde Palace or The Rehe Traveling Palace. It is seated in the northern part of the city of Chengde, along a narrow valley on the west bank of the Wulie River in Hebei province approximately 230 kilometers from Beijing. It was once used as a summer resort as well as a place for conducting state affairs by emperors during the Qing Dynasty.

The Mountain Resort began construction in the 42nd year of Emperor Kangxi's reign during the Qing Dynasty (1703 A.D.) and went through three generations of Emperors: Kangxi, Yongzheng, and Qianlong. It was eventually completed in the 55th year of Emperor Qianlong's reign (1790 A.D.) after 87 years.

The Emperor Kangxi discovered in his traveling to northern China that Chengde was not only excellent terrain, pleasant in weather, beautiful in scenery, but also a gateway for the emperors to the cradle of the Qing Dynasty. Moreover, it was a place on main land China that overlooked the interior

and allowed them to keep an eye on Mongolia. Naturally, Emperor Kangxi decided to build a palace here. In the 42nd year of Emperor Kangxi's reign (1703 A.D.), large-scale construction took place. Lakes were dredged and new roads and palaces were constructed. In the 52nd year of his reign (A.D. 1713), 36 scenic areas and the wall around the whole resort had been completed. During the reign of Emperor Yongzheng, construction was suspended, and resumed in the 6th year of the reign of Emperor Qianlong (1741 A.D.). Fi-

The Mountain Resort

nally, it was finished in the 57th year of Emperor Qianlong's reign (1792 A.D.). Thirty-six more scenic outposts and eight outer lying temples were added to the original, forming a resort of spectacular scale that housed unique imperial gardens. Originally, The Mountain Resort was named The Rehe Traveling Palace. The name was altered when Emperor Kangxi carved The Mountain Resort into the Meridian Gate.

Compared to the Forbidden City in Beijing, The Mountain Resort is a work of simple elegance. It adopts the innate qualities of natural landscapes, absorbing the scenic attributes of the southern and northern frontiers of China. It remains the largest ancient imperial palace in existence in China. The Mountain Resort is divided into four sections: palaces, lakes, plains, and mountains. The palace section is on the south bank of one of the lakes. The terrain there is flat and even. This area, where emperors managed state affairs, and held celebrations, also functioned as a temporary living palace of the emperor. It covers an area of about 100,000 square meters and is composed of four groups of buildings; The Main Palace, The Pine Crane Temple, The Palace of Ten Thousand Swaying Pines and the Eastern Palace. The lake section is seated to the north of the palace section. Islands included, the lakes occupy an area of 43 hectares. Eight islands divide the lakes into different regions, each having distinct elevations and smaller lakes strewn randomly throughout. The ripples on the surface of the clear water recall a utopia with an abundance of fish and rice (more specifically the remote southern Yangtze River area). In the northeast corner lies the famous crystal clear Rehe Spring. The flatland section is situated at the foot of mountains, with the lake section to the north. Within this vast terrain are countless gardens of trees, a dock for horses, jade-colored plants, lush forests, and boundless pasture. The mountain section occupies four-fifths of the entire grounds in the northwest of the Mountain Resort. A chain of mountains are undulating, forming ravines interspersed with several multi-storied pavilions and temples There are many bodies of water in the southeastern area and many mountains in the northwest. It is the embodiment of China's geography. Outside the confines of the grounds, magnificent temples and grandiose manor houses form a cosmos, encircling The Mountain Resort. The ring around the resort is symbol of national unity and the centralization of authority. The Eight Outer Temples are distributed in the north at the foot of the mountain, occupying an area of more than 400,000 square meters. Originally there were eleven temples. Presently remaining are the Temple of the Potraka Doctrine, The Temple Happiness and Longevity, The Temple of Universal Bliss, The Temple of Universal Peace, The Temple of Far Reaching Peace, The Temple of Universal Charity, and the Shuxiang Temple; all built of gold and jade in glorious splendor.

The Humble Administrator's Garden

The Humble Administrator's Garden is located along Northeast Street in the city Suzhou. It is the largest of its kind in the area and is one of Suzhou's four famous gardens, as well as a chief representative of the northern Chinese gardens. In the years of the Tang Dynasty, it was the private villa of poet Lu Guimeng. After the arrival of the Yuan Dynasty, it transformed into Dahong Temple. During the reign of Emperor Jiajing in the Ming Dynasty (1522–1566 A.D.), an administrator named Wang Xianchen, frustrated with his career in office, returned to Suzhou. He purchased the temple and employed the famous landscape artist Wen Zhengming to design the garden. He completed the task in

16 years. The lord named the garden The Humble Administrator's Garden after a verse in the poem Idle Life by poet Pan Yue of the Western Jin Dynasty: "Water the garden, sell the vegetables; offering meals morning and night... this also serves as the humble man's politics." Not long after the garden was finished, Wang Xianchen passed away. On one fateful night, his son, lost the entire garden to a bet. The owners of The Humble Administrator's Garden have changed quite often in the more than 400 years since its creation. It was once divided into 3 parts. The parts became a private garden, official garden, and a public area. It wasn't until the 1950's that the three parts were reunited and once again given the title The Humble Administrators's Garden. The garden covers an area of over 4 hectares.

The Humble Administrator's Garden

It can be divided into four sections: the east, middle, west, and the residential section. The middle section is the major attraction and the essence of the whole garden. This section covers an area of about 1.2 hectares, one third of it occupied by ponds. In the middle section, a number of structures surround the ponds and pools, such as lofty pavilions and elaborate terraces, decorated according to the elevation of the banks of the streams. Trees and hills set off one another, as the emerald green bamboo grow exuberantly. With the vast ponds and flourishing forests, the scenery is a spectacle to behold. The buildings facing the water are of varied architectural styles, and random heights. The western section, originally referred to as the courtesy garden, is the smallest part of the whole garden with an area of 8,400 square meters. In the western section the streams are roundabout, with a condensed layout. Hills are on one side and water on the other, flanked by pavilions. Exquisite verandas encroach the rippling waters of the snaking streams running through the mountain gorges. This is an excellent example of the artistic brilliance of Suzhou landscape gardening. The major building of the western section is The Hall of 36 Pairs of Mandarin Ducks. It is located near a structure used for giving banquets and listening to music. The ornamentation inside the central hall is something to ponder. The eastern section was once named Returning to the Fields Residence after the minister, Wang Xinyi, returned there in the fourth year of Emperor Chonzhen's reign during the Ming Dynasty (1631 A.D.). It occupies an area of about two hectacres. This part of the garden had long ago been deserted and barren but it has since been rebuilt. It is structured in accordance with the flat ridges, faraway hills, pine tree woods, grasses, bamboo docks, and roundabout streams. Combining with mountains, ponds, pavilions, and terraces, it forms a style that remains clear and bright. The major buildings are Snowy Orchid Hall, Lotus Terrace, Heavenly Spring Pavilion, and Auspicious Clouds and Mountains Peak, which were all removed from other places and brought here.

Although The Humble Administrator's Garden has undergone reconstruction for generations, its constructers have preserved the style of architecture characteristic of the Ming Dynasty. The garden is naturally spaced and made up mainly of water bodies; the quantity of which, make the landscape peaceful, simple, brilliant, and natural. At the center of the garden are pools surrounded by lofty rotating pavilions with carved windows. Winding pathways wing through mountain boulders, ancient trees, green bamboo, and other various flora and fauna, painting an elegant serene picture. This era was quite an inspiration to art and literature. The varied topography of lakes, pools, and gullies fueled the artistic concepts of the classic poetry and paintings of the period, that reveal the stark beauty as well as the reality of nature. One can appreciate the fish under the lotuses in summer, the plum blossoms and snow in winter. Spring's sunny days entice the blooming flowers, and fall brings the lush red reeds in the ponds. The passionate and poetic scenery is undauntedly implicit, the twisting paths revealing beauty every step of the way. Not only do the divisions in The Humble Administrator's Garden make use of and adapt to the natural environment, they depict great technique in the use of contrast. This allows for the creation of gardens within gardens, representative of typical gardens in the regions south of the Yangtze River. Some individuals have referred to it as the mother of all gardens under heaven.

The Lingering Garden

The Lingering Garden is located on the outskirts of Changmen Gate in Suzhou city. It was built during the reign of Emperor Jia Qing of the Ming Dynasty (1522–1566 A.D.) and was the private residence of Xu Shitai. During the Qing Dynasty, in the fifth year of the reign of another emperor similarly named Jia Jing (1800 A.D.), it belonged to Liu Rongfeng and was renamed Cold Mountain Villa. Since his surname was Liu, it was commonly known as The Liu Garden. Sheng Xuren obtained the grounds in the second year of Emperor Guangxu's reign, renaming it The Lingering Garden. The Lingering Garden takes up two hectares (others report more than 3.3 hectares), and can be divided into four sections: the middle, east, west, and north section. In each section there are distinct visual aspects of scenic mountains and rivers, pastoral landscapes, wooded areas, and courtyards. The middle section is famous for its aquatic scenery, which is the essence of the entire garden. The eastern section is famed for its' curved courtyards and winding corridors. There are more than ten struc-

tures, including the famed Worshipping Stone Pavilion, The Palace of the Spring, The Return-to-Read Pavilion, Cloud Capped Pavilion, and the Cloud Capped Tower. Three rock mountains stand behind the pools in the courtyard; Cloud Capped Peak in the center, with Auspicious Clouds Mountain and The Mountain of the Cloudy Cave by its two sides. The northern part of this section is pastoral landscape and newly developed potted plants. The western section, in all its' wildness, is the highest altitude of the garden. It is unique for the ornate human-made rock gardens interconnected with the natural landscape features. The original construction in the north has since been destroyed. In re-

The Lingering Garden

cent times bamboos, peach, and apricot trees have been widely cultivated. The Lingering Garden has the most buildings of all the gardens of Suzhou. There are dozens of courtyards containing halls, corridors, coral walls, arched doors, rock gardens, pools, flowers, and trees. The landscaping of The Lingering Garden fully embodies the superb technique and extreme intelligence of the ancient Chinese landscapers. It also features distinct artistic styles reminiscent of gardens in southern China.

In The Lingering Garden, there are three famous features. One is The Cloud Capped Peak. The so-called "mountains" are actually exquisite stones projecting from Lake Taihu. According to legend the magical stones were relics of Hua Shigang of the late Song Dynasty. The stones in Taihu Lake are of four very distinct qualities: thin, wrinkled, porous, and hollow. The Redwood Palace Hall in the same vicinity is named for the mighty Chinese cedar pillars that support it. A fossil of a fish is preserved in a natural marble slab that is housed in The Celestial Hall of the Five Peaks. The central part of the face of the slab shows the fish surrounded by hills and overlapping cliffs. The underside reveals running water and flowing waterfalls while the topside contains graceful flowing clouds. A white spot in the middle represents the sun or moon. These features synergistically form an exquisite landscape portrait. The marble originates from Yunnan province, it is about one meter in length and approximately 15 centimeters thick.

Residences

China is a multi-ethnic country. The style and architecture of the residences are rich and colorful. In this discussion we will only introduce some of most representative styles.

Hutong

Many foreign visitors in Beijing often ask, "Where in Beijing is Hutong located?" Indeed, the number of Beijing's hutongs (alleys) is extremely large. According to records, the quantity had reached as many as several thousand by the Ming Dynasty, more than nine hundred of which were inside the city and more than three hundred in the suburbs. During the Qing Dynasty, the number had increased to more than 1800. During the Republic of China residential alleys numbered over 1900. In the early stages of The People's Republic of China, the total topped 2550 in Beijing alone.

Beijing's alleys originated from the Yuan Dynasty. The Mongolians re-ferred to the streets of their capital as hutongs. It is believed that this word means water well in ancient Mongolian. People in Beijing generally refer to a road of south-north orientation as street. Being relatively wide, it was primarily used by horse carts, thus also called a horse road. The east-west oriented streets are called alleys. They are relatively narrow, and used mainly for foot travel. On the sides of the alleys are courtyard residences.

Hutong

There are many hutongs with distinctive features in Beijing such as the Banking Hutong, which is the shortest, with a distance of only about 30 or 40 meters.

It lies adjacent to the Zhubaoshi District outside Qianmen Avenue. The names of the alleys reflect the history of money exchange within the hutongs. In ancient China, it was traditionally said that there were seven things to obtain when one steps out of the house: firewood, rice, oil, salt, soy sauce, vinegar, and tea. It is no surprise then that in Beijing there was a corresponding hutong for each; Firewood Hutong, Rice Hutong, Oil Hutong, Salt Hutong, Soy Sauce Hutong, Vinegar Hutong, and the Tea Hutong. In this era people placed great value on the five precious metals; gold, silver, bronze, iron, and tin and consequently, there were hutongs named after each.

Some people think that hutongs are the product of the Yuan Dynasty. Their perfect relationship with the courtyard houses embodies the rulers' intelligence in residential planning and allocation. The hutong system is a work of urban managerial brilliance. The alleys are arranged in strict order with the well-proportioned courtyard houses. Some residential alleys are separated by dredging as Beijing had housed several military camps of no-madic tribes. An anonymous person gave this analogy: the city of Beijing is like a large piece of tofu that is cubed in shape. There are streets and hutongs amongst the city. Both of them are in accordance from south to north and from east to west. Therefore, inhabitants of Beijing must have a strong sense of direction.

Courtyard Residences

The courtyard is the traditional and the most typical style of residence in Beijing and throughout northern China. It is composed of the central structure, the east wing, and the west wing, surrounding a courtyard in the center. It is the oldest and most widely spread among Chinese residential living traditions mostly due to its connection with the Han, China's largest ethnic group. Some believe that courtyard residences have been around more than 3,000 years. As early as the Western Zhou Dynasty, the model had begun to take shape. The gate of the courtyard residence is generally in the southeast or northwest corner. The main room in the northern courtyard is built on a stone-mortared foundation. It is typically larger than the other rooms.

Courtyard Residences

The living room is reserved for the master of the house. The east and west wings are at the two sides of the courtyard where the younger generations reside. The corridors between the main room and wings are used for walking and resting. Windows adjacent to the street on the enclosing walls and rooms are generally not kept open, as the courtyards remain closed and secluded. Courtyard residences in Beijing are famous throughout China and around the globe. In Beijing there are various styles and sizes. Regardless of scale, it mainly consists of a courtyard with one-story residences on four sides. There is only one courtyard in the simplest residential areas, and two or three in the more complex ones. Mansions occupied by the wealthy are composed of several courtyards lying side by side with a wall separating in between. One distinctive feature of courtyard residences is the central structure and the symmetrically attached wings. What's more, they are multifunctional. As far as the large ones are concerned, it can be imperial palace or a prince's mansion. The smaller courtyards serve as residences for common people. Both the splendid Forbidden City and suburban houses of the working class are designs of this same mode of architecture.

Enclosed Residences

Due to wars and famine, the Hans, who occupied the basin of the Yellow River, were forced to migrate to the south (from the Western and Eastern Jin dynasties to the Tang and the Song periods of ancient China). During this period, there were a total of five large migrations, as consecutive populations departed for southern China. Since the flat area in the south was already inhabited, the arriving parties had no better option than to move to the northern mountains and hills. There is a saying from ancient times; where there are mountain peaks, there are guests. Where there are no guests, no mountains reside. At that time, the local officers would often register their residences as a place for guests or travelers to stay. They were often called keji or kehu, giving rise to the name Kejia that describes the Hakka ethnic group. In order to protect themselves from enemies and beasts, most Hakkas lived in groups, so the enclosed dragon house, walking horse residence, five phoenix structure, the warrior surrounded building, and fourcornered house came into being. A-

Enclosed Residences

mong these, the enclosed dragon house has existed the longest and is consequently the most famous. Thus it is commonly referred to as the enclosed residence or enclosed Hakka House. Such structures also convey the architectural culture of the Hakka. The enclosed dragon house originated in the Tang and Song dynasties and was popular throughout the Ming and the Qing eras. The Hakka people primarily built the enclosed dragon house with one entrance, three halls, two side rooms, and one surrounding wall. The enclosed house of the Hakka's are typically built similar to military barracks surrounded by a square rampart. The enclosed house is fortified with a one-meter thick wall that is 15 meters high. It is constructed of earth mixed with lime (calcium oxide), cooked glutinous rice, and egg whites; using lengths of bamboo, and wood pillars for strength. An ordinary enclosed dragon house covers an area of about one half to three-fourths of a hectare. Larger ones cover over two hectares. Generally it took five to ten years, and sometimes even more time to properly complete the structure. The enclosed dragon house is somewhat like the castle of the Hakka. Inside the residence, there are bedrooms, kitchens, various sized halls, wells, pigpens, henhouses, toilets, and storehouses. An enclosed house can accommodate dozens of people, sometimes even hundreds, lending itself to tight-knit, self-sufficient and enhanced social groups. Regardless of the size of structure, in front of the main gate, there must be a level area and half-moon pond. The level ground was used to dry the harvested grains and enjoy the cool shade among other activities. The pond served as a water reservoir, a place to raise fish, fire protection, and protection against drought. Inside the gate, there are upper, middle and lower halls and two or four wings at each side which are commonly known as horizontal rooms. This type of room extends straight back. The very end is where the enclosing wall is built to encircle the main rooms. A small-enclosed dragon house may contain over ten rooms, with larger ones occupied by twenty or more spaces. The middle room of the enclosed dragon house is referred to as the dragon hall. Smaller scale houses have one or two surrounding dragons, with four to six enclosing larger residences. These structures are still in existence and can be found in the Fujian and Jiangxi provinces. The Hakka's enclosed house, Beijing's courtyard residence, the dugout structures of Shangxi province, the pole-house style of Guangxi province, and the carved homes of Yunnan province make up the five characteristic residential architecture styles of China.

The Imperial Mausoleums

In ancient China, only the emperor's tomb was officially called a mausoleum. Numerous imperial mausoleums were constructed during all the past dynasties. Most of them are now submerged or destroyed, but many of them still stand.

The Mausoleum of the Yellow Emperor lies atop Qiao Mountain, north of Huangling county in Shanxi province. It is the resting place of Emperor Huang Di, known more commonly as the Yellow Emperor. He is said to be the earliest ancestor of the Chinese and is regarded as a great leader of the last phase of primitive society. After his death, he was buried on the majestic Qiao Mountain, which is surrounded by water at its base. Furthermore, the mountain is refuge to more than 80,000 cypress trees many of which have been standing for over a millennium. Throughout the four seasons the area is brimming with verdant and lush greenery. The Mausoleum of the Yellow Emperor sits deep in the forest of old cypress trees near the peak of the mountain. The mausoleum is 3.6 meters high and has a perimeter of 48 meters. It is a circular building constructed of black bricks and stones, but its walls are painted. In front of the mausoleum stands a carved stele from the 15th year of the reign of the Ming Emperor Jia Jing. The four Chinese characters qiao shan long yu (which translates to Qiao Mountain controls the dragon) are carved into the stele indicating the place from which the Yellow Emperor rode a dragon to heaven.

The Tomb of Yu the Great is at the foot of Kuaiji Mountain in the southeastern city Shaoxing in Zhejiang province. Da Yu (Yu the Great) became a famous hero by governing the waters of ancient China to prevent floods. The Tomb of Yu the Great is surrounded by mountains with many peculiar peaks standing amongst eastward flowing streams, enhancing the magnificence and dignity of the mausoleum. The mausoleum grounds are composed of three parts: The Tomb of Yu, The Temple of Yu, and The Shrine of Yu. The tomb faces The Pool of Yu, in front of which stands a monumental stone archway. At

Annually Sacrifice Ceremony at the Mausoleum of the Yellow Emperor

the end of a 100-meter walkway, one can see a stele pavilion carved with the words The Tomb of Yu the Great. The Temple of Yu stands in the northeast part of the grounds and faces south. This palatial building was first built in the early stages of the Liang period during the Northern and Southern Dynasties. The structures of the temple, namely, The Reflecting Walls, Stele Pavilion, Meridian Gate, The Hall of Worship, and The Main Hall, were constructed with reference to south and north and ascend the mountain terrain. The Main Hall, has rooftops of double eaves, and sits beside the hills and towers majestically among the clouds. There are four Chinese characters meaning serene land under heaven, inscribed by Emperor Kangxi on the back wall of the hall, which is decorated with wisps of dragons and owls piercing the clouds. The Temple of Yu is composed of two corridors and three rooms, and is located to the left side of the mausoleum. A serene mirrored pond reflects the temple and is known as the Liberating Life Pond.

The Mausoleum of Emperor Qin Shihuang is located 30 kilometers east of the foot of Li Mountain in Xi'an, Shaanxi province. The towering ridges and peaks of the structure join with Li Mountain in unsurpassed, harmonious unity. The size of the mausoleum park is quite imposing, occupying a total areal of 56.25 square kilometers. The mausoleum was originally constructed to be 115 meters high, but presently it is 76 meters in height. Inner and outer walls surround the grounds. The inner wall has a perimeter of 3840 meters, and outer wall has perimeter 6210 meters. The historic ruins of both walls presently stand 8 to 10 meters high. The burial mound is in the south of the grounds, and the Chamber Palace and The Hall of Expedience are constructed in the north. The Mausoleum of Emperor Qin Shihuang was built between 246 B.C. and 208 B.C. It is the first imperial cemetery in Chinese history. Large in scale and abundant in funerary objects, it is the precursor to all mausoleums in the successive later dynasties. The construction of the mausoleum was modeled after the Qin capital city of Xianyan, according to the wishes of Emperor Qin Shihuang as laid out in his will. The entire layout of the mausoleum resembles the written character (hui 一回). Today, the remaining structures are The Chamber Palace, The Hall of Expedience, The Temple Gardens, and ruins of the residences of minor officials. According to historical records, the tomb area is divided into two parts, the cemetery park and the imperial burial place. The tomb occupies approximately 56.25 square kilometers. It is 55.05 meters in height, with a perimeter of 2000 meters. The entire mausoleum covers an area of 220 square kilometers, on which the large scale palaces, pavilions, and other structures stand. The imperial burial sites are surrounded by two walls, an inside square wall with a perimeter of 2525.4 meters and a surrounding outside enclosure with a perimeter of 6264 meters. The sheer scale of the mausoleum far exceeds that of the distant Egyptian pyramids. The Great Pyramid of Giza is regarded as the world's largest mausoleum above ground, but The Mausoleum of Emperor Qin Shihuang is the largest subterranean tomb. Each of them is praised one of the Eight Wonders of the World.

The mausoleums known as The Ming Thirteen Tombs house the tombs of emperors of the Ming Dynasty. It is located near The Mountain of Heavenly Longevity, at the foot of Mountain Yan in Changping county of Beijing. It took over 230 years to build. Construction of the first mausoleum named Changling began in the fifth month of the 7th year of the Yongle period of Ming Dynasty (1409 A.D.). Construction of the mausoleums continued until the completion of the Si Mausoleum, built by the last

Emperor Chongzheng of the Ming Dynasty. A total of thirteen mausoleums serve as the final resting places of thirteen emperors, twenty-three empresses, two princes, thirty imperial concubines, and one court eunuch.

The Ming mausoleums are seated in a small basin, surrounded by foothills in the east, west, and north, and a plain in the central region. A stream meanders in front of the mausoleums, adding to the delightful and picturesque scenery with green hills and clear waters. The Thirteen Ming Tombs are named after the thirteen emperors of the Ming Dynasty. They are called: The Chengzu Lead Tomb, Renzong Tomb of Offering, Xuanzong Tomb of Brightness, Yingzong Tomb of Abundance, Xianzong's Luxuriant Tomb, The Xiaozong Tomb of Peace, The Wuzong Tomb of Health, The Perpetual Tomb of Shizong, The Muzong Clear Tomb, Shenzong's Tomb of Certainty, The Guangzong Tomb of Celebration, Xizong Tomb of Ethics, and the Sizong Tomb of Thought. The mausoleums, which were built in the east, west and north regions of the mountains, form a large, integrated system of majestic tombs. The Thirteen Ming Tombs, built between 1409 A.D. and 1644 A.D., have a history of over 300 to 500 years. The whole mausoleum, which covers forty square kilometers, is the largest in scale and contains the most imperial mausoleums in China and in the world.

Unit 2

I-go

The game of Go (also known as weiqi or I-go) is a game of strategy which originated from ancient China over 2,000 years ago.

It is said that in ancient times, after Emperor Yao settled disputes among various tribes brought peace and order, the capital of Pingyang entered an economic boom demonstrated by the prosperity of agriculture and societal living. But one thing worried Emperor Yao—his adolescent son, Dan Zhu of Empress Sanyi, not only idled about and was reluctant to attend his proper duties, but frequently provoked trouble, inviting disaster. In order to help his son become more useful, the imperial Yao couple racked their brains, but Dan Zhu

I-go

held fast to his usual ways. They suggested that he practice archery or study other skills, yet he had no interest whatsoever. Emperor Yao saw that his son was not making any progress, therefore he sighed, "I will make him learn the stone chess to understand marching formations and strategic military positions. After learning stone chess from a master, he will be rather productive." As Dan Zhu learned of his father's request, his views changed a little, stating, "It's so easy to learn how to play stone chess that I will understand it immediately." Thereupon he asked his father to teach him at once. Emperor Yao said to him, "You must practice something morning and night to master it, but if only you want to learn." In giving this advice, he used an arrow to inscribe dozens of lines, forming a grid on a flat stone, and then ordered the guards to gather a pile of stones and distribute half of them to Dan Zhu. As the ruling commander, he instructed Dan Zhu on the strategies of war by the depiction of stones, explaining the proper situation for advancement or retreat. Dan Zhu seemed to accept the knowledge and was very patient at this time. Emperor Yao taught his son the mechanics of Go until the sun set over the mountains. Only after the urging of the guards, did the father and son finish their first lesson. In the following days, Dan Zhu had taken the game to heart, constantly learning and never strolling about idly. Despite this, before long Dan Zhu once again returned to his offensive shortcomings. All day long he made troubles out of nothing, and even conspired snatch Emperor Yao's title. Upon seeing these circumstances, his mother Sanyi grieved endlessly, contracting illness and eventually dying full of remorse. Emperor Yao was also heartbroken and sent Dan Zhu to the South, never wanting to see this son again. Moreover, he abdicated and gave the crown to Yu Shun, who was intelligent and possessed both ability and political integrity through Emperor Yao's three years of strict observation. After Yu Shun had succeeded to the throne, he taught his son Shang Jun the strategies of Go to enlighten his intelligence as Yao as previously done. Later on, the lines of Go appeared in pottery. The story Emperor Yao Creates Go to Teach Dan Zhu was also recorded in history. Go in ancient times was called Yi and became the precursor to chess circles, with a time-honored tradition of more than 4,000 years.

Go presents people with a vivid analogy of the black and white contrasting world. It was a favorite activity of entertainment in ancient China and has the longest history of all the chess games. Due to its integration of science, art, and skill, it allows for the development of intelligence and the cultivation of one's will, as it forces the player to remain conscious and strategic in tactics. Consequently, the game has long been prosperous and has never declined, gradually developing into a culture of international competition. Asia presently holds millions of Go competitors, yet in Europe and in the Americas, there are also no lack of people who enjoy playing Go. The rules of Go are very uninvolved, nevertheless it employs a vast arena of many choices, making the game interchangeable and dynamic, and more complex than Xiangqi (Chinese chess). For these reasons, the enduring fascination with Go remains long and prosperous. The time consumed for a round of Go is extensively varies. A quick round may take only five minutes while a slow round may occupy several days, but it's more common for match to last one to two hours.

There are a total 19 pairs of equidistant horizontal and vertical intersecting parallel lines on the Go playing surface, which constitutes 361 intersections (generally called points). The surface of the board indicates several points called the star points. The middle point is called the heaven point or tianyuan. The playing pieces are black and white, and are all uniformly round. The optimum number of pieces is 181 of black and 180 of white.

In general, Go is played by two people. Before the game, it is determined who is to make the first move. The playing rules are as follows: Firstly, each opponent obtains the pieces of his or her respective color, with black going first and naturally followed by white, one piece at a time, in alternating turns. Secondly, the pieces are to be placed on the points formed by intersecting lines. Thirdly, after a decision has been made and the piece is placed on the board, the piece must not be moved. Fourthly, it is the right of two players to alternate turns, but it is also permitted for either player to waive this privilege.

Playing the game of Go is quite helpful in developing one's intelligence and strengthens the abilities of calculation, memory, originality, thought, judgment, and attentiveness. Go can also play an active role in the development of children. It is used to cultivate their analytical abilities and improve self-control.

Exorcising Dance

Exorcising Dance is also called Big Exorcism and Dancing Exorcism. It is also commonly known as ghost's drama and Dancing with the Exorcism Face. Regarded as the a foundation of primitive cultural faith, exorcising dance originated from the totem of the clans of ancient societies. As a part of a larger exorcism ceremony, this popular folk dance was used in ancient China to drive out the evil spirits while offering sacrifices. The exorcising dance which used to be danced for sacrificing is performed during the traditional Chinese Spring Festival. Dancers wear hideous masks and dress up as a Fangxiang, a warrior who was sent by the gods to expel ghosts. They dance and shout, "Nuo, Nuo…" with one hand holding a halberd and the other shield, jumping and dancing to every corner, searching for something inauspicious in order to drive out the ghosts and pray for protection during the whole year. The exorcising dance is still performed in the provinces of Jiangxi, Anhui, Guizhou, Guangxi, Shandong, Henan, Shaanxi, Hubei, Fujian, Yunnan, Guangdong. It is also called Jumping for Exorcism, Ghosts' Dance, and Enjoying the Happiness in various places of the country. There are two ways to perform this traditional folk dance. One involves four main performers wearing masks and fur and murmuring "Nuo, Nuo…" with a spear and shield in each hand. The other type requires twelve persons to wear red hair and painted fur. They noisily crack a long whip and shout the name of the deity who fights the evil spirits and savage beasts. The performance is always accompanied by music.

Exorcism Face

The origin and development of the exorcising dance can be traced far back in Chinese history. It is recorded in divination Ci (a form of classical literature in China) of Jia Gu Wen (Oracle Words), which are a set of inscriptions on bones or tortoise shells found in the ruins of the Yin Dynasty. The exorcising dance was called national exorcism or big exorcism in the Zhou Dynasty and villagers' exorcism in the countryside. According to records in Analects of Confucius Rural Party, Confucius once wore the full dress and stood reverently and respectfully to welcome the coming of an exorcism team. This folk dance was called villagers' exorcism by scholars after Qing dynasty and was cited in local or temple epigraphs. The custom of exorcising for sacrifice continued from Qin and Han dynasties to the Tang and the Song Dynasties and continued to develop during the Ming and Qing Dynasties. Although the exorcising dance has retained its own traditional meanings, it is also customarily performed for entertainment as a dramatic work and is locally called "exorcism hall drama" or "local drama". So far, the traditional style of the exorcising dance has been still preserved while some new elements have been added in the provinces of Jiangxi, Hunan, Hubei, and Guangxi among others. For example, in the counties of Wuyuan, Nanfeng, and Le'an of Jiangxi province, the exorcising dance is performed to represent the deity who cuts the mountain in the legend of Pangu's creation of heaven and earth,the rumor Two Fairies of Harmony and Unity and Liu Hai Playing Gold Toad. In the countryside, the dramas Meng Jiangnü and The Legend of White Snake are represented by the Jima dance. The making of masks and the performance style of the exorcising dance have had a great influence on lesser-known dances such as qiang mu from Zangs and sorcerers' dance from Zhuangs, Yaos, Maonans and Mulaos. All of these dances have absorbed the cultural elements and the techniques of the exorcising dance, but developed into new variations with the characteristics reflecting a particular nationality.

The villagers' exorcism recorded in *The Analects of Confucius ·Rural Party* has persisted among the Chinese people. Moreover, it has evolved into various forms of exorcising dance and exorcising drama by combining with religion, art and custom. The dance is still popular in rural areas of China, mainly in the provinces of Jiangxi, Hunan, Hubei, Shaanxi, Sichuan, Guizhou, Yunnan, Guangxi, Anhui, Shanxi, and Hebei.

Jiangxi is one of the birthplaces of Chinese exorcism culture. The off-spring of Miaos, who inhabited the Basin of Ganjiang River and Poyang Lake during the Shang and Zhou Dynasties, created the splendid bronze culture in Jiangxi province. The bronze mask of a deity with double angles that was excavated in Da Yang Zhou of Xin Gan County revealed information regarding exorcism in Gan (another name of Jiangxi). The earliest record of Jiangxi exorcism is *Jin Sha the Yus' Pedigree of a Clan: the Judgment Notes of Nuo Shen* (a god which is supposed to drive away pestilence) from Nan Feng county. It told that Wu Rui, the ruler of Changsha, was under order to go on a punitive expedition to Min (another name of Fujian province). He encamped the troops on the military mountain of Nanfeng in the early stage of the Han Dynasty. In order to avoid the war, the villagers were warned to practice exorcism to eliminate the demons. As the Tang Dynasty was at the height of its cultural splendor, the *Kai Yuan Ceremony* was a regular exorcising ceremony in prefectures and counties, which lead to the spread of rural exorcism in eight prefectures and thirty-seven counties of Jiangxi province. For example, exorcising temples were built and the Nuo Shen was sacrificed during the Tang Dynasty in the counties of Nanfeng, Pingxiang, and Xiushui areas. The economy and culture of Jiangxi province were prosperous in the Song Dynasty, which led to the proliferation of the exorcising dance. According to *Jin Sha the Yus' Pedigree of a Clan*,in order to find shelter from the turmoil of war, the Yus migrated to Nanfeng from Yugan at the end of the Tang Dynasty. During the early stages of the Song Dynasty, they moved a statue of Er Lang Shen, a legendary character from ancient China that worshiped by their ancestors, while from Guankou of Xichuan to Kingsha (present day village of Huansha in Zixiao County). They built a temple and burned joss sticks and candles for it each year. This practice was called Qu Nuo (the act of exorcising). Having flourished during the Ming and the Qing dynasties, exorcism in Jiangxi was recorded or remained in more than thirty cities and counties. Nanfeng topped all the others in its number in eastern Jiangxi. The exorcising classes were established in 180 villages from the end of the Qing Dynasty to the present. Today, 113 villages still perform the dance, which is also referred to as jumping for exorcising, jumping the bamboo horse, jumping for harmony, and dancing like the Eight Immortals. In Le'an county, there are classes in rolling the Nuo shen, playing the drums, and enjoying the happiness. In Yihuan county, there is jumping for exorcism. In Guangchang, there are Meng drama and jumping with chief star. In Lichuan there are jumping for harmony and jumping the eight shelves. Of all the counties in eastern Jiangxi, Pingxiang has the most variations of the exorcising dance. The exorcising dance is called Yang Nuo Shen (admiring the exorcising god) and Shua Nuo an (playing the exorcism board). The exorcising dance together with exorcism temple, exorcism mask are called three treasures. In Wanzai County, it is called Tiao Xiao (jumping mandrills) or Ban An (moving the case), and is divided into two genres, exorcising with mouth closed and exorcising with mouth open. These rural exorcisms were influenced by the Gan cultural groups and have Jiangxi characteristics.

Since the exorcising dance spread to varied regions, its performance styles differ from each other. There is civil exorcism which is characterized by complicated scenes, elegant performance, vibrant styles and graceful postures, and also acrobatic exorcism which has mighty and majestic momentum, lucid and lively rhythm, and powerful and vigorous actions. Such traditional types of exorcising dance are still popular in the stages, halls or in the farmlands in many counties like Dean, Wuning, Wuyuan, Nanfeng and Duchang of Jiangxi province. The performers generally put on masks to represent the many forms of Nuo Shen. Some represent a character in mythology, and others represent a common person or a historical celebrity. One who takes off the mask is a common person, and one who puts on the mask is a deity. The musical instruments used in the exorcising dance are very simple. They are generally percussion instruments like the drum and the gong. The organization formed by exorcising dancers is called exorcism class. It is composed of eight to ten or more participants and has strict rules. The exorcising dance is performed during the climax of the exorcism ceremony. The performances are deeply rooted in the culture in through-out the country, and have more of an impact when combined with sacrifice.

Nuo shen temple is the place where the performers rest and the exorcising ceremony is held. Seventeen temples exist in Pingxiang County of Jiangxi province and another seventeen in Nangfeng. The earliest recorded temple was built in Kingsha village during the North Song Dynasty. The temple in Ganfang village was rebuilt during the Yongle period of the Ming Dynasty (1403 — 1424 A.D.) and has been preserved well up to the present time. Another temple in Shiyou village that was rebuilt in Xinchou year of Emperor Qianlong's reign (1781 A.D.) possesses the strongest folk flavor. The exorcising ceremony follows a traditional sequence of performance. The exorcism in Gan follows the old traditions, which includes several basic procedures: start (opening the box, coming out of the cave, taking out the board), performance (jumping for exorcism, jumping with mandrills, jumping the evil spirit), expelling (searching and ridding, cleaning up the hall, processing), and end (sealing the box, blocking up the cave, putting away the case). The period of performance lasts from the first day in the first month of the lunar year to several days after the Lantern Festival (the minority exorcism troupes conclude in February). To expel the ghost is the objective of the whole ceremony, during which the performer drives out the pernicious demons by putting on a wry mask and holding the weapon along the gate by the light of a torch. As a major artistic form, exorcising dance is praised as the living fossil of Chinese dance. Now, there are over 200 traditional programs, more than 90 of which exist in Nanfeng County.

Due to the long course of its history and development, exorcism embodies Chinese anthropology, sociology, history, religion, folklore, drama, dance, aesthetics and plentiful cultural details. Since the Chinese nation has always laid emphasis on the protection of non-material cultural heritage, the exorcising dance was permitted by the State Council to be inscribed in the first list of national non-material cultural heritage on May 20, 2006.

Beijing Opera

Beijing Opera, called Jingxi and pingju (xi and ju meaning opera), National Opera and Pihuang, is the genuine quintessence of Chinese culture. It gets the name due to its formation in Beijing.

The original formation of Beijing Opera can be traced back to several ancient Chinese local operas. In the 55th year of Emperor Qian Long's reign during the Qing Dynasty, there were four local theatrical troupes from Anhui province: Three-Celebrations Troupe, Four-Happiness Troupe, Spring-Publicity Troupe and Spring Troupe. These troupes went to Beijing successively to put on performances. All of their performances had unprecedented success.

Garment of Beijing Opera

Beijing Opera came into being as a result of the classes from Anhui province constantly cooperating with artists in Han accent from Hubei opera. It absorbed the essence of local operas such as Kunqu opera, Shangxi opera, and Watchman's clapper mainly in style of Erhuang of the Hui dialect and Xipi of the Han dialect. It is generally thought that Beijing opera emerged from Guangxu period during the Qing Dynasty, since the name of Beijing Opera was first seen in *Shen News* (Shen was another name for Shanghai) during the second year of Guangxu's reign (1876 A.D.). Others believe that Beijing Opera came into being during Daoguang's reign of the Qing dynasty. It is popular from the south to north in countries and cities of China after its birth. Beijing Opera was the most popular type of opera in China, but it was especially popular

in the 1930s and 1940s. At that time it was called National Opera. Today,
it is still the quintessential Chinese art form with the greatest impact on the nation.

Beijing Opera embodies well-developed roles, is mature in performance, and has a magnificent and opposing manner. Beijing Opera is representative of modern opera in China. It tops other dramas throughout the country for its numerous productions, great number of artists, large groups of troupes, an a broad audience, showing great impact.

One reason is that the programs of the Beijing Opera are so abundant that there are over 1000 traditional programs. The most widespread and famous are The King Separating with His Lover, Gathering of Heroes Attacking the Zhus's Mansion Three Times, and The Junctions of Three Roads.

Secondly, Beijing Opera is a multi-disciplinary performing art, which integrates song (singing), soliloquy (reading), action (performing), fighting (acrobatic fighting) and dance (dancing) together. It depicts the stories and portrays the characters various forms of theatrics to express happiness, anger, grief, joy, surprise, fear, and sorrow. The reason why Beijing Opera is compared to Oriental opera, is that both operas are similar in form and are special forms of theater that integrate song, dance, music, art, and literature together. Meanwhile, these two kinds of stagecraft coming from different cultural backgrounds have obtained a traditional position within each cultural circle.

Thirdly, the types of roles in Beijing Opera fall into four categories: Sheng, Dan, Jing, and Chou. Sheng is the positive male character, while Dan is its female counterpart. Jing is the male supporting role, with a rough and straightforward disposition. Chou is the funny role or the villain of the piece.

Fourthly, each role in Beijing Opera has its own distinct facial makeup and appearance. The audience can recognize the identities of the roles as soon as they appear. Facial makeup is used to paint colors on one's face to indicate the disposition, quality, role, and fate. It is not only a major characteristic of the opera, but also the key to understanding the plot. Generally speaking, red face has a positive connotation and indicates loyalty and bravery. The black-faced character is neutral and stands for courageous wit. The blue and the green faces are both neutral and represent the uncultivated heroes. The yellow and white faces have a derogatory sense and represent the malicious characters. Gold and sliver faces are mysterious and stand for deities or demons. Besides the colors, the sketches of the facial makeup have similar meanings. For example, the powdered face that indicates the crafty and sinister has two forms: the fully powdered face and the partly powdered face (only on bridge of nose and eye sockets). The difference of coverage and position painted on the face indicates the different degrees of cattiness and craft. Generally, colors indicate the dispositions of the characters, while different facial makeup represent different degrees of the dispositions. In this way, the characters in Beijing Opera display loyalty to evil, beauty to ugliness, and righteousness to ferocity. The abundant numbers of famous artists in Beijing Opera is uncommon in common Chinese operas. Such artists include Cheng Changgeng, Yu Sansheng, Tan Xinpei, Ma lianliang, Mei Lanfang, Yu Shuyan, Cheng Yanqiu, and Shang Xiaoyun.

Since the Chinese nation has always placed emphasis on the protection of non-material cultural heritage. On May 20,2006, Beijing Opera was permitted by the State Council to be inscribed first on a list of national non-material cultural heritage.

Kunqu Opera

Few people know of the town of Qianshan in Kunshan city of Jiangshu province in China. On the other hand, many people are familiar with Kunqu Opera. In fact, as early as over 600 years ago, Kunqu Opera's predecessor Kun Shan Music originated in Qiandeng Town. Kunqu Opera, as an ancient Chinese type of drama music and, was originally called Kunshanqiang, and then shortened to Kunqiang (qiang means opera). It has been called Kunqu Opera since the Qing dynasty. Nowadays, it has another name of Kun Opera.

Kunshanqiang first emerged during the end of the Yuan Dynasty in Kunshan city of Jiangsu province. At that time, Kunshan Music was a branch of Southern opera. Before the reign of Wanli of the Ming Dynasty, it was only a kind of popular oratorio in Wuzhong. It underwent innovation and development after the middle stages of the Ming Dynasty, i.e. during the reign of Emperor Jiajing (1522-1566 A.D.) and Emperor Longqing (1567-1572 A.D.). During this period, Wei Liangfu, a citizen from Nanchang of Jiangxi province, came to Kunshan and devoted himself to the innovation of southern style music. He collaborated with artist Zhang Meigu who was quite apt at playing the dongxiao (a vertical bamboo flute). This caused great innovation and development to the music of Kunshan Music. Also known as the musical sage, Wei Lianfu summarized and developed the singing and performing techniques of Kunqu opera of the past 200 years. Using the original Kunshan song as a foundation and referring the strong points of Haiyan music and Yuyao music, meanwhile absorbing the singing methods of northern traditions. This led to the creation and publishing of The Water Millstone Song.

The year of 1543 was an extraordinary one for the development of Kunqu opera. It was at this time that Wei Liangfu completed his historic work—*Southern Prosody*. The publication of this work established the benchmark of Kunqu opera. However, Kunqu opera from only singing to developing into a staged drama was instigated by Kunshan local Liang Chengyu's *Washing the Silken Gauze* of the Ming period. This brilliant writer of traditional opera was proficient in poetry and tonality in much of the same way as the masters such as Zheng Sili, Chen Meiquan, and Tang Xiaoyu—all of whom have excellent command of musical theory and combined folkloric literature and new operatic tunes with performing arts, creating substantial works. In the opera *Washing the Silken Gauze*, the famous beauty Xi Shi is legendary as the main character. This was the first time that Kunqu opera was performed on the stage, maturing and taking on a different shape. The staging of Washing the Silken Gauze had a great impact on Chinese theater circles at that time. It reflected what the scholars of poetry had strived for in the tradition. Therefore many artists turned to studying and producing works of Kunqu opera. Kun opera, in conjunction with Yuyao opera, Haiyan opera, and Yiyang opera are referred to as the Ming Dynasty's four operas. Later, the styles diffused from Yangzhou into areas of Beijing and Hainan, even extending to regions such as Sichuan, Guizhou, and Guangdong; becoming a nationwide opera of great influence.

The instruments used in Kunqu Opera are mainly the flute, assisted by the bamboo pipes, reed mouth organ, zither, Chinese oboe, and stringed instruments. The music of Kunqu Opera belongs to a joint genre called qu, which is short for the qupai style. Qupai is the basic unit of Kunqu music. According to rough statistics, there are over 1,000 styles of qupai used throughout Kunqu opera. The performance of Kunqu opera has its own system and allure. The most prominent characteristic is the expression of deep emotion, exquisite acting, integrating singing and festive dancing, with emphasis on the costumes, colors, and facial makeup. Types of roles in the opera are on the basis of sheng, dan, jing, mo, chou, wai, and tie. Using the drama of the Yuan Dynasty for reference, it added the five other roles of xiaosheng, xiaodan, xiaomo, xiaowai, and xiaojing, equaling a total of twelve different roles.

Of these lengthy performances, there have survived several collected works of Kunqu opera, some of which have had great influence in theater. Commonly performed operas include Wang Shizhen's *Cry of the Phoenix*, Tang Xianzhu's *Peony Pavillion*, *The Purple Hairpin*, and *The Handan Dream*, as well as *A Dream Under the Southern Bough*, and *Memories of a Chivalrous Man* by Shen Jing. Besides the above mentioned operas, there are Gao Lian's *The Jade Hairpin*, *Mistakes of the Kite* by Li Yu, Zhu Sucheng's *Fifteen Strings of Coins*, Kong Shangren's *The Peach Blossom Fan* and *Longevity Hall* authored by Hong Sheng. Other famous highlighted Kunqu operas performed on stage include *Dreams of Wandering the Garden*, *Yangguan Pass*, *Three Drunks*, *Autumn River*, *Thinking of the Mundane*, and *The Broken Bridge*. Most of these operas have become the immortal masterpieces, especially Tang Xianzhu's *Peony Pavilion*, which was produced during the period of great prosperity of Kunqu opera and was destined as a great production to be handed down from generation to generation. For this reason, Tang Xianzhu is seen in the same light as William Shakespeare, exemplifying two of the world's greatest dramatists. Canadian professor Dr. Catherine Swatek spent 15 years researching before publishing the ethnographic work entitled *Peony Pavilion Onstage: Four Centuries in the Career of Chinese Drama*. This extensive account describes and analyzes performances throughout China and the world, as well as the history of its adaption into Western opera.

It is said that each nation has its own refined and exquisite performing art which symbolizes the spirit and aspiration of its people, such as the tragedy of Greece, the opera of Italy, the ballet of Russia, and Shakespeare's dramas of England. As for the China, this is undoubtedly Kunqu opera. Kunqu opera has a history of over 600 years and is praised as one of the three original forms of the world drama. Meanwhile, it is the ancestor of all other operas and the mother of all theater in China. Many regional theater styles in China such as Shanxi opera, Puzhou opera, Shandong opera, Hunan opera, Sichuan opera, Jiangxi opera, Guangxi opera, Nanning opera, Yue opera, Guangdong opera, Fujian opera, Wu opera, and Yunnan opera, are all nurtured and nourished by the many artistic elements of Kunqu Opera. Even Beijing opera, which is referred to as the quintessence of Chinese culture, permeates the artistic elements and inherits a series of perfor-mances from Kunqu opera, and it continuously applies its types of roles and modes of presentation.

Presently, as a representative of traditional Chinese culture, Kunqu Opera has extended across national boundaries. During 1980s and 1990s, opera troupes from all parts of China were sent abroad several to foreign countries to stage performances. Its refined interpretations have been retained in Europe, North America, Hong Kong, and Taiwan. Kunqu opera has been planted its roots in foreign countries by following the footprints of overseas Chinese artists. According to records, various Kunqu opera organizations have been established in countries such as the United States and Japan. For example, the Kunqu Opera Association founded by Zhang Huixin is one of the most influential overseas opera associations. Founded in Maryland in the United States in 1995, this association has attracted a number of relatively stable audiences. Whenever the theater companies hold performances, many audiences come to be members of the associations. Kunqu opera is a window for the local inhabitants of these areas to understand China and its rich culture and history.

On May 18, 2001 Kunqu opera was elected as the leading representative art of oral and non-mat erial cultural heritage by UNESCO with no objection. On May 20, 2006 the art was also recorded to be a high-ranking non-material cultural heritage by the approval of the State Council of the People's Republic of China.

Local Operas

Yu Opera

Yu opera is also known as Henan clapper opera, and Henan lofty tune. It is also called Henan ballad, as the early performers sang using distinct techniques of the throat and in falsetto when starting and ending the tunes. They voiced the syllable ou, meaning ballad at the end of phrases. Yu opera performed in the western mountainous regions of Henan relied on the flat areas amongst the hills for staging the productions. Therefore it is known in those regions as roaring beside the mountain Because of Henan province's term yu was popular to describe the performance, the regional drama was officially named Yu opera after the establishment of the People's Republic of China.

Yu opera firstly originated between the end of the Ming Dynasty and the early stages of the Qing Dynasty. It was greatly loved and appreciated by the masses, thus developing rapidly. The origin of Yu Opera is difficult to verify with written evidence, giving rise to various theories. One is that the art formed by combining the regional folk songs and music with Shanxi opera and Puzhou clapper opera that had spread to Henan province by the end of Ming Dynasty. Another theory is that it developed directly from stringed melodies of Northern opera. Yet some believe Yu Opera was formed on the basis of Henan traditional arts, especially the xiaoling (a short meter for poems that contains relatively few syllables), which was popular in the central plains during the middle and later stages of Ming Dynasty. These qualities combined with the absorption of stringed melodic music is believed to have created this style. Yu Opera has a long history of development. During the years of Emperor Qianlong's reign (1736-1795 A.D.), it was called tubang drama and bianliang opera and received great reviews.

Yu opera prevails in Henan province, northern parts of the Yangtze River, and provinces of the northwest, as well as regions such as Xinjiang, Tibet, and Taiwan. The types of the roles in Yu Opera are composed of sheng, dan, jing, and chou. There is generally four of each. The opera troupe is organized by casting the four male roles, four female roles, four painted-face roles, as well as four soldiers, four generals, four maids and eight stagehands, plus two officers and four mixed roles. Four male roles are the old man, the lead red-faced role, second red-faced role (military character), and the younger supporting male role. The four main dan female roles are da jing (black-faced role), the lead painted-face role, second painted-face role, and the third painted-face role (chou). There is another style that incorporates five female roles and five roles of painted faces. Performers generally specialize in one type of role. There are some performers who are quite apt in several roles; they may play a main part as well as being casted as other characters. There are a total of more than 1,000 traditional scripts of Yu opera, most of which draw from historical novels or romances, such as the dramas Granting Titles to Gods, The Three Kingdoms, Wagang Drama, Lord Bao's Drama, The Yang Family Drama, The Yue Family Drama, and other operas that depict marriage, love, and cultural ethics. The most famous operas are *Fighting with Short Spears*, *Three Times in the Sedan*, *Di Tang Ban*, *Catching the Thief*, *The Trial of Zha Mei*, and *Twelve Widows Travel to the West*. After the establishment of the People's Republic of China, many modern operas and newly-edited historical operas have since appeared, such as *Chaoyang Ravine*, *Litter Erhei's Marriage*, *Personal Joys and Blaring Horses*, *The Unlucky Uncle's Marriage*, *Testing Husband*, and *The Ripening Apple*.

Yu Opera focuses on singing aspects and using clapper vocal music which is fluent and clear cut in rhythmical arrangement with regards to key elements of the plot. It is full of and distinct oration of dialogue with merry and lively phrases, displaying a unique artistic charm, and is easy for audiences to comprehend. The attributes of Yu Opera are many. One, it is filled with bold and unrestrained passions of yang energy, being adept in expressing scenes of great momentum and intense emotions. Secondly, it has strong characteristics of regional culture which are simple, unadorned, and close to the daily life of people. Another aspect is the clear and intensive rhythms. The conflicts are sharp-pointed, as the plot has a distinct beginning and end while the characters are well developed. The major sects of Yu opera are composed of eastern theater and western theater. The eastern theater influenced by its counterpart of Shandong clapper opera in that the male voice is loud and sonorous, while the female voice is vivacious and pulsating, and is commonly used as comic relief. While the western style is adept in expressing tragedy, and has retained the lingering charms of Shanxi opera, such as the bleak, solemn, and stirring male voice and lingering sweet female voice. The representative characters of Yu Opera are the five famous female roles—Chang Xiangyu, Chen Suzhen, Cui Lantian, Ma Jinfeng, and Yan Lipin; each with a distinct style. Other common roles with various distinct characteristics are the male roles of xiaosheng, Zhao Yiting, Wang sujun, xusheng, Tang Xicheng, Liu zhonghe, Liu Xinmin, hei lian Li Sizhong, and chou Niu Decao.

Huangmei Opera

Huangmei opera, formerly known as Huangmei theater originated in China's Huangmei county of Hubei province and later developed in the Anqing prefecture region of in Anhui province. As early as the late 18th century, in the bordering area of Hubei, Anhui and Jiangxi provinces, traditional performances were based on the folk literature. The title Huangmei opera was first and formally proposed in the publication of *The Annals of Susong County* in 1921. In its history of over 200 years, Huangmei opera has become a wildly famous form of opera enjoying great popularity among Chinese audiences through many years development, particularly in the last several decades.

Being tactful and pleasant sounding, the music of Huangmei opera is divided into two categories—coloratura and tranquil verse. Coloratura is performed mainly in the form of short plays, and is rich in traditional cultural songs and poetry. Tranquil verse, or ping ci, is the major music of the voice for the original dramas, being used in many verses of narration and lyrics. It is euphemistic sounding, extending beyond the abundance of the lingering charm of floating clouds and flowing water. As a major form of musical voice of the original form of drama, the ping ci has been further strengthened with regard to the narration and lyrical aspects of the modern Huangmei opera. The innovation has broken through the restrictions of the coloratura by use of particular operas, absorbing the elements of folk ballads and other music, forming a new style of vocal and instrumental harmony. Huangmei opera relies mainly on the stringed accompaniment of the gaohu, coordinating with cymbals, drums, other folk instruments, of which are fit for expressing several themes throughout the performances.

According to records, there are a total of 36 full-length Huangmei operas, along with 72 different short dramas. The full-length dramas are con-sidered to express major themes of society, such as *The Story of Buck—wheat, Lawsuit of the Grain officer, and Marriage of the Immortal*. The short plays mirror fragments of daily life of laborers in the countryside, as portrayed in *The Barley, Spinning Cotton into Yarn*, and *Selling the Grain Baskets*. Since the establishment of People's Republic of China, many tra-ditional operas have been collected and adapted, as exemplified by *Marriage of the Goddess, The Emperor's Female Son-in-law, Tales of Hand—kerchief, Zhao Guiying, A Kind Mother's Tears*, and *The Three Searches in Mansion of the Father-in-law*. Furthermore, other operas have been adapted from myth, such as *The Cowherd and the Weaving Maid*, as well as the historical and modern operas of *Warm Spring and Blooming Flowers, Early Spring in the Little Shop*, and *The First Flower Blossoms*. Among them, *Marriage of the Goddess, Woman Emperor's Son-in-law*, and *The Cowherd and the Weaving Maid* have in successfully been presented on the silver screen, having great impact in China as well as the rest of the word. Well-known performing artists include Yan Fengying, Wang Shaofang, Wu Qiong, and Ma Lan.

Yue Opera

Yue Opera is a traditional form of Chinese opera that mainly prevails in the Shanghai municipality, it also is very familiar throughout the Zhejiang, Jiangsu, and Fujian provinces. The origins of Yue opera can be traced to Shengxian county of Zhejiang province's luo di chang shu (a genre of popular entertainment consisting mainly of dialogue and singing). In the spring of thirty-second year of Guangxu's reign during the Ming dynasty (1906 A.D.), it began to evolve into a form of theater staged on the rural grassland, and was referred to as small singing troupes, du troupes, or Shaoxing drama. The original performers were primarily males of the rural areas who were semifarmers and part-time artists. Therefore, in previous times it was commonly called male troupe theater. It wasn't until the start of female song troupes in Shi Jiatai of Shengxian county in 1923 that the style was renamed Shaoxing female opera, as it was vastly popular for female impersonators to play male roles. From then on, the male actors gradually became teachers and workers. The name of Yue Opera first appeared in the advertisement section of Shanghai's News Report on September 17, 1925.

Yue Opera focuses on expressing emotion, mainly in form of singing. The tone of the voice is beautiful, exquisite, and pleasant upon hearing. The performances are vivid and moving, embodying the sentiments of Jiangnan (the area south of the Yangtze River). The golden era of Shaoxing opera was in the period of the 1950s and the early years of the 1960s. Some of the most influential artistic treasures were created at this time, such as the *Butterfly Lovers*, *The Romance of Western Chamber*, and *A Dream of Red Mansions*, receiving great reviews in both China and throughout the world. The most popular works of *Butterfly Lovers*, *Love Detectives*, *Chasing the Fish*, *The Jade Pin*, and *Tales of Colored Buildings* had become the repertoire, which among them *Butterfly Lovers*, *Love Detectives*, *Chasing the Fish*, *The Jade Pin*, and *A Dream of Red Mansions* have been adapted for film. By means of such propagation, Shaoxing opera has become more and more popular in all parts of China, north and south of the Yangtze River. Popular actors of Yue opera include Yuan Xuefen, Fu Quanxiang, Qi Yaxian, Fan Ruijuan, Xu Yulan, Yi Guifang, Wang Wenjuan, Zhang Guifeng, and Mao Weitao.

Dunhuang Murals

Dunhuang Fresco

Dunhuang is located at the intersection of China's Gansu, Qinghai, and Xinjiang provinces. The Mandarin word dun means sincere, huang meaning brillance. This grand and majestic region of Dunhuang has a long history and splendid culture. The Dunhuang murals are not only the rare orchids of a time-honored and unique culture, but also an important part of Dunhuang study which attracts worldwide attention.

The Dunhuang Murals refer to the frescos painted in the Dunhuang Caves. The murals are housed in areas such as the Mogao Caves, The Western Buddhists Caves and the Anxi Elm Forest Caves, totaling 552 caves all together. Substantial in content, grand in scale, and exquisite in technical design, the total area of murals of all the past dynasties covers an area of over 50,000 square meters, containing the largest collection of murals in China and even in the world.

The Dunhuang murals are substantial and colorful in their artistic content. Compared to other religious arts, they mainly depict the images and activities of deities, and relationships among the deities or between deities and human beings. These images pacify the mind of the onlooker, as depicted in the famous Mogao Grottos.

The Mogao Grottoes, also referred to as Dunhuang Caves or the Thou-sand Buddhas Grotto, lie at the foot of Mount Mingsha, 25 kilometers southeast of Dunhuang county. The name is rendered from its location of nearby Mogao village. They are the largest and the most famous Buddhist art grottoes in China and are praised as the pearl of oriental art. The Mogao Grottoes are distributed throughout three or four levels of various degrees in the cliffs of Mount Mingsha, with an overall length of 1,600 meters. Presently remaining are 492 caves with 2,100 painted Buddhist sculptures. The murals cover a total area of 45,000 square meters. The grottoes vary in size and the statues differ in height. The larger caves are magnificent and vigorous, while the smaller ones are so exquisite and ingenious that their profound attainments and rich imagination are quite revealing. The murals often draw their content from Buddhist folklore and sometimes mirror the various traditions of agriculture, weaving, hunting, marriage, death, and festivals. These painted frescoes exhibit great skill and exquisite artisan-ship, therefore this treasured Buddhist art has been referred to by some as the acknowledgement of the dawn of the new era in human civilization. Dunhuang murals typically fall into the following general categories.

Buddhist Art

As the Buddhist art mostly prevails in the Dunhuang caves, mainly depicted are various statues depicting different eras such as that of third and seventh generations of Buddha and as well as Sakyamuni, being treasured images throughout history. Various Bodhisattvas, such as Manjusri, Samantabhadra, Avalokitesvara, and Shizi are also depicted. Also represented are the Eight Dragons of the Heavens—Heavenly King, Dragon King, Yaksha, Flying Apsara, Gandarva, Gardua, and Mahor-aga. Of these Buddhist depictions, the spirit of Avalokitesvara is of great presence. The Mogao Grottoes are home to nearly 933 paintings regarding the Buddhist doctrine, with approximately 12,208 statues of Buddhist images with varied expressions. Buddhist scripture murals mainly take advantage of the artistic modes of painting and literature to convey the profound Buddhist classics by means with are easy to comprehend. Such ways are referred to as bianjing. Similarly, expressing the contents of classical Buddhism through painting is commonly known as bianxiang or jingbian, while depictions of classic scriptures in writing is called bianwen. Paintings with the theme of traditional Chinese mythology are portrayed in the caves of late Northern Wei Dynasty. Here we can also witness influences of Chinese Taoist thought. For example, on the top of cave number 249 of the Western Wei Dynasty, besides the lotus well in the center, there are paintings of Asura and Cintama on both the west and east walls, and the north and south faces depict the Emperor of East and the Empress of the West traveling respectfully in chariots of the phoenix and dragon. On the top of the dragon and phoenix chariots are high-hanging canopies, while at the rear of the chariots, gonfalons flutter in the wind. A warrior is depicted in the foreground hoisting a banner while leading the way, Behind it, following the enlightened mythical beast with a man's head and the body of a dragon. Also included are the Vermillion Sparrow, the Black Tortoise, Azure Dragon, and the White Tiger, distributed throughout various the levels of the fresco. These paintings are quite vivid and animated. Lie Gong, the god of thunder, furiously beats a drum while the lighting strikes, splitting a rock with a flash as rain pours down from the endless mist. These images graphically depict a strong sense of distinct ethnic identity.

The Benefactor Image

The benefactors are the individuals who provided funds for the construction of the caves. In efforts to show their piousness and leave behind a good reputation for their later generations, these wealthy individuals had portraits of themselves, their families, relatives, and servants placed on the walls when they hewed the caves. Such portraits are called referred to as benefactor portraits.

The Decrotive Pattern

Among the Dunhuang murals, there are many rich and colorful vignettes which were primarily used for decorating cave walls, as well as tables, crowns, and vessels. The decorative patterns vary in form with the different periods and are everchanging, possessing superb painting skills and abundant imagination. They are mainly depicted in paintings of geometric designs, rafter patterns, and precise edging motifs.

Story Painting

Story paintings are aimed at attracting devotees and propagating Buddhist doctrine and scripture. In order to achieve this goal, the pictures needed express the abstract and profound Buddhist classics in a simple and terse way, in that the devotees will understand immediately and become inspired. Thus, they would devoutly believe and pay homage. Large quantities of pictures painted inside the caves educate the devotees unobtrusively and imperceptibly while they are admired. Substantial in content and moving in plots, these paintings reveal living glamour, exhibiting strong artistic force. The story paintings fall into five categories.

One category is that of depictions of the lifetime achievement of the founder of Buddhism, Siddhartha Gautama. Most of them are legends and folklore of ancient India. As Buddhism passed through a number of centuries, more importance was attached to the depictions of the Sakya-muni Buddha. Extremely prevalent are scenes of an elephant carrying a human baby and the story of jumping the wall at midnight. The pictures totaling 87 in the No. 290 cave of the Northern Zhou period depict all the details of Siddhartha, from his birth to becoming Buddhist. They are juxtaposed in a horizontal fashion, with every six pieces in structured in sequence. Such extensive and in depth forms of art are rare among Buddhist story paintings in China.

Paintings of Jataka stories describe the charity deeds of Siddhartha during his lifetime. The pictures spread the Buddhist thoughts of karma, bitter hardships, and ascetic practice through benevolence by uses of the vivid description of stories, such as the story of a Bodhisattva Sa Chuina feeding the tiger by sacrificing his body, Prince Sattva rescues the pigeon by cutting off his flesh, a nine-colored deer sacrificing itself to save others, and Xu Geti supporting his parents by cutting off his flesh. Although the pictures predominantly convey thought of Buddhism, they retain more or less the inherent qualities of legends, mythology, and popular folktales.

Story pictures of predestined relationships mainly tell the stories regarding delivering all living creatures from torment by Buddhist monks and nuns, Buddhist devotees, and Siddhartha. Such kinds of works differ from the pictures of Jataka stories in that the latter only describe the affairs of Siddhartha during his lifetime, while the former tell the stories of followers of Buddhism and Buddhist devotees in both prexisting and contemporary generations. These stories depict the "Five Hundred Thieves Attain Enlightenment," "The Novice Monk Commits Suicide Abiding by the Disciplines," and "Prince Shanyou Seeks the Treasures of the Sea." These stories are not only bewildering and complicated in plots, but are also rather dramatic.

Pictures of historical fact of Buddhism refer to the story pictures that draw their materials from written accounts. These include the holy deeds of Buddhism, influential stories, the achievements of eminent monks, pictures of auspicious images, and depictions of monastic disciplines. Such works contain historical characters and events which recur in the annals of Buddhism Historical pictures are painted mainly in the secondary positions such as the walls in the cave, the surface of a paved path, or the corners. Some of them are also painted on the front of the walls, such as Cave No. 323's picture of Zhang Qian being sent to the Western Regions on a diplomatic mission, Fotucheng (a Buddhist from the Western Regions), and Buddhist Liu Sae's depictions in Cave No. 72.

Metaphorical story pictures: Such category of works mainly selects the stories cited by Siddhartha explained the profound in simple terms to Buddhist monks, nuns, and devotees; revealing the doctrines of Buddhism. These various stories are primarily from ancient India and Southeast Asia. As folklore and fairy tales collected by followers, they have been recorded in Buddhist scriptures still preserved to this day. The typical ones are The Guard Elephant and the Golden Elephant and The Lion with the Golden Hair.

Landscape Painting

Abundant in subject matter and diversified in forms, the landscape paintings are dispersed among the Dunhuang Murals and throughout the grottos. These paintings integrate scripture murals and story paintings as whole, and also serving as contrast. Also portrayed are famous landscapes that make reference to Buddhist scriptures. This imaginative form of art commonly depicts scenes of the dynamic paradise of Sukhavati (Pure Land of Buddhism), with its verdant hills and green waters, birdsong and fragrant flowers. Other caves are independent of this style and solely depict landscapes, such as the painting of Mount Wutai in Cave No. 61. Except for the decorative patterns, the other six previously mentioned categories of murals encompass a general theme, especially the scripture murals and story paintings which reflect largely social life. Such scenes include: the journey of a high officials, banquets, trials, hunting, tonsure, and Buddhist Dharma. Among the depictions of commoners, we see the portrayal of agriculture, hunting, fishing, pottery making, metallurgy, animal slaughter, cooking, construction, and the actions of beggars. Furthermore, many social activities and roles in society are revealed, such as marriage, attending school, military drills, performing arts, traveling merchants, as well as renditions of distinct ethnic groups, and foreign ambassadors. Consequently, the Dunhuang Caves serve not only the function of depicting art, but also in the presentation of history.

Besides the five categories mentioned above, there are also paintings of architecture, vessels, birds, flowers, and animals included in the Dunhuang murals, exhibiting precious artistic value. The murals systematically mirror the historical physiognomy of China during various periods of artistic styles, historical involvement, and domestic and foreign artistic renditions with regards to the layout, sculpture, patterns, and vividly painted colors.

Jingdezhen Porcelain

Jingdezhen of Jiangxi province is considered the birthplace of porcelain. It is located in the transitional region of Mountain Huang, the residuals of the Huaiyu Mountain Range, and the plain of Lake Poyang, forming beautiful scenery surrounded by hills and rivers. In all four directions, lush green mountains embrace a small basin in the middle of undulating hills. Yet it is precisely in this inconspicuous region that the sub terrain contains all the necessary raw materials for manufacturing porcelain, such as magnetite, glaze, kaoline, feldspar, and limestone. They are not only tremendous in quantity, extremely varied, but also of superior quality. Pure as jade, thin as paper, bright as mirror, and rings like a bell, Jingdezhen porcelain has become a distinct cultural symbol of the Chinese nation. In English, the name China is used to describe the country as well as referring to porcelain of this origin.

History writes that pottery was first made in Xinping county during the Han Dynasty. Since Xinping was the earliest name for Jingdezhen, from this the town is claimed to be present from the inception of pottery. During the Song Dynasty, industry and commerce expanded vigorously as thriving cities prospered. The economy rapidly increased among the Yangtze River basin and the regions of southeastern China, which facilitated the unprecedented development of porcelain in ancient times. During the late Tang Dynasty and the Five Dynasties, artisans began firing celadon and the white porcelain of the Changnan district in the Raozhou prefecture. Later, the fine qualities of the two styles were combined to form the blue and white porcelain known as raoyu. Like mild smooth jade, the blue and white porcelain prevailed and became increasingly popular throughout the world upon its release. Reproductions of such porcelain sprung up in large quantities south of the Yangtze River, based on the methods of Jingdezhen manufactured wares. Moreover, great amounts of porcelain products sold well overseas. So far, the famous blue and white porcelain that has been excavated at archaeological sites throughout the world is quite commonly that of the Song Dynasty. Emperor Zhenzong of the Song Dynasty was so fond of this kind of porcelain that he would not let it go from his hands upon holding it. He immediately issued an imperial edict that requested variations of ceramic royal tribute, with the symbols meaning made in the year of Jingde in the bottom. Furthermore, he used his own reign title Jingde to name this small mountain town. Thus, this distinct blue and white glazed porcelain becomes the only porcelain that is bestowed with the title of an emperor's reign. In 1004, Changnan was renamed Jingdezhen, establishing the production center of ancient porcelain works. Jingdezhen ceramics unprecedentedly flourished during Emperor Shenzong's reign of the Song Dynasty. In fifth year and eighth month of Emperor Yuanfeng's reign (1082 A.D.), the feudal authorities established the Porcelain Exchange Center in Jingdezhen which specifically engaged in the affairs of the trade and taxes of chinaware. From then on, Jingdezhen had gradually become the ceramics capital of China, forming a unique subculture with extensive knowledge and profound scholarship in the processes of firing ceramics, selling goods, and managing expenditures.

During the Yuan Dynasty, a new kind of vitreous enamel had been developed in Jingdezhen. It was lighter in hue than the traditional blue and white porcelain, the combination of the gemlike glaze colors and the shining white finish resembling that of goose eggs. The development of such porcelain seemed to foreshadow the emergence of the blue-flowered porcelain which became immensely popular during the middle and late periods of the Yuan Dynasty. These porcelains are spotlessly white, thick, and heavy. The glazed surface is lustrous and perfectly clear. The colors of the flowers are verdant and gorgeous, with dazzling brightness like a hibiscus flower in clear water. Unadorned and magnificent, it is commonly referred to as the national color. From the Yuan period and over six hundred years to the present, the blueflowered porcelain has embodied the highest artistic achievement of porcelain in ancient China, thus being mainstream in the manufacturing and export of ceramic wares. Consequently, Jingdezhen porcelain has sold profitably all around the world, as people throughout the world are introduced to China by means of the exquisite porcelain wares.

Celadon Porcelain Vase Of Jingdezhen

During the Ming Dynasty, Jingdezhen had gradually developed the characteristics of a major center for ceramics. With the establishment of a porcelain factory by the imperial government in Jingdezhen, the expert potters from all over the country came here consecutively, forming a grand occasion known as artisans coming from all eight directions, the finished wares distributed throughout the world. Jingdezhen during the Ming era not only prospered from the government kilns, but brilliance arose from the civilian kilns also. After the middle period of the Ming dynasty, colored porcelain began to be fired large amounts. The colors of red, green, yellow, and purple added to the blue-flowered porcelain, were generally referred to as the five great Ming colors. The most representative multicolored porcelain in Ming Dynasty was produced during the reign of Emperor Chenghua—Chenghua Doucai, which was the newly developed artistic creation on the basis of the blue flowered and red hues in the early stages of that period. During the Qing Dynasty, the Jingdezhen ceramic industry reached its golden age of prosperity. Jingdezhen developed into a tenkilometer street consisting of half kiln factories and the other half houses. Smoke blanketed the sky during the daytime, while the flames glared deep into the night, as it remained the ceramics capital of the world. Three generations of emperors—Kangxi, Qianlong, and Yongzheng—considered Jingdezhen porcelain as national wares, placing great importance on the ceramic industry. At that time, Jingdezhen porcelain art had reached epic proportions, further advancing its development. Over 50 types of colored glazes were produced and fired, as well as reproductions of famous ancient ceramic wares of incalculable patterns and decor. The blue-flower tinted wares still retained their unique positions as newer artistic forms emerged, such as the five colors of Kangxi's reign, mixed glaze, enamel colors, and deep black pigments together pushed the Jingdezhen ceramic industry to its historical peak.

Arriving to modern times, the original techniques of Jingdezhen porcelain wares cannot be equaled to the Chinese cultural connotations bore inside them. It has achieved a breakthrough—an eruption revealing its longterm accumulated influence. The appearance of the flowing poetic ceramics of scholars and works such as Eight Friends on Mount Zhu, turned Jingdezhen porcelain art into another realm.

During the first third of July in 1965, Guo Moruo, Vice Chairman of the Standing Committee of the National People's Congress, and other deputies conducted an inspection visit in Jingdezhen. After visiting the exquisitely artistic porcelain factories, Guo Moruo scribed with good cheer the famous classical line, "China is praised as a nation of fine porcelain, and the peak of the porcelain industry is this city."

Unit 3

The Ancient Schools of Education

The earliest school of education in China probably began during the times of slave-owning society. According to the existing literature, there had already been schools during the Xia Dynasty, with a complete system of learning developed by the Western Zhou period. The schools can be classified in two categories: the Imperial Academy, and rural education, with regard to it different regions. Emperors in their capitals established the Imperial Academies during the period of vassal states. All encompassed the broad scope of the Five Studies—Biyong, Zhong, Dongxu, Chengjun, Guzhong, and Shangxiang. Among these, the structure that houses Biyong was the central core, surrounded by water on all four sides. Compared to this style of architecture, subordinate universities built by monarchs were less complex in design, with only one of the buildings half-facing the water. This was referred to as Pan Gong. Besides the Imperial Colleges, there were also schools throughout the rural areas established by administrative subdivisions. Due to the various magnitudes of different regions, rural universities are referred to by names such as lushu, dangxiang, zhouxu, and xiangxiao.

According to the records of *Zhou Rites*, the universities of the Western Zhou Dynasty educated students on the three virtues, the three behaviors of conduct, six rules of etiquette, and the six Confucian arts. Among these rich cultural connotations, the school of education stressed the concept of ethics. During the three periods of the Xia, Shang, and Zhou Dynasties, formal education was conducted by feudal officials. It wasn't until the Eastern Zhou Dynasty that the emperor's dethronement led to the poor management and decline of the official schools, changing the direction of education with regard to region. Therefore, the rising feudal states attracted talented individuals by all means, as the erudite officials drifted in amongst the commoners,and a-cademics gradually became private study. Laodan, a historian of the Zhou Dynasty, the musician Shixiang of the state of Lu, and the philosopher Confucius recruited a wide range of dis-ciples. It was the first time that the culture of education entered the general populace. However, at that time there was no regular location for Confucius and the other scholars to give the lectures and educate their students.

After the Emperor Qin Shi Huang unified China, he established the official system of court academia in order to change the trend of private education. Although the doctoral officials received salaries from the government, they were appointed the positions of advisors, never participating in the actual political decision-making. At the same time, they were obligated to recruit new disciples to retain their scholarly status as court academicians.

The court system of doctoral officials continued and wasn't abolished until the early stages of the Han Dynasty. Huge changes occurred during the reign of Emperor Wu as he established the Im-perial College—based on the doctoral officials' instruction of the Five Classics of Confucianism. Who were formally taught in the Imperial Colleges as the students were referred to as doctoral disciples. Emperor Wu of Han Dynasty attempted to revert to the former tradition of the government-spon-sored education of the Western Zhou Dynasty, therefore the subsidized education was no longer just of the aristocratic realm, but also intended for commoners. The emphasis on the system of education during the Western Han Dynasty aligned in combining the cultivation of talent with a selection of worthy individuals. In other words, the institutes were mutually compatible with the recruitment process, thus the government officials of the Han Dynasty were all from the Imperial College. Com-pared with that of former regimes, these new institutions showed great advancement. However, the Imperial College gradually deteriorated for various reasons among lack interested students. Scholars who truly wanted to pursue studies by heart returned to the private colleges. Therefore, the system of privatized education was revamped amongst the people.

Following the Eastern Han Dynasty, political power has disintegrated. During this period there emerged two forms of education—family education and monastery education, the prominent schol-ars at the time from either of a wealthy family or monastery. The Han Dynasty system of public edu-cation was revived with the unification of the Sui and the Tang dynasties. During the period of Taizong's reign during the Tang Dynasty, many foreign students were sent to China from places such as the three Korean kingdoms of Goguryeo, Baekje, and Silla, as well as Gaochang (Kharakhoja), and the Tibetan kingdom of Tubo, and the number of students reached over eight thousand. The Tang Dynasty implemented a system of examination apart from the institution of education. The process of attending school was relatively easy, but to run for public office was painstakingly difficult. Society regarded a Jinshi, or palace graduate in the highest regard, attaching little importance to the students of the Imperial College. Therefore, the state-run education at that time began to accomplished signifi-cantly less.

During the Tang Dynasty, there was an entrance examination was necessary, but lacking the schools to cultivate the talent. The educating of the student was dependent upon monastery or family

statue. While the talent cultivated in the monastery was not used for secular life, the candidates from family statues deceased daily. Despite this, there were
many palace graduates, yet they could merely recite poetry and compose the poetic essays with little
practical ability. Therefore, there was no universal school at that time. A great majority of learned individuals went to the monasteries to lay the foundation the Zen sect of Buddhism. In the later years
of Tang Dynasty emerged the academy of classical learning as the remnant and the shadow of the
family statue education, thriving during the Tang Dynasty. In order to rectify the malpractice of education of the Tang Dynasty, the Song Dynasty government implemented both public and private systems of education, with state-run colleges and private institutions. However, the Imperial College
controlled by government faced the corruption of politics and the short comings of education so that
the government-sanctioned education gradually lost confidence of the people. Although the government of Song Dynasty strived sedulously to promote education, the government-run schools still
could not reach the expectations of the private schools. Educators such as Zhou Dunyi, Cheng Jing,
Cheng Yi of the Northern Song Dynasty; and Zhu Xi and Lu Jingshan of the Southern Song Dynasty
gave personal lectures that exhibited great influence.

In the Yuan Dynasty, the Mongolians occupied the Central Plains with the Academies of Classical Learning spreading all over the country, which was more flourishing even more than that of the
Southern Song period. The first Ming Emperor Zu Yuanzhang, even before he seized power, established county schools in Wuzhou even before he had seized the state power. When he was on the
throne, he published the imperial edict to establish schools in counties all over the country. According to the statistics, there were a total of 4,100 educators among prefectures, government offices, administrative divisions, and places of garrison throughout country, which were several hundred times
more than that of the Yunfeng years of Northern Song Dynasty. The local students attended the national school which was originally called Guo Zi Xue (Imperial School) and later Guo Zi Jian (Imperial College).

As the Ming Dynasty was established, the two systems of education and examination were
merged together. Unlike the Tang era of recruiting according to one's ability to compose the poetry,
during the Ming period the selection was made through Jingyi, which involved writing an eight-part
essay. But afterwards the system was infested with malpractice, therefore many public lectures appeared in opposition. Wang Yangming and his disciples, as well as the scholars from the Dongling A-
cademy often amassed crowds to address the issue.

In the Qing Dynasty, state-run public schools and schools of the central authorities in all areas
existed only in name, as the Academies of Classical Learning continued uninterrupted. The Academy
of the Qing Dynasty mainly focused on contributions to the library collections and inscription.

In 1905, the government of the Qing Dynasty comprehensively abolished the imperial examination, opening a vast number of academies and establishing the central administrative authority to
conduct education—Xuebu, merging with the the Imperial College in order to exercise the control of
education nation wide. Although it had made a great progress of historic significance, judging from
its intrinsic quality, the educational system, whether in the teaching of philosophy, courses content,

or administration, at that time hadn't fully left the nest of the feudal code of ethics. The educational system at the time remained within the classification of a semi-colonial and semi-feudal society.

In 1912, the Xinhai Revolution (led by Dr. Sun Yat-sen) led to the overthrow of the Qing Dynasty, ending the over two thousand years of dominance by the feudal autocratic monarchy. Consequently, the development of education in China began to enter a new phase.

The Imperial Examination Culture

The Imperial Examination was held for intellectuals of ancient China as a means to select insightful individuals of talent. It was an integral system of recruiting government officials by feudal dynasties of the past. It was called keju, meaning subject selection, since it adapted methods of selecting talents through a range of different subjects. The system was implemented from the beginning of the Sui Dynasty until the end of the 31st year of Emperor Guanxu's reign (1905) of the Qing Dynasty, persisting for more than 1,300 years.

The ancient Chinese Imperial Examination System was originated during the Sui Dynasty. In the third year of his reign (605 A.D.), Emperor Yang established the jinshi exam to select successful candidates of the highest level of imperial examinations, which symbolized the official formation of the imperial examination. The system interconnected book study, testing, and stressed official conduct, opening up a new page in the annals of China's electoral system.

Emperors had followed the talent recruitment system of Sui Dynasty, taking it one step beyond. Consequently, the Imperial Examination System had gradually become complete. During this period, the imperial examination usually was composed to two main sections referred to as jieshi and xingshi—examination held by Ministry of Rites. One who passed the last phase was pronounced a Jinshi, or metropolitan scholar. Since the Jinshi examination was so extremely difficult that few could actually pass. Therefore, successful candidates generally went on to become elected officials. Upon evaluating the final examination, those who ranked first among all candidates were given the honorary title of Zhuangyuan. However, Zhuangyuan of the Tang Dynasty did not share the same priority as that of later periods. But the final examination of the Tang era was judged not only by the score, but also by the prominent person who gave the recommendation of the candidate. In 702 A.D., during this same dynasty, the Wuju examination was implemented to select military talents. Later, successive dynasties continued to use this system, eventually integrating with the Jinshi examination as one comprehensive test.

The imperial examination of the Song Dynasty was generally as same as that of Tang Dynasty except for the increasing number of successful candidates. Many individuals of common ancestry entered the bureaucracy through the system of examination and participated in the governing of the country. The Song Dynasty instituted that the examination was to be held once every three years in three levels: namely the rural, provincial, and court examinations. The candidates who successfully completed the final examination were immediately conferred a title without checking by the board of civil office. Jinshi during the Song era was divided into three strata: Jinshi Jidi of the first stratum, Jinshi Chushen of the second stratum, and the third-ranking Tong Jinshi Chushen. During the Song Dynasty, the Jinshi of the final examination enjoyed political superiority, lasting until the end of the Imperial Examination System.

In Yuan Dynasty, the imperial examinations were held occasionally for the Mongolians ruled the country. But during this time first appeared the complete examination based on the contents of The Four Books—*The Great Learning, the Doctrine of the Mean, the Analects of Confucius* and *the Analects of Mencius*. Furthermore, the Yuan against the Hans implemented a policy of racial discrimination with regards taking the examination.

The establishment of Ming Dynasty brought the downfall of the Yuan Dynasty. At this time, the Imperial Examination System entered a period of great prosperity. The authorities of the Ming Dynasty attached great importance to the system. The methods of selection were much stricter than that of any other past generation. Before the Ming Dynasty, the Imperial College was one of the ways to provide the candidates, while during the Ming Dynasty, one had to directly enter the Imperial Examination System. During the Ming era, the examination was formally divided into three levels: xiangshi (rural), huishi (provincial), and dianshi (court examination). First-place candidates of the rural examination were called Jieyuan, on the provincial test called Huiyuan, and of the court examination Zhuangyuan, which were collectively known as the Three Yuan. With regards to the court examination, in addition to the previously mentioned Zhangyuan, there was also the second and third ranking scholars that were respectively called Bangyan, and Tanhua. During the Ming Dynasty, the main contents of the imperial examination included a specific eight-part essay. The examination questions came from the verses of the Four Books and the Five Classics, which required the examinees to expound on the principals of these classical texts. The examinees were to answer the questions in the style of ancient writing, within a particular format. Furthermore, the number of words was strictly limited and the syntax required an antithesis. The eight-part essay brought forth great harm and seriously fettered the thoughts of people. Meanwhile, the Imperial Examination System led itself to a dead end.

During the Qing Dynasty, the imperial examination was generally as same as that of Ming era. However, the policy of the racial discrimination still existed. The Manchu enjoyed various priorities, becoming officials in absence of the examination. The Imperial Examination System declined day by day, with more and more disadvantages emerging, particularly with the onslaught of foreign aggressors, accelerating its extinction. In the 27th year of Emperor Guanxu's reign of the Qing Dynasty, after the imperial examination was administered for the last time, it was officially terminated in 1905.

In the over 1000 years implementation of the imperial exam-

The Imperial Examination Scene

ination, various relatively comprehensive systems had been set up in practice. For example, in order to discourage fraud, the avoidance system—relationships of kin were to be avoided between the examiners and the examinees, the concealed name system—the names and other information of the examinees should be covered, and transcription system that required the completed examination to be transcribed in the uniform handwriting by an official to avoid deception and to compose a clean copy. These systems have had far-reaching influence and have even played a role in modern society.

As an important invention of ancient China, over the years the Imperial Examination System has made a great impact on Chinese society and culture. Neighboring countries in Asia such as Vietnam, Japan, and Korea have all at one time introduced similar systems with which to select learned individuals. Sun Zhongshan believed the Chinese Imperial Examination System to be the world's oldest and most prestigious framework of assessment for the selection of expertise.

The Ancient Book-Collecting Culture

There were four major systems of cataloging books in ancient China: official libraries, private libraries, academic libraries and monastery collections. The history of book collection can be traced back to the pre-Qin era, when people used jiaguwen (oracle bone script) to record society, politics, the economy, and military issues, establishing halls to house the various tortoise shell and bone inscriptions, becoming the first archives of China. From this point on, China began its over three thousand year history of library collections. As the Zhou Dynasty came to power, the royal library, monastery, and vassal libraries were beginning to take shape with the appearance of the writing instruments such as inscribed wooden tablets, bamboo slips, and fine silk paper. During the Warring States period, the social atmosphere of a hundred schools of thought contending had broken down the government's monopoly of information, abolishing the practice that only allowed imperial historiographers to record oration and public affairs. This wrote a new chapter in the history of books collection as private libraries were established. During Qin and Han dynasties, the First Emperor Qin implemented the system of burning the books and burying the Confucians, which brought great destruction to Chinese cultural material as huge amounts of historical documents and classical works vanished. Fortunately, some private collectors protected their books with their upmost, there for preserving a few of the historical canonical texts for future generations. During the two periods of the Han Dynasties (Western Han and Eastern Han), the book collecting culture had been revived and further developed. According to documents, there were a total of twenty-two private collectors, most of them nobles, officials in high position, or families of learned scholars. The most famous collection are that of dignitaries such as Liu An, Liu Xin, Cai Yi, and Zheng Xuan.

During the Wei, Jin, the Northern and Southern Dynasties, the general contents of private libraries changed. In one aspect, the invention and the wide range of applications of paper greatly decreased the price of books. And in another aspect, book collecting enjoyed great popularity during this time among the class of ministers of a particular hierarchy. They circulated copies of books among each other, and even unselfishly donated volumes, allowing a small number of commoners to join the groups of books collectors. The number of private collectors had increased over one hundred, thus the quantity and quality of the libraries had been improved.

The period of the Sui and Tang Dynasties marked the peak of Chinese feudal society. There was a great demand for books, as the literate culture developed prosperously. This can likely be attributed to the invention and application of block printing. Block printing not only increased the speed and efficiency of publication, but also broke down the aristocratic exclusivity of books, enabling commoners to also read and accrue literature. Furthermore, the establishment of the Imperial Examination System propelled the book culture toward boom and prosperity, which brought forth many official librarians within the palace.

During the Tang Dynasty, a new cataloging system came into being—the academic library. The Imperial Academy established an archive, with abundant lists of books. There were over 100,000 volumes of books collected during the period of recruitment at the Academy of Classical Learning in Luoyang during this time. The library of collections was regarded as the spiritual homeland for the scholars and efficient for preserving traditional Chinese literary works and culture. It especially made an indelible contribution to the storage and protection of ancient books and records, and furthered the aspects of document research, textual criticism, and the publication of periodicals.

Ningbo's First Hall Under Heaven

The throughout the Song and Yuan periods great development took place among collections. This phase set a new precedent for the collating and cataloguing of subjects such as bibliography, annotated editions, textual criticism, and the study of publication. The quantity of the archives held edge on the previous generation, management during this period also became standardized.

During the period the Ming, society was relatively stable and flourishing in the aspect of politics, economy, and culture, therefore the book culture continued to expand. Particularly, the prospering of the block-printing industry and the emergence of bookstores and individual sellers furnished the favorable material basis for the development of the book industry. According to records, during the Ming Dynasty there were 869 book collectors who had accomplished much more than the collectors of the Song and Yuan dynasties with regards to the management of the materials. They were particular about the location and the name of buildings, paying particular attention to the three protections—fireproofing, moisture resistance, and insect deterrent. At the same time, great detail was given to discourage scattered or lost books. Ningbo city's First Hall Under Heaven assumes the responsibility as the leader of ancient book collections. As the oldest private library in Asia, it is also one of the three world's earliest existing book collections.

Throughout the Qing Dynasty, the amassing of literature took on an unprecedented turn of development. The government of Qing Dynasty attached the upmost importance to the collections of volumes of all the past generations. The achievement of the Qing Dynasty surpassed that of all the past generations with regards to the accumulation and archiving of books. In this period emerged the masterpiece edited by palace officials of Qing Dynasty—*The Complete Collection of Four Treasuries*.

Besides the above-mentioned imperial, private, and academic archives, there existed another distinct system of cataloging—the monastery collections, which emerged in accompaniment with the introduction of Buddhism and Taoism. During the period of the Six Dynasties of the Han and Wei, it emerged and began its development. As early as Emperor Ming of the Han Dynasty, ambassadors were sent to the Western Regions by the imperial government to obtain The Sutra in Forty-two Chapters and built the White Horse Temple to store and protect them. In the 11th year of Yong Ping's reign of Eastern Han Dynasty, in the holy land of Buddhism, Mount Wutai, the Dafu Lingjiu Temple was built, becoming the model of ancient Chinese monastery book collections as the circulation of literature increased by the effort of the devotees. During the last years of the Eastern Han Dynasty, Taoism emerged and developed into literary works, as books on the thought amassed in the temple collections. In order to protect and preserve the ancient books and records from natural and man-made calamities, the devotees adopted the methods of concealed storage—either carving them into the cliffs of the caves in remote mountainous regions, or hiding them in private rooms and Buddhist pagodas. Since many temples were local cultural centers in ancient times, as functioning to serve universal education by preserving the Buddhist and Taoist canonical texts, there were still other categories of books stored within the temples. The monastery collections was relatively stable and less disturbed.Certain individuals of higher thought were inclined to store their works in the temples. The four major systems of book collections helped each other make progress and were mutually complementary, greatly contributing to the inheritance of Chinese culture and tradition.

Confucianism

Confucianism refers to the doctrine of Confucian study that originated during the Spring and Autumn Period, encompassing a long and unbroken period of over 2,500 years. The rise of Emperor Wu of the Han Dynasty helped to integrate Confucian thought within Chinese culture. During this period, Confucian study expands its contents, forms, and social functions with the development of society. Its progress can be divided into four stages on the whole.

The primitive Confucian study during the pre–Qin era is presented by Confucius, Mencius, and Hsun Tzu

The founding concepts of Confucian doctrine mainly refers to the moral standards for cultivating people of virtue and principles for governing a country. People often refer to Confucian study as the study of benevolence, as a result of Confucius's conviction of benevolence as the fundamental moral standard required of a virtuous individual. *The Analects of Confucius* recorded many opinions of Confucius as he answered his students' questions with regard to the concept of benevolence. It contains various specific norms and principles to be followed in mundane practical activities.

Mencius made further development of Confucius' thought that men's mind should be cultivated benevolently. Besides, he introduced the doctrine of a benevolent government, which has become throughout the world. The requirements of benevolent governance were specific to the previous study of benevolence. For example, as stated, "the conduct of a benevolent government should begin with the management of its borders." The so-called management of boundaries refers to the belief that farmland should be evenly distributed and enacts a system that allows people to permanently be entitled to their property. Although the norms and principles proposed by Confucius and Mencius were specific, they were much too idealistic and placed great expectations on the realization of the innate nature of humans. Therefore, Confucius did his utmost to emphasize self-restraint and self-cultivation. Mencius promoted the theory of kinship by nature and placed further emphasis on intuitive knowledge and the instinctual generosity of human subjects.

Compared to Confucius and Mencius, Hsun Tzu was more inclined to realism. He not only gave priority over education on sense of righteousness and morality, but also accentuated the functions for corporeal punishment within the political and legal system. Hsun Tzu initiated the theory of immorality by nature, advocating the intuitive nature of people should be educated and guided by a sense of righteousness and law in so that the conduct would accord with the public standards and requirements of social groups.

The original Confucian study was one of the prominent primordial schools of thought which attached the concept of realism, making a great impact on society from the late Spring and Autumn to the Warring States periods. The theory of moral cultivation exhibited a heavy influence on the class of individuals of virtue. But, the ideal political and the state-run systems were not appreciated or adopted by the authorities in power since it lost touch with the current social reality of vassals seeking hegemony and rival warlord regimes competing for parts of the country. Thus, the primitive Confucian study differs from the thought developed later in that it was founded on the basis of the current political and social systems, incorporating the original notion of moral cultivation with political ideals.

Political and religion-oriented Confucian study in the Han Dynasty

Rulers during the early stages of the Han Dynasty adopted new policy forming a streamlined administration, governing by noninterference, and the rehabilitation of the people reducing taxes and levies so that the people can rest and financially recuperate in order to recover from the extreme financial destitution of people's livelihood caused by tyrannical government and the turmoil of war of the later stages of the Qin Dynasty. Correspondingly, they attached great importance to and advocated the Taoism of the Yellow Emperor. These circumstances continued until the initial changes during Emperor Wu's reign during the Han Dynasty.

A renowned scholar named Dong Zhongshu in Western Han Dynasty proposed that the authority should pay supreme tribute to Confucianism while banning all other schools of thought in order to accomplish national reunification. Emperor Wu adopted the proposal as Confucian study entered political institutions and religious places of worship. Dong Zhongshu studied the theory of Gong Yang (surname for Gong Yang Gao who was a scholar of the Warring States Period), which was a kind of theory closely related to societal norms. Gong Yang exemplifies in *The Spring and Autumn Annuals* the theories of the three systems (heaven, man, earth), the critical three months (periods of the lunar calendar) and the three eras (past, now, future). These ideals were aimed at expounding the establishment of Han Dynasty, while the various virtues and the estab-lished norms mentioned among these concepts could be emulated by the governmental realms of the Han Dynasty. *The Spring and Autumn Annals* is generally believed to be written by Confucius. Dong Zhongshu and Han scholars regarded Confucius as the Unadorned Emperor, namely a ruler without an actual throne. Therefore, the Confucian study associated closely with the practical social political system. It not only confounded the uninvolved theories of morality, ethical cultivation, and political idealism, but meanwhile functioned as articles of legality for the social system. The religious orientation of Confucian study greatly influenced political institutions, thus Confucius is praised as the King of Doctrine. The social political functions of Confucianism strengthened and developed, weakening its roles of moral ethical cultivation and political ideals

As the later period of the of Han Dynasty arrived, the governmental ethical code of Confucian brought about a fierce dissatisfaction among the masses, as it shackled and constrained the natural e-motions of individuals. Furthermore, it became the means of hypocrites to fish for fames and compliments. The study of metaphysics and Taoist philosophy and religion expounded the opportunity of this malpractice and replaced Confucianism in the realm of moral cultivation. After the periods of the Eastern Jin and the Northern and Southern Dynasties, the influence of Buddhism had surpassed that of metaphysics, attaching great importance to scholars with regards to moral cultivation. Therefore, in the 700 years from Wei, Jin, Northern and Southern Dynasties, to the Sui, Tang, and later stages of the period of the Five Dynasties, Confucian dogma which embodied the political institutions continued to function under the protection of the ruling authority.

The Confucian school of idealist philosophy of Song , Ming, and Qing Dynasties

The doctrines of the Buddhism and Daoism had great impact on the majority of scholarly officials in the aspect of self-cultivation, which arouse the dissatisfaction and uneasiness of Confucians. This sparked the revivalism of Confucian study. Wang Tong of the Sui and Tang Dynasties initiated this movement, followed by Han Yu, Li Ao, and Liu Zongyuan during the middle period of the Tang era. A more luminous view was presented during the Song Dynasty. Moreover, they strived to revive the main Confucian concepts of moral principles, ethics, and character development. As they hoped to give full play of its social functions in the aspect of moral cultivation, returning to the ideological fields that had been occupied by Buddhism and Taoism for the last 700 years.

Confucianism was called the School of Principal during Song and Ming Dynasties, including the Yuan and Qing periods, due to the fact that it greatly differed from the original Confucian theories. Generally speaking, the beginning stages of Confucian study only told us what and how in relation to conduct in daily life, but did not explain why. While an ideological system containing cosmic principles and conscience was established after the idealist philosophy, absorbing and amalgamating the theories of metaphysics, Buddhism, and Taoism. During the early phases of the Northern Song Dynasty, Hu Yuan, Sun Fu, and Shi Jie were know as the three teachers of the School of Principal. However, it was actually Zhou Dunyi, Shao Yong, Zhangzai, and the Cheng brothers who initiated the idealist philosophy. Zhu Xi of the Southern Song Dynasty epitomized the thought of this school, establishing a relatively complete objective idealist system as he proposed that the philosophy existed before the creation of the universe. Lu Jiuyuan, who opposed Zhu Xi's views of subjective idealism and proposed the doctrine that external reality is a product of human consciousness. In Ming Dynasty, Wang Shouren further developed the theory of Lu Jiuyuan. He thought that there was nothing or no reason outside man's mind. He even asserted that the soul was the origin of the universe.

Confucianism study in modern times

Neo-Confucianism emerged in the modern eras as a result of the influx of western culture into China, and the collision of the philosophical ideas of the East and the West. The narrow sense of modern Neo-Confucianism points to the works of Liang Shuming, Xiong Shili, Ma Yifu, Qian Mu, Feng Youlan, and He Lin. The broad sense of modern Neo-Confucian study refers to the doctrines of Confucianism's innovations that emerged after the Opium War. The modern school of thought aimed at promulgating the traditional cultural norms by means of modern interpretations so that it could play an active role in moral cultivation and the establishment of nationalized ideological principles.

As an embodiment of Chinese culture passed down for over 2000 years, the Confucianism is rich and profound in ideological connotations, with extensive influence in China and East Asia. Meanwhile, as one of the main representatives of oriental traditions, Confucianism, is mutually complimentary among Western cultures, becoming increasingly significant with the passage of time.

Taoism

Taoism is a school of thought reflecting ancient Chinese social, ideological, cultural values; using the Tao (the way),as its core concept. It emphasizes the effortless and spontaneous laws of wuwei, and the conformance of humanity in complying with these ways of nature. Taoism is primarily one of Hundred Schools of Thought during the pre-Qin period,afterwards it extended to include those who placed a premium on the doctrines of scholars Lao Tzu and Zhuang Tzu.

Tao is the core and the highest category of the school of thought, therefore Taoist scholars attach great importance to this concept. In general, Tao reflects the following aspects: the Tao is the source of a myraid of all things in nature, performs spontaneousness without action, is formless in existence; the Tao possesses ubiquity, is omnipresent, and timeless. As a genre of ideological and cultural thought, Taosim's essential characteristics revered by Taoist scholars are that of the doctrines of Zhuang Tzu, Lao Tzu and Emperor Huang. As the way of the Tao, is the central foundation among nature in the beliefs of Taoism, it also extends its ideological system from the framework of the relationship between humans and all things under the heavens, and the effortless and spontaneous ways of the cosmos, coupled with the acquiescence of humanity. They also regard worldly affairs with subtle and abstruse language, as such is the mindset of the recluse. In comparison to other schools of thought, Taoist scholars observe and record society by a more recollected, sober, and profound means, as well as having unique temperament of universal acceptance, possessing transcendence and freeness from vulgarity, abandoning benevolence and etiquette, and pursuing the unassuming aspects of nature.

Taoism shows diversity during different periods of its evolution, having passed through three historical phases.

The study of Emperor Huang and Lao Tzu in Qin and Han Dynasties is a school of philosophical political thought that emerged during the Warring States Period. In the term "Huang Lao", Huang refers to the Emperor Huang, and Lao naturally referrs to Laozi. During the Warring States period as study of the Five Elements circulated, Emperor Huang was not only considered himself to be one of the Five Elements, but also the legendary ancestor of Chinese culture, thus he became the object of worship relied upon by military strategists, legalist philosophers, the Yin and Yang school of philosophy, and even the Confucians.

Moreover, Emperor Huang is considered superior in thought in the passages of The Way of Chuang Tzu, a work reflecting the thoughts of Taoist master Chuang Tzu. In the late years of the Warring States period, the study of Emperor Huang and Lao Tzu is formed by the combination LaoTzu's influence from the state of Chu and the worship of Emperor Huang in the central plains of China. It marked a ideological trend of Taoism, thus developing to a new stage. Scriptures of the study of Emperor Huang and Lao Tzu are reflected in *The Book of the Yellow Emperor* and *The Way of Lao Tzu*.

During the period of the Wei and Jin dynasties, metaphysics became a prominent school of thought. The Taoist classical works: *The Way of Lao Tzu*, *The Way of Chuang Tzu*, and *The Book of Changes* (collectively known as the Three Profound Theories), reflect a kind of philosophy that integrates Confucian ideology on the basis of Taoist principle. The concept of xuan, meaning abstruse (modern era refers to metaphysics), emerges from chapter one in *The Way of Lao Tzu*. "The abtruse is within the abtruse, as the gateway to the multitude of the unfathomable." Metaphysics in the period of the Wei and Jin Dynasties went through a development in its history witnessed by scholars He Yan, Wang Bi, Ji Kang, Ruan Ji and Guo Xiang. This went from the ontology of valuing the concept of nothingness to theories of dignifying existence.

After the decline in the study of metaphysics, the vestigial residue of Taoist thought remained, which is revealed from the many annotated editions of *The Way of Lao Tzu* and *The Way of Chuang Tzu* emerging from the time of the Sui and Tang dynasties. But not long after the Sui and Tang era, the existing forms of Taoism took new shape, prospering mainly within the religious realms. Scholars of Taoism began establishing their own religious theories by interpreting and developing the thoughts of Chuang Tzu.

Nevertheless, Taoist philosophy and Taoist religion are two different terms, similar in some as-

pects, yet differing in others. The different periods of emergence of the
two schools of thought can account for contrasting views. The philosophy of Taoism
was founded by Lao Tzu in the last years of Spring and Autumn Period, while the religion was established during the late years of Eastern Han Dynasty. Secondly, the representatives for the two are different. Eventhough the same person represented, he is different in personality among the distinctions
of the two practices. Leading the philosophical school of thought are Lao Tzu, Chuang Tzu, and Lieh
Tzu; while the religion mainly relys on the teachings of Ge Hong, Tao Hongjing, and Cheng Xuany-
ing. The two types of persona mutually created by each cannot be interchanges. For example, Lao Tzu
is a realistic ideologist and founder of Taoist philosophy, while in a latter example, he is Supreme
Lord Lao Tzu as a religious leader. Both portray him in high regard, but are characteristically different. Thirdly, in the strict sense, the philosophy of Taoism is only a school of ideology and culture,
while Taoism as a religious group not only has ideological functions, but also has strict organization
and religious activities. One obvious connection between the two practices is that the religion of Taoism is established on Taoist philosophical prinicpals. Since after the Han and Wei Dynasties, no new
scholars nor school of thought appeared to support Taoist philosophy. Conversely, Taoism as a religion made considerable development during this time. Yet the philosophical schools of Taoism did
not completely vanish, one main reason being the continual growth and development of the religion.
Moreover, since the religion employs the principals of the philosophy as the theoretical pillars, it conveys philosophical thought and continues to develop as Taoist religious scholars annotate the classic
ideology of the scriptures of Zhuang Tzu.

As an indigenous religion, Taoism has contributed greatly to the development of traditional Chinese culture and it is considered as one of the Three Pillars—Confucianism, Buddhism, and Taoism—of traditional Chinese culture. Moreover, in the serious environmental crisis that exists in today's modern world, the Taoist thought of oneness of humanity and its wisdom of ecology give rise to
much needed enlightenment and respect for the earth.

Buddhism

Buddhism emerged during the 6th B.C. in India. At that time, India was going through periods
of major turmoil and great change resulting in continuous wars, social chaos, political corruption, and no way to make a living. Some disheartened people attempted to withdraw from social life,
becoming monks known as shramanas. They lived in the wild, wearing the bark of trees, eating a-
corns, drinking with their hands, remaining unmarried, bearing no children, and performed ascetic
practices, not moving throughout the day. The founder of Buddhism, Siddhartha Gautama was born
at this time. He had been in love with meditation since his childhood, and felt deeply upset with the
chopping and changing of the secular life that he wanted wholeheartedly to cast off. When he was 29
years old, he decided to abandon the superior material life and escaped from home late in the night,
shaving his head and bearing the live of a shramana. After years of penance and asceticism, at the age

of 35 he finally reached the realm of realizing all truths, becoming the Enlightened One.

Since he preached throughout the land, widely recruiting disciples to advance his ideals. With the emergence of Buddhism, the Buddhist arts, such as pagodas, sculptures, and painted murals, also appeared promoting Buddhism by use of images and metaphors.

In the following centuries, Buddhism and its arts followed the Silk Road and diffused to the north, west and east. Around the first century B.C. they were introduced to China. After longterm development, a form of Chinese Buddhism was formed with distinct cultural characteristics.

Due to the various periods of introduction, channels, regional and ethnic cultures, social and historical background; there were three major sects of Buddhism in the country, namely, Chinese Buddhism (Mandarin system), Tibetan Buddhism (Tibetan language system), and the Yunnan region's Theravada Buddhism (Pali Language system).

Chinese Buddhism: Buddhism is believed to have entered the Han regions of China, in Yong Ping years of Emperor Ming's rein during the Eastern Han Dynasty (58-75 A.D.), an envoy was sent on a mission to the Western Regions obtain The Sutra in Forty-two Chapters. Buddhism spread from the centers of Chang'an, and Luoyang regions. The first temple built on mainland China was the White Horse Temple, located 10 kilometers east of Luoyang. During the Eastern Han period, the vast majority of the Buddhist scriptures were translated.

During the periods of the Three Kingdoms, the Wei, and Western Jin Dynasties, a major aspect of dissemination was the translation of sacred Buddhist literature. The Weiduo district of the ancient capital of Luoyang and the capital of Wu, Jiangye, were the centers of Buddhist propaganda. The translation, dissemination, and research of the Buddhist doctrines laid a preliminary foundation for the development of the Buddhism during these periods. During the Eastern Jin to the Northern and Southern Dynasties periods, Buddhism was further developed, attracting people of all social strata, as pagodas and temples were built everywhere. The world famous ancient Buddhist grotto arts, such as Dunhuang Murals, Yungang and Dragon Gate began to be constructed during this period. The scholar Kumarajiva (c.a. 344-413A.D.) translated 384 volumes of sacred texts. Extremely accurate and concise, they have made substantial contributions to the development of Buddhism. On pilgrimage to the West for Buddhist scriptures, Fa Xian (337-422A.D.) toured more than 30 countries in regions of India and Sri Lanka. The sacred literature and travel log he composed has provided valuable materials for the development of Buddhism as well as historical research of Central and Southern Asia.

Emperor Liang Wu of the Northern and Southern Dynasties period faithfully believed in Buddhism. During the 14 years of his reign, he had entered the temple as a servant for four times, expounding on the texts of Buddhism and composing scriptures of his own. During the Liang Dynasty, there were a total of 2,860 temples and over 82,700 Buddhist monks and nuns.

During the Tang Dynasty, Chinese Buddhism was in its time of great prosperity. Emperor Taizong once received support from Buddhist monks to rid the land of separation and appease turmoil. He issued an imperial edict establishing temples all around the country, setting up places for explaining the scriptures and cultivating large quantities of eminent monks and scholars during his rule. One of the most famous monks was Xuanzang, who had spent 19

years trudging an over 100,000 kilometers long and difficult journey to India to

come into possession of the scriptures. He translated seventy-five Buddhist scriptures totaling 1,335

volumes and composed the Great Tang Records of the Western Regions. He was held in high esteem

by Emperor Tang Taizong as the leader that opened the gate of Buddhism, and an

individual that appears only once throughout the ages. His life stories were

recorded in all kinds of books that eventually evolved into mythological legends.

During the middle of the Tang period appeared the oral legends of Xuanzang. In

Song Dynasty, The Tang Record Xuanzang Obtaining the Scriptures emerged.

During the Ming Dynasty, Wu Cheng'en composed the novel *Journey to the West*,

making the Tang monk Xuanzang known to every household, and loved and rec-

ognized by all member of the family.

Xuanzang

The imperial government of Northern Song Dynasty adopted the protective

policy to the Buddhism so that both Chinese and Indian monks came and went in

an endless stream to share the dharma. In the fifth year of Emperor Tianxi's

reign, Buddhism was the zenith of its development with nearly 460,000 monks

and 40,000 temples throughout the region. The imperial government of Sothern

Song Dynasty was inclined to pacify the areas in the south of the Yangtze River.

Therefore Buddhism still maintained its grand occasion to some extent. Through-

out the Yuan Dynasty, the Mongolians advocated the Buddhism sect of Tibetan

nationality, simultaneously preserving that of the Han nationality. Before the establishment of the

Ming Dynasty, Emperor Zhu Yuanzhang was a monk. He proclaimed himself as the Great Preacher of

Daqing after he was enthroned. He passed on the Buddhist doctrines in person, performing tonsures

for the monks, and even made use of the support of Buddhism to consolidate his newly established

political power. The imperial government of Qing Dynasty practiced Tibetan Buddhism, while the

Chinese Buddhism prevailed among the nongovernment factions. During the later stages the Qing

Dynasty, there appeared many Buddhist researchers such as Yang Wenhui, Ouyang Jingwu, and Da

Xu. Modern thinkers like Kang Youwei, Tan Citong, Zhang Taiyan, and Liang Qichao were influenced

by Buddhist doctrine and propagated various new ideas, which brought Buddhist research to new stages.

The Buddhism of Tibetan nationality is also called the Buddhism of Tibetan Language System

and commonly known as Lamaism. Lama means seat of honor in the Tibetan language. Buddhism of

the Tibetan language began in the middle of the 7th century when the king of Tibet, Songsten Gampo,

escorted his brides Princess Bhrikuti Devi of Nepal and Princess Wengcheng of the Tang Dynasty,

both of them bearing Buddhist statues and scriptures. Songsten Gampo was converted to Buddhism

under the influence of the two princesses and built the Jokhang Monastery and Ramoche Monastery

in Lhasa. As the middle of 8th century arrived, Buddhism spread into Tibetan regions channeled di-

rectly from India. Buddhism of the Tibetan nationality was formally formed in the latter half of the

10th century. It began to spread throughout Mongolia during the middle of the 13th century. In the

over 300 years since then, all kinds of denominations with their own distinctions had been formed.

Followers at that time generally practiced the teachings of Tantric Buddhism (Mantrā yana). With the development of Buddhism in Tibet, Lamas in higher positions gradually controlled the local political power, which eventually formed the unique integration of Buddhism and government.

The most famous Buddhist construction is Potala Palace, built for Princess Wencheng as she entered Tibet in the 7th century. However, the one we see today was constructed during the 17th century.

The Pali language Buddhism circulates among the Dai nationality in the Yunnan province of China, the Bulang ethnic group, and other regions. The Buddhist traditions followed in these regions reflect that of Buddhist countries of southern Asian such as Tailand and Myanmar. Approximately in the middle of the 7th century, Buddhism dispersed into regions of the Dai nationality from Myanmar. People there had maintained the fine tradition for centuries according to the doctrines, disciplines, and further studies of the original teachings Buddhism. As the males of the Dai nationality enter school age, they must leave home to become monks. In the temples they study the literature until nearly the age of adulthood, thereupon returning to secular life.

Unit 4

A Dream of Red Mansions

A Dream of Red Mansions also called *The Story of the Stone*, *The Anecdotes of a Romantic Monk*, *The Treasured Mirror* of *Romantic Affairs*, and *The Twelve Beauties of Jinling* and *Baoyu's Fate*. It was written in the age of Emperor Qianlong during Qing Dynasty, and it is the representation of the highest achievement of novel, as one of the four greatest classical works of China.

The book contains 120 chapters, the previous 80 were written by Cao Xueqin, while the other 40 chapters are believed to be written by Gao E.

The author uses the four great families of Jia, Wang, Shi, and Xue as the story's background, the love tragedy of Jia Baoyu and Lin Daiyu as the main theme. The novel focuses on the process of the prosperity to the decline of the Rongguo Mansion and Ningguo Mansion. It not only displays a broad vision of multifarious life in society, but also includes distinct features of colorful common customs and human relationships.The book is claimed to reflect the history of an era, as an encyclopedia of the late feudal society.The language in the novel is exquisite and vivid. It paints as pictures of unique characters such as Jia Baoyu, Lin Daiyu, Wang Xifeng, Xue Baochai, and You Sanjie. Being well structured and immense in volume, the book is considered to be a high artistic achievement. It is not only the largest ancient Chinese novel, but also one of the most substantial classics of the world.

The writer Cao Xueqin (1715-1763A.D.) was a novelist in the Qing Dynasty. His great- grandfather Cao Xi, his grandfather Cao Ying, and the elder Cao Yong and Cao Fu had been in charge of the textiles in the Jiangning district for 60 years, they were all well trusted by the Emperor Kangxi, therefore Cao Xueqin grew up in a wealthy family. At the beginning of the reign of the Emperor Yong Zheng in Qing Dynasty, his family had suffered from the blows of the involvement in the inner struggle of the feudal ruling classes. Their property was confiscated, forcing the whole family to move to Beijing. Since then, they squandered in poverty. In this transformation, Cao Xueqin began to feel deeply concerned about the inconstancy of human relationships, awakening him to comprehend to the essence of feudal society. From then on, he lived his life devoid of money. He could not only write poems but could also paint. Being an excellent author, he had been thoroughly engaged himself in *A Dream of Red Mansions*, editing the novel for ten years. Eventually, he produced a magnificent literary work, pushing the creation of the Chinese classical novel to the summit.

A Dream of Red Mansions has become a great literary work of realism among the ancient novels in China. It is well known for an abundance of cultural content, dramatic plot twists, philosophical thoughts, and exquisite in artistic technique. *A Dream of Red Mansions* has become a masterpiece of realism among Chinese classical works. Tragically, in 1764 Cao Xueqin passed away, too poor to afford medical care.

A Dream of Red Mansions presents the whole picture of social norms by depicting society as family relations, and the transcendence over the traditional ways of thoughts and actions. In the story, the Jia family captures the zeitgeist of feudalism.

It depicts the rise and fall of four powerful families, which occur mainly within the Jia family. Furthermore it reveals various impenetrable conflicts, manifesting the degradation of feudal marriage, morality, culture, and education, setting up a series of the tragic emotional images regarding the roles of women. It presents a broad typical social environment of feudal society, reflecting the historical trend of the collapse.

The novel eulogizes the love between nobles who resist conforming to the feudal courtesy system. Also, it is an embodiment of preliminary thought of democracy, pursuing the freedom of the individual and deeply revealing of the social origin of marriage, becoming a tragedy among the families of Jia, Lin, and Xue.

However, owing to the historical limitation, while writing the fall of the feudal family, the writer also expressed sympathy and melancholy, with a tint of fatalism and nihilism.

After the book was published, with deep mental implications and exquisite artistic charisma, it had great influence on the mentality of readers for generations, crossing boundaries of space and time. There has been a trend of the study of the *A Dream of Red Mansions* in scholastic research fields; such is the group known as Red Study. After more than two hundred years of the wind and rain of history, Red Study never declined, even became more prosperous, better illustrating the artistic values of *A Dream of Red Mansions*.

With regards to the character development, *A Dream of Red Mansions* reached the point of perfection. The characters are all vividly portrayed, with unique personalities, and possess multiplicity; breaking the mold of earlier styles of novels. It sets up the various character depictions by precise description using the broad social background. It focuses on distinct personal psychological issues of the persona, forming a specific artistic atmosphere, reflecting the inner e-motions of the characters. Throughout the entire book, such imagery is conveyed by means of the characters Jia Baoyu, Lin Daiyu, Xue Baochai and so on are described in the whole book.

Jia Baoyu is the main character in the novel. As the descendent posterity of the official resi-dence of Rongguo Mansion, he is extremely intelligent and is the much hoped for heir of the Jia fami-ly. But his thoughts and temperament induce him to forsake the family.The core of his nature em-braced the equal treatment of others, respect to individualism, and the pursuance of freedom, caus-ing him to be a rebellious model towards feudal society, despite his aristocratic family background.

Lin Daiyu is an irreproachable noblewoman, who indulges in self-admiration, and is often de-pressed. She regards love as her life decision, but such love would not be tolerated, destroying the aristocratic family.

Jia Baoyu   Lin Daiyu

Xue Bao Chai is a faithful woman who scrupu-lously abides by the laws of feudal society, conform-ing to be the wise and virtuous woman as expected by the society. At the same time, she is also a victim to the system.

According to rough statistics, altogether *A Dream of Red Mansions* has more than sixty versions and has been translated into eighteen languages. It is a treasure of world literature, published in the coun-tries throughout the world.

Foreign scholars regard Red Study, the study of the oracle bone inscriptions, and the studies of Dunhuang as the three prominent fields of research. The great literary work of *A Dream of Red Man-sions* not only belongs to China, but to the world as a common spiritual treasure to the people all over the world.

Water Margin

Shi Naian wrote *Water Margin* during the late Yuan period and the onset of the Ming Dynasty. Since he was a child, he had been clever and studious, surpassing insight and acumen, conduct-ing himself in a righteous manner with regards to others.When he was 19 he became a licentiate, at 28 years old became a provincial graduate of the imperial examination, and at the age of 36, he and Liu Bowen both were listed as metropolitan graduates of the highest honor. He had been an officer for three years in the Qiantang region (modern day Hangzhou, Zhejiang province). Dissatisfied with the officialdom, unwilling to face the influential bureaucracy, he abandoned his government post and returned to the countryside.When Zhang Shicheng revolted against Yuan Dynasty, Shi Naian took part in military exercises and later actively participating in Zhang Shicheng's conspiracy. Ultimately,

Zhang Shicheng expressed his greed and was deaf to honest words. Consequently, Shi Naian, Lu Yuan, Liu Liang, and Chen Ji collectively grew disappointed, leaving the effort in succession.

Soon afterwards, Zhang Shicheng died sending his former country into peril. Shi Naian roamed throughout all the country, his footprints on the shore washed by waves. He traveled to such regions as Shandong and Henan province, eventually taking residence with the Xu family in Jiangyin, becoming the family's private teacher.Subsequently, he returned to the old white house, once again living in seclusion. Witnessing the decay of politics he authored *Water Margin* with respectable intent. Later, with a student of his, Luo Guanzhong, together wrote *Romance of Three Kingdoms*. He was also quite talented in the art of music and verse, but only a small amount has been preserved.In order to avoid the conscription of the Ming Dynasty, he secretly resided in Huai'an, contracting an illness and was buried there at the age of 75 years old.

In modern times people consider Shi Naian to be the writer of *Water Margin*, while some critics insist that he and his student Luo Guanzhong wrote the novel together.

Water Margin is based on the uprising led by Song Jiang in the final years of the Northern Song Dynasty.

The Song Jiang revolt began in the first year of the Xuanhe period in 1119, lasting more than three years, ending in 1121. The art of storytelling flourished in Song Dynasty. The tales of the outlaw Song Jiang and his thirty-six cohorts had been embraced as the fundamentals of the creation of a folktale. *Water Margin* originates during the initial stages of the Xuanhe period of the Northern Song. As the Southern Song era arrived, it has become a primary subject in the art of oral folk literature.

Song Jiang

At the beginning of Yuan Dynasty emerged a distinct literary form based on vernacular folk stories. *Matters of the Song Dynasty's Xuanhe Period*, portrays the story of thirty-six people, including the well known Chao Gai and Wu Jialiang (Wu Yong), having the gist of *Water Margin*. Throughout Yuan era theater, there were several variations of the *Water Margin* script, as Shi Naian emphasized nontraditional practices of constantly editing, compiling, and producing his works, eventually becoming a classical masterpiece.

Water Margin makes use of outstanding artistic conception, portraying a vivid description of the course of events of the peasant uprising against feudal society in China, lead predominantly by Song Jiang. The social significance of *Water Margin* lies in the deep revelation of the decadent life of feudal society, and the maliciousness of the ruling class. It conveys that the basic premise of uprising is the official force of the government causes the common people to revolt. With powerful artistic vision and vivid literary languages, Shi Naian has recounted several fascinating stories, depicting many unique heroic images.

The writer gives sufficient affirmation and passionate eulogy to the valiant characters, paying tribute not only to their spirit of resistance and righteous actions, but also to their outstanding martial arts skills and noble character.

The nature of the languages of the characters reaches a high plateau. It represents not only the visual features of the characters, but also the mentality and family background by use of regional languages of the characters. For example, the disposition of Ruan Xiaoqi's heart is impatient, the temperament of Wu Yong is resourceful, while the character of Song Jiang is of a modest person. The dialogues bring us into the presence of the characters in the novel, as we vividly hear their words and witness their actions.

The novel presents not only intense vivid plots, but also the rich descriptions of the details. Furthermore, on the basis of oral folk languages, it has created a simple, brief, and vivid style of literary language, full of expressive force.

After the novel is written, it spreads far and wide, being published in simplified character versions as well as traditional character texts.

Until the beginning of 1920s, it had yet to be translated into English. One particular English version emerged as Outlaws of the Marsh.

Among many other versions Pearl S. Buck translated the earliest in the late 1920's. The title, *All Men Are Brothers* makes reference to the verse in *the Analects of Confucius*. Within the confines of the four seas, all men are brothers. The book was published in 1933 as the first English translation, being a best seller in the United States at that time.

Hitherto, there exists a comparatively better English as *Outlaws of the Marsh*, translated by the Chinese born Jewish scholar Sidney Shapiro. Originally published during the period of the Cultural Revolution, he poured through numerous versions, remaining faithful to the original work and reflecting the verve of the authentic masterpiece.

There is also a French version translated as *Au bord de l'eau*, in addition to several Japanese versions, even including comic book, film, and television adaptations.

The Romance of the Three Kingdoms

*T*he *Romance of the Three Kingdoms* is China's first classic saga novel written in the style of chapters that dramatize historical events. The author Luo Guanzhong c.a. (1330 - 1400A.D.) was a noted opera writer of the late Yuan and early Ming period. It is the ancestor of the format of the chapter-based novels yet to come.

The Romance of the Three Kingdoms is the first saga novel in China. In general, the novels were short in length; some even had dozens of characters before *the Romance of the Three Kingdoms* was written. Stories of the famous Three Kingdoms were widely popular among the people in ancient China. It was performed on stage during the Song and Yuan dynasties, with more than 30 kinds of the programs performed during Yuan and Jin Dynasty.Luo Guanzhong integrated the folklore, operas and storyteller's scripts and combined Chen Shou's Records of the *Three Kingdoms* with historical materials annotated by Pei Songzhi to create the popular historical novel of *The Popular Romance of the Three Kingdoms*. This was mastered according to his own comprehension of society and norms during the late period of the Yuan and in the wake of the Ming Dynasty. During the reign of the Emperor Kang Xi in the Qing Dynasty, the father and son, Mao Lun and Mao Zonggang, edited the novel into the modern version of 120 chapters.

Zhuge Liang

The Romance of the Three Kingdoms depicts the conflicts and the battles among the political groups and the military blocs of the three kingdoms of Wei, Shu, and Wu, led respectively by Cao Cao, Liu Bei, and Sun Quan. Based on the broad social and historical background, it presents distinct complex political and military conflicts reflective of the times. Moreover, it is the epitome of the great change in the historical epoch and the creation of allconquering heroes from the aspect of the political and military strategy. It has brought the far-reaching effect towards the afterworld.With regards to the history of the Three Kingdoms, the writer reveals the conflict between Liu Bei and Cao Cao, being in favor of Liu Bei's actions, focusing on his bloc and eulogizing its main characters, while making supreme effort to reprimand Cao Cao.

The Romance of the Three Kingdoms includes a vividly descriptive cast of nearly two hundred characters. The most successful among them being Zhuge Liang, Cao Cao, Guan Yu, and Liu Bei.

In the author's mind, Zhuge Liang is the embodiment of a righteous minister. He has not only the virtue of integrity until his heart ceases to beat, but also the lofty ideals and great aspirations of recreating a time of peace and prosperity. Furthermore, the author endows him with the ability of superb stratagems.

Cao Cao was an unscrupulous careerist, his credo for life being, I would rather disappoint the masses, than have the masses disappoint me. He is of great skill and strategy, but brutal and devious nonetheless. As a cunning politician, his image rings forth through history.

Guan Yu is a man with virtue and fortitude. However, his righteousness is based on the premise of personal gratitude and resentment, not on the cardinal principles of the righteousness of the nation.

The author portrays Liu Bei as a representative humane monarch. He is not practices universal benevolence and shows respect for the wise, but is also a good judge of people and their abilities.The main artistic accomplishment of *The Romance of the Three Kingdoms* is the depiction of the war and the portraits of the character development. The novel is also adept at describing various wars, each battle having distinct traits. Great varieties of wars were described in the novel. With the grand design and various techniques we are able to vividly witness the gleaming sword and crimson blood of conflict.

Scenes such as the Battle of Guan Du and the Battle of Redcliff, unfold one culmination after another, with an opulent and varied in style. While the battles are commonly depicted, other activities are also described, such as the prelude to war or the fortification of armies. This exhibits the suspenseful intensity of a drawn bow and arrow, as well as the unstringing of the weapon in an attempt to sow discord. For example, prior to the Battle of Redcliff, it reveals the collaboration of the two families of Sun and Liu, the conflict between Zhuge Liang and Zhou Yu, the exploration of Cao Cao, the allied armies of the Sun and Liu and their strategy to lure the enemy in deep. In addition, the novel succeeds in the portrayal of well-developed characters.

More than 400 individuals are represented in the novel. Among these, the main characters are presented with the most distinct temperament and vivid imagery. While portraying the characters, the author is adept in capturing the fundamental traits and prominent features of the characters, by means of vaunted contrast, each with vividly unique qualities that bring life to the character.

For example, the treachery of Cao Cao, as every one of his actions is seemingly a scheme or intrigue. Zhang Fei is quite forthright and outspoken, as he is not nave to what is foreign, and has a rude and impetuous in disposition. Zhuge Liang however, is calm and unruffled, has amazing foresight, believing what the heart desires the hand accomplishes (idiom).There are several chapters that spread far and wide, such as the famous stories of Guan Yu, including The Wine is Warm as Hua Xiong is Beheaded and Guan Yu Slays Six Generals Through Five Passes. Zhang Fei is depicted in the chapter The Prestige of Chang Ban Bridge. Zhao Yun is described in The Sole Rescue of a Child, and Catching and Releasing Meng Huo Seven Times, invloving Zhuge Liang.

Structurally, the story development based on the main threads of the conflict of the Three Kingdoms, organizing a plot that is not only complex but also coherent throughout the entire book. Moreover, each section is independently distinct, artistically integrated a one complete work of art.

Throughout the book the language is not very profound, nor extremely secular, yet is clear and concise, with vigorous momentum and lifelike qualities, bringing about an upsurge of production of Chinese historical novels.

The Romance of the Three Kingdoms is the highest achievement in the realm of classical Chinese historical novels, as one of the most influential works. It has been widely circulated, its endless charm occupying a great portion of Chinese literary history, as well as profoundly moving the masses throughout their daily lives.

Journey to the West

The novel *Journey to the West* is traditional folklore based on the epics of the Buddhist monk Xuanzang and his quest to obtain the Buddhist sutras. It is written in a style with relations Song and Yuan vernacular folk dramas.

The beginning seven chapters describe the monkey Sun Wukong entering the world. Afterwards, he is depicted following Xuanzang on is travels to the Western Paradise to fetch the scriptures. By the wayside, they subdue countless demons and surmount numerous difficulties.

The book vividly portrays Xuanzang, Sun Wukong, Zhu Bajie, and Sha Wujing to a great extent, with complete intact composition.

The author Wu Cheng'en (c.a. 1500 - 1582A.D.) was a novelist in the Ming Dynasty. He was born of a small merchant family in decline, nevertheless he was quite fond of reading.

As a child, he was intelligent and studious and an acute individual who was well read. He was extremely fond of ancient myth and folklore, drafting his masterpiece with regards to his local culture.

The journey of the Tang Dynasty monk in search for the Buddhist sutras prevails throughout history. Approximately 1,300 years ago, in the year of 627 A.D. at only the age of 25, the youthful Buddhist monk Xuanzang left the capital of Chang'an with one of his disciples, with the intentions of study to the Indian subcontinent.In 645 A.D., he returned to Chang'an, bringing back 657 Buddhist texts. With the assistance of Emperor Tai Zong of the Tang period, the Dayan Pagoda was constructed to preserve the scriptures. His travels for the sutras lasted nineteen years, as a legendary journey or thousands of miles, causing quite a sensation at the time.

From then on, the story of the Tang Buddhist monk's search for the scriptures has spread far and wide. Based on the vernacular folklore of the Song and Tang eras as well as traditional opera, Wucheng'en has accomplished a monumental literary work through great effort, and by in large, admired by the people of China.

Journey to the West presents the reader a colorful world of the supernatural, as they marvel at the rich and audacious artistic imagination of the writer.

Yet any literary work is a reflection of the social life. With the novel's imaginary realms of demons, we can see the projection of the reality of society in various places.For example, the ideals of the writer are entrusted in the creation of Sun Wukong. Sun Wukong's unyielding struggle of the spirit and his dauntless battle of ghosts and demons, represent the strength of righteousness, displaying conviction of surmounting numerous difficulties. Another example is that along the journey the fantasized demons or catastrophes become metaphors for the sinister powers that be. Moreover, the Temple of Heaven ruled by the Jade Emperor and the Western Pure Land of Ultimate Bliss under the jurisdiction of the Buddha, both paint a dense vivid picture of society.

The Monkey King (Sun Wukong)

Journey to the West not only has deeply profound contents, but also possesses a lofty artistic accomplishment.With the peculiar artistic imagination, vivid plots, vivid and lifelike character images, and humorous language, it builds a unique artistic palace for *Journey to the West*.The greatest achievement in the aspect of the art in *Journey to the West* is the successful creation of two enduring artistic images, Sun Wukong (the Monkey King) and the pig-like Zhu Bajie.

Sun Wukong is the main protagonist of the novel, as an extraordinary hero. He is endowed with boundless skill, his unyielding spirit fears nothing in the heavens or on the ground. He has three-

Zhu Bajie

fold trait, which are the humanity, divinity and the nature of the monkey.

He is witty, brave and has unusual tolerance. However, he also has the defect that he likes to hear fair words. It is known to every household that he can change into 72 forms and could do a somersault that completes a distance of 180,000 miles.

Zhu Bajie's abilities are much less than that of Su Wukong, but his image is similarly starkly portrayed nonetheless. Zhu Bajie is a comic image, possessing strength, honesty, and is fearless in battling the demons. He is Sun Wukong's right-hand man. However, he had some shortcomings: he was fond of eating, took advantages of situations, was fond of women, and was sometimes afraid of the difficulties, often retreating. He also liked telling lies. Moreover, from time to time, he would ask Xuanzang to recite the spell of incantation that tightened a band around Sun Wukong's head, causing him to suffer. Though he had numerous faults, he still broke through brambles and thorns in their pilgrimage to the west, making nothing of hardships. Therefore he is not such as negative character. Readers of the novel are not disgusted with Zhu Bajie, on the contrary he is quite admired.

The description of Xuanzang is also in depth, but it as extensive as that of Sun Wukong or Zhu Bajie.

The character Sha Wujing even more lacks a vivid visual and mental description, it could be said that this is one of the novel's shortcomings.

Nevertheless, the artistic achievement of *Journey to the West* is still astonishing. With the distinct personalities, the two images of Sun Wukong and Zhu Bajie have established an immortal masterpiece of Chinese literature.

Journey to the West was written in the 16th century, during the middle period of the Ming Dynasty, which became the summit of the romantic saga novels at that time. Eventually, this sentimental epic infects the world history of literature.

The Encyclopedia Americana states that "the mythological novel boasts of sumptuous content and radiant ideas". The French Encyclopé die writes, "The entire story is brimming with humor and wit, giving the reader a deep sense of interest".

Since the beginning of the 19th century, it has been translated into more than ten languages, such as Japanese, English, French, German, and Russian. There are various kinds of the translations of the title. These include *The Pilgrimage of the Monk*, *A History of the Search for Buddhist Scriptures*, *The Monkey*, *The Monkey King*, and *The Chronicles of the Monkey* and *the Demons*.

In other countries, the earliest story about the story of the Tang monk's travels is the Korean version in the early stages of the Ming Dynasty, which is not entirely the same story as *Journey to the West*.

The earliest formal version is the Japanese edition published during the middle of the 18th century.

Sun Wukong, Xuanzang, Zhu Bajie, and Sha Wujing, are characters in popular stories such as Havoc in Heaven, Striking the White Bone Demon Three Times, and Mountain of Fire are greatly loved by people.

With the passage of several hundreds of years, *Journey to the West* has been adapted into a wide variety of media, including Chinese operas, films, teleplays, animated cartoons, and comic books.

In Japan and other Asian countries, there has also emerged several varied works of art brilliantly depicting the main character Sun Wukong.

Unit 5

The New Culture Movement

In the early stages of governance of the Northern Warlords (1912-1927A.D.), a New Culture Movement broke out in China. It was a great bolt of lightning from the dark cloudy skies, advocating science and opposing feudal superstitions. It attacked the outdated feudal code of ethics, which had lasted several thousands of years.

The New Culture Movement was the outcome of the integration of economy, politics, philosophy, and culture in a distinct historical period.

After the failure of the Xinhai Revolution, the imperialists or so-called Great Powers were in favor of Yuan Shikai, as they encroached on China, establishing a secret intelligence. Meanwhile, the advanced intellects were in search of a new way to positively change the situation. With regards to the economy, capitalism in China had further developed during the First World War, as the bourgeois pushed for the democracy of China to further expand capitalism. Among the culture of philosophers, the concept of enlightenment was introduced to China within the newly formed schools and from those studying abroad. The Xinhai Revolution influenced the ideals of a democratic republic and was held deeply in the hearts of the people. Yuan Shikai's yearning to return to the ancient ways of Confucian thought was not compatible with democracy and was opposed by the intellectuals. These are direct causes of the explosion of the New Culture Movement.

The journal *Youth* began its publication in September of 1915 by Chen Duxiu in Shanghai. With the printing of *Youth* (The name has been changed into *New Youth* since September 1916, and has been moved to Beijing in 1917), the New Culture Movement attacked feudalism under the banners of democracy and science.

The primary aim of the New Culture Movement was to promote democracy, science, and a new morality while opposing despotism, old superstitions, and feudalistic ideals.

Chen Duxiu had published an article called *Advice to the Youth* in the journal *Youth*, putting forward a slogan of democracy and science and attacking the feudalism and its ideology.

Chen Duxiu promoted faith, economic growth, new societal norms, and ethics, calling on the people to combat China's old ideology with the weapon of

Youth Journal

democracy. In regards to science, Chen Duxiu believed that anything is worthless if not fit for society, even though it may be cherished by the sages and advocated by the government. He called on the people to remain true to the scientific spirit to become the ruler and master of nature.

Chen Duxiu was the first to uncover the beginning of the New Culture Movement. Some other advocates such as Li Dazhao, Lu Xun, Hu Shi, and Qian Xuantong also promptly joined the movement.

The New Culture Movement not only defined a great ideological revolution, but also a great literary insurrection.

In January of 1917, Hu Shi published Tentative Suggestions for the Reform of Chinese Literature. He proposed a radical change in literature, advocating that vernacular Chinese should replace classical and ancient styles of literature. To do so, he proposed eight reforms. The first was to compose writings with substance. Secondly, writers were not to imitate the style of the ancients. Thirdly, one must respect grammar. Fourthly, refrain from melancholy that results in unproductive pose, and fifthly, exclude the old cliché s. The sixth reform was to avoid comparing the present to the past. The seventh proposition discourages writers from using parallelism or couplets. The final reform advocated using common words, characters, and expressions.

In February of that same year, Chen Duxiu published *A Thesis of the Literary Revolution*, clearly expressing his opposition towards the literature of the feudal periods. He put forward the three revolutionary ideas:toppling the aristocratic literature while constructing national literary styles; doing away with the classics and embracing realism in literature, and abolishing the writing of feudal times with the obscure content of mountains and rivers, while constructing a literature style that reflected society. These proposals raised the banner of a revolution in literature.

The article *Tentative Suggestions for the Reform of Chinese Literature*, written by Hu Shi, was the turning point of the Vernacular Movement.

These guiding principals of thought received a rapid response from Chen Duxiu.

In January of 1918, the vernacular writings were published in *New Youth*. In May, the publication of *Diary of a Madman*, written by Lu Xun, was symbolic of the Vernacular Movement, and became a crowning achievement.

The scholars, who favored the classical style of writing, attacked the ideology of the Vernacular Movement.

In 1919, The May Fourth Movement arose in opposition to imperialism and feudalism, advancing the Vernacular Movement by leaps and bounds. In 1920, the Education Ministry of the Northern Qing Beiyang government issued a decree that all textbooks in elementary school were to be written in vernacular Chinese.

New organizations such as the Literary Research Society sparked the emergence of multiple new literary associations.

The publication of Lu Xun's novella, *The True Story of Ah Q*, and the publication of a collection of Guo Moruo's poems entitled *The Goddesses*, established a solid foundation for vernacular literature.*The True Story of Ah Q* was the first masterpiece that gained world fame among modern Chinese vernacular literature.The New Culture Movement was an unprecedented campaign for ideology, enlightenment, and emancipation. It shook the ruling of feudal ethical standards, developing the disciplines of democracy and science. The New Culture Movement also laid the foundation of for the May Fourth Movement, paving the way for the spread of the Marxism in China.

However, some limitations inevitably existed. The advocates did not introduce the New Culture Movement to the masses, limiting it to only the circle of the intellects.Avoiding the struggle of the warlord government at that time, they did not directly oppose imperialism. Instead, they directly criticized classical literature along with Western thought and literature.

Hu Shi

Hu Shi, styled himself Shi-zhi, comes from Jixi of Anhui province. As a famous scholar, poet, historian, litterateur, philosopher in modern times, Hu Shi became one of the leaders of New Culture Movement since he advocated the literary revolution.

In 1910, Hu Shi went to United States studied under the famous philosopher John·Dewey, he was greatly influenced by the experimental philosophy. In January 1917, he published *Discussion on Literary Reformation* in *New Youth*, which elaborated Eight Proposals on literary reformation that aimed at the eight charges against former Chinese literature. Those proposals firstly came into contacts with a series of fundamental literature problems like the contents and forms of literature, its social functions, authenticity and times. It became the first declaration of the literary revolution.

Hu Shi

Hu Shi was not only the active advocator for the literary revolution theory, but also a practitioner. He was the first person to develop the free verse in vernacular Chinese. In February 1917, *Eight Pieces of Free Verse* in Vernacular Chinese which witnessed its beginning of new literary in Chinese history was published in *New Youth*, volume 2, No.6. New literary and stylistic revolution originated from such verse which acted as the forunner for the reform of other literary styles.

In March 1920, a collection of poems named *Collection of Attempts* was published by Hu Shi. It was the first collection of free verse in vernacular Chinese produced during the New Literary Movement. The name "attempts" was gotten from Hu Shi's believing that success came from attempts since ancient times. The collection demonstrated Hu Shi's great verve to rescue China. *The Collection of Attempts* exercised the proposal "liberty of the poetic styles", smashed the shackles of the rules and forms of the classical poetic composition and used the intelligible vernacular Chinese, without avoiding common words and spoken language and following antithesis and rhyme. Hu Shi proposed that all the former shackles of freedom should be smashed and to speak freely. As far as the contents of the poem, Hu Shi opposed to make a fuss, and proposed to replace the pedantic feudalism with democratism and humanitarianism thoughts. Some pieces in the collection like The *Old Crow Hope A Star Up to the Hill* were poems drawing inspiration from the scene or perceiving the sense from the happenings, using the techniques of direct description, luminous simile, symbolization and etc. Judged from the aspect of aesthetics, the artistic value of *the Collection of Attempts* is junior to its literary value. Hu Shi concluded, "What I review my poems of the past five years in retrospect now (1922) are just like a foot-binding woman reviewing her shoes year and year after she released her feet. Although the feet became bigger and bigger, the smell of the blood left from her foot-binding times always remained in it." So Hu Shi was a praiseworthy pioneer of the new free verse but not the founder.

Hu Shi successively served as: professor in Peking University, dean of college of Liberal Arts in Peking University, professor and director of Furen University, extraordinary and plenipotentiary of the Republic of China in the United States of America, honorary advisor of Eastern Division in the library of America Congress, president of Peking University, academician of central research institute, librarian of Gest East Asian Library in Princeton University, dean of central research institute (located in south of Taipei harbor)and so on. All of his life was greatly influenced by Huxley and Dewey. He always claimed that it is Huxley who taught him to doubt and it is Dewey who taught him to think. Hu Shi was the forerunner of liberalism in China, he advocated freedom throughout his life. In academic study, Hu Shi proposed that the right way to study was to assume boldly, to demonstrate carefully and to make words proved conclusively. He focused his academic activities in the field of history, literature, philosophy and etc. His major Works are *Outline of Chinese Philosophy History* (*Book* I), *Collection of Attempts, History on Literature in Vernacular Chinese* (*Book* I)and *Hu Shi Literary Depositss* (4 *volumes*) and so on. In his later years, Hu Shi devoted himself to the textual research of Water Channel Annotated, but had no time to finalize. He passed away in 1962 in Taipei.

Lu Xun

L u Xun was a great writer, thinker, and revolutionist. His original name was Zhou Shuren, as he styled himself as Yucai. Lu Xun was the pseudonym that he used when writing *Dairy of a Madman*, published in the journal *New Youth*.

Lu Xun was born to a downfallen feudal scholarly bureaucratic family in Shaoxing of Zhejiang province in 1881.

In his youth, his family fortunes declined, due to his father's declining health. His grandfather was imprisoned due to a legal case as his father's illness worsened. In a flash, his family plunged in a sea of financial difficulties as he anguished over the unfairness of life.

Lu Xun

Lu Xun's mother was from the countryside. As a child, therefore, he came to know and understand the rural areas and farmers.

In his early years of study, he was greatly influenced by the ideology of the evolution.

He went abroad to study in Japan on a state scholarship in 1902, attending Kobun Institute in Tokyo. After graduating in 1904, his ideals of curing disease and saving the lives of people led him study at the Sendai Medical Academy. While there, he found a mentor in a Japanese teacher named Dr. Fujino Genkuro. However, many Japanese students often discriminated against Lu Xun. He was stimulated by a slideshow of the war between Japan and Russia (1904-1905). In the presentation, the Japanese army had captured a Chinese man believed to be a spy for the Russians. When he was about to be beheaded by the Japanese army, a crowd of Chinese people gathered and bravely confronted the tragedy. He deeply believed, "Medicine is not crucial. Even if an individual is healthy, many insignificant practices can lead to unnecessary illne ss. Therefore, the primary task is to change their spirits and advance the movements of art and literature."

In 1906, Lu Xun returned to Tokyo after leaving Sendai and began to engage in literary activity. Shortly after, he published some important dissertations such as *The Annals of the Human*, *The History of Science*, *On Cultural Paranoia*, and *On the Power of Romantic Poetry*.

In 1908, Lu Xun and his younger brother, Zhou Zuoren, worked together translating foreign short stories. They compiled *An Anthology of Foreign Stories*, which had been published with assistance from their cohorts. In 1909, Lu Xun left Japan and returned to the motherland. He soon became a successful teacher in Hangzhou and then Shaoxing.

In 1911, he took an active role in the propaganda campaign when the Revolution of 1911 broke out.

From 1918, he began to participate in the activities of *New Youth* magazine. In May, the journal published Lu Xun's first vernacular novel, *Diary of a Madman*, making a significant impact on the history of modern literature in China. It had enormous influence due to its profound expression and a distinct format.

Meanwhile, he also published a great many essays in the column "Random Thoughts" on the journal *New Youth*. In addition to the creation of multiple literary works, he also organized the Yusi Society and The Weiming Organization (Modern Literary Group), which issued publications such as *Yusi*.

From 1925 to 1926, Lu Xun supported the mass struggle of the students in The Women Teachers Campaign at Normal University and the ideals that led to the March 18 Massacre.

In October of 1927, he settled in Shanghai and established The Chinese League of Left-Wing Writers in 1930, as one of the initiators and the leaders. He died in Shanghai on October 19, 1936.

Lu Xun is considered the founder of modern literature in China. His radical new style is expressed in various frameworks, including the novel, essay, prose, poetic prose, and the historical novel.

The collection of stories in *Call to Arms* and *Wandering* are the artistic summits of modern short stories in China. *The Diary of a Madman* is the first vernacular short story in the history of modern Chinese literature, reflecting the writing style of the May Fourth Movement.

Through the depiction of a man suffering from paranoia, it exposes the phenomenon of "eat people" from society to each family and attacks the essence of "Eat People" of the feudal clan system.

In terms of ideology, *The Diary of a Madman* is the embodiment of antifeudal tendencies. In its artistic form, it reflects both realism and symbolism, forming a unique artistic effect.

The True Story of Ah Q is not only a literary masterpiece in China, but it was also the earliest modern novel introduced to the world. Ah Q is such an image of a peasant that he is backward with the psychosis. The most prominent trait of the character is his spiritual victory. By the depiction of Ah Q, the writer describes the souls of the countrymen, exposing the weaknesses of the people, and achieving the effect of "reflecting the sickness to arouse attention of rescue." Meanwhile, the author combines the exploration of the issues of the Chinese peasants with the inspection of the issues of the revolutions in China. He gives a summation of the historical lesson of the failure for the Revolution 1911 by the depiction of Ah Q's fate.

Besides the novel, essay is another important contribution for Lu Xun to literature.

Lu Xun is not only the ideologist, but also the revolutionist. He fought the whole life. For him, the essay is the dagger, the javelin. He had said that the essay was the inductive nerve, "giving the immediate response towards the harmful things." His 15 collections of the essays are the phylogeny of the ideology and culture, which are the faithful records of the society from the May 4th to the middle times of the 1930s in China.

As a writer, Lu Xun was more concerned about the reaction and the change of the ideology, emotion, and psychology of the people during the historical event.

Lu Xun had said with self-confidence, "The souls of the masses are reflected in my essays."

While writing the novels of *Call to Arms* and *Wandering*, Lu Xun also produced the collection of prose *Dawn Blossoms Plucked at Dusk* and anthology of poetic prose *Wild Grass*. In his later years, he produced the short story collection, *Old Tales Retold* (published in 1936).

The collection of short stories portrays the mythology of ancient China, its folklore, and historical facts. However, he was not a stickler for formalities in depicting the original stories, often adding his own interpretations and imagination. His writing technique combined the ancient and modern styles of writing, using stark depictions to solemnly express the themes. This form of literature established set a new precedent in the composition of historical short stories.

Lu Xun is reputed by many to be the soul of the nation. Throughout his life, he strived for the survival and the development of the nation. The verse "Fierce-browed, I coolly defy a thousand pointing fingers, with my head bowed, I am an ox for the children." This quote exemplifies his artistic ways to express his ideology.

Mao Zedong is quoted as saying, "Lu Xun has the hardest bones. He hasn't the slightest amount of subservience or flattery. This is the most treasured temperament of the people in the colonial and semicolonial society." Furthermore, he found him to be "...a great literary artist, thinker, and revolutionist."

Guo Moruo

Guo Moruo was a famous litterateur archaeologist, paleographic expert, ideologist, and revolutionist of China.

His original name was Guo Kaizhen. Moruo was the pseudonym used when he began to publish the poetry in 1919.

Guo Moruo was born into a family of a landowners and businessmen in Leshan county, Sichuan province. In the spring of 1914, he left to study in Japan. At first, he studied medicine, but later changed his mind and began to study literature.

During this period, he read various classical works of the foreign writers, such as Tagore, Heine, and Goethe. The writings of the Dutch philosopher Spinoza greatly affected him by the thought of pantheism.

He was greatly inspired by the outbreak of the May Fourth Movement. He and some of his students studying in Japan worked together to form the organization Xia She, espousing opposition to Japanese imperialism.

Guo Moruo

He began to publishing poetry in September of 1919.

In 1921, various famous writers such as Guo Moruo, Yu Dafu, and Cheng Fangwu founded an organization called Creating Consortium. In August of that same year, Guo Moruo's first anthology of poems was published, entitled *The Goddesses*. This not only established the preeminent status of Guo Moruo in modern Chinese literary history, but also opened a new era for Chinese poetry.

In 1921 and 1922, Guo Moruo returned to his motherland three times. However, the reality and darkness of domestic society shattered his ideals. His poetry collection, *Starry Sky*, contains many heartfelt poems.

In 1923, he returned to China after graduating from the Medical School of Kyushyu Imperial University. Consequently, he continued to compile publications, engaging in new literary creations. At this time, his views on art, literature, and politics took on a heterogeeous appearance. The prose anthology, *The Forefront* is a distinct record of ideological change during that era.

In 1924, the previous activities of the organization Creating Consortium came to and end due to differences between several key writers. Throughout his trials and tribulations, he had gained an understanding of Marxism, reflecting a giant leap in thought.

In July of 1926, Guo Moruo took part in the Northern Expedition, advocating a proletarian revolutionary literary movement. The anthology *Restore* was his signature work of this period.

In February 1928, he left Shanghai for Japan because of the change of the political environment, living there for ten years.

After the war broke out against Japan, he returned to the motherland by himself, espousing resistance against Japanese aggression. He authored six historical plays. Among them are the famous *Qu Yuan* and *Tiger Tally*. In addition, he had created many works of poetry, prose, and the study of the historiography.

After the victory against Japan, Guo Moruo and vast numbers of the progressive individuals engaged in cultural work in areas such as Chongqing and Shanghai, striving for the peace and democracy of China, standing bravely in front for the democratic movement.

After the foundation of the People's Republic of China, Guo Moruo held posts of leadership in areas of the administration, science, and culture. Meanwhile, he also wrote a variety of publications, such as the poetry collection *Eulogy for New China* and the historical plays, *Cai Wenji*, and *Empress Wu Zetian*.

The Goddesses was not only Guo Moruo's first new anthology of poems, but also a production of great significance in the history of Chinese modern poetry, becoming the foundation of new poetry styles.

The Goddesses contained the writer's major poems written from 1919 to 1921. There were 57 pieces altogether including the preface, which was written when the writer studied abroad in Japan.

Literary critics divided the creative phases into three parts: the first phase included works such as *The Revival of the Goddess* and *The Flower of the White Poplar*. The poems of the climatic May Fourth Movement are expressed in *Phoenix Rising From the Ashes*, representative of the second phase. The third phase involves main poems from the early stages such as *The Temptation of Death*. Other wildly popular poems include *The Coal of the Stove*, *Sunrise*, *Earth, My Mother!*, *The Dog Star*, *Good Morning*, and *At the Edge of the Earth*.

The Goddesses conveys the spirit of May Fourth. Its contents focus on the following areas:

First, *The Goddesses* is the most intense reflection of democratic ideals and birth of the new world.

Phoenix Rising From the Ashes is a solemn song of the era, which was filled with a strong rebellious spirit and yearning for societal change. The writer expresses his deep nostalgia and dedication to the motherland through the metaphor of a phoenix rising from the dead to symbolize the revival of new China.

The story also expresses the poet's self-respect and appreciation of nature.

The celestial dog in the poem *Heavenly Dog* broke through the nets and destroyed all things of old. It conveys an unbridled passion and supernatural force, embodying the quest for personal liberation sought after in that era.

In *The Goddesses*, there are several poems depicting the nature's beauty. In Guo Moruo's heart, nature is not only the symbol of creation's force, but also the joy of life.

Third, it is the manifestation of the spirit that embodies bold innovation and destruction of the old ways.

The poet shows reverence for forces that bear destructive and creative powers such as the sun, mountains, rivers, oceans, birth, death, volcanoes, and the deep of night. All reflect the rebellious spirit of the May Fourth Movement.

In *The Praise for the Revolutionists*, the writer pays tribute to the revolutionists who were against the outmoded conventions. It also sings the praises of the revolutionists who took part in the political, social, religious, artistic, literary, and educational revolutions. In this work, he espoused his belief that only through complete destruction can a new creation arise.

In *The Goddesses*, the ideals of absolute freedom and complete independence were explicitly revealed; it's style of poetry relentless and challenging.

With vivid imagination, supernatural exploitation, and language with intense tone the brilliant language and elegant color, *The Goddesses* began a new style of romantic poetry in China.

Mao Dun

Mao Dun was not only a famous modern novelist and literary critic, but also an important cultural and social activist.

His original name was Shen Dehong; he also used the pseudonym Yanbing. He was born of a well-educated family in Wuzhen of Tongxiang county Zhejiang province on July 4, 1896. When he was ten years old, his father died, thus primarily his mother raised him.

In 1913, he was admitted to the preparatory school of Beijing University. Due to financial difficulties, he could not be able to continue in his studies. Consequently, he worked for the Shanghai Commercial Press, where he began translating and compiling Chinese and foreign books. He also wrote articles for several publications including *Student Magazine* and *Study Lamp*.

Mao Dun

In the period of the May Fourth Movement, as an active advocate and participant in the New Culture Movement, Mao Dun proposed literature for life.

In 1921, the Literature Study Group was founded. Mao Dun became the backbone.In that same year, he became chief editor of Fiction Monthly, making the publication express a firm position attacking feudalism.

Mao Dun was also the earliest revolutionary intellectual, taking part in the communist movement in China. In 1921, he became one of the first members of the Communist Party and took part in laying the foundation of the party. He was a very active participant in the social struggle led by the party.

After the struggling through blood and fire in the April 12, 1927, Mao Dun wrote the trilogy *Erosion*. This was Mao Dun's maiden novel. The pen name on the original manuscript was maodun, meaning contradiction, reflecting the political mood of the time. Later, Ye Shengtao had changed the word into the name Mao Dun. This is a profound work reflecting the true mentality of intellectuals in a turbulent era. It consists of three volumes: *Disillusion*, *Indecision*, and *Pursuing*.

In July 1928, Mao Dun went east to Japan. One reason was to escape persecution from the Kuomintang reactionaries; another reason was due to his depressed spirit.

While in Japan, he wrote the novel *Rainbow*.

The work displays the exploration of a new road of life for a young man under abroad historical background. It profoundly depicts one generation of intellectuals during the movement of May 4th to May 30th, 1919. The book embodies the collaboration of the masses, and their bitter struggle to break free from the prison that bound them.

In April of 1930, Mao Dun returned to China from Japan, actively taking part in the proceedings of the League of the Left-Wing writers and working together with Lu Xun. This promoted a prosperous development of left-wing literature.

The period from 1932 to 1937 was Mao Dun's period of great heights. The publication of the novel *Midnight* established Mao Dun in the history of the modern Chinese literature.

The "rural trilogy" (*Spring Silkworms*, *Autumn Harvest*, and *Winter Ruin*) and some of the short stories such as *The Lin Family's Shop* convey the creative vitality of Mao Dun as a writer of revolutionary realism.

During the period of the War of Resistance (1937-1945 A.D.), Mao Dun traveled to various places, such as Hong Kong, Xinjiang, Yan'an, Chongqing, and Guilin. During his travels, he produced many popular works, including the essays *A Discussion of Landscape*, and *Tribute to the Poplar*, lengthy novels such as *Putrefaction* and *February's Frosted Red Leaves Appear as Flowers* and *the Play Days of the Pure Brightness*.

After the foundation of the People's Republic of China, Mao Dun worked as the vice-chairman of the literary association, Minister of Cultural Affairs, and the chairman of the writers' association. In addition, he also worked as the vice-chairman of the Political Consultative Committee. He died in Beijing of illness on March 27, 1981.

He donated one of his entire salaries of 250,000 yuan to establish an award for writing that was later named The Mao Dun Prize of Literature.

Established in October of 1981, it was the first award for literature in China titled after an author's name. It has become one of the highest literature prizes in China. Every four years one novel is selected to receive the prize.

The Works of Mao Dun consists 40 volumes. It is a collection of all the writings of Mao Dun and has been continuously published by the People's Literature Publishing House since 1983.

Among these works is *Midnight*, published in June of 1933, marking the peak of his creativity. It shook literary circles in China. Its enormous influence is reflected in the fact that the politician Qu Qiubai called this one particular year Mid-night Year.

This novel depicts a broad picture of Chinese society in the early 1930's. It is a comprehensive portrayal of the intense conflict between the national capitalist Wu Sunfu and the competing capitalist Zhao Botao. The novel depicts workers on strike and the rioting of the peasants. Consequently, the reactionary authorities suppressed and destroyed the revolutionary movement. The government then annexed small and mediumsized national industries, creating a fierce fight for government bonds. Various proprietors struggled, creating a great deal of internal fighting within capitalist families. By means of framing these diverse ways of life, it reconstructed the struggles of the second domestic revolutionary war, and embodied the typical image of the national capitalist.

For more than half a century, *Midnight* has not only reached a wide range of readers in China, it has also been translated into several languages such as English, German, Russian, and Japanese displaying great influence internationally.

The famous Japanese literary researcher Hajime Shinodoa recommended *Midnight* as one of the world's literary masterpieces of the 20th century. He believed *Midnight* could be compared to epic works such as *In Search of Lost Time* written by Marcel Proust and *One Hundred Years of Solitude* written by Garcia Marquez.

Ba Jin

Ba Jin is one of the most influential writers since the May Fourth New Culture Movement. Modern Chinese literary circles have long known him to be a master artist.

His original name was Li Yaotang; his courtesy name was Feigan. Ba Jin became his pen name in 1928 after writing *The Destruction*.

Ba Jin was born in a feudal bureaucratic landlord family in Chengdu, Sichuan Province. He spent his childhood in the loving warmth of family life.

Ba Jin

His mother, Chen Shufen, was the first childhood teacher.

Her love for education was planted in the seeds of universal benevolence, which played a significant role in his later ideological development.

Sickness took the life of his mother and father in 1914 and 1917 respectively, radically changing his life.

The death of his father forced his once wealthy family into autocratic society. In the hypocritical feudal ethics prison, he saw his brothers and sisters struggling and suffering, killing the love in his heart. Suddenly, however, his affection turned to hate, as Ba Jin was awakened by the outbreak of the May Fourth Movement.

Among the various anarchisms and thoughts of the time, anarchism first broadened his worldview.

In 1923, Ba Jin left his ancestral home of Sichuan for the city centers of Shanghai and Nanjing to continue his studies.

In 1927, in efforts to further study anarchism, he attended a university in France. While living abroad in France, he was stimulated by two major events. One was the Chinese victory of Northern Expedition was short lived, and the execution of two Italian anarchists by the U-nited States government. In extreme pain and bitterness, Ba Jin wrote his first short novel *Destruction*, creating the hero Du Daxin, who despised the workings of society due to his desperation for love. The work marks the formal beginning of Ba Jin's literary career.

At the end of 1928, Ba Jin returned to his native country.

From 1929 to the end of 1949, Ba Jin had produced 18 novels, 12 collections of the short stories, and 16 volumes of essays, in addition to several translations. Among them, his epic novels became Ba Jin's main literary achievements prior to the foundation of China.

The Love Trilogy is Ba Jin's favorite work of his early writings. It consists of three chapters—*Fog*, *Rain* and *Lightning*, which is not only the summation of the intense and long reflections of the great social problem of revolution of his early years, but also a vivid demonstration of his early world views.

The Torrents Trilogy—*Family*, *Spring*, and *Autumn*, is one of Ba Jin's most representative collection of works. In particular, the first book, Family, displays an eternal artistic value.

In the preface of *The Torrents Trilogy*, Ba Jin writes, "What I want to convey to the reader is a picture depicting the past of more than ten years. This is naturally only a part of life. However, you can see the undulation of the torrents of life formed by love and hate, joy and pain."

The work portrays the complications of the heart. On one hand, was the collapse of the feudal patriarchal system, and the dying aristocratic ruling force frantically swallowing the fate of young lives. Yet in another aspect, the younger generation, attracted by the revolutionary trend, began the tragic course of the realization in the wake of the struggle of revolution. Among the various characters portrayed in *the Torrents Trilogy*, Gao Juehui is the most significant. From the sympathy towards the workers and the distrust of the feudal system, he came to embrace the bourgeois' reform and democracy, ultimately taking part in the social struggle. His writing brings forth a new wave of thought, awakening China at the beginning of the 20th century, and under the influence of the May Fourth Movement. He is not only a sharp critic of feudalism, but also the enthusiastic and young revolutionary. Through the portrayal of his character, Gao Juehui, the author unfurled his shared ideological thought of advanced intellectuals of China in last hundred years.

Cold Nights, written in 1946, was not only his last novel, but also another substantial work after *Family*, indicating a new stage of artistic development of the writer.

The novel describes the tragedy of death and destruction of the young functionary, Wang Wenxuan. Furthermore, by use of this character, the author reveals the fate of righteous and virtuous intellectuals, while exposing the dark reality of the war of resistance.

Upon victory in the war against Japan, Ba Jin was mainly engaged in the work of translation, editing, and publication. After the foundation of the People's Republic of China, Ba Jin went to the Korean front twice, writing two collections of dispatched essays, *Living Amongst Heroes* and *They Who Defend Peace*. Unfortunately, during the Cultural Revolution, Ba Jin was cruelly and unjustly persecuted.

After the Chinese Cultural Revolution,　Ba Jin began writing *Random Thoughts*, from 1978 and continuing until September of 1986, containing 150 chapters with 420,000 words.

Due to its profound ideological and cultural content, and unique style, *Random Thoughts* has become one of the most important creative productions of essays of this new period,　making it another great mile-stone in Ba Jin's literary road .

What moved people the most was his spirit of consciousness and reorganization of the ego,　reflecting his outstanding moral character and intellectualism . Combining personal introspection and the reflections of a nation, as well as personal and social criticism,　he marks a brilliant chapter in the annals of the intellectual and spiritual path of the Cultural Revolution,　showing great importance in the history of ideology and culture.

Lao She

The original name of Lao She was Shu Qingchun, his courtesy name being She Yu.　He was born into a poor Manchu family in Beijing that lived in an alley that collectively domesticated lambs.

In 1918, he graduated from Beijing Normal University, assuming an office of administration at a primary school.

The democratic,　scientific,　and liberating trend of thoughts reflective of the May Fourth Movement awakened him from the conscientious primary school,　with its deference to serve the　mother and the convention of getting married and having children.

The prosperity of the new literary revolution allowed him to indulge in art and literature, becoming a fresh starting point in his life and career.

In 1922,　Lao She worked as a Mandarin language teacher in the Nankai Middle School. In that same year, he published his first short novel *The Bell*.

Lao She

In 1924,　he went to England and served as lecturer of Mandarin in the School of Oriental studies at the University of London.　Apart from teaching,　he had read volumes of foreign literary works and began to formally launch his creative career.　During this time he consecutively published three satirical novels describing the life of the people. These include *The Philosophy of Old Zhang*, *Zhao Ziyue* and *Ma and Son*, which attracted the attention of literary circles.

In 1929, en route to returning home, he stayed in Singapore for several months, writing a fairy tale in the form of a novel called *The Birthday of Xiaopo*.

After returning to the motherland and before the outbreak of the war of resistance against the Japanese, he taught at Qilu University in Jinan, and Shandong University in Qingdao. Furthermore, during this period he created six novels, one novella, and three short stories, displaying vigorous creativity. *Cat Country*, *The Divorce*, and *Rickshaw Boy* are among his most famous works.

The Cat Country portrays an outer space engineer who drifts of course and ends up on Mars in a country ruled by cats. The depiction of what he sees and hears is analogous to the partisanship of the era, carrying the obvious meaning of political satire under the familiar guise of science fiction.

Through the depiction of the family troubles of several section members of a public finance office in Beiping (modern day Beijing), *The Divorce* criticized the entire social system of old China and created characters based on the culture of urban living.

Rickshaw Boy has also had an enormous impact. A rickshaw operator's whereabouts lead a trail of clues in Beiping, as it depicts incessant fighting between warlords and the dark rule of a country among the poor lower class. Displayed is the bitterness of the city residents and the light in the center of a dark abyss. By means of the auspicious protagonist it shows an unwillingness to accept defeat, as well as dissolution, and acceptance of destiny. This encourages the city residents to be their own masters and that no single person can exist alone in the city.

From the outbreak of the war of aggression to the liberation of the country, more than ten years passed. During this time, Lao She had created the novellas *This Life of Mine* and *The Crescent Moon*, in addition to novels such as *Four Generations Under One Roof*, and *The Drum Singers*.

In The Crescent Moon, the structure is delicate and the depiction is precise. It is a critique of the dark world by showing the miserable life of a mother and daughter and their deterioration into prostitution.

Four Generations Under One Roof-including *Anxious and Perplexed*, *To Live Without Purpose*, and *Famine*, is a boundary marker in the creative course of Lao She.

Selecting the common alley as the epitome of the western district of Beiping and centering the circumstances of old-fashioned businessman Qi Tianyou's family of four generations, it truly reveals the painful souls of people suffering under the rule of foreign invaders. It portrays the closed, perfunctory, and perplexed burden of the spirit. Moreover, it provides a reflection of the attitude of the people in the 1940s, conveying the quality of the national spirit and the psychological state of the inhabitants.

The work spans almost the entire process of the eight-year war against aggression, from the bombing of Pearl Harbor to the surrender of the Japanese; it portrays direct or indirect reflections. With regards to the space, it touched in various aspects, such as the small alley in Beijing, the residential compound, streets, the suburb, the countryside, the square, the theatres, execution grounds, the brothel, schools, even the Japanese puppet authority and the embassy... From the aspect of the breadth, depth, and vigor, the novel has a panoramic view that creates an epic with an imposing attitude.

After the foundation of China, the main works of Lao She including the novel, Beneath the *Red Banner*, the long reportage *The Nameless Highland Has the Name*, and the plays *Dragon Beard Ditch*, and *The Teahouse*.

The Teahouse is not only a representative work of Lao She's dramas, but also a classic work of modern China.

It uses a small teahouse representing local and national characteristics to vie the whole of society in China. It vividly depicts and defines three eras and three societies: the late Qing Dynasty after the coup by Dowager Empress Cixi, the society during the People's Republic of China and the civil wars instilled under the rule of the warlords after the failure of the Revolution of 1911; and the Kuomintang controlled areas after the war of resistance. In his work, he expresses the theme of burying the three old ages.

In reading Lao She's creations, you can see a basic premise, which is obviously the reflection and criticism of traditional culture.

In some aspects, Lao She inherits Lu Xun's concept of national character. Yet in other ways, he shows his own new development and characteristics.

Lao She Tea House in Beijing

Lao She grew up among the social strata of the urban Beijing population. Centering on the townspeople society in Beiping, his works of art have a dense local atmosphere and intense breath of life. Therefore, he is known to vividly depict city residents as well as sharply criticize the urban life of Beijing.

In 1951, the Beijing Municipal People's Government granted him the award of The People's Artist.

Cao Yu

Cao Yu is a renowned playwright who has made outstanding contributions to the development of Chinese modern drama.

His original name was Wan Jiabao. He was born in a declining feudal family of bureaucracy in Tianjin.

Because of the puerperal fever, his mother died three days after giving birth to him. Consequently, his mother's younger sister became his stepmother and raised him.

His stepmother enjoyed the theater very much. In his boyhood, he often went with her to see local plays, such as the Beijing opera, Kunqu opera, Hebei clapper opera, as well as the new cultural dramas that were popular at that time.

In 1922, Cao Yu attended Nankai Middle School in Tianjin.

During this period of study, he took an active part in theater. He

Cao Yu

played roles as the protagonist in various dramas, such as Henrik Ibsen's *A Doll's House*.

In 1929, he went to study in the Foreign Language Department in Tsinghua University. There he formed an extensive study from the tragedies of the ancient Greeks to the plays of Shakespeare, in addition to the works of Anton Chekhov, Henrik Ibsen, and Eugene O'Neill.

In 1933, the eve of graduation from the university, Cao Yu wrote a drama in four acts entitled *Thunderstorm*, which was published in the following year, rapidly evoking intense response. It was not only Cao Yu's maiden work, but also very famous and representative work.

In 1936 and 1937, Cao Yu respectively published two major plays, *Sunrise* and *The Wilderness*.

During the period of the War against Japanese, Cao Yu created *Peking Man*. Furthermore, he adapted Ba Jin's novel *Family* into a modern drama.

After the foundation of the People's Republic of China, the major creative plays of Cao Yu continue with *Courage and the Sword*, and *Wang Zhaojun*.

The fouract drama, *Thunderstorm*, depicts a distinguished family tragedy by the use of realism. The drama portrayed the period of time in one day (from morning to 2 a.m) and two settings (the Zhou family household and Lu the family residence). It depicted thirty years of complex conflicts between the Zhou and Lu families, as the drama showed precise and exquisite structural skills.

Zhou Puyuan was not only the main character of the *Thunderstorm*, but also the root cause of various dilemmas.

The author uses two major aspects in his portrayal. Firstly, the conflict between him and his wife Fanyi, displayed the internal dispute of the family. Secondly, the clash between him and the miner Lu Dahai revealed the contradiction between him and the workers. The two conflicts are closely to the character Shiping, making up of the complex discord of the drama.

Zhou Puyuan is depicted as a vicious and brutal capitalist. Furthermore, he was an autocratic and callous feudal patriarch. However, Cao Yu created him as an actual living person, not as a product of his class.

The novel also created another important character, Fanyi. She is known for her character that possesses the manner of a thunderstorm.

In the notes for the production, Cao Yu writes, "Her character has an irresistible unreasoned drive that causes her to make reckless decisions. If she loves someone, she will love him intensely like fire. While if she hates someone, she will use that fire to burn him."

Throughout the work, the author focuses on describing her struggle of an encaged animal due to the suffocating environment, as well as the interlaced the cruelest love and the most unbearable hate. She resists with despair and is filled with the blood and tears of an oppressed woman, showing bold contempt and rebelliousness against the feudal forces and the moral values. Her passion of a thunderstorm, not only destroys the order of the feudal family, but also ruins her own life. The tragic image of Fanyi is one contribution made by Cao Yu to modern drama, deeply conveying the May Fourth theme of anti-feudalism and the liberation of the personality.

After one year of the publication of the *Thunderstorm*, Cao Yu also created another work of realism as drama in four acts called *Sunrise*.

The background is the semi-colonial and semi-feudal city of Tianjin in 1930s. There are two specific locations—the luxuriant parlor of social butterfly Chen Bailu, and the third-class brothel of Cui Xi. It depicts two different living situations of upper and lower class society, revealing the unreasonable truth of the harm created by abundance.

Thunderstorm tries to reflect the oppression and slaughter of the feudal despotism, while the *Sunrise* exposes the poisoning, devouring, and killing people of the money-oriented society.

Cao Yu turned his view to the countryside and created successfully the psychological tragedy of a famer avenger who was under control of the thought of feudal clan in his third play the *Wilderness* (a three-act play).

The three-act play *Peking Man* is another artistic peak of the dramas for Cao Yu. He once again returns to his familiar subject of the outdated family, thoroughly criticizing feudalism.

As *Thunderstorm* focuses on the critique of the relation between ethics and morality, while *Peking Man* is an in depth analysis of feudal cultural traditions.

The Zeng family is portrayed as the epitome of the weak feudal society, as the era of prosperity had already passed.

The only happiness of Zeng Hao in his life was to repeatedly paint his own coffin, symbolizing the death of feudalism. The intelligent and benevolent feudal scholar Zeng Wenqing becomes a superfluous person with merely a hollow shell of life, as his spirit completely paralyzed.

The playwright opposed traditional culture, finding the spiritual strength to convey a new life.

第一单元

园林

中国园林历史悠久,早在西周时,王室贵族就开始兴建苑囿,秦汉时更是广建离宫别馆,像秦代的阿房宫、汉代的上林苑等都是中国古代著名的园林建筑。中国园林以兼供游玩欣赏及居住之用的城市山林型宅旁园最具特色,这种园林崇尚自然,但又不是简单地模仿自然,而是在追求中国山水画和诗词意境之中,以略带写意的手法,创造出更能够概括意境的景物。所以说,中国古典园林的构造,主要是在自然山水的基础上,辅以人工建造的宫、亭、廊、楼、台、阁、榭等建筑,以人工手段效仿自然,其中透视着不同历史时期的人文思想,特别是中国诗、词、绘画的艺术境界。中国古典园林在世界上有很高的声誉,代表作有号称中国四大古典名园的颐和园、避暑山庄、拙政园和留园。

颐和园

位于北京西北 15 公里处,为清代皇家避暑御用园林。这里泉泽遍野,群峰叠翠,水光山色,风景如画。从 11 世纪起,这里就开始营建皇家园林,清代乾隆十五年(1750 年)扩建为"清漪园",1860 年遭英法联军焚掠,1888 年,慈禧挪用海军军费重建,耗白银 3000 万两,工程历时十年,竣工后改名为"颐和园"。到清朝结束时,园林总面积达到了 1000 多公顷,如此大面积的皇家园林真可谓世所罕见。

颐和园由万寿山和昆明湖组成,其中四分之三是湖泊。环绕在山湖之间的宫殿、楼台、寺庙、廊榭等建筑有 3000 余间,这些建筑与山水交相辉映,浑然一体。颐和园有四大景区。最东边是东宫门区。这一带原为清朝皇帝从事政治活动和生活起居之所,包括朝会大臣的仁寿殿和南北朝房、寝宫、大戏台、庭院等。玉澜堂是光绪皇帝的寝宫,后来又成为囚禁他的地方,现在还能看到当时修筑的封闭通道的高墙。中间高耸的万寿山前山景区,建筑最多,也最华丽。整个景区由两条垂直对称的轴线统领,东西轴线就是著名的长廊,南北轴线从长廊中部起,依次为排云门、排云殿、德辉殿、佛香阁等。佛香阁是全园的中心,周围建筑对称分布其间,形成众星捧月之势,气派相当宏伟。最北部的后山后湖景区,尽管建筑较少,但林木葱茏,山路曲折,优雅恬静的风格和前山的华丽形成鲜明对比。一组西藏建筑和江南水乡特色的苏州街,布局紧凑,各有妙趣。颐和园的水面占全园面积的四分之三,特别是南部的前湖区,烟波浩渺,西望群山起伏、北望楼阁成群;湖中有一道西堤,堤上桃柳成行,6座不同形式的拱桥掩映其中;湖中3个小岛上,也有形式各异的古典建筑;十七孔桥横卧湖上,既是通往湖中的道路,又是一处叫人过目不忘的景点,造型十分优美。颐和园中的主体建筑是万寿山上的佛香阁。佛香阁建筑在高21米的方形台基上。阁高40米,有8个面、3层楼、4重屋檐;阁内有8根巨大铁梨木擎天柱,结构相当复杂,为古典建筑精品。回廊和角亭建筑是园林的常用形式。颐和园的长廊长约728米,为世界长廊之最。廊上绘有图画14000余幅,均为传统故事或花鸟鱼虫。昆明湖东岸的八角重檐廓如亭,也是中国最大的八角亭。巨大石舫,雕梁画栋,精彩无比。

颐和园集中了中国古典建筑的精华,容纳了不同地区的园林风格,堪称中国园林建筑的博物馆。

避暑山庄

又名"承德离宫"或"热河行宫"。坐落在中国河北省承德市区北部,武烈河西岸一带狭长的谷地上,距离北京约230公里。这里曾经是清代皇帝夏天避暑和处理政务的场所。

避暑山庄始建于清康熙四十二年(1703年),历经清朝三代皇帝:康熙、雍正、乾隆,至清乾隆五十五年(1790年)竣工,前后耗时87年。

当年康熙皇帝在北巡途中,发现承德这片地方不仅地势良好,气候宜人,风景优美,而且又直达清王朝发祥地——北方,是清朝皇帝家乡的门户。这里还可俯视关内,外控蒙古各部,于是,康熙皇帝决定在这里建行宫。康熙四十二年(1703年)开始在此大兴土木,疏浚湖泊,修路造宫,至康熙五十二年(1713年)已建成36景和山庄的围墙。雍正时期,避暑山庄暂停修建。从乾隆六年(1741年)开始,到乾隆五十七年(1792年)又继续修建直至完工,最后建成的避暑山庄又新增乾隆36景和山庄外的外八庙,最终形成了规模壮观、别具一格的皇家园林。避暑山庄最初称"热河行宫",因康熙皇帝在午门题"避暑山庄"而得名。

避暑山庄与北京紫禁城相比,以朴素淡雅的山村野趣为格调,取自然山水之本色,吸收江南塞北之风光,成为中国现存占地最大的古代帝王宫苑。避暑山庄分宫殿区、湖泊区、平原区、山峦区四大部分:宫殿区位于湖泊南岸,地形平坦,是皇帝处理朝政、举行庆典和生活起居的地方,占地约10万平方米,由正宫、松鹤斋、万壑松风和东宫四组建筑组成;湖泊区在宫殿区的北面,湖泊面积包括洲岛约占地43公顷,8个小岛将湖面分割成大小不同的区域,层次分明,洲岛错落,碧波荡漾,富有江南鱼米之乡的特色,东北角有清泉,即著名的热河泉;平原区在湖区北面的山脚下,地势开阔,有万树园和试马埭,是一片碧草茵茵,林木茂盛的草原风光;山峦区在山庄的西北部,面积约占全园的五分之四,这里山峦起伏,沟壑纵横,众多楼堂殿阁、寺庙点缀其间。整个山庄东南多水,西北多山,是中国自然地貌的缩影。避暑山庄之外,半环于山庄的是雄伟的寺庙群,如众星捧月,环绕山庄,它象征民族的团结和中央集权。承德"外八庙"分布在避暑山庄东北面山麓的台地上,面积达 40 多万平方米,原有寺庙 11 座,现存的有普陀宗乘之庙、须弥福寿之庙、普乐寺、普宁寺、安远庙、溥仁寺、殊像寺等。这些庙宇金碧辉煌,宏伟壮观。

拙政园

拙政园位于苏州市娄门内东北街,是苏州四大名园之一,为苏州园林中面积最大的古典山水园林,同时也是江南园林的代表。这里当年为唐代诗人陆龟蒙的住宅,元代改为大弘(宏)寺,明代嘉靖年间(1522—1566 年)御史王献臣因仕途失意,归隐苏州,将此地购买,并请著名画家文征明参与设计规划,前后历时 16 年始建成此园,园主借用西晋文人潘岳《闲居赋》中"灌园鬻蔬,以供朝夕之膳……此亦拙者之为政也"之语义,取园名为"拙政园"。拙政园建成不久,王献臣便去世,他的儿子在一夜毫赌中,竟把整个园子输掉。400 多年来,拙政园几易其主,曾经被一分为三,园名各异,或为私园,或为官府,或散为民居,直到 20 世纪 50 年代,才三园合一,恢复初名"拙政园"。

拙政园占地面积达 62 亩,分东、中、西和住宅四个部分。中区是拙政园的主区,也为全园精华之所在。面积约 18.5 亩,池水面积占总面积的三分之一。在中区,楼阁亭榭环绕池周,轩榭翼波,廊舍精巧,山林掩映,翠竹篁生;池广树茂,景色宜人,临水处建有形体不一、主次分明、高低错落的建筑。西区原为"补园",面积约 12.5 亩,在拙政园中面积最小。西区水面迂回,布局紧凑,依山傍水建以亭阁,起伏、曲折、凌波而过的水廊、溪涧则是苏州园林艺术的佳作。西部主要建筑为靠近住宅一侧的三十六鸳鸯馆,是当时园主人宴请宾客和听曲的场所,厅内陈设考究。东区原称"归田园居",是因为明崇祯四年(1631 年)拙政园东部归侍郎王心一而得名,占地约 31 亩,因归园早已荒芜,现全部为新建,布局以平冈远山、松林草坪、竹坞曲水为主。配以山池亭榭,仍保持疏朗明快的风格,主要建筑有兰雪堂、芙蓉榭、天泉亭、缀云峰等,这些建筑均为移建。

拙政园虽经历代改建,但仍然保留了明代建筑风格。全园布局疏密自然,以水为主是拙政园的主要特点,广阔的水面,景色平淡天真、疏朗自然。园中建筑以池水为中心,楼阁轩榭环绕在池水的周围,其间有漏镂刻窗、回廊相连,与园内的山石、古木、绿竹、花卉相融,构成了一幅幽远宁静的图画。拙政园形成的湖、池、涧等不同的景区,把景物诗、山水画的意境与自然中的实境再现于园中,使园景充满了浓郁的诗情画意,如夏季可观荷萍游鱼,冬季有梅影雪月,春季繁花丽日,秋季红蓼芦塘,真是处处有情,面面生诗,含蓄曲折,景随步移。而且拙政园的布局采用空间分割、利用自然、对比借景的手法,因而形成了"园中有园,景外有景"的特色,不愧为江南园林的典型代表,被人们誉为"天下园林之母"。

留园

在苏州市阊门外,始建于明代嘉靖年间(1522—1566 年),原为徐时泰私园,清代嘉庆五年(1800 年)归刘蓉峰所有,改称"寒碧山庄",因园主姓刘,所以俗称"刘园"。清光绪二年又为盛旭人所得,改称留园。留园占地约 30 亩(一说为 50 多亩),分中、东、西、北四个景区,在每个景区中都能领略到山水、田园、山林、庭园四种不同景色：中区以水景见长，是全园的精华所在；东区以曲院回廊的建筑取胜，有著名的佳晴雨快鱼之厅、林泉耆硕之馆、还我读书处、冠云台、冠云楼等十数处斋、轩，院内池后立有三座石峰，居中者为名石冠云峰，两旁为瑞云、岫云两峰；北部具乡村田园风光，并有新辟盆景园；西区则是全园最高处，有野趣，以假山为奇，土石相间，堆砌自然；北区原建筑已毁，如今这里广植翠竹桃杏。留园内的建筑数量在苏州各园林中居首位，厅堂、走廊、粉墙、洞门等建筑与假山、水池、花木等组合成数十个大小不等的庭园小品。留园在空间处理上，充分体现了中国古代园林艺术家的高超技艺、卓越智慧和江南园林建筑的艺术风格和特色。

在留园中，有号称"三绝"的佳景：冠云峰，所谓冠云峰实为太湖石中绝品，相传这块奇石还是宋末年花石纲中的遗物，此石集太湖石"瘦、皱、漏、透"四奇于一身；楠木殿，因殿柱所用都是上好的楠木而得名；鱼化石，保存在留园的五峰仙馆内，这是一幅大理石天然画，石头表面的中部，隐隐约约现出群山环抱，悬壁重叠，下部似流水潺潺，瀑布飞悬，上部则流云婀娜，正中上方，一轮白白的圆斑，仿佛一轮太阳或一轮明月……这是自然形成的一幅山水画，这块直径一米左右的大理石出产于云南，厚度也仅有 15 毫米。（夏汉宁编著）

民居

中国是一个多民族国家，其民居形式和风格多彩丰富。这里仅介绍几种最具代表性的民居。

胡同

不少外国游客到北京旅游，常常会问到的一个问题：是北京的胡同在哪里？的确，北京的胡同数量非常多，据文献记载，在明代就多达几千条，其中内城有 900 多条，外城 300 多条；清代增加到 1800 多条；中华民国时期有 1900 多条；中华人民共和国成立初期，北京共有胡同 2550 多条。

北京的胡同最早起源于元代，蒙古人把元大都的街巷叫做胡同——据说这个蒙古词的意思是指水井。北京人一般称南北走向的为街，相对较宽，又因为过去以走马车为主，所以也把这些街称为马路；称东西走向的为胡同，相对较窄，以走人为主，胡同两边一般都是住人的四合院。北京较有特色的胡同不少，如"钱市胡同"，这是北京最窄的胡同，长约三四十米，它位于前门外珠宝市大街，因为过去这条胡同里都是钱庄而得名。再如，中国古代有"开门七件事"——柴、米、油、盐、酱、醋、茶，所以，与此相对应，在北京也就有了"柴棒胡同"、"米市胡同"、"油坊胡同"、"盐店胡同"、"酱坊胡同"、"醋章胡同"和"茶儿胡同"人们在日常生活中经常要与金、银、铜、铁、锡这五种金属接触，于是，与此相对应，在北京也就有了"金丝胡同"、"银丝胡同"、"铜铁厂胡同"、"铁门胡同"和"锡拉胡同"。

有人认为，胡同作为元代的产物，它与四合院的完美组合，体现出元代统治者在城市建设与管理方面的聪明之处。胡同横平竖直，四合院错落有致，怎么看都像是军事化管理的结果。有了胡同的分割与疏通，北京城便成了一座由游牧民族安营扎寨的大军营。有人更是十分形象的比喻:北京城像一块大豆腐,四方四正。城里有大街,有胡同。大街、胡同都是正南正北,正东正西。这使得北京人的方位意识极强。

四合院

这是在中国北京及华北地区传统的最具代表性的院落式住宅。四合院是以正房、东厢房、西厢房围绕中间庭院形成平面布局的传统住宅,在中国民居中历史最悠久,分布最广泛,它也是汉族民居形式的典型代表。有人认为,四合院的历史已经有3000多年,在中国古代的西周时期,四合院的形制就已初具规模。四合院的大门一般开在东南角或西北角,院中的北房是正房,正房建在砖石砌成的台基上,比其他房屋的规模大,是院主人的住室。院子的两边建有东、西厢房,是晚辈们居住的地方。在正房和厢房之间建有走廊,可以供人行走和休息。四合院的围墙和临街的房屋一般不对外开窗,院中的环境封闭而幽静。北京四合院驰名中外,世人皆知。在北京有各种规模的四合院,但不论大小,都是由一个个四面房屋围合的庭院组成的。最简单的四合院只有一个院子,比较复杂的有两三个院子,富贵人家居住的深宅大院,通常是由好几座四合院并列组成的。中间还有一道隔墙。四合院的典型特征是外观规矩,中线对称,而且用法极为灵活——从大处扩展,它就是皇宫、王府;往小处收缩,它就是平民百姓的住宅;辉煌的紫禁城与郊外的普通农民家都是四合院。

围屋

在中国古代的两晋至唐宋时期,由于战乱饥荒等原因,原来居住在黄河流域的中原汉族人被迫南迁,这期间一共有五次人口大迁移,这些人先后流落南方。由于在南方平坦地区已有人居住,这些人只好迁居在南方的山区或丘陵地带,故有“逢山必有客,无客不住山”的说法流传。在当时,地方官员为这些移民登记户籍时,也常常把他们立为“客籍”,或为“客户”、“客家”,这就是客家人称谓的由来。为了防外敌及野兽侵扰,多数客家人聚族而居,由此形成了围龙屋、走马楼、五凤楼、土围楼、四角楼等,其中以围龙屋存世最多也最为著名,所以人们通常称这种围龙屋为“围屋”或“客家围屋”,这种建筑也是客家建筑文化的集中体现。围龙屋始于唐宋,盛行于明清。客家人多选择丘陵地带或斜坡地段建造围龙屋,主体结构为“一进三厅两厢一围”。客家围屋往往是营垒式住宅,以方形和圆形为主,围屋的建造是:在泥土中掺加石灰,以糯米饭、鸡蛋清作黏稠剂,用竹片、木条作筋骨,以此夯筑起墙厚1米,高15米以上的土楼。普通的围龙屋占地8亩至10亩,大围龙屋的面积占地约30亩以上,建好一座完整的围龙屋往往需要五年至十年的时间,有的甚至更长时间。一间围龙屋就是一座客家人的巨大堡垒。屋内分别建有多间卧室、厨房、大小厅堂及水井、猪圈、鸡窝、厕所、仓库等生活设施,适合几十个人、一百多人或数百人同居一屋,形成一个自给自足、自得其乐的社会小群体。围龙屋不论大小,大门前必有一块禾坪和一个半月形池塘,禾坪用于晒谷、乘凉和其他活动,池塘具有蓄水、养鱼、防火、防旱等作用。大门之内,分上、中、下三个大厅,左右分两厢或四厢,俗称横屋,一直向后延伸,在左右横屋的尽头,筑起围墙形的房屋,把正屋包围起来,小的十几间,大的二十几间,正中一间为“龙厅”,这也是“围龙屋”名称的由来。小围龙屋一般只有一至二条围龙,大型围龙屋则有四条五条甚至六条围龙。这种围屋在今天中国福建和江西省仍有保存。客家围屋与北京四合院、陕西窑洞、广西的“杆栏式”、云南的“一颗印”并称为中国五大特色民居建筑。(夏汉宁编著)

皇陵

在中国古代,只有皇帝的墓地才称为陵。中国历代皇陵很多,其中不少已经湮没或毁坏,但现存的皇陵仍有很多,最为著名的有以下几座:

黄帝陵相传是中华民族的始祖轩辕黄帝的陵园,它位于中国陕西省黄陵县城北的桥山顶上。黄帝是中国原始社会末期一位伟大的部落首领,是开创中华民族文明的祖先。黄帝崩,葬桥山,桥山山体浑厚,气势雄伟,山下有沮水环绕,山上有八万多棵千年古柏,四季常青,郁郁葱葱。轩辕黄帝的陵冢就深藏在桥山巅的古柏中。陵墓封土高 3.6 米,周长 48 米,环冢砌以青砖花墙,陵前有明嘉靖十五年(1536 年)碑刻"桥山龙驭"四字,意为黄帝"驭龙升天"之处。

大禹陵位于浙江省绍兴市东南会稽山麓,是中国古代治水英雄大禹的陵地。大禹陵周围群山环抱,奇峰林立,清流潺潺东去,使大禹陵更显凝重、壮观。大禹陵区由禹陵、禹庙、禹祠三大部分组成。大禹陵面临禹池,前有石构牌坊,过百米甬道,有"大禹陵"碑亭。禹庙在禹陵的东北面,坐北朝南,是一处宫殿式建筑,始建于南朝梁初,其中轴线建筑自南而北依次为:照壁、岣嵝碑亭、午门、拜厅、大殿。建筑依山势而逐渐升高。大殿为重檐歇山造,巍然耸立,殿背龙吻鸱尾直刺云天,背间"地平天成"四字,为清康熙皇帝题写。禹祠位于禹陵左侧,为二进三开间平屋,祠前一泓清池,悠然如镜,称"放生池"。

秦始皇陵位于陕西省西安市以东 30 公里的骊山脚下,高大的陵墓在巍巍峰峦环抱之中与骊山浑然一体,景色优美,环境独秀。秦始皇陵规模宏大,气势雄伟。陵园总面积为 56．25 平方公里。陵上封土原高约 115 米,现仍高达 76 米。陵园内有内外两重城垣,内城周长 3840 米,外城周长 6210 米,内外城郭有高约 8~10 米的城墙,今尚残留遗址。墓葬区在南,寝殿和便殿建筑群在北。秦始皇陵是中国历史上第一个皇帝陵园,建于公元前 246 年至公元前 208 年。其规模之大、陪葬物之丰富,堪称中国历代帝王陵之首。秦始皇陵按照秦始皇死后照样能够享受荣华富贵的原则,仿照秦国都城咸阳的布局建造,大体呈回字形,陵区内目前探明的大型地面建筑为寝殿、便殿、园寺吏舍等遗址。据史料记载,秦始皇陵陵区分陵园区和从葬区两部分,整座陵区总面积为 56.25 平方公里。秦始皇陵的冢高 55.05 米,周长 2000 米。整个墓地占地面积为 22 万平方米,内有大规模的宫殿楼阁建筑。陵寝的形制分为内外两城:内城为周长 2525.4 米的方形,外城周长 6264 米。秦始皇陵的规模之大远非埃及金字塔所能比。古埃及金字塔是世界上最大的地上王陵,中国秦始皇陵是世界上最大的地下皇陵,被誉为世界第八大奇迹。

位于北京昌平县境内的燕山山麓的天寿山,是中国明代皇帝的墓葬群。这里从明代永乐七年(1409 年)五月开始建造长陵,到明朝最后一个皇帝崇祯葬入思陵止,其间共经历了 230 多年,先后修建了 13 座皇帝陵墓、7 座妃子墓、1 座太监墓。明十三陵共埋葬了 13 位皇帝、23 位皇后、2 位太子、30 余名妃嫔和 1 位太监。十三陵地处东、西、北三面环山的小盆地之中,陵区周围群山环抱,中部为平原,陵前有小河曲折蜿蜒,山明水秀,景色宜人。这十三座皇陵依次是：成祖长陵、仁宗献陵、宣宗景陵、英宗裕陵、宪宗茂陵、孝宗泰陵、武宗康陵、世宗永陵、穆宗昭陵、神宗定陵、光宗庆陵、熹宗德陵、思宗思陵，故称明十三陵。十三座陵墓依山而筑，分别建在东、西、北三面的山麓上，形成了体系完整的、规模宏大、气势磅礴的皇帝陵寝建筑群。明十三陵建于 1409 年—1644 年，最后一座思陵距今已有 500 多年历史。陵区占地面积达 40 平方公里，是中国乃至世界现存规模最大、皇帝、皇后等陵寝最多的一处皇家陵墓建筑群。（夏汉宁编著）

第二单元

围棋

围棋是一种智力游戏，它起源于 2000 多年前的古代中国。

相传，在中国的上古时期，尧帝平阳在平息协和各部落方国以后，农耕生产和人民生活呈现出一派繁荣兴旺的景象。但有一件事情却让尧帝很忧虑，即散宜氏所生儿子丹朱虽长大成人，却游手好闲，不务正业，经常招惹祸端。为了让自己的儿子成器，尧帝夫妇真是伤透了脑筋，但丹朱仍是我行我素。让他学射箭，他不感兴趣；学其他的东西，他也不愿意。尧帝见丹朱如此不思上进，万般无奈，叹了一口气说："只好让他学行兵征战的石子棋吧，石子棋学会了，用处也大着哩。"丹朱听父帝叫他改学下石子棋，心里稍有转意："下石子棋还不容易吗？坐下一会儿就学会了。"于是要父亲立即教他。尧帝说："哪有一朝一夕就能学会的东西，你只要肯学就行。说着尧帝提起箭来，用箭头在一块平坡山石上用力刻画了纵横十几道方格子，让卫士们捡来一大堆山石子，又分给丹朱一半，他将自己在率领部落征战过程中如何利用石子表示前进后退的作战谋略讲解给丹朱。丹朱此时倒也听得进去，显得有了耐心。直至太阳要落山的时候，尧帝教子下棋还是那样的尽心尽力。在卫士们的催促下，父子们才结束了这第一次学棋课。此后一段时日，丹朱学棋很专心，也不到外边游逛。怎料，丹朱学棋不多久，老毛病便又犯了，他终日无事生非，甚至想用诡计夺取尧帝的王位经。散宜氏见状，痛心不已，大病一场，怏怏而终。尧帝也十分伤心，只好把丹朱迁送到南方，他再也不想看到这个不争气的儿子了，不仅如此，尧帝还把帝位禅让给经过他三年严格考察，不但有德且有智有才的虞舜。虞舜继位后，也学尧帝的样子，用石子棋教自己的儿子商均，以启发他的智力。于是，在以后的陶器上便出现了围棋方格的图形，史书里面也有了"尧造围棋，以教丹朱"等记载。

围棋，在中国古代称为弈，在整个古代棋类中可以说是棋之鼻祖，相传已有 4000 多年的历史，被人们形象地比喻为黑白世界的围棋，是中国古代为人们所喜爱的一项娱乐竞技活动，同时也是人类历史上最悠久的一种棋戏。由于它将科学、艺术和竞技三者融为一体，有着发展智力，培养意志品质和机动灵活的战略战术思想意识的特点，因而，几千年来长盛不衰，并逐渐地发展成了一种国际性的文化竞技活动。今日，在亚洲的围棋爱好者有数千万人，在欧美等国家也有不少人喜欢下围棋。围棋的规则十分简单，却拥有十分广大的空间可以落子,这使得围棋变化多端,比中国象棋更为复杂。这也是围棋魅力长盛不衰的原因所在。下一盘围棋的时间没有规定,快则五分钟,慢则要几天,多数时候下一盘棋需要一到两个小时。

围棋的棋盘盘面有纵横各 19 条等距离、垂直交叉的平行线,共构成 361 个交叉点(一般称为"点")。在盘面上标有几个小圆点。称为星位,中央的星位又称"天元"。棋子分黑白两色。均为扁圆形。棋子的数量以黑子 181、白子 180 个为宜。

围棋一般为两人对局,对局前确定谁先走。其下法有以下几点:一、对局双方各执一色棋子,黑先白后,交替下子,每次只能下一子。二、棋子下在棋盘的点上。三、棋子下定后,不得向其他点移动。四、轮流下子是双方的权利,但允许任何一方放弃下子权。

下围棋对人脑的智力开发很有帮助,可增强人的计算和记忆能力、创意和思维能力、判断和注意能力。下围棋对儿童可以起到积极作用,能够培养他们对事物的分析能力,同时还能够增强他们的自我控制能力。

傩舞

傩舞,又叫"大傩"、"跳傩",俗称"鬼戏"或"跳鬼脸"。傩舞渊源于上古氏族社会中的图腾信仰,为原始文化信仰的基础。它广泛流传于中国各地的一种具有驱鬼逐疫、祭祀功能的民间舞蹈,是傩仪式中的舞蹈部分。傩舞一般在中国传统节日春节的大年初一到正月十六期间表演,原是古代祭祀性的原始舞蹈,舞者佩戴形象狰狞的面具,装扮成传说中的"方相氏",一手持戈、一手持盾,边舞边"傩、傩……"地呼喊,舞者奔向各个角落,跳跃舞打,搜寻不祥之物,以驱除疫鬼,祈求一年平安。现存傩舞主要分布在中国的江西、安徽、贵州、广西、山东、河南、陕西、湖北、福建、云南、广东等地,各地分别有"跳傩"、"鬼舞"、"玩喜"等地方性称谓。这种历史悠久的民间舞蹈,一般有两种表演形式:一种由主角四人表演,表演者头戴面具如冠,身着兽皮,手执戈盾,口中发出"傩、傩"之声;另一种由十二人组成,每人朱发画皮,手执数尺长的麻鞭,甩动作响,并高呼各种专吃恶鬼、猛兽之神名,起舞时各有音乐伴奏。

傩舞源流久远,殷墟甲骨文卜辞中已有傩祭的记载。周代称傩舞为"国傩"、"大傩",乡间也叫"乡人傩"。据《论语·乡党》记载,当时孔夫子看见傩舞表演队伍到来时,曾穿着礼服站在台阶上毕恭毕敬地迎接。由此典故引申而来,清代以后的许多文人,多把年节中的各种民间歌舞表演,泛称为"乡人傩",并为一些地方和寺庙碑文中引用。傩祭风习,自秦汉至唐宋一直沿袭下来,并不断发展,至明、清两代,傩舞虽古意犹存,但已发展成为娱乐性的风俗活动,并向戏曲发展,成为一些地区的"傩堂戏"、"地戏"。至今,在中国的江西、湖南、湖北、广西等省区农村,仍保存着比较古老的傩舞形式,并增添了一些新的内容。例如:江西的婺源、南丰、乐安等县的"傩舞",有表现盘古开天辟地的"开山神"、传说中的"和合二仙"、"刘海戏金蟾",戏剧片段的"孟姜女"、"白蛇传",以及反映劳动生活的"绩麻舞"等。傩舞的表演形式与面具的制作,对中国许多少数民族的舞蹈产生了影响,如藏族的"羌姆",壮族、瑶族、毛南族、仫佬族等民族的"师公舞",就是吸收了傩舞的许多文化因素和表演手法,从而发展成为有本民族特色的舞蹈形式。

《论语·乡党》中记载的"乡人傩"一直在民间延续,并与宗教、文艺、民俗等结合,衍变为多种形态的傩舞、傩戏,至今仍在中国广大农村流行,以江西、湖南、湖北、陕西、四川、贵州、云南、广西、安徽、山西、河北等省区遗存较多。这里仅以江西傩为例:

江西是中国傩文化的发祥地之一。商周时聚居于赣江和鄱阳湖流域的三苗后裔,创造了灿烂的江西青铜文化。江西新干县大洋洲商墓出土的青铜双角神人面具,透露了赣傩滥觞的信息。记载最早的赣傩是南丰县《金砂余氏族谱·傩神辨记》,其中说汉初长沙王吴芮奉命征伐闽越,驻兵南丰军山。为避兵之灾,告诫乡民要敬傩以此消除妖孽。唐代文化鼎盛,《开元礼》对州县傩礼的统一规定,推动了江西 8 州 37 县"乡傩"的传播,如在江西的南丰、萍乡、修水等地,都流传着唐代建傩庙、供傩神的传说。宋代江西经济文化发达,赣傩盛行。南丰《金砂余氏族谱》记载,余氏为避唐末战乱,由余干迁徙南丰,宋初将祖先在四川为官时崇奉的西川灌口二郎清源真君神像迁至金砂(现紫霄镇黄沙村),立庙奉祀,岁时香火,并将这种制度称为"驱傩"。明清两代是赣傩繁荣时期,江西 30 多个县市有乡傩记载或遗存:赣东以南丰为最,清末至今有 180 多个村庄组建过傩班,现仍有"跳傩"、"跳竹马"、"跳和合"、"跳八仙"等 113 班;乐安有"滚傩神"、"戏头鼓"和"玩喜"等;崇仁有"面仈公"和"跳八仙"等;宜黄有"跳傩"、广昌有"孟戏"和"跳魁星"、黎川有"跳和合"与"跳八架"等等。赣西数萍乡最多,傩舞称"仰傩神"或"耍傩案",并称傩庙、傩面、傩舞为"三宝";万载称"跳魈"或"搬案",分"闭口傩"和"开口傩"两种流派……各地乡傩构成了具有江西特色的赣傩文化群。

由于傩舞流传地区不同,其表演风格也各异,既有场面变化复杂,表演细致严谨,生活气息浓厚,舞姿优美动人的文傩流派;又有气势威武磅礴,情绪奔放开朗,节奏热烈明快,动作刚劲有力的武傩流派。这种古老传统傩舞之花,至今仍流行于江西的德安、武宁、婺源、南丰、都昌等县的舞台、厅堂和村镇田头。傩舞表演时一般都佩戴某个角色的面具。其中有神话形象,也有世俗人物和历史名人,由此构成庞大的傩神谱系,"摘下面具是人,戴上面具是神"。傩舞伴奏乐器简单,一般为鼓、锣等打击乐。表演傩仪傩舞的组织称为"傩班",成员一般有八至十余人,常有严格的班规。傩舞常在傩仪仪式过程中的高潮部分和节目表演阶段出现,各地的傩舞节目丰富,兼具祭祀和娱乐的双重功效。

傩神庙是众神(面具)栖息之地,也是举行傩仪的主要场所。江西的萍乡现存 17 座,南丰亦存 17 座,其中北宋金砂村傩神庙记载最早。明永乐年间(1403—1424 年)迁建的甘坊村傩神殿保存完好,清乾隆辛丑年(1781 年)迁建的石邮村傩神庙民俗风味最浓。傩仪是傩基本形态。赣傩仪式沿袭古礼,有起傩(开箱、出洞、出案)、演傩(跳傩、跳魈、跳鬼)、驱傩(搜除、扫堂、行靖)、圆傩(封箱、封洞、收案)等基本程序。时间一般从农历正月初一开始,至元宵后几天结束(少数傩班在二月间结束)。"驱傩"是整个仪式重点,傩人戴着狰狞面具,拿着武器,在火把照耀下沿门驱疫,将危害人类的邪魅赶走。傩舞是赣傩的主要表演形式,素有中国舞蹈"活化石"之称。现有 200 多个传统节目,其中南丰 90 多个。

傩在漫长的传承和发展过程中,融合了人类学、社会学、历史学、宗教学、民俗学、戏剧学、舞蹈学、美学等多种学科内容,积淀了丰厚的文化底蕴。国家非常重视非物质文化遗产的保护,2006 年 5 月 20 日,傩舞经国务院批准列入第一批国家级非物质文化遗产名录。(夏汉宁编著)

京剧

京剧,又称"京戏"、"平剧"、"国剧",也称"皮黄",是地地道道的中国国粹,因形成于北京而得名。

京剧形成的源头还要追溯到中国几种古老的地方戏剧。清代乾隆五十五年(1790 年),安徽的四大地方戏班——三庆班、四喜班、春公班和春班先后进京演出,这四个戏班的演出,在北京获得了空前的成功。由于"微班"常与来自湖北的汉调艺人合作演出,于是,一种以微调"二簧"和汉调"西皮"为主,兼收昆曲、秦腔、梆子等地方戏精华的新剧种便诞生了——这就是京剧。一般认为,京剧正式诞生于清代的光绪年间,因京剧之名始见于清光绪二年(1876 年)的《申报》。也有人认为诞生于清代道光年间。京剧诞生后,便广泛流行于中国的大江南北、城乡各地。20 世纪三四十年代尤为盛行,是中国最大的戏曲剧种,当时就有"国剧"之称。直至今天,京剧仍是具有全国影响的大剧种。

京剧行当全面、表演成熟、气势宏美,是近代中国戏曲的代表。其剧目之丰富、表演艺术家之多、剧团之多、观众之多、影响之深均为全国之冠。之所以这样说,是基于以下几个方面的理由:

一、京剧剧目丰富,据统计,京剧传统剧目有 1000 多个,流传较广的著名剧目有《霸王别姬》《群英会》《三打祝家庄》《三岔口》等等。

二、京剧是综合性表演艺术,集唱(歌唱)、念(念白)、做(表演)、打(武打)、舞(舞蹈)为一体,通过程式的表演手段来演绎故事、刻画人物,以表达"喜、怒、哀、乐、惊、恐、悲"的思想感情。所以有人将京剧称作"东方歌剧",是因为两个剧种都是集歌唱、舞蹈、音乐、美术、文学等于一体的特殊戏剧形式,在形式上极为类似;同时,这两种产生在不同文化背景中的舞台表演艺术,都在各自生存的文化圈中获得了经典性地位。

三、京剧角色分为"生、旦、净、丑"四大行当,这其实就其是京剧的角色分类,"生"是男性正面角色;"旦"是女性正面角色;"净"是性格粗犷鲜明的男性配角,"丑"是幽默滑稽或反面角色。

四、京剧每种角色都有表明身份的脸谱和扮相等,只要演员一上场,观众通过脸谱或扮相一看便知角色身份。脸谱,就是在人的脸上涂上某种颜色以象征这个人的性格和品质、角色和命运。这是京剧的一大特点,也是理解剧情的关键。一般来讲,红脸含有褒义,代表忠勇者;黑脸为中性,代表猛智者;蓝脸和绿脸也为中性,代表草莽英雄;黄脸和白脸含贬义,代表阴险狡诈者;金脸和银脸是神秘的象征,代表神妖。除颜色之外,脸谱的勾画形式也具有类似的象征意义,例如:象征阴险狡诈的粉脸,就有满脸都白的粉脸,也有只涂鼻梁眼窝的粉脸,白粉面积的大小和部位的不同,标志着阴险狡诈的程度不同,通常来说,面积越大就越狠毒。总之,颜色代表性格,而不同的勾画法则表示性格的程度。所以,在京剧中,人物有忠奸之分、美丑之分、善恶之分,而这种区分通过角色的脸谱即可识别。

五、京剧表演艺术家之多，在中国戏曲剧中之中是罕见的，如程长庚、余三胜、谭鑫培、马连良、梅兰芳、余叔岩、程砚秋、尚小云等人，都是著名的京剧表演艺术家。

中国政府非常重视非物质文化遗产的保护，2006 年 5 月 20 日，经中华人民共和国国务院批准，京剧被列入第一批国家级非物质文化遗产名录。（夏汉宁编著）

昆曲

提起中国江苏省昆山市千灯镇，知道的人也许不多；但是提起昆曲，知道的人一定不少。其实，600 多年前，昆曲的前身昆山腔就是从千灯镇发源的。昆曲是中国古老的戏曲声腔和剧种，原称"昆山腔"，简称"昆腔"，从清代开始又称"昆曲"，现在也称"昆剧"。

昆山腔始于元代末年中国苏州的昆山一带。在当时，昆山腔是南曲的一个支派。明代万历之前，它只是流行于吴中的一种清曲，其变革和发展是在明代中叶以后，也就是明代的嘉靖（1522—1566 年）、隆庆（1567—1572 年）年间。在此期间，一位名叫魏良辅的江西南昌人来到了昆山，他致力于南曲改革，与善吹洞箫的张梅谷等人合作，对昆山腔作了很大的改进与发展。号称"乐圣"的魏良辅对过去两百年间的昆曲演唱技巧进行了整理和总结，在原昆山腔的基础上，参考海盐腔和余姚腔的优点，同时吸收北曲中的一些唱法，建立了昆山腔的歌唱体系，昆山腔"水磨调"由此问世。

公元 1543 年是昆曲发展史上非同寻常的一年。正是在这一年，魏良辅完成了他那部具有历史意义的著作——《南词引正》。这部著作的问世，确立了昆曲的正声地位。但昆曲真正从清唱演变为舞台戏剧，却是从明代昆山人梁辰鱼的《浣纱记》开始。这位精诗词、通音律的著名戏曲作家，与精通音理的郑思笠、陈梅泉、唐小虞等人一道，把传奇文学与新的声腔和表演艺术结合在一起，创作了以西施为主要人物的《浣纱记》传奇，第一次将昆曲搬上了舞台，这也成为昆曲定型和成熟的标志。《浣纱记》的上演，扩大了昆山腔在当时中国戏曲界的影响，形成了文人学士争相运用昆腔创作传奇的局面，学习昆腔的人也日益增多。于是，昆腔与余姚腔、海盐腔、弋阳腔一起并称为明代的"四大声腔"。后来，它经扬州传入北京、湖南等地，并由此蔓延到四川、贵州、广东等地，从而发展成为一个有很大影响的全国性剧种。

昆曲使用的乐器以笛为主，同时辅以箫、笙、琴、琵琶、唢呐、弦子等乐器。昆曲音乐属于联曲体结构，简称"曲牌体"。曲牌是昆曲演唱中最基本的单位。据不完全统计，昆曲所使用的曲牌，大约有 1000 种以上。昆曲的表演，也有它独特的体系和风格，其最大特点就是抒情性强，动作细腻，载歌载舞，将歌唱与舞蹈结合得相当巧妙和完美，对服装、色彩以及脸谱也非常讲究。角色行当以生、旦、净、末、丑、外、贴七行为基础角色，同时借鉴元杂剧中的小末、小旦等设置法，增设了小生、小旦、小末、小外、小净五行，共十二行。

昆曲在长期的演出活动中，积累和保留了大量的剧目，其中影响较大而且又经常演出的剧目有：王世贞的《鸣凤记》；汤显祖的《牡丹亭》《紫钗记》《邯郸记》《南柯记》；沈璟的《义侠记》等等。除此之外，还有高濂的《玉簪记》李渔的《风筝误》朱素臣的《十五贯》孔尚任的《桃花扇》洪升的《长生殿》。《游园惊梦》《阳关》《三醉》《秋江》《思凡》《断桥》等著名折子戏,也常在昆曲舞台上表演。这些剧目有不少已经成为不朽经典,如产生于昆曲鼎盛时期的汤显祖的《牡丹亭》,就堪称是中国古代文学和戏剧中的传世佳作。汤显祖也因此和英国的莎士比亚一样,被公认为世界上最伟大的戏剧家之一。加拿大人史凯蒂,曾经用了15年的时间,写作并出版了一部关于《牡丹亭》演出史的著作,内容包含《牡丹亭》在中国以及世界各国的演出史,还包含它被改编成歌剧版的经过。

有人说,每个民族都有一种高雅精致的表演艺术,它能深刻地表现出那个民族的精神与心声,希腊人有悲剧,意大利有歌剧,俄国人有芭蕾,英国人有莎士比亚戏剧。我们中国人的高雅艺术是什么? 是昆曲。昆曲至今已有600多年历史,被誉为世界戏剧的三大源头之一,同时也被称为中国戏曲的"百戏之祖"、"百戏之母",中国许多地方剧种如晋剧、蒲剧、上党戏、湘剧、川剧、赣剧、桂剧、邕剧、越剧和广东粤剧、闽剧、婺剧、滇剧等等,都受到过昆剧艺术多方面的哺育和滋养,就连被称为当今"国粹"的京剧,也渗透着大量的昆剧艺术元素,它从昆曲中继承了一批演出曲目,基本沿用了昆曲的行当和表演体系。

今天,昆曲作为中国传统文化的代表,已经跨越了国界。20世纪八九十年代,中国各地昆曲剧团经常赴海外演出。欧洲、北美以及香港和台湾地区都留下了中国昆曲美妙的身影。昆曲也伴随着海外华人的足迹,在异国他乡生根发芽。据有关资料记载,美国和日本等地,都有昆曲曲友自发成立的曲社。如张惠新所在的昆曲艺术研习社团就是最有影响的海外曲社之一。它于1995年在美国马里兰州成立,拥有一批相对固定的观众群。曲社的每一次公开演出,都会有大批观众赶来捧场。对当地人而言,昆曲是他们了解中国、了解中国历史和文化的一个窗口。

2001年5月18日,中国昆曲以全票入选联合国教科文组织首批"人类口述和非物质遗产代表作"。2006年5月20日,经中华人民共和国国务院批准,昆曲被列入第一批国家级非物质文化遗产名录。(夏汉宁编著)

地方戏

豫 剧

豫剧,又称河南梆子、河南高调。因早期演员用本嗓演唱,起腔和收腔时都用假声翻高,尾音带"讴",所以又叫"河南讴"。豫剧在河南西部山区演出时,多凭借山的平土为舞台,所以在当地称豫剧为"靠山吼"。因为河南省在中国简称"豫",所以在中华人民共和国成立后,将这种地方戏曲正式定名为豫剧。

豫剧最早产生于明末清初,初时以清唱为主,深受老百姓的喜爱,因而发展非常迅速。豫剧起源已经很难考证,说法不一。一说明末秦腔与蒲州梆子传入河南后,与当地民歌、小调相结合而成;一说由北曲弦索调直接发展而成;一说是在河南民间演唱艺术,特别是自明代中后期,在中原地区盛行的时尚小令基础上,吸收"弦索"等艺术成果发展而成。总之,豫剧发展历史较长,在清代乾隆年间(1736—1795 年),被称为"土梆戏"或"汴梁腔"的豫剧,就相当兴盛了。

豫剧主要流行于中国的河南全省、长江以北和西北各省,以及新疆、西藏、台湾等省、区。豫剧的角色行当,主要由"生、旦、净、丑"组成。按一般的说法是四生、四旦、四花脸。戏班组织也是按照"四生、四旦、四花脸,四兵、四将、四丫环;八个场面两箱官,外加四个杂役"来搭建的。"四生",即老生、大红脸(红生)、二红脸(武生)、小生;"四旦",即大净(黑头)、大花脸、二花脸、三花脸(丑)。也有五生、五旦、五花脸的说法。演员一般都有自己专工行当,也有一些演员一专多能,工一行外,兼演他行。豫剧的传统剧目有 1000 多个,其中很大一部分取材于历史小说和演义。如封神戏、三国戏、瓦岗戏、包公戏、杨家将戏和岳家将戏,还有很大一部分描写婚姻、爱情、伦理道德的戏。比较有代表性的是《对花枪》《三上轿》《地塘板》《提寇》《铡美案》《十二寡妇征西》等等。中华人民共和国成立之后,出现了不少描写现实生活的现代戏和新编历史剧,如《朝阳沟》《小二黑结婚》《人欢马叫》《倒霉大叔的婚事》《试夫》《苹果,红了》等。

豫剧一向以唱见长,在剧情的节骨眼上都安排有大板唱腔,唱腔流畅、节奏鲜明、极具口语化,一般吐字清晰、行腔酣畅、易为听众听清,显示出特有的艺术魅力。豫剧的风格首先是富有激情奔放的阳刚之气,善于表演大气磅礴的大场面戏,具有强大的情感力度;其次是地方特色浓郁,质朴通俗、本色自然,紧贴老百姓的生活;再次是节奏鲜明强烈,矛盾冲突尖锐,故事情节有头有尾,人物性格鲜明。豫剧主要流派分为豫东调与豫西调。豫东调因受其邻近的兄弟剧种山东梆子的唱腔的影响,男声高亢激越,女声活泼跳荡,擅长表现喜剧风格的剧目;豫西调因遗留了部分秦腔的韵味,如男声苍凉、悲壮,女声低回婉转,故擅长表现悲剧风格的剧目。豫剧的代表人物有常香玉、陈素真、崔兰田、马金凤、阎立品等"豫剧五大名旦",代表五大风格旦角流派,小生赵义庭、王素君,须生唐喜成、刘忠河和刘新民,黑脸李斯忠,丑角牛得草也成为各具特色的名演员。

黄梅戏

黄梅戏,原名"黄梅调",起源于中国湖北省黄梅县,发展于安徽省安庆地区。最早是 18 世纪后期在湖北、安徽、江西三省毗邻地区形成的一种民间小戏。在 1921 年出版的《宿松县志》中,第一次正式提出了"黄梅戏"这个名称。已有 200 多年历史的黄梅戏,经过多年的发展,特别是近几十年的发展,已成为深受中国观众喜爱的著名剧种。

黄梅戏唱腔委婉清新,分花腔和平词两大类。花腔以演小戏为主,富有浓厚的生活气息和民歌风味,多用"衬词";平词是正本戏中最主要的唱腔,常用于大段叙述和抒情,听起来委婉悠扬,韵味丰富,有如行云流水。现代黄梅戏在音乐方面增强了"平词"类唱腔的表现力,常用于大段抒情和叙事,是正本戏的主要唱腔。这一改革突破了原有"花腔"专戏专用的限制,吸收了民歌和其他音乐成分,创造了与传统唱腔相协调的新腔。黄梅戏以高胡为主要伴奏乐器,加以其他民族乐器和锣鼓配合,适合于表现多种题材的剧目。

黄梅戏在剧目方面,有"大戏三十六本,小戏七十二折"之称。所谓大戏,是指表现较大题材的剧目,如《荞麦记》《告粮官》《天仙配》等;所谓小戏,则大都表现的是农村劳动者的生活片段,如《点大麦》《纺棉纱》《卖斗箩》等。中华人民共和国成立以后,先后整理改编了

《天仙配》《女驸马》《罗帕记》《赵桂英》《慈母泪》《三搜国丈府》等一批大小传统剧目,创作了神话剧《牛郎织女》、历史剧《失刑斩》、现代戏《春暖花开》《小店春早》《蓓蕾初开》等。其中《天仙配》《女驸马》和《牛郎织女》相继搬上银幕,在中国乃至国际上都产生了较大影响。严凤英、王少舫、吴琼、马兰等是黄梅戏的著名演员。

越剧

越剧,是中国传统的戏曲形式。主要流行于上海、浙江、江苏、福建等地。越剧的前身是浙江嵊县一带流行的说唱形式"落地唱书",清代光绪三十二年(1906年)春,开始演变为在农村草台演出的戏曲形式,曾称小歌班、的笃班、绍兴文戏等。艺人初始基本上是半农半艺的男性农民,故称男班。1923年在嵊县施家岙开办了女子小歌班,后改名为"绍兴女子文戏",以女子反串男角,盛极一时,从此男演员逐渐转为教师或工作人员。1925年9月17日上海《新闻报》演出广告中首次以"越剧"称之。

越剧长于抒情,以唱为主,声腔清悠婉丽,优美动听,表演真切动人,极具江南地方色彩。20世纪50年代和60年代前期,是越剧的黄金时期,在这个时期创造出了一批有重大影响的艺术精品,如《梁山伯与祝英台》《西厢记》《红楼梦》等,在中国国内和国际上都获得了巨大声誉,《情探》《李娃传》《追鱼》《碧玉簪》《彩楼记》等成为优秀保留剧目,其中《梁山伯与祝英台》《情探》《追鱼》《碧玉簪》《红楼梦》还被摄成电影,借助这种传播方式,使得越剧风靡中国的大江南北。越剧著名演员有袁雪芬、傅全香、戚雅仙、范瑞娟、徐玉兰、尹桂芳、王文娟、张桂凤、茅威涛等。(夏汉宁编著)

敦煌壁画

敦煌位于中国甘肃、青海、新疆三省(区)的交汇点。敦,是大的意思;煌,是盛的意思。盛大辉煌的敦煌有着悠久的历史,灿烂的文化。敦煌壁画就是这悠久灿烂文化中的奇葩,也是世人瞩目的敦煌学中的一个重要组成部分。

敦煌壁画,泛指存在于敦煌石窟中的壁画。敦煌壁画包括敦煌莫高窟、西千佛洞、安西榆林窟共有石窟552个,有历代壁画50000多平方米,是中国也是世界壁画最多的石窟群。敦煌壁画内容丰富,规模巨大,技艺精湛。

敦煌壁画内容丰富多彩,和其他宗教艺术一样,它主要是描写神的形象、神的活动、神与神的关系、神与人的关系,通过这些壁画寄托人们善良的愿望,以达到安抚人们心灵的目的。敦煌壁画以莫高窟最为著名。

莫高窟,又名敦煌石窟、千佛洞,位于敦煌县城东南25公里的鸣沙山下,因地处莫高乡而得名。它是中国最大、最著名的佛教艺术石窟,素有"东方艺术明珠"之称。莫高窟分布在鸣沙山崖壁上三四层不等,全长一千六百米。现存石窟492个,壁画总面积约45000平方米,彩塑佛像等造型2100多身。石窟大小不等,塑像高矮不一,大的雄伟浑厚,小的精巧玲珑,其造诣之精深,想象之丰富,是十分惊人的。题材多取自佛教故事,也有反映当时的民俗、耕织、狩猎、婚丧、节日欢乐等的壁画。这些壁画彩塑技艺精湛无双，被公认为是"人类文明的曙光"、世界佛教艺术的宝库。敦煌壁画主要有以下几种类型：

佛像画

作为佛教艺术的敦煌壁画，佛像画是其主要部分，这些佛像画包括各种佛，如，三世佛、七世佛、释迦牟尼佛、多宝佛等；各种菩萨，如文殊、普贤、观音、势至等；天龙八部，如，天王、龙王、夜叉、飞天、阿修罗、迦楼罗、紧那罗、大蟒神等。这些佛、观音、神的像大都画在说法图中。仅莫高窟壁画中的说法图就有933幅，各种神态各异的佛像12208身。经变画主要利用绘画、文学等艺术表现手法，将深奥的佛教经典用通俗易懂的方式来表现，这种表现方法被称为"变经"。仅用绘画的手法来表现佛教经典内容的称为"变相"，也就是"经变画"；用文字、讲唱手法来表现佛教经典内容的叫"变文"。以中国民族传统神话为题材的绘画在北魏晚期的洞窟里，我们可以看到具有中国道家思想的神话题材作品。例如，在西魏249窟顶部，除中心画莲花藻井外，其东西两面画有阿修罗与摩尼珠，南北两面画有东王公、西王母驾龙车、凤车出行。龙、凤车上重盖高悬，车后旌旗飘扬，前有持节扬幡的方士开路，后有人首龙身的开明神兽随行。另朱雀、玄武、青龙、白虎分布在各壁之中。飞廉振翅而风动，雷公挥臂转连鼓，霹电以铁钻砸石闪光，雨师喷雾而致雨。这些画形象生动，具有浓郁的民族特色。

供养人画像

供养人，是指由信仰佛教而出资建造石窟的人。这些供养人为了表示自己虔诚信佛，同时为了留名后世，他们在开窟造像时，在窟内画上自己和家族、亲眷和奴婢等人的肖像，这些肖像，被称为"供养人画像"。

装饰图案画

在敦煌壁画中，有丰富多彩的装饰图案，这些图案主要是用于石窟建筑的装饰，也有用于桌围、冠服和器物等的装饰。图案的装饰花纹随时代而异，千变万化，具有高超的绘画技巧和丰富的想象力。图案画主要有藻井图案、椽间图案、边饰图案等。

故事画

故事画的主要目的是为了广泛吸引信众，大力宣传佛经佛法。要达到这一目的，就必须把抽象、深奥的佛教经典及史实用通俗、简洁、形象的形式表现出来，使一般的信众一看即懂，从而感召信众，使他们笃信朝拜。在敦煌洞窟内，就绘制了大量的故事画，这些画可以让信众在观赏的过程中，受到潜移默化的教育。故事画内容十分丰富，情节也生动感人，而且生活气息浓郁，具有很强的艺术魅力。故事画主要可分为五类。

佛传故事画：以宣扬释迦牟尼的生平事迹为主。其中许多是古印度的神话故事和民间传说，佛教徒经过若干世纪的加工修饰，附会在释迦身上。一般以画"乘象人胎"、"夜半逾城"的场面为多。第290窟（北周）的佛传故事作横卷式六条并列，用顺序式结构绘制，共87个画面，描绘了释迦牟尼从出生到出家之间的全部情节。这样的鸿篇巨制连环画，在中国佛教故事画中是比较少见的。

本生故事画：也是以描绘释迦牟尼生前的各种善行为主，通过这些生动故事的描绘，宣传"因果报应"、"苦修行善"的佛教思想。如"萨埵那舍身饲虎"、"尸毗王割肉救鸽"、"九色鹿舍己救人"、"须阇提割肉奉亲"等。这些画虽然都打上了佛教的烙印，但它们仍或多或少地保留了神话、童话、民间故事的本色。

因缘故事画：主要表现的是佛门弟子、善男信女和释迦牟尼度化众生的故事。这类作品与本生故事的区别是，本生故事画只描述释迦牟尼生前故事，而因缘故事画则讲佛门弟子、善男信女前世或今世的故事，如"五百强盗成佛"、"沙弥守戒自杀"、"善友太子入海取宝"等。这类作品所选故事，内容离奇，情节曲折，颇有戏剧性。

佛教史实故事画：是指取材于史籍记载而画成的故事画，其中包括佛教圣迹、感应故事、高僧事迹、瑞像图、戒律画等。这类作品包含着历史人物和历史事件，是佛教历史文献的形象再现。佛教史实故事画多绘于洞窟龛内四披、甬道顶部和角落处等次要地方，但也有绘于正面的墙壁，如第323窟的"张骞出使西域图"、"佛图澄"和第72窟的"刘萨诃"等。

比喻故事画：这类作品主要选取释迦牟尼深入浅出、通俗易懂地给佛门弟子、善男信女讲解佛教教义所列举的故事。这些故事大都是古印度和东南亚地区的寓言、童话，被佛教徒收集记录在佛经里，而且保存至今。典型作品有"象护与金象"、"金毛狮子"等。

山水画

敦煌壁画中的山水画几乎遍布石窟，其内容丰富，形式多样。这类作品大多与经变画、故事画融为一体，起着陪衬的作用。敦煌壁画中的山水画，有的是按照佛教典籍中的山水，参照现实景物，经过艺术想象，描绘出"极乐世界"中青山绿水、鸟语花香的美丽自然风光；有的是以山水为主体的独立画幅，如第61窟的"五台山图"等。以上五类壁画作品，除了装饰图案外，一般都有情节，尤其是经变画和故事画，大都反映了大量的现实社会生活，如：贵族高官的出行、宴会、审讯、游猎、剃度、礼佛等；普通民众的农耕、狩猎、捕鱼、制陶、冶铁、屠宰、炊事、营建、行乞等；还有嫁娶、上学、练武、歌舞百戏、商旅往来、少数民族、外国使者等等各种社会活动。因此，敦煌石窟，不仅是艺术，也是历史。

敦煌壁画的内容除了以上五类外，还有建筑画、器物画、花鸟画、动物画等，其艺术价值弥足珍贵，在结构布局、人物造型、线描勾勒、赋彩设色等方面系统地反映了中国各历史时期的艺术风格、传承演变、中外艺术融汇的历史面貌。（夏汉宁编著）

景德镇陶瓷

景德镇，似乎是一块为瓷而生的土地。它位于黄山、怀玉山余脉与鄱阳湖平原过渡的地带，这里山环水绕，景色秀丽。四周翠绿的山峦包围着中间小小的盆地，盆地上丘陵起伏。就是这块不起眼的地方，底下竟蕴藏着制作瓷器必须的所有原料：磁石、釉泥、高岭土、耐火土、石灰石等，不仅数量大，品种多，而且质量优。景德镇陶瓷以"白如玉、薄如纸、明如镜、声如磬"的特点成为中华民族一个特殊的文明符号。英语中的"中国"与"瓷器"是同一个单词。

史载"新平冶陶，始于汉世"。新平即景德镇最早的名称；可见从汉世起，景德镇就开始制瓷了。宋代时，工商业的蓬勃兴起、城市的高度繁荣和长江流域及东南地区经济的快速增长，促成了中国古代瓷业的空前发展。在晚唐和五代已开始烧制青瓷和白瓷的饶州昌南镇，于此时结合二者之长，创烧出被称为"饶玉"的青白瓷。温润如玉的青白瓷一经问世，便风靡天下，深受海内外市场的欢迎。不仅长江以南大量地区出现仿烧，形成一个以景德镇为中心的青白瓷窑系，而且大量产品远销海外，迄今为止，青白瓷仍是海内外考古发掘中出土最多的中国宋代瓷器品种之一。宋真宗初见青白瓷，简直爱不释手，立刻下一道圣旨，诏令由昌南镇烧造和进贡御器，器底一律标上"景德年制"款识，并用自己的年号"景德"为这山区小镇命名。青白瓷成为历史上赢得以皇帝年号命名的唯一瓷种。1004 年，昌南改名景德镇，奠定了其作为中国古代陶瓷生产中心的基础。景德镇制瓷业发展到宋神宗时代，已是空前地发达和昌盛。元丰五年（1082 年）八月，官府在景德镇设"瓷窑博易务"，专事瓷器交易及其税收等事宜。至此，景德镇开始逐渐成为全国制瓷业中心，在陶瓷的烧造、销售、消费过程中，形成了博大精深的景德镇陶瓷文化。

元代的景德镇，继青白瓷之后，又研烧出一种比青白瓷更白、胎釉结合紧密、釉汁莹润、色泽似鹅蛋的卵白釉瓷。它似乎是为青花瓷的出现作先期技术条件铺垫的。元代中晚期，景德镇开始烧造出极其成熟的青花瓷。这些青花瓷洁白厚重，釉面光润透亮，青花料色青翠艳丽，光彩焕发，如清水芙蓉，素雅大方，被称为"国色"。从元代至今的 800 年间，青花瓷成为最能体现中国古代瓷业艺术成就的品种，也一直是中国瓷器生产和外销的主流。从此，景德镇陶瓷产品畅销世界，世界也以景德镇陶瓷来认识中国。

明代时，景德镇已越来越多地具有瓷城的色彩。随着朝廷在景德镇建立御器厂，全国各地制瓷高手先后流向景德镇，出现了"工匠来八方，器成天下走"的盛况。明代景德镇不仅官窑兴旺，民窑也生机勃勃。明代中期以后，彩瓷开始大量烧造。常见彩料有红、绿、黄、紫，加上青花烧成的蓝色，一般统称为大明五彩。明代彩瓷最有代表性的是成化斗彩，这是在明初青花红彩的基础上发展而开拓的崭新艺术天地。清代时，景德镇瓷业进入黄金时代。景德镇发展成为"廿里长街半窑户"、"昼间白烟掩盖天空，夜则红焰烧天"的世界瓷都。清代康熙、雍正、乾隆三朝帝王均视景德镇瓷器为"国器"，对制瓷业高度重视。这时的景德镇制瓷技艺业已达到炉火纯青、出神入化的地步，创烧了 50 多个品种的色釉、仿名窑古瓷及无法计数的各类器型和装饰纹饰。青花仍然独步当朝，与光彩夺目的康熙五彩、粉彩、珐琅彩、墨彩等崭新工艺，共同将景德镇制瓷业推向了历史的高峰。

到了近代，景德镇陶瓷原有的工艺形式已无法胜任它所承载的中国文化内涵。它需要寻找一个突破口，一个喷发点，释放出积聚已久的力量。浅绛彩文人瓷画和"珠山八友"的出现，将景德镇陶瓷艺术推向了另一座高峰。

1965 年 7 月上旬，全国人大常委会副委员长郭沫若一行来景德镇视察。在参观了艺术瓷厂后，郭沫若欣然提笔，写下了"中华向号瓷之国，瓷业高峰是此都"的经典名句。（倪爱珍编著）

第三单元

古代的学校教育

中国最早的学校教育大约始于奴隶社会。从现有文献看,夏代已有学校,西周时,学校制度已比较完备。从设置上看,分为两类,国学和乡学。国学建在王城及诸侯国都,由天子设立,规模较大,有"五学"之称,即辟雍(中)、东序(东)、成均(南)、瞽宗(西)、上庠(北)。其中辟雍是中心,四面环水。诸侯所设的大学,规模比较简单,仅有一学,半面临水,称"泮宫"。国学之外,又有乡学。乡学是地方学校,按地方行政区划设立。由于地方区域的大小不等,乡学也有不同名称,如闾塾、党庠、州序、乡校等。

据《周礼》记载,西周大学教育有"三德"、"三行"、"六艺"、"六仪",内容丰富,其中又以德为主。夏商周三代,都是"学在官府"。到了东周,周天子失去了"共主"地位,官学也因此动摇。"天子失官,学在四夷",蜂起的诸侯国纷纷延揽人才,世守专职的官学文化官员流入民间,学术授受转向私门。周守藏史老聃、鲁国乐师师襄、儒家鼻祖孔丘等,广收门徒,文化教育第一次走近平民。但当时孔子等人私家讲学,是没有固定教学场所的。

秦统一中国后,意欲扭转私人教育的风气,设置了博士官制度。博士官受政府禄养,但不负实际政治责任,只起顾问、参议的作用,同时必须收纳弟子,所以仍不失学者身份。

汉初时博士官制沿袭不废。待到汉武帝时,来了一次大改变。他建立太学,设五经博士,由他们在太学中正式任教,太学生又称博士弟子。汉武帝企图恢复西周官立教育的旧传统,不过这时的官立教育已不是贵族教育,而是平民教育。西汉教育制度的重要性,在于育才与选贤双轨并进。换言之,就是教育制度与选举制度配合实行。所以,汉代政府成员都是太学出身。与以前历史上所有旧政府相比,显示了巨大进步。但由于种种原因,太学逐渐变质,官学也因此不受人重视,真心求学之人,重新转归私学,民间又开始设教授徒。

东汉以下,政治解体,这一时期出现了两种教育形式,即门第教育和寺院教育。当时世之杰出之人,不在门第,即在寺院。隋唐统一,汉代公立教育制度也随之复起。唐初太宗时,高丽、百济、新罗、高昌、吐蕃等国都派留学生来中国,太学生多至8000余人。唐代实行教育考试分开制度,学生接受学校教育容易,但入仕途难。社会看重进士,不看重太学生。所以当时的国立教育,并没有大的作为。

唐代虽有考试取才,却无学校养才。养才仍依赖于寺院与门第。寺院所养不为世用,门第出身人员数量日渐减少,进士虽然很多但又仅会吟诗作赋,并没多少实际才能。所以,那时举世无才,有才之人大多数都去寺院做禅宗祖师了。唐末出现了书院教育,它是门第教育的残波余影。书院真正的兴旺,是在宋代。宋代为了矫正唐代教育的弊端,公私教育都推行,既有私家教育,也有国立太学。然而太学既由政府官办,政污则学敝,官办教育也因此渐渐不为人重视。所以宋代政府虽刻意兴学，但官学仍比不上私学。北宋的周敦颐、程颢、程颐，南宋的朱熹、陆象山等私人讲学，影响广泛。

元代，蒙古入主中原，书院遍布全国，较之南宋时更加繁荣。明太祖未定天下，即在婺州开郡学。等到他来做皇帝时，诏令天下郡县都设立学校。据统计，全国府、州、衙、所共有教官4100百余员，比北宋元丰时多近百倍。地方生员升至国学，初称国子学，后称国子监，一律受到朝廷重用。

到了明代，学校与考试两制度融合为一。与唐代以诗赋取士不同，明代以经义取士，后来演变为八股，流弊更甚，因此出现了与之相对的民间讲学，王阳明及其弟子、东林书院的学者等都经常聚众讲学。

清代时，政府公立学校无论在中央还是在地方，均已名存实亡，而书院制度则禅续不绝。清代书院的主要贡献在于藏书与刻书。

1905年，清朝全面废除科举，广开学校，成立中央教育行政机关——学部，合并国子监，统辖全国教育。这虽然是一个历史性的巨大进步，但从本质上看那时的教育无论是教学理念、教学内容，还是教学管理方式等，都没有完全摆脱封建思想的窠臼，仍属于半封建半殖民地性质的教育。

1912年，辛亥革命推翻了清王朝，结束了中国2000多年的封建帝制，中国的教育也开始了一个全新的发展历程。（倪爱珍编著）

科举文化

科举是中国古代读书人所参加的人才选拔考试。它是历代封建王朝通过考试选拔官吏的一种制度。由于采用分科目选举人才的办法，所以叫做科举。科举制从隋代开始实行，到清光绪三十一年（1905年）科举制度结束，经历了1300多年。

中国古代科举制度最早起源于隋代。隋炀帝在大业三年（605年）开设进士科，用考试办法来选取进士。这标志着科举制度的形成。它把读书、考试和做官三者紧密结合起来，揭开了中国选举史上崭新的一页。

在唐朝，唐朝的皇帝承袭了隋朝的人才选拔制度，并做了进一步的完善。因此，科举制度逐渐完备起来。唐朝的进士考试一般要依次经过"解试"、"省试"（或"礼部试"）两个阶段。在后一阶段中考取的就称为进士。唐朝的进士考试非常难，能够考取进士的并不多，所以考取进士的一般能获得好的官职。在进士考试中第一名的称为状元。但是，唐朝的状元不像以后的状元那样具有优先权。但是，唐代的进士考试，除看考试成绩外，主要的还是要有名人的推荐。在公元702年，在唐朝还出现了武举考试，以此来选拔军事人才。此后各个朝代沿用，并与进士考试共同存在。

宋朝的科举，大体同唐代一样，但选取的人数有很大的增加。大量平民通过科举考试进入官僚阶层，参与国家的管理。宋朝确立了三年一次的三级考试制度，即依次为：乡试、省试和殿试的三级科举考试制度。殿试以后，不需再经吏部考试，直接授官。宋朝进士分为三等：

一等称进士及第;二等称进士出身;三等称赐同进士出身。在宋朝,在进士考试第一的状元已经在政治上具有优先权了。这种优先权一直延续到科举制度的结束。

元朝时期,蒙古人统治中国,科举考试有时举行有时停废。但是,"四书"为科举考试的主要内容却是首先在元朝出现。并且在科举考试时,元朝对汉族人还实行民族歧视政策。

元朝灭亡后,明朝建立,科举制进入了鼎盛时期。明代统治者对科举高度重视,科举方法之严密也超过了以往历代。明朝以前,学校只是为科举输送考生的途径之一。到了明朝,进学校却成为科举的必由之路。在明朝,正式将科举考试分为乡试、会试、殿试三级。乡试第一名叫解元,会试第一名叫会元,殿试第一名叫状元,合称三元。在殿试考试中,第一名称状元,第二、三名分别称榜眼和探花。明朝科举考试中的主要内容是"八股文"。它是以"四书"、"五经"中的文句做题目,考生只能依照题义阐述其中的道理。要用古人的语气,结构有一定程式,字数有一定限制,句法要求对偶。"八股文"的危害极大,严重束缚人们的思想,同时也将科举考试制度本身引向绝路。

清朝的科举制度与明朝基本相同,但在科举考试中存在着民族歧视政策。满族人享有种种特权,做官不必经过科举途径。科举制发展到清代,日趋衰落,弊端也越来越多。特别是在外国侵略者的冲击下,更加速了科举制度的消亡。清光绪二十七年(1901年),在举行最后一次科举考试之后,科举制度于1905年宣告结束。

科举考试实行了1000多年,在实践中,逐渐形成了一些比较好的制度。比如,为了防止考生舞弊,发明了回避制度(考官与考生之间有亲属关系需要回避)、糊名制度(将考生的姓名及其他信息遮蔽)、誊录制(为防止在笔迹上舞弊,由人用统一笔迹誊录考生试卷)等等。这些制度影响深远,至今在我们的社会生活中发挥着作用。

科举制度是古代中国的一项重要发明,它对中国的社会和文化产生了巨大影响。邻近中国的亚洲国家如越南、日本和朝鲜也曾引入了这种制度来选拔人才。孙中山先生曾认为,中国的科举制度是世界各国中所有以选拔真才实学之最古、最好的制度。(黎清编著)

古代的藏书文化

中国古代的图书收藏有四大系统:官府藏书、私人藏书、书院藏书、寺观藏书。藏书的历史可以上溯到先秦时期,那时候的人们便用甲骨文详细记载了商王朝的社会、政治、经济、军事情况,并且设有专藏甲骨的龟室,那应该算是中国最早的国家图书档案馆了。由此算起,中国藏书事业的历史已有3000多年。到了周代,随着木牍、竹简、缣帛等书写工具的出现,王室宗庙以及诸侯的藏书开始初具规模。战国时期,百家争鸣的社会氛围打破了官学对知识的垄断,打破了只有史官才能记言记事的陈规,也因此而开始了私人藏书的历史新篇章。秦汉时期,秦始皇的"焚书坑儒"给中国文化带来了巨大的灾难,不少历史文献和经典著作因此消失。幸好有一些私人藏书家的竭力保护,一部分历史典籍才得以流传下来。两汉时期,藏书事业得以恢复并开始发展,有史可查的私人藏书家有22位。他们多是贵族高官或鸿儒世家,其中著名的有刘安、刘歆、蔡邕、郑玄等。

到了魏晋南北朝,私人藏书的主体开始转变。一方面,由于纸的发明和广泛应用使书的价格大大降低;另一方面,藏书成为当时士大夫阶层的一种时尚,他们相互传抄借阅,甚至无私捐赠,这使得少数平民百姓也有机会加入到藏书家群体之中。私人藏书家的数量增加到 100 多人,所藏书籍的数量和质量也有很大提高。

隋唐时期是中国封建社会发展的黄金时期,藏书事业也蓬勃发展。这与雕版印刷技术的发明和应用分不开。它的意义不仅在于极大地提高了书籍的印刷传播速度和效率,更在于打破了皇家贵族对书籍的垄断,使寻常百姓也可以读书藏书。此外,科举制度的确立也极大地推动了藏书事业的兴旺发达,造就了一批"官"藏书家。

唐代还出现了一种新的藏书体系——书院藏书。书院设有藏书楼,所藏书目非常丰富,当时洛阳的集贤书院藏书达 10 万卷左右。藏书楼是读书人的精神家园,对于中国传统文化的传承起着重要作用,特别是在古代典籍的收藏、保护,乃至古文献的研究、校勘、刊布发行等方面作出了不可磨灭的贡献。

宋元时期是中国藏书史上大放异彩的时期。它创造性地开启了目录学、版本学、校勘学、刊刻学等藏书整理编目活动之先河。藏书楼不仅在数量上远胜于前朝,而且管理上也开始往规范化方向发展。

明代社会的政治经济文化相对稳定和发达,藏书业也达到了一个新的高峰。尤其是刻书业的发达和书肆书商的出现,为藏书事业的发展提供了有利的物质基础。据统计,明代有藏书家 869 人,他们在书籍管理上比宋元时期更胜一筹,讲究楼的选址、取名,尤其注重"三防",即防火、防潮、防虫,同时还考虑如何防止书籍的散佚。此类藏书楼首推宁波天一阁。它是世界上现存最早的三个私家藏书楼之一,也是亚洲最古老的私家藏书楼。

到了清代,藏书事业出现了前所未有的兴盛局面。在历代封建王朝中,清朝政府对图书事业最为重视。在图书的收集、典藏等方面,清代的成就超过了历代。清代官修书目的集大成之作是《四库全书总目》。

除上述的官府藏书、私人藏书、书院藏书外,还有一种比较特殊的藏书体系,即寺观藏书。它伴随着佛教和道教的传入而出现。汉魏六朝时期是它的产生和发展时期。早在东汉明帝时,朝廷就遣使赴西域取回《四十二章经》,并建白马寺保存。东汉永平十一年(68年),佛教圣地五台山兴建大孚灵鹫寺,经过历代信徒的努力,其藏书不断增加,成为中国古代寺院藏书的典范。东汉末年,道教产生并得到一定程度的发展,道教书籍也逐渐向道观集中。为了使一些重要的典籍免遭天灾人祸,信徒们采用秘藏的方法,或者把它凿刻在深山洞窟的石壁上,或者把它藏在密室、佛塔中。由于古代有相当一部分寺观是当时地方上的文化中心,客观上担任着普及教育的功能,所以寺观藏书中除佛经道藏外,还有一小部分其他类书籍。寺观藏书稳定性较强,受外界因素干扰少,一些志士仁人有意将自己的著作送到寺观收藏。寺观藏书与官府藏书、私人藏书、书院藏书之间相互促进,相互补充,共同为中国文化的传承作出了重要贡献。(倪爱珍编著)

儒学

儒学即儒家学说的简称,起源于春秋时期,绵延至今已有 2500 余年的历史。自汉武帝时起,儒学成为中国社会的正统思想。儒学的内容、形式和社会功能随着社会的发展而发展,大致可分为四个阶段。

孔子、孟子、荀子等为代表的先秦原始儒学

原始儒学的主要内容是关于"士"的修身方面的道德规范和从政方面的治国原则。人们常把孔子之学称为"仁学",就是因为孔子把"仁"作为"士"的最根本的道德规范来要求。《论语》中记载着许多孔子回答弟子们问"仁"的言论,其内容都是实际行为中所要遵循的各种具体规范和原则。

孟子除了进一步发展孔子以"仁"修身的思想外,又以推行"仁政"学说而著称于世,而其"仁政"内容,同样也是十分具体的。如:"夫仁政,必自经界始。"而所谓的"正经界",就是"分田制禄","制民恒产"。孔子、孟子提出的规范和原则,虽然都很具体,但同时又带有浓厚的理想主义成分,更多地寄希望于人的本性的自觉。所以,孔子竭力强调"克己"、"修身",孟子倡导"性善论",强调人的"良知"、"良能"。

与孔、孟相比,荀子的思想具有更多的现实主义倾向。他在重视礼义道德教育的同时,也强调政法制度的惩罚作用。荀子倡导性恶论,主张用礼义法度教化引导人的自然本性,以使人的行为合乎群体社会的公共原则和要求。

原始儒学在春秋末至战国时期,是社会上具有广泛影响的"显学"之一。它所提倡的道德修养学说在"士"阶层中有着深远的影响。但他们设计的理想政治制度和治国原则,由于太脱离当时诸侯称霸、群雄割据的社会现实,因而始终没能得到当权者的赏识和采用。所以,原始儒学与以后成为实际社会制度依据的儒学不同,它还只是一种关于道德修养和政治理想的一般性学说。

两汉政治制度化宗教化的儒学

汉初统治者为医治秦末苛政、战乱造成的社会民生极度凋敝的状况,采用了简政约法、无为而治、与民休息的治国政策。与此相应,在文化思想上则推崇和提倡黄老道家学说。这种情况一直延续到汉武帝时才有所变化。

汉武帝采纳了西汉大儒董仲舒提出的"春秋大一统"和"罢黜百家,独尊儒术"的主张,从而把儒学推向政治制度化和宗教化的方向。董仲舒研究的春秋公羊学,是一种密切联系社会现实的学说。公羊学认为,《春秋》中所说的"三统"、"三正"、"三世"等理论,都是为汉王朝的建立作论证的,而《春秋》中所提到的各种礼义法度也都可以为汉王朝所效法。《春秋》被认为是孔子所作,董仲舒与汉儒们于是称孔子为"素王",即一位没有实际王位的王。这样,儒学就开始与当时实际的社会政治制度联系起来。它已不再是单纯的伦理道德修养和政治理想的学说了,而是同时具有一种社会制度上的律条的作用。与儒学的政治制度化密切

相关的是儒学的宗教化,孔子被称为"教王"。儒学社会政治层面功能的形成和加强,导致它在伦理道德修养和政治理想层面功能的削弱。

到了汉末,政治制度化了的儒学礼教(名教),一方面成为束缚和压制人的自然感情的东西,一方面又成了一些伪君子沽名钓誉的工具,因而引起了人们的强烈不满。玄学或道家(以及道教)乘此流弊而起,取代了儒学在思想修养层面的功能。东晋南北朝以后,佛教思想的影响又超过了玄学,在士大夫的思想修养方面起着重要作用。所以,从魏晋南北朝至隋唐五代末约 700 年间,儒学只有那些体现为政治制度化方面的东西,在统治阶层的维护下继续起着作用。

宋、明、清时期性理之学的儒学

佛道学说对广大士大夫修养身心方面的巨大影响,引起了一部分儒者的不满与不安。于是一场复兴儒学的运动开始了。隋唐之际的王通发其先声,唐代中期以后的韩愈、李翱、柳宗元诸人继其后续,至两宋时期蔚为大观。不过,他们所要复兴的儒学,主要是伦理道德、身心修养层面的儒学。他们希望重新充分发挥儒学道德修养方面的社会功能,夺回被佛、道占据了 700 年优势的思想领域。

宋明(包括元及清)时期的儒学之所以被称之为理学,是因为它在理论上与原始儒学存在着巨大差异。通俗地说,原始儒学仅仅告诉我们日常行为中应该做什么和怎么去做,但没有告诉我们为什么要这样做。而理学在吸收和融合玄学、佛教、道教和道家的理论后,从形而上高度构筑起一套"天理"、"良知"的思想理论体系。北宋初的胡瑗、孙复、石介被称为"理学三先生"。然而理学实际创始人为周敦颐、邵雍、张载、二程兄弟,南宋的朱熹则是理学的集大成者。他建立了一个比较完整的客观唯心主义体系,提出"理"先于天地而存在。与朱熹对立的是陆九渊的主观唯心主义,他提出"宇宙便是吾心"的命题。明代,王守仁进一步发展了陆九渊的学说,认为"心外无物"、"心外无理",断言心之"灵明"为宇宙万物的根源。

近现代的新儒学

新儒学又称新儒家,是近代西方文明输入中国以后,在中西文明碰撞交融中产生的新的儒家学派。狭义的新儒学,是指梁漱溟、熊十力、马一浮、钱穆、冯友兰、贺麟等人所提倡的新儒学。广义的新儒学则可上溯到鸦片战争以来关于儒学变革的所有学说。新儒学希望通过对儒学的现代阐释,发扬民族传统文化,使其在当代人的思想道德修养和民族主体意识的确立方面发挥积极作用。

儒学作为中国 2000 余年来流传不息的文化主体之一,具有丰富而深邃的思想内涵,不仅对中国,而且对东亚各国都有着广泛的影响。同时,儒学作为东方文化的主要代表之一,在与西方文化的互补性发展中,也越来越显示出它的重要意义。(倪爱珍编著)

道家学

道家是古代中国社会思想文化体系中以道为核心观念,强调天道自然无为、人道顺应天道的一个流派。它最初是先秦时期诸子百家中的一家,后来有所扩展,凡是崇尚老庄黄老之学的人都被称为道家。

"道"是道家思想的核心,是它的最高范畴,为所有的道家学者所推崇。一般说来,道家的"道"具有以下几个方面的意义:道是天地万物的本源;道自然而无为;道无形而实存;道具有普遍性,无所不在,无时不在。道家作为一个思想文化流派,其基本特征为:崇尚老庄黄老之学;以道作为该学派的思想核心和最高范畴;在天道自然无为、人道顺其自然的天人关系的架构中展开自身的思想体系;以幽深微妙的言语,以高蹈隐逸之士的心态关怀世情。与其他各家相比,他们对社会的观察和体认更冷静、更清醒,也更深刻,具有独任清虚、超迈脱俗、绝礼去仁、追求返璞归真这样一种独特的精神气质。

道家在历史上的不同时期表现出丰富的多样性,它的演变大致经历了三个阶段:

秦汉时期的黄老之学:黄老之学是战国时期兴起的哲学政治思想流派。黄指黄帝,老指老子。战国时期五行学说流行,黄帝既是五行之一,同时又是传说中的华夏始祖,因此而便成为兵家、法家、阴阳家乃至儒家崇拜和依托的对象。

道家文化的集大成者庄子在其《庄子》一书中多处以黄帝为寓言中的高人。战国末年,楚文化的老学与北方中原的黄帝崇拜相结合形成黄老之学,它标志着道家思潮发展到一个新的阶段。黄老之学的经典是《黄帝书》和《老子》。

魏晋时期的玄学:魏晋时期,玄学成为显学。它是以道学的典籍《老子》《庄子》和《周易》(谓之"三玄")为本,综合儒道而形成的一种哲学思想。"玄"一词出现于《老子》第一章"玄之又玄,众妙之门"。魏晋玄学自何晏、王弼、嵇康、阮籍至郭象,经历了从贵"无"的本体论到崇"有"的存有论的发展过程。

隋唐及其之后的道家:玄学衰落之后,道家思想仍余绪未绝从隋唐及其之后注释《老子》《庄子》的数量之众,可窥见一斑。不过,隋唐之后,道家的存在形式发生了变化。它主要是在道教的阵营中蓬勃发展。道教学者通过对老庄思想的阐释和发挥来建立自己的宗教理论。

不过,道家与道教是两个不同的术语,既有区别又有联系。其区别主要在于:一、道家与道教产生于不同的时代。道家由老子在春秋末年创立,而道教则形成于东汉末年。二、道家与道教各有不同的代表人物。即使同一个人物,在道家与道教之中也具有不同的个性特征。道家的代表人物有老子、庄子、列子等,道教的代表人物有葛洪、陶弘景、成玄英等,这两类人物相互之间是不能替代的。以老子为例,道家中的老子是一个现实的思想家,道家的创始人,道教中的老子则是太上老君,是一个宗教教主,两者的性质显然是不一样的。三、从严格的意义上来说,道家仅仅是一种思想文化流派,而道教则是一个宗教团体,它不仅具有意识形态功能,同时还有严密的组织与宗教活动。二者间的联系在于:道教是依托道家思想建立起来的。汉魏以后,道家再没有形成有影响的学派,也没有出现杰出的道家学者,而道教此时却得到了长足的发展。道家之所以没有湮灭,一个重要的原因就在于它借助于道教的发展而延续。道教既然以道家思想作为理论支柱,因而必然包含道家,老庄的著述被作为道教经典,道教学者在进行注释时对其有所发展。

作为土生土长的宗教,道教曾为中国传统文化的发展作出过巨大贡献,被认为是中国传统文化的"三大支柱"(儒、释、道)之一。在生态危机日益严重的今天,道家文化中关于天人合一、道法自然的生态智慧对我们有很大的启发意义。(倪爱珍编著)

佛学

佛教大约产生于公元前 6 世纪的印度。当时的印度正处于一个大动荡、大变革的时代,战争频仍,社会混乱,政治腐败,民不聊生,有些人心灰意冷,企图退出社会生活,便出家做"沙门"。他们住在野外,"穿树皮,吃橡子,用手捧水喝,不结婚,不生子,行苦行,枯坐终日不动"。佛教的创始人释迦牟尼就诞生在这样的时代。他自幼爱沉思,深感世间人事变化无常,一心想摆脱人生的苦恼,29 岁时,毅然放弃优越的物质生活,在一个夜晚逃出家门,削发剃须,做了"沙门"。经过多年的苦修和思索,35 岁时,他终于达到大觉大悟的境界,修成了圣人——"佛陀"。

从此他四处布道,广收门徒,弘扬自己的思想。伴随着佛教的产生,用形象和比喻的方法宣扬佛教教理的佛教艺术,佛塔建筑、佛像雕刻、彩绘壁画等也随之出现。

在以后的几个世纪里,佛教及其艺术沿着丝绸之路向北、西、东面传播,大约在公元前 1世纪时,传入中国,经长期发展,形成了具有中国民族特色的中国佛教。

由于传入的时间、途径、地区和民族文化、社会历史背景的不同,中国佛教形成三大系,即汉地佛教(汉语系)、藏传佛教(藏语系)、云南地区上座部佛教(巴利语系)。

汉地佛教:佛教传入中国汉族地区,历来均以东汉明帝永平年间(58—75 年)派使去西域取回《四十二章经》为佛法传入中国之始。传播地区以长安、洛阳为中心。中国内地营建的第一座寺院是洛阳市东 10 公里处的白马寺。东汉时绝大部分佛经都是在这里翻译的。

佛教在中国的三国、魏、西晋时期,主要传播活动仍是佛典翻译,魏都洛阳和吴国都城建业是传播活动的中心。这阶段的译经工作和对佛教教义的宣传、研究,为以后佛教发展打下了初步基础。到了东晋南北朝时期,佛教得到进一步发展,各阶层人普遍信仰,佛塔、寺院到处都是。举世闻名的佛教石窟艺术,如敦煌、云冈、龙门等古代的雕塑、壁画,都是这一时期开始建造的工程。佛经翻译家鸠摩罗什(344—413 年)所译的佛典有 384 卷,内容正确,技巧精湛,对佛教发展贡献极大。西行取经的法显(337—422 年),游历了印度、斯里兰卡等南亚 30 余国,他取回的佛典和撰写的见闻,为佛教发展和研究古代中亚、南亚诸国历史提供了宝贵的资料。

南北朝时的梁武帝笃信佛教。他在位 14 年中,曾 4 次舍身入寺院为寺奴。梁武帝亲自讲经说法,撰写经文。梁朝有寺院 2860 所,僧尼 82700 余人。

唐朝是中国佛教发展的鼎盛时期。唐太宗在清除割据、平息骚乱时曾得到僧兵的援助。他即位后下诏在全国建立寺院,设释经处,培养了大批佛教高僧、学者。这时最著名的僧人之一是玄奘(600—664 年)。他历时 19 年,长途跋涉 5 万余里去印度取经,共翻译佛经 75 部 1335卷,并写出了《大唐西域记》。唐太宗推崇玄奘为"法门之领袖","千古而无对"。他的生平事迹被写入各种书籍中,后来逐渐演变为神话故事。唐中叶产生了有关玄奘的传说,宋代出现《大唐三藏取经诗话》,明代吴承恩又把他撰写成小说《西游记》,使唐僧玄奘成为家喻户晓、妇孺皆知的人物。

北宋朝廷对佛教采取保护政策,中国和印度的僧人间传法交往络绎不绝。天禧五年(1021年),北宋佛教发展到顶峰,全国僧尼近46万人,寺院近4万座。南宋朝廷偏安江南,佛教仍保持一定盛况。元朝蒙古民族崇尚藏传佛教,但对汉地佛教也采取保护政策。明朝开国皇帝朱元璋出身僧侣,即位后自封"大庆法王",亲自讲佛法,度僧道,利用佛教帮助他巩固刚刚建立的明朝政权。清朝皇室崇奉藏传佛教,汉语系佛教在民间流行。清朝末年中国出现了一批著名的佛学研究学者,如杨文会、欧阳竟无、大虚等。近代思想家如康有为、谭嗣同、章太炎、梁启超等都曾受过佛学影响,并对其提出了新的见解,把佛学思想研究发展到一个新的水平。

藏传佛教,或称藏语系佛教,俗称"喇嘛"教。喇嘛藏语意为"上师"。藏语系佛教始于7世纪中叶,当时的藏王松赞干布迎娶尼泊尔尺尊公主和唐朝文成公主时,两位公主都带去了佛像、佛经。松赞干布在两位公主影响下皈依佛教,建大昭寺和小昭寺。到8世纪中叶,佛教又直接从印度传入西藏地区。10世纪后半期藏传佛教正式形成。10到13世纪中开始流传于蒙古地区。此后的300多年间,形成了各具特色的教派,普遍信奉佛法中的密宗。随着佛教在西藏的发展,上层喇嘛逐步掌握地方政权,最后形成了独特的政教合一的藏传佛教。

西藏最著名的佛教建筑布达拉宫,始建于7世纪文成公主入藏时为其建的宫室,但建成现在的规模,是到17世纪才完成的。

巴利语系佛教(上座部佛教)流传于我国云南省傣族、布朗族等地区。那里人民的佛教传统信仰与南亚佛教国(泰国、缅甸等)大致相同。大约在7世纪中叶,佛教从缅甸传入中国云南傣族地区。那里若干世纪以来,都能保持依照原始佛教的佛法、戒律和进修学的优良传统。傣族男童到了入学年龄必须出家为僧,在寺院学习文化知识,接近成年再还俗。(倪爱珍编著)

第四单元

《红楼梦》

《红楼梦》,又名《石头记》《情僧录》《风月宝鉴》《金陵十二钗》《宝玉缘》等,成书于清代乾隆年间,代表了中国古代长篇小说的最高成就,中国古典小说四大名著之一。

全书120回,前80回是曹雪芹所作,后40回据说由高鹗续写。

内容以贾、王、史、薛四大家族为背景,以贾宝玉、林黛玉的爱情悲剧为主线,着重描写贾家荣国府和宁国府由盛到衰的全过程,展示了广阔的社会生活视野,森罗万象,囊括了多姿多彩的世俗人情。人们称《红楼梦》包含着一个时代的历史容量,是封建末世的百科全书,作品语言优美生动,善于刻画人物,塑造了贾宝玉、林黛玉、王熙凤、薛宝钗、尤三姐等个性鲜明的人物。该书规模宏大,结构严谨,具有很高的艺术成就,是中国古代最伟大的长篇小说之一,也是世界文学经典巨著之一。

作者曹雪芹,清代小说家,生于 1715 年,卒于 1763 年。曹雪芹的曾祖父曹玺,祖父曹寅,父辈的曹颙和曹頫相继担任江宁织造达 60 余年之久,很受康熙帝宠信。曹雪芹在富贵荣华中长大。雍正初年,由于封建统治阶级内部斗争的牵连,曹家遭受多次打击,家产抄没,举家迁回北京,家道从此日渐衰微。这一转折,使曹雪芹深感世态炎凉,更清醒地认识了封建社会制度的实质。从此他生活一贫如洗。他能诗会画,擅长写作,以坚忍不拔的毅力专心致志地从事小说《红楼梦》的写作和修订,披阅 10 载,增删 5 次,写出了这部把中国古典小说创作推向巅峰的文学巨著。

《红楼梦》以其丰富的内容,曲折的情节,深刻的思想认识,精湛的艺术手法成为中国古典小说中伟大的现实主义作品。1764 年,曹雪芹因贫病无医而逝世。

《红楼梦》突破了传统的取材和构思方式,将社会高度浓缩于家庭范围内作整体展现,贾府实际上是整个社会的缩影。它描写了以贾家为代表的四大家族的兴衰,揭示了封建大家庭的各种错综复杂的矛盾,表现了封建的婚姻、道德、文化,教育的腐朽、堕落,塑造了一系列贵族、平民以及奴隶出身的女子的悲剧形象,展示了极其广阔的封建社会的典型生活环境,曲折地反映了那个社会必然崩溃、没落的历史趋势。

作品还歌颂了贵族的叛逆者和违背封建礼教的爱情,体现出追求个性自由的初步的民主主义思想,并深刻而全面地揭示了贾、林、薛之间爱情婚姻悲剧的社会根源。

但由于历史的局限,作者在写出封建大家族没落的同时,也流露出惋惜和感伤的情绪,蒙有一层宿命论和虚无主义的色彩。

该书问世后,以其深进的思想意蕴与精湛的艺术魅力,震撼着一代代读者的心灵,产生了跨越时空的巨大的影响,在学术研究领域形成了声势浩大的“红学”。在经历了 200 多年风风雨雨之后,“红学”不但没有衰微,反而更为兴盛,这足以说明《红楼梦》所具备的艺术价值。

在人物塑造方面,《红楼梦》达到了炉火纯青的地步,所描写的人物皆栩栩如生,个性鲜明,具有多重性格,打破了以往小说写人类型化的特征,在广阔的社会背景上,以精雕细刻的工夫,塑造不同的人物形象;注意人物的个性化,心理描写具体而简洁;把人物放在特定的艺术气氛里,烘托人物的内心情绪。全书塑造了贾宝玉、林黛玉、薛宝钗等生动的人物形象。

贾宝玉是小说的中心人物,作为荣国府嫡派子孙,他聪明灵秀,是贾氏家族寄予众望的继承人。但他的思想性格却促使他背叛了家庭。其性格的核心是平等待人,尊重个性,追寻自由,是一位贵族家庭乃至封建制度的叛逆典型。

林黛玉是一位冰清玉洁、孤高自许、多愁善感的贵族小姐,她视爱情如同她的生命,但她的爱情却因不容于贵族家庭而被摧毁。

薛宝钗是一位遵奉妇道、恪守妇规的封建淑女,她同样是封建制度的牺牲品。

据不完全统计,《红楼梦》迄今已有 18 种文字、60 多种译本,在世界各国发行,它是世界文学宝库中的珍品。国外学者把“红学”与“甲骨学”、“敦煌学”一起列为关于中国的三门世界性的显赫学问。《红楼梦》这部伟大作品是属于中国的,也是属于世界的,它是世界人民共同的精神财富。(刘双琴编著)

《水浒传》

《水浒传》，元末明初施耐庵撰。施耐庵自幼聪明好学，才气过人，为人仗义。19岁中秀才，28岁中举人，36岁与刘伯温同榜中进士。其曾在钱塘（今浙江省杭州市）为官三年，因不满官场黑暗，不愿逢迎权贵，弃官回乡。张士诚起义抗元时，施耐庵参加了他的军事活动，后来又在张士诚幕下参与谋划。后因张士诚贪享逸乐，不纳忠言，施耐庵与鲁渊、刘亮、陈基等大为失望，相继离去。

不久，张士诚身亡国灭。施耐庵浪迹天涯，漫游山东、河南等地，后寓居江阴徐氏初，为其塾师。随后还旧白驹，隐居不出，感时政衰败，作《水浒传》寄托心意，又与弟子罗贯中撰《三国志演义》等。他还精于诗曲，但流传极少。施耐庵为避明朝征召，潜居淮安，染病而殁，就地高葬，享年75岁。

今人一致认为施耐庵是《水浒传》作者。也有人认为是同弟子罗贯中合著或者由罗贯中续写。

《水浒传》取材于北宋末年宋江起义的故事。

宋江等起义的年代大约在宣和元年（1119年）至宣和三年（1121年），前后三年多。宋代说书技艺兴盛，民间流传的宋江等36人故事，很快就被说书人采来作为创作话本的素材，《水浒传》的故事最初起源于北宋宣和年间，从南宋开始就成了民间口头文学的主要题材。

元朝初年，出现了话本《大宋宣和遗事》，描述了晁盖、吴加亮（吴用）等36人的故事，初步具有了《水浒传》的故事梗概。元朝，元杂剧中还出现了一些水浒故事剧本。施耐庵正是把这些在不同地区流传的故事，汇集起来，经过选择、加工、再创作，写成这部优秀的，古典名著《水浒传》。

《水浒传》以它杰出的艺术描写手段，生动形象地描述了中国封建社会中以宋江为首的农民起义的发生、发展和失败过程，深刻揭露了封建社会的黑暗和腐朽、统治阶级的罪恶，说明造成农民起义的根本原因是"官逼民反"。

施耐庵以其高度的艺术表现力，生动丰富的文学语言，叙述了许多引人入胜的故事，塑造了众多可爱的个性鲜明的英雄形象。作者对于这些英雄人物，予以充分的肯定和热情的讴歌，歌颂了这些人物的反抗精神、正义行动，也歌颂了他们超群的武艺和高尚的品格。

《水浒传》人物语言的性格化，达到了很高的水平，通过人物的语言不仅表现了人物的性格特点，而且对其出身、地位以及所受文化教养而形成的思想习惯有时也能准确地表现出来，如阮小七的心直性急，吴用的足智多谋，宋江的谦虚下人，通过他们的对话，无不令人如闻其声，如见其人。

小说不单以情节的生动紧张取胜，还有较丰富真实的细节描写，并在民间口语的基础上创造出一种通俗、简练、生动、富于表现力的文学语言。

《水浒传》成书后，流传广泛，并有简体本、繁体本等多个版本问世。

20世纪 20 年代初以来,还被翻译成英文。英文版通常将《水浒传》翻译成 *Water Margins* 或 *Out laws of the Marsh*。

众多译本中,最早的当属赛珍珠女士在 1920 年代中后期翻译的 *All Men Are Brothers*(《四海之内皆兄弟》)。书名出自《论语》"四海之内,皆兄弟也"。1933 年出版的 *Outlaws of the Marsh*,是《水浒传》的第一个英文全译本,当时在美国颇为畅销。

迄今为止《水浒传》被认为比较好的英文版本,应该是中国籍的美国犹太裔学者沙博理先生在"文革"期间受命译的 100 回版的 *Out laws of the Marsh*(《水泊好汉》)。其译本,被认为更忠实于原著,且很贴切地反应了原文的神韵。

法语版则将其直译为 *Au bordde l'eau*。日文版的《水浒传》的版本非常之多,甚至被改编和演绎成了许多漫画、电影、电视作品。(刘双琴编著)

《三国演义》

《三国演义》,是中国古代第一部长篇章回小说,是历史演义小说的经典之作。作者罗贯中(约 1330—约 1400 年),元末明初著名小说家、戏曲家,是中国章回小说的鼻祖。

《三国演义》是中国第一部长篇小说,在《三国演义》全书出现以前,中国各类小说一般都篇幅短小,有些甚至只有几十个字。

三国故事在中国古代民间颇为流行。宋元时代即被搬上舞台,金、元演出的三国剧目达 30 多种。元末明初罗贯中综合民间传说和戏曲、话本,结合陈寿《三国志》和裴松之注的史料,根据他个人对社会人生的体悟,创作了《三国志通俗演义》。清康熙年间,毛纶、毛宗岗父子辨正史事、增删文字,修改成今日通行的 120 回本《三国演义》。

《三国演义》描写了公元 3 世纪以曹操、刘备、孙权为首的魏、蜀、吴三个政治、军事集团之间的矛盾和斗争。在广阔的社会历史背景上,展示出那个时代尖锐复杂又极具特色的政治军事冲突,在政治、军事谋略方面,概括了这一时代的历史巨变,塑造了一批叱咤风云的英雄人物,对后世产生了深远的影响。在对三国历史的把握上,作者表现出明显的拥刘反曹倾向,以刘备集团作为描写的中心,对刘备集团的主要人物加以歌颂,对曹操则极力揭露鞭挞。

《三国演义》刻画了近 200 个人物形象,其中最为成功的有诸葛亮、曹操、关羽、刘备等人。

诸葛亮是作者心目中的"贤相"的化身,他具有"鞠躬尽瘁,死而后已"的高风亮节,具有经世济民再造太平盛世的雄心壮志,而且作者还赋予他呼风唤雨、神机妙算的奇异本领。曹操是一位奸雄,他生活的信条是"宁教我负天下人,不教天下人负我",既有雄才大略,又残暴奸诈,是一个政治野心家阴谋家。这与历史上的真曹操是不可混同的。关羽"威猛刚毅","义重如山"。但他的义气是以个人恩怨为前提的,并非国家民族之大义。刘备被作者塑造成为仁民爱物、礼贤下士、知人善任的仁君典型。

《三国演义》的艺术成就主要是在战争描写和人物塑造上。小说最擅长描写战争,并能

写出每次战争的特点。其中描写了大大小小的战争,构思宏伟,手法多样,使我们清晰地看到了一场场刀光剑影的战争场面。

官渡之战、赤壁之战等战争的描写波澜起伏、跌宕跳跃。在写战争的同时,兼写其他活动作为战争的前奏、余波,或者战争的辅助手段,使紧张激烈、惊心动魄力的战争表现得有张有弛,疾缓相间。如在赤壁之战前描写孙、刘两家的合作、诸葛亮、周瑜之间的矛盾,曹操的试探,孙、刘联军诱敌深入的准备等等。

此外,它成功地塑造了众多的人物形象。全书写了400多人,其中主要人物都是性格鲜明、形象生动的艺术典型。作者描写人物,善于抓住基本特征,突出某个方面,加以夸张,并用对比、衬托的方法,使人物个性鲜明生动。如曹操的奸诈,一举一动都似隐伏着阴谋诡计;张飞心直口快,无处不带有天真、莽撞的色彩;诸葛亮神机妙算,临事总可以得心应手,从容不迫。著名的关羽"温酒斩华雄"、"过五关斩六将"、张飞"威震长坂桥"、"赵云"单骑救幼主"、诸葛亮"七擒孟获"等,更是流传极广的篇章。

在结构上,以三国的矛盾斗争为主线,组织全书的故事情节,既曲折多变,又前后连贯,井井有条,脉络分明,各回能独立成篇,全书又是一个完整的艺术整体。

全书的文不甚深,言不甚俗,简洁明快,气势充沛,生动活泼,带来中国历史小说创作的热潮。

《三国演义》是古代历史小说中成就最高、影响最大的一部作品,它广泛流传,魅力无穷,在中国文学史上和人民生活中都有着难以估量的深远影响。(刘双琴编著)

《西游记》

《西游记》,以民间传说中唐僧取经的故事和有关话本及杂剧为基础创作而成。本书讲述了孙悟空出世、随唐僧西天取经,沿途除妖降魔、战胜困难的故事。

书中唐僧、孙悟空、猪八戒、沙僧等形象刻画生动,规模宏大,结构完整。

作者吴承恩(约1500—约1582),中国明代小说家。他出身一个世代书香后败落为小商人的家庭,虽身为商人,却喜读书。吴承恩自幼敏慧好学,聪明过人,博览群书,喜欢读野言稗史,熟悉古代神话和民间传说,年轻时即以文名著于乡里。

唐僧取经是历史上一件真实的事。大约距今1300多年前,即公元627年,年仅25岁的青年和尚玄奘带领一个弟子离开京城长安,只身到天竺(印度)游学。645年,玄奘回到了长安,带回佛经657部。为防止经文被盗,玄奘在唐王的帮助下修筑了大雁塔,保存经文。他这次西天取经,前后19年,行程几万里,是一次传奇式的万里长征,轰动一时。

后来,唐僧取经的故事开始在民间广为流传。吴承恩正是在民间传说和话本、戏曲的基础上,经过艰苦的再创造,完成了这部令中华民族为之骄傲的伟大文学巨著。

《西游记》向人们展示了一个绚丽多彩的神魔世界,人们无不为作者丰富而大胆的艺术想象惊叹不已。

然而,任何一部文学作品都是一定社会生活的反映,通过《西游记》中虚幻的神魔世界,我们处处可以看到现实社会的投影。如在孙悟空的形象创造上,就寄托了作者的理想。孙悟空那种不屈不挠的斗争精神,横扫一切妖魔鬼怪的大无畏气概,代表了一种正义的力量,表现出战胜一切困难的必胜信念。又如取经路上遇到的那些妖魔,或是自然灾难的幻化,或是邪恶势力的象征。不仅如此,玉皇大帝统治的天宫、如来佛祖管辖的西方极乐世界,也都浓浓地涂上了人间社会的色彩。

《西游记》不仅有较深刻的思想内容,艺术上也取得了很高的成就。它以丰富奇特的艺术想象、生动曲折的故事情节,栩栩如生的人物形象,幽默诙谐的语言,构筑了一座独具特色的《西游记》艺术宫殿。《西游记》在艺术上的最大成就,是成功地创造了孙悟空、猪八戒这两个不朽的艺术形象。

孙悟空是《西游记》中第一主人公,是个非常了不起的英雄。他有无穷的本领,天不怕地不怕,具有不屈的反抗精神。他有着人性、神性和猴性三重特点。大英雄的不凡气度,对师父师弟有情有义,也有爱听恭维话的缺点,机智勇敢又诙谐好闹。他的七十二变,一个跟头十万八千里,已是家喻户晓。

猪八戒,他的本事就比孙悟空可差远了,更谈不上什么光辉高大,但这个形象同样刻画得非常好。猪八戒是一个喜剧形象,他憨厚老实,有力气,也敢与妖魔作斗争,是孙悟空第一得力助手。但他又满身毛病,如好吃,好占小便宜,好女色,怕困难,常常要打退堂鼓,有时爱撒谎,还时不时地挑拨唐僧念紧箍咒,让孙悟空吃点苦头。他的毛病实在多,但他在西天取经路上披荆斩棘,当开路先锋,不辞辛苦污臭,所以他并不是一个被否定的人物,因此人们并不厌恶猪八戒,相反却感到十分真实可爱。

唐僧的形象刻画得也不错,但比起孙悟空、猪八戒来,则要逊色得多。

沙僧更是缺少鲜明的性格特点,这不能不说是《西游记》的缺憾。

尽管如此,《西游记》在艺术上取得的成就仍是十分惊人的,孙悟空、猪八戒这两个形象,以其鲜明的个性特征,在中国文学史上立起了一座不朽的艺术丰碑。

《西游记》成书于 16 世纪明朝中叶,是古代长篇小说浪漫主义的高峰,在世界文学史上,它也是浪漫主义的杰作。《美国大百科全书》认为它是"一部具有丰富内容和光辉思想的神话小说"。《法国大百科全书》说:"全书故事的描写充满幽默和风趣,给读者以浓厚的兴味。"从 19 世纪开始,它被翻译为日、英、法、德、俄、等十多种文字流行于世,译名也有多种,如《圣僧的天国之行》《一个佛教徒的天国历程》《猴》《猴王》《猴与诸神魔历险记》。

在其他国家,最早关于唐僧取经故事是明代前期的朝鲜文译本,不过那是取经故事,与《西游记》不完全是一回事。《西游记》最早的正式译本是 18 世纪中叶的日文译本。

孙悟空、唐僧、猪八戒、沙僧等人物和"大闹天宫"、"三打白骨精"、"火焰山"等故事也因此广为流传,为人熟悉。

几百年以来,西游记被改编成了各种地方戏曲及电影、电视剧、动画片、漫画,版本繁多。

在日本等亚洲国家也出现了以孙悟空为主角的文艺作品,样式众多,数量惊人。(刘双琴编著)

第五单元

新文化运动

北洋军阀统治前期,在中国满布阴霾的天空中,响起一声春雷,爆发了一场崇尚科学、反对封建迷信、猛烈抨击几千年封建思想的文化启蒙运动——新文化运动。

新文化运动是特定历史经济、政治、思想文化诸因素综合作用的产物。

政治方面,辛亥革命失败后,列强支持袁世凯称帝,加紧侵略中国,中国先进知识分子为改变这种局面积极地寻找新的出路;经济方面,中国资本主义在一战期间进一步发展,资产阶级强烈要求在中国实行民主政治,以更好地发展资本主义;思想文化方面,随着新式学堂的建立和留学风气的日盛,西方启蒙思想进一步被介绍到中国。辛亥革命使民主共和的思想深入人心,袁世凯尊孔复古的逆流为民主知识分子所不容,这是新文化运动发生的最直接原因。

新文化运动以1915年9月陈独秀在上海创办《青年》杂志(1916年9月起改名为《新青年》,1917年初迁到北京)为起点和中心阵地,以民主和科学("德先生"和"赛先生")两面旗帜,向封建主义展开了猛烈的进攻。

它的主要内容是:提倡民主,反对专制、独裁;提倡科学,反对愚昧、迷信;提倡新道德,反对旧道德;提倡新文学,反对旧文学。

陈独秀在《青年》创刊号上发表《敬告青年》一文,提出民主和科学的口号,向封建主义及其意识形态发动了进攻。

陈独秀提出政治民主、信仰民主、经济民主、社会民主和伦理民主的主张,号召人们拿起民主这个武器和旧的意识形态进行斗争。关于科学,陈独秀认为,不论什么事物,如果经科学和理性判定为不合于现今社会的,即便它是祖宗所遗留的,圣贤所深爱的,政府所提倡的,都一文不值。他号召人们坚持科学的精神,成为自然界的统治者和主人。

陈独秀首先举起大旗,揭开了新文化运动的序幕,李大钊、鲁迅、胡适、钱玄同等人也迅速加入其中。

新文化运动不仅是一场伟大的思想革命,也是一场伟大的文学革命。

1917年1月,胡适在《新青年》上发表《文学改良刍议》,首先提出文学改良的主张,提倡以白话文代替文言文,以白话文学代替仿古文学,并提出了著名的八大主张:一是需言之有物;二是不模仿古人;三是需讲求文法;四是不做无病之呻吟;五是务去滥调套语;六是不用典;七是不讲究对仗;八是不避俗字俗语。2月,陈独秀发表《文学革命论》,明确提出反对封建主义的文学,并把文学革命的内容与形式统一起来,提出了著名的"三大主义",即推倒贵族文学,建设国民文学;推倒古典文学,建设写实文学;推倒山林文学,建设社会文学,真正举起了文学革命的旗帜。

文学革命的一个重要组成部分是白话文运动。胡适的《文学改良刍议》一文是白话文运动的公开信号。这个纲领性的意见,很快就得到陈独秀的响应。1918 年 1 月,《新青年》实现自己的主张,全部改用白话文。5 月,鲁迅在《新青年》上发表《狂人日记》,标志着白话文运动在文艺方面首先突破,显示出卓越的实绩。

白话文运动口号的提出,遭到一些支持文言文的学者的猛烈攻击,引起一场关于白话文和文言文的论战。

1919 年反帝反封建的"五四"运动爆发,白话文运动得到突飞猛进的发展。1920 年,北洋政府教育部命令,小学教科书改用白话文。

新文学团体如文学研究会、创造社等也相继成立。

鲁迅的中篇小说《阿 Q 正传》的发表,郭沫若诗集《女神》的出版,为白话文学奠定了坚实的基础。《阿 Q 正传》是中国现代白话文学中赢得世界声誉的第一部杰作。

新文化运动是一次前所未有的思想解放和启蒙运动。它动摇了封建思想的统治地位,使民主和科学的思想得到了弘扬。新文化运动还为五四运动的爆发作了思想准备,为马克思主义在中国的传播开辟了道路。

但它不可避免地存在着一定的局限性。运动的倡导者没有把新文化运动同广大群众结合起来,使新文化运动仅仅局限在知识分子的圈子里。他们回避当时对军阀政府的实际斗争,没有正面提出反帝的任务。他们对中国古典文学的一味批判以及对西学的全盘肯定也具有片面性。(倪爱珍编著)

胡适

胡适,字适之,安徽绩溪人,现代著名学者、诗人、历史学家、文学家、哲学家。因提倡文学革命而成为新文化运动的领袖之一。

胡适 1910 年赴美国留学,师从著名哲学家杜威,深受其实验主义哲学的影响。1917 年 1 月在《新青年》上发表了《文学改良刍议》,针对中国旧文学的八大罪状,具体地阐述了他改良文学的"八大主张"。这些主张初步接触到了文学的内容与形式、文学的社会功能、真实性与时代性等一系列文学根本问题,成为文学革命的第一篇宣言。

胡适不仅是文学革命理论的积极倡导者,还是身体力行的实践者,是用白话创作新诗的第一人。1917 年 2 月,他在《新青年》第 2 卷第 6 号发表了《白话诗八首》,这是中国新文学史上白话文学的滥觞之作,中国新文学文体革命就是这样从诗歌开始的。它为其他各种文体的变革充当了开路先锋。

胡适于 1920 年 3 月出版的诗集《尝试集》是新文化运动中第一部白话新诗集。取名"尝试"是因为他相信"自古成功在尝试"。从这个诗集的名字可以见出胡适敢为天下先的气魄。《尝试集》实践"诗体大解放"的主张,破除旧格律的束缚,采用明白晓畅的白话语言,不避俗字和口语,不求对仗和押韵。胡适主张"把从前一切束缚自由的枷锁镣铐,一切打破;有什么话,说什么话;话怎么说,就怎么说"。在诗歌内容上,胡适反对无病呻吟,主张以民主主义、人道主义思想的新内容代替迂腐的封建主义的旧内容。诗集中的《老鸦》《希望》《一颗星儿》《上山》等多是即事感性、即景生情之作,常用直接描写、浅显的比喻、象征等手法。若从审美角度看,《尝试集》的艺术价值低于它的文学史价值。正如他自己的总结:"我现在(1922年)回头看我这五年来的诗,很像一个缠过脚后来放大了的妇女回头看她一年一年的放脚鞋样,虽然一年放大一年,年年的鞋样上总还带着缠脚时代的血腥气。"所以,胡适是新诗难能可贵的开拓者,但不是真正的奠基人。

胡适历任北京大学教授、北大文学院院长、辅仁大学教授及董事、中华民国驻美利坚合众国特命全权大使、美国国会图书馆东方部名誉顾问、北京大学校长、中央研究院院士、普林斯顿大学葛思德东方图书馆馆长、中华民国中央研究院(位于台北南港)院长等职,一生深受赫胥黎与杜威的影响,自称"赫胥黎教他怎样怀疑,杜威教他怎样思想"。胡适毕生宣扬自由主义,是中国自由主义的先驱。在学术上,他倡导"大胆的假设,小心的求证"、"言必有证"的治学方法,主要学术活动集中在史学、文学和哲学等几个方面,主要著作有《中国哲学史大纲》(上)《尝试集》《白话文学史》(上)和《胡适文存》(四集)等。晚年潜心于《水经注》的考证,但未及写出定稿。1962年在台北病逝。(倪爱珍编著)

鲁迅

鲁迅是中国伟大的文学家、思想家和革命家。原名周树人,字豫才,"鲁迅"是他1918年5月在《新青年》上发表《狂人日记》时使用的笔名。

鲁迅1881年出生于浙江绍兴一个没落的封建士大夫家庭。少年时代,正值家道式微,祖父因科场案入狱,父亲患病不起,一家人的生活从小康转瞬间坠入困顿,鲁迅也因此深深领略到了世态的炎凉。鲁迅母亲的娘家在农村,这使他从小有机会接触了解农村和农民。

鲁迅早年读书时受到进化论思想的影响。1902年公费留学到日本,就读于东京的弘文学院。1904年毕业后,抱着治病救人的理想去仙台医专学医。在那里,鲁迅一方面得到日本老师藤野先生公正无私的关怀与帮助,另一方面也受到一些日本学生的民族歧视。特别是在一次放映记录日俄战争的幻灯画片后,鲁迅受到很大刺激:画面上是一个被日军捉住据说是为俄军当侦探的中国人,在他行将被日军砍头时,周围站着看热闹的同样是一群中国人,他们面对惨剧却神情麻木。这使鲁迅深深感到:"医学并非一件紧要事,凡是愚弱的国民,即使体格如何健全,如何苦壮,也只能做毫无意义的示众的材料和看客,病死多少是不必以为不幸的。所以我们的第一要著,是在改变他们的精神,而善于改变精神的是,我那时以为当然要推文艺,于是想提倡文艺运动了。"

1906年,鲁迅离开仙台回到东京,开始了他的文学活动。先后发表《人之历史》《科学史教篇》《文化偏执论》《摩罗诗力说》等重要论文。

1908年起,和弟弟周作人一起翻译外国短篇小说,合编为《域外小说集》,并在朋友的帮助下出版。1909年鲁迅离开日本返回祖国。回国后鲁迅曾先后在杭州、绍兴任教。

1911年辛亥革命爆发,鲁迅积极参加宣传活动。

1918年起,鲁迅开始参与《新青年》活动。5月,在《新青年》上发表在中国现代文学史上具有划时代意义的第一篇白话小说《狂人日记》,以其"表现的深切和格式的特别"引起巨大反响。同时,鲁迅还在《新青年》"随感录"栏目中发表许多杂文。

除文学创作外,鲁迅还先后支持和组织了语丝社、未名社,编辑出版《语丝》等刊物。

1925至1926年,鲁迅在先后发生的"女师大风潮"和三一八惨案中声援学生,支持群众斗争。1927年10月定居上海。1930年,中国左翼作家联盟成立,鲁迅成为发起人和领导者之一。1936年10月19日,鲁迅在上海逝世。

鲁迅是中国现代文学的奠基人。他在小说、杂文、散文、散文诗、历史小说等各种类型的创作中,都有自己全新的创造。

小说集《呐喊》和《彷徨》是中国现代小说的艺术高峰,其中的《狂人日记》是中国现代文学史上第一篇白话小说,标志着五四新文学创作的伟大开端。它通过一个"迫害狂"患者的精神状态和心理活动的描写,揭露了从社会到家庭的"吃人"现象,抨击了封建家族制度和礼教的"吃人"本质。在思想上,它体现了彻底的反封建倾向;在艺术形式上,它大胆采用现实主义与象征主义相结合的创作方法,形成了独特的艺术效果。

《阿Q正传》是中国现代小说史上的一个杰出创造,也是最早被介绍到世界去的中国现代小说。阿Q是一个落后不觉悟的、带有精神病态的农民形象,其思想性格中最突出的特点是精神胜利法。作者通过阿Q画出了国人的灵魂,暴露了国民的弱点,达到了"揭出病苦,引起疗救的注意"的效果。同时,作者也通过小说把探索中国农民问题和考察中国革命问题联系在一起,通过对阿Q的遭遇和阿Q式的革命的描写,深刻地总结了辛亥革命之所以归于失败的历史教训。

除了小说,鲁迅对于文学的另一个重要贡献是杂文。鲁迅是思想者,也是革命者,他的一生都在战斗。杂文对于他来说,是匕首,是投枪。鲁迅曾说,杂文是"感应的神经","是在对于有害事物,立刻给以反响或抗争"。他的15本杂文集,是从五四前后到20世纪30年代中期中国社会的忠实记录,是一部思想文化发展史。

作为一个作家,鲁迅更为关注的是在历史事变背后人的思想、情感、心理的反应与变动。鲁迅曾充满自信地说:"'中国大众的灵魂',现在是反映在我的杂文里了。"

在写作《呐喊》《彷徨》的同时,鲁迅还创作了散文集《朝花夕拾》和散文诗集《野草》,晚年时完成了一部富有独创性的小说集《故事新编》(1936年出版)的写作。

这部小说集取材于中国古代神话、传说和历史事实,但它没有拘泥于原故事,而是加进了自己的理解和想象,有些还采取古今交融的写作手法,以荒诞的形式表现严肃的主题,创立了一种完全新型的历史小说写法。

鲁迅被誉为"民族魂"。他一生为中华民族的生存和发展挣扎奋斗,其诗句"横眉冷对千夫指,俯首甘为孺子牛"就是他的形象真实写照。

毛泽东说,"鲁迅的骨头是最硬的,他没有丝毫的奴颜和媚骨,这是殖民地半殖民地人民最可宝贵的性格",并对鲁迅作出"伟大的文学家、思想家和革命家"的高度评价。(倪爱珍编著)

郭沫若

郭沫若是中国著名的文学家、考古学家、古文字学家、思想家和革命活动家。原名郭开贞，"沫若"是他 1919 开始发表新诗时用的笔名。

郭沫若 1892 年出生于四川省乐山县的一个地主兼商人家庭。1914 年春赴日本留学，先学医，后从文。

留学期间他接触了泰戈尔、海涅、歌德等外国作家的作品，又由歌德导引到荷兰哲学家斯宾诺莎的著作，受到泛神论思想的影响。

五四运动爆发，身居异邦的郭沫若受到极大鼓舞，同部分留日学生一起组织"夏社"，从事反对日本帝国主义的宣传工作。

1919 年 9 月郭沫若开始发表新诗。

1921 年，郭沫若与郁达夫、成仿吾等组织成立"创造社"。同年 8 月，第一部诗集《女神》出版。它不仅确立了郭沫若在中国现代文学史上的卓越地位，同时也为中国新诗开辟了一个崭新的时代。

1921 年和 1922 年，郭沫若曾三次回国。但国内黑暗的现实把他美好的理想击得粉碎。诗集《星空》中那些含着"深沉的苦闷"的诗篇就是这种思想情绪的反映。

1923 年，郭沫若从九州帝国大学医科毕业后回国，继续创办刊物，从事文学创作。郭沫若此时的文艺观与政治观呈现出相当驳杂的面貌。诗集《前茅》是这一时期思想变化的鲜明记录。

1924 年，创造社前期活动因几个主要作家的离散而告一段落。郭沫若在进退维谷的苦闷中接触和认识了马克思主义，他的思想因此而有了一个巨大的飞跃。

1926 年 7 月，郭沫若参加北伐战争，积极倡导无产阶级革命文学运动。诗集《恢复》是这一时期的作品。

1928 年 2 月，郭沫若因政治环境的变化离开上海赴日本，一住就是十年。

抗日战争爆发，郭沫若别妇抛雏，只身回国，投入抗日文化宣传工作，并创作了《屈原》《虎符》等六部历史剧，此外还有众多的诗歌、散文及史学研究著作。

抗日战争胜利后，郭沫若在重庆、上海等地与广大进步文化人士一起，勇敢地站在民主运动的前列，为争取和平民主的新中国而斗争。

新中国成立后，郭沫若长期担任多种国家行政、科学文化方面的领导工作，同时还写下了诗集《新华颂》、历史剧《蔡文姬》《武则天》等多部作品。

《女神》是郭沫若的第一部新诗集，也是中国现代新诗史上具有划时代意义的作品，是中国新诗的奠基之作。

《女神》收入作者 1919 年到 1921 年之间的主要诗作，连同序诗共 57 篇，多为诗人留学日本时所作。

按诗人创作阶段分为三辑：第一辑收入《女神之再生》《棠棣之花》等作品；第二辑收入《凤凰涅槃》等五四高潮期的诗作；第三辑收入《死的诱惑》等早期主要诗作。其中代表诗篇有《凤凰涅槃》《女神之再生》《炉中煤》《日出》《笔立山头展望》《地球，我的母亲！》《天狗》《晨安》《立在地球边上放号》等。

《女神》是诗化了"五四"精神。它的思想内容集中表现在以下几个方面：

一、最强烈而集中地体现了诗人呼唤新世界诞生的民主理想。

《凤凰涅槃》是一首庄严的时代颂歌，充满了彻底反叛的精神和对光明新世界的热切向往。作者借古典神话中凤凰死而复生的原型意象来象征新中国的再生，表达了诗人对祖国的深沉眷恋和愿意为之献身的赤诚。

二、充分表达了诗人对自我的崇尚和对自然的礼赞。

《天狗》中的天狗敢于冲决一切罗网，破坏一切旧事物，具有无法遏制的激情和无比神奇的力量，这正是那个时代个性解放要求的极度体现。

《女神》中有大量描写自然、讴歌自然的诗篇。郭沫若心中的自然，是力的象征，是创造的结晶，充满着欢乐高昂的情调。

三、显示了彻底破坏和大胆创新的精神。

诗人对太阳、山河、海洋、生、死、火山、黑夜等一切具有破坏与创造力量的事物，都无比崇拜，充分张扬了五四时代的反抗、叛逆精神。

《匪徒颂》中作者对历来备受污蔑的敢于反抗陈规旧俗的革命者，对一切投身政治革命、社会革命、宗教革命、文艺革命、教育革命的"匪徒们"都予以热烈歌颂。破坏的目的是为了创造，只有彻底的破坏，才可能有全新的创造。

《女神》在形式上，实践了诗人"绝对的自由、绝对的自主"的艺术主张，使诗的形式得到完全的解放。

丰富的想象、神奇的夸张、激越的音调、华赡丰美的语言和浓烈瑰丽的色彩，使《女神》成为中国浪漫主义新诗的开山之作。（倪爱珍编著）

茅盾

茅盾是现代著名小说家、文学评论家、文化活动家和社会活动家。原名沈德鸿，字雁冰，1896年7月4日生于浙江桐乡县乌镇的一个书香门第之家，十岁时父亲去世，由母亲一手教育长大。

1913年考入北京大学预科，读完后因家境困难，无力升学，进入上海商务印书馆工作，并开始翻译、编纂中外书籍，在《学生杂志》《学灯》等刊物上发表文章。

五四运动时期，茅盾以新文学运动的积极拥护者和参加者的姿态为之呐喊助威，大力提倡"文学为人生"的艺术主张。

1921年，文学研究会成立，茅盾成为中坚力量。同年，他接手《小说月报》的主编工作，使得这个刊物成为向封建文学进攻的坚固阵地。茅盾还是最早从事中国共产主义运动的革命知识分子,1921年成为中国共产党的第一批党员,参与了党的筹建工作,并积极地投身于党所领导的社会斗争。

1927年四一二政变,茅盾在经历了血与火的斗争后,很快完成了三部曲《蚀》的创作。这是茅盾小说的处女作,原稿笔名为"矛盾",可见其当时的心境,后由叶圣陶改为"茅盾"。这是一部反映动荡年代里知识分子真实心态的深刻之作,由三个中篇组成:《幻灭》《动摇》《追求》。

1928年7月,茅盾东渡日本,一方面是为了逃避国民党反动派的迫害,另一方面是因为精神上的苦闷。长篇小说《虹》就是在日本撰写的。作品在较为广阔的历史背景下表现了知识青年对新的生活道路的探索,深刻描摹了一代知识分子从五四到五卅这段时期如何冲破囚笼,走上与人民大众携手战斗的艰难心灵历程。

1930年4月,茅盾从日本回国,积极参加左联的活动,与鲁迅并肩作战,促进了左翼文学的蓬勃发展。

1932年到1937年,是茅盾创作的鼎盛时期。

长篇小说《子夜》的问世,奠定了茅盾在中国现代文学史上举足轻重的地位。

"农村三部曲"(《春蚕》《秋收》《残冬》)和《林家铺子》等短篇小说则进一步展示了茅盾作为一个革命现实主义作家强大的创作生命力。

抗战时期,茅盾辗转于香港、新疆、延安、重庆、桂林等地,创作了散文《风景谈》《白杨礼赞》长篇小说《腐蚀》《霜叶红似二月花》和剧本《清明前后》等。

建国后,茅盾历任文联副主席、文化部长、作协会主席,并任全国政协副主席,1981年3月27日,病逝于北京。

他将自己的25万元稿费全部捐献出来设立文学奖金,后定名为"茅盾文学奖"。它是中国第一次设立的以个人名字命名的文学奖,于1981年10月正式启动,现已成为中国长篇小说的最高文学奖项之一,每四年评选一次。

人民文学出版社自1983年起陆续出版的40卷本的《茅盾全集》收录了茅盾的全部文学著作。在这些著作中,出版于1933年6月的《子夜》标志着其创作的一个高峰。它震动了中国文坛,瞿秋白把这一年称为"子夜年",可见它的影响之大。这部长篇围绕着民族资本家吴荪甫与买办资本家赵伯韬之间的尖锐矛盾,全方位、多角度地描绘了30年代初中国社会的广阔画面:工人罢工,农民暴动,反动当局镇压和破坏人民的革命运动,帝国主义掮客乘机活动,中小民族工业被吞并,公债场上惊心动魄地斗法,各色地主拼命挣扎,资本家家庭内部矛盾重重……通过这些多姿多彩的生活画面,艺术地再现了第二次国内革命战争时期的风云,成功地塑造了民族资本家吴荪甫的典型形象。

半个多世纪以来,《子夜》不仅在中国拥有广泛的读者,且被译成英、德、俄、日等十几种文字,产生了广泛的国际影响。日本著名文学研究家筱田一士在推荐十部20世纪世界文学巨著时,便选择了《子夜》,认为这是一部可以与普鲁斯特的《追忆逝水年华》、加西亚·马尔克斯的《百年孤独》相媲美的杰作。(倪爱珍编著)

巴金

巴金是五四新文化运动以来最有影响的作家之一,中国现代文坛的巨匠。原名李尧棠,字芾甘,"巴金"是他 1928 年写完《灭亡》时开始使用的笔名。

巴金出生于四川成都一个封建官僚地主家庭。童年时代的巴金基本上是在一种"充满父母的爱,人间的爱,家庭生活的温暖"的环境中度过的。母亲陈淑芬,是他童年时代的第一位先生。她的"爱的教育"在巴金幼小的心田里埋下了"博爱"的种子,对巴金后来的思想发展起到了重大的启蒙作用。

1914 年母亲的病逝和 1917 年父亲的病逝是巴金人生道路上的一大激变。父亲的死使这个富裕的大家庭变成了一个专制的大王国。在虚伪的封建礼教的囚牢中,巴金看到了自己的兄弟姐妹在挣扎、受苦以致死亡。

于是,接着"爱"来的便是"恨"。五四运动爆发,唤醒了巴金。在各种广泛传播的"主义"与思潮中,最先打开巴金心扉的是无政府主义。

1923 年,巴金离开闭塞的四川来到上海、南京求学。

1927 年,为了进一步研究无政府主义,巴金赴法国留学。旅法其间,两件大事使巴金深受刺激。一是国内北伐战争的胜利成果被葬送,一是两个意大利无政府主义者被美国政府判处死刑。在极度的痛苦之中,巴金写下了第一部中篇小说《灭亡》,塑造了一个因爱的绝望而恨人类的主人公——杜大心。它标志着巴金文学生涯的正式开始。

1928 年底,巴金离法回国。

从 1929 年到 1949 年底,巴金一共创作了 18 部中长篇小说,12 本短篇小说集,16 部散文随笔集以及大量的翻译作品。其中,中长篇小说最能代表巴金建国前创作的主要成就。

《爱情三部曲》是巴金自己前期创作中最喜爱的作品,它由《雾》《雨》《电》三个中篇组成,是巴金早年对"革命"这一重大社会问题进行痛苦紧张而又持久思索的总结,也是他早期世界观的形象化展示。

《激流三部曲》(包括《家》《春》《秋》)是巴金的代表作,特别是第一部《家》,具有永恒的艺术价值。

巴金在《〈激流〉总序》中说,"在这里我欲展示给读者的乃是描写过去十多年的一幅图画,自然这里只有生活的一部分,但已经可以看见那一股由爱与恨、欢乐与痛苦所组织成的生活之激流是如何地动荡了"。

作品所描写的正是这样一股生活的激流:一方面,随着封建宗法制度的崩溃,垂死的封建统治力量疯狂地吞噬年轻的生命,另一方面,为革命潮流所吸引的青年一代开始了觉醒、挣扎与斗争的悲壮历程。

在《激流三部曲》所塑造的众多人物形象群中,高觉慧无疑是最具有重要意义的一个。他从朴素的对劳动者的爱和对封建制度的恨出发,走到资产阶级改良主义和民主主义,最后又走向社会斗争。他是 20 世纪初在新思潮冲击下由五四运动首先唤醒的中国人,是封建主义大胆的、勇敢的叛逆者,也是满怀热情的、不成熟的革命者。作者通过他展示了近百年来中国先进知识分子所共同经历的思想历程。

巴金 1946 年完成的《寒夜》是他的最后一部长篇,也是继《家》之后的又一部力作,标志着作家在艺术上进入了一个新的发展阶段。小说写了一个小公务员汪文宣的生离死别、家破人亡的悲剧,并且通过他揭示了旧中国正直善良的知识分子的命运,暴露了抗战后期国统区的黑暗现实。

抗战胜利后巴金主要从事翻译、编辑和出版工作。建国后,巴金曾两次赴朝鲜前线,写出了《生活在英雄们中间》《保卫和平的人们》两本散文通讯集。"文革"中,巴金遭到了残酷的迫害。文革结束后,从 1978 年起,巴金开始"随想录"的系列写作,至 1986 年 9 月完成,共 150 篇,合 42 万字。

《随想录》以其博大精深的思想文化内容和独特的文体意义,成为新时期乃至当代最为重要的散文创作成果之一,是巴金以散文的形式在自己的文学道路上竖起的又一座丰碑。它最撼人心魄的是作者那种严于责己、解剖自我的强烈自审意识和自省精神,表明了巴金作为一个正直作家所具有的高尚的人格风范和知识分子的良知良心。

他把个人内省与民族反思结合,将个人批判与社会批判结合,是一部摄照"文革"时代知识分子心灵轨迹的史册,具有重要的思想文化史的价值。(倪爱珍编著)

老舍

老舍,原名舒庆春,字舍予,1899 年出生于北京西城小羊圈胡同的一个满族城市贫民家庭。

1918 年,老舍毕业于北京师范学校,担任过小学校长等职。五四新文化运动掀起的民主、科学、个性解放的思潮,把他从"兢兢业业办小学,恭恭顺顺地侍奉老母,规规矩矩地结婚生子"的人生信条中惊醒。文学革命的勃兴,又使他醉心于新文艺,由此开始生命和事业的新起点。

1922 年老舍任南开中学国文教员。同年发表了第一篇短篇小说《小铃儿》。

1924 年赴英国,任伦敦大学东方学院中文讲师。教学之余,他读了大量外国文学作品,并正式开始创作生涯,陆续发表了《老张的哲学》《赵子曰》和《二马》三部描写市民生活的讽刺长篇小说,引起文坛注目。

1929 年老舍回国途中在新加坡逗留数月,写作了一部童话体长篇小说《小坡的生日》。

回国后到抗战爆发前,老舍执教于济南齐鲁大学和青岛山东大学,并创作了六部长篇、一部中篇和三个短篇作品,显示出旺盛的创作力,其中著名的有《猫城记》《离婚》《骆驼祥子》等。

《猫城记》写一个漂流到火星上猫国里的机师在猫国都城的所见所闻,在类似科幻小说的外衣下寄寓着明显的政治讽刺意味。

《离婚》通过对北平财政所几个科员家庭风波的描写，批判了整个旧中国的社会制度和形成市民性格的文化系统。

《骆驼祥子》的影响非常大。它以北平（今北京）一个人力车夫的行踪为线索，向人们展示军阀混战、黑暗统治下的北京底层贫苦市民生活于痛苦深渊中的图景，通过主人公祥子"精进向上——不甘失败——自甘堕落"的命运三部曲，告诉人们，城市贫农要翻身做主人，单靠个人奋斗是不行的。

从抗战爆发到全国解放这十几年时间，老舍创作出了中篇《我这一辈子》《月牙儿》和长篇《四世同堂》《鼓书艺人》等作品。

《月牙儿》结构精致玲珑，描写精到入微，通过展示母女两代人相继沦为暗娼的悲剧控诉非人的黑暗世界。

《四世同堂》（包括《惶惑》《偷生》《饥荒》）在老舍的创作历程中是一块高耸的界碑。

它选取北平西城一条普普通通的小羊圈胡同作为故都这座"亡城"的缩影，以旧式商人祁天佑一家四代的境遇为中心，真实地反映了北平人在外族侵略者的统治下灵魂遭受凌迟的痛史，剖示了他们封闭自守、苟且敷衍、惶惑偷生的思想精神负累，并进而对民族精神素质和心理状态进行了清醒剔透的反省，为人们提供了映现 20 世纪 40 年代沦陷区人民心态的一面镜子。这部作品几乎跨越了八年抗战的全过程，从珍珠港事件爆发到日本侵略者缴械投降，都有直接或间接的反映；空间上，它触及北京的小胡同、大杂院、街头、城郊、乡村、广场、戏院、监狱、刑场、妓院、学校乃至日伪机关、大使馆……全景式、多线索的描写，使这部小说在广度、深度、力度和气势上都具有史诗的气魄。

建国后，老舍的主要作品有长篇小说《正红旗下》、长篇报告文学《无名高地有了名》、剧本《龙须沟》《茶馆》等。

其中《茶馆》不仅是老舍戏剧的代表作，也是中国当代戏剧的经典之作。

它通过最具地方特色和民族特色的小茶馆来透视整个大中国的风云，生动而精炼地描绘了三个时代和三个社会：戊戌政变后的清末社会、辛亥革命失败后各派系混战中的军阀统治的民国社会和抗战后国民党统治下的国统区，表达了"埋葬三个旧时代"的主题。

纵观老舍的创作，可以看到一个似断实续的基本主题，那就是对于民族传统文化的反思、批判。

老舍继承了从鲁迅开始的关于"国民性"的思考，在某些方面还显示了自己新的开拓与特色。

老舍自幼生长于北京的市民阶层，他的作品多以北京市民社会为中心，具有浓郁的地方色彩和强烈的生活气息，因而被称为"北京市民社会的表现者和批判者"。1951 年北京市人民政府授予老舍"人民艺术家"的光荣称号。（倪爱珍编著）

曹禺

曹禺是一位对中国现代戏剧发展做出杰出贡献的剧作家。原名万家宝,出生于天津一个没落的封建官僚家庭。母亲生下他三天即患产溽热去世,母亲的胞妹做了他的继母,并把他抚养长大。继母喜欢看戏,少年时代的曹禺经常跟着她观看京戏、昆曲与河北梆子等许多地方戏以及当时流行的文明新戏。

1922年曹禺进入天津南开中学。学习期间参加戏剧活动,曾担任易卜生《玩偶之家》等剧的主角。

1929年曹禺考入清华大学外文系,刻苦钻研从古希腊悲剧到莎士比亚戏剧以及契诃夫、易卜生、奥尼尔的剧作。

1933年大学即将毕业前夕,曹禺创作了四幕话剧《雷雨》,于次年公开发表,很快引起强烈反响,它不仅是曹禺的处女作,也是他的成名作和代表作。

1936年和1937年,曹禺分别出版了他的重要剧作《日出》和《原野》。

抗战期间曹禺创作了《北京人》,并把巴金的小说《家》改编成话剧。

新中国成立后,曹禺创作的剧本主要有《胆剑篇》《王昭君》等。

四幕话剧《雷雨》是一部杰出的现实主义家庭悲剧。戏剧在一天时间(从上午到午夜两点)、两个场景(周家和鲁家)里,集中展开了周、鲁两家前后30年错综复杂的矛盾冲突,显示了作者严谨而精湛的戏剧结构技巧。

周朴园是《雷雨》的中心人物,也是剧中各种悲剧的根源。作品以他为中心,安排了两条主要线索:一是他与妻子繁漪的冲突,以表现家庭内部的矛盾;一是他与矿工鲁大海的冲突,以表现他与工人的对立,这两条线索又通过侍萍紧密地联系在一起,构成尖锐复杂的戏剧冲突。周朴园是一个狠毒凶残的资本家,更是一个专制冷酷的封建家长。但曹禺并没有把他作为一个阶级的典型,而是作为一个活生生的“人”来塑造的。

《雷雨》还成功塑造了另一个重要人物——“繁漪”,她具有“雷雨式”的性格。曹禺在剧本的“舞台提示”中这样写道,“她的性格中有一股不可抑制的‘蛮劲’,使她能够忽然做出不顾一切的决定。她爱起人像一团火那样热烈;恨起人来也会像一团火,把人烧毁”。在创作中,作者着力描写她因“环境的窒息”而做出的一次“困兽的搏斗”,以及在这一过程中生命里所交织的“最残酷的爱和最不忍的恨”。她绝望中的反抗,充满着一个被压迫女性的血泪控诉,表现出对封建势力及其道德观念的勇敢蔑视与反叛。她“雷雨式”的激情摧毁了封建家庭秩序,也毁灭了她自己。繁漪这一悲剧形象,是曹禺对现代戏剧的一大贡献,深刻地传达出反封建与个性解放的五四主题。

《雷雨》发表一年后,曹禺又创作了一部现实主义力作——四幕话剧《日出》。

它以20世纪30年代具有中国特色的半封建半殖民地都市天津为背景,以“交际花”陈白露的华丽客厅和翠喜所在的三等妓院“宝和下处”为具体地点,展示了上层社会与下层社会两种完全不同的生存状态,揭示出"损不足以奉有余"的不合理现象。

《雷雨》着力反映封建专制主义对人的压迫与虐杀,《日出》则揭露了金钱化社会对人的毒化、吞噬与残杀。

曹禺在第三个剧本《原野》(三幕剧)中将创作视野转向农村,成功开掘出一个在封建宗法思想下农民复仇者的心理悲剧。

三幕剧《北京人》为曹禺剧作的又一艺术高峰。他再一次回到自己所熟悉的旧家庭题材,对封建主义作了抽筋剔骨的批判。假如说《雷雨》侧重于伦理道德关系的批判,《北京人》则企图对整个封建文化传统作清算。曾家是衰弱的封建社会的缩影,曾经有过的诗书礼仪的鼎盛时代已经过去。家长曾皓生活中唯一的"快慰"就是一遍遍油漆为自己准备的棺材,这正是一个封建僵尸的象征。曾文清这位天资聪敏心地善良的封建士大夫,精神上已完全瘫痪,成了徒有"生命空壳"的"多余人"。

剧作家力图对传统文化进行反思,找到通往新生活的精神力量。(倪爱珍编著)

A Brief Chronology of Chinese History
中国历史年代简表

Xia Dynasty 夏朝			2070–1600 B.C.
Shang Dynasty 商朝			1600–1046 B.C.
Zhou Dynasty 周朝	Western Zhou 西周		1046–771 B.C.
	Eastern Zhou 东周		770–256 B.C.
	Spring and Autumn Period 春秋		770–476 B.C.
	Warring States Period 战国		475–221 B.C.
Qin Dynasty 秦朝			221–206 B.C.
Han Dynasty 汉朝	Western Han 西汉		206 B.C.–25 A.D.
	Eastern Han 东汉		25–220
Three Kingdoms 三国	Wei 魏		220–265
	Shu Han 蜀汉		221–263
	Wu 吴		222–280
Western Jin Dynasty 西晋			265–317
Eastern Jin Dynasty 东晋			317–420
Northern and Southern Dynasties 南北朝	Southern Dynasties 南朝	Song 宋	420–479
		Qi 齐	479–502
		Liang 梁	502–557
		Chen 陈	557–589
	Northern Dynasties 北朝	Northern Wei 北魏	386–534
		Eastern Wei 东魏	534–550
		Northern Qi 北齐	550–577
		Western Wei 西齐	535–556
		Northern Zhou 北周	557–581
Sui Dynasty 隋朝			581–618
Tang Dynasty 唐朝			618–907
Five Dynasties 五代	Later Liang 后梁		907–923
	Later Tang 后唐		923–936
	Later Jin 后晋		936–947
	Later Han 后汉		947–950
	Later Zhou 后周		951–960
Ten Kingdoms 十国			891–979
Song Dynasty 宋朝	Northern Song 北宋		960–1127
	Southern Song 南宋		1127–1279
Liao Dynasty 辽代			907–1125
Jin Dynasty 金代			1115–1234
Yuan Dynasty 元朝			1206–1368
Ming Dynasty 明朝			1368–1644
Qing Dynasty 清朝			1616–1911
Republic of China 中华民国			1912–1949
People's Republic of China 中华人民共和国			Founded on October 1, 1949

Postscript

After two years work in subject selection, writing, translation, illustration and editing, we finally bring our conception of *The Fundamentals of Chinese Culture* into reality. We rewrite and revise the draft for several times because we know a good book is the result of continuing language refinement. Particularly, it is a comprehensive survey of Chinese culture issued overseas for university students who are interested in Chinese. In such a sense, we become the propagandists of Chinese civilization and deliverers of the cultural exchange between China and the West. And that sharpens our awareness of the mission's value and urges us to be more discreet about the compilation.

Research Group of the Jiangxi Provincial Academy of Social Science undertakes the whole writing task:

Liu Shuangqin: Chapter 1—Sections 1, 2, 3, 5 and 6 of Unit 1, Unit 2, Section 18 of Unit 3; Chapter 2—Sections 1, 2, 4, 5 of Unit 1, Sections 7, 8, 9 of Unit 2, Sections 17, 19, 21, 22 of Unit 4; Chapter 3—Units 2 and 3.

Li Qing: Chapter 1—Section 4 of Unit 1, Units 4 and 5; Chapter 2—Sections 10, 12, 13, 14, 15 of Unit 3; Chapter 3—Section 1 of Unit 1, Units 4 and 5.

Ni Aizhen: Chapter 1—Sections 11–17 of Unit 3; Chapter 2—Section 3 of Unit 1, Section 6 of Unit 2, Section 11 of Unit 3, Sections 16, 18, 20 of Unit 4; Chapter 3—Sections 2–4 of Unit 1, Section 10 of Unit 2, Units 3 and 5.

Xia Hanning: Chapter 2—Unit 5; Chapter 4—Unit 1, Sections 4–9 of Unit 2, Unit 4.

The teachers of Jiangxi University of Finance and Economics undertake the whole translating task:

Wuke: Chapter 1 ; Collates Chapter 1,3,4.

Yuan Zhimei: Chapter 3(fifty thousand words)

Lin Ying: Chapter 4, units 1,2,3 (thirty two 3.2 thousand words)

Yuan Zhen: Chapter 4, units 4, section 16—26 (eighteen thousand words)

You Jiajuan: Chapter 2, units 1,2,3

Li Jian: Chapter 4, units 4,5

Chinese culture is famed for its well—established and long standing history, as well as its all—embraciveness and profundity. It's no easy job to cover the most representative components and to explicate them with plain and concise language within a book of this scope and this length. Despite all our wholehearted efforts, inaccuracies and mistakes are unavoidable partly due to our limited competence. We hope to receive criticisms and suggestions from our dear readers.

Editorial Board of *Fundameutals of Chinese Culture*

2010.3.1

后 记

　　《中国文化ABC》这本书从选题、写作、翻译、插图到编辑出版历经两年,中间几易其稿,反复修改。这不仅是因为一本书,特别是一本好书的诞生本来就要历经千锤百炼,更是因为它是一本特殊的书。它在国外发行,主要读者是热心汉语的大学生们,因此我们也就顺理成章地成了中国文化的宣传者和中西文化交流的使者,这无疑增加了我们肩头的责任感,整个编撰的过程便慎之又慎了。

　　本书的写作主要由江西省社会科学院课题组承担。其中,刘双琴同志编著:第一章的第一单元(1、2、3、5、6)、第二单元、第三单元(18);第二章的第一单元(1、2、4、5)、第二单元(7、8、9)、第四单元(17、19、21、22);第三章的第二单元、第三单元。黎清同志编著:第一章的第一单元(4)、第四单元、第五单元;第二章的第三单元(10、12、13、14、15);第三章的第一单元(1)、第四单元、第五单元;倪爱珍同志编著:第一章的第三单元(11—17);第二章的第一单元(3)、第二单元(6)、第三单元(11)、第四单元(16、18、20);第三章的第一单元(2—4)、第二单元(10)、第三单元、第五单元;夏汉宁同志编著:第二章的第五单元;第四章的第一单元、第二单元(4—9)、第四单元。

　　本书的翻译主要由江西财经大学外国语学院的教师承担,其中,吴可同志翻译:第一章,校对第一、三、四章;袁志美同志翻译:第三章和第四章的第四单元(计5万字);林颖同志翻译第四章的一、二、三单元(计3.2万字);袁真同志翻译第四章第四单元的16—26章节(计1.8万字);尤佳娟同志翻译第二章的一、二、三单元;李健同志翻译第二章的第四、五单元。

　　本文所选取图片部分来自网络,在此对作者表示感谢。某些图片作者现无法联系,如方便可联系我们。

　　五千年中国文化源远流长,博大精深,要遴选出其中最具中国特色的文化已非容易之事,何况还要用最平易、最凝练的语言来叙述。所以,尽管我们尽心尽力,但由于水平有限,书中难免有疏漏和不当之处,恳请读者朋友们批评指正。

《中国文化ABC》编委会

2010年3月1日

图书在版编目(CIP)数据

中国文化 ABC/朱法元等主编;吴可等译.—南昌:江西人民出版社,2010.8

ISBN 978-7-210-04589-2

Ⅰ.①中… Ⅱ.①朱… ②吴… Ⅲ.①汉语—阅读教学—对外汉语教学—教材 Ⅳ.①H195.4

中国版本图书馆 CIP 数据核字（2010）第 165065 号

中国文化 ABC

朱法元 吴琦幸 夏汉宁 （美）高汉 主编

江西人民出版社出版发行

江西省南昌市红星印刷有限公司印刷 新华书店经销

2010 年 8 月第 1 版 2011 年 10 月第 2 次印刷

开本:787 毫米 × 1092 毫米 1/16 印张:24

字数:600 千

ISBN 978-7-210-04589-2 定价:70.00 元

赣版权登字-01-2010-61

江西人民出版社 地址:江西省南昌市三经路 47 号附 1 号

邮政编码:330006 传真:0791-6898827 电话:0791-6898501(发行部)

网址:www.jxpph.com

E-mail:jxpph@tom.com web@jxpph.com

（赣人版图书凡属印刷、装订错误,请随时向承印厂调换）